Juvenile Justice

Juvenile Justice

International Perspectives, Models, and Trends

Edited by
John A. Winterdyk

CRC Press
Taylor & Francis Group
Boca Raton London New York

CRC Press is an imprint of the
Taylor & Francis Group, an **informa** business

CRC Press
Taylor & Francis Group
6000 Broken Sound Parkway NW, Suite 300
Boca Raton, FL 33487-2742

Printed on acid-free paper
Version Date: 20140715

International Standard Book Number-13: 978-1-4665-7967-5 (Hardback)

Library of Congress Cataloging-in-Publication Data

Juvenile justice : international perspectives, models, and trends / edited by John A. Winterdyk.
    pages cm
  Includes bibliographical references and index.
  ISBN 978-1-4665-7967-5 (hardback)
  1. Juvenile delinquency. 2. Juvenile justice, Administration of. I. Winterdyk, John, editor.

HV9069.J88 2014
364.36--dc23   2014024228

Visit the Taylor & Francis Web site at
http://www.taylorandfrancis.com

and the CRC Press Web site at
http://www.crcpress.com

Contents

Contributors   vii

1   **Introduction: Juvenile Justice in the International Arena**   1

JOHN A. WINTERDYK

2   **Of Justice and Juveniles in Austria: Achievements and Challenges**   25

KARIN BRUCKMÜLLER AND STEFAN SCHUMANN

3   **Youth Justice and Youth Crime in Australia**   55

MICHAEL O'CONNELL AND ELIZABETH O'CONNELL

4   **Administration of Juvenile Justice in Brazil: Recent Advances and Remaining Challenges**   89

ALINE YAMAMOTO, JULIANA CARDOSO BENEDETTI, KARYNA BATISTA SPOSATO, MARISA MENESES DE ANDRADE, AND NATÁLIA LAGO

5   **Juvenile Justice and Young Offenders: A Canadian Overview**   107

JOHN A. WINTERDYK AND ANNE MILLER

6   **China's Juvenile Justice: A System in Transition**   137

RUOHUI ZHAO, HONGWEI ZHANG, AND JIANHONG LIU

7   **The Iranian Juvenile Criminal Justice System: An Overview**   163

TAHMOORES BASHIRIYEH AND MOHAMMAD ALI RAJAB

8   **Juvenile Justice and Juvenile Crime: An Overview of Japan**   179

YOKOYAMA MINORU

9   **Child Justice in Namibia: Back to Square One?**   209

STEFAN SCHULZ

10   **Juvenile Justice and Juvenile Crime in the Netherlands**   **239**
         HENK B. FERWERDA

11   **The Scottish Juvenile Justice System: Policy and Practice**   **263**
         LESLEY McARA AND SUSAN McVIE

12   **Juvenile Justice in Slovakia**   **295**
         DAGMAR KUSA AND ANNE M. NURSE

13   **South Africa's New Child Justice System**   **321**
         ANN SKELTON AND R. MORGAN COURTENAY

14   **Juvenile Justice: England and Wales**   **343**
         LORAINE GELSTHORPE AND VICKY KEMP

15   **Juvenile Justice in the United States**   **369**
         PETER J. BENEKOS AND ALIDA V. MERLO

Index   **395**

Contributors

Tahmoores Bashiriyeh
Department of Criminal Law and Criminology
University of Tehran (Formerly)
Tehran, Iran

Juliana Cardoso Benedetti
Chief International Advisor
Secretariat for Human Rights of the Presidency of
    the Republic
São Paulo, Brazil

Peter J. Benekos
Department of Criminal Justice and Sociology
Mercyhurst University
Erie, Pennsylvania

Karin Bruckmüller
Department for Criminal Law
Criminal Procedure Law
Philosophy and Sociology of Law
Ludwig-Maximilians-University
Munich, Germany

and

Department for Criminal Justice Practice and
    Medical Criminal Law
Johannes Kepler University
Linz, Austria

R. Morgan Courtenay
Centre for Child Law
University of Pretoria
Pretoria, South Africa

Marisa Meneses de Andrade
Universidade Tiradentes
Aracaju, Brazil

Henk B. Ferwerda
Bureau Beke
Arnhem, The Netherlands

Loraine Gelsthorpe
Institute of Criminology
University of Cambridge
Cambridge, England

Vicky Kemp
School of Law
University of Nottingham
Nottingham, England

Dagmar Kusa
Bratislava International School of Liberal Arts
Bratislava, Slovakia

Natália Lago
Youth Project Advisor in the NGO
    "Ação Educativa"
São Paulo, Brazil

Jianhong Liu
Department of Sociology
Faculty of Social Sciences and Humanities
University of Macau
Macau, China

Lesley McAra
School of Law
University of Edinburgh
Old College, South Bridge
Edinburgh, Scotland

Susan McVie
School of Law
University of Edinburgh
Old College
Edinburgh, Scotland

Alida V. Merlo
Indiana University of Pennsylvania
Department of Criminology
Indiana, Pennsylvania

Anne Miller
Constellation Consulting Group
Calgary, Alberta, Canada

Yokoyama Minoru
Faculty of Law
Kokugakuin University
Tokyo, Japan

Anne M. Nurse
Department of Sociology and Anthropology
The College of Wooster
Wooster, Ohio

Elizabeth O'Connell
Helping Young People Achieve (HYPA)
SYC Ltd.
Adelaide, South Australia, Australia

Michael O'Connell
Commissioner for Victims' Rights
Adelaide, South Australia, Australia

Mohammad Ali Rajab
Department of Criminal Law and Criminology
University of Tehran
Tehran, Iran

Stefan Schulz
Department of Legal Studies
School of Human Sciences
Polytechnic of Namibia
Windhoek, Namibia

Stefan Schumann
Institute for Criminal Law and Criminal Procedure
Johannes Kepler University
Linz, Austria

Ann Skelton
Centre for Child Law
University of Pretoria
Pretoria, South Africa

Karyna Batista Sposato
Department of Law
Federal University of Sergipe
Sergipe, Brazil

and

Universidade Tiradente
Aracaju, Brazil

John A. Winterdyk
Department of Justice Studies
Mount Royal University
Calgary, Alberta, Canada

Aline Yamamoto
Lawyer and Coordinator of Access to Justice and
    Violence Against Women at Brazil's Secretariat
    for Policies for Women
São Paulo, Brazil

Hongwei Zhang
Law School
Guangxi University
Nanning, China

Ruohui Zhao
Department of Sociology
Faculty of Social Sciences and Humanities
University of Macau
Macau, China

Introduction
Juvenile Justice in the International Arena

1

JOHN A. WINTERDYK[*]

Contents

Delinquency as a Growing International Enigma 3
Models of Juvenile Justice 7
International Standards and Guidelines for the Treatment of Young Offenders 8
   Highlights of the UNCRC 12
Rationale for Comparative Studies 17
   Sentencing Polices 18
   Juvenile Crime: A Global Phenomenon 18
Challenges with Comparative Studies 19
Organization of This Book 20
Acknowledgment 21
Review/Discussion Questions 21
References 22
Internet Sources 24

> Although some countries have experienced a decline of juvenile offending, others have reported an intensification, and "As the potentially real and perceptual problem of youthful misconduct grows in the world's societies, the question of how to respond to youth crime has also become ever more significant."
>
> **Hartjen (2008, xv)**

It is a fairly universally acknowledged fact that young people represent a subservient class and are comparatively powerless and that concerns about the welfare and discipline of young persons have plagued societies for centuries. Even Socrates is reported to have commented on the plight of young people. Furthermore, if we were to examine the history of child-rearing/disciplinary patterns throughout, then we would find that our ideas about how to raise and discipline children have been fraught with ambiguity, inconsistency, and fundamental ignorance concerning the nature of youth. deMause (1974) and Ariès (1962) offer insightful reviews as well as opposing perspectives on the evolution of views of children and youth throughout the ages (see Box 1.1). For example, deMause asserts that "the history of childhood is a nightmare from which we have just begun to awaken" (1974, 1). In spite of their different approaches, deMause and Ariès share a perspective that speaks to the challenges societies have faced in trying to raise children into adults regardless of social class or culture as well as what constitutes appropriate social

---

[*] Matthew Dunnette, a former student, assisted by researching sources, facts, and details for this chapter.

justice for youth at risk. The plight of young persons throughout the ages and even today remains an issue of power and the powerless between the state and young persons (see, for example, Whyte 2009). The issue of juvenile justice is a global phenomenon whose issues transcend borders.

Conversely, others have focused their attention on delinquency in the aftermath of the "child-saving" movement of the late 1800s, the key proponents of which in North America included Lewis Pease, Samuel Gridley Howe, and Charles Loring Brace. The phrase *child saver*, popularized by Anthony Platt (1977), points out that in North America, our concern with youth emerged from a group of middle- and upper-class citizens who imposed their values on delinquent youth (see Box 1.2). As Platt notes, the individuals in this movement began to use such terms as *disease* and *illness*, implying that delinquency is some kind of pathology and that delinquents need to be treated "like irresponsible, sick patients" (1977, 45).

BOX 1.1   THE MANY FACES OF CHILD-REARING

Child-rearing practices have been slowly evolving towards more nurturance. As a result, we have taken momentous strides toward greater democracy, justice and equality.

Grille (2009, 4)

The notion of how we respond and treat our young people is often linked to how we raise them. Just as there are a number of different models of juvenile justice systems, there is considerable variation in how we raise our children—even today. For example, although there have been both similarities and differences among countries regarding ideas of child-rearing, various studies have displayed substantial differences regarding child-rearing values throughout many European countries (Tulviste and Ahtonen 2007). Some of these variations include differences in personal achievement, self-direction, benevolence, tradition, hard work, and conformity. Moreover, the parents of children might also convey bad habits and criminal propensity (Tulviste and Ahtonen 2007). For example, a study conducted by Hämäläinen, Kraav, and Raudik (1994) found that both Estonian and Finnish mothers were much more concerned with teaching the values of respect, social justice, peace, and equality than fathers were. Conversely, Estonian fathers were more concerned with financial welfare and self-direction of their children (Tulviste and Ahtonen 2007). In addition, a similar study by Park and Cheah (2005) found that Korean mothers are much more likely to have a higher expectation of the social behavior of girls than that of boys (Tulviste and Ahtonen 2007).

Although general child-rearing ideologies have undergone many changes over the years, there are still many culture-based differences in the values of child-rearing. Moreover, based on the fact that each parent provides differing values, single parents may highly influence their children's behavior in one particular direction over another, since there is a lack of variation in child-rearing values.

BOX 1.2   THE ROOTS OF CHILD WELFARE

One of the first comprehensive attempts to explain delinquency was initiated by social work pioneer Jane Addams, a member of the well-meaning "society" of women in Chicago (i.e., Hull House) who recruited psychiatrist Dr. William A. Healy (1869–1963) in the early 1900s to conduct a longitudinal study of several hundred young offenders. In his 1915 book *The Individual Delinquent: A Textbook of Diagnosis and Prognosis for All Concerned in Understanding Offenders*, Healy focused on a wide range of potential causes of delinquency, from "the influence of bad companions" to "the love of adventure, early sex experiences and mental conflict" (see Krisberg and Austin, 1978, 31). As Jones (1999) observes, however, Dr. Healy's efforts and ideas failed to eliminate delinquency or the troublesome behavior of youth.

Delinquency as a Growing International Enigma

Never give up on a child

C.A. Robinson-Easley (2012, 206)

Although the circumstances of the past may be somewhat blurred with respect to how accurately they have been reported and how we choose to interpret them, the fact remains that we have been dealing with the dilemma of youth crime for a very long time. Even in 2014, the mass media and the public continue to focus on youth crime and violence among youth. In Canada, for example, public reaction to several violent crimes committed by adolescent boys and girls in the 1990s was instrumental in the forging of new legislation, in April 2003, for young offenders: the Youth Criminal Justice Act. Moreover, the Conservative Government has recently passed Bill C-10, which, among other legislative changes, sets out to amend the Youth Criminal Justice Act. Yet, while Canada struggles to find a balance between accountability and rehabilitation, other countries (including a number of Latin American nations) continue to resort to less tolerant measures (see Chapter 5 for further discussion). Some countries, such as Nepal, still allow mentally ill children to be jailed and chained (see generally, Khatiwada n.d.), in clear violation of Article 37 of the United Nations Convention on the Rights of the Child (UNCRC) (UNCRC; see Box 1.3). And although the legal systems in most countries recognize that young persons (i.e., children and adolescents) are different from adults, there are notable disparities in how various nations respond fiscally, legally, politically, and socially to these differences.

Furthermore, if official and unofficial crime data are any indication, we would be somewhat hard pressed to deny the fact that, irrespective of formal differences among nations, the issue of juvenile delinquency has grown into a significant contemporary social problem. Even though it is difficult to make simple statistical comparisons among countries because of differences in recording and reporting methods, terminology, and languages, when the majority of reporting countries draw similar conclusions, the nuances of any limitations become moot. Also perplexing are the diverse ways in which nations have evolved control, intervention, prevention, and treatment strategies to handle young offenders—all this in

BOX 1.3   ARTICLE 37 OF THE UNCRC

Article 37 of the UNCRC provides the child with the right to be protected from the following kinds of treatment:

- Torture
- Other cruel, inhumane, or degrading treatment or punishment
- Capital punishment
- Life imprisonment without possibility of release
- Unlawful or arbitrary deprivation of liberty

BOX 1.4   SUMMARY OF THE MAJOR U.N. CONVENTIONS TO FACILITATE A BALANCE OF YOUTH JUSTICE AND WELFARE

1985, the Beijing Rules—Standard Minimum Rules for the Administration of Juvenile Justice: Its primary focus addresses the administration of justice and includes such rules/recommendations as age of responsibility, although it does not specify any specific age limits and recommends diversion over incarceration when and where feasible, the right to legal counsel, and so on (see Box 1.5 in the following text).

1990, the Riyadh Guidelines—Directing Principles for the Prevention of Juvenile Delinquency: The primary focus of the guidelines was on early intervention and diversion and dealing with juvenile transgressions from a multidisciplinary perspective and within a crime prevention framework.

1990, the Havana Rules—Rules for the Protection of Juveniles Deprived of their Liberty: The rules emphasize the independence of the judiciary process and promote diversion from the prosecution of youth under the age of 18.

1990, the Tokyo Rules—Standard Minimum Rules for Non-custodial Measures: The rules call attention to the need for greater community involvement and community-based responses to crime.

1996, the Vienna Guidelines—Economic and Social Council Guidelines for Action on Children in the Criminal Justice System: The guidelines point out and reemphasize the need for young persons' rights to be respected and that states should strive to establish and maintain a child/youth-oriented youth justice system.

Do you think a justice and welfare approach to juvenile justice system is feasible?

spite of international agreements, in the 1990s, that have established standards and norms for the handling, processing, and treatment of such offenders (see Box 1.4).

At the Eighth and Ninth United Nations Congresses on the Prevention of Crime and the Treatment of Offenders, aside from the recognition of conventional and nonconventional crimes as a growing problem, participants also reported that youth crime is increasing around the world—especially in countries experiencing economic and political transition (Crime Congress 1995). A U.N. report published in 1995 noted that the average age of the onset of delinquent behavior was dropping (also see Farrington et al. 2003).

These observations, combined with the fact that in the year 2000, more than 50% of the world population was under the age of 15, serve to further "highlight the seriousness of the problem of juvenile delinquency and youth crime" (United Nations 1995). Furthermore, the UNCRC acknowledges that one of its challenges is the fact that "some States are moving toward increasingly punitive systems of juvenile justice, with children beaten and arbitrarily detained by police and forced to share prisons with adults in inhumane conditions" (see UNICEF n.d.).

At the Tenth United Nations Congress on the Prevention of Crime and the Treatment of Offenders, a statistic was stated that over 50% of the urban populations in developing countries are under the age of 19, and the trend is likely to continue for many more decades (United Nations 2005). This is a concerning figure since males between the ages of 15 to 24 are most likely to either commit crimes or become victims of crime (United Nations 2010). However, the International Centre for the Prevention of Crime has indicated that there appears to be somewhat of a growing level of stability regarding youth criminality on a global scale (United Nations 2010).

Although not all countries are experiencing the pragmatic concerns about youth crime that seem to accompany certain social, economic, and political changes, it is important that we recognize, examine, and understand the significance and relevance of the diverse ways in which young offenders are treated within their nations' respective justice systems (Muncie and Goldson 2006; Winterdyk 2002; see also Table 1.1). For example, some countries still use the death penalty (e.g., Saudi Arabia Sudan, Iran, China, and Nigeria),* many still exercise corporal punishment (e.g., Bolivia, Bangladesh, Mali, Taiwan, and some states in the United States), while others have no separate legislation and/or no juvenile court system for young offenders (e.g., Burundi, Denmark, Russia, Sweden, Kenya, among others) (also see Table 1.2 in the following text).

Youth crime is not by definition transnational in its scope, but it is an international problem, and it raises cross-national concerns. Furthermore, the issue of how nations should respond formally to youth crime has been addressed by the United Nations, the Human Rights Convention, and Amnesty International, as well as at national and even continental levels for some time now. There are several key U.N. initiatives that have served as benchmarks to guide its signatory members to standardizing their approach to juvenile justice. However, as the reader will discover or want to explore, compliance with the various international agreements, declarations, and standards is, to borrow from Freeman's (2011, 61) work on human rights, largely "carried out by diplomats and lawyers, prompted and assisted by activists."

In an effort to complement the focus of this anthology, in this Introduction, we provide an overview of the six key models of juvenile justice that can be found around the world. We also provide an overview of the various U.N. guidelines and conventions that pertain to the rights of children and young persons. This is followed by a rationale for engaging in comparative criminal justice research as well as reviewing some of the key articles of the UNCRC and several other key international documents that have created standards and guidelines by which all nations (or at least member states) have agreed to abide.

---

* Some countries like China abolished the death penalty of children under the age of 18, but due to insufficient efforts taken to determine the age of the offenders, older juveniles are still being put to death. Further information can be found at such sites as Amnesty International (see http://www.amnesty.org/en/death-penalty/executions-of-child-offenders-since-1990).

Table 1.1 Summary of the Features of Juvenile Justice Models

Features	Participatory Model	Welfare Model	Corporatist Model	Modified Justice Model	Justice Model	Crime Control Model
General	Informality Minimal formal intervention Resocialization	Informality Generic referrals Individualized sentencing Indeterminate	Administrative decision-making Offending Diversion from court/custody programs	Due process Informality Criminal offenses Bifurcation: soft offenders diverted, hard offenders punished	Due process Criminal offenses Least restrictive alternatives/ sanctions/ educational concerns	Due process/discretion Offending/status offenses Punishment/ retribution Determinate sentences
Key personnel	Educators	Childcare experts	Juvenile justice specialists	Lawyers/childcare experts	Lawyers	Lawyers/criminal justice actors
Key agencies	Community agencies/ citizens school and community agencies	Social work agencies	Interagency structure	Law/social work agencies	Law	Law
Tasks	Help and education team	Diagnosis	Systems intervention	Diagnosis/ punishment	Punishment	Incarceration/ punishment
Understanding of client behavior	People basically good	Pathology/ environmentally determined	Unsocialized	Diminished individual responsibility	Individual responsibility	Responsibility/ accountability
Purpose of intervention	Reeducation	Provision of treatment (*parens patriae*)	Retraining	Sanctioning of behavior/provision of treatment	Sanctioning of behavior	Protection of society/ retribution, deterrence
Objectives	Intervention through education	Respond to individual needs/rehabilitation	Implementation of policy	Respect individual rights/respond to special needs	Respect individual rights Punishment	Order maintenance
Countries (sample)	Japan	Austria, The Netherlands, India, South Korea, Italy, Scotland, Belgium	England/Wales, Hong Kong	Canada, South Africa, Ireland	Germany, Russia, China, Namibia	United States, Hungary

Source: Adapted from Winterdyk, J. (Ed.). (2002). Juvenile Justice Systems: International Perspectives (2nd ed.). Toronto: Canadian Scholars Press.

Note: As indicated in the text, no country's juvenile justice model is absolute or mutually exclusive; the designations shown here are intended to reflect general character-istics of the listed countries' juvenile justice systems. For example, in recent years an increasing number of countries have taken steps to embrace the United Nations Convention on the Rights of the Child (UNCRC) and other international standards that share many of the characteristics of the welfare model of juvenile justice. Therefore, despite their allocation in the book, the models used to characterize the juvenile justice system of a country are meant to be definitive.

Models of Juvenile Justice

While working in a Mesopotamian valley, archaeologists found a clay tablet in a tomb some 6000 years old.

The inscription on the tablet reads:

> Our earth has degenerated in these latter days; there are signs that the world is coming to an end. Children no longer obey their parents. The end of the world is manifestly drawing near.

Burrows (1967)

In partial response to the diverse range of explanations of juvenile crime and the varied perceptions and beliefs as how best to respond to juvenile crime, the legal implementation of criminal proceedings against juvenile/young offenders varies significantly around the globe. As a result, there exists considerable commentary and controversy about the appropriate legal responses to juvenile crime and how best to deter juvenile offenders from reoffending. Therefore, there is considerable divergence in how different jurisdictions deal with juvenile offenders. These different procedural systems are based on diverse theoretical approaches, which emerged over the years within the legal and criminal justice/criminological community.

Ever since the emergence of the welfare model of juvenile justice in 1899, with the establishment of the first juvenile court in the United States, there have been ongoing concerns and debates about which correctional philosophies (e.g., "just deserts," rehabilitation–treatment, and legalistic versus participatory and corporatist versus crime control) offer the most appropriate societal responses to youth crime (see Table 1.1 for a summary of the features of the various models). Although no individual country can be characterized as being truly representative of any one model, the models provide frameworks that are useful for describing and differentiating among nations' treatment of youthful offenders and allow for objective comparative analysis. For example, in Canada, we have what has been described as a *modified justice model* (Corrado et al. 1992; Hoge 2008; Winterdyk 2002) because while the Youth Criminal Justice Act is a federal piece of legislation, the provinces have some discretion in how they interpret the act (see, e.g., Carrington, Roberts, and Bala 2013). The province of Quebec, for instance, tends to embrace a welfare approach, whereas some of the western provinces tend to follow a justice model (Cournoyer et al. 2013). Yet all Canadian provinces are required to follow the general provisions declared in the act. Similarly, since the 1980s, Australia has moved away from a dichotomized justice and welfare approach to a more welfare-based model, yet Western Australia's Crime (Serious and Repeat Offenders) Sentencing Act of 1992 has been criticized for breaching a number of UN conventions (Atkinson 1997). However, when one considers the juvenile justice system in Australia, it is important to recognize that each of that nation's six states and two territories is responsible for its own juvenile justice system, and, as O'Connor, Daly, and Hinds (2002) point out, "The answer to the question 'Who is a juvenile?' differs between jurisdictions" (2002, 225). Even so, South Australia is commonly credited with establishing the world's first children's court and was the first state in Australia to introduce family conferencing on a formal basis.

Hence, a close examination of the juvenile justice systems in most countries will reveal that the laws on which these systems are based (that is, in those countries that have dedicated juvenile justice legislation) tend to be subject to interpretation. In some cases, the laws may be interpreted in ways that do not reflect the characteristics generally associated with particular countries' identified juvenile justice models.

It is beyond the scope of this Introduction to provide a comprehensive overview of the juvenile justice models in use in various countries, but the information in Table 1.2 serves to illustrate the diversity among nations. This table also indirectly illustrates the challenge that international recommendations and guidelines face within member countries attempting to fulfill their commitment to the UNCRC and other conventions.

International Standards and Guidelines for the Treatment of Young Offenders

Interestingly, neither the U.N. Declaration of the Rights of the Child in 1924 nor its Declaration of the Rights of the Child in 1959 made any specific reference to juvenile justice. Even the Standard Minimum Rules for the Treatment of Prisoners issued by the United Nations in 1955 made no reference to the handling of juvenile offenders. It was not until the 1980s that the United Nations began to consider juvenile justice as a subject matter. At the Seventh U.N. Congress on the Prevention of Crime and the Treatment of Offenders, held in Beijing, China, in May 1984, the United Nations endorsed the Standard Minimum Rules for the Administration of Juvenile Justice. These standards, commonly referred to as the Beijing Rules, are widely viewed as the most important (but not the only) guidelines for improving the quality of juvenile justice globally. Unfortunately, given the diversity in economic, political, and social factors among the world's nations, it is questionable whether such ideas can be universally embraced. However, this does not excuse countries from attempting to follow the essential recommendations. For example, the Centre for Europe's Children and the former Oisin program of the European Commission published a newsletter, *JUMPletter*, which in June 2002 examined the initiatives from within the European Union to address juvenile crime through social prevention. The Oisin program was established in 1996 by the European Parliament under the field of Justice and Home Affairs. During its tenure, the objective was to "promote exchange and training of, and co-operation [among], law enforcement authorities" in Europe. The program ended on December 31, 2002 and was subsequently replaced by AGIS. Similar to the Oisin program, the objective of AGIS was, "to help legal practitioners, law enforcement officials and representatives of victim assistance services from the EU Member States and Candidate Countries to set-up Europe-wide networks, exchange information and best practices in the field of cooperation in criminal matters" (European Union n.d.). Although stated to end in 2007, the AGIS program ended in 2006 for new security and justice programs to take effect until the end of 2013.

In 1998, the United Nations Children's Fund (UNICEF) incorporated the Beijing Rules into the *Implementation Handbook for the Convention on the Rights of the Child*. Other significant U.N. declarations pertaining to juvenile justice include the United Nations Guidelines for the Prevention of Juvenile Delinquency (known as the Riyadh Guidelines) and the United Nations Rules for the Protection of Juveniles Deprived of their Liberty, both of which were issued in 1990 (see Box 1.4).

The following section examines some of the key standards and explores the extent to which signatories of the standards have been able to actualize them.

Table 1.2   Juvenile Delinquency: Country Profiles

Country	Minimum[†]–Maximum Age of Criminal Responsibility	Justice Model[‡]/Conditions (International agreements)/ Transfer to Adult Court an Option
		North America
Canada	12–18	**Modified justice model;** includes provisions to transfer juvenile offenders to adult court (**see Chapter 5**)
United States	7–15+ (varies depending on state)	**Crime control model;** upper limit can range up to age 20 in some states, for most it is 17; includes provisions to transfer juvenile offenders to adult court (**see Chapter 15**)
South and Central America		
Argentina	16–18 (however, there is some debate about changing the minimum to age 14)	Recent model reform in 2005; legal system for juveniles has been described as similar to that of Italy; youth regulated under the Penal Regulations for Youth Law 22.778, 1980; very little research on youth crime/**justice model***
Bolivia	12–15 and 16–18 (two different jurisdictions, depending on age)	Youth court for ages 12–15, adult court for 16+
Barbados	7–16	Juvenile Offenders Act 1932; although system is modeled after British tradition, it includes heavy reliance on police cautioning; little research on the effectiveness of the system/ **corporatist model**
Brazil	12–17 for juvenile detention centers; 18 for criminal responsibility (however, there is some debate about changing the minimum to 16)	**Modified welfare–justice model (see Chapter 4)**
Cayman Islands	8–17	Children ages 8–13 classified as young persons, ages 14–17 classified as juveniles/**welfare model**
Chile	16–18	There is no formal legislation children and juveniles but if found guilty between the ages of 16–18, the young person can be deprived of his/her liberty. **Modified welfare-justice model.**
Colombia	14–18	Introduced the Code for Minors in 1990 and recently exploring restorative justice options. **Modified justice model.**
Cuba	6–16	Progressive **welfare-based model** introduced by Castro regime in 1959 for "children with conduct problems"; no formal provisions for transfer to adult court
Jamaica	7–14	New legislation was introduced in 2001/the new legislation resembles a **corporatist model**
		Europe
Austria	14–19	Juvenile Justice Act 1988, amended 1993; from 1981 to 1991, youth conviction rates dropped (1799 to 763)/**modified justice model/welfare model;** no provision to transfer young offenders to adult court (**see Chapter 2**)
Belgium	16–18	Children ages 6–15 dealt with informally/**welfare model with penal** exceptions; includes provisions to transfer juvenile offenders to adult court

(Continued)

Table 1.2 (*Continued*)   Juvenile Delinquency: Country Profiles

Country	Minimum†–Maximum Age of Criminal Responsibility	Justice Model‡/Conditions (International agreements)/ Transfer to Adult Court an Option
Bulgaria	14–17	Influence of Roman civil and criminal law/**modified welfare–justice model**
England and Wales	10–18	**Corporatist–mixed model (see Chapter 14);** includes provision to transfer juvenile offenders to adult court
Denmark	15–18	No formal juvenile justice system, but young offenders handled by combination of the penal system and the social welfare system
Finland	15–21	Three important age limits—15, 18, and 21; under 15 not liable, penal code recommends lighter sentences for children younger than 18, 17 and younger considered "child," 18 to 21 considered "juvenile"; 1991 proposal to lower minimum age to 14 in response to increase in youth crime/**justice model**
France	13–18	Problem youth addressed under Ordinance No. 45-174 of February 2, 1945, modified 1958 and 1970; specially trained children's judges/magistrates and social services for educational help; compared with most western European countries, rate of increase among the lowest (2% from 1992 thru 1993)/**welfare model** (social defense system); no provisions to transfer juvenile offenders to adult court
Germany	14–17	Youth 18–20 may be transferred to juvenile court/**justice model;** includes provisions to transfer juvenile offenders to adult court
Hungary	14–18	No separate juvenile legislation/**crime control model**, no provisions to transfer juvenile offenders to adult court
Ireland	12–14	In 2006, the minimum age was raised from 7 to 12 under Section 126 of the new Criminal Justice Act; detention to be used as a last resort; **modified justice model** with a strong community-based focus
Italy	14–18	**Welfare–justice model;** no provisions to transfer juvenile offenders to adult court
Israel	13–18	Juvenile Offenders Section (JSO), 1959; ethical code of JSO personnel goes beyond the limits established by the Youth Act stressing protection/**corporatist model**
Republic of Macedonia	14–18	In 2013, the country introduced new legislation, which relies heavily on restorative principles and is reflective of a **participatory model**
The Netherlands	12–18	**Modified justice model (see Chapter 10);** includes provisions to transfer juvenile offenders to adult court
Norway	15–18	Minimum age raised from 14 to 15 in 1990; 18-year-olds most frequently represented; recidivism rate continues to climb (41% among young offenders)/**welfare-modified justice model;** no provisions to transfer juvenile offenders to adult court
Poland	13–17	Responsibility based on mental and moral ability; 16- to 17-year-olds can be held criminally responsible/**justice model**
Russia	14–18	**Justice model** (but attempting to embrace **welfare** principles); no provisions to transfer juvenile offenders to adult court

(*Continued*)

Table 1.2 (*Continued*)   Juvenile Delinquency: Country Profiles

Country	Minimum[†]–Maximum Age of Criminal Responsibility	Justice Model[‡]/Conditions (International agreements)/ Transfer to Adult Court an Option
Scotland	8–16	Upper age limit 18 if already under supervision/**welfare model with penal exceptions** applied for ages 8–15; **justice model** elements with **welfare exceptions** applied for ages 16–18; no provisions to transfer juvenile offenders to adult court (**see Chapter 11**)
Slovakia	14–18	Youth under the age of 15 must undergo a psychological examination to ensure they can be held accountable for their transgression(s); **modified justice model;** no provision to transfer juvenile offenders to adult court (**see Chapter 12**)
Sweden	15–20	Known as "juvenile criminals," youth aged 15–18 given special consideration/**justice model;** no provisions to transfer juvenile offenders to adult court
Switzerland	15–18	Youth aged 7–14 considered children, 15–17 considered adolescent, 18–25 considered young adults (treated less severely than older adults)/**crime control model**
Asia		
China	14–25	Children partially responsible officially until age 18; law requires limited punishment; between 1977 and 1991, steady increase in crime, with proportionate number of young offenders; **participatory model** with justice elements (**see Chapter 6**)
Hong Kong	16–20	Children ages 7–15 classified as juveniles/**corporatist model**
India	7–16 for boys; 18 for girls	Espouse a **welfare–justice model** under the Juvenile Justice (Care and Protection of Children) Act 2000, but in the aftermath of the Nirbhaya gang rape case on December 16, 2012, which received worldwide attention, there has been a call for reassessing the Indian juvenile justice system
Japan	14–20	**Participatory model. (see Chapter 8)**; includes provisions to transfer juvenile offenders to adult court; juveniles have no right to an attorney
Philippines	12–17	Youth offenders aged 12–17 receive suspended sentences, offenders 18–20 are criminally responsible but entitled to leniency/**welfare–justice model**; in June 2013, the Supreme Court lowered the minimum age to 12 from 15
Singapore	7–16 (16–21 are considered young adults)	Islamic law sets minimum age of criminal responsibility at puberty/**welfare–justice model**.
South Korea	13–18	**Justice–welfare model**
Africa and Middle East		
Egypt	15–18	Juvenile Law No. 31 (1974); youth are segregated by age (12 and under, 13–14, 15–18); under 15 required to attend school, over 15 must receive vocational skills; judge aided in deliberation by two (appointed) experts, one of whom must be female/**corporatist model**
Namibia	15–18	**Justice model** (although still very much in developmental stage) (**see Chapter 9**)

(*Continued*)

Table 1.2 (*Continued*)   Juvenile Delinquency: Country Profiles

Country	Minimum[†]–Maximum Age of Criminal Responsibility	Justice Model[‡]/Conditions (International agreements)/ Transfer to Adult Court an Option
Israel	13–18	JSO, 1959; ethical code of JSO personnel goes beyond the limits established by the Youth Act stressing protection/ **corporatist model**
Kenya	8–18	Kenya ratified the United Nations Convention on the Rights of the Child in 1990 and introduced their Children's Act in 2001; system still evolving and not considered well suited to young persons' needs; for example, Kenya has one of the highest street and homeless population of young persons whose needs are not being met
Nigeria	7–12; 14–17	Modeled after the early British approach to juvenile justice, there is a greater emphasis on a **crime control model** rather than prevention or intervention attributed to a breakdown in the traditional extended family system
South Africa	15–18	**Modified justice model (see Chapter 13)**
Tanzania	7–15	Relatively new legislation/elements of **welfare model**
Australia and New Zealand		
Australia	10–16/17	Two jurisdictions have minimum age lower than 10; includes provisions to transfer juvenile offenders to adult court; access to legal counsel varies by state; **welfare model (see Chapter 3)**
New Zealand	14–17 (10 for murder and manslaughter)	**Welfare model**; includes provisions to transfer juvenile offenders to adult court and has a strong restorative component as well

Source: The information in this table comes primarily from data supplied by foreign embassies and/or relevant juvenile departments. In some cases, insufficient information is available to describe the model of justice or any other characteristics.

Although not included in Table 1.2 some countries (e.g., Cambodia, Bhutan, Democratic Republic of the Congo, and Senegal), do not recognize a minimum age of criminal responsibility; hence no age is given here. In 1804, the Napoleonic Code in France was one of the first laws to prescribe limited responsibility to offenders under the age of 16 (Terrill, 2009).

* The models (identified by bold type in this table) are the models found in Table 1.1.

† Between 2005 and 2008, there have been five countries involved in capital punishment of juvenile offenders. This includes Iran, Saudi Arabia, Sudan, Yemen, and Pakistan (Human Rights Watch 2008, 2). Between 2009 and 2011, the only reported executions of juvenile offenders were from Iran and Saudi Arabia. During this time frame, a reported total of 11 people who were juveniles at the time of the offence had been executed (Amnesty International n.d.). The United States had also allowed the execution of juvenile offenders until a Supreme Court decision deemed it unconstitutional in 2005 (*Roper v. Simmons* 543 U.S. 551 [2005]).

‡ Names of models are provided only for countries in which sufficient information is available to allow a description of their juvenile justice practices.

Highlights of the UNCRC

> Mankind owes to the child the best that it has to give.
>
> **U.N. Declaration of the Rights of the Child, 1924**

In accordance with a welfare model of juvenile justice (see Table 1.1), the Beijing Rules state that the objectives of a nation's juvenile justice legislation should focus on furthering the well-being of the juvenile and her or his family (1.1) and on developing conditions that will ensure a meaningful life in the community for the youth (1.2); in addition, the administration of juvenile justice should represent an integral part of the natural development process of the country. If countries are to meet these objectives, why is it that the United Nations has fair-to-excellent information on adult offenders, yet very limited data on young offenders (see Hamilton 2002)? This lack of central information makes a cross-national comparative study of juvenile justice very difficult.

The broad nature of the U.N. principles allows for considerable latitude of interpretation and may account in part for some of the diversity witnessed among those countries that claim they are trying to adhere to the guidelines. For example, juveniles in Sudan, Zimbabwe, and Singapore can still face flogging, amputation, and execution, and juveniles in Kenya are locked up regularly with adults because the country has only one juvenile court. Several years ago, some Iranian teenagers were sentenced to 10 lashes and a fine of 100,000 rials (approximately $30) each for attending a dance party that included both boys and girls (this mixing of the genders among unmarried persons is forbidden under Islamic laws; see *Calgary Herald*, August 25, 1999). According to the U.S. Department of Justice, even in the United States some 75% of the juvenile facilities "lack adequate health care, security, and access to suicide-prevention programs" (cited in Prince 1997). Meanwhile, in the Caribbean, due to economic factors, many juveniles remain unrepresented by legal counsel at trial (Singh 1999; Wright 2010). The countries in these examples would seem to fall short of U.N. standard 2.3 (a), which says that "efforts shall be made to establish in each national jurisdiction... provisions... to meet the varying needs of juvenile offenders, while protecting their basic rights."

As Table 1.2 illustrates, there is considerable variation among countries concerning the age of criminal responsibility. The Beijing Rules (i.e., 4.1) simply state that the beginning age shall not be fixed at too low an age level (see Box 1.5). The rules recommend that in determining the lower limit, legislators should keep in mind the factors of emotional, mental, and intellectual maturity. Consequently, we see the minimum age of responsibility ranging from as low as 6 in Mexico and 7 in Thailand and Kenya to as high as 16 in Argentina. Ironically, the rules offer even fewer guidelines for the upper limit of juvenile responsibility. This would appear to reflect a clear lack of social, psychological, and biological understanding of adolescent development. For example, most related studies show that whereas adolescence begins between the ages of 10 to 13 and peaks around age 15, the neurological and social development of individual adolescents can vary depending on a wide array of factors. Therefore, rather than trying to clarify such matters, the Beijing Rules speak for legislative consideration in this case.

The aim of juvenile justice, according to the Beijing Rules (i.e., 5.1), should be that any reaction to juvenile offenders should always be in proportion to the circumstances of both the offender and the offense. However, any action should emphasize, foremost, the well-being of the juvenile. This section of the rules represents conflict between the classical doctrine of criminology and the positive doctrine of criminology. Appreciating that the principle is meant as a guideline, it is both vague and untenable, given that no legislation can equitably apply a fair reaction at an individual level. Rather, for any juvenile/youth justice system to work effectively, it must apply general standards that are consistent in their ideology and grounded in empirical evidence.

Again, when we look at the aims of the countries that are signatories of the UNCRC standards, we see that the scope for interpretation is excessively broad and appears to

BOX 1.5   HIGHLIGHTS OF THE BEIJING RULES (1984)

Fundamental perspectives

1.1: To further the well-being of the juvenile and his or her family

1.2: To develop conditions that will ensure a meaningful life in the community for the juvenile

1.4 To make the administration of juvenile justice an integral part of the natural development process of each country

Age of responsibility

4.1 To not fix the beginning age at too low an age level, bearing in mind the facts of emotional, mental, and intellectual maturity

Aim of juvenile justice

5.1 To emphasize the well-being of the juvenile and ensure that any reaction to juvenile offenders shall always be in proportion to the circumstance of both the offender and the offence

Scope and discretion

6.2 To make efforts to ensure sufficient accountability at all stages and levels in the exercise of any such discretion

Protection of privacy

8.1 To respect the right to privacy at all stages to avoid harm being caused by undue publicity or by the process of labeling

8.2 To not publish any information that may lead to the identification of a juvenile offender (U.N. 1986)

For further details on the Beijing Rules see; http://www.un.org/documents/ga/res/40/a40r033.htm

be more reflective of political agendas than of any intent to represent the true needs of young persons. In Honduras several years ago, two 16-year-old street children escaped a government-run youth center and were found dead 2 days later. The police were suspected of committing the killings even though Honduras has ratified the UNCRC (Prince 1997). In Canada, the Youth Criminal Justice Act aims to command the respect of Canadians by holding young offenders responsible for their actions and ensuring meaningful consequences for those who commit certain offenses while still attempting to fulfill its commitment to the various international conventions and agreements it has signed (see Chapter 5).

The scope of discretion (Section 6) laid out in the Beijing Rules calls for "sufficient accountability at all stages and levels in the exercise of any such discretion." A number of countries have taken notable steps to broaden their scope of discretion when dealing with young offenders. India, even though representative of a welfare model of justice, has taken additional steps to embrace the fundamental principles of its model. In 2000, India's new Juvenile Justice (Care and Protection of Children) Act introduced provisions that make the juvenile justice system more child friendly in promoting opportunities for proper care and protection of young persons. The act also makes a clear distinction between juvenile offenders and neglected children. Perhaps most impressively in a country with limited resources, the new act requires that all cases relating to juveniles be completed within a 4-month period (T. Chakraborty, personal communication, 2012). The act was subsequently amended in 2006 to include both clarification of various sections and additional regulations regarding the children in need of protection, and not just juvenile offenders.

Further evidence of the general lack of participation of member states in implementing the U.N. standards and norms is the fact that in 1999 the U.N. Committee on the UNCRC issued a recommendation calling on member states to give priority attention toward full implementation of Articles 37, 39, and 40 (see Box 1.6) of the convention. The committee also urged the United Nations High Commission for Human Rights to do what it could to encourage and/or assist member countries to implement the standards fully. For example, it seems ironic that the most powerful country in the world, the United States, signed the UNCRC in 1995, but (along with Somalia) is yet to ratify its signature. The only other U.N. member state that has not ratified the UNCRC is the African country of Somalia. Somalia currently has no functioning government and so is unable to ratify anything. In spite of its intention to ratify, the United States has allowed some 9 years to pass since it signed the convention. Therefore, the United States is not obliged, nor has it made any overt effort, to make this legal commitment to children or to embrace international customary law. The American absence is a significant statement that undermines the goodwill and positive intentions of the rest of the members of the international community as they strive to reach some uniformity in the treatment and handling of young offenders. Moreover, since the creation of the UNCRC in 1990, there have been 193 countries that have accepted and implemented its provisions aside from some reservations; no country has withdrawn from the agreement (United Nations Treaty Collection 2013).

One recommendation that has been put forth to assist in the implementation of the UNCRC and the monitoring of compliance is that member countries should regularly

---

BOX 1.6   HIGHLIGHTS OF ARTICLE 40 OF THE UNCRC

After the Beijing Rules were incorporated into the *Implementation Handbook for the Convention on the Rights of the Child* in 1998, several key articles (i.e., 37, 39, and 40) dealt with the treatment of young persons and their rehabilitation and recommended reintegration strategies. Article 40 focuses on the legal rights of young persons and it recommends that ALL countries should

- Establish a minimum age of criminal responsibility
- Not take any action against a young person unless there are provisions within the law
- Presume a youth is innocent until proven guilty
- Not compel a youth to give testimony or to confess
- Ensure that all persons have access to legal counsel
- Provide a variety of alternative dispositions to incarceration and/or institutional care (Convention on the Rights of the Child, 1990)

Source: http://www.sccyp.org.uk/resources/uncrc-illustrated-guide/images-young-people.

submit statistics on their juvenile justice systems and on juvenile offenders. According to a report prepared by Hamilton (2002), however, at present, participation in such data collection is all but absent, with the modest exception of a few countries. Even though such statistics may not provide reliable figures on youth crime, they would provide a basis on which some comparisons could be made, and then steps could eventually be taken to streamline recording methods and practices. In the meantime, the rhetoric concerning the rights of the child will continue until the public and governments are prepared to embrace the reality of the plight of children. For example, the United Nations has reported that in 2012 some 300,000 children served as soldiers (aka "nonstate actors") of whom 40% are estimated to be girls (*The Independent*, December 23, 2012),* and in 2013 the KAISER Family Foundation estimated the percent of children under the age of five who are malnourished to be just over 16% (see Prevalence of Child 2013).

What becomes evident when we evaluate the application of international guidelines and standards to countries that are signatories of the UNCRC is that, irrespective of any models of juvenile justice, no country is able to implement and/or actualize the guidelines and standards uniformly. Furthermore, many of the states that can be characterized as developing nations simply have not had the resources or the political will to implement juvenile justice systems (or have been inordinately slow in doing so). What becomes evident is that each country's juvenile justice system has evolved since it was first introduced, and, although nations might strive to honor the UNCRC, pragmatic factors such as social values and norms, economic standards, cultural ideologies, and political and public opinion continue to compromise the establishment of universal standards for juvenile justice.

Hamilton (2002) concludes that the member states of the UNCRC have "been notoriously slow at implementing Articles 37, 39, and 40" (2002, 1). In fact, she further notes that virtually all states have been, or could be, criticized for their "failure to fully implement them" (2002, 1). These are daunting accusations, but they are based in reality. As I have already noted, for most countries, the failure to follow or to establish a system of juvenile justice that embraces the UNCRC standards and norms is rooted in an inability to inform and educate citizens properly about the true nature and extent of juvenile offending, the administration of juvenile justice, and the efforts being made in some nations to curb offending or to rehabilitate offenders. Even though juvenile offending and juvenile justice are universal concerns, countries continue to legislate models of justice that are often dictated by political agendas and public opinion even as they attempt to acknowledge the standards of the UNCRC.

As noted above, and as illustrated in Table 1.2, it is evident that the administration of juvenile justice is more a reflection of the social and political will of the state than of the universal interests of young persons in conflict with the law. When the administration of justice is dictated by political (i.e., human-made) laws instead of scientific/natural laws, we typically end up with a legal system that is consistent with the conflict model. Political laws are based on political power and have no stability, whereas scientific laws are based on common law principles and reflect consensus. Therefore, the more juvenile justice systems move away from scientific laws, the more thinly protected the rights of children and young offenders will be. As will be evidenced throughout the contributions in this

---

* Every year, February 12 is Red Hand Day. The day is used to commemorate, campaign, and draw international attention to the plight of child soldiers, which is primarily limited to war-torn African countries.

collection, there are as Whyte (2009:12) points out "inevitable tensions in all systems" and each system and/or model struggles to "managing the 'mix' between social and protective measures, punitive responses and sanctions."

Rationale for Comparative Studies

Are juveniles in Iran more violent than those in Namibia? Is juvenile gang activity more prevalent in some parts of the world than others? If so, why? How does the juvenile justice system compare between countries with similar or different legal, religious, and/or political systems? Is juvenile crime less/more serious in countries where criminal responsibility starts at age 7 (e.g., Sudan, Jordan and Pakistan) versus countries whose age of criminal responsibility starts at 18 (e.g., Belgium, Peru and Panama)? How do the different justice models compare in terms of their relative effectiveness and efficiency?

While the vast majority of criminological and sociological literature on crime has been based on a nonlinear model—"focused within countries and without pretense to being general"—this has continued to evolve (Teune 1992: 35). The interest in comparative research would seem closely aligned to macroglobal changes as well as advances in technology. For example, in the aftermath of the Great Depression (the 1930s), many researchers turned their focus inward, while in the aftermath of World war II it became necessary to do comparative research as a necessary part of decentralizing the world order (see Nelken 1994; Tuene 1992). The process, as Marsh (1967) observed, emerged rather slowly, especially with respect to the phenomena of crime. But since the mid-1980s, there has been increased attention directed toward comparative research.

As can be seen in Tables 1.1 and 1.2, the level of attention that different systems and societies pay to the "age of responsibility" reflects major practical and theoretical differences between systems and countries. For example, of the countries listed in Table 1.2, Switzerland has the lowest age of criminal responsibility at 7 while Belgium has the highest minimum age at 16 or 18, depending on the nature of the offense. Also in Tables 1.1 and 1.2, it can be seen how countries vary in their definition of what legally constitutes a "juvenile" or "young offender." The variations reflect different cultural, historical, political, and social differences that can make comparisons challenging. Furthermore, not only are there variations between countries but even within countries (see, e.g., the coverage of Canada—Chapter 5 and the United States—Chapter 15). As discussed in Chapter 15, 36 states in the United States have no minimum age of criminal responsibility. A question that could be explored through a comparative analysis is: What are the implications of high versus low minimum ages? How do countries with high minimum ages of responsibility respond to youth at risk and what are the comparative benefits or challenges?

As countries strive to address the plight of youth crime, it is possible through comparative analysis to explore and examine the relative impact and effectiveness of different models of juvenile justice and applications of these models. For example, by examining juvenile crime, trends and reactions to youth crime may provide insight into how one can address juvenile crime situations better in one's own country, or between different legal systems, and/or between different models of justice. As several researchers (see Reichel 2012; Dammer, Fairchild, and Albanese 2014) have commented, comparative information can provide a practical window of opportunity to gain new insights and adopt, adapt, and develop new responses. For example, why is it that not only are there differences between northern and southern European countries in juvenile crime rates but also variations between these countries in the importance, in some instances, of sociodemographic factors (see Junger-Tas 1994; Walgrave and Mehlbye 1988)? In a number of countries (e.g., Austria, France, Hungary, and Switzerland), it is not possible to transfer juvenile offenders to adult court, while in Canada though it is now not possible, for very serious offences, the young offender can receive an adult sentence. What are the implications of such an option and what lessons might we be able to learn by examining the different procedural differences? Similarly, how do countries that practice common law as opposed to civil law compare in their approach to juvenile justice?*

Another theme that cross-cultural comparisons allow for is the comparison of how different societies use different criminological explanations and/or ideological perspectives to justify their response to juvenile crime. For example, both France and Italy use a conciliatory model of restorative justice. Disagreements between juvenile offenders and their victims are commonly resolved through agreement and assent (Yenisey 2007). The Dutch meanwhile rely more on diversion-based programs (see Chapter 10).

Sentencing Polices

Canada has historically had a fairly lenient juvenile justice system, but in 2011, the federal Conservative government introduced legislation that represented a dramatic shift toward more punitive sentencing policies that represent a shift toward a jail-intensive approach. Paperny (2011) points out that countries such as Australia, Britain, and the United States, whose systems share many similarities to that of Canada, are puzzled as to why Canada is going down this path when there is rather compelling evidence that such a punitive approach simply does not work (the issue will be discussed at greater length in Chapter 5).

Juvenile Crime: A Global Phenomenon

Although every country has a legal system to control crime and enhance public safety, it is evident that not all juvenile justice systems work as well as they are designed. For example, Japan has historically had comparatively low juvenile crime rates. But as discussed in Chapter 8, juvenile crime, and in particular violent juvenile crime, is no longer a rarity. Why is this happening and what, if anything, can be done? Conversely, in a country like Namibia (see Chapter 9) where they still do not have a juvenile justice system, the system struggles with trying to uphold its commitment to the various U.N. agreements and conventions it signed.

Finally, as juvenile delinquency is a universal phenomenon and all the countries represented in this collection have ratified the U.N. Declaration of the Rights of the Child, it is interesting to explore why some of the nations are more willing to follow the U.N. standards than others. It is also interesting to note that while most of the countries have legislated additional policies to protect youth, why is it that some still commit violations of their own laws and the U.N. standards? For example, why is it that some of the countries still allow

---

* For a broader illustration of how different legal systems can be used to engage in comparative criminal justice research, see Dammer, Fairchild, and Albanese (2014) and Terrill (2009). Conversely, for a broader comparative approach that focuses on key aspects of the criminal justice system (e.g., law enforcement, courts, and corrections, see Reichel 2012).

capital punishment, detain young offenders in inhumane conditions, and/or fail to provide access to proper education or essential care; moreover, as Bailleau and Cartuyvels (2010) have questioned in their edited book on juvenile justice in Europe, Turkey, and Canada, is there evidence to suggest that countries are becoming increasingly more reliant on criminalizing their young offenders (as Hastings argues in the book, Canada is an exception to this growing trend)?

Although this collection does not address the issues directly, the reader is encouraged to explore any range of comparative issues that might enrich our/your understanding of the complexity of how best to respond to juvenile crime—be it within a national context or from a global perspective.

Challenges with Comparative Studies

Until only a couple of decades ago, a number of researchers believed that comparative studies generally resulted in fragmented knowledge since the comparisons tend to use "temporal and/or spatial logic" (Teune 1992:8). Similarly, Beirne (1983) argued that comparative criminal justice typically has to contend with significant methodological and epistemological challenges; Newman (1977) identified several other key obstacles, some of which include

- Language barriers: An obvious limitation if you do not have access to an interpreter.
- Definition barriers: Known offences vary from country to country. For example, in the United States, the Uniform Crime Reports provide compilations of known offenses for eight categories of crime, called index offenses (Part 1). Yet, in England and Wales, the Criminal Statistics includes 64 known crimes that are further divided into eight major categories. Finally, in Canada, the Crime and Traffic Enforcement Statistics lists 25 known offenses that are divided into several subcategories.
- Reporting and recording practices: How crime data is collected and recorded, as Bayley (1990:18) points out, "cannot be trusted" due to a range of cultural and systemic factors. Developing countries are notorious for having inefficient record systems (see, e.g., Clinard 1978). Cultural differences among countries also has an impact on how delinquency/crime is defined, enforced, and catalogued.
- Administrative variations: There are numerous factors such as law enforcement, the judicial system, corrections, or public support that can affect how justice is administered, as illustrated by the different contributions in this book.

In spite of these apparent hurdles, the academic and technological study of crime and criminal justice has become increasingly international and comparative. In recognizing the challenges, nonequivalent concepts, and an array of other possible unknown intervening factors, it is possible, if not necessary to engage in an objective analysis that may provide new insights into a complex global issue such as juvenile delinquency. In fact, a few years ago, Maguire, Howard, and Newman (1998) called for a universal index for criminal justice, a performance index, which quantitatively measures the performance of national criminal justice systems in three key areas: equity, effectiveness, and efficiency.

Organization of This Book

> When there is crime in society there is no justice.
>
> **Plato**

This book comprises 15 chapters. The selection of the contribution was based on several criteria. First, we wanted to ensure that each of the main models of justice was represented. We also wanted to include countries, which have different legal systems as well as different social–cultural and/or religious differences. And while it was not practically possible to include countries to cover all the various combinations, there is sufficient diversity to allow the learner to explore a variety of critical issues as they pertain to juvenile justice.

Rather than asking the authors to address a strict set of criteria, all the contributors were asked to try and provide an overview of their juvenile justice system bearing the following key points in mind:

- Social and legal definition of delinquency
- Nature and status of delinquency
- Identification of the model of juvenile justice, as defined in Table 1.1, that best describes the country's administration policies
- Description of the role of law enforcement, (juvenile) courts, corrections, and the broader community in administering juvenile justice
- The general philosophy and practice of juvenile justice administration
- Identification of the current theoretical models used to explain and justify responses to young offenders
- Discussion of the current issues, legally and socially, confronting young offenders
- Review/discussion questions, helpful Web links that would allow the reader to follow-up on key issues discussed and/or to keep current with any development issues presented throughout the chapter

The format is designed to enable the reader to accomplish several tasks. First, countries or juvenile justice models can be examined on an individual basis. Second, two or more countries/justice models can be compared, based on a variety of criteria ranging from descriptive information to comparing juvenile justice models. And third, a transnational approach can be adopted in which all countries are examined in the light of the larger international phenomena of delinquency. As Kohn (1989) observed, each approach may produce different practical and theoretical outcomes. Finally, throughout this book, the terms juvenile delinquency and youth crime are used interchangeably because in some countries one term may be used more commonly than the other.

Since this book is intended to serve a wide international audience, the contributors were also asked not to make any direct comparisons to any specific country(ies) other than those they might feel comfortable discussing in relation to the specific theme under discussion.

In summary, while this book is composed of 15 chapters representing 14 countries covering North America, South America, Africa, Australia, Europe, and Asia, all the six different juvenile justice models are included. We have intentionally not drawn any direct comparisons with any one country or any one model of juvenile justice. With this objective in mind, it is hoped that the book will generate discussion and comparisons as best meet the needs of the reader and/or classroom. Learners and instructors are encouraged to use the material presented in the book to draw comparisons as best suits their respective interests. To this end, I hope that the contributions are both general enough to provide a robust overview and yet specific enough to allow, where appropriate, for a deeper level of analysis. Naturally, a limitation in this regard is the sole responsibility of the editor, as I defined the chapter format and pedagogy for the contributors.

Finally, should you have any constructive comments or suggestions for any future editions, I would appreciate hearing from you. I can be reached at

Professor John Winterdyk
Department of Justice Studies
Mount Royal University
4825 Mount Royal Gate, SW
Calgary, AB, Canada T3E 6K6

In the meantime, thank you for selecting this book, and I trust that you will find the book as informative and useful to read as I found it interesting and challenging to revise and update.

Acknowledgment

I would like to acknowledge the invaluable assistance of one of my former students, Matthew Dunnette, in helping to track down various sources, facts, and details for this chapter.

Review/Discussion Questions

1. To what extent do/have historical factors influenced the development of youth justice models and legislation? What appear the significant factors that have influenced the development of the different models of justice?
2. How have the major United Nations conventions impacted the welfare and justice of young offenders? To what extent does your country comply with these underlying principles of the various conventions?
3. Which of the six juvenile justice models do you feel is 'the best'? Explain your answer.
4. As illustrated in Table 1.2 there is considerable variation between the minimum and maximum age of criminal responsibility. Explore why this might be the case and discuss whether you agree with such variations or should there be one international standard?
5. Despite most countries experiencing a decline in youth crime, how might we explain a shift towards a law and order approach and what has been described by some as a more comprehensive and integrated approach?
6. What do you see as the major advantages of engaging in comparative juvenile justice research/studies?

References

Amnesty International. (n.d.). Recorded executions of child offenders since 1990: Statistics. Available at: http://www.amnesty.org/en/death-penalty/executions-of-child-offenders-since-1990.

Ariès, P. (1962). Centuries of Childhood: A Social History of Family Life. New York: Vintage.

Atkinson, L. (1997). Juvenile justice in Australia. In Juvenile justice systems: International perspectives, Ed. J. Winterdyk, pp. 29–54. Toronto: Canadian Scholars Press.

Bailleau, F. and Cartuyvels, Y. (Eds.). (2010). The Criminalization of Juvenile Justice in Europe, Turkey, and Canada. Brussels: Vub Press.

Beirne, P. (1983). Cultural relativism and comparative criminology. Contemporary Crises 7:371–391.

Burrows, B.L. (1967). The role of the New Zealand police: Prevention, detection and prosecution. In Juvenile Delinquency in New Zealand, Ed. P. J. Blizard. Wellington: Social Science Section of the Royal Society of New Zealand.

Clinard, M. (1978). Comparative crime victimization surveys: Some problems and results. International Journal of Criminology and Penology 6:221–231.

Convention on the Rights of the Child. (1990). Available at: http://www.ohchr.org/en/professional interest/pages/crc.aspx.

Corrado, R.R., Bala, N., Linden, R., and LeBlanc, M. (Eds.). (1992). Juvenile Justice in Canada. Toronto: Butterworth.

Cournoyer, L.-G., Dionne, J., Goyette, M., and Hamel, P. (2013). Quebec's Experience Keeping Youth Out of Jail. In Youth at Risk and Youth Justice: A Canadian Overview, Eds. J. Winterdyk and R. Smandych. Toronto: Oxford University Press. (Chapter 14).

Crime congress targets terrorist crimes, firearms regulations, and transnational crime. (1995). CJ International 11:4–6.

Dammer, H.R., Fairchild, E., and Albanese, J.S. (2014). Comparative Criminal Justice Systems (5th ed.). Belmont, CA: Wadsworth Thomson Learning.

deMause, L. (Ed.). (1974). The evolution of childhood. In The History of Childhood. New York: Peter Bedrick.

European Union. (n.d.). European commission on freedom, security and justice—Programs 2004–2007. Available at: http://collection.europarchive.org/dnb/20070702132253/http://ec.europa.eu/justice_home/funding/intro/funding_2004_2007_en.htm#AGIS.

Farrington, D.P., Jolliffe, D., Hawkins, D., Catalano, R.F., Hill, K.G., and Kosterman, R. (2003). Comparing delinquency careers in court records and self-reports. Criminology 41:933–958.

Freeman, M. (2011). Human Rights (2nd ed.). Cambridge: Polity Press.

Grille, R. (2009). Parenting for a Peaceful World. Gabriola Island: New Society Publishers.

Hamilton, C. (2002). Juvenile justice: The role of statistics and public perception. Paper prepared for the Office of the High Commissioner for Human Rights, The European Institute for Crime Prevention and Control, affiliated with the United Nations (HEUNI), Helsinki, Finland.

Hartjen, C. (2008). Youth, Crime, and Justice: A Global Inquiry. New Brunswick, NJ: Rutgers University Press.

Hoge, R.D. (2008). Advances in the Assessment and Treatment of Juvenile Offenders (From UNAFEI: Annual Report for 2007 and Resource Material Series No. 75, pp. 81–104). Washington, DC: NCJRS.

Human Rights Watch. (2008). Enforcing the international prohibition on the juvenile death penalty. A Human Rights Watch submission for the Secretary-General's report on follow-up to General Assembly resolution 62/149 on a death penalty moratorium. Available at: http://www.crin.org/docs/FileManager/HRWEnfIntProhibJuvDPenalty08EN.pdf

Iranian teens to be whipped for dance party [electronic version]. (1999, August 25). Calgary Herald. Available at: www.calgaryherald.com (subscription required) and www.csmonitor.com (fee access).

Jones, K. (1999). Taming the Troublesome Child: American Families, Child Guidance, and the Limits of Psychiatric Authority. Cambridge, MA: Harvard University Press.

Khatiwada, I. (n.d.). Nepalese juvenile justice system: An overview. Available at: www.ksl.edu.np/cpanel/pdf/ishwors.doc.

Krisberg, B. and Austin, J. (1978). The Children of Ishmael. New York: Mayfield.

Maguire, E.R., Howard, G., and Newman, G. (1998). Measuring the performance of national criminal justice systems. International Journal of Comparative and Applied Criminal Justice 22:31–59.

Muncie, J. and Goldson, B. (2006). State of transition: Convergence and diversity in international youth justice. In Comparative Youth Justice, Ed. J. Muncie and B. Goldson. London: Sage Publications.

O'Connor, I., Daly, K., and Hinds, L. (2002). Juvenile crime and justice in Australia. In Juvenile Justice Systems: An International Comparison of Problems and Solutions, Eds. N. Bala, J. P. Hornick, H. N. Snyder, and J. J. Paetsch, pp. 221–254. Toronto: Thompson Educational Publishing.

Paperny, A.M. (2011, July 19). Canada's youth crime plans bewilder international observers. The Globe and Mail. Available at: http://www.theglobeandmail.com/news/national/time-to-lead/canadas-youth-crime-plans-bewilder-international-observers/article592992/.

Platt, A.M. (1977). The Child Savers (2nd ed.). Chicago: University of Chicago Press.

Prevalence of child malnutrition (Percent underweight under age five). (2013, January). Henry J. Kaiser Family Foundation. Available at: http://kff.org/global-indicator/child-malnutrition/

Prince, C.J. (1997, October 22). Justice lags for world's juveniles. Christian Science Monitor International. Available at: www.calgaryherald.com (subscription required) and www.csmonitor.com (fee access).

Reichel, P. (2012). Comparative Criminal Justice Systems: A Topical Approach (6th ed.). Upper Saddle River, NJ: Prentice Hall.

Robinson-Easley, C.A. (2012). Our Children, Our Responsibility: Saving the Youth We Are Losing to Gangs. New York: Peter Lang Pub.

Roper v. Simmons, 543 U.S. 551 (2005).

Singh, W. (1999). A regional report: Latin America. Paper presented at the International Penal Reform Conference, London.

Ten facts about child soldiers that everyone should know. (2012, December 23). The Independent. Available at: http://www.independent.co.uk/voices/comment/ten-facts-about-child-soldiers-that-everyone-should-know-8427617.html.

Terrill, R. (2009). World Criminal Justice Systems: A Survey (7th ed.). New Providence, NJ: LexisNexis.

Tulviste, T. and Ahtonen, M. (2007). Child-rearing values of Estonian and Finnish mothers and fathers. Journal of Cross-Cultural Psychology 38:137–155.

UNICEF. (n.d.). Introduction. In Convention on the Rights of the Child. Available at: http://www.unicef.org/crc/crc.htm.

United Nations. (1995). Ninth United Nations Congress on the Prevention of Crime and the Treatment of Offenders (A/CONF.167/7), Vienna: U.N. Crime Prevention and Criminal Justice Branch.

United Nations. (2005). Eleventh United Nations Congress on Crime Prevention and Criminal Justice (A/CONF.203/11), Bangkok: U.N. Crime Prevention and Criminal Justice Branch.

United Nations. (2010). Twelfth United Nations Congress on Crime Prevention and Criminal Justice (A/CONF.213/4), Salvador: U.N. Crime Prevention and Criminal Justice Branch.

Whyte, B. (2009). Youth Justice in Practice: Making a Difference. Bristol: The Policy Press.

Winterdyk, J. (Ed.). (2002). Juvenile Justice Systems: International Perspectives (2nd ed.). Toronto: Canadian Scholars Press.

Wright, K. (2010, June 04). Teen unrepresented in court. http://www.caribarena.com/antigua/news/police/9420-teen-unrepresented-in-court.html.

Yenisey, F. (2007). Age of criminal responsibility in terms of comparative law and alternate sanctions for children under the age of criminal responsibility. Bahcesehir University School of Law, Istanbul, Turkey.

Internet Sources

The following websites represent a sample of international organizations that champion the cause and plight of children and young persons who are young offenders or youth at risk.

http://www.ipjj.org/about-us/ipjj/.

http://www.oijj.org/en. The International Juvenile Justice Observatory includes among other links, specific links to juvenile justice in each of the five main continents.

http://www.unicef.org/ceecis/protection_7704.html. This UNICEF website includes all the relevant UN standards and guidelines on juvenile justice as well as a link to the Council of Europe Guidelines on Child-Friendly Justice.

http://www.unodc.org/pdf/criminal_justice/UN_Standard_Minimum_Rules_for_the_Admin_of_ Juvenile_Justice_Beijing_Rules.pdf. The United Nations Standard Minimum Rules for the Administration of Juvenile Justice ("the Beijing Rules").

Of Justice and Juveniles in Austria: Achievements and Challenges

2

KARIN BRUCKMÜLLER AND
STEFAN SCHUMANN

Contents

Overview of the Juvenile Justice Framework in Austria   28
  Adaptations of Penal and Procedural Laws   28
  A Gradated Concept of Criminal Responsibility and Intervention When Needed   29
    The Age of Criminal Responsibility   29
    Delayed Maturity as a Reason for Immunity   29
    A Need to Intervene?   29
  No Penalization of Status Offenses   30
A Brief History of Juvenile Justice in Austria   30
  Early Rules   30
  Juvenile Court Act from 1928: The First Separated Codification of Juvenile Justice
    in Austria   30
  The Juvenile Court Act from 1961: Establishing a Gradually Increasing Structure
    of Response   30
  The Linz Model of Diversion with the Aim of Avoiding Public Trial and
    Stigmatizing Conviction   31
  Juvenile Court Act from 1988: The Backbone of Today's Juvenile Justice System in
    Austria   31
  Recent Adaptations of the Juvenile Court Act from 1988   32
The Sanctions System: Types of Informal and Formal Interventions   32
  Diversion   33
    Nonintervention   33
    Interventional Diversion   33
  Conviction without Sentence or with Suspended Sentencing Decision   34
    Conviction without Sentence   34
    Conviction with Suspended Sentencing Decision   34
  (Suspended) Fines and Imprisonment   35
    Reduced Penalty Ranges   35
    Deferred Prison Sentences   35
    Suspension of Fines or Imprisonment   35
  Nonpunitive Reactions   36
    Preventative Measures   36
    Orders Based on Family and Youth Welfare Law   36
Juvenile Criminal Procedure   37
  Offender Protection and Support during the Proceedings   38
    Specialized Judges and Prosecutors   38

Strengthening the Young Offender's Procedural Rights 38
Rebalancing of Victim's and Suspect's Rights 38
Supporting Offender's Personal Development and Advancement in Future 38
Avoiding Pretrial Detention: Law and Practice Falling Apart 38
Restricting Publicity 39
Establishing Youth Inquiry Reports to Support Courts' Decisions 39
Avoiding Financial Burdens Affecting the Offender's Personal Development in
Future 39
Rules on Juvenile Imprisonment 39
Facts and Figures about Juvenile Delinquency and Juvenile Justice in Austria 40
Causal Factors for Juvenile Delinquency in Austria 40
Increasing Public Preparedness to Report 40
Juvenile and Young Adult Delinquency as a Phenomenon of Coming-of-Age 41
Conviction Rates 41
Trends in Juvenile and Young Adult Delinquency 43
Typical Offenses: Theft, Damages, and Criminal Assault 44
(Extensive Use of) Pretrial Detention and Imprisonment Rate 44
Sanctioning Practice 45
Public Prosecutors' Decisions 45
Court Dispositions 46
Conditions of Imprisonment 46
Compliance with International Recommendations: The Beijing Rules 48
Emerging Issues 49
Pretrial Detention 49
Juvenile Legislation and Practice 50
Juvenile Center in Vienna 50
Summary: The Austrian Juvenile Justice Model 50
Review/Discussion Questions 51
References 51
Internet Sources 53

FACTS ABOUT AUSTRIA

Basic facts: Austria is a relatively small country located in the middle of Europe, extending from the eastern and northern parts of the Alps in the west to the Pannonia lowland in the east. It is populated by approximately 8.4 million people of whom 2.4 million live in the capital Vienna and its surroundings. The official language is German. **History and European integration:** Founded as a republic in 1918 after the end of World War I and the collapse of the Austro-Hungarian Monarchy, Austria today is a federal democratic parliamentarian republic. Austria forms part of the Council of Europe human rights regime characterized by the European Convention on Human Rights and Fundamental Freedoms and the jurisprudence of European Court of Human Rights. A founding member of the European Free Trade Association since 1960, Austria entered the European Union (EU) in 1995. The EU not only guarantees the free movement of goods, services, workers, and capital within the internal market but also provides for closer internal and external political cooperation and enhanced police and judicial cooperation in criminal matters. In addition, in 2007, Austria formed part of the Schengen Free Travel Area Agreement where internal border controls were abolished, a common external border check was established, and a coordinated policy on visa, asylum, and migration was developed. **Population, demographic, and cultural factors:** The European internal market currently consisting of 28 member states and nearly 507 million inhabitants and the Schengen Free Travel Area significantly influence not only the Austrian economic and political situation but also its demographic characteristics as a multiethnic society. Additionally, Austria was a destination country for refugees and immigrants from southeast Europe, especially during the Balkan Wars, after the fall of the Iron Curtain and the failure of the former Yugoslavian state. Nearly 20% of the population has a recent migration background: 1.2 million are migrants of first generation; additionally, 0.4 million were born in Austria as children of migrants. More than one-third of those first- or second-generation migrants came from other EU member states, nearly one-third migrated from former Yugoslavia (excluding Slovenia), and more than 17% of the migrants have their roots in Turkey. Although Austria is a multiethnic society, its culture seems to be dominated by its Catholic tradition. Official statistics report that in the year 2001, nearly 6 million Austrian inhabitants were Catholic, followed by 0.38 million Evangelicals and 0.34 million Islamics. The average age in Austria is rising; currently it is 42. Roughly 0.8 million children are aged below 10, and 0.335 million children are between 10 and 14 years old; 0.377 million minors are aged 14 to 18, and 0.309 million are so-called young adults aged 18 to 21 years. **Economy and education:** The Austrian economy is dominated by the service sector contributing to nearly two-thirds of the Austrian gross domestic product (GDP) and the industrial sector contributing one-third. Only 2% of the GDP is based on agriculture. Austria is renowned for its tourism sector, forming an integral part of the service sector. In 2012, the unemployment rate in Austria was 4.3% on average, based on the International Labour Organization definition (national definition: 7%). In the age group of 15–24, the unemployment rate is 8.7%. The level of educational achievement is rising: Whereas in the early 1980s, only 4.5% of the Austrian inhabitants in the age group between 25 and 64 had graduated from universities or colleges, by 2009 this figure had risen to 14.6%.

Democracy, humanity, solidarity, peace and justice as well as openness and tolerance towards people are the elementary values of the school, based on which it secures for the whole population, independent from origin, social situation and financial background a maximum of educational level, permanently safeguarding and developing optimal quality. In a partnership-like cooperation between pupils, parents and teachers, children and juveniles are to be allowed the optimal intellectual, mental and physical development to let them become healthy, self-confident, happy, performance-oriented, dutiful, talented and creative humans capable to take over responsibility for themselves, fellow human beings, environment and following generations, oriented in social, religious and moral values. Any juvenile shall in accordance with his development and educational course be led to independent judgment and social understanding, be open to political, religious and ideological thinking of others and become capable to participate in the cultural and

(Continued)

FACTS ABOUT AUSTRIA (*Continued*)

economic life of Austria, Europe and the world and participate in the common tasks of mankind, in love for freedom and peace.

Article 14 § 5a Austrian Federal Constitutional Law

Overview of the Juvenile Justice Framework in Austria

The standards and guidelines for the handling of juvenile delinquents were mainly established in the Austrian Juvenile Court Act of 1988. The act contains both substantive and procedural norms dealing with juvenile delinquent behavior, including regulations on the use of imprisonment. However, the Penal Code and the Code of Criminal Procedure remain applicable if the Juvenile Court Act does not contain specific provisions. In the case of conflict of laws, the special rules of the Juvenile Court Act prevail over those established in the latter two codes.

The main objective of the Juvenile Court Act is to take into account the special development-related characteristics of juvenile delinquents. Therefore, the Austrian juvenile justice system follows a step-by-step approach from no criminal liability for those under the age of 14 to an adapted system of substantive and procedural rules for those between the ages of 14 and 18. In some cases, the act can also be extended and applied to young adults up to the age of 27 (see "Rules on Juvenile Imprisonment" (pp. 30 et seq.)). Additionally, the act allows for the exclusion of the criminal liability of juveniles under specific circumstances, and in addition to that, the range of sanctions provided for juveniles under the Juvenile Court Act goes beyond those sanctions provided for adults (including young adults) in the Penal Code.

Adaptations of Penal and Procedural Laws

The Austrian Juvenile Court Act 1988 (*Jugendgerichtsgesetz*) contains special rules for those juveniles who come into conflict with the law. These rules are adapted to the transitional stages that characterize the development from childhood to adolescence. In principle, the rules focus on supporting the young offender's future good conduct.

First, and most notably, a gradated system of sanctions is implemented to provide for adequate measures in each particular case; see "The Sanctions System" (pp. 33 et seq.). This system is analogous to the concept of *parens patriae* often expressed in North American discourse (see, e.g., Chapters 5 and 15).

Second, the Juvenile Court Act is also characterized by provisions to protect the juvenile offender during criminal proceedings. For example, juvenile proceedings have to be handled by specialized prosecutors and judges, and the act demands the presence of the juvenile offender's legal representative during the proceedings. Usually, the offender's parents will be the legal representatives. If the parent(s) do not participate, then the law enforcement judiciaries or the judiciaries must provide for other legal representation that will help to ensure that the interests of the juvenile are protected. Finally, the act aims to avoid a stigmatizing (e.g., labeling) effect that could affect the young offender's future development (see especially the section on the sanction system in the following text).

A Gradated Concept of Criminal Responsibility and Intervention When Needed

The Age of Criminal Responsibility

The Juvenile Court Act is primarily applicable to *juveniles*, defined as persons from 14 to 18 years of age at the time they (allegedly) committed the offense. Most of the procedural rights of the act also apply to the so-called young adults, persons between 18 and 21 years of age. In exceptional cases, some provisions on serving a prison sentence are even applicable to persons up to the age of 27; we will come back to this in the section on rules on juvenile imprisonment. Since minors (i.e., persons not yet 14 years of age) are below the age of criminal responsibility, they can only be subject to measures (e.g., institutional care) according to the provisions of the Federal Child and Youth Welfare Act 2013 *(Bundes-Kinder- und Jugendhilfegesetz 2013—B-KJHG 2013)*, which recently replaced the former Youth Welfare Act of 1989 (*Jugend- und Wohlfahrtsgesetz*).

Delayed Maturity as a Reason for Immunity

As mentioned earlier, criminal responsibility in Austria starts at the age of 14. However, § 4 (2) of the Austrian Juvenile Court Act points out that juveniles cannot be held culpable for any crime if their maturity is delayed, as they are then considered incapable of realizing the wrongfulness of their acts. To determine whether the juvenile in question is delayed in his/her maturity, an expert opinion is usually sought (see Box 2.1).

A Need to Intervene?

In addition to the issue of maturity, a young offender shall not be held liable for a misdemeanor if he/she committed the offense while under the age of 16 years, and there are no exceptional reasons that specifically call for the application of juvenile criminal law to prevent further offending by the young juvenile. The introduction of proceedings merely for general preventative reasons, namely, for reasons of deterrence or to support public confidence in the laws is illegal.

BOX 2.1   DELAYED MATURITY AS AN EXCLUSION TO CRIMINAL RESPONSIBILITY

"A juvenile, who commits a punishable offence, shall not be held liable, if
    1. for specific reasons he is not sufficiently mature in order to realize the wrongfulness of his act or to act according to this insight,"

§ 4 (2) of the Austrian Juvenile Court Act

"Embittered family circumstances after the divorce of the parents and poor performance at school are not enough indications for the delayed maturity of a young offender. To approve a case of delayed maturity, the delay must have been the result of physical or psychiatric illness, gross neglect or severe social problems."

Austrian Supreme Court Decision: 15 Os 184/08k, 21/01/2009

No Penalization of Status Offenses

In Austria there are no so-called status offenses. For example, truancy is not classified as a criminal offense. These problems have to be confronted by youth welfare authorities. For example, measures to be taken focus both on the minors or juveniles and on their parents. Yet, all the measures are outside the scope of Austrian criminal laws.

A Brief History of Juvenile Justice in Austria

Early Rules

Adapted rules on the sanctioning of young offenders date back to the *Constitutio Criminalis Carolensia* from 1532, when limited criminal responsibility for young persons was recognized (Bogensberger 1992). The Penal Code from 1852 represents the foundation of today's Austrian Penal Code. It ruled that those under the age of 10 cannot be held liable, while those between the ages of 10 and 14 were held liable only for severe crimes, but were placed in correctional facilities separate from adults. Meanwhile, for minor offenses, punishment of juveniles was left to the discretion of their family.

Juvenile Court Act from 1928: The First Separated Codification of Juvenile Justice in Austria

The first attempts to establish a special legal framework on how to deal with juvenile delinquents dates back to 1928 when the first separated Juvenile Court Act was introduced. The act embraced the philosophy that young juveniles required correction (i.e., education and guidance) rather than punishment. In fact, the approach of using conventional punishments, mainly fines and imprisonment, was seen as a measure of last resort (Neumair 1996). During the Nazi reign (1938–1945), the Juvenile Court Act only nominally remained in force; in practice, it was rendered inoperative by a large number of special provisions (Jesionek 2003, 2007). In 1945, however, it became an active part of the Austrian legal system.

The Juvenile Court Act from 1961: Establishing a Gradually Increasing Structure of Response

The 1961 Juvenile Court Act restructured the system of responses and sanctions applicable to juvenile delinquency. Mainly based on measures already available under the former Juvenile Court Act, a gradually increasing system of responses and sanctions were established. They ranged from refraining from proceedings by the public prosecutor authorities to warnings by the court, convictions with suspended sentencing decisions, suspended sentences, right up to fines and imprisonment. In line with the special characteristics of Austrian juvenile laws, which are rooted in the Juvenile Court Act from 1928, the court was established to determine only the minimum and maximum terms of imprisonment. The actual end term had to be determined by the executing authorities depending on the (re)education progress of the juvenile during imprisonment. In theory, this concept was based on the idea of education through the use of punishment.

Significant to the system of responses and sanctions provided for by the Juvenile Court Act was that any actions, aside from refraining from proceedings (which had only limited scope for application), could only be taken after the main trial. All these measures were to be registered as convictions in the criminal record. The harm of even a simple warning issued to the juvenile could potentially have a long-lasting impact on his or her development.

The Linz Model of Diversion with the Aim of Avoiding Public Trial and Stigmatizing Conviction

To avoid the disadvantages of public trial and formal conviction, in the 1980s, a model project for an out-of-court offense solution, the so-called Linz model, was developed. The stakeholders involved must have commonly agreed to this out-of-court offense solution. In cases of successful settlement, the public prosecutors made use of their option to refrain from further proceedings extensively. The model project has been successful, and it has been used as a blueprint for the new Juvenile Court Act from 1988 (Jesionek 2013; Schroll 2002).

Juvenile Court Act from 1988: The Backbone of Today's Juvenile Justice System in Austria

The most extensive amendments to Austrian laws on juvenile justice were made in 1988. This reform was based on the intention to promote decriminalization and rehabilitation of juvenile offenders (Jesionek 1990, Bogensberger 1992, Jesionek and Edwards 2010). It focused on measures intended to prevent the particular juvenile offender from further offending (i.e., special preventative effect). In doing so, the Juvenile Court Act set limits on the educational aims (Jesionek and Edwards 2010, Burgstaller 1997, Triffterer 1988, Köck 1999) of juvenile criminal law: Although the Juvenile Court Act originated from educational thinking, nowadays, it only allows considerations of educational needs with regard to sentencing to the extent as is justified and necessary within the legal framework of what is deemed to be a "special" prevention measure. This means that a sentence is only justified if deemed necessary to prevent the possibility of reoffending. However, it should be noted that neither grounds of deterrence nor protection of public confidence can be used as reasons to increase the severity of the sentence.

To find the most effective response for each young offender, cooperation between the courts and youth welfare authorities was enforced. This cooperative approach in the interest of the juvenile resulted in broadening the tasks of judges in juvenile criminal proceedings: They were no longer exclusively concerned with criminal matters, but were also in charge of related aspects of youth welfare. The latter measures were not based on penal law but were regarded as extrapenal, that is, those not strictly of a criminal nature. It was intended to provide criminal courts with the possibility to react as quickly as possible to a specific endangerment of the minor (Jesionek and Edwards 2010) by way of issuing respective orders (e.g., supporting the legal guardian or placing the child in a home). Moreover, a system of specialized juvenile courts was established in the larger cities, in particular in Vienna (Vienna Juvenile Court [*Jugendgerichtshof Wien*]). At these courts, the offices of judges, youth welfare courts, youth welfare agents, and Juvenile Court Assistance (*Jugendgerichtshilfe*) were all located in the same building to assure close cooperation.

The 1988 Juvenile Court Act accomplished additional important goals. The age of full criminal majority was raised from 18 to 19 years. Juveniles aged 14–15 years were granted immunity from punishment for misdemeanors in cases of delayed maturity (see "The Juvenile Court Act from 1961:Establishing a Gradually Increasing Structure of Response"). The range of dispositions for juvenile delinquents was dramatically improved. For example, measures of nonintervention and diversion were introduced as new and innovative ways (including victim–offender mediation) to reduce considerably the use of punishment as the primary response for juvenile offenders (see in detail the section on the sanctions system). Finally, for those cases where nonintervention or diversion is considered to be inappropriate, but punishment is deemed necessary, the law no longer stipulated for minimum sentences and minimum fines (see Box 2.2 in the following text).

Recent Adaptations of the Juvenile Court Act from 1988

Since 1988, the juvenile justice legislation has partly shifted back toward a more punitive-oriented approach. Two major achievements of 1988 have been undone. First, the age of majority was lowered again in 2001 to 18 years (Fuchs 2002). The rationale was that the reforms of 1988 had granted an age group, commonly associated with a great deal of criminality, undue access to the juvenile justice system. However, the procedural regulations for juveniles were expanded to young adults as compensation, recognizing that levels of crime in the age group of 18–21 can rise temporarily due to the difficulties associated with adjusting to adulthood. This approach, however, is too narrow to meet the needs of this age group and demand exists for a comprehensive criminal law for young adults (at least for those up to the age of 21; some researchers demand for those up to 25) (Miklau 2002).

The Vienna Juvenile Court was closed down in 2003. Its remit was spread out over several district courts (*Bezirksgerichte*) and the Vienna Regional Court for Criminal Matters (*Landesgericht für Strafsachen Wien*), respectively. As a result, the formerly well-established network for the exchange of information between the court and youth welfare organizations—especially the Youth Welfare Authority (*Jugendwohlfahrtsträger*)—was considerably reduced. Solely continuing cooperation between juvenile judges and the Juvenile Court Assistance was prolonged by way of relocating the Court Assistance to the building of the Vienna Regional Court for Criminal Matters. Some years ago, the (re)establishment of a *Juvenile Competence Centre* (*Jugendkompetenzzentrum*) was planned in Vienna (Jesionek 2007), but has been postponed for financial reasons.

Second, in 2007, the legal provisions of the Juvenile Court Act on criminal judges handling youth welfare issues were abolished and a strict separation of juvenile justice responsibilities of the criminal court and youth welfare authorities was undertaken. In the past few years, however, practical measures have been developed as pilot projects to renew cooperation between the courts and the other agencies involved in juvenile cases. The objective is to try and meet the best interests of the child.

The Sanctions System: Types of Informal and Formal Interventions

The sanctions provided for juveniles (but not for young adults) under the Juvenile Court Act cover a wide range of possibilities. In addition to the traditional sanctions such as fines and prison sentences, the Juvenile Court Act also includes provisions for convictions without punishment and extended forms of suspended sentences. Hence, alternatives for penalizing juvenile delinquents range from nonintervention to detention.

When deciding upon a sanction, consideration must be given to the sanction that has the best special preventative effect and, at the same time, offers the least severe consequences for the juvenile's lifestyle (Jesionek and Edwards 2010, Löschnig-Gspandl 2002). Fines and prison sentences are to be used as a measure of last resort (*principle of ultima ratio*). The Austrian juvenile justice system rejects the concept of a so-called short sharp shock, whether it be weekend arrest or short-term detention. It is considered common sense that the stigmatizing effect of those measures would outweigh any preventative effect on the juvenile's lifestyle in the future (special preventative effect).

Next, we will review and summarize the various sanctions that are available for juvenile offenders in Austria.

Diversion

Both the prosecution* and the court can decide on diversion.[†] As a precondition to a diversion order, the circumstances of the case have to be investigated to prove that the alleged offense was committed by the suspect. Diversionary measures for juveniles can be noninterventional or interventional.

Nonintervention

Nonintervention is particularly recommended in cases of petty offenses (e.g., shoplifting things of low value) committed by nonproblematic juveniles for whom already the mere reaction of authorities has a special preventative effect. But, it is not limited to petty crimes: Nonintervention is applicable if the maximum penalty for the offense committed is a fine or imprisonment of up to a maximum of 5 years (hence also the offenses of robbery and extortion are included), with the explicit specification that the crime did not lead to the death of any person (§ 6 Juvenile Court Act). Prosecutors and judges have to drop the case where interventional measures appear unnecessary to prevent the juvenile from reoffending. However, aspects of deterrence and public confidence in laws have to be taken into account by the discretionary decision (more details in Jesionek 2007, Schroll 2010, Schwaighofer 2001).

Interventional Diversion

Interventional diversion is compulsory where it is not possible to simply drop the charge, whereas the other forms of punishment do not seem necessary to prevent the juvenile from reoffending (§ 7 Juvenile Court Act). Conceptual measures of interventional diversion are—other than in cases of nonintervention—also applicable if the penalty range exceeds imprisonment of a maximum of 5 years or when ordering a fine. However, the juvenile's level of guilt must not be severe, and the culpable act must not have resulted in the death of

---

* The prosecutor in Austria has the obligation to be neutral: He/she is obliged to investigate both incriminatory and exonerative circumstances of the case.
† Notably, the concept of diversion was first introduced for dealing with juvenile offenders; after it was proven to be a valuable means, it was extended to general penal law and thus, with adoptions, also an option for offending adults.

a person other than a family member (Schütz 1999). If the penalty range exceeds imprisonment of a maximum of 5 years, then the guilt will typically be seen as severe. In such cases, specific mitigating circumstances are needed to opt for measures of diversion (Schroll 2010). Additionally, the juvenile suspect has to give his or her consent to the diversional proceeding (Höpfel 2002).

In addition to the above-mentioned disposition options, there are several other interventional measures available to the prosecutor or court.* For example, a probation order can be linked with other special obligations; victim–offender mediation that requires the victim's consent, community services, and fines without conviction. Such a fine may only be ordered if the juvenile can pay the money without causing undue hardship. In the case of narcotic drug offenses, health-related measures must be ordered by the public prosecutor or the courts if the offender is using illegal drugs, and/or meets the preconditions of the Austrian Narcotic Act. However, to use the treatment option, the offender's consent is required (Bruckmüller 2006; Bruckmüller et al. 2011a, Soyer and Schumann 2012, 2013).

When a juvenile is given a diversion disposition, it will not be included in a Police Clearance Certificate. This is an important point since police certificates have to regularly be provided when applying for a new job. Thus, public prosecutors may prevent a potential stigmatizing effect of a conviction by applying measures of diversion instead of indicting the young offender.

Conviction without Sentence or with Suspended Sentencing Decision

Conviction without Sentence

In cases where only a minimal sentence would be applicable, the court may convict a juvenile offender, but at the same time abstain from passing a sentence (Schroll 2010). In so doing, the young offender will have been given a warning without having been stigmatized with a formal prosecution. The rationale is analogous to the "labeling theory." A conviction without sentence is only applicable if the official conviction itself is considered sufficient to deter the offender from reoffending, and no general preventative considerations indicate the need for passing the sentence (§ 12 Juvenile Court Act) (Schroll et al. 1986). Any convictions that are accompanied without a sentence while being entered into the official criminal records are expunged after 3 years.

Conviction with Suspended Sentencing Decision

Where the court does not, or cannot, make use of a conviction without sentence, it may reserve the sentence in favor of a probation order. In accordance with § 13 of the Juvenile Court Act, the order can be between 1 and 3 years. The sentencing decision can only be suspended if neither special preventative needs of reoffending nor general preventative considerations of deterrence and public confidence in laws call for a sentence. The probation order can be combined with a personal directive and/or probation. Administering a sentence in retrospect remains possible in certain circumstances, especially if the offender disregards or

---

* § 7 of the Juvenile Court Act refers to § 90 of the Code of Criminal Procedure. The court is not mentioned explicitly in the Juvenile Court Act; there is a legal loophole contrary to duty (Schroll 2010).

breaches the order. The conviction with suspended sentencing decision will be entered into the criminal records but—as is true for a conviction without sentence—it will be expunged after 3 years, hence earlier than records of sanctions would be.

(Suspended) Fines and Imprisonment

Under the Juvenile Court Act, fines or imprisonment are proscribed as measures of last resort (*ultima ratio*) when dealing with juvenile delinquents. If they are unavoidable (e.g., in case of serious offenses such as murder), the court has to choose the particular sanction that seems to fit best the needs of the particular offender (hence, the sentence has to focus solely on special preventative aspects). When deciding on prison sentences for juveniles and their enforcement, general preventative considerations must not be taken into account. Furthermore, instead of short prison terms, fines can be determined.

Reduced Penalty Ranges

In Austria, the prevailing system of fines is measured by units that are based on the offender's daily net income. Since juveniles frequently have no income of their own, the limits are in such cases usually determined by their pocket money with additional considerations to the part of the family income spent on the juvenile and potential sources of income, such as summer or seasonal jobs (Platzgummer 1980, Lässig 2010). As prescribed under Section 5 of the Juvenile Court Act, a fine for a juvenile offender is half that of an adult (see Box 2.2).

In cases of prison sentencing of juveniles, the penalty ranges are also shorter than those for adults. The shortest possible prison sentence is 1 day. Any time spent in police or pretrial detention must be deducted from the total sentence.

Deferred Prison Sentences

An important option under § 52 of the Juvenile Court Act is the provision for juvenile offenders to defer the enforcement of prison sentence to complete his/her professional qualification. This is limited to remaining prison terms of up to 1 year (regardless of whether the sentence in total has been longer). The deferral itself can exceed 1 year. There are additional possibilities to defer an enforcement of prison sentences in line with the laws on imprisonment and with drug laws. Such deferrals can be granted to undergo medical treatment (e.g., § 39 et seq. Austrian Drug Laws) for family reasons (e.g., marriage, divorce, etc.), or to support the professional status of the convict. As regards § 39 Austrian Drug Law, it is noteworthy that if the convict undergoes a quasi-compulsory treatment ordered by the court, the convict will be granted a pardon (Bruckmüller et al. 2011b; Bruckmüller and Forstner 2012, Soyer and Schumann 2012).

Suspension of Fines or Imprisonment

For juvenile offenders, fines and prison sentences can be suspended either in their entirety (§ 43 Penal Code) or a portion thereof (§ 43a Penal Code). Unlike standard cases of adult convicts, where suspensions are limited to prison sentences of no more than 2 or 3 years, the unrestricted possibility to suspend a sanction or part thereof for juvenile offenders exists. When doing so, a probation order ranging from 1 to a maximum of 3 years can be issued.

BOX 2.2   REDUCED PENALTY RANGES FOR JUVENILES (§ 5 JUVENILE COURT ACT) IN COMPARISON TO THE PENALTY RANGES FOR ADULTS AS STATED IN THE AUSTRIAN PENAL CODE

For serving time in prison, maximum sentences are halved for juveniles, and there are no minimum sentences.

- For example, robbery: For adults, there is a penalty range of 1 up to 10 years of imprisonment applicable; for juveniles it ranges from 1 day up to 5 years of imprisonment

There are, however, two exceptions:
- If the penal code provides for a particular offense

  - lifetime imprisonment, or
  - lifetime imprisonment, or a penalty range of 10–20 years of imprisonment for adults, then the penalty range for juveniles is reduced to
    - 1–15 years of imprisonment, if the juvenile committed the offense when he/she was 16 years or older, and
      - 1–10 years of imprisonment, if the offense was committed under the age of 16
- A possible prison sentence of 10–20 years for an adult is replaced by a sentence of 6 months up to 10 years for the juvenile

For example, the possible sentence for committing an offense against life and limb (§ 83 Criminal Code) is a prison sentence up to 1 year or a fine up to 360 daily rates for adults. For juveniles, the possible sentence is a prison sentence up to 6 months or a fine up to 180 daily rates.

A and B injure C. The court convicts the two juveniles to a fine of 80 daily rates. A has a net income of EUR 420 per month, and B has a net income of EUR 1,200 per month (neither have any children). A will have to pay (EUR 420/30) = EUR 14 × 80 daily rates = EUR 1,120 as a fine. B will have to pay (EUR 1,200/30 =) EUR 40 × 80 = EUR 3,200 as a fine.

Nonpunitive Reactions

Preventative Measures

Other than the Juvenile Court Act, the Austrian Penal Code provides for so-called preventative measures (§ 21 et seq.) where this is necessary due to the dangerousness of the offender. But these measures, namely, the compulsory placement of insane or drug-addicted offenders into a treatment facility, are rarely applied in juvenile criminal proceedings.

Orders Based on Family and Youth Welfare Law

Additionally, the Federal Child and Youth Welfare Act determines how to administratively respond to juvenile offenders. These acts include family and youth welfare orders, as directives to minors who have committed a crime under the age of 14 years but also govern the

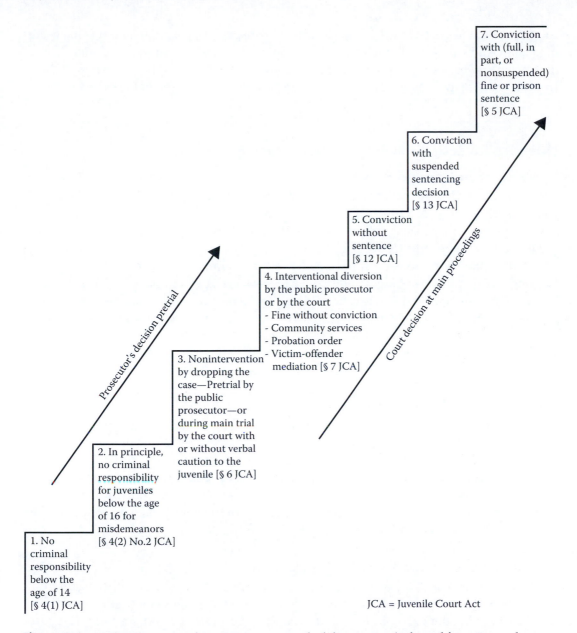

Figure 2.1 Gradated system of responses to juvenile delinquency. (Adapted from Bogensberger, W. (1992). *Jugendstrafrecht und Rechtspolitik: Eine rechts- und sozialwissenschaftliche Studie zur Genese des österreichischen Jugendgerichtsgesetzes.* Graz. p. 162.)

support of legal guardians of delinquent juveniles, or the removal of the minor from the family, and bringing the young person to a home or apartment-sharing community. The jurisdiction belongs to the youth welfare authorities and family courts (see Figure 2.1).

Juvenile Criminal Procedure

The special procedural provisions in the Juvenile Court Act are mostly applicable for both juveniles (aged 14<18) and young adults (18<21). These changes and amendments to the

Austrian Penal Code and the Code of Criminal Procedure are geared to two specific needs of juvenile and young adult offenders: They are aimed at strengthening the offender's legal protection and providing support during the court proceedings. In the meantime, stigmatization shall be avoided as far as possible, and the offender's personal development and advancement in the future shall be protected.

Offender Protection and Support during the Proceedings

Specialized Judges and Prosecutors

Specialized departments for juvenile cases have been established at the district and regional courts. Judges and prosecutors in charge of juvenile criminal matters are—according to law—required to be pedagogically skilled and to have a certain expertise in psychology and social work (§ 30 Juvenile Court Act). Where a court of lay judges or a jury is to decide, at least half of the lay persons must be experienced in dealing with juveniles. So, a court of lay judges consists of two judges and two lay judges, one of whom has to be or have been a teacher or someone working in youth welfare. The same accounts for at least four (out of eight) members of each jury. Moreover, at least one lay judge or two jury members, respectively, must be of the same gender as the accused (§ 28 Juvenile Court Act). The court in charge is determined by the young offender's usual place of residence to not unduly disrupt the young person's life during the trial (§ 29 Juvenile Court Act).

Strengthening the Young Offender's Procedural Rights

Some of the provisions of the Juvenile Court Act are particularly designed to afford increased protection: The young offender is entitled to have a confidante present during the entire proceedings (§ 37 Juvenile Court Act). Important procedural rights—for example, the right of access to the files (§ 38 Juvenile Court Act)—are expanded to the legal guardians of juveniles, however, not so for young adults. Yet, the applicability of mandatory defense and the access to free legal aid extended to the benefit of the young offender are granted to both juveniles and young adults (§ 39 et seq. Juvenile Court Act).

Rebalancing of Victim's and Suspect's Rights

Regardless of the recent improvements of victim's rights, in general the conflicting interests of victims and offenders are mostly resolved in the young offender's favor. "Private suits" or "subsidiary suits," for example, are inadmissable; some victim's rights such as joining the proceedings as a private party are altogether suspended (§ 44 Juvenile Court Act).

Supporting Offender's Personal Development and Advancement in Future

Avoiding Pretrial Detention: Law and Practice Falling Apart

The Juvenile Court Act calls for avoidance of arrest or pretrial detention of juveniles whenever possible. It is considered to be a measure of last resort, and it is only applied if the perceived drawbacks for the development and advancement of the juvenile's personality are not disproportionate to the impact of the alleged offense and the sentence to be expected. However, in practice, extended use of pretrial detention creates huge problems. Pretrial detention of juvenile (alleged) offenders came under discussion in the course of the year (2013). We will come back to this when discussing emerging issues of the juvenile justice system in Austria.

Restricting Publicity

The principle of publicity of trials can be restricted in the interest of the juvenile (§ 42 Juvenile Court Act). For example, if public proceedings might reflect negatively on the development of the accused, then the trial will be closed to the public and media (Schroll 2010). Furthermore, the young person's identity is particularly protected from being revealed under media law (§ 7a *Mediengesetz*).

Accordingly, the release of information on juvenile criminal cases is closely restricted to protect the young offenders and their future development (§ 33 Juvenile Court Act). At the same time, access to police records on juveniles is also restricted. The retention period for this data is reduced; usually, it will be automatically deleted after 5 years (§ 3 *Tilgungsgesetz*). Together, these measures are intended to encourage reintegration into society and to avoid any stigmatization that might occur.

Establishing Youth Inquiry Reports to Support Courts' Decisions

In Austria, it is typical for a so-called juvenile court assistance unit to be established. However, where this is not the case, those tasks are taken on by youth welfare organizations. They provide the court with youth inquiry reports. Those reports contain important information on the defendant's social, educational, and health-related situation and his/her background in general (§ 47 et seq. Juvenile Court Act). The information is intended to support the court especially in choosing the most effective sanction. Juvenile court assistance is also involved where diversionary measures are agreed upon.

In the case of youths who reoffend, their probation officer is entitled to be present and to be heard at the main trial (§ 40 Juvenile Court Act). In this way, the probation officer is able to provide necessary information to the court on which to base the most effective sanction (Schroll 2010). At the same time, he/she is also entitled to abstain from any statement in court to protect his/her client.

In addition to these reports, medical or psychological expert opinions can be obtained to help in establishing the young offender's situation and to support court decisions.

Avoiding Financial Burdens Affecting the Offender's Personal Development in Future

Alongside the limitations to fines mentioned earlier, the provisions on reimbursement of costs of the proceedings are limited in favor of juveniles and young adults (§ 45 Juvenile Court Act).

Rules on Juvenile Imprisonment

The Juvenile Court Act states that young offenders should serve their sentence in special institutions, or at least in a prison section away from adults, to avoid "criminal contagion."

Juvenile offenders up to the age of 18 have to be brought into juveniles' sections/prisons. Offenders who are not yet 22 years of age may start serving their sentence in the juvenile penal system, if there will be no negative effects on juvenile inmates. Subject to this condition, he/she can remain in the special juvenile section/prison up to the age of 24. If the inmate has a sentence that goes beyond that age, they may remain in the juvenile system if the remainder of the sanction does not exceed 1 year, or if the transfer to the adult system would entail substantial setbacks for the young person. Inmates, who are older than 27 years have to be transferred to a prison for adults.

For young prisoners, there are special enforcement regulations such as nutritional requirements, which must be appropriate to their physical development, and they should receive ample exercise and fresh air. In addition, school education and job training must be given special importance within the juvenile prison system. The objective is to enable the prisoner to complete any compulsory schooling.

Staff members in youth prisons are required to have special pedagogical skills and an understanding of the basics of psychology and psychiatry to support the inmates in the best possible way.

Facts and Figures about Juvenile Delinquency and Juvenile Justice in Austria

Causal Factors for Juvenile Delinquency in Austria

As is the case in most other European countries, in Austria no prevailing single causal factor causing juvenile delinquency has been identified. Rather, it is arguably considered to be common sense that juvenile criminal delinquency is rooted in a wide range of risk factors and circumstances that are at times unique to each particular case. For example, biological factors, especially any disturbances of personal development, social factors such as problems in the family, at school, unemployment, difficulties due to different cultural backgrounds, and issues of migration are mentioned. A recent Austrian study on shoplifting indicates that in groups, peer pressure has a significant role to play (Hirtenlehner and Leitgeöb 2012). More details are not known because there have been no comprehensive studies done to examine the potential causal factors (besides the one mentioned ongoing study) in Austria. Researchers adapt general findings from studies in Germany due to the comparable cultural and legal situation in both countries.

In general, juvenile delinquency is considered to be mainly a phenomenon during a time when juveniles are coming of age and juveniles are still searching for their own personal and separate identity.

Increasing Public Preparedness to Report

Again, as is the case in most countries, in Austria, police statistics are often used to prove the alleged rise of juvenile delinquency. Research indicates, however, that registered offenses in the official statistics of police reports are influenced by internal and external factors that are not directly linked to an increase or decrease in actual delinquency.

The official police-registered accounts of juvenile delinquency significantly depend upon the public's willingness to report alleged criminal behavior. However, it is assumed that the increasing trend to report does not correlate to an increasing danger of falling victim to crime (Fuchs and Krucsay 2011). This assumption is supported by statistics on juvenile convictions, which show that there has not been any increase in the same. Having said that, it is important to bear in mind that since 1988, legal options for diversion measures to close proceedings have been extended considerably.

Table 2.1   Police-Reported Alleged Offenders per Age Group

Year	Total No	Total BKBZ	<10 No	<10 BKBZ	10–14 No	10–14 BKBZ	14–18 No	14–18 BKBZ	18–21 No	18–21 BKBZ
2002	210,713	2,591	773	89	3,737	992	21,561	5,659	26,011	8,706
2003	229,143	2,845	801	93	4,427	1,147	25,804	6,815	28,736	9,678
2004	247,425	3,048	778	92	4,721	1,213	28,700	7,511	30,962	10,440
2005	243,493	2,979	709	85	5,033	1,287	27,678	7,159	30,784	10,393
2006	238,111	2,892	1,099	132	7,044	1,818	28,683	7,314	28,726	9,682
2007	247,021	2,983	676	82	5,496	1,441	33,068	8,343	30,092	10,119
2008	240,554	2,893	656	81	6,913	1,844	35,912	9,010	28,261	9,445
2009	246,378	2,955	724	90	6,074	1,661	33,063	8,289	30,571	10,145
2010	239,954	2,869	741	93	5,736	1,608	29,306	7,441	27,927	9,167
2011	259,028	3,088	771	97	5,565	1,601	28,045	7,251	30,486	9,914
2012	259,923	3,087	811	102	5,482	1,622	26,549	6,988	28,467	9,200

Source: BMI. Austrian Crime Reports (*Kriminalitätsberichte*).

Note: Police-reported alleged offenders per age group in absolute numbers (No) and per 100,000 inhabitants of the peer group in Austria (*Besondere Kriminalitätsbelastungszahl* [BKBZ]).

Table 2.1 shows how many offenses, respectively, alleged offenders, have been reported by the police between 2002 and 2012. In detail, the table provides data for all police-reported alleged offenses in Austria per year, as well as a breakdown of the data for minors, which is divided into two groups of child offenders below the age of 10 years and those from this age up to the age of 14. As noted earlier, criminal responsibility begins in Austria on the day of the 14th birthday. Hence, the next group of offenders—ranging from the age of 14 years up to the age of 18—will be held liable based on the Code of Austrian Juvenile Justice. Finally, the table includes data on young adults from the age of 18 up to 21, the so-called young adults.

To compare this data with other countries, the total figures (column marked No) are of limited value. Rather, it is helpful to focus on the number of police-reported alleged offenders of an age group per 100,000 inhabitants of this age group (the so-called *Besondere Kriminalitätsbelastungszahl*, abbreviated as *BKBZ*). This data is also included in Table 2.1.

Juvenile and Young Adult Delinquency as a Phenomenon of Coming-of-Age

The figures in Table 2.1 show that the delinquency rate of juveniles is two times higher than the average criminal delinquency rate in Austria. The delinquency rate of young adults (i.e., 18- to 21-year-olds) is even two times more than the average criminal delinquency rate. This data underlines the understanding of juvenile delinquency as being primarily a temporary phenomenon in the coming-of-age period. It demands for rules that account for and adapt to that fact.

Conviction Rates

Table 2.2 shows the total numbers of criminal convictions in Austria between 2002 and 2012, regardless of the offender's age in comparison to the total numbers and percentages of juvenile offenders and young adult offenders. In general, a slight decrease in the number of convictions can be seen. While interpreting the data of 2002 and 2003, one has to keep in

Table 2.2 Convictions per Age Group (Absolute Numbers and Percentages)

Year	Total		14–18			18–21		
	No	%	No	%		No		%
2002	41,078	100	3,278	8.0	(10.2)*	2,103	5.1[†]	(12.3)*
2003	41,749	100	3,178	7.6	(11.3)	3,745	9.0[2]	(12.5)
2004	45,185	100	3,336	7.4	(11.6)	5,500	12.2	(12.5)
2005	45,691	100	2,953	6.5	(11.4)	5,999	13.1	(12.6)
2006	43,414	100	2,889	6.7	(12.0)	5,594	12.9	(12.1)
2007	43,158	100	3,084	7.1	(13.4)	5,916	13.7	(12.2)
2008	38,226	100	2,988	7.8	(14.9)	5,259	13.8	(11.7)
2009	37,868	100	3,155	8.3	(13.4)	5,257	13.9	(12.4)
2010	38,394	100	3,063	8.0	(12.2)	5,246	13.7	(11.6)
2011	36,461	100	2,747	7.5	(10.8)	5,152	14.1	(11.8)
2012	35,541	100	2,562	7.2	(10.2)	4,903	13.8	(11.0)

Source: BMJ. Austrian Security Reports (*Sicherheitsberichte*), *Teil Strafjustiz.*
*   For reasons of comparison, the percentages of police-reported offenses per age groups are included.
†   The rising figures from 2002 to 2004 are likely to be explained by the decrease in the age of criminal majority from 19 to 18 years in 2002.

mind that in 2001, the range of age groups in the Austrian Juvenile Court Act was changed: Until December 31, 2001, those of 18 years were seen as juveniles; due to legislative changes from January 1, 2002 onward, they were now considered to be young adults. In doing so, the legislator adapted the Juvenile Court Act to lower the legal age from 19 to 18 years. The ensuing shift in changes of conviction rates in both age groups is due to the fact that the classification is bound by the *lex mitior* principle. This principle is understood to mean that if the law relevant to the offense of the accused has been amended, the less severe law shall be applied. The rules on criminal minority or criminal majority influence the sentencing range that is to be applied. Hence, the less stringent laws governing minors' criminal responsibility will remain applicable to offenders who committed an offense before 2002 at the age of 19. This is regardless of the fact that at the time they were sent to trial (most likely in 2002 or 2003), the age of criminal majority had already begun at the age of 18. The aftermath of this legislative change, which saw the increase of the age of criminal majority in 2001, resulted in a transition period that was likely to see the figures of convictions of young adults increase, whereas the figures of convictions of juveniles would decrease. And, in fact, both did so, as Table 2.2 proves for the period of 2002–2005.

Table 2.2 includes not only figures on convictions. Rather—for reasons of comparison—we also included the percentages of police-reported offenses per age group. If one compares both these rates of alleged juvenile offenses based on police report accounting and of convictions of juveniles, it becomes obvious that the conviction rate remains relatively constant (in fact, it even decreased temporarily), whereas, by contrast, the rate of alleged juvenile offenses temporarily increases from 10% to nearly 15% in 2008 (see Figure 2.2).

How could this difference be explained? To our mind, it can be assumed that the increased possibilities for measures of diversion to settle juvenile criminal proceedings—which were implemented in 2001 (see the section on the sanctions system in the preceding text)—have been effectively applied. The figures for young adults support this presumption as no comparable divergence is to be seen there—and, in fact, the new measures of

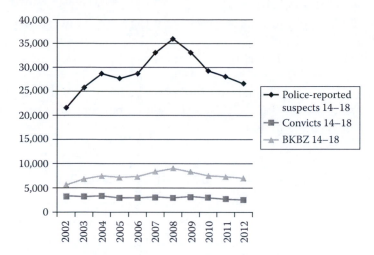

Figure 2.2 Development of police-reported juvenile suspects and convicts. (For database see Tables 2.1 and 2.2.)

diversion replacing conviction were limited to juvenile offenders and were not applicable to young adults.

Trends in Juvenile and Young Adult Delinquency

Juvenile delinquency and its handling by the criminal justice and welfare system in Austria has been repeatedly debated by professionals, researchers, and politicians for the past couple of decades (see among others, Burgstaller 1977, Schroll 1986, Triffterer 1988, Jesionek 2007, Fuchs and Krucsay 2011). In the meantime, juvenile delinquency remains a recurring topic of public interest in Austria. In recent years, public discussion has been mostly driven by high-profile cases (such as a rape of a juvenile detainee by other juvenile inmates in the Viennese prison of Josefstadt, see "Emerging Issues / Pre-trial Detention") or trends (allegedly) supported through statistical data being used by the media and/or by various political stakeholders. Yet, the role of media is neither uniform nor one dimensional. For example, media support for the implementation of alternatives to imprisonment for juvenile offenders mitigated the implementation of the present Juvenile Court Act in 1988 (Bogensberger 1992).

When examining trends and patterns, one must ask the question whether there is actually an increasing trend of delinquency of minors and young adults as often claimed in public discussion.

On average between 2002 and 2012, the data in Table 2.1 shows that there is an increase from 5,659 alleged offenses per 100,000 juveniles aged 14–18 years in 2002 to 6,988 alleged offenses per 100,000 juveniles aged 14–18 years in 2012. This represents an increase of 23%. In terms of young adults (18–21 years), the figures increased 6% from 8,706 alleged offenses in 2002 to 9,200 in 2012. These trends remain in line with the development of all alleged offenses per 100,000 inhabitants in Austria. This figure increased 19% from 2002 to 2012 from 2,591 to 3,087.

By contrast, the figures for delinquency by minors seem to paint another picture. The number of alleged offenses per 100,000 minors aged 10–14 years increased from 992 in 2002 to 1622 in 2012—an astonishing increase of 64%. Yet, an Austria-wide police obligation to register all alleged offenses by minors who are under the age of criminal responsibility was not established until 2008 (Grafl 2009). So, it is very likely that these figures are influenced by the peoples' willingness to report the offenses and of the police to officially record the alleged offenses.

Generally, the data has to be chosen and interpreted carefully. Not only are the trends influenced by external factors and by legislative changes but they also depend on the year chosen as a basis for such evaluation.

Typical Offenses: Theft, Damages, and Criminal Assault

The typical offenses (allegedly) committed by juveniles are property-related offenses (e.g., property damage and theft) and personal offenses such as assaults (see Table 2.3).

(Extensive Use of) Pretrial Detention and Imprisonment Rate

In 2013, sexual offenses, including rape, of other juvenile detainees became public and thus initiated a public and professional debate on pretrial detention and imprisonment of juveniles (e.g., BMJ 2013). Both the very application of pretrial detention against juveniles and the conditions of pretrial detention and imprisonment have been heavily criticized.

Figure 2.3 shows the number of detained juveniles each year over the last decade. It includes both pre- and posttrial detention.

Neither fluctuations over the years nor the average length of detention is included in Figure 2.3. Those factors might be indicated by the total number of juveniles detained at any given point in time in a particular year. In the course of 2012, 593 juveniles were imprisoned in Austria, most of them in the detention facilities of Vienna—Josefstadt and Gerasdorf; the latter being the only juvenile correction facility in Austria (BMJ 2013).

Table 2.3   Typical Offenses of Juveniles*

Year	Total	Life and Limb	Property
2002	5659	1573	4036
2003	6815	1614	3979
2004	7511	1739	4423
2005	7159	1712	3915
2006	7314	1854	4189
2007	8343	2174	4768
2008	9010	2270	5355
2009	8289	2135	4662
2010	7441	1997	4195
2011	7251	1987	3925
2012	6988	1846	3590

Source: BMI. Austrian Crime Reports (*Kriminalitätsberichte*).

* Police-reported alleged juvenile offenders (all offenses; offenses against life and limb; property offenses) per 100,000 inhabitants of the peer group in Austria (*Besondere Kriminalitätsbelastungszahl* [BKBZ]).

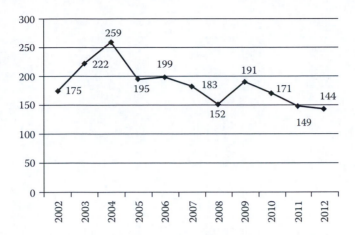

Figure 2.3 Detention of juveniles (reference date September 1). (BMJ (2013). *Untersuchungshaft für Jugendliche. Vermeidung, Verkürzung, Vollziehung. Abschlussberichts des Rundes Tisches.* http://www.justiz.gv.at/web2013/file/2c948486422806360142c82f9ac124b8.de.0/bericht.pdf.)

The juvenile percentage of the prison population in Austria is relatively high by comparison to European countries (BMJ 2013). In Austria, 1.6% of all prisoners are juveniles. The overall imprisonment rate per 100,000 inhabitants in Austria is 104.3 (this data refers to 2011). The percentage of juvenile detainees in Austria is comparable to Germany (1.4%) or Romania (1.5%), yet the former has a lower overall imprisonment rate of 86.8 per 100,000 inhabitants, whereas in the latter country, the overall imprisonment rate is 139.3. The percentage of detainees in Austria who are juveniles is far above France (1.0%/imprisonment rate 111.3), Belgium (0.7%/107.5), Slovenia (0.7%/62.1), and Poland (0.7%/an overall imprisonment rate of 211.2; twice as much as Austria), Switzerland (0.5%/77.1), Czech Republic (0.4%/220.9), Denmark (0.2%/71.0), and Norway (0.2%/71.8) (BMJ 2013; Aebi ans Delgrande 2013).

About one-third of all juvenile detainees in Austria are, or have been, in pretrial detention. In the aftermath of the rape that took place among juvenile pretrial detainees during the summer of 2013, which initiated an enormous public debate, this figure then decreased from about 60 juveniles on average to 40 juveniles in pretrial detention in October 2013. In December 2013, a task force initiated by the Minister of Justice tabled a proposal on how to avoid the pretrial detention of juveniles and how to improve conditions of imprisonment, where this measure seems to be unavoidable (BMJ 2013; see "Emerging Issues").

Sanctioning Practice

This section of the chapter provides a brief overview on the application of the sanctions system as described earlier.

Public Prosecutors' Decisions

Figure 2.4 shows the sanctioning practices of public prosecutors during the charge of pretrial proceedings. Upon reviewing, Figure 2.4 shows that more than 60% of the proceedings against juveniles are dismissed, whereas decisions for diversion or for indictment are roughly equal.

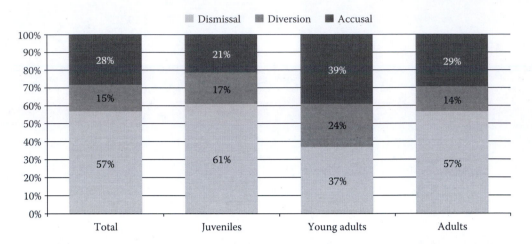

Figure 2.4 Overview of decisions by public prosecutors in 2010. (BMJ (2012). *Responses of Justice to Urban Violence. Urban Violence—Juveniles—New Media. Tackling the current challenges in Austria* [Country Report, Austria, of the 31st Council of Europe Conference of Ministers of Justice] http://www.coe.int/t/dghl/standardsetting/minjust/mju31/Country-Report-Austria-Final-09-08-2012.pdf.)

Table 2.4 shows that in terms of diversion, the majority of the decisions for diversion in 2010 by public prosecutors are for drug-related offenses under § 35 Austrian Drug Law. If a suspect is known to be a drug user, then the diversion disposition will usually be accompanied with a quasi-compulsory treatment order (Bruckmüller 2012; Soyer and Schumann 2012). The second-most common decision by public prosecutors is the use of community service, and probation orders without specific duties are preferred options.

Court Dispositions

Figure 2.5 shows that the most common disposition used by the juveniles courts is the use of a suspended prison sentence (i.e., 41%), followed by the ordering of a fine (18%). By contrast, both conviction without sentence (§ 12 Juvenile Court Act) and suspended fines are rarely administered by the courts.

Conditions of Imprisonment

Conditions of imprisonment are extremely dependent on the type of detention facility. In Austria, there is only one specialized youth prison in Gerasdorf—a little village—in Lower Austria near Vienna. Only male juveniles and young adults (and in exceptional cases, inmates up to 27 years, see the section on rules of juvenile imprisonment in the preceding text) are imprisoned in Gerasdorf. Although the prison is quite large, about six hectares, it only has 122 beds. Because there is only one cell block, the other areas are used as a school as well as for sports and workshop activities. The rest of the grounds include a large garden and sports ground.

At Gerasdorf, education and physical activity are given high priority. Therefore, school lessons for all ages are offered, as well as computer courses. In addition to formal education, the school also provides training for professions in such areas as bakery, automotive

Table 2.4   Decisions by Public Prosecutors in 2010 in Detail

	All Ages 2010		Juveniles 2010	
Total final decisions	**250,838**	**100.0%**	**25,355**	**100.0%**
Total dismissals	**142,853**	**57.0%**	**15,531**	**61.3%**
§ 190 Z 1 StPO No crime	45,594	18.2%	2,162	8.5%
§ 190 Z 2 StPO No evidence	71,563	28.5%	3,992	15.7%
§ 4 Abs. 1 JGG Under 14 years	5,879	2.3%	0	0.0%
§ 4 Abs. 2 JGG Lack of maturity	3,125	1.2%	3,124	12.3%
§ 6 JGG Diversion without intervention	5,552	2.2%	5,522	21.8%
§ 191 Abs. 1 StPO Minor offense	11,140	4.4%	731	2.9%
Total diversions	**36,957**	**14.7%**	**4,402**	**17.4%**
§ 35 SMG Drugs	7,955	3.2%	1,249	4.9%
§ 198 Abs. 1 Z 1 StPO Fine	11,344	4.5%	187	0.7%
§ 198 Abs. 1 Z 2 StPO Community service	1,770	0.7%	998	3.9%
§ 198 Abs. 1 Z 3 StPO Probation without duties	10,441	4.2%	869	3.4%
§ 198 Abs. 1 Z 3 StPO Probation with duties	725	0.3%	172	0.7%
§ 198 Abs. 1 Z 4 StPO Victim–offender mediation	4,722	1.9%	927	3.7%
Accusals	**71,028**	**28.3%**	**5,422**	**21.4%**

Source: BMJ (2012). *Responses of Justice to Urban Violence. Urban Violence—Juveniles—New Media Tackling the current challenges in Austria* (Country Report, Austria, of the 31st Council of Europe Conference of Ministers of Justice). http://www.coe.int/t/dghl/standardsetting/minjust/mju31/Country-Report-Austria-Final-09-08-2012.pdf.

Abbreviations: JGG, *Jugendgerichtsgesetz* (Juvenile Court Act); SMG, *Suchtmittelgesetz* (Narcotics Substance Act); StPO, *Strafprozessordnung* (Austrian Federal Code of Criminal Procedure).

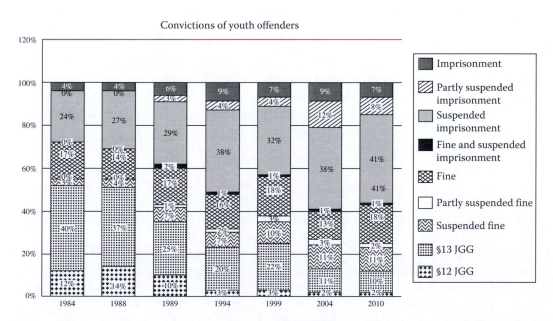

Figure 2.5 Overview of convictions of juvenile offenders in 2010. (BMJ [*Bundesministerium für Justiz*] (2012). *Responses of Justice to Urban Violence. Urban Violence—Juveniles—New Media. Tackling the current challenges in Austria* [Country Report, Austria, of the 31st Council of Europe Conference of Ministers of Justice] http://www.coe.int/t/dghl/standardsetting/minjust/mju31/Country-Report-Austria-Final-09-08-2012.pdf.)

**BOX 2.3   THE TYPICAL DAILY SCHEDULE IN THE
PRISON FOR YOUNG OFFENDERS AT GERASDORF**

6:30 a.m. Wake-up
7:00 a.m. to 7:30 a.m. Breakfast
7:30 a.m. to 2:45 p.m. Work or school
12:30 p.m. Lunch
3:00 p.m. to 5:00 p.m. Outdoor activities
3:00 p.m. to 6:00 p.m. Visitors
5:45 p.m. Dinner
6:00 p.m. to 8:00 p.m. Monitored recreational activity
8:00 p.m. All prisoners placed under lock, night shift begins

BMJ 2013

training, cooking, and gardening. In addition to providing educational services, the facility also offers therapy (e.g., individual and group psychotherapeutic treatment, and anti-aggression training), which plays an important role. Additionally, the young inmates are encouraged to use their leisure time in productive ways such as participating in various sports or theater plays (for further details and pictures of Gerasdorf, visit: http://strafvollzug.justiz.gv.at/einrichtungen/justizanstalten/justizanstalt.php?id=5).

As shown in Box 2.3, the inmates have a well-structured schedule comparable with a daily routine outside (especially with short lockup times) to avoid recidivism after release.

Outside of Gerasdorf, young offenders may be located in separate areas of a penitentiary so that they are kept separate from adult prisoners. The major challenge for such facilities is to be able to provide the necessary and/or appropriate support to meet the needs of the juveniles placed in them. This is especially true at the Josefstadt prison in downtown Vienna. In particular, the lockup times are quite long, because of administrative problems and the working schedule of the staff members. In Josefstadt, juveniles will typically be locked in their cells from early afternoon until the following morning without any out-of-cell time. Hence, the young inmates have a lot of time—in mostly overcrowded cells—to engage in inappropriate conduct.

Compliance with International Recommendations: The Beijing Rules

Austria ratified several international documents dealing with the protection of children who are in conflict with the law. To a large extent, the Austrian provisions dealing with juveniles are largely in accordance with the United Nations Beijing Rules, which constitute the internationally consented minimum standards for dealing with young offenders (http://www.un.org/documents/ga/res/40/a40r033.htm).

There are, however, some areas in which either the law itself or its practical implementation should be further adapted.

The age group of young adults constitutes the most important issue of law. Regarding the same, changes to Austrian legal provisions on juvenile justice should be discussed.

The Beijing Rules recommend extending the applicability of principles for juveniles to young adults as well. In Austria, however, this is not implemented comprehensively in national law. As explained earlier, only special procedural rules for juveniles apply to young adults as well; most of the other provisions, for example, concerning the sanctions, do not. The working group *Jugend im Recht* calls for the expansion of the stage-by-stage system of sanctions for juveniles, to apply to young adults also.

In addition to the need for changing the law, there is also a need for improvement in various aspects in practice. According to the Beijing Rules, those persons in charge of discretionary measures are to be specifically qualified. Accordingly, Austrian law demands such prerequisites for the judges and prosecutors who are dealing with juvenile cases. As noted earlier in this chapter, particular pedagogical comprehension or even special skills in the fields of psychology and social work are legal preconditions for becoming a judge or a prosecutor in charge of juvenile proceedings. However, failure to fulfill these requirements is not penalized. If a person without these special skills is appointed, no sanctions or other consequences will follow. Assumedly, in Austria, this explains why these rules are often ignored by those responsible for recruiting executives (Jesionek and Edwards 2010).

Pretrial detention is another topic that calls for improvement. The Beijing Rules postulate the need for nondiscrimination (2.1) also in cases of pretrial detention (13.1). In Austrian practice, however, more foreign juveniles are in pretrial detention than young Austrian perpetrators in similar cases. This phenomenon in ordering pretrial detention seems to result from legal requirements: Danger of absconding is stated as a reason for imposing pretrial detention. Hence, it should be discussed whether this is a just reason or rather a discrimination of foreigners.

The Beijing Rules (13.2) also call for alternatives to pretrial detention such as placement with families or in homes. In fact, Austrian law provides for "milder" measures. Yet, on the one hand, the authorities sometimes tend not to make use of these legal alternatives, and on the other hand, the factual possibilities of alternatives provided in Austria are very limited.

Emerging Issues

Pretrial Detention

Currently pretrial detention is the most widely discussed issue in Austria. Whereas experts were criticizing the situation for years, it was not until the case of a rape in juvenile pretrial detention in the summer of 2013 that the broader public and politicians picked up on this problem: A 14-year-old boy, who had been in pretrial detention in a Vienna detention facility for alleged robbery, became a victim of rape in the cell by three older inmates. During investigations already conducted, the report of the Juvenile Court Assistance had contained allusions to obvious developmental disorders of this juvenile. Nevertheless, the pretrial detention was ordered and adhered to. It is questionable, whether in this case it was permissible to order pretrial detention or if milder measures would have been sufficient and more adequate.

This case of rape received much public and media attention, and a task force was established by the Ministry of Justice. Consisting of practitioners involved in juvenile cases, this working group was asked to develop suggestions on how to avoid the deficits of ordering and enforcement of pretrial detention. In its recommendations, the task force argued for strictly ordering pretrial detention of juveniles as a measure of last resort (*ultima ratio*). Preferentially, the court should order—to the extent possible—alternatives to detention, for example, preliminary probation. New possibilities of alternatives should be created, such as placing juvenile suspects in an apartment-sharing community that is controlled and supervised by social workers. Additionally, community services should replace pretrial detention. To enable the judge to choose the best possible alternative for each young suspect, case conferences should be held by judges together with staff members of the Juvenile Court Assistance (BMJ 2013).

Juvenile Legislation and Practice

This case illuminated the problem of violation in prison (BIM 2013), which is also a challenge for the future.

A task force was set up that developed proposals for improvements and, alongside other (academic) working groups, proposed further reforms of the Juvenile Court Act. It demanded that cells in juvenile prisons generally be occupied by no more than two people and that more solitary cells be established. As mentioned already, the lockup time should be as short as possible not only to avoid violence in prison but also to enable the juveniles a daily routine comparable to life outside prison. In juvenile facilities, social workers should be appointed in addition to enforcement officers. Furthermore, corresponding training for staff members should be offered.

Moreover, the sanctions for juveniles should be expanded to young adults (Birklbauer 2011, Working Group *Jugend im Recht* 2012).

Juvenile Center in Vienna

Immediately after the closing of the Viennese Juvenile Court, the discussion to reopen it began. Today, there is still the demand for a specialized juvenile justice center in Vienna to reduce the problems especially in prisons (e.g., Working Group *Jugend im Recht* 2012). A variety of models are discussed; however, there is stagnation especially because of financial reasons.

Summary: The Austrian Juvenile Justice Model

Prior to the abolition of possibilities for criminal law judges to order family or youth welfare legal measures in 2007 (see "Orders Based on Family and Youth Welfare Law" (p. 36)), the Austrian juvenile criminal law could—at least to some extent—be considered as a *welfare-oriented model* (see Table 1.1 in the Introduction to this book). Now with the explicit separation of penal and nonpenal sanctions and the exclusion of nonpenal measures from criminal legal proceedings, the Austrian model has changed toward a *justice* or a *modified justice model*. Primarily, sanctions are ordered by the court or, as regards diversionary measures, also by the prosecution.

Overall, the Austrian Juvenile Court Act can be seen as a best practice model in protecting juveniles in conflict with the law within Europe. Throughout all the stages of proceedings, its rules focus on the juvenile and his/her future development and advancement.

Conversely, in cases concerning young adults, the act requires improvement. First of all, there is a need to provide for a more suitable response range for young adults, and it remains to be seen whether the political sphere will endorse this in the future.

Review/Discussion Questions

1. Is the Austrian law and practice sufficient to reduce recidivism of young offenders?
2. Why is it so important to shorten the lockup time for juveniles in prison?
3. Should all rules for juveniles also be in force for young adults?
4. Can you identify any best practice example in juvenile justice in Austria?

References

Aebi, M. and Delgrande, N. (2013). *Council of Europe Annual Penal Statistics. SPACE I. Survey 2011.* http://www3.unil.ch/wpmu/space/space-i/annual-reports/.

BIM (Bolzmann Institut für Menschenschrechte). (2013). Ending violence in custody. http://www.violencefreecustody.org.uk/; for the Austrian country report in particular, see also http://www.weisser-ring.at/Aussendung_Broschuere_Gewaltschutz_im_Jugendvollzug.pdf.

Birklbauer, A. (2011). Jugendkriminalität als Herausforderung? Antwortversuche aus Sicht der Strafrechtswissenschaft. *Journal für Strafrecht.* pp. 157–167.

BMI (Bundesministerium für Inneren Austrian Ministry of Interior). (annually). *Kriminalitätsberichte* (Austrian Crime Reports), Vienna.

BMI (Bundesministerium für Inneren/Austrian Ministry of Interior). (annually). *Sicherheitsberichte* (Austrian Security Reports), Vienna.

BMJ (Bundesministerium für Justiz/Austrian Ministry of Justice). (2012). *Responses of Justice to Urban Violence. Urban Violence—Juveniles—New Media Tackling the current challenges in Austria* (Country Report Austria for the 31st Council of Europe Conference of Ministers of Justice). http://www.coe.int/t/dghl/standardsetting/minjust/mju31/Country-Report-Austria-Final-09-08-2012.pdf.

BMJ (Bundesministerium für Justiz/Austrian Ministry of Justice). (2013). *Untersuchungshaft für Jugendliche. Vermeidung, Verkürzung, Vollziehung. Abschlussberichts des Rundes Tisches.* http://www.justiz.gv.at/web2013/file/2c948486422806360142c82f9ac124b8.de.0/bericht.pdf.

Bogensberger, W. (1992). *Jugendstrafrecht und Rechtspolitik: Eine rechts- und sozialwissenschaftliche Studie zur Genese des österreichischen Jugendgerichtsgesetzes.* Vienna Hanz.

Bruckmüller, K. (2006). Austria: A protection system. In Junger-Tas, J. and Decker, S. H. (Eds.), *International Handbook of Juvenile Justice.* Dordrecht Springer, pp. 263–294.

Bruckmüller, K. et al. (2011a). Juvenile justice system in Austria. In Dünkel, F. et al. (Eds.), *Juvenile Justice Systems in Europe—Current Situation, Reform, Developments and Good Practices.* Mönchengladbach, Forum Verlag Godesberg, pp. 41–98.

Bruckmüller, K. et al. (2011b). Medizinische und juristische Beurteilung substanzabhängiger (mutmaßlicher) Täter. *Journal für Rechtspolitik* pp. 267–278.

Bruckmüller, K. and Forstner, K. (2012). Gesundheitsbezogene Maßnahmen im Suchtmittelrecht. In Soyer, R. and Schumann, S. (Eds.), *Gesundheitsbezogene Maßnahmen bei Substanzabhängigkeit und Suchtmittel(straf)recht.* Vienna, NWV, pp. 45–77.

Bundes-Kinder- und Jugendhilfegesetz 2013—B-KJHG. (2013). http://www.ris.bka.gv.at/Dokumente/BgblAuth/BGBLA_2013_I_69/BGBLA_2013_I_69.pdf. BGBl. I Nr. 69/2013.

Burgstaller, M. (1977). Ist der Einsatz des Strafrechts eine sinnvolle Reaktion auf delinquentes Verhalten Jugendlicher? *Österreichische Juristen-Zeitung.* pp. 113–121.

Fuchs, H. (2002). Reif mit 18? In Moos, R. et al. (Eds.). *Festschrift für Udo Jesionek zum 65. Geburtstag.* Vienna, NWV. p. 67.

Fuchs, W. and Krucsay, B. (2011). Zählen und Verstehen: Jugenddelinquenz, erfahrungswissenschaftlich betrachtet, Bundesministerium für Wirtschaft, Familie und Jugend (Ed.), *6. Bericht zur Lage der Jugend in Österreich.* Vienna.

Grafl, C. (2009). Kinderkriminalität in Österreich—Grund zur Sorge? *Journal für Strafrecht.* pp. 192–199.

Hirtenlehner, H. et al. (2012). Ladendiebstahlskriminalität von Jungen und Mädchen. Der Erklärungsbeitrag der Power-Control-Theory. *Monatsschrift für Kriminologie und Strafrechtsreform* Vol. 95. pp. 307–330.

Hirtenlehner, H. and Leitgöb, H. (2012). Zum empirischen Status der Power-Control-Theory. Eine Replikationsuntersuchung. *Zeitschrift für Jugendkriminalrecht und Jugendhilfe* Vol. 23. pp. 175–185.

Höpfel, F. (2002). Das Freiwilligkeitselement bei der Diversion. In Moos, R. et al. (Eds.), *Festschrift für Udo Jesionek zum 65. Geburtstag.* Vienna, NWV. pp. 329–338.

Jesionek, U. (1990). Zum Jugendgerichtsgesetz 1988. *Österreichische Juristen-Zeitung.* p. 51.

Jesionek, U. (2003). 80 Jahre Jugendgerichtsbarkeit in Österreich—Rückblick and Ausblick (Parts I–IV). *Österreichische Richterzeitung.* pp. 66 (Part I); pp. 94 (Part II); pp. 118 (Part III); pp. 142 (Part IV).

Jesionek, U. (2007). Jugendgerichtsbarkeit in Österreich. *Zeitschrift für Jugendkriminalrecht und Jugendhilfe.* pp. 121–128.

Jesionek, U. (2013). Modellversuch ATA für Jugendliche. Das Linzer Modell (Oral History—ein sehr persönlicher Bericht). In Loderbauer, B. (Ed.), *Kriminalität, Gesellschaft und Recht. 40 Jahre interdisziplinärer Kriminalpolitischer Arbeitskreis.* Linz Traunu. pp. 78–88.

Jesionek, U. and Edwards, C. (2010). *Das österreichische Jugendgerichtsgesetz.* Vienna Hanz.

Köck, E. (1999). Der Erziehungsgedanke im Jugendgerichtsgesetz. *Journal für Rechtspolitik.* pp. 269–278.

Lässig, R. (2010). Kommentierung zu § 19. In Höpfel, F., Ratz, E. (Eds.), *Wiener Kommentar*, 2nd ed. Vienna Hanz.

Löschnig-Gspandl, M. (2002). Österreich. In Albrecht H. -J., Kilchling M. (Eds.), *Jugendstrafrecht in Europa.* Freiburg im Breisgau, Germany. pp. 269–302.

Miklau, R. (2002). Junge Menschen und das Strafrecht—Perspektiven eines Heranwachsendenstrafrechts in Österreich. In Moos, R. et al. (Eds.), *Festschrift für Udo Jesionek zum 65. Geburtstag.* Graz/Vienna, NWV. pp. 137–148.

Neumair, M. (1996*). Erziehung und Strafe. Rechtshistorische Untersuchung über Herkunft und Entstehung des österreichischen Jugendgerichtsgesetzes 1928.* Doctoral dissertation. University of Vienna.

Platzgummer, W. (1980). Probleme der Geldstrafe. *Österreichische Juristen-Zeitung.* pp. 29–35.

Schroll, H.-V. (2002). Die strafrechtlichen Sanktionen bei jungen Erwachsenen in Österreich. In Moos, R. et al. (Eds.), *Festschrift für Udo Jesionek zum 65. Geburtstag.* Vienna, NWV. pp. 189–204.

Schroll, H.-V. (2010). *Kommentierung zum Jugendgerichtsgesetz.* In Höpfel, F., Ratz, E. (Eds.), *Wiener Kommentar*, 2nd ed. Vienna.

Schroll, H.-V. et al. (1986). Das Linzer Konfliktregelungsmodell. *Richter Zeitung.* pp. 98–104; 124–128.

Schütz, H. (1999). Das schwere Verschulden als Diversionsgrenze. In Miklau R. et al. (Eds.), *Diversion. Ein anderer Umgang mit Straftaten.* Vienna Österreich, pp. 19–28.

Schwaighofer, K. (2001). Zum Anwendungsbereich der Diversion bei Jugendstraftaten. *Richterzeitung.* pp. 60–62.

Soyer, R. and Schumann, S. (Eds.). (2012). *Therapie statt Strafe. Gesundheitsbezogene Maßnahmen und Suchtmittel(straf)recht.* Vienna/NWV.

Soyer, R. and Schumann, S. (2013). Suchtmittelstrafrecht auf dem Prüfstand. Ausgewählte Ergebnisse einer internationalen Vergleichsstudie und Schlussfolgerungen für Österreich. In Loderbauer, B. (Ed.), *Kriminalität; Gesellschaft und Recht. 40 Jahre interdisziplinärer Kriminalpolitischer Arbeitskreis.* Linz. Traunu, pp. 337–346.

Trifferer, O. (1988). Dogmatische und kriminalpolitische Überlegungen zur Reform des Jugendstrafrechts. Juristische Blätter. pp. 342–353.

Working Group "Jugend im Recht" (2012). Thesen zu einer Reform des Jugendstrafrechts in Anlehnung an die "Tamsweger Thesen." *Journal für Strafrecht.* pp. 221–223.

Internet Sources

A report of violence in youth prisons in Austria: http://www.violencefreecustody.org.uk

About the Juvenile Court Assistance (but only in German) http://strafvollzug.justiz.gv.at/einrichtungen/jugendgericht/

Austrian Country report for the 31. Council of Europe Conference on Ministers of Justice: http://www.coe.int/t/dghl/standardsetting/minjust/mju31/Country-Report-Austria-Final-09-08-2012.pdf (especially interesting are the activities of the probation service "Neustart").

Details and pictures of the youth prison Gerasdorf in Austria: http://strafvollzug.justiz.gv.at/einrichtungen/justizanstalten/justizanstalt.php?id = 5

Youth Justice and Youth Crime in Australia

3

MICHAEL O'CONNELL AND
ELIZABETH O'CONNELL

Contents

The Welfare Approach   57
The Justice Approach   58
The Restorative Justice Approach   60
Age of Criminal Responsibility   62
Causes of Young Offending in Australia   63
The State of Young Offenders' Offenses in Australia   64
   Gender Issues in the Youth Justice Systems   64
   Type of Offense   65
   Youth Courts   66
   Youth in Detention   66
   Young Offenders under Supervision   67
   Overrepresentation of Indigenous Young People 67
Australia's Youth Justice Systems   69
   Australian Capital Territory   70
      Responsible Institution   70
      Courts   70
      Detention   71
   New South Wales   71
      Responsible Institution   71
      Courts   71
   Northern Territory   73
      Responsible Institution   73
      Courts   73
      Detention Facilities for Young People 73
   Youth Diversions Scheme   73
   Queensland   74
      Responsible Institution   74
      Courts   74
      Detention   74
      Bail Support Program   74
   South Australia   75
      Responsible Institution   75
      Courts   75
      Youth Training Centre   75
      Community Protection Panel   75
   Tasmania   77

     Responsible Institution   77
     Courts   77
     Custodial Youth Justice Services   77
  Victoria   78
     Responsible Institution   78
     Courts   78
     Youth Detention Services   78
  Western Australia   79
     Responsible Institution   79
     Courts   79
     Youth Bail Service and Intensive Supervision Program   80
Future Directions in Dealings with Young Offenders   80
Conclusion   81
Acknowledgment   81
Review/Discussion Questions   82
References   82
Internet Sources   87

FACTS ABOUT AUSTRALIA

Area: Australia, the great southern land, is the largest island in the world (7,692,024 sq. km), surrounded by the Indian and Pacific Oceans. **Population:** It has an estimated population of 23,240,102 (2013), with 4.29 million being under the age of 15. People who identify as Aboriginal people make up approximately 2.5% of the total population (2007). **Language:** The national language is English. **Capital:** Canberra is the nation's capital and the seat of the federal parliament, although Sydney is the largest city and capital of the New South Wales that has more people than any other state or territory. **Climate:** Being the driest inhabited continent, conditions vary—semiarid, desert, and tropical. **Economy:** Australia is an industrialized and affluent welfare-conservative state. Unemployment is 5.3% (2012). Australia has a social service system, including a universal health scheme known as Medicare and state-funded primary and secondary education. Its gross domestic product is about A\$998.265 billion. **Government:** Australia is a parliamentary democracy and constitutional monarchy.

Australia is a federation comprising six states and a Commonwealth, as well as two self-governing territories. Each state and territory has its own legal framework, which has evolved in a local context. There are, however, many commonalities and fundamental principles that underpin, for instance, the eight youth justice systems. The philosophy underpinning Australia's youth justice systems has shifted from the welfare approach to the justice approach, and more recently to the restorative justice approach, which has been impacted by the emergence of right-wing pragmatism.

In Australia, young people are often labeled *youth*. Youth can refer to a broad cohort of young people aged 12–25 years and sometimes in Australia, the word is associated exclusively with males (White 1990). The youth justice systems, however, deal with the young who have not attained 18 years in age. In this chapter, young people means those aged

10 years and above (i.e., the age of criminal responsibility) but below 18 years (i.e., the age of adulthood). The average national rate of detention of these young people in Australia is 31 per 100,000 youth, but there are marked variations in the rate of youth detention across jurisdictions. In New South Wales, for instance, the rate is 38 per 100,000, whereas in Western Australia, it is 56, and in the Northern Territory, the rate is 99. This compares starkly with the rate in Victoria, that is, 9 per 100,000 youth (AIHW 2012). The variations reflect the differing emphasis in policy and practice.

As this chapter will show, Australia has proved to be a "fascinating laboratory" in terms of the development and operation of youth justice systems (Seymour 1988; see also Wundersitz 2000). The chapter begins with an overview of the philosophies that have influenced and continue to influence the administration of youth justice, as well as points to some challenges for youth justice in increasingly conservative political and social contexts. Next, it profiles young offenders who come into contact with Australia's youth justice systems and then outlines the different laws that provide for and govern these systems. The chapter also highlights an important strategy or initiative in each jurisdiction and concludes with some observations about future directions for youth justice in Australia.

The Welfare Approach

On settlement by the British, Australia's colonies inherited the common law, adversarial criminal justice system. Like Britain at the time, there was no unique youth justice system—young people accused of crime were dealt with in the same way as adults. With the exception of South Australia, the colonies were convict settlements, so, many young people were transported to Australia as convicts; for instance, over 5 years, beginning in 1812, 916 young people were sent to Australia (Muncie 1984: 33).

Since its founding as a nonconvict settlement in 1836, South Australia has served as a "social laboratory" (Newman 1982: 5). It was one of the first places in the world to deal separately with children in law. In 1869, under pressure from public opinion, the colonial parliament debated the Minor Offences Bill that provided for magistrates sitting summarily to hear and determine charges against child defendants (Caldwell 1961). Rather than brand guilty children as criminals and send them to prison, the emphasis was on keeping child offenders in the community and rehabilitating them. In 1892, the colonial government instructed the police that all boys under 16 years and girls under 18 years should be detained in premises maintained by the Children's Department and tried in one of its rooms set aside for that purpose. The practice of dealing with children in a "special court" rather than the police court became law in 1895.

As happened in South Australia, in the other colonies also, the pendulum, impacted by a shifting social consciousness, swung in favor of a separate youth justice system. Young people's offending came to be understood as a "cry for attention" (Clifford 1978) by "incompetents" who had been neglected or abandoned, or who were victims of dysfunctional familial circumstances. Young people came to be looked upon as vulnerable and dependent, as lacking the mental capacities of adults, as impressionable and socially disabled. Crudely put, over time, "nobody's child became everybody's child." Reformers felt care and protection of young people should be paramount, and where not upheld, the state should intervene.

A better understanding of the psychosocial factors associated with young offenders informed those in government and nongovernment who urged rehabilitation as the prime objective of youth justice (Wundersitz 2000). The previous focus on young people's behaviors was replaced by an emphasis on the needs of the young. Courts were empowered to order young offenders into treatment intended to foster proper growth and development and resocialize the young offender (O'Connor 1997). Some rehabilitative interventions designed to reform young offenders, however, may be viewed as archaic when considered in the light of what is known today about what works in changing behaviors and reducing recidivism.

The essence of a "welfare" approach—punishment should be accompanied by care and guidance—prevailed for over one hundred years. Reflecting on the role of the Children's Court, the Full Court of South Australia concluded in 1979 that "the Court is trying to find out what is the best means of turning this delinquent juvenile into a responsible law-abiding adult, and that has really got nothing to do with the seriousness of the crime or the degree of complicity quote some other companion in crime, and no useful comparison can be made between an order made under a non-punitive system and a sentence imposed on an adult" (*R v Homer* 1979 SASR 377 @ 382).

Australia did not embrace the "child-saving" philosophy as happened in the United States (see Chapter 15). Bracey (1988) claims that philosophy was detrimental for many young people who, according to Platt (1977; see also Kupchik 2006) became victims of "class control" and a cheap source of labor. It is, however, evident that in Australia, like in the United States and other places, the ideals of welfare and care and protection were often a cloak of injustice on young people (Mullighan 2008). As Starrs (1967: 290) observed, the youth justice system could be an "instrument not only of arbitrariness but of oppression as well. Informality and compassion are not necessarily running mates. We may be doubly misled—first, into thinking that a benevolent purpose automatically ensures a beneficial result, and, second, into believing that the court always acts to benefit and protect juvenile charges."

The Justice Approach

During the 1970s, Australia's legislation providing for youth justice systems came increasingly under review. In 1971, South Australia in many ways led the reform when it completely redrafted its legislation. Later, several reports in New South Wales drove change in law and procedures (Comparative Youth Project 2013). A Committee of Enquiry in Victoria also reported youth justice law and procedures (Child Welfare Practice and Legislation Review 1984; Freiberg, Fox, and Hogan 1989), and in Queensland, a Law Reform Commission and an inquiry (Commission of Inquiry into Youth 1975) contributed to the prevailing debate. Likewise, committees reviewed the law in Western Australia and Tasmania (Blackmore 1978). Common to all, the welfare approach was much criticized. Australia's youth justice systems stood accused of being too permissive and of being preoccupied with controlling young people whose behavior threatened middle-class values (Freiberg, Fox, and Hogan 1988). Other accusations included that the existing systems failed to protect a young person's due process (such as the presumption of innocence) and failed to distinguish clearly young offenders from neglected young people (Warner 1993; O'Connor 1997). Thus, some young people, whether offenders or not, were able to be detained for acts or omissions for which an adult received little, if any, sanction (O'Connor 1997). Furthermore, it also became common to challenge the effectiveness of programs intended to rehabilitate offenders (Fischer 1978; Martinson 1974). Such influences on policy and practice stimulated considerable legislative change throughout Australia; however, that change was not as extreme as happened in the United States (Law Enforcement Assistance Administration and National Institute of Law Enforcement and Criminal Justice 1973).

Classical and neoclassical criminological thinking were ingrained in the justice approach that emerged (Murray and Borowski 1986). For example, procedural formality, due process rights and administrative regularity, as well as limited judicial discretion became common features of youth justice systems (O'Connor 1997). Unlike the welfare focus on young people's needs, the justice approach focused on youths' antisocial and criminal behavior, and certain and proportional punishment (Murray 1985; Chrzanowski and Wallis 2011). The dominant aims of such punishment became "deterrence" and "just deserts." As a result, young offenders were held to a higher degree of accountability for their actions as happened under the welfare approach and more punitive sanctions were imposed (Freiberg, Fox, and Hogan 1989; Wundersitz 2000). Consistent with the justice approach, legislation was introduced throughout Australia during the 1980s and early 1990s that removed noncriminal behavior from youth justice systems.

Although the welfare approach was discounted, its central concerns were not entirely disregarded in the justice approach. Rather, criminal justice concerns for the prevention and control of crime were melded with the welfare desire to respond humanely and understandingly to young people's particular needs (Seymour 1983). Thus, alongside the justice approach, the evolution of special measures continued. Innovative diversionary mechanisms were devised and implemented, such as the Juvenile Aid Bureau established by the Australian Capital Territory Police and staffed by male and female police officers whose duties included enquiries into missing children; liaison with school authorities and welfare services; counseling children; apprehending neglected or uncontrollable children; investigating offenses allegedly committed by children; and commencing court action at the request of the Welfare Branch (Young 1978).

Similarly, Juvenile Aid Panels in South Australia were established to provide an alternative to court proceedings for those young people accused of minor offenses, truancy, or uncontrollable behavior; to offer support and assistance to the young accused within his or her family; and to use formal "undertakings" and "agreements" to offer the young accused the opportunity to develop appropriately within his or her family and community (Owen 1978; Seymour 1983). Panels operating in South Australia were proclaimed a success when in the mid-1980s it was reported that the panel reduced the number of young people coming into contact with the criminal justice system and 8 in 10 young people who appeared before a Children's Aid Panel did not reoffend (Potts 1985; see also Wundersitz 1992 on the net-widening effect).

Law and procedures adopted in the Australian Capital Territory and South Australia did not differ greatly from those in other jurisdictions. Police and welfare workers who costaffed Children Aid Panels and Screening Panels in several jurisdictions, for instance, were tasked with the objective of reducing or eliminating further offenses by young people and also with protecting young accused people from being stigmatized and penalized for the rest of their life for offenses committed when they were young (Owen 1978; White and Haines 1996). Such panels were in addition also intended to improve relations between the police and welfare workers (Potts 1985).

By the 1980s, the justice approach coupled with welfare-oriented solutions for youth justice attained more prominence as worry about law and order and demand for stronger social regulation dominated discourse on dealing with young people's antisocial behavior and young people as offenders. Politically, the justice approach was an attractive way to counteract a "moral panic" stirred by media reporting on young people that was skewed and fed a nervous public. It also was a manifestation of the right-winged pragmatism that became a dominated element in the shift toward "conservatism" and the rise of right-winged think tanks (White 1990; Cunneen and White 2011).

As happened with the welfare approach, questions began to be asked about the efficacy of core elements of the justice approach. Some criticized it for not catering adequately to the demands of law enforcement and instead, giving too much ground to lawyers whose views were influential in bringing about change in the operation of the reformed systems (Seymour 1988). Meanwhile, others criticized the approach for failing to address the needs of young people satisfactorily, in particular, their personal problems and circumstances (Seymour 1993; Cunneen and White 2011).

The Restorative Justice Approach

Since the 1990s, the majority of jurisdictions across Australia have undergone some transformation with greater attention being paid to diversion underpinned by the principles of restorative justice. Australian studies have examined youth offending and recommended that diversionary programs, such as informal and formal cautioning and family conferencing, be implemented to prevent young people entering the court end of the criminal justice process, especially the formality of courtroom justice (Potas, Vinning, and Wilson 1990; New South Wales [NSW] Standing Committee on Social Issues 1992; Moore 1993; O'Connell 1993).

Consistent with the findings and recommendations of such studies, diversion is a central aspect of youth justice across Australia. Diversion takes a number of forms including informal cautioning by police and referral to services outside the justice system, such as drug and alcohol treatment services. Other diversion from youth courts include formal cautioning by police and conferencing.

Both formal cautioning for young offenders who commit minor offenses and youth justice conferencing, which are provided for in legislation in every Australian state and territory, embed elements of restorative justice. In other words, conferences involve the offender, the victim, the police, and other key stakeholders as appropriate in a process to examine the objective elements of the offense and identify ways to deal with the aftermath of the offense, such as the harm done. Youth justice conferences represent an attractive alternative to the problems that beset the legalistic and procedural aspects of the justice approach to youth justice (Seymour 1993).

Although youth justice conferences have become both desirable and attractive, it is unclear whether the promise matches the reality. Sometimes offenders, victims, and other participants are unwilling to act in restorative ways (Daly 2003). Sometimes offenders remain unmoved by victims' stories and withhold apologies, and sometimes victims remain angry and/or fearful (Hayes 2006; see also Pemberton, Winkel, and Groenhuijsen 2007). Another concern centers on low victim attendance rates in some jurisdictions (see, e.g., Office of Crime Statistics and Research, South Australia, 2000, 2005). Other evidence suggests that, compared to offenders, victims who attend conferences remain less satisfied with outcomes (O'Connell and Hayes 2012). Several evaluations show that smaller proportions of victims compared with offenders are satisfied with conference outcomes (Trimboli 2000; Strang 1999; Strang et al. 1999). Several other studies, however, show offender and victim satisfaction is high immediately following a youth justice conference (Palk, Hayes, and Prenzler 1998) and remains high even after 4 months (Wagland, Blanch, and Moore 2013), and some victims feel conferences are worthwhile even after a year (Daly and Hayes 2001). On balance, O'Connell and Hayes (2012) concluded that offenders and victims emerge from youth justice restorative conferences across Australia with a positive view of the process. That view, however, becomes less positive if young offenders' undertakings are not fulfilled.

There is also controversy regarding the effectiveness of youth conferences. One study was unable to find a significant difference in reoffending outcomes between youth justice conferences and the youth court (Smith and Weatherburn 2012; on recidivism see also Vignaendra and Fitzgerald 2006). Another study however, demonstrated that, over all, youth justice conferencing appear to be more cost-effective than youth (or children's) courts (Webber 2012).

Despite declines in youth offending and the purported success of diversions, especially conferences, Australia is facing a creeping conservatism. The focus of law and order activists and media on "habitual young offenders" and on particularly heinous offenses committed by a minority of young offenders has fueled the demand for stricter bail conditions and stronger enforcement; prosecution of young offenders as adults; and stronger emphasis on detention as deterrence. The old adage, "old enough to do the crime, old enough to do the time" has been popularized, notwithstanding the flaws in many of the assumptions upon which it rests. For example, it is assumed that adult criminal courts function differently from youth criminal courts, yet there is a paucity of evidence to prove this. It is evident, however, that adult courts are more offense oriented and tend to conduct proceedings more formally than youth courts. It is also notable that adult courts are looked upon to punish offenders, whereas youth courts are seen to be preoccupied with rehabilitating offenders (see Box 3.1).

BOX 3.1 CAN YOUNG DEFENDANTS WHO ARE CHARGED WITH SERIOUS OFFENSES (E.G., MURDER, RAPE, AND ARMED ROBBERY) BE TRIED IN A COURT SUPERIOR TO THE YOUTH COURT?

Jurisdiction	Other Court?	Governing Act
ACT	Yes	Children and Young People Act
NSW	Yes	Children (Criminal Proceedings) Act
NT	Yes	Juvenile Justice Act
QLD	Yes	Children's Court Act
SA	Yes	Young Offenders Act
TAS	Yes	Youth Justice Act
VIC	Yes	Children and Young Persons Act
WA	Yes	Young Offenders Act

Abbreviations: ACT, Australian Capital Territory; NSW, New South Wales; NT, Northern Territory; QLD, Queensland; SA, South Australia; TAS, Tasmania; VIC, Victoria; WA, Western Australia.

Although understanding of the ineffectuality of punishment in the treatment of young offenders has improved, the concept of "crushing" prolific young offenders and those who commit horrific violence prevails in Australia. There is a constant tension between that concept and the concept of "rehabilitating" young offenders. The former is popularized in tabloid media proclamations that "punishment should fit the crime" (Bessant and Hill 1997; White 2007), whereas the latter shifts the emphasis from exiling young offenders by detention to programs devised to tackle criminogenic factors peculiar to the individual and his or her social conditions. Two other concepts also feature in the debate on dealing with youth crime as a social problem: "deterring" potential (i.e., general deterrence) and actual deterrence of young offenders (i.e., specific deterrence), and "caring" for those young offenders who are in custody or guardianship of the state (i.e., protecting the individual from him or herself and from the community). That said, throughout Australia, there are elements of all four concepts in approaches dealing with young offenders found guilty of their crimes.

Age of Criminal Responsibility

There is currently uniformity across all states and territories with respect to the young people's criminal responsibility. A child under the age of 10 years cannot be charged with a criminal offense in any jurisdiction. Likewise, across all jurisdictions, a child aged between 10 and 14 years is presumed incapable of committing an offense, although this is a "rebuttable presumption." Thus, if a young accused person pleads not guilty, the onus is on the prosecution to prove that the child knew at the time of the alleged offense that what he/she was doing was seriously wrong. Further, in all jurisdictions, except Queensland, if a child aged 14 years and above commits an offense before their 18th birthday, they will be dealt with in the youth justice system. In Queensland, young accused persons are dealt with in the youth justice system until their 17th birthday.

There are also laws that govern the transition of a young offender into Australia's adult criminal justice systems. In the Northern Territory, for instance, if a young detainee turns 18 years while on remand in detention or serving a sentence in detention, within 28 days, he/she must be transferred to an adult prison to serve the period of remand or the remainder of the sentence (s164, Youth Justice Act 2006). Similarly in South Australia, any person aged 18 years or older remanded in detention and serving a sentence in a youth detention center, can be transferred to an adult prison for the duration of the remand or to complete the sentence (s63, Young Offenders Act 1993). In Tasmania, if a young person is jointly charged with an adult, the youth should be dealt with in the adult system (s27A, Youth Justice Act 1997). In New South Wales, if a person under 18 years of age has co-offended with an adult, then both might be dealt with in the youth justice system; however, on a finding of guilt, the adult will be sentenced in accord with adult sentencing rules (s29, Children (Criminal Proceedings) Act 1987). As explained below, the law in Victoria provides that a guilty adult offender aged 18–20 years at the time of the criminal offense can be dealt with in the adult justice system, but the court also has the option to sentence him or her to a youth detention center rather than to imprisonment in an adult prison (s32, Sentencing Act 1991).

All of Australia's legislation providing for youth justice systems imparts the notion that young people should be detained only as a last resort, which is consistent with the United

> **BOX 3.2   THE APPLICATION OF THE UNITED NATIONS STANDARD MINIMUM RULES FOR THE ADMINISTRATION OF JUVENILE JUSTICE IN AUSTRALIA**
>
> The Australasian Juvenile Justice Administrators (AJJA) is composed of Australian and New Zealand youth justice administrators. A minimum of one senior executive officer from each of the Australian states or territory departments and New Zealand who is responsible for the delivery of youth justice services forms the membership of the AJJA. The AJJA does not have statutory powers; however, the primary function is to work collaboratively across jurisdictions. Successes have included publishing an agreed minimum standard for practice that youth justice service agencies aspire to meet (AJJA 2009) and a process for young people who are under the supervision of a state youth justice agency to move temporarily or permanently to another jurisdiction.
>
> Further, in 2009, Australia signed, but has not yet ratified, Operational Protocol to the Convention against Torture and Other Cruel, Inhuman and Degrading Treatment or Punishment. The Operational Protocol allows for international inspection of all places of detention. The then federal attorney general Robert McClelland noted that a "national preventative mechanism" will be required so that all detention facilities are monitored by an independent body.
>
> Since 2006, Guardian for Children and Young People in state care in South Australia commenced regular visits to young offenders resident in the youth training centers. Advocates from the office visit these residents each month, and since 2012, the office now combines visiting residents once a month with an audit of records.

Nations Convention on the Rights of the Child Article 37(b) (Office of the United Nations High Commissioner for Human Rights 1989). It is also consistent with the United Nations Standard Minimum Rules for the Administration of Juvenile Justice (often referred to as the Beijing Rules) (Office of the United Nations High Commissioner for Human Rights 1985) (see Box 3.2).

Causes of Young Offending in Australia

Research demonstrates that while a significant proportion of young people will at some time commit some type of offense, it is only a small proportion that do so on an ongoing basis. Most young people who do offend will stop without any form of intervention and without ever coming into contact with the criminal justice system (Fagan and Western 2005). There is, however, a small group of young offenders who continue to engage in criminal behaviors, and this group has been found to be accountable for a disproportionate amount of crime (Weatherburn and Baker 2001). Research shows that the earlier a young person comes into contact with the criminal justice system, the more likely that they will continue offending for longer (Chen et al. 2005).

An Australian study (Salmelainen 1995) distinguished "high-rate" young offenders from "low-rate" young offenders. Lifestyle factors rather than developmental factors were the most important correlates of offending frequency. Drug use and the income needed to maintain this lifestyle factor were the most important correlates of such frequency.

BOX 3.3   YOUNG PEOPLE AS VICTIMS OF CRIME IN AUSTRALIA

Young people are not just overrepresented as offenders; they are also overrepresented as victims of crime. This is often overlooked in debate on young people and crime in Australia. The Australian Bureau of Statistics data on victims of crime show in 2010–2011:

- More than any other age group, 10–14 year olds were victims of sexual assault
- More than any other age group, 15–19 year olds were victims of robbery

Other data show that young people aged between 15 and 24 years are overrepresented as victims of assault (Australian Bureau of Statistics 2013a). Being subject to violence can have serious repercussions for a young person's physical and mental health.

The risk of apprehension was the only risk or punishment factor to be related to offending frequency. Notably, the study also showed that young offenders' attitudes toward the effects of their offenses on the victim had little association with their rate of offending. Conversely, see Box 3.3 regarding young people as victims of crime.

The State of Young Offenders' Offenses in Australia

Gender Issues in the Youth Justice Systems

Data collected by the Australian Bureau of Statistics depicts the rates of youth offending. In the year 2011–2012, within the juvenile age range, rates were highest for those aged 17 with 60 per 1000 young people charged with an offense (ABS 2013a). At all ages, males are more likely to be involved in crime than females (Beikoff 1996; Holmes 2010; AIHW 2012). Research does, however, show that young females' involvement in crime has increased since the 1960s (Fitzgerald et al. 2012). In 1960, for instance, young females were involved in about 1 in 13 criminal matters, whereas in 2007, they were involved in about 1 in 4 (Carrington and Pereira 2009). Further, research shows that over the past two or so decades, the increase in the number of young females charged with violent offenses in New South Wales is greater than the increase for young males (Holmes 2010) (see Table 3.1). Carrington and Pereira (2009) offer several explanations for such a trend, including the participation of young females in youth subcultures (e.g., street-based youth culture) and the role of social media as a facilitator of offending such as cyberbullying. The authors also point to the impact of legislative amendments that have, among other things, led to a shift away from the welfare approach (see The Welfare Approach above).

Notwithstanding, young males are more likely to enter the youth justice system than young females. For example, in 2010–11, the police were approximately twice as likely to proceed against young males compared to young females; young males were about three times more likely to be found guilty in the youth/children's courts and five times more likely to be in detention (see Youth Detention below). Alternatively, young females were more likely than young males to be supervised in the community as well as spend less time under supervision than young males (AIHW 2012).

Table 3.1   Rates of Offending by Age and Gender

	Male	Female
10	3019.4	693.7
11	4804.1	1391
12	9369.6	3568.6
13	18416.3	8811.1
14	29359.3	15372.9
15	41810.5	17803.6
16	52995.6	21259.6
17	65571.8	24127.7

Source: ABS. (2013b). Recorded Crime-Offenders, 2011–12, 4519.0. Canberra, Australia: ABS. Online http://www.abs.gov.au/AUSSTATS/abs@.nsf/Lookup/4519.0Main+Features12011-12?OpenDocument.

Table 3.2   Principal Offenses by Young People Aged 10–19 Australia-Wide in Year 2011–2012

Offense Type	Total Number
Homicide	26.9
Acts intended to cause injury	4,457.9
Sexual assault	370.0
Dangerous/negligent acts	102.2
Abduction/harassment	280.5
Robbery/extortion	496.4
Unlawful entry with intent	2,276.6
Theft	5,243.2
Fraud/deception	341.1
Illicit drug offences	2,925.1
Prohibited/regulated weapons	663.8
Property damage	1,816.5
Public order offences	5,908.3
Offences against justice	717.4
Miscellaneous offences	909.6

Source: ABS. (2013a). 4510.0 - Recorded Crime - Victims, Australia, 2012. Canberra, Australia: ABS On-line: http://www.abs.gov.au/AUSSTATS/abs@.nsf/Previousproducts/4510.0Main%20Features1 2012?opendocument&tabname=Summary&prodno=4510.0&issue =2012&num=&view.

Type of Offense

ABS data also shows that young people in Australia have been more likely than adults to be proceeded against by police for allegedly committing an offense. In 2010–11, there were about 300 young people aged 10–17 (the primary group in the youth justice system) proceeded against by police for every 10,000 in the population, compared with about 180 per 10,000 among those aged 18 and over (ABS 2013a). Table 3.2 shows the types of offenses (by principal offense) perpetrated by young people aged 10–19 throughout Australia in 2011–2012. In that year, the principal offense that was most prevalent for youth offenders varied in each selected jurisdiction. The most prevalent principal offense for which offenders aged

10–19 years were proceeded against in 2011–2012, as measured by the Australian Bureau of Statistics (ABS) for offender rates per 100,000 people aged 10–17 years, was

- Public order offenses in Tasmania (2076) and the Australian Capital Territory (623)
- Theft in Victoria (976) and Queensland (823)
- Acts intended to cause injury in the Northern Territory (954) and Western Australia (456)
- Illicit drug offenses in South Australia (891)

Youth Courts

In 2011–2012 in Australia, children's or youth courts heard and determined matters involving 33,604 young offenders as defendants, which is a decrease of 7% from 2010 to 2011. Defendants were most likely to be finalized for acts intended to cause injury (21% or 7065 defendants), followed by theft (20% or 6767 defendants). Of those defendants finalized in the children's or youth courts, 83% were finalized by adjudication (by a guilty plea, which almost three-quarters of defendants entered, or a court determination of their guilt or innocence). Almost 9 in 10 guilty defendants were sentenced to a noncustodial order (ABS 2013b).

A report by the Australian Productivity Commission (2013) depicts the ability of the courts to "clear" cases against the objective of providing court services in an efficient manner. Finalizations represent the completion of matters in the court system, incorporating adjudication, transfer, settlement, or withdrawal of the matter. Lodgments are a reflection of demand for court services (see Box 3.4).

Figure 3.1 depicts the ability of the children's courts in each Australian jurisdiction to finalize cases. Clearance rates higher than 100% indicates that during the reporting period, the court finalized more cases than were lodged, and the pending caseload should have decreased. Only Tasmania and the Northern Territory had clearance rates less than 100%, indicating that during the reporting period, the children's courts in these jurisdictions finalized fewer cases than were lodged, and the pending caseload most likely increased.

Youth in Detention

One of the more worrying trends is the number of young people in detention on remand waiting for their cases to be heard. This seems contrary to the principle that detention should be a "last resort"; however, an analysis of the relevant data indicates that many of those end up on remand in detention because they do not have anywhere to live. There are some notable variations when the data is broken down by jurisdiction, which can be attributed to differences in youth justice policies and programs across Australia that are elaborated on later in this chapter. For example, providing accommodation for homeless young people at risk of remand can help keep youth out of detention (Thompson and O'Connell 2008). Looking closer at commonalities for young people in detention, there are also blatant personal, educational, and familial disadvantages (Jesuit Social Services 2013). For example, in a study on youth in detention in New South Wales:

- Eighty-seven percent suffered at least one psychological disorder
- Seventy-seven percent were of below average intellectual ability

BOX 3.4	ARE YOUTH COURTS OPEN TO THE PUBLIC?	
Jurisdiction	Open to Public?	Governing Act
ACT	No	Children and Young People Act, s 61
NSW	No	Children (Criminal Proceedings) Act, s 10
NT	Yes*	Juvenile Justice Act, s 22
QLD	No	Children's Court Act, s 20
SA	No, but the victim of the youth's crime is permitted to be in court unless the court orders him or her to leave.	Youth Court Act, s 24
TAS	No	Youth Justice Act, s 30
VIC	Yes*	Children and Young Persons Act, s 19
WA	Restricted	

Abbreviations: ACT, Australian Capital Territory; NSW, New South Wales; NT, Northern Territory; QLD, Queensland; SA, South Australia; TAS, Tasmania; VIC, Victoria; WA, Western Australia.

* Unless otherwise ordered

		NSW	VIC	QLD	WA	SA	TAS	ACT	NT
Lodgements	'000	10.57	19.75	12.31	7.16	5.97	2.13	0.53	1.84
Finalizations	'000	11.16	20.06	12.53	7.77	6.08	2.02	0.57	1.64
Clearance rate	%	105.6	101.6	101.8	108.5	101.9	94.8	107.6	88.9

Figure 3.1 Youth/children's court clearance of criminal matters, 2011–2012. (Productivity Commission 2013. *Report on Government Services: 2012,* Canberra, Australia.)

- Seventy percent were diagnosed with a behavioral disorder
- Almost 50% had at least one parent imprisoned at some time (Indig et al. 2011)

Young Offenders under Supervision

Table 3.3 shows the number of young people (10–17) under supervision (community-based supervision and detention) of the youth justice systems by jurisdiction, gender, and indigenous status on an average day throughout Australia.

Overrepresentation of Indigenous Young People

Indigenous youth overrepresentation under community and custodial supervision is a consistent issue across Australia (see Table 3.3). Although the national indigenous juvenile imprisonment rate has declined by 33% since 1997, over half of the people aged 10–17 years in youth corrective institutions were indigenous. A range of diversionary alternatives to imprisonment (cautioning, conferencing, etc.) have proven to be effective in reducing reoffending but indigenous young offenders are less likely to be diverted than nonindigenous offenders. For example, indigenous young females are more likely than nonindigenous

Table 3.3   Rates of Indigenous and Non-Indigenous Young People under Supervision of the Youth Justice Systems in Australia on an Average Day

	Indigenous Male	Non-Indigenous Male	Indigenous Female	Non-Indigenous Female
RATE per 1,000 of applicable population	36.83	2.47	8.69	0.54

Source: ABS. 2013b. Criminal Courts, Australia, 2011-12, 4513.0. Canberra, AUST: ABS. Online http://www. abs.gov.au/ausstats/abs@.nsf/Products/4513.0~2011-12~Chapter~Children's+Courts?Open Document.

Abbreviations: ACT, Australian Capital Territory; NSW, New South Wales; NT, Northern Territory; QLD, Queensland; SA, South Australia; TAS, Tasmania; VIC, Victoria; WA, Western Australia.

Table 3.4   Number of Young Offenders under Supervision (Community-Based Supervision and Detention): Indigenous/Nonindigenous; Male/Female

	Indigenous Male	Non-Indigenous Male	Indigenous Female	Non-Indigenous Female	Unknown
ACT	25	85	9	21	0
QLD	575	631	145	143	4
NSW	685	890	150	164	121
NT	n/a	n/a	n/a	n/a	n/a
SA	125	195	29	51	24
TAS	50	227	14	59	1
VIC	164	1149	37	166	11
WA	n/a	n/a	n/a	n/a	n/a

Source: ABS 2013b. Criminal Courts, Australia, 2011-12, 4513.0. Canberra, AUST: ABS. Online http://www. abs.gov.au/ausstats/abs@.nsf/Products/4513.0~2011-12~Chapter~Children's+Courts?Open Document.

young females to be involved at every stage of Australia's youth justice systems. They were also more likely to be found guilty. As with indigenous young males, young indigenous females were overrepresented on supervision and in detention (AIHW 2012). Moreover, the "level of Indigenous over-representation among young [females] was higher than the level among young men" (AIHW 2012, 18) (see Table 3.4).

Despite variances in the dealings of Australia's jurisdictions with youth offenders, all operate consistent with the Beijing Rules under the principle that detention is the "last resort." Available data shows that on an average day, the vast majority, around 82%, of young people serving an order of supervision were doing so in the community rather than in detention (AIHW 2012). With detention being the last resort for sentencing of a young offender, it is interesting to note the seemingly high number of young people held in detention on remand. In Queensland, 71% of young people in detention on an average day were found to be there without sentence. The only Australian jurisdiction where the majority of those in detention were there serving a sentence was Victoria, where 25% of those in detention were held on remand (AIHW 2012). Furthermore, Australian research shows that approximately 65% of the juveniles reoffend within 6 months of release from detention, and more than half are imprisoned as adults (AIC 2013).

Australia's Youth Justice Systems

Governments for each state and territory determine the policy on youth justice in Australia and that policy is implemented by government agencies and nongovernment organizations. There are common policy directions of which some of the most common include (see also Figure 3.2)

- Greater use of police discretion to make informal cautions (or warnings) and formal cautions
- Precourt interventions such as bail assistance for young people suspected of committing offenses
- Alternatives to court proceedings in particular conferencing for young offenders who admit the objective elements of minor offenses
- Adaption of adult problem-solving courts such as the drug court and indigenous courts
- Preference for evidence-based programs to address offending while young offenders are under supervision in the community

Youth Justice Outcomes and Orders	ACT	NT	NSW	QLD	SA	TAS	VIC	WA
Pre-Court Diversion Options								
Informal caution	•	•	•	•	•	•	•	•
Formal caution	•	•	•	•	•	•	•	•
Restorative Justice/Family Conferences	•	•	•	•	•	•		•
Nominal Court Sanctions								
Reprimand	•	•	•	•	•	•	•	•
Fine	•	•	•	•	•	•	•	•
Good Behavior Bond	•	•	•	•	*	•	•	•
Restorative Justice/Family Conference	•	•		•	†	•	•	•
Court Imposed Community Based Supervision Orders								
Community Service	•	•	•	•	•	•	•	•
Suspended Detention	•	•	•	•	•	•		•
Community based supervision	•	•	•	•	•	•	•	•
Court Imposed Detention Orders								
Home Detention		•			•			
Detention	•	•	•	•	•	•	•	•
Supervised Release (parole)		•	•	•	‡	•	•	•

* In the Youth Court, South Australia, an order equivalent to a "good behaviour bond" is referred to as an "obligation" (s.26 *Young Offenders Act* 1993 (SA))

† The Youth Court, South Australia, has referred matters for family conference and has deferred sentencing while a victim-offender impact conference is held.

‡ In South Australia the Training Centre Review Board will sit as the Youth Parole Board when dealing with declared recidivist young offenders (s39 *Young Offenders Act* 1993 (SA)).

Figure 3.2 Options for diversion and sentencing in Australia's youth justice systems.

- An emphasis on deterrence by providing for the prosecution of recidivist or violent young offenders as adults or by threatening mandatory imprisonment
- Investment in detention facilities to enhance rehabilitation but also facilitate transition of young offenders who due to the length of their sentences, will be transferred to adult prisons
- More attention paid to pre- and postrelease assistance, such as life skills training and accommodation support, for young people leaving detention

These policies have not happened in a vacuum but rather complement growing concern for child protection resulting from inquiries into child abuse in institutional care; housing policy that has seen the disposal of public housing assets in preference for public funding for private housing; greater attention to educational attainment and school retention; and endeavors to reign in the costs of welfare and tackle the growth of social dependency.

The next section of this chapter presents a jurisdiction-by-jurisdiction overview of key features of the respective youth justice system. Each table identifies the relevant law, and the lead agency and court responsible for young offenders; moreover, a commentary on a matter particular to the jurisdiction follows each table. The section does not give a comprehensive report on the operation of Australia's youth justice systems.

Australian Capital Territory

Principal Act(s)	Key Objectives and Principles	Youths to Be Treated Differently from Adults	Youths to Be Diverted Where Appropriate	Youth Detention as Last Resort
Children and Young People Act (CAYPA) 2008 and Crimes (Restorative Justice) Act (CRJA) 2004	S 94 CAYPA; s 6 CRJA	S 94(1)(b), (g) CAYPA	S 7 CRJA	S 94(1)(f) CAYPA
Other Relevant Act(s)				
Bail Act 1992				
Crimes (Sentence Administration) Act 2005				
Crimes (Sentencing) Act 2005				

Responsible Institution
The lead agency for youth justice in the ACT is the Office of Children, Youth and Family Support, within the Department of Disability, Housing and Community Services.

Courts
There is the Children's Court for minor offenses; serious indictable or prescribed offenses are heard before the Supreme Court with a youth justice court officer present.

The Australian Capital Territory (ACT) has the most highly educated workforce in Australia (Canberra Women in Business 2013). In November 2013, ACT (4.2%) recorded the lowest trend in unemployment rate (ACT Chief Minister and Treasury Report 2013). The median household income per week for households in ACT in 2009–10 was $2008 compared to $1320 nationally. ACT has also the highest gross household disposable income per capita in Australia (Peake 2013).

The majority of young people in ACT do not have any contact with police or the youth justice system. In 2009–10, ACT had the lowest number of offenders (1%) of the Australian offender population aged 10 years and over. ACT also had the lowest offender rate with 933 offenders per 100,000 population aged 10 years and over. There are, however, a small proportion of young people in ACT who come into contact with the police and youth justice system as a result of offending behavior or alleged offending behavior. Of those young people who do come into contact with the police, the majority are proceeded against by police only once. In 2009–2010, only about 20% of offenders were proceeded against by police more than once (ABS 2011).

Detention

Bimberi Youth Detention Centre is a modern, purpose-built, 40-bedded, youth detention facility staffed and managed by the Department of Disability, Housing and Community Services (ACT Department of Disability, Housing and Community Services, Office for hildren, Youth and Family Support n.d.). The opening of Bimberi in 2009 signaled a new direction in the care of young people in the ACT youth justice system as it was based on the principles of active engagement with young people and their families, and a human rights framework and philosophy (see also ACT Human Rights Commission 2011).

New South Wales

Principal Act(s)	Key Objectives and Principles	Youths to Be Treated Differently from Adults	Youths to Be Diverted Where Appropriate	Youth Detention as Last Resort
Children (Criminal Proceedings Act) (CCPA)1987; Young Offenders Act (YOA) 1997	S 7 YOA; S 6 CCPA	S 6(b) CCPA	S 7 (c) YOA	S 33 CCPA
Other Relevant Act(s)				
Children (Community Services Orders) Act 1987				
Children (Detention Centres) Act 1987				
Children (Detention Centre) Regulation 2005				
Children (Interstate Transfer of Offenders) Act 1988				
Criminal Procedure Act 1986				

Responsible Institution

The Department of Attorney General and Justice is the lead agency regarding youth justice in New South Wales.

Courts

The Children's Court deals with the following types of cases across New South Wales (NSW) involving children and young people:

- Criminal cases where the defendant/s were under the age of 18 at the time of the alleged offense
- Care and protection cases that involved children and young people under 18 years

- Traffic cases where the defendant is not old enough to hold a driver's license or where involved with another criminal offense
- Application for apprehended violence order where the defendant is under 18 years of age
- Breaches of, or eligibility for, parole of children and young people
- Applications for compulsory schooling orders

There are seven juvenile detention facilities in NSW, all of which offer health, education, and spiritual and personal development services. Cobham Juvenile Justice Centre is the principal remand center for males aged 15 and over. Juniperina Juvenile Justice Centre is the only facility for young women in NSW and is also the only facility to exclusively accommodate young women in Australia. Reiby Juvenile Justice Centre accommodates males under 16 years and operates a dedicated unit for the males aged 10–16 with extreme behavioral difficulties. Frank Baxter Juvenile Justice Centre is NSW's largest facility and accommodates males aged 16–21 years. Orana Juvenile Justice Centre is the smallest and accommodates males from the central and far west areas of NSW. Riverina Juvenile Justice Centre accommodates low-to-medium risk males from the Riverina and southwestern areas of NSW. Acmena Juvenile Justice Centre accommodates young males from the far north and midcoastal areas of NSW.

There are a number of government-funded services and programs that aim to address the various needs of young people; however, most commonly it is not until a court orders supervision that an assessment of a young person's criminogenic risk and need is undertaken. Therefore, it is only after a young person has had multiple and increasingly serious contact with the criminal justice system that he/she receives an intervention aimed at reducing criminal behavior.

NSW Department of Attorney General and Justice have recently introduced a new approach to early intervention for 10- to 17-year-old young offenders. Named *Youth on Track*, this voluntary program provides the police and education system with an avenue to refer young people who are known to be at high risk of offending to support without requiring a mandate (NSW Government n.d.).

Youth on Track is provided through formalized partnership with a nongovernment organization. Young people, who fit the cohort, and their families are engaged in case work support and programs targeted at addressing a young person's identified offending-related needs. Evidence demonstrates that working intensively with young people together with their families can achieve significant shifts in behavior (Richards, Rosevear, and Gilbert 2011; Thompson and O'Connell 2008).

This new approach facilitates coordinated, intensive interventions for young people and families before they become entrenched in the juvenile justice system.

For young offenders at the other end of the offending spectrum, the Serious Young Offenders Review Panel (SYORP) is an independent body, which makes recommendations on the reclassification of and the granting of leave to young people in custody for serious indictable offenses (Juvenile Justice, Attorney-General and Justice NSW 2013). The SYORP was established as a recommendation under the NSW Juvenile Justice Advisory Council's (JJAC) Green Paper (published in 1993). The panel must balance he safety and punishment expectations of the community with needs and expectations of the young people and their families, while maintaining accordance with legislation.

Northern Territory

Principal Act(s)	Key Objectives and Principles	Youths to Be Treated Differently from Adults	Youths to Be Diverted Where Appropriate	Youth Detention as Last Resort
Youth Justice Act 2006	S 4	S 4 (b), (d), (r)	S 4(q)	S 4 (c)
Other Relevant Act(s)				
Care and Protection of Children Act 2007				
Cross-border Justice Act 2009				
Youth Justice Regulations 2005				

Responsible Institution

The Department of Attorney-General and Justice as well as the Department for Correctional Services share responsibility for youth justice in the Northern Territory. The Department for Correctional Services operates both adult prisons and youth detention centres.

Courts

The Youth Justice Court is established by the Youth Justice Act and hears charges against young people who were under 18 years at the time of being charged or appearing before the court. The Supreme Court may be referred to for trial or sentence if the offense is considered to be particularly serious.

Detention Facilities for Young People

Alice Springs Juvenile Detention Centre operates within the Alice Springs Correctional Facility.

Youth Diversions Scheme

The Northern Territory Police Youth Diversions Scheme provides a structure for police provision of diversionary programming including warnings, cautions, restorative conferencing, and community-based skill development programs. Alongside a range of structured programs for youth at risk, police also provide formal case management.

Family Responsibility Orders hold parents accountable for the repeat offending behavior of their children. Parents are provided with support to make lifestyle changes for themselves and their children, while adhering to imposed conditions. Among other things, parents may be obligated to participate in rehabilitation programs; to ensure their child attends school or other educational institution; and, to enforce a curfew or non-association order. An inability to abide by a Family Responsibility Order can result in a fine or the seizure of nonessential household items.

Despite these measures, in 2011–2012, the Northern Territory had the highest rate (143 per 100,000) of incarceration of young offenders in Australia. Indigenous young offenders account for 90% of those held in custodial centers; 60% of these are sentenced (Northern Territory Criminal Justice Research and Statistics Unit 2013).

Queensland

Principal Act(s)	Key Objectives and Principles	Youths to Be Treated Differently from Adults	Youths to Be Diverted Where Appropriate	Youth Detention as Last Resort
Youth Justice Act 1992	Sch 1	Sch 1: 12, 14, 18	Sch 1: 5	Sch 1: 17
Other Relevant Act(s)				
Bail Act 1980				
Children's Court Act 1992				
Child Protection (Offender Prohibition Order) Act 2008				
Child Protection (Offender Reporting) Act 2004				
Criminal Code				
Police Powers and Responsibilities Act 200				
Youth Justice Regulation 2003				
Young Offenders (Interstate Transfer) Act 1987				

Responsible Institution

In Queensland the Department of Attorney-General and Justice in the lead agency in accordance with the Youth Justice Intervention Framework.

Courts

Apart from the Children's Court of Queensland, serious indictable and prescribed offenses can be directed to the District Courts or the Supreme Court.

Detention

There are two custodial centers in Queensland, the Brisbane Youth Detention Centre and Cleveland Youth Detention Centre.

Bail Support Program

Queensland offers a Bail Support Program that is primarily aimed at reducing the number of young people held on remand. The program provides support for young people to meet their bail conditions (including obligations) alongside some behavioural interventions. It has the capacity to both support young people with existing accommodation and to provide accommodation for those who may otherwise be held in custody due to lack of accommodation.

Indigenous support officers have recently been introduced to work within the conferencing unit and community and custodial centers in several areas with a high proportion of Aboriginal and Torres Strait Islanders in contact with the youth justice system. The roles involve facilitation of communication between the indigenous communities and youth justice staff and providing culturally appropriate programs and services.

South Australia

Principal Act(s)	Key Objectives and Principles	Youths to Be Treated Differently from Adults	Youths to Be Diverted Where Appropriate	Youth Detention as Last Resort
Young Offenders Act (YOA) 1993	S 3	S 3 (1)	S 3(2a), (3)	S 23(4) YOA
Other Relevant Act(s)				
Bail Act 1985				
Criminal Law (Sentencing) Act 1988				
Family and Community Services Act 1972				
Youth Court Act 1993				

Responsible Institution

The Youth Justice Directorate, Department for Communities and Social Inclusion is the lead agency for youth justice in South Australia, although the Courts Administration Authority operates the Youth Court, including the Family Conferencing Unit (see Box 3.5)

Courts

There is the Youth Court of South Australia; serious indictable or prescribed offenses can be referred to the Supreme Court.

Youth Training Centre

After years of intense criticism about the conditions of its youth detention facilities, in 2012, South Australia built and began operating the Adelaide Youth Training Centre. This facility operates over two campuses, separating the majority of those held in police custody from sentenced offenders, and young people with intensive support needs from the general population. In establishing the Adelaide Youth Training Centre, the department took the opportunity to modify its management of incarcerated youth and implemented a "client outcome framework" and "behavior management framework" conducive with diffusion of emotional or aggressive behaviors within detention. This new service approach involves an open-campus design for the detention facility, along with adoption of contemporary evidence-based approaches and individualized programming toward "young person outcomes."

Community Protection Panel

In January 2009, consistent with a recommendation of an inquiry into "breaking the cycle" of youth offending, a Community Protection Panel was established to provide an interagency response to serious, repeat young offenders as well as to enhance community safety. Currently, the targeted offender cohort is aged mostly between 14 and 18 years, and each offender is comprehensively assessed and then intensively managed. Yet a review of court data pertaining to 38 frequent, repeat offenders revealed that about two-thirds of these offenders are 14 years of age or younger; almost one-half are under the Guardianship of the Minister, and almost one-half are identified as of indigenous descent. Based on this and other data, an unpublished evaluation recommended earlier intervention and targeting 10–14 years before they become chronic, long-term offenders. For this purpose, a suite of evidence-based interventions have been devised to tackle individual risk factors as well as address other factors pertaining to family, education, peers, and the community. The Community Protection Panel will also employ culturally appropriate responses for Aboriginal young offenders.

BOX 3.5 SOUTH AUSTRALIA AS AN EXAMPLE OF AUSTRALIA'S YOUTH JUSTICE SYSTEMS

Not all young people who come into contact with South Australia Police will appear in the Youth Court. Police can divert young offenders away from the courts by way of informal and formal cautions and family conferences. Furthermore, the Youth Court can also initiate programs as part of the court process by transferring young defendants to intervention programs, such as specialist courts (e.g., Youth Drug Court). Some defendants may be referred to a program as an "undertaking" made during a family conference or as a sentencing outcome (e.g., the "Mary Street" Treatment Programme for young sex offenders).

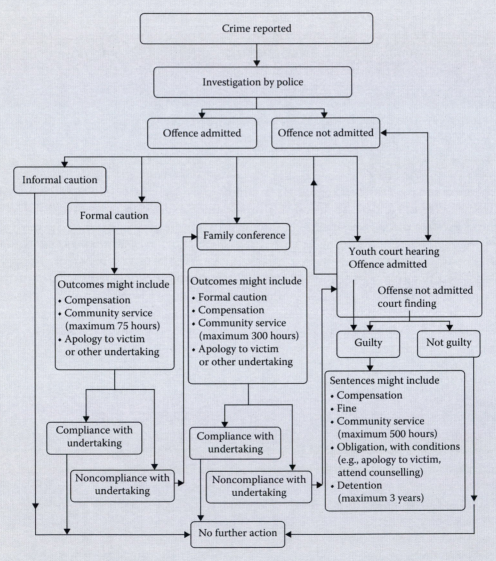

Source: Commissioner for Victims' Rights. (2011). *Information for Victims of Crime.* Adelaide, South Australia: Government of South Australia. Online http://www.voc.sa.gov.au/Publications/Booklet/Victims%20of%20Crime%20book%20web2.pdf.

Tasmania

Principal Act(s)	Key Objectives and Principles	Youths to Be Treated Differently from Adults	Youths to Be Diverted Where Appropriate	Youth Detention as Last Resort
Youth Justice Act 1997				
Other Relevant Act(s)				
Bail Act 1994				
Child, Young Persons and Their Families Act 1997				
Child Welfare Act				
Police Offences Act 1935				
Sentencing Act 1997				
Youth Justice Amendment Act 2003				
Youth Justice Regulations 1999				

Responsible Institution

The lead agency in Tasmania is the Disability, Child, Youth and Family Services (DCYFS) within the Department of Health and Human Services (DHHS).

Courts

The Magistrate's Court (Youth Justice Division).

Custodial Youth Justice Services

Custodial Youth Justice Services are provided at the Ashley Youth Detention Centre. The center provides a range of drug and alcohol, employment, life skills, and other programs that take account of participants' cultural needs.

Tasmania has combined the responsibility for disability, parenting, community development, adoption, child protection, family violence counseling and support, sexual assault, and youth justice into one government department with the intention of overcoming gaps and overlaps in service delivery and communication.

The Youth Justice Act 1997 outlines a set of principles intended to meet the criminogenic needs of young people who offend through diverting them from a criminal pathway. The act objectifies an integrated and collaborative method of service delivery for young people, families, and services, through formalizing partnerships with the Magistrate's Court, Tasmania Police, government, and the nongovernment sector.

The delivery of diversionary programs provides an example of the workings of formalized partnership in the Youth Justice directorate. The U-Turn Program provides an example of the partnership between DCYFS and the nongovernment sector. U-Turn is a structured automotive training course for young people who are involved or are at risk of becoming involved in motor vehicle thefts. The program combines formalized training with recreational activities to redirect "thrill-seeking behaviors." All young people are also provided with case management and personal development support with the aim of linking young people to employment and further education. Successes demonstrated through formal evaluation have included reduction in antisocial and offending behaviors, along with improvements in personal and social skills and awareness (TILES 2005).

Victoria

Principal Act(s)	Key Objectives and Principles	Youths to Be Treated Differently from Adults	Youths to Be Diverted Where Appropriate	Youth Detention as Last Resort
Children, Youth and Families Act 2005 and Courts Legislation (Neighbourhood Justice Centre) Act (CLNJCA) 2006	Pt 5.3, Div 1; S 360–s 362	S 362(1)	S 361 resentencing hierarchy; s 1 CLNJCA	S 361, S 412(1)(C)
Other Relevant Act(s)				
Bail Act 1977				
Crimes Act 1958				
Sentencing Act 1991				

Responsible Institution

The Department of Human Services (DHS) is the lead agency in Victoria, although the Department of Justice is responsible for some youth justice matters.

Courts

In Victoria there are the Victorian Children's Court, Magistrates Court, County Court and Supreme Court. This State also operates a Children's Koori Court for Aboriginal or Torres Strait Island young people. It replicates the Koori Division of the Victorian Magistrates Court. These Koori Courts are enabled under Magistrates Court (Koori Court) Act 2002, which provides for the courts to ensure "greater participation of the Aboriginal people in the sentencing process through the role to be played in that process by the Aboriginal elder or respected person and others" (section 1(b)).

Elders and respected persons provide the sentencing court with cultural advice and also speak directly with the young person about the circumstances that have led to their offending. To have their case dealt with in the Koori Court, the young person must first enter a guilty plea or be found guilty of an offense and consent to their involvement. The Koori Court does not deal with sex offenses. The sentencing options available to the presiding judicial officer are the same as mainstream criminal courts; however, the judge or magistrate should, if relevant, take into account what has been discussed with the Koori community representatives and the young offender.

Youth Detention Services

There are three youth detention facilities in Victoria. Melbourne Youth Justice Centre accommodates young men aged 15–18 years, either on remand or serving a custodial sentence generally from the Children's Court. Parkville Youth Residential Centre accommodates males aged 10–14 years on remand or sentenced by the Children's Court to a youth residential center. It is also the only center to accommodate females of age groups of 10–18 and young women aged 18–21 (*dual track*), who have been sentenced by either the Children's Court or an adult court. Malmsbury Youth Justice Centre accommodates males aged 17–20 years who have been sentenced to a youth justice center order by the Magistrate's Court, County Court or Supreme Court through the *dual track system*.

Under Victoria's unique dual track system, adult courts can, in certain circumstances, sentence young offenders (defined in the Sentencing Act 1991 (Vic) as those aged under 21 years at the time of sentencing) to serve a custodial sentence in a youth detention facility rather than an adult prison. The system is intended to prevent vulnerable young offenders from entering the adult prison system at a young age. Victoria's Sentencing Advisory Council (2012) analyzed Magistrates' Court and County Court data from 2005 to 2009 and found that approximately half of the offenders aged from 18 to 20 years for whom a custodial sentence was deemed appropriate were sent to a youth detention facility rather than an adult prison. Once sentenced, the young person falls within the jurisdiction of either the Adult Parole Board or the Youth Parole Board, which have power to transfer the person either to or from adult prison.

Victoria also operates an Afterhours Bail Placement Support Service to reduce inappropriate remands in custodial centers. The afterhours service engages a worker to provide support and information to children and young people aged from 10 to 18 who are being considered for remand. The worker is also responsible for conducting an assessment for suitability of bail placement, placing the young person in suitable accommodation, and assisting with accessing appropriate accommodation for those who need accommodation options to access bail.

Western Australia

Principal Act(s)	Key Objectives and Principles	Youths to Be Treated Differently from Adults	Youths to Be Diverted Where Appropriate	Youth Detention as Last Resort
Young Offenders Act 1994	S 7	S 7(a), (c), (i), (k), (l), and (m)	S 7 (b)	S 7 (h)

Other Relevant Act(s)

Bail Act 1982

Children's Court of Western Australia Act 1988

Child Welfare Act 1947

Court Security and Custodial Services Act 1999

Inspector of Custodial Services Act 2003

Sentence Administration Act 2003

Young Offenders Amendment Act 2004

Young Offenders Amendment Regulations 1995

Responsible Institution
The Department of Corrective Services is responsible for administering both adult community corrections and juvenile corrections under the Community Justice Services Directorate as well as juvenile remand and detention services under the Juvenile Custodial Services Directorate.

Courts
There is the Children's Court of Western Australia.

Youth Bail Service and Intensive Supervision Program

Western Australia has two youth justice detention facilities for young people remanded in custody or sentenced to a period of detention. Rangeview Remand Centre accommodates young people charged with an offense who are not granted bail by the courts.

The rate at which young people are placed in custody in Western Australia is 56 per 100,000. Further, indigenous Australians constitute 75% of all juvenile inmates across the state. To avoid unnecessary remand of young people within custodial centers, Western Australia operates the Metropolitan Youth Bail Service. This service is available for young people where a court has deemed them to be eligible for bail but a responsible adult cannot be found to sign the bail undertaking. Prevention and Diversion Officers act as "responsible persons" and signatories to the bail undertaking. These officers also ensure that the young person abides by their bail conditions, attends future court proceedings, and has access to suitable safe accommodation. Young people in regional Western Australia are also able to access bail and accommodation support. Regional Youth Justice Services provides an extended-hours bail service to assist police to assess suitability for bail and locate "responsible adults." This service operates in partnership with nongovernment agencies to ensure that short-term accommodation is also available in regional areas 7 days a week for young people on bail.

Western Australia's Intensive Supervision Program (ISP) is a specially designed program for the state's most serious repeat young offenders. The ISP operates under license from the U.S. Multisystemic Therapy (MST) model, which has been applied in a number of international jurisdictions and which numerous studies have found to be effective in reducing recidivism and producing significant savings to taxpayers (Schaeffer and Borduin 2005). Under the program, ISP teams work with serious and repeat juvenile offenders (and their families) with complex personal circumstances associated with their delinquent behavior.

Future Directions in Dealings with Young Offenders

It is difficult to compare the effectiveness of youth justice initiatives among Australia's jurisdictions due to the general lack of evidence and formal evaluations concerning state and territory youth justice systems and programs. This is unfortunate, given the impact that youth justice systems have on the lives of young offenders, their families, and communities. Studies conducted in Australia (as in other places) reveal that the "get tough" methods of young people's crime, including overly strict bail conditions and overpolicing young suspects, and strong reliance on deterrence by detention are not effective in addressing the causes of youth crime. Furthermore, such methods reinforce public stereotypes about young people, thus negatively impacting sensible debate on how to prevent the onset of antisocial and criminal behavior and tackle recidivism among youth offenders (see Alder et al. 1992; White and Haines 1996). In addition, these methods have proven to be costly in a social and financial context of dealing with youth crime (Potas, Vinning, and Wilson 1990).

Conversely, an evolving body of research suggests (Noetic Solutions 2010; Richards et al. 2011; Little and Allard 2011) that certain interventions with young offenders can reduce reoffending. Features of these interventions include

- Community-based strategies that incorporate family and significant others
- Building on existing strengths such as individual and family resilience, cultural traditions, and values
- Addressing youth offending in a holistic way that targets the multiple correlates (or risk factors) of such offending and magnifies the protective factors
- Addressing youth offending through collaborative approaches (across government agencies and nongovernment organizations) between indigenous and nonindigenous individuals, including young offenders, and communities

Australian research has also highlighted the implications for selection, training, and the roles of youth justice workers. According to Trotter, (2012: 8) "There is potential for widespread reductions in recidivism if juvenile justice organisations prescribe a counselling role to supervisors and employ staff with relevant qualifications." To enhance such potential, it is important to provide ongoing training and supervision that pays attention to effective practice skills. Moreover, skill development should incorporate regular observation and analysis of interviews between youth justice workers and their supervisors, feedback and frank discussion, and coaching.

Conclusion

Since colonization, Australia has achieved a considerable reputation among western nations for the innovative approaches to dealing with young offenders. This chapter has shown how Australia's policy-makers, criminal justice practitioners, and others have pondered the attitudes and behaviors of youth in general and appraised and responded to young people's offending behaviors in particular. Contrary to popular belief, only a small percentage of young people come into contact with the youth justice systems. It is evident, however, that the "get tough" attitude has been influential in recent decades resulting in, among other demands, that young offenders who commit "adult crimes be tried as adults." However, research shows that strategies such as increasing the severity of punishment are unlikely to have much effect on the offending behavior of young people already involved in crime.

On the other hand, all Australian states and territories have devised ways to divert young offenders who would otherwise be headed to the youth/children's court. The success of diversion, such as family conferencing, has been mixed. It is also evident that despite reductions in youth crime, indigenous young people continue to be grossly overrepresented. Australia's experiences in dealing with youth crime confirm that there is no single solution to reducing such crime in society.

Acknowledgment

The authors thank Sarah Fletcher, Program and Policy Officer for the Commissioner for Victims' Rights, for proofreading the drafts of this chapter and her invaluable feedback.

Review/Discussion Questions

1. The philosophy underpinning Australia's youth justice systems has shifted from welfare to justice to restorative justice. Compare and contrast these underpinnings.

2. Are diversions being used as an effective alternative to court proceedings, or do they provide a rationale for processing young people who, without them, would not have been processed at all?

3. Should the ways of responding to young people who have been involved in "victimless" crime such as the use of drugs and alcohol be the same as the ways of responding to violent crime?

4. Does the option to avoid formal court proceedings by admitting the objective elements of the alleged offense put pressure on young people to plead guilty? Does the option encourage a young person to choose the most convenient option despite the possibility of long-term consequences?

5. In Australia, arrest and detention have their place in tackling crime perpetrated by young people; however, there are better ways to deal with young offenders. What should be the core elements of a strategy for the prevention and reduction of youth crime?

References

ABS. (2011). Corrective services, Australia, September quarter 2011, 4512.0. Canberra, Austraila: ABS.

ABS. (2013a). 4510.0 - Recorded Crime - Victims, Australia, 2012. Canberra, Australia: ABS On-line: http://www.abs.gov.au/AUSSTATS/abs@.nsf/Previousproducts/4510.0Main%20Features12012?opendocument&tabname=Summary&prodno=4510.0&issue=2012&num=&view.

ABS. (2013b). Recorded Crime-Offenders, 2011–12, 4519.0. Canberra, Australia: ABS. Online http://www.abs.gov.au/AUSSTATS/abs@.nsf/Lookup/4519.0Main+Features12011-12?OpenDocument.

ABS. (2013c). Criminal Courts, Australia, 2011–12, 4513.0. Canberra, Austraila: ABS. Online http://www.abs.gov.au/ausstats/abs@.nsf/Products/4513.0~2011-12~Chapter~Children's+Courts?OpenDocument.

ACT Chief Minister and Treasury Report. (2013). Labour Force—November 2013. ACT: ACT Government.

ACT Department of Disability, Housing and Community Services, Office for Children, Youth and Family Support. (n.d.). Welcome to the Bimberi Youth Justice Centre. Online http://www.dhcs.act.gov.au/ocyfs/bimberi.

ACT Human Rights Commission (2011). *The ACT Youth Justice System 2011: A Report to the ACT Legislative Assembly*. Australian Capital Territory: ACT Human Rights Commission. http://www.hrc.act.gov.au/res/Volume%20One%20Low%20Res.pdf.

AIC (Australian Institute of Criminology). (2013). Juvenile Justice—In Focus. Online http://www.aic.gov.au/crime_types/in_focus/juvenilejustice.html.

AIHW (Australian Institute of Health and Welfare). (2012). *Juvenile Justice in Australia 2010-2011*. Juvenile Justice Series No. 10. Canberra, Australia: AIHW.

AJJA (Australasian Juvenile Justice Administrators) (2009). Juvenile Justice Standards. Australia: AIJA. Online http://www.ajja.org.au/.

Alder, C., O'Connor, I., Warner, K., and White, R. (1992). *Perceptions of the Treatment of Juveniles in the Legal System*. Hobart, Australia: National Clearinghouse for Youth Studies.

Beikoff, L. (1996). Queenland's juvenile justice system: Equity, access and justice for young women. In C. Alder and M. Baines (Eds.), *And When She Was Bad? Working with Young Women in Juvenile Justice and Related Areas*. Hobart, Australia: National Clearing House for Youth Studies. 15–25.

Bessant, J. and Hill, R. (Eds.). (1997). *Youth, Crime and the Media*. Hobart, Australia: Clearinghouse for Youth Studies.

Blackmore, R.D. (1978). Some aspects of the juvenile justice system. Presentation at the Juvenile Justice Conference, 4–6 July, Australian Institute of Criminology.

Bracey, D. (1988). Issues and trends in juvenile justice. *Australian Crime Prevention Council Journal*, 10 (1):4–7.

Caldwell, R.G. (1961). The Juvenile Court: Its development and some major problems. *Journal of Criminal Law, Criminology and Police Science*, January-February, 51(5):493–511.

Canberra Women in Business. (2013). Snap Shot of Canberra. Online http://www.cwb.org.au/.

Carrington, K. and Pereira, M. (2009). *Offending Youth: Sex, Crime and Justice*. Leichhardt, Australia: Federation Press.

Chen, S., Matruglio, T., Weatherburn, D., and Hua, J. (2005). *Crime and Justice: Contemporary Issues in Crime and Justice* No.86. Sydney NSW:NSW Bureau of Crime Statistics and Research. http://www.bocsar.nsw.gov.au/agdbasev7wr/bocsar/documents/pdf/cjb86.pdf.

Child Welfare Practice and Legislation Review Committee (Carney Report). (1984). Equity and social justice for children, families and communities—Final report. Melbourne, Australia: Government of Victoria.

Chrzanowski, A. and Wallis, R. (2011). Understanding the youth justice system. In A. Stewart, T. Allard, and S. Dennison (Eds.), *Evidence Based Policy and Practice in Youth Justice*. Chapter 2. Annandale, Australia: The Federation Press. pp. 7–27.

Clifford, W. (1978). Juvenile justice before and after the onset of delinquency. Opening address at the Juvenile Justice Conference, 4–6 July, Australian Institute of Criminology.

Commissioner for Victims' Rights. (2011). *Information for Victims of Crime*. Adelaide, South Australia: Government of South Australia. Online http://www.voc.sa.gov.au/Publications/Booklet/Victims%20of%20Crime%20book%20web2.pdf.

Commission of Inquiry into Youth (Demack Report). (1975). The nature and extent of problems confronting youth in Queensland. Queensland, Australia: Government of Queensland.

Comparative Youth Project. (2013). Chronological Summary 1970–2008. University of New South Wales. Online http://cypp.unsw.edu.au/.

Cunneen, C. and White, R. (2011). *Juvenile Justice: Youth and Crime in Australia*. Melbourne, Australia: Oxford University Press.

Daly, K. (2003). Mind the gap: Restorative justice in theory and practice. In A. von Hirsch, J. Roberts, A. Bottoms, K. Roach, and M. Schiff (Eds.), *Restorative Justice and Criminal Justice: Competing or Reconcilable Paradigms*. Oxford, UK: Hart Publishing.

Daly, K. and Hayes, H. (2001). Restorative Justice and Conferencing in Australia. Trends and Issues in Crime and Criminal Justice, No. 186. Canberra, Australia: Australian Institute of Criminology. Online http://www.aic.gov.au/publications/current%20series/tandi/181-200/tandi186.html.

Fagan, A. and Western, J. (2005). Escalation and deceleration of offending behaviours from adolescence to early adulthood. *Australian and New Zealand Journal of Criminology*, 38 (1):59–76.

Fischer, J. (1978). Does anything work? *Journal of Social Science Research*, 1 (3):215–243.

Fitzgerald, R., Mazerolle, P., Piquero, A., and Ansara, D. (2012). Exploring sex differences among sentenced juvenile offenders in Australia. *Justice Quarterly*, 29 (3):420–447.

Freiberg, A., Fox, R., and Hogan, M. (1988). Sentencing young offenders. Sentencing research paper no. 11. Sydney, Australia: Australian Law Reform Commission and Commonwealth Youth Bureau.

Freiberg, A., Fox, R., and Hogan, M. (1989). Procedural justice in sentencing Australian juveniles. *Monash University Review*, 15 (3/4):279–301. Online http://www.austlii.edu.au/cgi-bin/download.cgi/au/journals/MonashULawRw/1989/17.

Hayes, H. (2006). Apologies and accounts in youth justice conferences: Reinterpreting research outcomes. *Contemporary Justice Review*, 9 (4):369–385.

Holmes, J. (2010). Female offending: Has there been an increase? *Crime and Justice Statistics, No. 46.* Sydney, Australia: Bureau of Crime Statistics and Research.

Indig, D., Vecchiato, C., Haysom, L., Beilby, R., Carter, J., Champion, U., Gaskin, C., Heller, E., Kumar, S., Mamone, N., Muir, P., van den Dolder, P., and Whitton, G. (2011). 2009 NSW young people in custody health survey—Report. Sydney, NSW: Justice Health and Juvenile Justice.

Jesuit Social Services. (2013). Thinking outside—Alternatives to remand for children. Richmond, Australia: Jesuit Social Services.

Juvenile Justice, Attorney-General and Justice NSW. (2013). Serious young offenders review panel (SYORP). Sydney, Australia: NSW Government.

Kupchik, A. (2006). *Judging Juveniles: Prosecuting Adolescents in Adult and Juvenile Courts.* New York, USA: New York University Press.

Law Enforcement Assistance Administration and National Institute of Law Enforcement and Criminal Justice. (1973). New approaches to diversion and treatment of juvenile offenders. *Criminal Justice Monograph.* Washington, USA: US Department of Justice.

Little, S. and Allard, T. (2011). Responding to offending—Youth justice system responses. In A. Stewart, T. Allard, and S. Dennison (Eds.), *Evidence Based Policy and Practice in Youth Justice.* Annandale, Australia: The Federation Press. pp. 152–168.

Martinson, R. (1974). What works?—Questions and answers about prison reform. *The Public Interest*, 35: 22–54.

Moore, D. (1993). Facing the consequences. In L. Atkinson and S. Gerull (Eds.), *National Conference on Juvenile Justice, Conference Proceedings No. 22.* Canberra, AUST: Australian Institute of Criminology. 203–220.

Mullighan, E. (2008). Inquiry—Commission of Inquiry Report (Children in State Care). Adelaide, Australia: Government of South Australia. Online https://www.sa.gov.au/topics/ crime-justice-and-the-law/mullighan-inquiry/children-in-state-care.

Muncie, J. (1984). *The Trouble with Kids Today: Youth and Crime in Post-War Britain*, London, UK: Hutchinson.

Murray, J.M. (1985). The development of contemporary juvenile justice and correctional policy. In A. Borowski and J.M. Murray (Eds.), *Juvenile Delinquency in Australia.* Sydney, Australia: Methuen.

Murray, J.M. and Borowski, A. (1986). Perspectives on juvenile crime and justice in Australia. In D. Chappell and P. Wilson (Eds.), *The Australian Criminal Justice System—The Mid-1980s.* Adelaide, Australia: Butterworths.

New South Wales (NSW) Standing Committee on Social Issues. (1992). *Juvenile Justice in NSW.* Sydney, Australia: Government Printer.

Newman, L.K. (1982). Delinquents and schools—A view point from the Bench. *Forum*, 6 (2):5–11.

Noetic Solutions. (2010). Review of effective practice in juvenile justice: Report for the Minister for Juvenile Justice. Sydney, Australia: New South Wales Department of Human Services. Online http://www.djj.nsw.gov.au/pdf_htm/publications/general/Juvenile%20Justice%20Effective%20 Practice%20Review%20FINAL.pdf.

Northern Territory Criminal Justice Research and Statistics Unit. (2013). An analysis of the association between criminal behaviour and experience of maltreatment as a child in the Northern Territory. Presentation for the Australasian Conference for Child Abuse and Neglect, 10–13 November, Melbourne. Online http://www.nt.gov.au/justice/policycoord/researchstats/researchstats/2013/ child_maltreatment_and%20criminal%20behaviour.pdf.

NSW Government. (n.d.). Youth on Track—Fact Sheet. Sydney, Australia: Attorney-General and Justice. Online http://www.youthontrack.lawlink.nsw.gov.au/agdbasev7wr/_assets/yot/m771002l2/yot_ fact_sheet.pdf.

O'Connell, M. and Hayes, H. (2012). Victims, criminal justice and restorative justice. In T. Prenzler and H. Hayes (Eds.), *An Introduction to Crime and Criminal Justice.* Sydney, Australia: Pearson. 329–347.

O'Connell, T. (1993). Wagga Wagga juvenile cautioning program: "It may be the way to go!" In L. Atkinson and S. Gerull (Eds.), *National Conference on Juvenile Justice, Conference Proceedings No. 22*. Canberra, AUST: Australian Institute of Criminology. 221–232.

O'Connor, I (1997). Models of juvenile justice. In A. Borowski and I. O'Connor (Eds.), *Juvenile Crime, Justice and Corrections*. Sydney, Australia: Longman. 1–11. Online http://www.aic.gov.au/media_library/conferences/juvenile/oconnor.pdf.

Office of Crime Statistics and Research. (2000). *Crime and Justice in South Australia—Juvenile Justice*. Adelaide, Australia: Office of Crime Statistics and Research. Online http://www.ocsar.sa.gov.au/docs/crime_justice/JJ_Text2000.pdf.

Office of Crime Statistics and Research. (2005). Juvenile justice in South Australia: Where are we now? *Information Bulletin*, (40) January. Online http://www.un.org/documents/ga/res/40/a40r033.htm.

Office of the United Nations High Commissioner for Human Rights. (1985). United Nations Standard Minimum Rules for the Administration of Juvenile Justice ('the Beijing Rules'). Online http://www2.ohchr.org/english/law/beijingrules.htm.

Office of the United Nations High Commissioner for Human Rights. (1989). Convention on the Rights of the Child. Online http://www.ohchr.org/en/professionalinterest/pages/crc.aspx.

Owen, P. (1978). Juvenile Aid Panels. Presentation at the Juvenile Justice Conference, 4–6 July, Australian Institute of Criminology.

Palk, G., Hayes, H., and Prenzler, T. (1998). Restorative justice and community conferencing: Summary of findings from a pilot study. *Current Issues in Criminal Justice*, 10 (2):138–155.

Peake, R. (2013). ACT Economy on the Rise Despite Public Sector Cuts. *Canberra Times*, November 29. Online http://www.canberratimes.com.au/act-news/act-economy-on-the-rise-despite-public-service-cuts-20131128-2yehc.html#ixzz2pn0qk2pA.

Pemberton, A., Winkel, F., and Groenhuijsen M. (2007). Taking victims seriously in restorative justice. *International Perspectives in Victimology*, 1 (1):4–13.

Platt, A. (1977). *The Child Savers: The Invention of Delinquency* (2nd edition). Chicago, USA: University of Chicago Press.

Potas, I., Vinning, A., and Wilson, P. (1990). *Young People and Crime: Costs and Prevention*. Canberra, Australia: Australian Institute of Criminology.

Potts, R. (1985). Juvenile crime prevention programs. In H.G. Weir (Ed.), *Issues in Police Administration*. Adelaide, Australia: Techsearch for South Australian Institute of Technology. 92–98.

Productivity Commission. (2013). Report on government services: 2012. Canberra, Australia: Productivity Commission.

Richards, K., Rosevear, L., and Gilbert, R. (2011). Promising interventions for reducing Indigenous juvenile offending. Research brief no. 10, March. Sydney, Australia: Indigenous Justice Clearinghouse.

Salmelainen, P. (1995). *The Correlates of Offending Frequency: A Study of Juvenile Theft Offenders in Detention*. Sydney, Australia: NSW Bureau of Crime Statistics and Research.

Schaeffer, C.M. and Borduin, C.M. (2005). Long-term follow-up to a randomized clinical trial of Multisystemic Therapy with serious and violent juvenile offenders. *Journal of Consulting and Clinical Psychology*, 73 (3):445–453.

Seymour, J. (1983). *Juvenile Justice in South Australia*. Sydney, Australia: Law Book Company and Australian Institute of Criminology.

Seymour, J. (1988). *Dealing with Young Offenders*. Sydney, Australia: Law Book Company.

Seymour, J. (1993). The need to ask the right questions. In L. Atkinson and S. Gerull (Eds.), *National Conference on Juvenile Justice, Conference Proceedings No. 22*. Canberra, Australia: Australian Institute of Criminology. 25–33.

Smith, G. and Weatherburn, D. (2012). Youth justice conferences versus children's court: A comparison of re-offending. *Crime and Justice: Contemporary Issues in Crime and Justice* No160. Sydney NSW:NSW Bureau of Crime Statistics and Research. http://www.bocsar.nsw.gov.au/agdbasev7wr/bocsar/documents/pdf/cjb160.pdf.

Starrs, J.E. (1967). Southern juvenile courts. *Crime and Delinquency*, 13 (2): 289–306.

Strang, H. (1999). Recent research on conferencing: The Canberra experiments. In A. Morris and G. Maxwell (Eds.), *Youth Justice in Focus: Proceedings of an Australasian Conference held 27–30 October 1998*. Wellington, New Zealand: Institute of Criminology, Victoria University of Wellington. pp. 27–30.

Strang, H., Barnes, G., Braithwaite, J., and Sherman, L. (1999). *Experiments in Restorative Policing: A Progress Report on the Canberra Re-integrative Shaming Experiments*. Canberra, Australia: Australian Federal Police and Australian National University.

Thompson, E. and O'Connell, E. (2008). A recipe for success: How independent living skills can prevent accommodation breakdown in young offenders exiting secure care. *Parity*, 21 (4):33–34.

TILES (Tasmanian Institute of Law Enforcement Studies). (2005). Evaluation of U-turn project in Tasmania—Final report. Hobart, Australia: University of Tasmania.

Trimboli, L. (2000). *An Evaluation of the NSW Youth Justice Conferencing Scheme*. Sydney, Australia: New South Wales Bureau of Crime Statistics and Research, Attorney General's Department.

Trotter, C. (2012). Community based supervision for young offenders. *Trends and Issues in Crime and Criminal Justice,* no. 448. Australian Institute of Criminology. http://www.aic.gov.au/publica tions/current%20series/tandi/441-460/tandi448.html.

Victoria Sentencing Advisory Council. (2012). *Sentencing Children and Young People in Victoria*. Melbourne, Australia: Sentencing Advisory Council.

Vignaendra, S. and Fitzgerald, J. (2006). *Reoffending among Young People Cautioned by Police or Who Participated in Youth Justice Conference*. Sydney, Australia: New South Wales Bureau of Crime Statistics and Research.

Wagland, P., Blanch, B., and Moore, E. (2013). Participant satisfaction with youth justice conferencing. *Crime and Justice Bulletin, Contemporary Issues in Crime and Justice*, (170). Sydney NSW: NSW Bureau of Crime Statistics and Research. http://www.bocsar.nsw.gov.au/agdbasev7wr/_ assets/bocsar/m716854l2/cjb170.pdf.

Warner, K. (1993). The Courts, the Judiciary and new directions: The limits of legislative change. In L. Atkinson and S. Gerull (Eds.), *National Conference on Juvenile Justice, Conference Proceedings No. 22*. Canberra, Australia: Australian Institute of Criminology. 43–52.

Weatherburn, D. and Baker, J. (2001). Transient offenders in the 1996 secondary school survey. *Current Issues in Criminal Justice*, 13 (1):60–73.

Weber, A. (2012). Youth justice conferences versus children's court: A comparison of cost-effectiveness. *Crime and Justice Bulletin, Contemporary Issues in Crime and Justice,* No. 164, August. Sydney, Australia: NSW Bureau of Crime Statistics and Research.

White, R. (1990). *No Space of Their Own—Young People and Social Control in Australia*. Cambridge, UK: Cambridge University Press.

White, R. (2007). *Youth Gangs, Violence and Anti-social Behaviour*. Hobart, Australia: Australian Research Alliance for Children and Youth.

White, R. and Haines, F. (1996). *Crime and Criminology: An Introduction*. Oxford, UK: Oxford University Press.

Wundersitz, J. (1992). The net-widening effect of Aid Panels and Screening Panels in the South Australia Juvenile Justice System. *Australian and New Zealand Journal of Criminology*, 25 (2):115–134.

Wundersitz, J. (2000). Juvenile justice in Australia: Towards the new millennium. In D. Chappell and P. Wilson (Eds.), *Crime and the Criminal Justice System in Australia: 2000 and Beyond* (5th edition). Sydney, Australia: Butterworths. pp. 102–118.

Young, B.J. (1978). Juvenile justice: Juvenile Aid Bureau. Presentation at the Juvenile Justice Conference, 4–6 July, Australian Institute of Criminology.

Internet Sources

Australian Bureau of Statistics—Provides statistics on a wide range of economic, environmental, and social issues, such as annual and occasional reports on criminal justice, including youth justice and victims of crime. www.abs.gov.au.

Australian Institute of Criminology—The national research and knowledge center on crime and criminal justice. www.aic.gov.au.

Australian Legal Information Institute—A joint venture that maintains Australia's largest online database on Australian legislation and case law. http://www.austlii.edu.au/.

Australian Health and Welfare Institute—The national agency for information and statistics on Australia's health and welfare that also publishes a juvenile justice series. https://www.aihw.gov.au/.

Administration of Juvenile Justice in Brazil: Recent Advances and Remaining Challenges

4

ALINE YAMAMOTO, JULIANA CARDOSO BENEDETTI,
KARYNA BATISTA SPOSATO, MARISA MENESES DE ANDRADE,
AND NATÁLIA LAGO

Contents

Introduction	90
Historical Overview	91
Juvenile Justice Procedure	96
Juvenile Justice Model in Brazil	99
Current Trends and Patterns	101
Conclusion	104
Summary	105
Review/Discussion Questions	105
References	105
Internet Sources	106

FACTS ABOUT BRAZIL

Area: The Federative Republic of Brazil is a country in South America, bordering the Atlantic Ocean in its east side. It is also bordered, on its western side, by Argentina, Bolivia, Colombia, French Guiana, Guyana, Paraguay, Peru, Suriname, Uruguay, and Venezuela. Brazil is the largest country in South America and the fifth-largest country in the world with a total area of 8,514,877 sq. km. **Population:** The last census survey conducted in Brazil, in 2010, indicated that the country's population exceeded 190 million[*] inhabitants.[†] Of these, more than 30 million (or about 17% of the population) are adolescent girls and boys who are between 12 and 18 years old. Most of these adolescents reside in urban areas (81.9%), and the ethnic composition of this group is white (42.3%), black (56.2%), yellow (1%), and Indians (0.5%). Brasilia is the capital. **Climate:** Brazil's climate is predominantly tropical. However, due to its enormous landmass, the country's weather is quite diversified. There is a significant weather difference between the south, with temperate conditions, and the north and northeast of the country, with its equatorial climate conditions.

(Continued)

[*] Source: Instituto Brasileiro de Geografia e Estatística (IBGE; Brazilian Institute of Geography and Statistics), Censo 2010.
[†] The Brazilian Institute of Geography and Statistics, which is responsible for the census, estimates that the Brazilian population, now, has surpassed 200 million inhabitants.

FACTS ABOUT BRAZIL (*Continued*)

Economics: The Human Development Index (HDI), which measures progress in the long term in relation to income, health, and education, ranks Brazil in the 85th place (with 0.730 in an evaluation between 0 and 1). While this position does not place the country among those with the highest human development, it is important to recognize that Brazil is moving forward regarding the population's access to human rights. In addition, the gross domestic product (GDP) has been growing, and in 2012, GDP per capita was 22,402 reais, which is currently equal to 11,747 U.S. dollars.* In a survey conducted by Brazil's Institute of Geography and Statistics (*Instituto Brasileiro de Geografia e Estatística*—IBGE), citizens from Brazil can expect an increase in access to formal employment and higher wages,† as a result of changes related to Brazil's rapid economic growth. **Government:** Brazil is a presidential democratic republic with a multiparty system. The President of Brazil is not only the chief of state, but also the head of government who is elected by direct popular vote for a 4-year term. There is the possibility of reelection for a second consecutive term. The Federative Republic of Brazil is constitutionally based upon five fundamental principles: sovereignty, citizenship, dignity of human beings, the social values of labor and freedom of enterprise, and political pluralism. Portuguese is the official language.

* Source: Instituto Brasileiro de Geografia e Estatística—IBGE (2012).
† Data are for the period 2004–2009. Source: IBGE (2013).

Introduction

Brazil occupies the seventh position in the 95 countries of the world with homogeneous data provided by the World Health Organization on homicides (between 2007 and 2011), with a rate of 27.4 murders per 100,000 inhabitants and 54.8 per 100,000 young people (Waiselfisz 2013).

A significant portion of the adolescents in Brazil present some vulnerability, whether due to economic problems or education, teenage pregnancy, drugs, or violence. Different studies have shown that this age group is marked by varied manifestations of violence, affecting their physical and mental health directly and indirectly. In these studies, adolescents appear to be not only the aggressors but also direct and indirect victims (Doriam and Ignácio 2012).

There are, in Brazil, 435 socio-educational institutes for adolescents in conflict with the law, which corresponds to 179 institutes for the socio-educational measure of institutionalization, 110 institutes for the socio-educational measure of semifreedom, 10 institutes for initial care, and 136 institutes that are mixed. According to a document of the National Council of Justice (CNJ), published in the year 2012, in Brazil there are more adolescents deprived of liberty in the internment units than its capacity.

The National Survey—Socio-Educational Treatment of the Adolescents in Conflict with the Law, published by the Human Rights Secretariat, showed that 17,703 adolescents were restricted or deprived of liberty in 2010. This number, when compared with that from 2009, represents a 4.50% increase (see Figure 4.1).

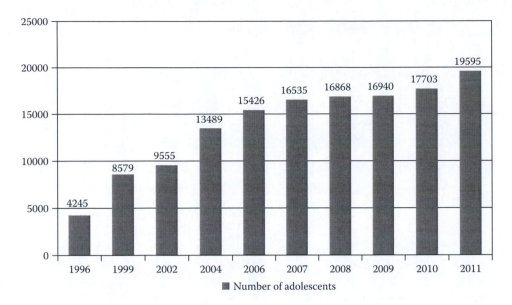

Figure 4.1 Number of adolescents deprived of liberty in Brazil. (Brazil. Presidency of Republic. Secretariat for Human Rights. 2011. *Levantamento Nacional—Atendimento Socioeducativo ao Adolescente em Conflito com a Lei.* Brasília: SDH/PR.)

The most recent official figures on adolescents in conflict with the law are from 2011 (National Council of Justice, 2012). Back then (when the adolescent population amounted to 30 million), almost 40,000 adolescents were serving sentences for criminal offenses. Despite the lack of reliable updated data, it is safe to assume that this number has increased over the past few years. Although only 14% of juvenile offenders have committed serious violent crimes (i.e., murder, robbery with murder and/or rape), nearly half of the total number of adolescents in conflict with the law are serving custodial sentences (National Council of Justice 2012). This reveals the punitive practices of Brazilian judges and over-burdens the existing custody infrastructure (see Figure 4.2).

In 2013, the National Council of the Public Prosecutors inspected 287 of the 321 Brazilian custodial institutions and discovered that they held 18,378 adolescents, albeit their capacity was 15,414. Therefore, there is a serious issue of overcrowding of adolescent offenders in prisons throughout Brazil. This is a direction violation of international standards. Data from the Secretariat for Human Rights from the Presidency of Republic. (2011) show that there was an alarming 461.6% increase in the number of adolescents being detained in custody from 1996 to 2011 (see Figure 4.1).

According to the National Council of Justice (2012), from the total number of adolescents restricted or deprived of liberty, the majority were boys (95%), and 72% of them declared that they were attending school regularly when they committed the offense for which they were convicted. Their average age was 17–18 years (see Figure 4.3), which means that some of them would reach adult legal age before deinstitutionalization.

Historical Overview

Brazil was "discovered" in 1500 by Portugal, and until the year 1822, it was the main Portuguese colony. In 1889, the monarchical regime established after independence was

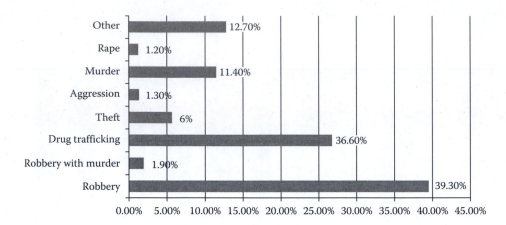

Figure 4.2 Types of crimes commited by juvenile offenders. (National Council of Justice. 2012. *Panorama Nacional: a execuçao das medidas socioeducativas de internaçao.* Brasília: CNJ.)

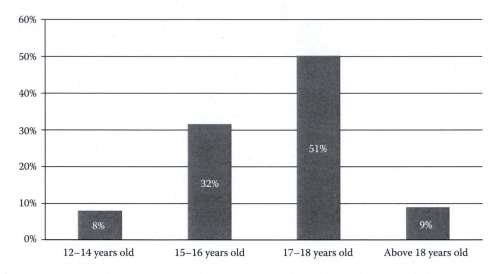

Figure 4.3 Average age of juvenile offenders deprived of liberty. (National Council of Justice. 2012. *Panorama Nacional: a execuçao das medidas socioeducativas de internaçao.* Brasília: CNJ.)

overthrown and Brazil became a republic. Although the Empire's Criminal Code did not include many details about the state's intervention on crimes committed by children and adolescents, it mentioned that children under 14 who had committed a crime would not be judged, except if they demonstrated discernment about their actions. At that time, the model of penal responsibility was in force, which determined that the criminal codes of the nineteenth century excluded children under 7 years from criminal responsibility. In Brazil, that rule goes back to the law in force during the Iberian Union (1580–1640), and it was reinforced by the Empire's Criminal Code, which dates back to the year 1830.

The establishment of the child and adolescent law or juvenile law takes us necessarily to the origins of the welfare state. With the new law, the changes included formal government provisions that made it clear that it was not only enough for individual liberties and rights to be recognized but also and, more importantly, that they be protected (Bobbio *apud* Sposato 2006). In Brazil, the child and adolescent law built a parallel penal system, which had three different approaches since independence: the penal stage, the protection stage, and the guaranteeism stage.*

The Empire's Criminal Code also stated that offenders aged between 14 and 21 years would be punished for their crimes, but such punishment would be attenuated when compared with the punishment imposed to adults.

With the advent of the nineteenth century, the economic, political, and social transformations, which were taking place in Brazil had an impact on the treatment meted out to children and adolescents. The shift from a monarchy to a republic resulted in a different and complex medical–legal care approach toward the treatment of children and adolescents, which conflated prevention, education, recuperation, and restraint (Sposato 2006).

The Republican Penal Code of 1890 discharged children under 9 years of age from any criminal responsibility. When it came to the age range of 9–14 years, criminal responsibility was conditional to the demonstration of the capacity of discerning. Through the ages of 14–17 years, the capacity of discerning was presumed, yet the penalty was lowered to two-thirds the punishment attributed to adults. Anyone from 17 to 21 years of age who committed a crime would receive the same punishment as an adult. However, they could benefit from mitigating circumstances (see Box 4.1).

In Brazil's newborn republic (the so-called Old Republic lasted from November 1889 to November 1930), children and adolescents who were homeless or were abandoned by their relatives began to be identified as little bandits and were subjected to punishment. The indifferent penal stage treated offenses and situations of social vulnerability indiscriminately and had a notable positivist conception of crime and punishment (Sposato 2006).

The 1920s witnessed the emergence of the protective stage. The adoption of the Federal Law n. 4.242/1921, the creation of the first Brazilian Minor's Court, in 1923, and the promulgation of the first Minors Code, in 1927, ushered in the protective stage of Brazilian Juvenile

---

BOX 4.1   CHILDREN AND ADOLESCENTS' CRIMINAL RESPONSIBILITY IN THE REPUBLICAN PENAL CODE OF 1890

Children and Adolescents' Age Range	Criminal Responsibility
<9 years	They were discharged from any criminal responsibility
9–14 years	They would be held responsible if discernment was shown regarding their criminal conduct
14–17 years	They were responsible for their actions; however, the penalties were lowered to two-thirds when compared with adults
17–21 years	They received the same punishment as an adult; there were nonetheless mitigating circumstances

---

* Guaranteeism, which is a new term conceived by the italian jurist Luigi Ferrajoli, designates a legal model oriented to guarantee legal rights. It is linked to the classical tradition of liberal thought on criminal law and it demands the minimization of the punitive power, the same power that was described as horrible by Montesquieu. Such minimization materializes through the submission to the law itself, as it was said by Ferrajoli, the law's submission to the law: which means, the submission of the Judiciary Power to criminal law and the submission of the Legislative Power to the constitutional rules. Therefore, garantism and minimal criminal law are almost synonymous terms designating a theoretical and normative model of criminal law able to minimize the violence of punitive intervention. This minimization occurs due to criminal warranties that reduce the range of offences and also due to procedural safeguards that serve to lower the Judiciary's will.

Penal Law. The protective stage granted the juvenile judge the power to decide what was the best for the child or adolescent—this was similar to what is referred to as *parens patraie* in the Western world. The child and adolescent law began to be perceived as separate legislation from the criminal law, but it did not result in juvenile offenders being treated any less harshly than adults. Many arbitrary decisions were taken in the name of protection of the society (Sposato 2006).

As demonstrated by Emilio Garcia Mendez, the history of social control of children and adolescents is a paradigmatic example of creating a weak citizenry for whom protection was more of an imposition than a right (Garcia Mendez 1998).

It is not a casual observation that one of the most important books on this subject is called *The Child Savers: The Invention of Delinquency* written by the American sociologist Anthony M. Platt in the 1960s.

Since criminal law principles were not applicable under the novel "Minors Law," the period was characterized by a number of setbacks in terms of formal due process guarantees. The judge's discretion was considered to be an appropriate mechanism to control children and adolescents who were perceived as *potential* offenders. Emilio Garcia Mendez clarifies that "the dominant mentality understood that moral and material abandonment constituted a step toward criminality" (*apud* Sposato 2006). One's physical structure, clothes, and skin color became reason for arbitrary institutionalization, which was justified as a method to remove children and adolescents from "irregular situations" (Sposato 2006).

The Minors Code of 1927 determined that no one under 14 years (i.e., children) could be held responsible for committing a criminal offense. If the child or adolescent was abandoned or neglected, or was likely to be, the competent authority could act in two different ways. They could either resort to institutional sheltering or put them under the care of someone who could ensure their education, for as long as it took, until they were 21 years of age.

Criminal responsibility was attributed to the age range of 14–18 years and they were submitted to a special process. If the adolescent had committed an infraction and was regarded "dangerous," the judge was authorized to imprison him/her in the same institutes that were meant for adults. it means that, the imprisonment in the institutes meant for adults would only rely on the judge's perspective, in what his/her thoughts were about the adolescent. When the Penal Code came into force in 1940, the age of criminal responsibility was raised to 18. Though the Penal Code of 1940 made some alterations to the Minors Code of 1927, it did not change the nature of the state intervention (Sposato 2006).

The protective stage allowed a largely repressive attitude toward poor children and adolescents, in which "irregular situations" legitimated state intervention. The imprisonment of children and adolescents was allowed just because they were poor or abandoned or had an appearance that authorities did not like.

New institutions were designed for a temporary custody of teenagers between 14 and 18 years of age, in 1963. One year later, the Foundation for the Welfare of Minors (*Fundação Nacional de Bem-Estar do Menor* - Funabem) was created by the newly instated military regime, which was propelled by the political interests to advertise the concern of the new government with a focus on the well-being of adolescents. Brazil's military dictatorship lasted from April 1964 to March 1985, and during this period, a new Minors Code was crafted. The code created provisions for the establishment of specialized centers for reception, triage, and observance. In addition, new custodial facilities for juvenile offenders were built (Sposato 2006).

"The institutionalization and the incarceration were presented as the only possible and effective solution to refrain the 'little monsters' [...]. It is known that, on the one hand, minors were safeguarded against the application of the ordinary penal law; on the other hand, their situation as objects of study and intervention favored the exercise of power under the name of the Irregular Situation Doctrine" (Sposato 2006).

According to the Minors Code of 1979, there were six types of "irregular situations" in which a child or adolescent could be found: (a) deprived of conditions essential to his/her subsistence, health, and education, (b) as a victim of mistreatment, (c) in moral danger, (d) deprived of legal representation or assistance, due to the loss of his or her parents or of another person responsible for his or her welfare, (e) misconduct, due to familiar or community unsuitability, and (f) as perpetrator of a criminal offense.

There were different measures for each case of an "irregular situation," the most punitive being custody. It is important to highlight that in some cases, an adolescent could be imprisoned in penal institutions for adults: If he or she had reached 21 years of age and the judge did not dismiss the custody measure, the minor would be transferred to the ordinary jurisdiction of adult penal execution, and deprivation of liberty could be maintained until the moment when the reason that justified the measure was over (Sposato 2006).

Experts in children's law in Latin America do not hesitate to characterize the advent of the Convention on the Rights of the Child, in 1989, as a legal breakthrough in the region (that process is thoroughly analyzed by Mendez and Beloff 1999). The negotiations that led to the adoption of the convention ran, in Brazil, in parallel with the legislative debates that led to the promulgation of a new constitution, in 1988, and of the Statute of the Child and Adolescent (*Estatuto da Criança e do Adolescente*—ECA), (Brazil 1990), which faithfully reflected the spirit of the convention. These legal landmarks represented a profound shift of paradigms, prompting the transition from the so-called irregular situation doctrine to the "integral protection doctrine."

The irregular situation doctrine viewed the child more as an object of intervention as opposed to a person deserving of having his/her human rights protected. By elevating the legal status of children and regarding them as rights holders, the integral protection doctrine operated a transformation that the Argentinian jurist Emilio Garcia Mendez described as a "French Revolution" of children that came 200 years late (Mendez 1997). Under the irregular situation doctrine, everything that concerned children and adolescents fell under the private realm of the family, from which the state was to keep away unless exceptional, or "irregular," situations—such as orphanhood, negligence, or delinquency—required its intervention, which often oscillated between compassion and repression, conflating charity and correctional elements.

Conversely, the integral protection doctrine acknowledges the care of children and adolescents as a shared responsibility of family, society, and the state and attributes to the state, an active role in ensuring their welfare. In doing so, there are two postulates to be observed: the absolute priority of children and adolescents in the formulation of public policies, the allocation of budgetary resources, the provision of services, and the respect for the special condition of persons in development, which demands services that are tailored to their needs and contribute to their psychological and social development.

Within the justice system, the postulates are translated into the establishment of special courts for children and adolescents. As noted earlier, the courts for "minors" already existed under the irregular situation doctrine but no distinction was made among the different "irregular" situations brought before them. Today, however, their jurisdiction is quite comprehensive. For example, a specific procedure is followed in the trial of criminal offenses committed by young persons.

Juvenile Justice Procedure

The ECA distinguishes between children—persons under 12 years of age—and adolescents—people from 12 to 18 years of age. The most important legal repercussion of the distinction has to do with the imposition of legal sanctions in the event of a criminal offense. Only adolescents are legally responsible for their actions, even though such responsibility is not established as being of a penal nature. The age of criminal responsibility is set by the Brazilian Constitution at 18 years—in a clause that, for the majority of constitutionalists, cannot be amended, since individual liberties are not subject to modification. Nonetheless, the socio-educational measure of institutionalization may last until the adolescent reaches the age of 21 and where the case in question began when the young offender was at least 17 years of age.

In the event of an offense committed by a child, only "protection measures" (*medidas de proteção*) can be applied (either by a judicial authority or by the Guardianship Council).* It is important to clarify that the Guardianship Council or the judge may apply protection measures to both children and adolescents, regardless of the commitment of an act of infraction, if there is need to protect the child or adolescent from situations that could be harmful to their physical and/or emotional development. If, however, the crime is perpetrated by an adolescent, there is a special procedure (*medida socioeducativa*). Such measures combine disciplinary and pedagogical components and it is only applied by the special courts in the event of an act of infraction committed by an adolescent—never in other circumstances. Socio-educational measures can be applied jointly with protection measures (see Table 4.1).

Since adolescents are criminally irresponsible, crimes or contraventions committed by them are treated as "acts of infraction" (*atos infracionais*). According to the ECA and the Brazilian Constitution, the apprehension of adolescents is only admitted when he/she is caught committing an offense or when there is a written and substantiated order by a judicial authority.

The statute demands that the apprehension of any adolescent and the place where he/she is taken be communicated to his/her family, or to a person indicated by him/her, and to a judicial authority. If the adolescent's parents agree to sign a term of responsibility committing themselves to present him or her to a public prosecutor, the adolescent must then be released by the police. The nonliberation of the adolescent is limited to a number of circumstances: (a) commitment of a serious act of infraction, (b) serious social repercussions or threat to the adolescent's personal security, and (c) need to maintain public order. If the adolescent is detained, he/she must be presented to a public attorney within 24 hours (see see Figure 4.4).

The public prosecutor (*Ministério Público*) may request the filing of the case if there is not sufficient evidence to support the prosecution, grant an unconditional or conditional remission (i.e., accompanied by the imposition of a protection or a noncustodial socio-educational measure), or present a representation order that will set the judicial procedure in motion. In the third case, if there is sufficient evidence of authorship and reason to keep the adolescent detained, the adolescent can be held in a provisional institutionalization unit for up to 45 days, but this term is hardly adhered to; there are cases of teenagers who were held for more than 7 months.

---

* Guardianship Councils (Conselhos Tutelares) are nonjudicial bodies responsible for safeguarding the rights of children and adolescents. They are composed of five members, elected by their communities, for a mandate of 4 years. Besides the prerogative to apply protection measures, they have the power to demand public services in favor of children and adolescents and to notify a public attorney or a judicial authority of violations committed against them.

Table 4.1   The Different Kinds of Protection and Socio-Educational Measures

Protection Measures	Socio-Educational Measures
Devolution of the child or adolescent to her or his parents or guardians, accompanied by the signing of a responsibility term	Advertence: a verbal reprimand given by the judge
Guidance or temporary follow-up	Obligation to repair damages: a compensation paid to the victim or any other action to restore the harm suffered as a result of the act of infraction
Mandatory enrolment and attendance at an official education institution	Community service: mandatory work at a public institution
Inclusion in social welfare programs	Assisted freedom: mandatory attendance before an assisted freedom official to receive guidance or to be directed to educational, professionalization, or psychological services
Requisition of health, psychological, or psychiatric services, hospitalization or outpatient treatment	Semifreedom: mandatory institutionalization by night (with professional or educational activities outside the institution during the day)
	Institutionalization: custody in socio-educational institutions, exclusive to perpetrators of violent offenses

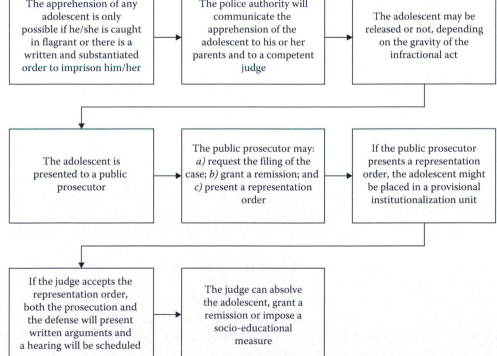

Figure 4.4 Flow of the case in the juvenile justice system.

If the judge accepts the representation order, both the prosecution and the defense will present written arguments, and a hearing will be scheduled. The judge will hear the adolescent and the witnesses appointed by the parties and peruse the available evidence. If there is need, the judge can hold a continuation hearing to gather more information; if not, he/she can absolve the adolescent, grant a conditional or unconditional remission, or impose a socio-educational measure. The statute does not set a fixed term to any of these procedural acts, but if the adolescent is provisionally detained, all the procedures usually take up to 45 days, considering that it is the maximum period of the provisory detention established by law (see Figure 4.4).

Overall, in theory, the process is quite simple (see Figure 4.4), but serious problems persist in practice. To begin with, the absence of specialized juvenile courts and public defense bodies (*Defensoria Pública*) is an issue in many jurisdictions. In addition, Brazil's legal culture is still immersed in obsolete concepts about childhood and adolescence (aggravated by the fact that the curricula of most law schools still lack a mandatory subject on the rights of children and adolescents and the juvenile justice process), and it results in violations of due process-related safeguards. Unfortunately, public prosecutors and judges still see themselves as "pseudo-fathers" whose role is to strive for the "best interest" of the adolescent—regardless of evidence thresholds, appropriate technical defense, and due process rights. The outcome is the inadequate and excessive use of institutionalization measures (which should only be imposed on juveniles who commit violent offenses, but are widely applied in drug-related cases), leading to overcrowded and poorly managed institutions in which retributive concerns surpass, by far, educational ones.

The execution of a sentence is followed by a different judge who will evaluate the social and psychological reports prepared by technical teams. And since the term of the measure is not fixed in the sentence, the presiding judge can decide whether to dismiss or to extend it up to the maximum of 3 years.

Since this model of juvenile justice was established, groups of law practitioners and civil society organizations have been advocating the establishment of legal parameters for the implementation of socio-educational measures considering that ECA is silent on the issue. Although national guidelines for the execution of socio-educational measures have existed since 2006, they only became legally binding parameters in 2012 when the "SINASE Act" was enacted. Almost 20 years after ECA, the "SINASE Act" established the "Socio-Educational Measures National System" (*Sistema Nacional de Atendimento Socioeducativo*; SINASE).

SINASE's main objective is to coordinate the roles of the different levels of government regarding the financing, implementation, monitoring, and evaluation of socio-educational measures, as well as to assign them clear responsibilities in terms of the provision of education, health, security, and social assistance services to adolescents in conflict with the law (see Box 4.2).

SINASE stresses the importance of municipalities in the implementation of noncustodial modalities of socio-educational measures, thus making local governments responsible for the management of community service and assisted freedom measures. The proposal is to engage the municipalities in the needs of adolescent's local specificities when it comes to measures based on the proximity between adolescents in conflict with the law and their community, such as the assisted freedom measure.

The document also provides educational guidelines that reaffirm the predominantly educational nature of these measures. In so doing, the law requires that the execution of both custodial and noncustodial measures is preceded by the development of an Individual Assistance Plan (*Plano Individual de Atendimento*—PIA), which should guide all the activities undertaken by the adolescent throughout the duration of the measure. Therefore, reports presented by technical teams to judiciary authorities should always refer to the adolescent's PIA, and his or her progress will be measured by the goals set therein. The PIA

BOX 4.2   SINASE'S MAJOR AXES

Act n. (Brazil, 2012), which established the Socio-Educational Measures National System (*Sistema Nacional de Atendimento Socioeducativo*; SINASE), addresses the following issues:

- Distribution of prerogatives among the different levels of government (federal, state, and local)
- Provisions on the establishment of assistance programs
- Assessment, monitoring, and management of social assistance and education services
- Accountability and charging of managers, operators, and service entities
- Funding and priorities on the fulfillment of policies
- Implementation of the socio-educational measures (procedures, individual rights, Individual Assistance Plan [PIA], disciplinary procedures, and rights of adolescents deprived of liberty)

Source: http://www.planalto.gov.br/ccivil_03/_ato2011-2014/2012/lei/l12594.htm.

---

aims at ensuring that various individual needs of the adolescent (i.e., education, health, family, and community life, etc.) are properly addressed.

The PIA is prepared by the technical staff, but it requires the participation of the adolescent and her or his family since the outcome should not respond only to the socio-educational process but should ultimately seek the restoration of broken family and social ties that might have prompted the offense.

Despite these improvements, young persons in conflict with the law still face stark discrepancies between their stated legal rights and the actual reality of the treatment they receive, especially in institutionalization contexts. In a recent research project, the Brazilian National Council of Justice indicated that 28% of adolescents deprived of liberty claim to have been victims of physical aggression committed by the state personnel. The data from the research project demonstrates that violations of the rights of adolescents in conflict with the law are still recurrent and often perpetrated by those who should watch over their socio-educational process.

Notwithstanding persistent violations, the establishment of SINASE is a long-awaited accomplishment that renders different levels of government—federal, state, and local—accountable for the implementation of policies and reaffirms the priority constitutionally conferred on children and adolescents. It also sets clear criteria that allow for better monitoring and stronger social control of the implementation of socio-educational measures and the identification of violations.

Juvenile Justice Model in Brazil

The ECA created a special system of accountability for adolescents who commit an offense (defined as a crime or a criminal misdemeanor under criminal law) that is most

Table 4.2   Juvenile Justice Models in Brazil

Justice Model	Welfare Model
Differential treatment to adolescents who commit crimes as compared to those who are at risk (vulnerability)	
Guarantee of due process, legal defense, and setting of a list of individual rights on behalf of the accused	
The principle of proportionality in the application of the sanction is limited to the definition of the type of measure, which should consider not only the seriousness and circumstances of the act but also the ability of the adolescents to comply with the measure; the law establishes some criteria for the application of the most severe measure (institutionalization), and it must comply with the principles of exceptionality and brevity and be the last option of the system	The length of the socio-educational measure is not established in the sentence, and the law only defines the maximum period of 3 years for custodial measures
The judge extinguishes the socio-educational measure based on the reports made by a multidisciplinary staff, after hearing the parts	The multidisciplinary staff that prepares the periodical reports about the adolescent during the compliance of the socio-educational measure has a great importance in defining the length of the sanction

closely related to the *justice model* (see the Introduction to this anthology). Some of its characteristics, nonetheless, resemble features of the *welfare model* (see Table 4.2).

Although the ECA has made notable advances in ensuring the rights of children and adolescents in Brazil, it has left gaps and given the judges a wide margin of interpretation on various devices concerning, among other things, the limitation of the state's punitive power.

One of the gaps related to the ECA refers to the incipient regulation of the implementation of the socio-educational measures, which in practice amounted to the lack of clear parameters for the execution of custodial measures, a lack of structured programs to undertake alternative measures to incarceration, and a lack of coordination among the different governmental bodies involved in the development of comprehensive policies to protect the rights of juvenile offenders. One example of vagueness can be found in the provision, which states that the provisional custodial measure, imposed before the sentence, can only be applied if there is an "imperious necessity," without fixing any objective parameter to avoid the abuse of this measure, in line with the Beijing Rules (see Box 4.3).

The hybridity of the juvenile justice model in Brazil reveals the dichotomies that are present in the social movements involved in the drafting and passage of the bill. The creation of SINASE, through Act n. 12.594/2012 two decades after the establishment of the ECA is not exempt from this same dichotomy between the models of welfare and justice. In spite of seeking to restrict the arbitrariness and violation of rights in the implementation of socio-educational measures, the law does not change the rule that states that the time of the sanction will depend on the performance of the adolescent throughout the measure. Rather, it gives prominence to the multidisciplinary staff in the preparation and monitoring of the PIA. However, the final decision is up to the judge after hearing the parties. In practice, the law gives margin to the juvenile justice system to be more oriented either to the welfare or to the justice model according to the interpretation that practitioners make of it. In this sense, there is a dispute between the social psychologists and the legal scholars, and the prevalent discourse may vary. For example, it is not clear as to who has the power

> ### BOX 4.3 BEIJING RULES AND THE BRAZILIAN CONTEXT
>
> The Beijing Rules were adopted by the United Nations in 1985. The Rules define the minimum rules for the administration of justice of the child and adolescent. The document proposes that juvenile justice must ensure to adolescents in conflict with the law the same rights observed in criminal justice as the presumption of innocence, the right to information about the charges, and the right to technical defense. The Beijing Rules also consider that the deprivation of liberty of adolescents in conflict with the law should be a measure of outstanding character.
>
> Although the Beijing Rules have not been formally incorporated into Brazil's domestic law, the outlines contained in the document served as inspiration for the ECA. Law practitioners usually invoke the Beijing Rules whenever the Brazilian Law is silent or insufficient to ensure a certain right, and judicial authorities normally welcome arguments based on the Beijing Rules.

to define the meaning of the "best interest of the adolescent" considering the "peculiar condition of development"* in each case.

Finally, the debate on the model of restorative justice in the country is very recent since the few existing initiatives involving restorative justice principles only began at the turn of the new millennium. These initiatives were mostly driven by the Secretariat of the Judicial Reform of the Ministry of Justice.[†] Existing experiences are incipient and have emerged within the judiciary as measures to increase accountability and not necessarily as ways to avoid the judicialization of the conflict. In the state of Rio Grande do Sul, restorative practices involve adolescents who have already been sanctioned with custodial measures.[‡] The Act n. 12.594/12, which created SINASE, paves the way for restorative initiatives by reaffirming the principles of exceptionality of judicial intervention and of the imposition of socio-educational measures by favoring alternative mechanisms of conflict resolution and by conferring priority to restoratives measures or practices, whenever possible, to meet the needs of victims.[§]

Current Trends and Patterns

The main criticism against the welfare model before the ECA entered into force referred to the discriminatory and arbitrary manner through which state intervention targeted children and adolescents from lower classes, and it was tainted by a racist bias that led to an early institutionalization of such social strata in the name of their protection.

Although there has been a significant change in the structure of the juvenile justice system since the ECA, it appears that in practice, the same adolescents—poor, Afro-Brazilian,

---

* Cf. Article 227, par. 3, Clause V of the Federal Constitution and Article 6 of the Child and Adolescent Act (Estatuto da Criança e do Adolescente [ECA]).
† In 2005, the Ministry of Justice published the first Brazilian publication on the subject to stimulate and enhance the debate in the legal and academic community.
‡ More information about this experience is available at http://www.justica21.org.br/
§ Cf. Article 35, clauses II and III of the Federal Law 12.594/2012.

BOX 4.4   YOUTH VICTIMIZATION RATES

Although much has been discussed about crimes perpetrated by young offenders in Brazil, less attention has been devoted to their situation as victims. Recent surveys (see Waiselfisz 2013) show alarming homicide rates among young persons 15–24 years of age. Although they represent only 18% of the total population, figures of homicides related to that age group correspond to 36% of the total number of homicides registered in the country. Between 2001 and 2011, 203,225 young persons were victims of murder in Brazil, which amounts to a death rate of 53.4 per 100,000 population in 2011. A racial cleavage is evident in the registered figures: Victimization rates of young black persons are 237.4% higher than the ones related to white young persons (13,405 homicides against 6,596 in 2011). In 2007, the National Programme to reduce lethal violence against children and adolescents was created by Brazil's Secretariat for Human Rights, the United Nations Children's Emergency Fund (UNICEF), and Favela's Observatory in association with the Laboratory for the Analysis of Violence (LAV-UERJ). The program aims to promote awareness, political articulation, and production of monitoring mechanisms to ensure that the violent deaths of young people are treated as priority on the public agenda. Under the program was created the Index of Homicides in Adolescence (IHA), which was launched in 2009. The IHA was created to estimate the risk faced by adolescents (i.e., aged between 12 and 18 years) who lose their lives due to acts of violence and evaluate factors that may amplify this risk (e.g., race, gender, the age, and their social environment). The data from 2009 reveals that for every 1000 people of 12 years 2.61 will be murdered before reaching 19 years of age. This value increased to 2.98 in 2010, and it represents a disturbing increase in lethal violence against adolescents in Brazil. From this index, it is possible to estimate that if the conditions that prevailed in 2010 do not change, a total of 36,735 teenagers will be murder victims by 2016. The IHA also showed that in 2010, male adolescents had an 11.5 times higher risk of being murdered than female adolescents, and black teenagers ran a 2.78 times higher risk than whites. Moreover, teens had a 5.6 times greater risk of being killed by firearms than by any other instrument. In 2012, these figures led the Government to launch the Alive Youth Plan (*Plano Juventude Viva*), which comprised a set of initiatives aimed at preventing violence against young persons and fighting racism, creating opportunities for social inclusion and autonomy, supplying equipment, utilities, and living spaces in areas that concentrate high homicide rates, and improving the performance of the state by means of confronting institutional racism and awareness of public officials. By March 2014, the Alive Youth Plan has been implemented in the states of Bahia, Alagoas, Paraiba, Federal District and the Metropolitan Region and the city of São Paulo.

Source: Index of Homicides in Adolescence (IHA). Available at http://www.unicef. org/brazil/pt/br_indiceha10.pdf and www.juventude.gov.br/juventudeviva

or coming from communities with less access to justice and fundamental rights—still fill custody institutions. The high levels of incarcerated youth and adolescents along with high levels of victimization within the same age groups (see Box 4.4) highlight three features of Brazilian society: (a) It shows how the cycle of urban violence disproportionately affects this age group (and specifically a certain social profile), (b) it portrays the use of deprivation of liberty as a strategy to mediate social conflicts, and (c) it underlines the pervasive culture of discrimination, which dominates the processes of imprisonment and detention.

Given this scenario, we cannot avoid posing some questions. Is the ECA being applied according to constitutional principles and international norms? Is the justice model able to curb arbitrariness, excessive punishment, and the selectivity of criminal justice institutions? What are the future directions of juvenile justice in Brazil?

One of the existing trends aims at strengthening the justice model through the recognition of "juvenile criminal law" principles. Advocates of the "juvenile criminal law" argue that despite the special nature of socio-educational measures, they are still a state response to the commission of an offense, have coercive features, and restrict the fundamental rights of adolescents. Because of this, the advocates claim that adolescents in conflict with the law are entitled to all due process safeguards that are applicable in any given criminal procedure, wielding the conceptual repertoire of the theory of Penal Guaranteeism (which uses a critical theoretical approach to examine law and reason and the impact of the globalization process in its structure) and the minimum penal law of the Italian author Luigi Ferrajoli.

Those who oppose this perspective raise questions about the need to resort to criminal law concepts to ensure the rights of adolescents in conflict with the law. The opposing trend, which is mostly linked to social workers and psychology professionals, argue that the proposal of "juvenile criminal law" may strengthen Law and Order debates. In doing so, it opens the doors for harsher treatment of the juvenile offender, which could even include lengthier sanctions—according to ECA, the deprivation of liberty of the adolescent cannot last for longer than 3 years. Lately, the sensational coverage given by the mass media to the violent crimes committed by adolescents has given rise to calls for stricter sanctions of young offenders. Meanwhile, the socio-educational system is perceived increasingly as excessively lenient *vis-à-vis* increasing crime rates. Advocates for harsher punishments propose lowering the age of criminal responsibility from 18 to 16 years or even less. In fact, recent opinion polls show that over 90% of Brazilians support the reduction of the current criminal age, which currently stands at 18 by force of a constitutional provision. Currently, there are over 20 different amendment proposals to the constitution under discussion in Parliament, though the predominant line of constitutional interpretation restrains the possibility of legal changes, stating that as a civil liberty-related provision, the established criminal age of responsibility is not subject to modification within the current constitutional framework and would only be allowed if a whole new constitution-making process was set in motion.

In an attempt to derail these initiatives, advocates for children's rights are expressing alternative reform proposals aimed at responding to popular claims while still maintaining a socio-educational system apart from the adult penal system for all offenders below 18 years of age. One of the alternate proposals posits the establishment of different stages of socio-educational responsibility for young persons who have committed violent crimes, which would entail shorter or longer institutionalization sentences depending on the age of the offender. The underlying idea of modulating the time frame of the socio-educational measure according to the age of the offender assumes that older offenders have a higher degree of discernment that would justify a harsher treatment (and, thus, a longer institutionalization sentence, which could go up to 8 years).

There is, for sure, a laudable advantage of avoiding an abrupt transition from socio-educational responsibility to criminal responsibility, which could establish a *de facto* young adults' liability system. However, those who oppose the idea argue that extending the institutionalization period represents a backlash in terms of children's rights and legal safeguards, since it could result in a more detrimental punishment to the adolescent than the one devoted to an adult in a similar situation. Moreover, they add that it is not compatible with the principles of the integral protection doctrine and will not have a palpable effect on criminality figures.

Within specialized circles, however, criticisms are tied not to the rigor (or lack of) of the socio-educational system but to the absence of public policies that are essential to its effectiveness. In that sense, the Ten-Year Plan of the National Socio-educational System, which was launched by the government in 2013* will be key to bridge crucial policy gaps. Proposals contained in the preliminary versions of the plan, such as establishment within the juvenile justice system, of a specialized branch to deal with offenses committed by adolescents may result in a better administration of justice. Also important is the definition of clear standards (in terms of architecture, management, security, and pedagogical program) to the functioning of socio-educational institutions accompanied by the design of tools (such as the PIA) to follow the institutional trajectory of each adolescent. The Ten-Year Plan will also encourage the adoption of restorative justice practices, which are still very weak in the country (for more information regarding pilot restorative initiatives in Brazil, see Raupp and Benedetti 2007), and hopefully institute favorable conditions for the decentralization of noninstitutional socio-educational measures whose absence or precariousness in some municipalities are invoked by judges to determine institutionalization measures.

Conclusion

The Brazilian juvenile justice system is based on the ECA, put in force in 1990, inspired by international guidelines. Its rules reveal a hybrid model of juvenile justice, as a result of the dichotomies that were present in their development processes. The promulgation of the SINASE in 2012 aimed to fill the voids of legislation, especially relating to procedures for the implementation of these measures. Although the SINASE has incorporated some guarantees to avoid the institutional violence committed against adolescents in conflict with the law, it could not avoid some negative judicial practices followed in the name of the protection of the superior interest of the adolescent.

In spite of the priority constitutionally conferred on children and adolescents in Brazil, our legal culture is still immersed in obsolete concepts about childhood and adolescence, and it results in violations of due process-related safeguards combined with several episodes of institutional violence. The outcome is the inadequate and excessive use of institutionalization measures, leading to overcrowded and poorly managed socio-educational institutions in which retributive concerns surpass, by far, educational ones.

Despite all the controversies, it is important to note that the profound changes introduced by the 1988 Constitution and the ECA are still in dispute and will certainly take more time to be fully assimilated by the judiciary and by the Brazilian society as a whole.

---

* See   http://www.sdh.gov.br/assuntos/criancas-e-adolescentes/plano-nacional-de-atendimento-socioedu-cativo-diretrizes-e-eixos-operativos-para-o-sinase

Meanwhile, it is up to the advocates in Brazil to champion the rights of children and adolescents to safeguard the advances achieved so far and to block regressive reform attempts.

Summary

This chapter aims to present an overview of the juvenile justice system in Brazil. The authors present the main points related to the changes in the system and the rules governing Brazilian juvenile justice and its workflow to address the distance between legislation and socio-educational practice—exemplified by information about the execution of socio-educational measures, including custodial. Despite the attempt to align Brazilian legislation with international guidelines, there is a gap between theory and practice that violates the rights of this population. This gap is especially strong when we direct our attention to adolescents in conflict with the law. Moreover, it is important to note that the profound changes introduced by the 1988 Constitution and the ECA are still in dispute in Brazil.

Review/Discussion Questions

1. What are the main differences between the "Irregular Situation Doctrine" and the "Integral Protection Doctrine"?
2. In your opinion, is Brazil's juvenile justice closer to the *justice model* or to the *welfare model*? Explain your answer.
3. The duration of socio-educational measures is not fixed by the sentencing judge in Brazil. Elaborate arguments for and against the use of indeterminate measures.
4. Would you support the formulation of a "criminal juvenile law?" Explain your answer.
5. Name a few normative and practical challenges still facing Brazil's juvenile justice.

References

Brazil. 1990. *Lei nº 8.069 de 13 de julho de 1990. Dispõe sobre o Estatuto da Criança e do Adolescente e dá outras providências*. Brasília: Presidência da República.

Brazil. 2006. *Sistema Nacional de Atendimento Socioeducativo—SINASE*. Brasília: Conanda.

Brazil. 2012. *Lei nº 12.594, de 18 de janeiro de 2012*. Brasília: Presidência da República.

Brazil, Presidency of Republic. Secretariat for Human Rights. 2011. *Levantamento Nacional—Atendimento Socioeducativo ao Adolescente em Conflito com a Lei*. Brasília: SDH/PR.

Doriam, L.B.M. and Ignácio, C. (orgs.). 2012. *Índice de homicídios na adolescência: IHA 2009-2010*. Rio de Janeiro: Observatório de Favelas.

http://www.planalto.gov.br/ccivil_03/_ato2011-2014/2012/lei/l12594.htm.

Index of Homicides in Adolescence (IHA). http://www.unicef.org/brazil/pt/br_indiceha10.pdf.

Méndez, E.G. 1997. *Derecho de La Infancia-Adolescencia en America Latina: de la situación irregular a la protección integral* (2nd ed.). Santafé de Bogotá: Fórum Pacis.

Méndez, E.G. and Beloff, M. (orgs.). 1999. *Infancia, ley y democracia: análisis crítico del panorama legislativo en el marco de la Convención Internacional sobre los Derechos del Niño* (2nd ed.). Bogotá: Temis/Depalma.

National Council of Justice. 2012. *Panorama Nacional: a execução das medidas socioeducativas de internação*. Brasília: CNJ.

Pratt, J. 1993. Welfare and justice: Incompatible philosophies. In *Juvenile Justice: Debating the Issues*. Sydney: Allen and Unwin.

Public Prosecution Service National Council. 2013. *Um olhar mais atento às unidades de internação e semiliberdade de adolescentes: Relatório da Resolução no. 67/2011*. Brasília: CNMP.

Raupp, M. and Benedetti, J. 2007. A implementação da justiça restaurativa no Brasil: uma avaliação dos programas de justiça restaurativa de São Caetano do Sul, Brasília e Porto Alegre. São Paulo: *Revista Ultima Ratio*, 1(1):3–36.

Sposato, K.B. 2006. *O Direito Penal Juvenil*. São Paulo: Editora Revista dos Tribunais.

Yamamoto, A. and Lago, N. 2010. Teenagers in conflict with the law and justice in Brazil. *Freedom from Fear Magazine*. Accessed at: http://f3magazine.unicri.it/?p=74

Waiselfisz, J.J. 2013. *Mapa da Violência 2013: Homicídios e juventude no Brasil*. Rio de Janeiro: CEBELA, FLACSO.

Internet Sources

ANDI: A news agency specialized in the promotion of the rights of children and adolescents. ANDI´s website has a good coverage of news related to juvenile justice and other subjects. http://www.andi.org.br/

Observatory for Rights of Children and Adolescents: A government website that contains information about official policies, legislation, and news about rights of children and adolescents in Brazil. http://www.obscriancaeadolescente.gov.br/

Rights of Children and Adolescents Monitoring Project: Developed by the National Forum for the Rights of Children and Adolescents (an association of civil society organizations), this website presents reports on the situation of children and adolescents in each Brazilian state. http://www.monitoredireitos.org.br/

Juvenile Justice and Young Offenders: A Canadian Overview

5

JOHN A. WINTERDYK AND
ANNE MILLER

Contents

The Birth of Juvenile Justice in Canada   109
    Creating the JDA   109
    The Long Road to Reform   110
    Creating the YOA   111
    New Millennium, New Act: YCJA   114
The Dimensions of the Delinquency Problem   115
    What Are the Official Trends?   116
    Types of Crimes Committed   118
    Profile of Young Offenders   118
    Victimization   120
    "Causes" of Youth Crime   120
    Repeat Offenders   121
    The Financial Burden of Youth Justice   122
The Youth Justice Process   122
    Initial Contact   124
    Youth Court Proceedings   124
    Sentencing Options   125
    Postsentencing: "Corrections"   125
       Youth in Court   125
       Youth in Custody   126
Current Issues Facing Canadian Youth Today   128
    Youth Gangs   128
    Runaways and Street-Involved Youth   128
    Teenage Suicide   130
    Female Delinquency   130
    Aboriginal Youth   131
Summary   132
Review/Discussion Questions   133
References   133
Internet Sources   136

FACTS ABOUT CANADA

Area: With an area of 3,851,792 sq. miles or approximately 10 million sq. km, Canada covers six time zones. **Population:** Its population was in excess of 35.1 million in 2013. Outside of the province of Quebec, approximately 80% of Canadians are English speaking, 6% French, with other denominations including Chinese, East Indian, Ukrainian, and German. Seven out of 10 citizens are urban dwellers. Approximately 85% crowd into a 200-km-wide strip along the U.S. border. Major cities include Montreal, Toronto, and Vancouver. Ottawa is the nation's capital. Canada's population characteristics are changing rapidly and will continue to do so well into the future. Life expectancy in 2009 was 81.1 years of age. **Climate:** Climate varies widely by region and latitude. Winters are cool to cold (avg. 0°C to −15°C), while summers can average temperatures from 18°C to mid-20s. **Economy:** Canada hosts a wide range of natural resources: fishing, pulp and paper, farming, mining (e.g., gold, silver, zinc, coal, asbestos, uranium, hydroelectric), as well as manufacturing. **Government:** A parliament and 10 provincial legislatures and 3 territories guide the government. In 2013, the Conservative Party was the federal party. Other major parties include the National Democratic Party; Bloc Québécois, Green Party, and the Liberal Party. The ruling party has a 4-year term.

Every juvenile delinquent shall be treated ... as a misdirected and misguided child.

Juvenile Delinquents Act, 1908

Young persons who commit offences should ... bear responsibility.

Young Offenders Act, 1984

By international standards, Canada is a fairly young nation. It is also one of the few countries in the world, which gained nationhood without a revolution. It was first permanently settled by Europeans in 1608, by Samuel de Champlain of France and then by the English circa 1660s around the Hudson Bay area. Although England and France were interested in colonization, their primary investment in the "New Land" was fur trading. Within a few years, the rivalries over trading routes and territory began to escalate. This culminated in the Seven Years' War (1756–63) in which the French were defeated, but in the Quebec Act of 1774, French Canadians were granted a certain amount of autonomy in Quebec. However, the Quebec Act said that for criminal law, the law of England would apply.

Since early times, Canada has been influenced by the different political orientations of its European heritage. And while the Canadian criminal justice system is primarily influenced by England, remnants from the French accusatorial model are still felt—an adaptation of the Code of Napoleon in 1804—and French-speaking Canadians are well represented in federal politics as it is well defined and guaranteed under the Constitution. In addition, Quebec has retained its French legal heritage by modeling its civil code after that of France. Another legal area of note concerns jurisdictional powers. In accordance with the British North America Act (1867) (replaced by the Constitution Act, 1982 wherein the first 35 sections of the act form the Canadian Charter of Rights and Freedom), Canada adopted a political model in which there is a demarcation between federal jurisdiction and provincial jurisdiction. This division of power has had a profound impact on the administration of juvenile/youth justice in Canada.

This chapter will begin by tracing the historical development of the juvenile justice system in Canada after presenting an overview of the Juvenile Delinquents Act (JDA), an outline of the tumultuous transition, which led to the Young Offenders Act (YOA) in 1984, and then the Youth Criminal Justice Act (YCJA) in 2004. Here, the key elements of the act will be covered before describing some of the past and present trends and patterns in youth crime. Next, an overview of how young offenders are officially handled by the major elements of the young offenders system will be described. The chapter will conclude with a discussion of some of the major issues currently confronting the handling of young offenders in Canada today.

The Birth of Juvenile Justice in Canada

Creating the JDA

During the early pioneer days, Canada's young people were likely given considerable freedoms given the frontier spirit that prevailed. However, due to both economic and physical hardships, life was difficult on both families and the youth. As Carrigan (1991) notes, numerous young persons were being abandoned, abused, or simply neglected. These wayward youth slowly became a growing concern until the mid-1880s when the government found it necessary to intervene. One of the first steps taken in an attempt to control the problem involved making school attendance compulsory in 1871. However, growing urbanization and dramatic increases in the number of "homeless British waifs and street urchins" only helped to fuel the youth problem during the late 1800s (West 1984, 29).

Sutherland (1976) reports that, toward the end of the 1890s, people felt that more drastic measures were required. The public felt that somehow the state needed to intervene to help ensure that rehabilitation principles could be enforced for the benefit of those involved in delinquent behavior. An Act Respecting Arrest, Trial and Imprisonment of Youthful Offenders was passed on July 23, 1894, as a measure to permit the state to intervene when families failed to raise their children "properly" (Carrigan 1991). The essence of the legislation was that a juvenile delinquent not be treated as an adult criminal in need of punishment "but as a misdirected and misguided child." This reform and family-centered system led to the development of the children's court. The supposition was to keep young persons away from the influence of the adult judicial process. Given the varying sentiments at the time, little was done until 1908 when primarily through the stewardship of J.J. Kelso and W.L. Scott, the JDA was passed.

In addition to setting out the guidelines for juvenile courts, the JDA encompassed a number of key philosophical elements, which strongly reflected the treatment philosophy. This treatment philosophy is widely referred to as *parens patriae*.*

---

* A Latin expression, which means the state has the power to act on behalf of the child/youth and provide care and protection equivalent to that of a parent. The term reflects a paternalistic philosophy emphasizing treatment and which sees delinquent youth as misguided and in need of special consideration and help.

It embodied the essential elements of the positivist school of criminology and is described as representing a **welfare model** (Winterdyk 2002). For example, Section 2 of the JDA defined a juvenile delinquent as

> any child who violates any provision of the Criminal Code or any federal or provincial statute, or any by-law or ordinance of any municipality, or who is guilty of sexual immorality or any similar form of vice, or who is liable by reason of any other act to be committed to an industrial school or juvenile reformatory under any federal or provincial statute.

The general features of the JDA can be summed up as follows:

Informality of handling (e.g., while the minimum age of delinquency was 7, the upper limit varied among provinces from 17 to 18), individualized sentencing (i.e., provincial responsibility), and indeterminate sentencing—based on the rationale of *parens patriae.*

Reliance on childcare experts, social workers, and probation officers.

Emphasis on diagnosing problems (e.g., social, family, school, personal, and physical environment).

Individualized treatment over punishment; for example, Section 38 of the JDA stated: "The care and custody and discipline of a juvenile delinquent shall approximate as nearly as may be that which should be given by his parents."

While the act was revised in 1929 and had a number of amendments made to it in subsequent years, criticism grew over whether the principle of *parens patriae* violated basic constitutional rights (Currie 1986). This issue drew widespread attention after 1967 when the U.S. Supreme Court heard the case of *In Re Gault,* the first juvenile case to be decided on constitutional grounds. Furthermore, throughout the 1960s and into the early 1970s, there was increasing disillusionment over the rehabilitative philosophy of the Canadian juvenile system and its programs. This general sentiment was epitomized in Robert Martinson's classic 1974 paper in which he proclaimed "nothing works" in the area of community-based corrections. Subsequent support, for this view, came from Empey (1982), Lundman (1984, 1994), and Trojanowicz (1978). Also during this time, a number of researchers called for greater accountability of young offenders (e.g., Wilson 1975). The seeds for reform had begun to germinate. But, as deMause (1988) questioned, were the seeds planted in the interest of the youth in conflict with the law or did the reforms simply represent a tactic for extending state control (i.e., "net-widening") over our youth? This is a pedagogical issue for which there is no clear answer.

The Long Road to Reform

The following synopsis offers a chronological overview of the major legislative proposals, which led to the proclamation of the YOA in 1984.

1965: The Federal Committee on Juvenile Delinquency began to actively campaign to reform the JDA.

1970: Bill C-192 introduced a measure to repeal the JDA.

1975: "Young Persons in Conflict with the Law" proposals were circulated. Each province was asked to review elements for the new act. Key elements included title of the act (Young Offences Act vs. YOA); ages (12–17); jurisdiction of administration; the importance of diversion and use of alternative social and legal measures; detention and general matters pertaining to sentencing and custody; setting the minimum age for transfer to adult court from 14 to 16; legal representation; and federal–provincial financial implications.

1977: The YOA was first introduced. But, between 1977 and 1981, it was revamped several times.

February 16, 1981: The Young Offenders Bill was tabled in the House of Commons. Seventy-three years after the JDA, the then Solicitor General of Canada, Bob Kaplan tabled the new act declaring that the existing act (JDA) "was seriously out of date with contemporary practices and attitudes regarding juvenile justice and inadequate to meet the problems presented today by young people in conflict with the law" (Solicitor General of Canada 1981).

1982: The YOA was passed by the Parliament with unanimous support from all three major political parties.

April 1, 1984: The YOA was proclaimed law.

Creating the YOA

As demonstrated above, the transition from the JDA to the YOA was a drawn-out process. Political debates for reform began in 1965, and it took nearly 20 years before the JDA was replaced with the YOA. And while the political argument was that delinquency rates had been increasing significantly throughout the 1960s and 1970s, several Canadian researchers suggested that any increase might be largely attributable to more effective police surveillance and a greater determination to bring young people to justice (McDonald 1969). Furthermore, the period was marked by high unemployment rates and other social problems such as role ambiguity, which in accordance with the General Strain Theory (Akers and Sellers 2013), generates stresses and strains that can leave adolescents feeling lost when they are unable to meet or attain the basic goals common to others in their age group. Some youths may feel the only way to resolve their anger, frustrations, and other adverse emotional states is by resorting to deviant and criminal acts.* Akers and Sellers (2013) identify three sources of strain: (a) strain resulting from the failure to achieve positively valued goals (e.g., wealth, fame, and social acceptance); (b) when a youth's positively valued stimuli are removed (e.g., the loss of a girl/boyfriend, move to a new town, and the divorce or separation of parents), strain can result; and (c) strain arising with the presentation of negative stimuli (e.g., child abuse, criminal victimization, and school failure).

The combination of dramatic social changes, public pressure for accountability of young offenders, the frustration of police with youth courts because they felt the courts interfered with their work, and the political momentum behind the need for reform finally brought the new act to fruition. The act brought new legal principles and fundamentally

---

* This theme was reiterated in a feature article of the Alberta Report. Dr. Genuis, executive director of the National Foundation for Family Research and Education in Edmonton, Alberta, was quoted as saying: "There is also a cultural crisis among teens... Too many of their other anti-social behaviours are on the rise to believe they are not also committing more crimes" (Verburg 1995, 31).

different philosophies for handling of juvenile offenders into force. The YOA represented a shift from the positivist school and a welfare model to the neo-classical school and the "**Modified Justice Model**" (Corrado et al. 1992) that Hagan, Alwin, and Hewitt (1979) generally described as a "**loosely coupled system**" (see Box 5.1; also see Hagan 1995).

BOX 5.1   BILL C-10: GETTING "TOUGH ON CRIME"

The Safe Streets and Safe Communities Act, or Bill C-10, was passed by the Parliament on March 12, 2012. Taking a "tough-on-crime" approach to justice in Canada, the bill combined a number of different bills to address several areas of justice the presiding Conservative government felt should be addressed through harsher punishments, including increased incarceration. According to the Department of Justice, the areas addressed through this large, multifaceted bill include the protection of children and youth from sexual predators; penalties for organized drug crime; ending house arrest for serious crimes; the protection of the public from violent young offenders; the elimination of pardons for serious crimes; enshrinement in law of a number of additional key factors in deciding whether an offender would be granted a transfer back to Canada; offender accountability and support for victims of crime; support for victims of terrorism; and the protection of vulnerable foreign nationals against abuse and exploitation.

Specifically in relation to young offenders, Bill C-10 put forward amendments to the YCJA designed to

- Change pretrial detention rules to keep violent and repeat young offenders in custody while they await trial
- Facilitate the sentencing process to ensure violent and repeat young offenders can be sentenced to custody; specifically, to create principles of sentencing based on "deterrence" measures, to expand the definition of "violent offense," and to allow more custodial sentences to be imposed if patterns of offending emerge under other sanctioning measures
- Require the Crown to consider seeking adult sentences for youth convicted of the most serious violent crimes (murder, attempted murder, manslaughter, and aggravated sexual assault)
- Facilitate the lifting of publication bans on the names of young offenders convicted of "violent offenses"
- Require police to keep records when informal measures are used to make it easier to track offenders

Despite international trends away from harsher punishments for young offenders, this new development in Canada's approach to youth justice provides for both increased incarceration time for youth committing crimes as well as the potential for harsher sentences and greater shaming. Critics of the bill have expressed concern that the changes shift Canada's approach to youth justice away from rehabilitation and toward the "protection of society," with the potential of resulting in punishing young offenders rather than steering them away from deviant behavior. Further, longer and harsher sentences are argued to transform convicted youth into hardened criminals, thereby undermining the potential for rehabilitation. With the increased emphasis on incarceration brought about through this approach, some are concerned that young Aboriginal and black Canadians, who are already disproportionately represented in the justice system, will be increasingly disproportionately affected by the changes. Finally, critics argue that encouraging the names of young offenders to be released by the courts to the media and public will result in unproductive stigmatization of these youth.

The concerns already mentioned come not only internally from members of the Canadian public, but they have also been highlighted internationally by the United Nations. Finishing a 10-year review of how Canada treats its children according to the Convention on the Rights of the Child, the UN Committee on the Rights of the Child expressed concerns about the punitiveness enhanced through the changes to the YCJA through Bill C-10. The United Nations Children's Emergency Fund (UNICEF) Canada even went as far as to submit a Brief to the House of Commons Standing Committee on Justice and Human Rights outlining concern over the bill. Considering that the preamble to the YCJA states that "Canada is a party to the United Nations Convention on the Rights of the Child and recognizes that young persons have rights and freedoms, including those stated in the Canadian Charter of Rights and Freedoms and the Canadian Bill of Rights, and have special guarantees of their rights and freedoms" it seems essential to examine critically the recent move toward harsher punishment for youth crimes (see Smandych 2006).

The most important provisions of the YOA may be summarized as follows:

The YOA (Section 2(1)) defines a "young person" as someone who is 12–17 years of age, inclusive. All jurisdictions are required to comply with this uniform age range in applying the act.

Those youth under 12 years of age were not to be dealt with by the criminal justice system. Each province maintained its own child welfare legislation to handle any youth requiring special attention (in most provinces, the two bodies worked closely together—see Bala, Hornick, and Vogl 1991 for a detailed review).

Youthful offenders were now referred to as "young offenders" rather than juvenile delinquents to reflect the change in status and philosophical orientation.

As recommended under Rule 1.3 of the UN Standards (1986), young offenders under the YOA were entitled to due process, and ideally the process was to be conducted informally.

Like adult offenders, youth crimes were considered criminal in nature and were handled in a similar manner. These principles appear under Rule 25 of the United Nations (UN) Standards (1986).

Young offenders who were suspected of violating any federal legislation, such as the Criminal Code, the Food and Drugs Act, and the Narcotic Control Act came under the jurisdiction of youth courts.

The youth court could also hear the cases of young persons accused of provincial
offenses such as traffic violations.

Sentencing was to be determinant with a minimum and maximum range. This principle can also be found under Rule 3.1 of the UN Standards (1986).

Because of their "special" status, offending youth were to be entitled to childcare/
youth-care experts as well as lawyers for counsel.

Sentencing was to reflect a greater level of accountability. Hence, under the YOA there
was a greater emphasis on accountability. However, due to their age, maturity, and
history of offending behavior, delinquent youth are not generally accountable in
the same manner as adults. These concepts are also found in the UN Standards
(1986) under Rules 13.1 and 19.1.

The primary purpose of intervention was a balance between sanctioning criminal/
deviant behavior and providing appropriate treatment.

The primary objective of the act was to provide greater accountability while still
respecting the individuals' rights and taking into account their "special needs."

To address the needs of young offenders, a system of separate and specialized youth
courts and correctional programs was maintained.

In essence, the shift was toward due process of law and as Ted Rubin in 1976 noted
(cited in Milner 1995, 67): "The future is clear: law and due process are here to stay in juvenile court... rehabilitation efforts will be pursued in a legal context." However, as indicated
in the preceding text, as controversial as the YOA has been, it does include many of the
guidelines put forth by the United Nations (1986).

New Millennium, New Act: YCJA

The YCJA came into force in 2003, replacing the YOA. The YCJA is notably longer than
the YOA. It has 165 substantive sections in comparison to 70 sections in the YOA (see
Green 2012). Although more complex and arguably more comprehensive than the YOA,
Barnhorst (2004, 233–235) has summarized the main components of the act in six main
points. They include

1. **Restraint**, encompassing both sentencing and the decision of whether to use the
   formal court process in the first place
2. **Accountability**, with a focus on holding youth accountable for their actions by
   imposing meaningful consequences that will promote the rehabilitation and reintegration of the youth into society.
3. **Proportionality**, meaning that consequences imposed on young people be proportionate to the seriousness of the offense and the youth's degree of responsibility.
4. **Protection of the public**, which the system can contribute to through holding
   youths accountable in a fair and proportionate manner, while acknowledging that
   "there are many factors outside the youth justice system that can have as much
   effect, or greater effect, on public protection than the activities of the youth justice
   system."
5. **Rehabilitation and addressing needs**, ensuring that the "seriousness of the offence
   sets the degree of intervention, and efforts to address the rehabilitative needs of
   youths fit within the proportionate response."

6. **Structured discretion**, reflecting the Parliament's view that officials in the youth justice system be given more legislative direction on how to exercise their discretion in a way that is consistent with the act's objectives.

As reflected in the points in the preceding text, the YCJA strives to reduce its former reliance on the use of custody and limit its use to only the most serious of cases. And as will be discussed in the following text, the new provision for extrajudicial measures for less serious offenses have availed the system of a host of new alternative options (e.g., conferencing and other expressions of restorative justice practices). Yet, the act still ensures that young offenders are held accountable for their offenses and, where possible, encourages a multidisciplinary approach to youth justice.

Having now been in effect for over 10 years, the act has gained reasonable respect, although some argue that it could also benefit from various amendments. Yet, Bala, Carrington, and Roberts (2012) conclude that when passed, the act "represented an astute political compromise" as the act has attempted to balance public anxiety about alleged escalating incidents of violent crimes with the disproportionate number of youth being processed through the formal criminal justice channels.

Having presented an overview of the past and present legislative measures used to address young offenders, we will now examine some of the trends and patterns of youth crime. Thereafter, we will provide an overview on how the key actors of the youth justice system handle young offenders.

The Dimensions of the Delinquency Problem

> Many Canadians, afraid and frustrated, succumb to the temptation of quick fixes served up by ever-willing politicians and the media. Lock them up and throw away the key! Send them to boot camp! Bring back the cane! Zero tolerance! Adult time for adult crime!
>
> **Youth Justice, 1994**

In collaboration with the provinces and territorial departments responsible for youth courts, the Canadian Centre for Justice Statistics (CCJS) currently collects information on young persons in Canada's justice system.* However, from time to time, some jurisdictions have been unable to submit their data. Also because of variations among provincial reporting practices, data are considered suggestive rather than definitive.† Notwithstanding these qualifiers, it is possible to present a general picture of youth crime in Canada that comes to the attention of the police and of how the cases are disposed of. That is, in addition to examining official statistics, where possible, reference will be made to self-report and victimization studies to provide a more realistic account of the "true" youth crime picture.

---

* In 1962, the federal government introduced, nationwide, the Canadian Uniform Crime Report (UCR) system. This measure helped to minimize many of the limitations of the previous approach. The Canadian UCR was modeled after the American UCR system. In the late 1980s, Statistics Canada created the national institute, The Canadian Centre for Justice Statistics, which is now responsible for collecting, aggregating, and disseminating official crime statistics. The first reports were published in 1991. This model is similar to what the Home Office does for England and Wales.

† While 12 became the minimum age requirement for charges under the YOA in 1984, it was not until April 1984 that the maximum age of 17 (inclusive) was established across all of Canada. Therefore, reliable comparisons cannot be made prior to 1986–87.

What Are the Official Trends?

Measuring the prevalence and nature of crime in Canada is an important issue, as the amount of crime in a country can be seen as a reflection of the overall safety and well-being of the population (HRSDC 2012). Statistics Canada uses two methods to measure crime in Canada: self-reported victimization surveys and police-reported data. The Uniform Crime Reporting (UCR) Survey collects data on all criminal incidents that Canadian police have substantiated from reports. Statistics Canada has been collecting this data since 1962, providing long-term data on police-reported crime statistics in the country. The survey captures changes in the number and rate of individual offenses reported by police, including homicide, robbery, sexual offenses, break-ins, and motor vehicle thefts. It also provides information to determine trends in the volume and severity of both violent and nonviolent offenses at the national, provincial/territorial, and census metropolitan area levels.

Juristat is a publication from Statistics Canada that presents findings on justice-related topics in Canada. Articles from this publication are useful in providing data on crime, homicide, youth and adult courts, and correctional services.

Juristat's "Police-Reported Crime Statistics, 2011" indicates that the crime rate in Canada (the total volume of crime per 100,000 in the population) has been steadily decreasing for the past 18 years after peaking in 1991. In 2011, the crime rate had reached its lowest point since 1972.

The same police-reported statistics can be used to assess the *severity* of crimes rather than just focusing on the *volume* of these crimes (the crime rate) (see Figure 5.1). This is assessed using the Crime Severity Index (CSI) (for further details on the CSI see Brennan 2012). Over the past decade, not only has the number of crimes decreased in Canada, but the severity of these crimes has also decreased (with the exception of the year 2003). Overall, there has been a 26% decrease over the past decade up to 2011 (Brennan 2012). This data only speaks of the Canadian population as a whole and does not offer any breakdown for Canada's younger citizens. However, as of July 1, 2010, in Canada, there were approximately, 3.7 million children under the age of 10; 1.9 million youths aged 10–14; and 2.2 million youths between 15 and 19 years of age. In 2006, 48% of the Aboriginal people were less than 25 years old, compared to 31% for non-Aboriginals; young Aboriginals is one of the fastest growing demographic categories in the nation (Statistics Canada 2010).

In the past decade, following the trend in the general population, crime committed by youth in Canada has been on the decline according to police-reported statistics. This trend is seen both in terms of the youth crime rate, which measures the number of criminal incidents involving youth, as well as the youth CSI, which measures the seriousness of youth crime. Figure 5.2 illustrates this trend.

Another way to measure youth crime in Canada is through self-reported crimes. The International Youth Survey found that in total, 37% of the youth self-reported having engaged in one or more delinquent behaviors over the course of their life. These delinquent behaviors could be acts of violence, acts against property, or the sale of drugs. It also found that delinquent behavior reported for foreign-born youth was lower than that for their Canadian-born peers (15% and 23% respectively) and that there was no significant difference in the prevalence of delinquency between Canadian-born children of immigrant parents (22%) and Canadian-born children whose parents were not immigrants (24%) (Savoie 2007).

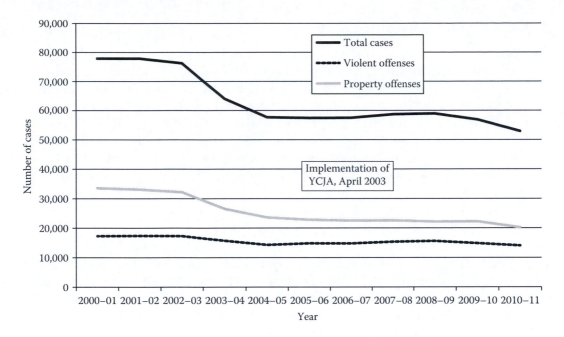

Figure 5.1 Cases completed in Youth Court, Canada, 2000/2001 to 2010/2011. Note: Total cases include violent offenses, property offenses, administration of justice offenses, other Criminal Code offenses, Criminal Code traffic offenses, and other federal statutes. (Statistics Canada. (2012). *Integrated Criminal Court Survey, 2010/2011.* Statistics Canada, Canadian Centre for Justice Statistics.)

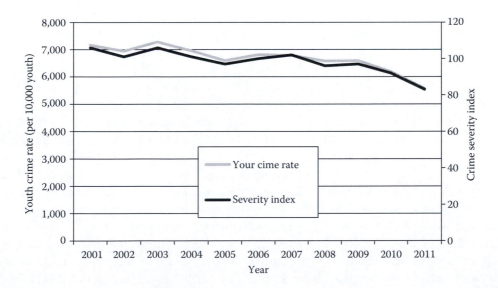

Figure 5.2 Police-reported youth crime rate and Crime Severity Index. Note: The Youth Crime Index has been standardized to a base year of 2006, which is equal to 100. Youth refers to individuals aged 12–17 years. The crime rate includes youth who were formally charged by police (or recommended for charging) as well as youth who were cleared by other means (e.g., alternative measures). (Statistics Canada, Canadian Centre for Justice Statistics. (2011). Uniform Crime Reporting Survey.)

Types of Crimes Committed

The decade-long decrease in youth crime outlined in the preceding text was seen in all types of crime, including the most serious offenses like homicide, assault, or robbery. For example, there were 46 youth accused of homicide in 2011, 10 fewer than in 2010, which resulted in a 16% drop in the youth homicide rate. Further, the rate of major assault and robbery dropped 4% from 2010. Declines were also seen in the rate of youth accused of most nonviolent crimes, including break-ins (−5%) and motor-vehicle theft (−4%). In 2006, around 5% of all Criminal Code violations committed by youth involved a weapon, most commonly a knife. Table 5.1 in the following text outlines the change in youth violent crime rate by province from 2010 to 2011 and Table 5.2 the overall youth crime rate by province and territory as well as the change in the crime rate between 2010 to 2011. Overall, the youth crime rate has dropped as has been the case since the late 1990s (see Box 5.2 in the following text).

In 2008, the most common locations for youth crime were private residences (32%); commercial establishments (23%); and outdoor public spaces (23%). The peak times for youth crime were after-school hours (3–6 p.m.) for violent (22%) and nonviolent (20%) crime; early afternoon (noon–3 p.m.) for drug offenses (24%); and nighttime (9 p.m. to midnight) for youth traffic violations (28%).

Profile of Young Offenders

In 2010, nearly 153,000 youths were accused of committing a crime. This represents approximately 6% of the Canadian youth population 12–17 years of age. Youth crime, however, continues to represent a small proportion of overall crimes. In 2010, of the 494,621 persons charged for **Criminal Code** violations (excluding traffic), 64,800 (13.1%) were youths. In 2010, the peak age for offending, in terms of those accused of a Criminal Code offense, was 18 years of age, and generally decreased with increasing age. In addition, the rate of persons accused increases sharply from age 12 to age 18 where it peaks. The rate then decreases throughout the 20s, leveling off in the 30s, and then decreases continuously to age 55 (see http://www.publicsafety.gc.ca/cnt/rsrcs/pblctns/ststclsnpsht-yth/index-eng.aspx).

As evidenced in virtually every other country, there has continued to be a gender split in terms of the youth who are committing crimes in Canada, with females accounting for only about one-quarter of youth accused by police of having committed a **Criminal Code** offense in 2009. Overall, the rate of offending of female youth is still less than half of that of male youth (4,011 per 100,000 vs. 9,700 per 100,000). Further, young males (30%) were twice as likely as young females (15%) to have engaged in violent behavior, and they were also slightly more likely than young females to report that they had committed acts against property (30% vs. 26%). Typically, young females are charged most frequently with shoplifting offenses, mischief, and administrative offenses (e.g., failure to comply with decisions of youth court—failure to comply with decisions of the youth justice) (see Hotton 2011). These trends are not dissimilar from those expressed in other chapters throughout this book.

A popular explanation for female underrepresentation in the official statistics draws on three related factors: gender role socialization, differential social control, and variations in opportunity (Hagan, Simpson, and Gillis 1979). As mentioned in the previous section, crimes committed by foreign-born youth were lower than by their Canadian-born peers (15% and 23%, respectively), and there was no significant difference between

Table 5.1   Change in Youth Violent Crime Rate, 2010–2011, by Province

Province or Territory	Youth Violent Crime Rate (per 100,000)	Change in Rate (2010–2011)
Alberta	1793	⇩ 10%
British Columbia	1217	⇩ 6%
Manitoba	3160	⇩ 12%
Newfoundland and Labrador	2032	⇩ 4%
Northwest Territories	7418	⇩ 3%
Nova Scotia	2649	⇩ 4%
Nunavut	5882	⇩ 27%
Ontario	1549	⇩ 3%
Prince Edward Island	1477	⇩ 9%
Quebec	1662	⇧ 2%
Saskatchewan	3404	⇩ 12%
Yukon	4071	⇩ 13%
CANADA	**1756**	**⇩ 5%**

Source: Statistics Canada, Canadian Centre for Justice Statistics. (2011). Uniform Crime Reporting Survey.

Note: Youth refers to individuals aged 12–17 years. The crime rates are based on the number of youth who were either charged (or recommended for charging) by police or diverted from the formal criminal justice system through the use of warnings, cautions, referrals to community programs, etc. Counts are based upon the most serious violations in the incident. Violent crimes include murder, robbery, major assault, etc.

Table 5.2   Change in Youth Crime Rate, 2010–2011, by Province

Province or Territory	Youth Crime Rate (per 100,000)	Change in Rate (2010–2011)	
Alberta	6,918	13%	⇩
British Columbia	4,623	14%	⇩
Manitoba	9,330	15%	⇩
Newfoundland and Labrador	6,327	5%	⇩
Northwest Territories	36,168	15%	⇩
Nova Scotia	8,985	2%	⇩
Nunavut	25,235	24%	⇩
Ontario	4,561	9%	⇩
Prince Edward Island	5,303	13%	⇩
Quebec	3,800	6%	⇩
Saskatchewan	16,997	4%	⇧
Yukon	18,133	20%	⇩
CANADA	5,564	10%	⇩

Source: Statistics Canada, Canadian Centre for Justice Statistics. (2011). Uniform Crime Reporting Survey.

Note: Youth refers to individuals aged 12–17 years. The crime rates are based on the number of youth who were either charged (or recommended for charging) by police or diverted from the formal criminal justice system through the use of warnings, cautions, referrals to community programs, etc. Counts are based upon the most serious violations in the incident. Crimes include break and enter, motor vehicle theft, property crime, etc.

Canadian-born children of immigrant parents (22%) and Canadian-born children whose parents were not immigrants (24%).

When looking at youth crime on Aboriginal reserves, however, there is a stark contrast with the rest of the Canadian population. The youth crime rate on reserves was three times the national average in 2004, with about one-quarter of on-reserve youth offenses being violent crimes, compared with one-fifth elsewhere in Canada. Young offenders on reserves were accused of committing homicides about 11 times more often than youth elsewhere in Canada and were seven times more likely to be accused of break and enter and disturbing the peace. The higher rates of crime, particularly violent crime, among youth on reserves highlight the need to understand the socioeconomic, cultural, and historic experience of Canada's Aboriginal peoples.

Victimization

About 60% of the victims of a youth crime are youth themselves (children or youth under the age of 18). Individuals within the 18–24, 25–34, and 35–44 age ranges each make up about one-tenth of youth crime victims, with victims aged 45 and over constituting the remaining tenth (http://www.publicsafety.gc.ca/cnt/rsrcs/pblctns/ststclsnpsht-yth/index-eng.aspx). The General Social Survey (GSS) measures many different elements of social interaction in Canadian society. Included in the GSS are measures of violent victimization. This is measured by gathering information on three violent crimes—sexual assault, robbery, and physical assault. In addition to measuring the prevalence of violent victimization in Canada, the 2009 GSS provides information on the sociodemographic characteristics of victims of violence, as well as information about offenders. In 2009, younger Canadians were more likely than older Canadians to indicate that they had been violently victimized within the previous 12-month period. This can be broken down into people between the ages of 15 and 24 years, who were almost 15 times more likely than those aged 65 and older to report being a victim of a violent victimization (http://www.statcan.gc.ca/pub/85-002-x/2010002/article/11340-eng.htm). Based on these 2009 GSS survey results, Northcott (2011) explored the implications of these greater rates of victimization in her 2010 study *Understanding the Experiences of Youth Victimization*. She found that youth are more likely to seek support from friends and family rather than from more formal supports, such as the police or counselors and that the victimization experienced by individuals at a young age can have many negative consequences, ranging from effects on self-esteem to drug and alcohol use and other forms of self-harm. She highlighted that "finding ways to reach and educate youth is therefore essential in mitigating these negative outcomes."

"Causes" of Youth Crime

Why do young people break criminal rules and commit status offenses? This is a question not only asked and studied by many Canadian criminologists but also by scholars around the world. The range of explanations can often appear overwhelming. In this section, we will only focus on several key studies conducted on Canadian young offenders.

If one can use Canadian textbooks and Canadian journal articles as an indicator of theoretical preference, then it would appear that sociological/macro perspectives are the most popular for explaining causes of youth crime. Factors that have been studied to explain delinquent involvement include the following:

- Based on the Social Learning Theory (Akers and Sellers 2013), peer influence and peer pressure has been studied by some scholars in Canada. Using secondary data, Brownfield and Thompson (1991) were able to support the social learning/control theory. They concluded that "measures of peer involvement in delinquency are strongly and positively associated with self-report delinquency" (1991, 57).
- Using a conceptualization of class and family that focuses on the power relations in the workplace and the home, Hagan, Simpson, and Gillis (1987) argue that delinquency rates are a function of class differences and economic conditions that in turn influence the structure of family life. Their Power-Control Theory has been reasonably effective in explaining the relative increase in female delinquency since it recognizes the effects of social changes such as the decline of the patriarchal family and changing gender roles (Baron 2012).
- Drawing on ecological concepts and presuming the rationality of offenders, the Routine Activity Theory, developed by Cohen and Felson in 1979, has attempted to link the increase in delinquency to increased suitability of targets and a decline in the presence of guardians (e.g., friends, family, and neighbors). In Canada, Kennedy and Baron (1993) demonstrated that choices, routines, and cultural milieu interact to affect one another to create opportunities for delinquency.
- Gottfredson and Hirschi's recent General Theory of Crime (earlier version entitled Propensity-Event Theory) has also received recent attention in Canada. This approach represents an attempt to integrate classical and positivist principles into a general model of crime. The theory represents a revision of Hirschi's Control Theory. The new version suggests that people naturally act in a self-interested fashion. However, our socialization can affect our level of self-control. Delinquency is largely a result of low self-control. However, unlike Hirschi's earlier theory, the new model focuses more on the individual traits than external sources of control. In his study on delinquency and school dropouts, Creechan (1995, 238) found the "general theory of crime produced a remarkably accurate prediction of who is normal."
- Other factors commonly studied and used to explain Canadian youth crime include substance abuse (Diplock and Plecas 2012), abuse and neglect (Horner 1993), breakdown in values and norms, and various personality problems.

Overall, the cause(s) of youth crime in Canada might best be illustrated in a quote from the Canadian Criminal Justice Association (CCJA) which concluded, "Causal relationships among these behaviors cannot be determined accurately, nor can we affirm which comes first in time or importance" (CCJA 1992, 3).

Therefore, while the phenomena of youth crime has been around since Europeans first began to colonize Canada, our legal efforts and theoretical approaches have not had a positive impact on youth crime rates. This has been reflected in our youth crime data as well as our in our recidivism counts.

Repeat Offenders

It has been suggested that the success, or failure, of punishment can be measured by recidivism. While the concept is not that straightforward, nevertheless, such rates are considered a reasonable measure of how effective the youth justice system is in deterring and rehabilitating young offenders.

Recidivism rates on young offenders in Canada are not regularly recorded. However, there have been a number of studies that offer a glimpse into the repeat offending patterns of young offenders. In the early 1990s, about 18.6% of young offenders who appeared in court had five or more prior convictions (Moyer 1992). By the late 1990s, nearly 42% of cases with convictions involved repeat offenders (Carrieree 2000). And although there have been a few isolated studies since then, there is a need for more comprehensive research into the subject area as it has the potential to "provide a deeper understanding of criminal career trends and provide evidence-based insight into how to better address youth crime" in Canada (Winterdyk 2012, 44).

The Financial Burden of Youth Justice

One of the ongoing concerns the provinces have had since the 1970s has been the increased cost to the provinces to provide the services needed to meet the conditions of the new act. Based on the most recent available data, crime costs Canadians approximately $59 billion each year. For 2011–12, the federal and provincial criminal justice budget was $20.3 billion (1.1% nominal gross domestic product [GDP]) on criminal justice (Story and Yalkin 2013). This represents a 23% real-time increase per capita.

This is up significantly from 1992 to 1993 when criminal justice spending was $9.57 billion or approximately $300 per Canadian per year (CCJA 1996). The largest allotment for youth justice has been and still remains youth corrections. For example, in 2011 it cost, on average, $95,826.37 to imprison a young person for a year. Unfortunately, only 2 of the 10 provinces (Ontario and Alberta) provide any recent data on youth justice expenditures, and therefore any observations are limited (Story and Yalkin 2013).

Although corrections still account for a significant proportion of the youth justice budget, the area that has been most impacted by the YCJA is legal aid. First introduced in 1971, legal aid is a shared federal and provincial responsibility that is intended to promote access to justice and protect rights under the **Canadian Charter of Rights and Freedom**. Even though young offenders are entitled to legal representation, they are often unable to retain their own counsel. Hence, they become dependent on legal aid—one of the reasons for its inception. Between 1988–89 and 1992–93, Legal Aid expenditures went up 70.3%. By 1994–95, expenditures for Legal Aid were greater than that for the entire young offenders' budget. In fact, the federal government became so concerned that in the early 1990s, they placed a ceiling on how much Legal Aid lawyers could charge per type of case (Hung and Bowles 1995). However, Statistics Canada Legal Aid Survey stopped collecting related information in 2010. Nevertheless, based on the available data, it lends further support to the general observation that the YCJA is placing a large burden on tax payers as reflected through its legalistic orientation. It further begs the questions, how much "justice" can be afforded and are these the most appropriate ways of addressing youth crime?

The Youth Justice Process

The Canadian criminal justice system can generally be characterized as lacking coordination (Larsen 1995; Cowper 2012). Critics of the CCJS point out that the system does NOT share a common goal, a common philosophy, or a centralized decision-making authority. And while it can be argued that the system does share the generic goal of crime control and protection of society, there is little agreement as to how these goals can be attained. However, although one could argue that the young offender system is also lacking a clear degree of coordination, the new act has been successful in reducing the use of custody for minor offenses while ensuring harsher penalties for those youth who commit more serious and repeat offenses. Additionally, more resources have since been directed to community alternatives for youth, including restorative justice measures. And perhaps most notably under the YCJA, more resources have been allocated to young persons in the justice system with mental health issues/concerns and expressing a history of abuse (Caputo and Vallee 2010).

Figure 5.3 provides a graphic illustration of what happens once a youth comes into contact with the young offender system. As noted earlier, the history of the juvenile justice system in Canada has undergone a number of dramatic changes in recent years. Today, the model reflects a due process model in which an accused youth is entitled not only to legal representation but also given special consideration; hence the description "modified justice model" (see Box 5.1).

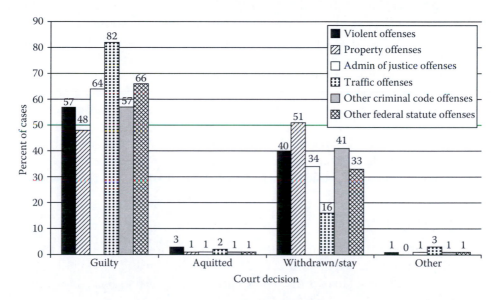

Figure 5.3 Cases completed in youth court, by type of offense and decision, Canada, 2010/2011. Note: Violent offenses include homicide, attempted murder, robbery, sexual assault, other sexual offenses, major assault, common assault, uttering threats, criminal harassment, and other violent offenses. Property offenses include theft, break and enter, fraud, mischief, possession of stolen property, and other property crimes. Administration of justice offenses include failing to appear, breach of probation, being unlawfully at large, failing to comply with order, and other administration of justice offenses. Traffic offenses are Criminal Code traffic offenses including impaired driving and other Criminal Code traffic offenses. Other Criminal Code offenses (which exclude traffic offenses) include weapons offenses, prostitution, disturbing the peace, and residual Criminal Code. Other Federal Statute Offenses include drug possession, other drug offenses, YCJA, and other federal statutes. "Other" includes final decisions of found not criminally responsible, waived in province/territory, and waived out of province/territory. This category also includes any order where a conviction was not recorded, cases where the court accepted a special plea, cases that raise Charter arguments, and cases where the accused was found unfit to stand trial. (Statistics Canada. (2013). *Integrated Criminal Court Survey. 2010/2011.* Ottawa: Canadian Centre for Justice Statistics.)

Initial Contact

The police are usually the first representatives of the formal system youths come into contact with. Under the YCJA, all Criminal Code provisions from the point of arrest to applying for bail apply equally to young persons. The Act and Section 10(a) of the Charter of Rights provides that all youths suspected of committing an offense **must be** informed about their rights by the attending police officer before they are apprehended and/or arrested.

Given that most of the crimes committed by young offenders are minor in nature, discretion is often exercised when handling such cases. Again, there is the notion of *parens patriae*, which was discussed at the beginning of this chapter.

Should the incident warrant formal measures, the police will then use a formal form recommending the laying of a charge. Again, because of provincial jurisdictional authority, the extent to which discretion is exercised varies considerably.

The final decision on the laying of information rests with either the police or the Crown. Again, it varies across jurisdictions. What is consistent, however, is that before giving a statement to the police, Section 32 of the YCJA provides the safeguard that a youth be entitled to be advised of the option of having either a lawyer or a parent/guardian present. This provision is intended to ensure that there is no improper questioning by authorities. Under Section 113 of the YJCA, should the youth be charged with a serious (indictable) offense, he/she may be photographed, palm-printed, or fingerprinted.

While the basic tenets of the criminal law are entrenched into the YCJA, sections such as 3(1)(f) have raised considerable debate as to how much discretion—accountability—can be exercised. Section 4 refers to the young person's right to the least possible interference with freedom. Hence, given that enforcement of the act rests with each province and police department, the use of informal procedures (i.e., extrajudicial measures) varies widely among provinces and even among police jurisdictions within provinces. This practice is virtually unchanged from how youth were handled under the JDA and the previous YOA.

Youth Court Proceedings

As was the case under the former legislations, legal proceedings under the YCJA are conducted in specially designated "youth courts." Depending on the jurisdiction, in some provinces it is the Family Court while in other provincial jurisdictions a branch of adult Provincial Court.

While the YCJA stipulates that proceedings in youth court approximate the rules governing summary conviction offenses in adult court, the proceedings for indictable offenses are less complex and intended to be more expeditious. For example, unlike in the adult system, there are no preliminary inquiries, and all trials are conducted by a judge alone (there are no jury trials in Family Court/Provincial Court).

Relatively few cases actually end up in youth court. However, should young offenders be required to attend court, Section 25 of the YCJA requires that they be advised of their rights and that if they cannot afford to retain counsel, one will be provided by the state. And although it is possible to have a guardian or parent (see Section 26) attend in place of a lawyer, given the formal legal procedure and potential risk for punishment, youths are encouraged to seek legal counsel.

In Canada, even though young offenders are meant to be held accountable for their actions, there are provisions under the YCJA (e.g., s. 110 and 111), which do not allow the youth's name or identity to be published unless he/she is considered "dangerous to others" and/or if the young person is receiving an adult sentence. Also, Section 128 includes provisions for the destruction of records and prohibition on the use and disclosure of youth court records. Again, the objective is to minimize the impact of the young persons' future prospects of rehabilitation and reintegration back into society.

Sentencing Options

In accordance with Section 20 of the YCJA, available dispositions include
Retained sentences from the former YOA:

- Absolute discharge—no record after 1 year
- Conditional discharge—no record after 3 years if conditions are met
- Fine—up to $1000.00 based on time needed and ability to pay
- Restitution—return of goods to the victim
- Compensation—repayment for loss suffered by the victim
- Community service—work hours done without pay in the community
- Probation—period of supervision with conditions
- Intermittent custody—noncontinuous custody
- Custody
- Concurrent sentences
- Consecutive sentences—served one after the other

New youth sentences:

- Judicial reprimand—stern lecture by the judge
- Program Attendance order—specific to the youth's needs
- Intensive support and supervision program (ISSP)—closer monitoring than probation
- Deferred custody and supervision order—similar to adult suspended sentence, that is, no custody if conditions followed
- Custody and supervision—custody always to be followed by supervision in the community
- Intensive rehabilitation custody and supervision (IRCS)—greater control and guaranteed treatment for serious violent offenders

Although the options may appear straightforward, there is considerable variation among jurisdictions as each province tries to consolidate its disposition philosophy for young offenders. For example, following the enactment of the act, there was a significant increase in the number of custodial dispositions, but it varied among provinces.

Postsentencing: "Corrections"

Youth in Court

In sentencing youth for crimes, there has historically been, and continues to be, a division between adult courts and youth courts. This is the same in incarceration practice in

Canada. For over a century, from the introduction of the Juvenile Delinquents Act in 1908 to the enactment of the YCJA in 2003, it has been recognized that different principles of justice (e.g., intent) should apply to youth and to adults. While the total number of cases processed through the formal justice system in Canada has decreased since implementing the YCJA, a significant number of youth continue to move through the formal court system.

Overall, there were more than 52,900 cases completed in youth court in 2010/2011; however, there has been an overall decline in the number of cases completed in youth court (down 7% from the year prior). Figure 5.1, in the following text, illustrates this trend.

The majority of cases completed in youth court deal with nonviolent crimes, theft being the most common crime addressed, followed by YCJA infractions (e.g., failure to comply with an order), and then break and enter. The decline seen in the number of completed youth court cases in 2010/2011 occurred, however, across all major offense categories. Cases involving traffic offenses showed the greatest decline, decreasing by 16% from the previous year. On the other hand, cases involving other federal statute offenses (e.g., drug possession) showed the smallest decline at 2% (Statistics Canada 2012).

Looking at statistics from 2008/2009, it is apparent that youth who go through the court process are more often male (which fits with the greater proportion of males committing crimes, as discussed p. 117), and on the older end of "youth" (also discussed above with respect to average age of young offenders). In 2008/2009, 72% of the accused youth in court were male, of whom 57% were 16–17 years old. Again, Aboriginal youth are disproportionately represented when it comes to crime as well as the court process, with 27% of remanded youth being of Aboriginal descent, while only representing 6% of the overall youth population (A statistical snapshot 2010).

Youth who proceed through the court process are most likely to experience one of three common outcomes: guilty (either pleading guilty or being found guilty); stay/withdrawal/dismissal (interrupted proceedings); or acquittal. In 2010/2011, 57% of the youth court cases resulted in a guilty outcome, while 42% of cases were stayed, withdrawn, or dismissed. In these years, very few cases were acquitted (1%).

As a general trend over the past 10 years, there has been a shift in youth court decisions, with the proportion of cases resulting in guilty outcomes decreasing, and those being stayed or withdrawn increasing. For example, in 2000/2001, 67% of cases resulted in a decision of guilt, compared to 57% of cases in 2010/2011. On the other hand, the number of cases being stayed or withdrawn increased from 31% in 2000/2001 to 42% in 2010/2011 (Statistics Canada 2012).

In the youth court process over the past 10 years, the average length of time to process cases has increased. In 2010/2011, the average time to complete a youth court case was 113 days, over a month longer than the average of 70 days in 2000/2001. The largest increase in processing times occurred between 2002/2003 and 2003/2004; however, since then, the length of time to process cases in youth court has remained within a similar range (Statistics Canada 2012).

Youth in Custody

On any given day in 2010/2011, there were, on average, about 163,000 adult offenders (18 years or over) in Canada's correctional system compared with 14,800 youth (ages 12–17). This represents 12% less than 5 years ago and 6% less than the previous year. Youth in the correctional system include both youth in custody (incarcerated or in remand) as well as youth serving supervised community sentences (e.g., probation). Most youth (90%) involved in Canada's correctional system are under community supervision (Dauvergne 2012).

Youth in sentenced custody include those found guilty of a crime and who are detained either in open or secure custody. This may include community residential centers; childcare institutions; group homes; forest or wilderness camps; or separate sections within a secure facility. Remand is a type of temporary custody (detention) for young offenders awaiting trial or sentencing. Just over 1500 youth in 2010/2011 (10% of those in the correctional system) were in custody. Of those youth in custody, 54% were in remand, while 44% were in sentenced custody. Overall, the youth incarceration rate has been declining since 2008/09. The decreases seen were both in youth in remand (−5%) as well as youth serving an open custody sentence (−7%) and youth serving a secure custody sentence (−3%) (Munch 2012).

The largest group of youth involved in correctional services in Canada reflects the same demographic as the youth most represented in the court system, namely, older (16–17 year old) male youth. Figure 5.4, in the following text, illustrates this trend.

Aboriginal youth are significantly overrepresented within the corrections system in Canada. While these individuals make up around 6% of Canadian society, they make up 26% of the youth admitted to the correctional system in Canada. There is an even greater discrepancy in the case of female Aboriginal youth, who make up 34% of the female youth in the correctional system (while still comprising about 6% of the female youth of Canada overall) (Statistics Canada 2012). Once again, this opens the debate to the cultural, historical, and societal reasons (including racism) that have contributed to this trend (see Satzewich 1998).

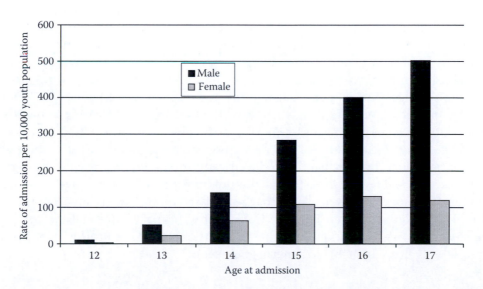

Figure 5.4 Youth admissions to Canadian correctional services, 2010/2011. Note: Youth refers to individuals aged 12–17 years. This chart excludes individuals whose age was unknown and individuals 18 years of age or older who were 12–17 at the time the offense was committed. An admission is counted each time a person begins any type of custody or community program. The same person can be included several times in the admission counts where the individual moves from one type of legal status to another or reenters the system in the same year. (Statistics Canada. (2013). *Integrated Criminal Court Survey. 2010/2011.* Ottawa: Canadian Centre for Justice Statistics.)

Current Issues Facing Canadian Youth Today

It seems that every generation and every country has its issues to deal with (see Box 5.2). Canada is no exception. Today, Canadian youth are involved in several forms of behavior, which are a concern for either criminal justice personnel or society as a whole. With this in mind, the following summaries are not exhaustive; rather, they are intended to provide a synopsis of some of the key "problem" areas Canadians are facing in recent years regarding young offenders.

We will only touch on a few of the current issues facing Canadian youth today. We begin with the ever-present concern with youth gangs.

Youth Gangs

While street/youth gangs have been around in Canada since the late 1920s, during the late 1980s and into the 1990s, we have witnessed a flurry of gang activity, which has been accompanied with a number of articles on an otherwise sparsely covered topic (Gordon 1995; Totton 2012). Recent studies suggest that, notwithstanding definitional problems, the problem has escalated and diversified. For example, Asian organized crime groups (e.g., triads and tongs) since the mid-1980s have become a growing concern (Totton 2012). Aside from being more violent than "traditional" youth gangs, they engage in a wide variety of crimes ranging from home invasion robbery to extortion, protection rackets, and distribution of drugs among other offenses. The primary attraction of gang activity seems to be related to material and psychological rewards and because of these temptations, some youth seem to "drift" (Matza 1964) into gang-related activities. As a result of their associations, they learn techniques that enable them to neutralize the values and beliefs taught by law-abiding citizens. To date, most gang activities seem to be primarily limited to major metropolitan areas, and many metropolitan police forces have established special youth gang units to monitor and counter this growing problem. Since 2007 through Public Safety Canada, the government has established a National Crime Prevention Centre (NCPC), which is committed to "disseminating knowledge to address the problem of youth gangs" (Youth gang involvement 2013). The NCPC focuses on articulating risk factors and various prevention strategies. Since the inception of the project, various jurisdictions have introduced gang intervention/prevention programs, and the research evidence suggests that the programs have been relatively successful. One of the more successful models/approaches is based on the American program developed by David Kennedy from John Jay College of Criminal Justice at New York's City University known as "Operation Ceasefire" or as the "Boston Gun Project," which is now referred to as "Cure Violence" (see Internet Sources).

Runaways and Street-Involved Youth

Even though being a runaway or street-involved youth (i.e., being under the age of 25 and not having a safe place to reside) is not a crime in Canada, the number of youths running away from home has allegedly increased significantly throughout the 1980s and into the new millennium (MacLaurin and Worthington 2012). However, given the nature of the behavior, there is no reliable data on the true extent of the problem. The

BOX 5.2   CYBERBULLYING

"I think kids today listen to a story and if that's the most sensational story to go with they jump on that and they don't care how it hurts other people. It's just too easy to Facebook and text, to say and do mean things..." (Nova Scotia 2013). These are the words of the mother of Rehtaeh Parsons. Rehtaeh committed suicide in April 2013 at the age of 17 after being bullied online over an incident of sexual assault perpetrated against her at a party. While this is a recent Canadian example, it is not the only example of cyberbullying leading to real-life trauma and tragic outcomes. All across the world, young people are spending more of their lives online, and within this sphere, bullying can be extremely dangerous.

The online Oxford Dictionary defines cyberbullying as "the use of electronic communication to bully a person, typically by sending messages of an intimidating or threatening nature." This can include threatening e-mails or instant messages, and hateful comments spread through social media sources, e-mails, or instant messages. It can also include using another's identity to make posts or spread hateful or threatening materials electronically.

While bullying has always existed in schools and among young peers, the increasing amount of social interaction that happens on the Internet means that this aspect of youth behavior is increasingly developing online. In the 2009 GSS conducted by Statistics Canada, adults were asked whether any children (aged 8–17) living in their household had been victims of cyberbullying. Approximately 10% of adults surveyed knew of cyberbullying happening to children in their household. Of the bullying that these adults knew about, 74% involved receiving threatening or aggressive e-mails or instant messages. Most often, the adults surveyed knew of incidents involving female youth (71% of the cases reported in the survey) (Dauvergne 2012).

Many different responses to this trend have begun to emerge. Online, there are help sites and resources available for victims of cyber bullying to access. For example, the *It Gets Better* project was started by Dan Savage and his husband Terry Miller, in response to several suicides of gay teenagers in the United States who had been bullied with respect to their sexuality. This campaign has since spread across the Internet and includes a broader message outside just the gay community, that bullying is not acceptable. While campaigns like the *It Gets Better* project provide support to victims of bullying and shames perpetrators of bullying, it does not set a legal framework for addressing this issue for young people (It Gets Better project 2013).

In response to the tragic death of Rehtaeh Parsons, the Canadian government is currently investigating whether legislative gaps exist in Canada, which should be addressed to properly punish perpetrators of extreme cyberbullying (Nova Scotia 2013). The application of current laws in Canada in addressing this serious issue area also being investigated; however, if significant gaps are found, new laws may be the answer.

highest-risk category is those between the ages of 14 and 15. A combination of a lack of employment opportunities and limited social and marketability skills results in an increasing number of these youths turning to crimes, prostitution, substance abuse, and joining militant groups as a means of trying to survive on the streets. Girls are more likely than boys to run away and in a substantial number of cases, those who run away from home have done so more than once. These chronic runaways become vulnerable to being victimized physically and sexually and risk engaging in substance abuse as a coping mechanism (Tyler and Johnson 2006) and risk contracting HIV. Other related risks that affect this sector of the street-involved population include increased problems of physical and mental health problems and sexually transmitted infections (MacLaurin and Worthington 2012).

Teenage Suicide

It is a well-established fact that the adolescence years are marked by many dramatic and challenging changes. The expectations to succeed in school and to adjust to changes in the home, society, and life can be difficult for young people. Therefore, mental health problems such as anxiety, depression, self-worth, and so on, can become overwhelming, and in the worst-case scenario, the young person may seek to escape the pressure through suicide. In his seminal work on suicide, Durkheim referred to this type of suicide as "anomic suicide"—characterized by an individual's sense of moral confusion and lack of social direction. A case that recently captured international attention and has raised new concerns about ("anomic") suicide among Canadian youth involved the case of 15-year-old Rehtaeh Parsons who after being sexually assaulted at a party, had pictures of herself posted on Facebook and other social media. The strain and depression led her to commit suicide as a way to end her pain (Nova Scotia 2013). Her story is but one example of the risk many young people face today.

According to recent data from Statistics Canada, for young people in Canada, suicide is the second leading cause of death, preceded by accidents (including motor vehicle accidents) (Navaneelan 2012). This should be of significant concern in Canadian society as it can be seen as a reflection of the turmoil and emotional distress many youth are experiencing. Hence, the "problem" is seen as a barometer of youth in conflict or youth *at risk*. They may then choose to act out in deviant ways to draw attention (e.g., dropping out of school, teenage pregnancy, alcohol and substance abuse). Suicide rates may also be linked with the number of youth at risk (e.g., street-involved youth), those who are vulnerable to the negative consequences of school failure, substance abuse, poor job prospects, early sexuality, and the pressures to assume greater responsibility at earlier ages.

Female Delinquency

Even though in 1895, Cesare Lombroso and William Ferrero wrote the first book on female offenders: *The Female Offender*, Artz, Stoneman, and Reitsma-Street (2012) observed that this area has received little attention in Canada. In fact, Sangster (2002) has written one of the few academic books on female delinquency. Nevertheless, official data show that young females, as is the case in most parts of the world, commit far fewer offenses than do their male counterparts. However, in a study by Fisher (1993), it was observed that between 1987 and 1991, the rate of increase in violent crime charges for females was higher than that of the males. More recently, Kong and AuCoin (2006) not only reported that female offending peaks at around 15 years of age, but that the incident rate of "serious violence crime" more than doubled between 1986 and 2005. The rate now stands at 132 per 100,000 females. As to why young females are committing more offenses, Reitsma-Street (1993) found that there was a marked increase in the number of charges of noncompliance with the administration of youth justice by females. In terms of explaining the increase in serious violent crimes among young women, there are a range of explanations including reactive behavior as a result of their own victimization (e.g., sexual abuse), witnessing violence in the home, personality pathologies, and so on (see Bottos 2007). The key to understanding is that the trends that appear to be the risk factors predisposing young women to offend tend to be different from those for young males. There remains much work to be done in this area as female offending continues to increase.

Aboriginal Youth

One of the most enduring issues confronting the Canadian criminal justice system is the overrepresentation of Aboriginal people in the system. While Aboriginal youth (12–17 years of age) represent approximately 6% of the total youth population in Canada, they represent approximately and 24% of youth who admitted to remand, 36% of youth admitted to custody, and of youth who received probation (Calverley et al. 2010 cited in Greenberg, Grekul, and Nelson 2012, 236). Their representation in the systems varies geographically, with some regions having a greater representation than others. Adolescent Aboriginal youth are no exception to this trend.

Much has been written over the years about how Canada's historical policies and (mis) treatment of Aboriginal people have "resulted in severe and entrenched trauma among generations of Aboriginal people" (Greenberg, Grekul, and Nelson 2012, 230). And the unfortunate fact is that the Aboriginal youth of today have not escaped the intergenerational effects of having been colonized in a manner that undermined their culture, their spirit, and their person. Common terms that are used to describe the generational effects of colonization, marginalization, and subjugation is "trauma" and "victimization."

Minaker and Hogeveen's (2009) research has shown a significant relationship between Aboriginal youth who have been victimized and future criminal activity. And a range of different studies show that Aboriginal youth—both male and female—are more likely to be victims of violent crime than are non-Aboriginal youth. A host of risk/causal factors of criminalization have been well documented in the literature. They include such factors as poor self-esteem, relative isolation within their own culture and broader social community, relative poverty, and the comparatively high incident rate of fetal alcohol spectrum disorder (FASD).

As noted at the outset of this section, Aboriginal youth gangs represent a major concern, and researchers such as Totton (2012) have documented numerous Aboriginal youth gangs across the country with such names as Red Alert, Native Syndicate, Native Blood, Cree Boys (a name of an Aboriginal tribe), and so on.

Fortunately, the plight of Canada's Aboriginal people has received increasing attention, and in recent years, we have seen a growing number of initiatives and crime prevention programs oriented specifically at helping Aboriginal youth who are at risk.

Summary

Canada is a relatively young nation that has already had three major reforms to its juvenile justice legislation, the most recent being the YCJA in 2003. Canadian youth justice legislation is a federal act, but one, which is administered by the provinces and territories. The current act has been described as a **modified justice** model (see Table 1.1—Introduction), which attempts to balance the perceived special needs of young people with a measured degree of accountability.

In the second section of the chapter, it was shown how, since the enactment of the YCJA, the overall youth crime rate has modestly, but steadily, declined. While the decrease cannot be assumed to be directly attributable to the YCJA, this trend has raised considerable debate about the effectiveness of the act (see Reid and Gilliss 2012). It seems quite clear that the YCJA has attempted to strike a better balance between accountability and providing young offenders alternative options that facilitate reintegration, rehabilitation, and resocialization. But, research evidence continues to question whether anyone punishing anyone who hurts another is an effective way to demonstrate that hurting is wrong! This is a fundamental issue that all societies (must) grapple with.

The third major section of the chapter provided an overview of how youth justice is administered by the major actors in the system. Aside from the cases following a similar format, the key issues pertain to how the YCJA is administered somewhat differently between the provinces and territories and that there is variation among the provinces in terms of such options as alternative measures, use of restorative justice, use of detention, and so on. As suggested, these variations, while understandable to an extent, further indicate the general differing cultural, political, and social views about the objectives of the YCJA as well as the varying financial realities of the provinces and territories. The fourth section offered a descriptive overview of youth at risk in Canada, and it is noted that while youth crime has declined in recent years, there remain a number of anomalies, which point to the need for continued research and exploration for alternatives that might prove more fruitful.

The final major section identified several of the key areas of current concern regarding youth at risk in Canada. When placed within the context of the international community, outside of the persisting challenges around the criminal activity of Aboriginal youth, the challenges are fairly universal. However, what is not explored in this chapter are the risks and protective factors similar to those in other countries.

Overall, several scholars have been quite supportive of the YCJA (see Bala et al. 2012). However, while not all may be in agreement, the evolution of youth criminal justice in Canada has and continues to reflect a system that evolved from a punitive system to one that lends itself to an increasing number of opportunities and initiatives that champions alternatives to custodial sentences—or at least tries to limit their use for only the most grievous of cases. To this end, there has also been a shift to empowering youth by giving them a voice (Reid and Gilliss 2012). What lies ahead for the administration of juvenile justice in Canada is not clear, but it might serve us well to look beyond our limited frame of reference to examine what other countries are doing, perhaps, to provide alternative political and etiological insights. The youth are our future, and they deserve our fullest attention and support, and as Robinson-Easley (2012) recently commented: "Our children are our responsibility."

Review/Discussion Questions

1. Although this chapter focuses on youth at risk in Canada, what can we learn from studying the history of childhood that may be relevant to understanding the development and operation of the juvenile justice system?
2. What types of youth crime activities appear to be the most problematic for Canadians today? How might they compare and/or differ from some of the other countries presented in this book?
3. How well does the Canadian juvenile justice system appear to fulfill international juvenile justice standards (e.g., CRC)? Explain your answer.
4. Explore and discuss the potential implications for Aboriginal youth programs that are based on values for Aboriginal youth versus those for non-Aboriginal youth.
5. How do the current issues confronting Canadian young offenders/youth at risk compare with your country (or other countries in this collection)? What kind of conclusions might you be able to draw from your observations?

References

Akers, R. and Sellers, C. (2013). *Criminological Theories: Introduction, Evaluation and Application.* (6th ed.). NY: Oxford University Press.

Artz, S., Stoneman, L., and Reitsma-Street, M. (2012). Canadian girls and crime in the twenty-first Century. In J. Winterdyk and R. Smandych (Eds.), *Youth at Risk and Youth Justice: A Canadian Overview*. Don mills, ON: Oxford University Press, 130–155.

Bala, N., Hornick, J.P., and Vogl, R. (Eds.). (1991). *Canadian Child Welfare Law*. Toronto: Thompson Educational Publishing.

Bottos, S. (2007). *Women and Violence: Theory, Risk, and Treatment Implications*. Ottawa: Correctional Service Canada.

Brennan, S. (2012). Police-reported crime statistics in Canada, 2011. Retrieved from: http://www. statcan.gc.ca/pub/85-002-x/2012001/article/11692-eng.htm#r3.

Brownfield, B. and Thompson, K. (1991). Attachment to peers and delinquent behaviour. *Canadian Journal of Criminology*, 33(1): 45–60.

Caputo, T. and Vallee, M. (2010). A report prepared for the review of the roots of youth violence. Report prepared for the Ontario Ministry of Children and Youth Services. Toronto, Ontario. Retrieved from: http://www.children.gov.on.ca/htdocs/English/topics/youthandthelaw/roots/volume4/comparative_analysis.aspx.

Carrigan, D.O. (1991). Juvenile Delinquency. *Crime and Punishment in Canada* (Chapter 5). Toronto: McClelland and Stewart Inc. 201–224.

Cowper, G. (2012). A criminal justice system for the 21st Century. Report prepared by the BC Justice Reform Initiative for the Minister of Justice and Solicitor General. Vancouver, BC: Ministry of Justice and Solicitor General of British Columbia.

Creechan, J.H. (1995). A test of the general theory of crime: Delinquency and school dropouts. In J.H. Creechan and R.A. Silverman (Eds.), *Canadian Delinquency*. Scarborough: Prentice Hall Canadian Inc, 77–87.

Currie, D. (1986). The transformation of juvenile justice in Canada: A study of Bill C-61. In B.D. MacLean (Ed.), *The Political Economy of Crime*. Scarborough: Prentice Hall, 56–72.

Dauvergne, M. (2012). Adult correctional statistics in Canada, 2010/2011. Retrieved from: http://www.statcan.gc.ca/pub/85-002-x/2012001/article/11715-eng.htm.

deMause, L. (Ed.). (1988). *The History of Childhood*. New York: Peter Bedrick Books.

Diplock, J. and Plecas, D. (2012). Issues of substance abuse and related crime in adolescence. In J. Winterdyk and R. Smandych (Eds.), *Youth at Risk and Youth Justice: A Canadian Overview*. Don Mills: Oxford University Press, 204–227.

Empey, L.T. (1982). From optimism to despair: New directions in juvenile justice. In C.A. Murray and L.A. Cox Jr. (Eds.), *Beyond Probation: Juvenile Corrections and the Chronic Delinquent*. Beverly Hills, CA: Sage, 62–79.

Fisher, M. (1993, May 19). Rising crime linked to girls. *The Calgary Sun*. p. 29.

Gordon, R.M. (1995). Street gangs in Vancouver. In J.H. Creechan and R.A. Silverman (Eds.), *Canadian Delinquency*. Scarborough: Prentice Hall, Chapter 20, 311–321.

Greenberg, H., Grekul, J., and Nelson, R. (2012). Aboriginal youth crime in Canada. In J. Winterdyk and R. Smandych (Eds.), *Youth at Risk and Youth Justice: A Canadian Overview*. Don Mills: Oxford University Press, 228–252.

Hagan, J. (1995). Good people, dirty system: The Young Offenders Act and organizational failure. In N. Larsen (Ed.), *The Canadian Criminal Justice System*. Toronto, ON: Canadian Scholars' Press Inc. pp. 389–418.

Hagan, J., Alwin, D., and Hewitt, J. (1979). Ceremonial justice: Crime and punishment in a loosely coupled society. *Social Forces*, 58(2): 506–527.

Hagan, J., Simpson, J., and Gillis, A.R. (1979). The sexual stratification of social control: A gender based perspective on crime and delinquency. *British Journal of Criminology*, 30(1): 25–38.

Hagan, J., Simpson, J., and Gillis, A.R. (1987). Class in the household: A power-control theory of gender and delinquency. *American Journal of Sociology*, 92(4): 788–816.

Horner, B. (M.P. Chairman). (1993, February). *Crime Prevention in Canada: Towards a National Strategy, 12th Report of the Standing Committee on Justice and Solicitor General*. Ottawa: Solicitor General of Canada.

Hotton, M.T. (2011). Women and the criminal justice system. In *Women in Canada: A Gender-based Statistical Report*. (6th ed.). Ottawa: Statistics Canada. Catalogue no. 89-503-X.

HRSDC (Human Resources and Skills Development Canada). (2012). *Indicators of Well-being in Canada*. Ottawa: HRSDC.

Hung, K. and Bowles, S. (1995). Public perception of crime. *Juristat*, 15(1): 17.

It Gets Better Project. (2013). Retrieved from: http://www.itgetsbetter.org/.

Juristat's Police Reported Crime Statistics, 2011. Retrieved from: http://www.statcan.gc.ca/pub/85-002-x/2012001/article/11692-eng.htm#n1.

Kennedy, L. and Baron, S.W. (1993). Routine activities and a subculture of violence: A study of violence on the street. *Journal of Research in Crime and Delinquency*, 30(1): 88–112.

Larsen, N. (Ed.). (1995). *The Canadian Criminal Justice System: An Issues Approach to the Administration of Justice*. Toronto: Canadian Scholars' Press.

Lundman, R.J. (1984). *Prevention and Control of Juvenile Delinquency*. New York: Oxford University Press.

Lundman, R.J. (1994). *Prevention and Control of Juvenile Delinquency*. (2nd ed.). NY: Oxford University Press.

MacLaurin, B. and Worthington, C. (2012). Street-involved youth in Canada. In J. Winterdyk and R. Smandych (Eds.), *Youth at Risk and Youth Justice: A Canadian Overview*. Don Mills: Oxford University Press, 279–306.

Matza, D. (1964). *Delinquency and drift*. New York: Wiley.

McDonald, L. (1969, November). Crime and punishment in Canada: A statistical test of the 'conventional wisdom'. *Canadian Review of Sociology and Anthropology*, 6(4): 212–236.

Milner, T. (1995). Juvenile Legislation. In J.H. Creechan and R.A. Silverman. (Eds.), *Canadian Delinquency*. Scarborough: Prentice Hall Canada.

Minaker, J.C. and Hogeveen, B. (2009). *Youth, Crime, and Society: Issues of Power and Justice*. Toronto: Pearson Prentice Hall.

Moyer, S. (1992). Recidivism in youth courts, 1990-91. *Juristat*, 12(2).

Munch, C. (2012). Youth correctional statistics, 2010/2011. Retrieved from: http://www.statcan.gc.ca/pub/85-002-x/2012001/article/11716-eng.htm.

Navaneelan, T. (2012). Suicide rates: An overview. Retrieved from: http://www.statcan.gc.ca/pub/82-624-x/2012001/article/11696-eng.htm.

Northcott, M. (2011). Victims of crime: Research digest. Justice report 10. Retrieved from: http://www.justice.gc.ca/eng/rp-pr/cj-jp/victim/rd4-rr4/rd4-rr4.pdf.

Nova Scotia teen Rehtaeh Parsons was 'disappointed to death': Editorial. (2013, June 12). Retrieved from: http://www.thestar.com/opinion/editorials/2013/04/14/nova_scotia_teen_rehtaeh_parsons_was_disappointed_to_death_editorial.html; http://www.cbc.ca/news/canada/nova-scotia/story/2013/04/09/ns-rehtaeh-parsons-suicide-rape.html.

Reid, S.A. and Gilliss, S. (2012). Key challenges in hearing the voice of youth in the youth justice system. In J. Winterdyk and R. Smandych (Eds.), *Youth at Risk and Youth Justice: A Canadian Overview.* Don Mills: Oxford University Press, 379–399.

Reitsma-Street, M. (1993). Canadian youth court changes and dispositions for females before and after implementation of the Young Offenders Act. *Canadian Journal of Criminology,* 35(4): 437–458.

Robinson-Easley, C.A. (2012). *Our Children, Our Responsibility.* New York: Peter Lang.

Sangster, J. (2012). *Girl Trouble: Female Delinquency in English Canada.* Toronto: Between the Lines.

Satzewich, V. (Ed.). (1998). *Racism and Social Inequality in Canada: Concepts, Controversies and Strategies of Resistance.* Toronto: Thompson Educational Publishing Inc.

Savoie, J. (2007). Youth self-reported delinquency, Toronto—2006. *Juristat,* 27(6).

Smandych, R. (2006). Canada: Repenalization and young offenders rights. In J. Muncie and B. Goldson (Eds.), *Comparative Youth Justice.* London: Sage. pp. 21–32.

Solicitor General of Canada. (1981, February 16). *News Release. Young Offenders Bill Tabled in House of Commons.* Ottawa: Solicitor General of Canada.

Statistical snapshot of youth at risk and youth offending in Canada. (2010). Retrieved from: http://www.publicsafety.gc.ca/cnt/rsrcs/pblctns/ststclsnpsht-yth/ssyr-eng.pdf.

Statistics Canada. (2010). *Annual Demographic Estimates: Canada, Provinces and Territories.* Ottawa: Statistics Canada. Catalogue no. 91-215-X.

Statistics Canada. (2012). *Integrated Criminal Court Survey, 2010/2011.* Statistics Canada, Canadian Centre for Justice Statistics. Ottawa, ON.

Statistics Canada. (2013). *Integrated Criminal Court Survey. 2010/2011.* Ottawa: Canadian Centre for Justice Statistics.

Statistics Canada, Canadian Centre for Justice Statistics. (2011). Uniform Crime Reporting Survey.

Story, R. and Yalkin, T.R. (2013). Expenditure analysis of criminal justice in Canada. Retrieved from: http://www.pbo-dpb.gc.ca/files/files/Crime_Cost_EN.pdf.

Sutherland, N. (1976). *Children in English-Canadian society: Framing the Twentieth Century Consensus.* Toronto: University of Toronto Press.

Totton, M. (2012). An overview of gang-involved youth in Canada. In J. Winterdyk and R. Smandych (Eds.), *Youth at Risk and Youth Justice: A Canadian Overview.* Don mills: Oxford University Press, 253–278.

Trojanowicz, R. (1978). *Juvenile Delinquency: Concepts and Control.* Englewood Cliffs, NJ: Prentice Hall.

Tyler, K.A. and Johnson, K.A. (2006). Pathways in and out of substance use among homeless-emerging adults. *Journal of Adolescent Research,* 21(2): 133–157.

United Nations. (1986). *United Nations Standard Minimum Rules for the Administration of Juvenile Justice.* New York: Department of Information.

Verburg, P. (1995, May). Rebels without consciences. In *Alberta Report.* pp. 30–36.

Walker, R. (1996, December 13). Drop in health concerns seen. *Calgary Herald.* p. A9.

West, G. (1984). *Young Offenders and the State: A Canadian Perspective.* Toronto: Butterworths.

Wheeler, S. (1967). Criminal statistics: A reformulation of the problem. *Journal of Criminal Law, Criminology and Police Science*, 58(3): 317–324.

Wilson, J.Q. (1975). *Thinking about Crime*. New York: Vintage Books.

Winterdyk, J. (Ed.). (2002). *Juvenile Justice Systems: International Perspectives*. Toronto: Canadian Scholars' Press.

Youth gang involvement: What are the risk factors? (2013). Retrieved from: http://www.publicsafety.gc.ca/prg/cp/bldngevd/2007-yg-2-eng.aspx.

Youth justice: A better direction for our country. (1994, Fall). Ottawa: The Church Council of Justice and Corrections.

Internet Sources

www.bgccab.com Boys and Girls Club Canada. The official website for the Boys and Girls Club of Canada that serves young people in the community as they become adults. Many of the clubs also provide services for street/runaway youth.

http://cureviolence.org/ Cure Violence (formerly Ceasefire). Although an American based initiative, it has been adopted by a number of Canadian jurisdictions because of its relative success in addressing areas plagued by youth violence.

www.justice.gc.ca/eng/pi/yj-jj/YCJA-Isjpa/back-hist.html Department of Justice: The Youth Criminal Justice Act: Summary and Background. This site offers a summary and background of the YCJA.

www.not4me.ca National Anti-Drug Strategy drugsnot4me Youth Drug Prevention. This government site provides the most recent anti-drug messages to young people.

www.publicsafety.gc.ca Public Safety Canada. When navigating this site, you can find information on youth gang involvement and strategies for addressing youth gangs problems in Canada.

www.statcan.gc.ca Statistics Canada. The official website for Statistics Canada, where the reader can find a wealth of official data on youth crime from the police, youth courts, etc. Links can also be found to *The Daily* and *Juristat* reports which provide regular reports on a wide range of official information on youth justice.

China's Juvenile Justice: A System in Transition

RUOHUI ZHAO, HONGWEI ZHANG,
AND JIANHONG LIU

Contents

Juvenile Crime Trends and Patterns	138
Juvenile Crime Trends	139
Juvenile Crime Patterns	140
Cultural and Historical Contexts	143
Cultural and Social Contexts	143
Historical Evolutions	145
Origins	145
Early Developments	145
Further Struggles	146
New Approaches	147
Legislative Attempts to Address Juvenile Delinquency and Crime	148
Areas of Juvenile Delinquency and Crime	148
Operational Mechanisms	149
Age Restrictions on Jurisdiction of Juvenile Courts	150
Components of the Juvenile Justice System	150
Policing and Juveniles	151
Juvenile Court and Procuratorate	152
Defense Attorney and Legal Representation	154
Juvenile Proceedings	154
Juvenile Pretrial Detention	154
Juvenile Arrest	155
Juvenile Prosecution	155
Adjudication and Sentencing	156
Juvenile Rehabilitation	157
Conclusion	158
Review/Discussion Questions	159
References	159
Internet Sources	162

FACTS ABOUT CHINA

Area: China is situated in east Asia and has a land size of 9.6 million square kilometers, which makes it the largest country in Asia. **Population:** According to the latest official statistics from the National Bureau of Statistics of China (2012), China has a population of close to 1.35 billion, of whom 0.691 billion (51.26%) are male and 0.657 billion (48.74%) are female. Although China is traditionally classified as an agricultural country, its rural population for the first time made up less than 50% (48.73%) of the overall population by the end of 2011 due to rapid urbanization processes. China has 56 ethnic groups altogether, of which the Han ethnic group accounts for more than 90% of the overall population. **Administrative divisions:** China has 23 provinces (including Taiwan, which has been under a separate administration since 1949), 5 ethnic minority autonomous regions (equivalent to provinces), 4 municipalities (i.e., Beijing, Shanghai, Tianjing, and Chongqing) directly under the central government, and 2 special administrative regions (Hong Kong and Macao, which were previously colonies of Great Britain and Portugal, respectively). Beijing is the capital city of China. **Government:** The Chinese government is led by the Communist Party, the ruling party, whose work is assisted by eight non-Communist parties. The People's Congress has legislative authority. **Economy:** China's economy is developing rapidly. The annual growth rate (from 2001 to 2011) of the gross domestic product (GDP) was 10.4%. In 2011, the GDP reached 364.5002 billion yuan, which was the second highest in the world. China's annual GDP per capita, however, was 35,181 yuan, which ranked China 114th out of 213 economies around the world (1 U.S. dollar = approximately 6.1 Chinese yuan). **Education:** China implements 9-year compulsory education. The latest official statistics show that by the end of 2011, the net enrollment ratio in primary school was 99.8%. The transfer rate from primary schools to junior secondary schools was 98.3%, the transfer rate to senior secondary schools was 88.9%, and the transfer rate to higher education was 88.3% (including transfers to regular classes of TV universities). **Culture:** Confucian philosophy plays a dominant role in shaping Chinese customs as well as legal tradition. Various religious customs including Buddhism, Taoism, Islam, and Christianity are practiced. The official language is Mandarin, and there are numerous local dialects.

Juvenile Crime Trends and Patterns

Of China's population of approximately 1.35 billion, 222 million (16.5%) are children under the age of 15, 1 billion are between the ages of 15 and 64, and the remainder are elderly, aged 65 or more (National Bureau of Statistics of China 2012). Regarding juveniles under the age of 18, the most recent statistics by the China Adolescents Research Center (2009) show that this group accounts for approximately a quarter of the nation's population (26.1% or 341 million). Juveniles are in the transitional period from teenager to adult, and their behavior in puberty may have a long-term impact. Western literature consistently suggests that juveniles and young adults are at a crime-prone age (Sampson and Laub 2003).

Although the official (Chinese) crime statistics have been criticized for having many shortcomings, they are still the most systematic source of data available (Liu 2008). The *Law Yearbook of China* (China Law Society 1991–2012) and the *China Statistical Yearbook* (National Bureau of Statistics of China 2012) are the major sources of statistics on crime, including juvenile crime. They mainly report the number of juvenile offenders, the percentage of juvenile offenders among all offenders, and the number of juvenile offenders incarcerated. No statistics on types and patterns of juvenile offenses are reported. Such information can only be obtained from academic research and from some local reports on the criminal justice system. Furthermore, academic research often involves a limited sample size and typically covers only a small geographical area, of several provinces at the most. The current paper will make use of both official crime statistics and academic research results to provide an enriched overview of juvenile crime in China.

Juvenile Crime Trends

Official crime statistics show that in the past 20 years, the overall number of criminals (including both juvenile and adult offenders) has steadily increased. The number reached more than one million in 2011. In comparison, the total number of juvenile (under the age of 18) and young (aged 18 and 25) offenders has fluctuated and shows a downward trend since 2008. The number of young offenders aged between 18 and 25 shows a similar trend. The number of juvenile offenders under the age of 18, however, has increased from approximately 42,000 in 1990 to approximately 67,000 in 2011 (see Figure 6.1). This is an increase in 20 years of approximately 60%. At the same time, China's overall population increased

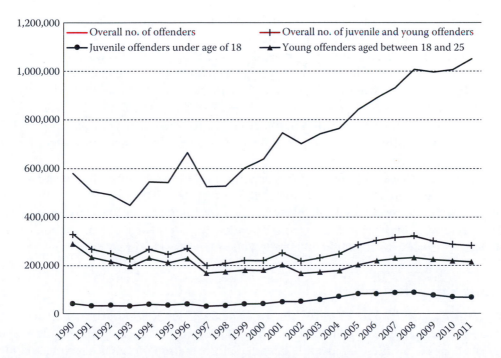

Figure 6.1 Number of juvenile and young offenders, 1990–2011. (China Law Society. (1991–2012). *Law Yearbook of China*. Beijing: Press of Law Yearbook of China.)

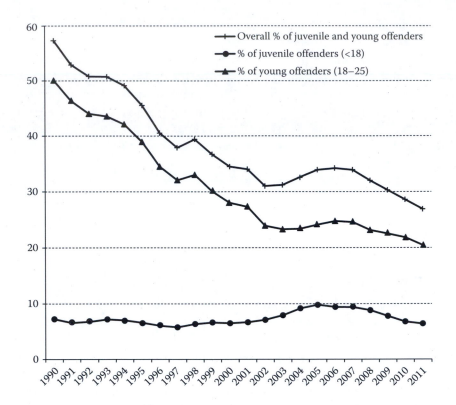

Figure 6.2 Percentage of juvenile and young offenders among all offenders, 1990–2011. (China Law Society. (1991–2012). *Law Yearbook of China*. Beijing: Press of Law Yearbook of China.)

approximately 18.15% from about 1.16 billion to about 1.37 billion during the 1990–2010 period (National Bureau of Statistics of China 1990, 2010).

Although the overall number of juvenile and young offenders has fluctuated since the 1990s, the number of juvenile and young offenders as a percentage of all offenders has steadily decreased, from approximately 57% in 1990 to 26.9% in 2011. The decrease is mainly in the number of young offenders aged between 18 and 25. The percentage of juvenile offenders under the age of 18 has fluctuated and reached its peak of 10% in 2005; it has since steadily decreased. In 2011, juvenile offenders (under the age of 18) accounted for 6.49% of all offenders (see Figure 6.2).

The *Law Yearbook of China* also reports the number of juvenile offenders who are incarcerated. The available statistics show that, in line with the trend in the overall number of offenders, the number of all offenders who are incarcerated has been increasing since 2003. The number of incarcerated juvenile offenders (under the age of 18), on the contrary, decreased from close to 20,000 in 2003 to 16,700 in 2011 (see Figure 6.3).

Juvenile Crime Patterns

Neither the *Law Yearbook of China* (China Law Society 1991–2012) nor the *China Statistical Yearbook* (National Bureau of Statistics of China 2012) provides specific information on the types of crimes committed by juvenile offenders. Information on types of crime and juvenile crime patterns can only be obtained through limited local law enforcement reports and empirical/academic research. Previous studies conducted in various geographical

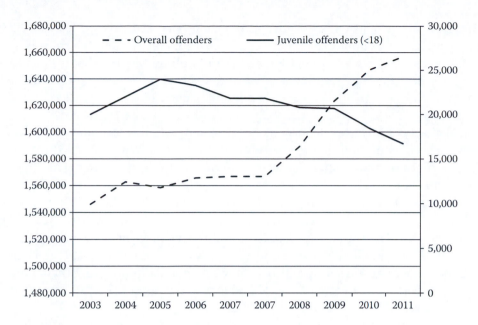

Figure 6.3 Incarcerated juvenile offenders, 2003–2011. (China Law Society. (1991–2012). *Law Yearbook of China*. Beijing: Press of Law Yearbook of China.)

locations* consistently show that since around 2000 or so, juvenile crime in China has the following patterns:

- In terms of types of crime committed, most crimes committed by juveniles are property-related crimes including primarily robbery and theft (Hao 2012; Hu 2012; Fu 2011; Bing 2010; Shao 2010; Wu 2010; Chen 2009a; Chen 2009b; Yang 2009; Zhang 2009; Zou 2008; Li 2007; Ma, Fang, and Wan 2006; Hainan Prosecutions Office 2002; Chen 2001); violent crimes account for relatively a small percentage (Wu 2010; Yang 2009); the number of drug-related crimes, such as drug abuse and drug trafficking, has been increasing (Qiao 2010; Wu 2010; Zou 2008; Ma, Fang, and Wan 2006); many crimes are committed to obtain money for drug abuse (Hainan Prosecutions Office 2002); the number of sexual assaults has increased (Bing 2010; Qiao 2010); and juvenile organized crime has also tended to increase (Shao 2010).
- Although violent crimes account for a small percentage, the consequences are becoming more serious. The number of crimes such as rape and homicide, which were rarely committed by juveniles, has tended to increase (Hu 2012; Fu 2011; Bing 2010; Chen 2001; Hainan Prosecutions Office 2002); in many cases, deadly weapons are involved (Hao 2012; Lu 2002).
- The majority of crimes committed by juveniles are opportunistic crimes. Very few are premeditated cases (Hao 2012; Fu 2011; Yu 2010; Du 2009).
- Most crimes are committed by juveniles in groups. This is especially the case for property-related crimes, such as theft and robbery (Hao 2012; Yu 2007; Li 2007; Li 2006; Ma, Fang, and Wan 2006; Hainan Prosecutions Office 2002; Chen 2001).

* Previous studies include studies conducted in more than 10 municipalities or provinces, such as Beijing, Anhui, Jiansu, Hunan, Shandong, Guangzhou, Ningxia, Zhejiang, Guangxi, Inner Mongolia, Sichuan, Tianjin, Xinjiang, and Jiangxi.

- The average age of juvenile offenders is reducing (Hao 2012; Bing 2010; Wu 2010; Shao 2010). For example, the official statistics from Guangzhou, the third largest Chinese city with a population of more than 12 million, showed that the peak age for juvenile crime was 16–18, but it reduced to 14–16 in recent years. From 2000 to 2007, the average age for juvenile crime has decreased by 2 years (Yang and Lv 2008).
- The majority of juvenile offenders have only received junior secondary school or a lower level of education (Hu 2012; Qiao 2010; Shao 2010; Wu 2010; Yu 2010).
- The number of school students who commit crimes is increasing (Hu 2012; Li 2006). Juvenile recidivists and female juvenile offenders account for only a small percentage (Henan Provincial High Court 2012; Shao 2010; Wu 2010); the number of female juvenile offenders has tended to increase (Bing 2010; Shao 2010). According to a recent judicial report issued by Henan Provincial High Court, a total of 687 female offenders were under juvenile trial from 2007 to 2011 in Henan, the most populous agricultural province with a population of more than 93 million. The percentage of female juvenile offenders increased from 1.91% in 2007 to 3.04% in 2011 (Henan Provincial High Court 2012).
- Most juvenile crimes occur in public areas such as plazas, bus stops, railway stations, entertainment centers, and so on (Ma, Fang, and Wan 2006).
- High technology is involved in many juvenile crimes (Hao 2012; Shao 2010). For example, the use of network in crime commission and cybercrimes such as computer intrusion, cyber stalking, or identity theft are not uncommon.
- Accompanying the rapid urbanization processes, which demand a large labor force, many farmers left their land and now work in the cities, as a result of the surplus rural labor force and the shrinking of farmland in rural areas. Some of the rural workers took their children with them when they went to work in the cities. Meanwhile, many youths who dropped out of school or failed to further their studies also joined the labor forces in the cities. Studies show that in urban areas, the majority of juvenile offenders prosecuted or imprisoned are children of rural workers or young people belonging to a "migrant/floating population" (Hu 2012).
- In rural communities, because many farmers work in the cities, their children are "left behind" without being taken care of by their parents. A number of studies have shown that the number of juvenile offenders who are left behind is increasing (Shu and Hao 2009; Wang and Han 2009; Cao 2007).

Overall, official crime statistics, along with empirical studies show that, although the number of juvenile offenders has been increasing over the last 20 years, juvenile offenders account for no more than 10% of all offenders. Comparatively, Hong Kong's juvenile offenders (those aged between 10 and 20) accounted for approximately 16.9% of overall crimes (Hong Kong Police Force 2012); Macau's juvenile offenders (aged between 13 and 20) accounted for approximately 4.5% of overall offenders (Macau Education and Youth Affairs Bureau 2013).* In other east Asian countries, Korean juvenile offenders (under age of 18) accounted for as less as 3.6% of all offenders (Korean Statistical Information Service

---

* The percentages are calculated using available statistics.

2010);* in Japan, juvenile arrestees (under age of 18) accounted for approximately 25.6% of all arrestees (Japan Statistics Bureau 2013).†

Most crimes committed by juveniles are property-related crimes including, primarily, robbery and theft; the numbers of drug-related crimes and sexual assaults have tended to increase; the majority of juvenile offenders have received only junior secondary school or a lower level of education; and many juvenile crimes involve the use of high technology. In many urban areas, juvenile members of the "migrant/floating population" and children of rural immigrants have become the most likely juvenile offenders, and in rural places, the number of juvenile offenders who are "left behind" by their parents has been increasing.

It is worth noting that the official crime statistics should be interpreted with caution. First, official juvenile crime statistics report only juvenile crimes with a certain level of severity, and leave out minor criminal cases. In China, crime is defined as behavior that reaches a certain level of severity (Liu 2008). Many examples of minor criminal behavior, such as the intentional damage of public property and the theft of a small amount of money or item of equivalent value, are not classified as crimes. These types of minor criminal behavior are defined as public order violations and are regulated by the Security Administration Sanction Law. In other words, these types of minor criminal behavior are subject to administrative penalties, which are handled by the Public Security Police instead of the courts. Second, although official crime statistics report the number of juvenile offenders and the percentage of juvenile offenders among all offenders, they do not take into consideration changes in the juvenile population over the years. It is therefore difficult to estimate the true juvenile crime rate in China. Because of the aforementioned shortcomings and the intrinsic limitations in the official crime statistics and the fact that definitions of crimes are different from one jurisdiction to another, cross-national comparisons using the official juvenile crime statistics in China are difficult, if not almost impossible.

Cultural and Historical Contexts

Cultural and Social Contexts

Deeply affected by both traditional ideology and Western thought, Chinese juvenile justice is the product of a mixture that bridges Confucianism, Maoism, and the doctrine of *parens partiae* (see Boxes 6.1 and 6.2). Throughout almost the entire span of Chinese history, juveniles have not had an independent legal personality. However, this does not mean that juveniles were completely ignored. The theoretical framework for juvenile justice in China can be traced back to Confucianism. Confucianism plays an important role in the legal philosophy and the moral codes of Chinese culture (Liu and Palermo 2009). The code offers abundant advice on how to prepare young people to serve the state as well as the family (Marr and Rosen 1998). The main content of Confucianism includes affectionate

---

* Korean Statistical Information Service (2010) reported that in 2009, the number of juvenile offenders (under age of 18) was 91,537, and the overall number of offenders was 2,519,237. The percentage of juvenile offenders among all offenders is calculated using available statistics.

† Japan Statistics Bureau (2013) reported that in 2010, the number of juvenile arrestees (under age of 18) was 87,048, and the overall number of arrestees in all age groups was 340,347. Juvenile arrestees accounted for approximately 25.6% of all arrestees in Japan in 2010. The percentage of juvenile arrestees among all arrestees is calculated using available statistics.

BOX 6.1   CONFUCIANISM

Traditional Chinese culture is represented by Confucianism. Confucianism is an ethical and philosophical system developed from the teachings of the Chinese philosopher Confucius (Kung-fu-tzu 551–479 BCE). It emphasizes three cardinal principles (ruler guides subject, father guides son, and husband guides wife) and the five constant virtues (benevolence, righteousness, propriety, wisdom, and fidelity). Along with rapid economic development and social change, China has been experiencing a renaissance of Confucianism.

BOX 6.2   MAOISM

Formally known as Mao Zedong Thought, Maoism is an ideological system derived from the teachings of the Chinese political leader Mao Zedong (1893–1976) and his communist associates. Maoism stresses the theory of guerrilla warfare and emphasizes peasantry as a revolutionary force.

fathers and respectful children, and respected elders and humble youngsters. Influenced by Confucianism, the Chinese juvenile justice system emphasizes "caring tenderly for the young" and "protecting infants" doctrines.

In addition to Confucianism, the establishment of the juvenile justice system was dominated by Communist ideology. The Chinese government drew on Communist theory and practice when formulating programs aimed at socializing young people (Marr and Rosen 1998). Along with the reform and opening up in the late 1970s, pluralistic concepts of values arose. The uniform Communist thoughts, once enforced by the method of simple and brute force, gradually waned and were marginalized. Despite this, the ideological influence on Chinese youth and juvenile justice will not suddenly disappear, but will be combined with other cultural factors to play an important role in shaping juvenile behavior and the juvenile justice system. For instance, the "temper justice with mercy" doctrine is a new development in juvenile delinquency policy in China, which calls for consideration of the juvenile and societal needs for forgiveness to soften the need for justice.

A couple of recent high-profile juvenile incidents highlight a shift away from traditional Confucian values. In a time of prevalent violence, social sentiment in China is in favor of punishment and institutionalization. In the face of increasing public concerns over juvenile crime and violence, Chinese juvenile criminal justice has to take these complaints seriously, while also taking serious action with respect to the special demands and needs of juveniles. Wong (1999) identifies four cultural factors that stand out as relevant to the nature of a modern juvenile justice system: positive punishment and forgiveness, the logic of interdependency, the attractiveness of gang brotherhood, and social disadvantage and delinquency. Beyond that, the principles of the criminal justice laws are also endowed with new implications. For example, the severe penalty doctrine, as the guiding principle of criminal law, had reflected the Criminal Code in both ancient and communist China. The severe penalty doctrine and compassion are a pair of inconsistent but concomitant philosophies, and form part of Chinese juvenile justice. Moreover, restorative justice is playing an increasingly important role in Chinese juvenile justice. The ideas and practices of Western restorative justice were introduced into China at the turn of the twenty-first century. In the most recent decade, an increasing number of translated restorative justice texts and research provided Chinese scholars and practitioners a better understanding of the concept and its practice in juvenile justice (Zhang 2013). Compared with adult offenders, Chinese people naturally feel more empathy for juveniles and therefore are more oriented toward reconciliation between juvenile offenders and victims and community.

Historical Evolutions

Origins

Although the concept of juvenile justice is new in China, some of the fundamental ideas can be traced back to a century ago. After the first Opium War with Great Britain (1840–1842), China was invaded and reduced to the status of a semicolony with a semifeudal society, and clans gradually disintegrated when encountering unprecedented dilemmas and challenges. From the law reform of the late Qing Dynasty (1636–1911), the criminal justice system began its modern historic revolution, and many Western laws were translated into Chinese legislation. The first-ever juvenile court was established in Illinois in the United States in 1899 (see Chapter 15) and is regarded as the beginning of the independent juvenile justice system and a model for other nations, including Japan, to follow. But Chinese reformists failed in the **Hundred Days' Reform** movement to make a radical change to society in 1898, and China has not kept pace with modern juvenile justice.

Slowly but surely, the New Qing Imperial Criminal Code of 1911 was the most significant achievement in this historical period. The law provided that children under 12 years of age could not be charged with a crime (Article 11), and that those under 16 years of age could have light, or reduced, sentences (Article 60). Most strikingly, given its status as the first law to be revised in the late **Qing Dynasty**, the law first proposed that children under 12 years of age should receive reformatory education (Article 11).

Early Developments

The New Qing Imperial Criminal Code of 1911 was scheduled to be implemented in 1913, but the victory of the 1911 Revolution and the subsequent establishment of an interim republican government overturned the rule of the Qing Dynasty, making the implementation impossible. However, the new government soon made an official announcement proclaiming that the articles of the Criminal Code could be applied temporarily, except any that contravened republican doctrine. Based on this law, the Criminal Code of the Chinese Nationalist Party (or the Kuomintang, hereinafter referred to as the "KMT") became law in 1928, raising the age of criminal responsibility to 13; delinquents aged from 13 to 16 could have their sentences reduced by half. Seven years later, the Criminal Code of 1935 revised the threshold to 14, and provided for those aged from 14 to 18 to have their sentences reduced (Article 18). This code was admired by some foreign observers for its treatment of juveniles because it "very logically deals with" juvenile delinquents with both protective measures and criminal responsibility (van der Valk 1936).

In the absence of direct provision for the special treatment of juveniles, the Department of Justice issued an order on May 9, 1936, noting the differences in the characteristics

BOX 6.3   CHINA'S SOCIAL POLITICAL SHIFT SINCE 1912

China's last dynasty, the Qing Dynasty (1636–1911) gradually collapsed in the early 1900s. It led to the establishment of the Republic of China, a democratic regime, in 1912. Since then, the social–political shift has been in the transition from feudalist tradition to modernization. The road to modernization had been tough because it was full of natural disasters and frequent civil wars. The nation's crisis deepened when Japan invaded China during 1937 and 1945. Later, the civil war with Kuomingtang (the nationalist party) lasted for another 4 years. In 1949, the Communist Party of China asserted its control over China and established the People's Republic of China (PRC). The 10-year Cultural Revolution (1966–1976), which traumatized Chinese traditional values, was followed by the market economic reform that put to an end to the ideology of class struggle as one of the core objectives of PRC. Since then, China has been working on market economic reform and strengthening of its legal systems, among which juvenile justice receives increasing attention.

between adult and juvenile offenders, and requesting that specially trained judges with rich experience and patience deal with juvenile cases. The department also included a detailed statement entitled *The Fifteen Points on Juvenile Trials*. In addition to criminal responsibility, the KMT government had dealt with institutionalized treatment for juveniles. For example, the Prison Law of 1946 provided that children under the age of 18 should be kept in separate juvenile prisons.

The progress toward the rule of law for juveniles was plagued by civil war because of endless disputes between warlords and confrontations occurring one after another. The civil war between the KMT government and the Communist Party of China (hereinafter referred to as the "CPC"), which had begun in the 1920s and abated during the Japanese occupation, resumed between 1945 and 1949. The rise of the CPC marked the collapse of the KMT, and the gradual preliminary establishment of a communist juvenile justice system. On April 8, 1934, the Chinese Soviet Republic issued the *Regulations for Suppression of Counterrevolution*, which provided that children under the age of 16 could have a reduced punishment and that offenders under the age of 14 should receive reformatory education (see Box 6.3).

During this period, and particularly in the early 1930s, juvenile delinquency was largely seen as being much less severe than adult crime. In a paper published in 1934, comparing Chinese with American juvenile delinquency, Ching-Yueh Yen (1934) optimistically thought that delinquency was not a problem in Chinese cities except for Shanghai, and observed that the courts in Beijing had not sent a single delinquent to reformatory school for 2 years. When using China's official crime figures, some scholars warned that there might be a large gap between official statistics and actual crimes and that such statistics might have hidden crime figures (Zhang and Liu 2007).

Further Struggles

On February 28, 1949, 7 months before seizing state power, the CPC announced the abolition of the KMT's six laws (the Constitution, Civil Law, Commercial Law, Criminal Law, Civil Procedure Law, and Criminal Procedure Law) and replaced them with new ones.

As a result, China has been "the subject of a significant legal experiment" (Cohen 1966, 469). Apparently, the relevant regulations related to juvenile suspects and offenders were included in the list of what was abolished. One of the most important tasks for the new regime would be to restore social order and construct a socialist legal system. Under these circumstances, given that China did not have a systematic approach to juvenile justice, a few juvenile policies began to appear in scattered rules.

The reason for the slow development of juvenile justice during this period also lies in the alleged low juvenile crime rate. Through the 1950s and 1960s, the juvenile crime rate among those aged 14–18 amounted to only 0.2%–0.4% (Bakken 1993). Through the tumultuous Cultural Revolution (1966–1976), Western legal thought was regarded as a product of the degeneracy and decayed tastes of the Western bourgeoisie. In addition, the class-conflict theory caused legal nihilism. This was a disturbing and worrying phenomenon. However, it was believed that juvenile delinquency and the crime rate were low and "posed no threat to social order" (Wong 1999, 27). An American judge noted, after his visit to China in 1975, "Juvenile delinquency is nearly non-existent" (cited by Chiu 1977, 375). One of the main reasons for this disproportionately low juvenile crime rate might have been due to Mao Zedong's policy of sending educated youths to settle in rural areas (Chiu 1977). As a result, not much attention has been given to the nature or extent of delinquency in China (Wong 2001).

New Approaches

After prolonged stagnation and despair, China embraced juvenile justice with gusto. Rapid social changes originating from the economic reform in the late 1970s have been making juveniles' lives more stressful and therefore contributing to juvenile delinquency and crime (Bao and Haas 2009). As a result, the juvenile crime rate rapidly increased to 1.4% in 1977, 2.2% in 1978, and 3.3% in 1979, and then reached 23.8% in 1985 (Bakken 1993). Until the late 1970s, China had not enacted a criminal code or criminal procedure code, although there were a few statutes governing criminal justice (Leng 1982). Plagued by soaring juvenile delinquency and crime, the CPC's Central Committee soon issued its *Report Addressing the Problem of Juvenile Delinquency* on June 10, 1979, which focused the nation's attention on this issue and called for urgent action.

Through the 1980s, China has experienced an alarming increase in crime and a high proportion of juvenile crime (Epstein 1986; Bakken 1993). The increasing worry about juvenile delinquency has raised concerns in China about the new approach toward dealing with juvenile delinquency. As a result, laws and programs have sprung up around China. The first official juvenile court was established in Changning district, Shanghai, in 1984, and marks the beginning of the Chinese juvenile justice system. In the first 3 years after this court was set up, 45 juveniles were tried there and only one committed another crime (Kang 2012). The National People's Congress has focused on adopting important laws to underpin juvenile protection and rehabilitation. Influenced by those laws and regulations, one sees here the acceleration of the establishment of juvenile courts and the rapid growth of the juvenile justice system. In 2007, the Chinese Supreme Court began a pilot program to establish specialized juvenile tribunals in 17 big cities. In July 2010, the Professional Committee for Juvenile Trials was set up by the Chinese Association of Adjudication Theory, a semiofficial research group initiated and supported by the Chinese Supreme Court.

Legislative Attempts to Address Juvenile Delinquency and Crime

Social control in China is a mixture of formal and informal control. As formal control becomes more influential, it has been widely concerned with how to strengthen legal control over juvenile offenders. Because juveniles are not considered as adults who are fully responsible for all of their actions, special regulations have been established that pertain only to them. The various laws relating to juvenile offenders include the Constitution and criminal justice laws, as well as a specialized juvenile protection law and a juvenile delinquency prevention law. The Chinese Constitution of 1982 proclaims that the state promotes the all-round moral, intellectual, and physical development of children and young people (Article 46). However, a specialized law was not enacted until the late 1980s. On June 20, 1987, Shanghai introduced the Shanghai Youth Protection Ordinance, the first significant legislative attempt in China to protect juveniles, and the most notable achievement of this was to establish a juvenile tribunal. The more important laws dealing with juveniles found to be in breach of the criminal law are contained in the Criminal Code and Criminal Procedure Code, among others. The laws and regulations of juvenile justice make no distinction between the terms child and juvenile. Compared with *child, juvenile* is largely seen as a more appropriate term within juvenile justice. In China, juvenile justice law is applicable to those under 18 defined as juvenile.

The various laws recognize that juveniles are inherently different from adults and that it is the state's responsibility to protect and rehabilitate young offenders. They further define juvenile delinquency and set out rules with which juvenile court procedures and punishments must comply. In addition, the Chinese Supreme Court and the Chinese Supreme Procuratorate have given various judicial interpretations for the better implementation of national laws affecting juveniles. The Convention on the Rights of the Child has been ratified by the National People's Congress, thus making it legally effective in China and a part of Chinese law.

Among all these laws, the Juvenile Protection Law of 1991 and the Juvenile Delinquency Prevention Law of 1999 are of great importance. The Juvenile Protection Law of 1991 sets out the standards for juvenile justice, stating that education is the primary means and punishment is the secondary means for handling delinquency. This is the first such set of national regulations ever adopted in China. The purpose of the law is to regulate the procedures and principles for protecting juveniles who are in need of protection or who are driven to crime, and ensuring that their rights and well-being are protected. But the daily operation does not seem to meet all requirements. The Juvenile Protection Law of 1991 was revised in 2006, and the revision of the Juvenile Delinquency Prevention Law of 1999 is underway.

In 2012, China added a new chapter on juvenile criminal procedure to its Criminal Procedure Code, addressing such issues as free legal aid, appropriate adult presence during questioning, conditional nonprosecution, nonpublicizing of trials, the sealing of juvenile criminal records, and the compilation of background reports on young people. These 11 articles aim to enhance the judicial protection of juvenile criminal suspects and defendants further, causing practitioners to "jump for joy."

Areas of Juvenile Delinquency and Crime

The general range of Chinese juvenile delinquency is not much different from that of China's Western counterparts. Juvenile delinquents are defined and described, as well as the types of offenses they commit. The Chinese juvenile justice system has jurisdiction over two distinct categories of offenders, delinquents and offenders. Certain offenses such as curfew violations, running away, disobeying parents, and school truancy are not punishable under the criminal code. As a matter of fact, the majority of juvenile delinquency consists of offenses such as theft, shoplifting, vandalism, being out at night while underage, underage drinking, and simple assault. The minor offenses could be regulated through other noncriminal mechanisms, such as the management of public security. The Juvenile Delinquency Prevention Law of 1999 makes a distinction between bad misbehavior and serious misbehavior. For example, the law lists a few types of misbehavior such as school truancy, curfew violation, carrying a knife illegally, assault, verbal abuse of others, demanding the property of others, theft, vandalism, participating in gambling, watching or listening to erotic material, pornographic videos, or books, and entering places not fit for juveniles (Article 14). The law further lists serious misbehavior such as forming a gang and disturbing the peace, repeatedly carrying an unrestrained knife, reckless or repeated gang violence or forcible demands for property, disseminating obscene books and/or obscene audio material, sexually promiscuity, pornography or prostitution, frequent theft, repeated gambling, and drug abuse (Article 34). Most of the bad misbehavior and serious misbehavior could be seen as having the status of offenses from a Western point of view.

By contrast, juvenile crime, particularly school violence and gang violence, is often perceived to be extensive and serious. The more lenient laws such as the Security Administration Sanction Law of 2005 might not be sufficient to handle serious juvenile crimes.

Operational Mechanisms

Considering that a young offender, in China, has diminished accountability and legal understanding, the general idea of giving priority to education and supplementing this with punishment has served as a fundamental principle in Chinese juvenile justice. It is fair to say that Chinese juvenile justice is a hybrid between prevention and sanctions.

Generally speaking, China does not currently have a distinct justice system for juveniles from the perspective of a Western juvenile justice framework. Unlike in the United States or Canada, where juveniles alleged to have committed serious offenses can be transferred to an adult court, the current Chinese juvenile justice system could be seen as part of the general criminal justice system. The premise of the Criminal Procedure Code of 2012 for juveniles clearly stipulates that it will implement educational, reformative, and redemptive guiding principles for juvenile offenders and uphold the principle of education first, and punishment second (Article 266). The top Chinese judicial bodies, the Supreme Court and the Supreme Procuratorate, repeatedly call for criminal cases to be handled with "justice tempered with mercy," and this mostly refers in passing to the handling of juvenile delinquency. The doctrine is in line with the United Nations Standard Minimum Rules for the Administration of Juvenile Justice ("the Beijing Rules"), which stipulates that "the juvenile justice system shall emphasize the well-being of the juvenile and shall ensure that any reaction to juvenile offenders shall always be in proportion to the circumstances of both the offenders and the offence" (Rule 5.1). Moreover, more rules drawn from various international standards, including the United Nations Guidelines for the Prevention of Juvenile Delinquency ("The Riyadh Guidelines"), are introduced into China's juvenile justice practice and relevant research.

Age Restrictions on Jurisdiction of Juvenile Courts

Many crimes are committed by individuals who have not come of age. The characteristics of juveniles' physical and mental development determine the adoption of different rules of criminal responsibility. The jurisdiction of juvenile courts over young people depends upon established legislative definitions. Until the introduction of the Juvenile Protection Law of 2006, many expressions were used to define the term *juvenile*. According to the Juvenile Protection Law of 2006, any individual who has not yet come of age is defined as a juvenile (Article 2). The age of 18 is the legal age of majority in China.

By comparison, the age of criminal responsibility is covered by the Criminal Code of 2011. Under the Chinese Criminal Code of 2011, the general age of criminal responsibility is 16 (Article 17), which indicates that for certain illegal actions, juveniles are subject to criminal proceedings from the age of 16. Moreover, if a juvenile aged between 14 and 16 commits a serious crime, he or she needs to bear criminal responsibility. According to the code, these crimes include intentional homicide, intentionally hurting another person so as to cause serious injury or death, rape, robbery, drug trafficking, arson, explosion, or poisoning (Article 17). This means that children who have not reached the age of 14 cannot be prosecuted for any offence. The code further provides that a juvenile aged below 18 could be given a lighter or mitigated punishment. A juvenile delinquent between the ages of 14 and 18 is subject to punishment, but to a lighter degree (Article 17).

Components of the Juvenile Justice System

From a global perspective, there are several models that inspire the administration of juvenile justice including, but not limited to, the welfare model, the justice or retributive model, and the restorative model. Some scholars argue that neither the welfare model nor the retributive model could be used to describe the Chinese juvenile control system (see Wong 1999). Wong also observed that "developments in the juvenile justice system of China reveal a shift from an informal 'societal' to a formal 'juridical' model of justice" (Wong 1999, 35). Generally speaking, the main components of contemporary juvenile justice are historically influenced by criminal justice and therefore operate as an integral part of the latter. Although many restorative elements have been introduced to the Chinese juvenile justice system (as evidenced by the revisions of Juvenile Protection Act of 2006 and Criminal Procedure Code of 2012), it might be safer to say that juvenile justice in China could be viewed largely as a crime control model at the core with an increasing emphasis on more education and less punishment. As the incidence and severity of crimes committed by juveniles remain high, the emphasis on juvenile rehabilitation is and will continue to be under attack from both the criminal justice professionals and the general public. It takes time and effort to transform the main focus from a crime control model to a complete justice model.

As part of general criminal justice, Chinese juvenile justice is composed of policing, procuratorate, court, correction, and social welfare agents who provide young people with diverse services. The development of juvenile justice is the result of the social interaction of these various components. Although all these components have something in common,

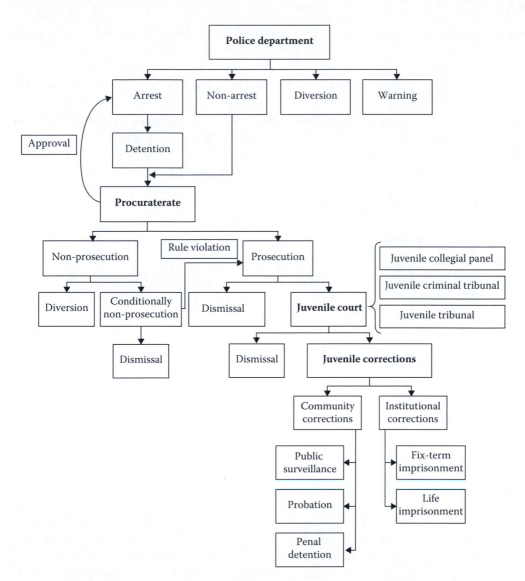

Figure 6.4 Juvenile case flow. Note: The figure is developed based on relevant provisions of the Criminal Law of 2011 and the Criminal Procedure Law of 2012. (Adapted from National Bureau of Statistics of China. (2012). *China Statistical Yearbook*. Beijing: China Statistics Press.)

such as a common set of core principles for handling juvenile cases, this does not distinguish them from the regular criminal justice system for adult offenders.

The processing of cases in the juvenile justice system involves a series of decisions by police officers, procurators, and judges. To achieve the desired effect of the prevention of juvenile delinquency, these people decide at each stage whether the case will move on to the next stage or be dropped from the system (see Figure 6.4).

Policing and Juveniles

A Chinese juvenile's first contact with juvenile justice is usually with the police. A police officer usually has considerable discretion in dealing with juvenile matters. In addition to regular contact because of criminal activity, there might be some additional contacts between the police and juveniles. The passage of the Security Administration Sanction Law of 2005 strengthens the function of the police in handling these juvenile matters. This law covers the illegal behavior of stirring up fights and causing trouble, but does not deem those types of delinquency to be criminal. For example, many clauses provide that juveniles are prohibited from hanging out at night and that a police officer can stop and question them. The Juvenile Delinquency Prevention Law of 1999 stipulates that parents, guardians, and schools bear the responsibility of guiding juveniles so that they do not hang around on the street at night. This is often considered to be a juvenile curfew law. When juveniles have gone out at night, the law further prescribes that their parents, guardians, or boarding school should look for them without delay, or approach the police for help (Article 14). The law, however, does not provide specific stipulation on a time frame for the curfew, which makes it difficult to carry out in practice. The law also warns that anyone taking in underage young people for the night must get permission from the young people's parents, guardians, or boarding schools, or report them to the police department within 24 hours (Article 16). The lack of related statistics makes it difficult to assess whether this has been strictly implemented.

Like other jurisdictions, however, the meaning of policing in China is undergoing change. Some scholars like Dutton (2000) argued that the Western concept of policing did not arrive until the post-Mao reforms. As the most visible officials in juvenile justice, the police are expected to play a more prominent role in solving the problems that lead to juvenile delinquency and crime. However, at present, the specialized juvenile policing experience to deal with juvenile crime and delinquency has not been acquired.

Juvenile Court and Procuratorate

Unlike other nations, the Chinese judicial system includes the **procuratorate system** in addition to the court system. There are therefore two corresponding basic types of judicial bodies with the responsibility for overseeing the implementation of juvenile justice: the juvenile courts and the juvenile procuratorate. Similarly, both juvenile judges and juvenile procurators advocate that juveniles are different because of their diminished juvenile accountability and legal understanding and their amenability to treatment.

The Chinese courts include the local courts at various levels, military courts, other special courts, and the Supreme Court. The local courts are divided into grassroots courts at county court or urban district court levels, intermediate courts at prefectural levels, and higher courts at provincial levels. Yet, the meaning of juvenile court in China might be quite different from its Western counterpart, and it is more appropriate to refer to a juvenile tribunal. The Supreme Court and the local courts have established the juvenile courts with different forms. For example, the Supreme Court has set up the steering division for juvenile tribunals within its research office, whereas several higher courts such as the Beijing Higher Court have set up juvenile tribunals.

The first juvenile trial chamber was created in Shanghai's **Changning District Court**, to separate cases against juveniles from those faced by adults, in November 1984. This particular year is often marked as the year the juvenile court was born (Zhang 2008). Since then, juvenile tribunals have gradually formed into three general types, the criminal tribunal's juvenile collegial panel, the juvenile criminal tribunal, and the juvenile tribunal. In the early stages of development, a juvenile collegial panel affiliated to a criminal tribunal was the sole trial chamber for hearing juvenile criminal cases. As the juvenile collegial panels expanded and grew, the specialized juvenile criminal tribunals emerged from the criminal tribunals. For the better protection of juveniles' interests, especially their civil and administrative interests, some juvenile criminal tribunals have been upgraded to juvenile tribunals and, further, include certain civil and administrative cases relating to the protection of juveniles within their jurisdictions. Each tribunal changes as it develops, but this does not necessarily mean that it disappears or is transformed into another one. On the national scale, these types of tribunals might therefore coexist in a stable fashion over a long period of time. By 2012, there were 2331 juvenile courts over the whole country, including 1584 juvenile collegial panels, 390 juvenile criminal tribunals, and 357 juvenile tribunals, with 7450 juvenile judges (Hu 2013). Influenced by both *parens partiae* and Confucianism, the emphasis in all juvenile tribunals is upon the rehabilitation of youthful offenders rather than punishment. To date, almost all juvenile criminal cases have been handled by one of these tribunals.

In spite of all this, all the tribunals are affiliated to ordinary courts and are divisions within those courts. Over the past 10–20 years, however, there has been an increasing number of calls to organize an independent juvenile court to hear juvenile cases including, but not limited to, delinquency matters, juvenile crime, and care and protection proceedings, exclusively (Xu 2001; Ding 2001). For example, since 2001, efforts to establish an independent juvenile court in Shanghai have been actively underway. If that happens, there might be another opportunity for setting up a juvenile court.

The Chinese court system is paralleled by a hierarchy of prosecuting officers called procuratorates. The Chinese procuratorates include local procuratorates at various levels, that is, military procuratorates, other special procuratorates, and the Supreme Procuratorate. The local procuratorates are divided into grassroots procuratorates at county court or urban district court levels, prefectural procuratorates, and provincial procuratorates. Although the procuratorate is regarded constitutionally as a judicial organ, it in fact carries out various tasks such as crime control and prevention. The Constitution of 1982 prescribes that the procuratorates are state organs for legal supervision (Article 129). Because of their uniqueness, the procuratorates oversee cases involving juveniles. The Supreme Procuratorate has established the Office of Juvenile Prosecution within its Bureau of Public Prosecution. Some provincial, prefectural, and county/district procuratorates have set up their own offices for juvenile prosecutions. Furthermore, they can put forward procuratorial suggestions to relevant organizations and individuals, to prevent and reduce juvenile delinquency. As a kind of supervision function for prosecutions, these suggestions have some particularity in content, scope, and forms to some extent. They are regarded as a form of soft judicial order, and the respondents are normally requested to act accordingly.

A Chinese procurator usually has considerable discretionary authority in cases referred to them by the police and often has several options at the arrest-decision stage. It is their duty to decide whether to keep a juvenile in custody or to allow the youth to go home while waiting for further court action. The procurator is primarily responsible for the prosecution decision. In addition, they could make a decision not to prosecute first-time offenders, attempted offenders, offenders who have been influenced by others, and offenders who have committed acts of criminal negligence, whose crimes are juvenile and who exhibit true repentance. Recently, sentencing suggestions by procurators have been given close attention. When putting forward sentencing suggestions, the procurator could put forward a motion with respect to sentencing together with the indictment to the court.

Defense Attorney and Legal Representation

The Constitution of 1982 and the relevant laws provide that an accused juvenile is entitled to be represented by counsel. The Criminal Procedure Code of 2012 further provides that the courts have the obligation to ensure that the accused obtains a defense and sets forth specific procedures so that any suspect or accused may, in addition to exercising their right to defend themselves, appoint one or two representatives to defend them. Note that, in real life, many juveniles do not have a full understanding of the legal proceedings against them as could be seen elsewhere. The defense counsel could be either a private or a public defender from a legal aid agent. The Criminal Procedure Code of 2012 requires that where a juvenile criminal suspect or defendant has not appointed a legal representative, the court, the procuratorate, or the police department should notify the legal aid agency to designate a lawyer to undertake the defense (Article 267). However, lawyers in China are often poorly trained, resulting in variable professionalism (Landsberg 2011).

The Criminal Procedure Code of 2012 further requires that, the legal representative of the juvenile suspect or defendant should appear in the interrogation or trial of the juvenile. In the case of failure to notifying the legal representative, or when the legal representative is an accomplice, another adult relative of the juvenile criminal suspect or defendant, a representative of the school, unit, grassroots organization in the place of residence, or organization for the protection of juveniles may also be notified, and the relevant matters shall be kept on record (Article 270). The legal representative at the trial may exercise litigation rights on behalf of the juvenile criminal suspect or defendant.

Juvenile Proceedings

The concern for the rights of due process of a juvenile is more critical than ever, and this can be seen by the number of new legal provisions. In the United States and many other nations, juvenile courts are civil proceedings exclusively designed for juveniles, while criminal courts are criminal proceedings designed to try adults (Champion, 2010). Unlike American "quasi-civil" proceedings, Chinese juvenile court proceedings are considered largely as criminal proceedings. Overall, the juvenile proceedings demonstrate the protection of the juvenile and the focus on his/her interests throughout the juvenile process, from detention to arrest, prosecution, court trial, and rehabilitation. Although juvenile offenders might be treated slightly differently from adults, the divergence is not remarkable.

Juvenile Pretrial Detention

After a juvenile has been questioned, the police officer has notable discretion on whether or not to take the youth into custody. Pretrial detention could be used for certain juveniles, particularly those showing serious violent behavior. Releasing the juvenile to his or her parents/guardians is the most favored decision, while placing the juvenile in a local jail is another alternative. This involves locking up a certain number of juveniles in a secure facility while waiting for a court trial or a decision not to prosecute. In certain circumstances, the juvenile could probably be placed under house detention or be out on bail. In judicial practice, the application of bail pending trial of juveniles varies greatly from one jurisdiction to another. For instance, while juvenile bail has been rare in many jurisdictions, in Zhenjiang city's Jinkou district, one of the most flourishing economic areas in east China's Jiangsu province, application of juvenile bail steadily increased from 17% in 2000 to 31% in 2007 (Zhang 2007). The Criminal Procedure Code of 2012 requires that juveniles who are detained, arrested, or are being punished for a crime should be locked up, supervised, and educated separately from adults (Article 269). This means that a juvenile cannot be detained or confined in any institution in which they would have contact with adults.

Juvenile Arrest

Unlike most Western counterparts, the Chinese procuratorate is entrusted with the authority to issue an arrest warrant. The Chinese Constitution of 1982 prescribes that no citizen may be arrested except with the approval or by the decision of a procuratorate, or by the decision of a court, and that arrests must be made by the police department (Article 37). In juvenile criminal justice, however, it is the procurator who shoulders the heavy responsibility of approving an application for arrest from the local police department. The police refer the juvenile criminal case to the procurator, who uses a file-based system to examine and approve the arrest; this results in a high rate of arrests. Since police departments are under considerable pressure of performance evaluation, high rates of juvenile arrest are not surprising.

According to the Criminal Procedure Code of 2012, lesser juvenile offenders who have effective guardianship or access to proper education and help, and who pose little or no danger to society, can avoid being arrested. The code requires that arrests of juvenile criminal suspects or defendants be rigorously restricted (Article 269). The code further stipulates that where the procuratorate examines and approves an arrest, or the court decides on an arrest, they shall interrogate the juvenile criminal suspect or defendant and hear the opinions of the defense lawyer. In 2011 alone, the approval rate for arrests of juvenile suspects by procuratorates at various levels was down 5% from its level of the previous year (Huang 2012).

Juvenile Prosecution

As is the case with the police, juvenile procurators have broad discretionary powers in China. Based on the nature of the crime and the degree of harm, the procurator has a wide discretion over those who may be criminally responsible by declaring certain conditions and requirements that the suspects must fulfill during a certain test period; depending on their performance in this period, the procurator will decide whether to prosecute. In recent years, the *nolle prosequi* (declination of prosecution) rate of prosecuting offices has been very low. In 2012, the procuratorates nationwide posted a 1% decrease in the juvenile prosecution rate from the previous year (Huang 2012).

Conditional nonprosecution is modeled on the Western practice that allows young people who commit juvenile offenses to avoid spending time in jail by successfully completing a certain period of time under supervision. This is a very important function for the procurator, for considerations of public interest and the best interests of children. The Criminal Procedure Code of 2012 specifies that for those juveniles on whom a criminal punishment of not more than 1 year of fixed-term imprisonment may be imposed, and who meet the requirements for being prosecuted but have demonstrated repentance, the procuratorate may make a decision of conditional nonprosecution. Prior to making such a decision, the procurator should hear the opinions of the police department and the victim (Article 271). The code further states that juvenile suspects who are under a conditional nonprosecution decision shall observe the following actions: abiding by laws and regulations and obeying supervision; reporting their activities, according to the provisions, to the supervising agent; obtaining approval from the observing organ if they decide to leave the city or county where they reside or move to another area; and accepting rectification and education required by the supervising agent (Article 272). If, during the probation period of a conditional nonprosecution, the juvenile criminal suspect does any of the following, the procuratorate shall cancel the decision of conditional nonprosecution and bring a public prosecution: committing a new crime or being found to have committed, prior to the conditional nonprosecution decision, other crimes for which they should be prosecuted, or seriously violating the provisions for the administration of public security or the provisions concerning conditional nonprosecution made by the observing organ on supervision and administration (Article 273).

Adjudication and Sentencing

Cases begin in the juvenile court with the issuance of a criminal complaint, either by the public procurator or by a private citizen, stating the law that has been violated and the facts that support the allegation. The Criminal Procedure Code of 2012 states that the onus of proof that a defendant is guilty is on the procurator in a public prosecution case and on the private procurator in a private prosecution case (Article 49). The court of second instance has the final decision, as the juvenile criminal procedure is a two-tier system. A juvenile criminal trial of first instance at a grassroots court (county or district court) can be heard by a bench or a single judge, while such cases of first instance in the intermediate court could only be heard by a bench.

Since a juvenile tribunal is largely seen as part of a criminal court, the court proceedings are formal and adversarial. Despite this, juvenile court proceedings are closed to the public since juvenile matters are confidential. The Criminal Procedure Code of 2012 requires criminal cases involving juvenile defendants under the age of 18 not to be tried publicly (Article 274). However, with the consent of the juvenile defendant and the legal representative, the school attended by the juvenile defendant and the juvenile protection organization may send representatives to the trial (Article 274).

Before hearing the evidence, the juvenile court judge will first determine whether the juveniles understand their legal rights as most of them are not aware of their rights in the legal proceedings. The typical juvenile hearing involves brief introductions by both the procurator and the defense counsel, followed by the presentation of evidence, testimony, confrontation, and cross-examination. Article 270 of the Criminal Procedure Code of 2012 requires, in the trial of a juvenile in a criminal case, that after the juvenile defendant has made his/her final statement, his/her legal representative may make a supplementary statement. After a juvenile has been found guilty, a deposition will be made based on legal variables such as the seriousness of the offense and the juvenile's prior record, and individual and social factors. The court relies on a social investigation report prepared by a police officer, the procurator, or another agent. This report may include information such as family history, attendance, grades and behavior in school, peer relationships, community relationships, and previous court record. The code further requires that, in dealing with crimes committed by juveniles, the police department, the procuratorate, and the court may, depending on the circumstances, conduct an investigation into such matters as the young person's childhood experiences, his/her reason(s) for committing a crime, and the education offered by his or her guardians (Article 268). The social investigation report is an important reference document for the juvenile's sentence.

Prior convictions play a vital yet variable role in sentencing. From the perspective of starting over, an opportunity might be presented to juvenile offenders who want to correct their errors and make a fresh start when they reach the age of majority. In line with the practices followed abroad, the Criminal Procedure Code of 2012 requires that if a juvenile has committed a crime and has been sentenced to a criminal punishment of not more than 5 years of fixed-term imprisonment, the relevant criminal record shall be sealed (Article 275). Juvenile criminal records are confidential and can only be released to officers of the court or specific agencies. The sealed criminal record is not provided to any unit or individual unless a judicial organ needs it to handle cases or a relevant unit is permitted to consult it according to state regulations. A unit, which may consult it in accordance with the law shall keep the information in the sealed criminal record secret.

The sentencing alternatives available to the juvenile court vary considerably, and the primary options include dismissal, probation, and imprisonment. At present, while most nations have abolished the death penalty, it can still be imposed in China. The Criminal Code of 2011 states that the death penalty shall not be imposed on a person who had not reached the age of 18 at the time the crime was committed or on a woman who was pregnant at the time of trial (Article 49). Therefore, the death penalty cannot be applied to a juvenile. Life imprisonment can, however, be imposed on juvenile offenders. In other words, life imprisonment is the severest possible punishment for a juvenile. Although various sources question the independence of the Chinese justice system (this is especially the case for adult criminal justice system), when it comes to juveniles, the laws such as the ones that prohibit death penalty and requires juvenile criminal records to be kept confidential are strictly followed, mostly without interruption by any third party.

Juvenile Rehabilitation

Punishment, as an instrument of deterrence, has traditionally been an important element in Chinese correctional philosophy. Although juvenile courts are more focused on rehabilitation, many juveniles are placed in detention. The establishment of modern prisons was initiated in 1909 (Wang 1917). And since then, model prisons, including juvenile prisons, have been set up in most of the provincial capitals, and some special treatment has been given to juvenile inmates. The institutional approach to dealing with criminals has remained a salient feature in the judicial system. A juvenile sentenced to life imprisonment or a prison term will be put into a juvenile reformatory. According to the Prison Law of 1994, criminal punishments for juvenile delinquents are to be carried out in reformatories for juvenile delinquents (Article 74), which indicates that the juvenile reformatory is seen as a prison. Provincial reformatories house delinquents and apply reform through labor (see Box 6.4)

Juvenile offenders aged 16 who are frequently subject to little or no responsible parental supervision or control are often placed within the control of a governmental rehabilitation center. The Criminal Code of 2011 provides that when persons are not criminally punished

BOX 6.4   REFORM THROUGH LABOR

Modeling it after the Soviet *Gulag*, reform through labor came to effect in the early 1950s. It is used to punish and reform criminals through laborious work and economic gain. Nowadays, reform through labor places more emphasis on rehabilitation, urging the criminals to rehabilitate themselves, learn labor skills and resocialize through labor.

because they have not reached the age of 16, the family or guardian is to be ordered to subject them to discipline; when necessary, they may also be given shelter and rehabilitation by the government (Article 17).

In addition to the institution-based sentences, community-based sentences for juveniles have become a hot topic for discussion. In China, juvenile offenders eligible for community correction include those who have been sentenced to public surveillance, probation, and parole, and to serve a prison term outside prison. Among these, probation is one of the favored alternatives for juvenile court judges for juvenile first-time offenders who have committed nonviolent crimes. If the juvenile does not comply with the terms of probation/parole or commits a new crime, the probation or parole can be revoked after a hearing in court.

Conclusion

For most of China's history, Chinese juvenile offenders have been dealt with under the same laws and systems as adults. The historical development of Chinese juvenile justice is full of twists and turns. Rapid social change after the Cultural Revolution has witnessed an increase in the overall number of juvenile offenders and juvenile delinquency,* which threaten the existing social order. Chinese juvenile justice has developed since the early 1980s with a number of differences that distinguish it from Western juvenile justice. The first recognized juvenile court was established in Changning, Shanghai, in 1984, 85 years after the first-ever juvenile court in Chicago. Through nearly 30 years of development, the Chinese juvenile justice system has slowly been formed to deal with juvenile offenders.

As in other jurisdictions, the juvenile justice system in China is also facing a multitude of challenges and arguments about its rationale, including parens partiae, punishment, deterrence, and child welfare. Generally, Chinese juvenile justice is still dominated by the institutions dealing with juvenile criminal justice. The change in the Chinese juvenile justice system in recent year does not match the Western trend, which indicates a sharp contrast to Western systems. While the Western counterparts have argued about legal procedures, rehabilitation goals for juveniles, and an emphasis on punishment, Chinese juvenile legislation and judicial practice have advocated the principles of the "best interests

---

* Although official statistics (1990–2012, see Figure 6.2) showed an increase in the number of juvenile offenders, China's overall population including juvenile population also increased during the same time period. Due to the lack of statistics on juvenile population, the question as to whether juvenile crime rates have increased remains unanswered.

of the child" and have focused more on juvenile rehabilitation. Some new types of community-based programs, although still rare, have been created. For example, the first halfway house, which targets mainly the nonlocal youth, was recently introduced into Guangzhou City in 2013. It serves not only as a means of correction but also creates job opportunities for the newly released nonlocal juvenile inmates and helps them reenter the community (Zhao et al. 2013).

China's response to the emerging juvenile delinquency over the past few decades has garnered considerable attention. China's juvenile justice system is in a process of reform and improvement, and the system is still suffering from shortages of qualified personnel, heavy caseloads, and the absence of a system of in-service training for professionals. Meanwhile, the ritualistic and moralistic persuasion advocated through juvenile proceedings, especially in court trials, is challenged and questioned by some scholars and practitioners. For example, Wong criticized the fact that "in China, there is a marked tendency for judges and prosecutors to indulge in moralistic lecturing to offenders during the trial rather than concentrate on the legal aspects of the case" (Wong 1999, 36).

China surpassed Japan as the world's second-largest economy in 2010. But, with prosperity, the number of cases of juvenile delinquency and crime has also soared. The new communist leadership transition in late 2012 and early 2013 took place at the time of a growing awareness of a realistic necessity to adjust the juvenile criminal justice policy to address the increasing social conflicts. China still does not have a formal juvenile justice system; so there are calls for an independent juvenile justice system in reaction to the increase in the number of juvenile offenders and crime, and the diverse components of the juvenile justice system are expected to be more closely coordinated.

Review/Discussion Questions

1. What constitutes a "juvenile" in China? Is it different from your country?
2. What are the juvenile crime trends in China? What are the juvenile crime patterns in China? Do the official crime statistics provide a full picture of juvenile crime in China?
3. Chinese procuratorate has its unique function in dealing with juveniles. What is it?
4. How does Chinese court handle juvenile crime? What are the historical evolutions in dealing with delinquent juveniles in China?
5. What are the major types of Chinese courts to try juveniles?

References

Bakken, B. (1993). Crime, juvenile delinquency and deterrence policy in China. *Australian Journal of Chinese Affairs*. 30(3), 29–58.

Bao, W. and Hass, A. H. (2009). Social change, life strain, and delinquency among Chinese urban adolescents. *Sociological Focus*. 42(3), 285–305.

Bing, X. (2010). The current status, characteristics, and prevention measures of juvenile delinquency—The case of Xinjiang Uygur Autonomous Region. *Journal of Hunan Financial and Economic College*. 26(123), 136–138.

Cao, H. (2007). Analysis of rural juvenile crime and its prevention [in Chinese]. *Journal of Southern Forum*. 87(4), 61–71.

Champion, D. J. (2010). *The Juvenile Justice System: Delinquency, Processing, and the Law* (6th edition). Upper Saddle River, NJ: Prentice Hall, Inc.

Chen, Y. (2001). New ideas on prevention of juvenile delinquency—Investigation and insights on juvenile delinquency in Liaocheng [in Chinese]. *Journal of China Youth College for Political Sciences*. 20(5), 17–19.

Chen, Y. (2009a). Insights on juvenile delinquency and legal education—The case of Cangnan [in Chinese]. *Legal System and Society*. 5, 320–320.

Chen, Z. (2009b). Practice and exploration of juvenile corrections in new era [in Chinese]. *Beijing, Guangdong, Hong Kong, Macao Prison Forum Proceeding*. Unpublished.

China Adolescent Research Center. (2009). Chinese juvenile rights protection report [in Chinese]. Retrieved on June 20, 2013, from http://www.cycs.org/Article.asp?Category=1andColumn=130andID=8250.

China Law Society. (1991–2012). *Law Yearbook of China*. Beijing: Press of Law Yearbook of China.

Chiu, H. (1977). Criminal punishment in mainland China: A study of some Yunnan Province documents. *Journal of Criminal Law and Criminology*. 68(3), 374–398.

Cohen, J. A. (1966). The criminal process in the People's Republic of China: An introduction. *Harvard Law Review*. 793(3), 469–533.

Ding, F. (2001). Setting up juvenile courts is the inevitable of juvenile trial development in China. *Issues on Juvenile Crime and Delinquency*. 5, 15–18.

Du, X. (2009). An analysis of juvenile intentional assault in the first half a year of 2009 [in Chinese]. *Legal System and Society*. 10, 263–263.

Dutton, M. (2000). The end of the (mass) line? Chinese policing in the era of the contract (1). *Social Justice*. 27(2), 61–105.

Epstein, I. (1986). Children's rights and juvenile correctional institutions in the People's Republic of China. *Comparative Education Review*. 30(3), 359–372.

Fu, G. (2011). A study on the patterns, causes, and countermeasures of juvenile delinquency [in Chinese]. *Legal System and Economy*. 272(4), 126–127.

Hainan Prosecutions Office. (2002). Analysis of juvenile crimes in Hainan in recent years [in Chinese]. *Legal System and Society*. 1, 36–38.

Hao, F. (2012). On juvenile crime patterns, causes, and countermeasures—Using 100 criminal cases in Inner Mongolia as an example. *Journal of Inner Mongolia University of Technology*. 21(2), 15–18.

Henan Provincial Higher Court. (2012). Judicial report on juvenile crime prevention in Henan province (2007–2011) [in Chinese]. Retrieved on September 19, 2013, from http://www.hncourt.org/public/detail.php?id=137219.

Hong Kong Police Force. (2012). Police statistics [in Chinese]. Retrieved on September 20, 2013, from http://www.police.gov.hk/info/doc/2012_police_in_fig.pdf.

Hu, L. (2012). Contemporary juvenile delinquency patterns, causes, and countermeasures—The case of juvenile delinquency in Huadu, Guangzhou [in Chinese]. *Legal System and Society*. 5, 281–282.

Hu, Y. (2013). Juvenile trials summary [in Chinese]. Retrieved on June 20, 2013, from http://www.chinacourt.org/article/detail/2013/03/id/907165.shtml.

Huang, H. (2012). The modifications of criminal procedure law and construction of juvenile criminal prosecution [in Chinese]. *Juvenile Delinquency Prevention Research*. 5, 16–19.

Japan Statistics Bureau. (2013). *Japan Statistical Yearbook 2013*. Retrieved on September 26, 2013, from http://www.stat.go.jp/english/data/nenkan/index.htm.

Kang, S. (2012). Development and perfection of the juvenile justice system in Communist China [in Chinese]. *Journal of Jiangxi Police College*. 152(2), 82–86.

Korean Statistical Information Service. (2010). *Korea Statistical Yearbook*. Retrieved on September 20, 2013, from http://kostat.go.kr/portal/english/help/1/index.board?bmode=readandbSeq=andaSeq= 252785.

Landsberg, B. K. (2011). Promoting social justice values and reflective legal practice in Chinese law schools. *Pacific McGeorge Global Business and Development Law Journal.* 24(1), 107–114.

Leng, S. (1982). Criminal justice in post-Mao China: Some preliminary observations. *Journal of Criminal Law and Criminology.* 73(1), 204–237.

Li, B. (2007). Current status, patterns, and countermeasures of juvenile delinquency in Yuanzhou District, Guyuan City [in Chinese]. *Journal of Ningxia Teachers College (Social Sciences).* 28(4), 114–117.

Li, X. (2006). Juvenile delinquency is getting serious in Hunan [in Chinese]. *Police Officer Literature.* 1, 10–12.

Liu, J. (2008). Data sources in Chinese crime and criminal justice research. *Crime, Law and Social Change.* 50(3), 131–147.

Liu, J. and Palermo, G. B. (2009). Restorative justice and Chinese traditional legal culture in the context of contemporary Chinese criminal justice reform. *Asian Pacific Journal of Police and Criminal Justice.* 7(1), 49–68.

Lu, X. (2002). The current situation, patterns, and countermeasures of juvenile crime [in Chinese]. *Social Sciences and Economic Information.* 350(5), 99–101.

Ma, J., Fang, Z., and Wan, X. (2006). Research report on juvenile delinquency patterns in Liangzhou Prefecture [in Chinese]. *Journal of Xichang College* (Social Science). 18(3), 63–72.

Macau Education and Youth Affairs Bureau. (2013). Macau youth indicators. Retrieved on September 20, 2013, from http://www.dsej.gov.mo/ijm/stat/pdf/yim_07.pdf.

Marr, D. and Rosen, S. (1998). Chinese and Vietnamese youth in the 1990s. *China Journal.* 40, 145–172.

National Bureau of Statistics of China. (1990). *China Statistical Yearbook.* Beijing: China Statistics Press.

National Bureau of Statistics of China. (2010). *China Statistical Yearbook.* Beijing: China Statistics Press.

National Bureau of Statistics of China. (2012). *China Statistical Yearbook.* Beijing: China Statistics Press.

Qiao, Q. (2010). An exploratory study on juvenile delinquency and its prevention [in Chinese]. *Legal and Economy.* 233(3), 18–20.

Sampson, R. J. and Laub, J.H. (2003). Life-course desisters? Trajectories of crime among delinquent boys followed to age 70. *Criminology.* 41(3), 555–592.

Shao, J. (2010). Study on juvenile crime prevention and correction mechanism in Tianjin [in Chinese]. *Tianjin Legal Science.* 103(1), 83–89.

Shu, R. and Hao, M. (2009). Rural family "empty nest phenomenon" and crimes of "left-behind" children [in Chinese]. *Journal of Shandong Youth Administrative Cadres College.* 141(5), 13–15.

van der Valk, M. H. (1936). The new Chinese criminal code. *Pacific Affairs.* 9(1), 69–77.

Wang, C. (1917). Law reform in China. *Chinese Social and Political Science Review.* 2(2), 13–21.

Wang, S. and Han, Z. (2009). A study on current status and prevention of rural juvenile crime [in Chinese]. *Legal System and Society.* 12, 249–249.

Wong, D. S. (1999). Delinquency control and juvenile justice in China. *Australian and New Zealand Journal of Criminology.* 32(1), 27–41.

Wong, D. S. (2001). Changes in juvenile justice in China. *Youth Society.* 32(4), 492–509.

Wu, D. (2010). Thoughts about juvenile judicial protection—The case of Longwan [in Chinese]. *Merchandise and Quality.* 7, 92–93.

Xu, J. (2001). On conditions and the necessity of establishing juvenile courts in China. *Issues on Juvenile Crime and Delinquency.* 4, 15–21.

Yang, H. (2009). Juvenile crime patterns and correctional strategies in Beijing [in Chinese]. *Beijing, Guangdong, Hong Kong, Macao Prison Forum Proceeding.* Unpublished.

Yang, M. and Lv, N. (2008). Guangzhou: Average age for juvenile crime decreases two years [in Chinese]. *Guangzhou Daily*, March 1, 2008.

Yen, C. (1934). Crime in relation to social change in China. *American Journal of Sociology*. 40(3), 298–308.

Yu, Y (2007). Research on juvenile delinquency in Beijing [in Chinese]. *Journal of Shanxi College for Youth Administrators*. 20(4), 11–14.

Yu, Y. (2010). Reports on study of juvenile delinquency—Social causes and crime prevention [in Chinese]. *Legal System and Society*. 3, 87–87.

Zhang, H. (2013). Revisiting people's mediation in China: Practice, performance and challenges. *Restorative Justice: An International Journal*. 1(2), 244–267.

Zhang, L. (2008). Juvenile delinquency and justice in contemporary China: A critical review of the literature over 15 years. *Crime, Law and Social Change*. 50(3), 149–160.

Zhang, L. and Liu, J. (2007). China's Juvenile Delinquency Prevention Law: The law and the philosophy. *International Journal of Offender Therapy and Comparative Criminology*. 51(5), 541–554.

Zhang, X. (2009). Current status, causes, and countermeasures of youth crime in Qingyang [in Chinese]. *Economic Research Guide*. 41(3), 291–292.

Zhang, Y. (2007). A study on juvenile bail [in Chinese]. Retrieved on September 16, 2013, from http://old.chinacourt.org/html/article/200711/16/274929.shtml.

Zhao, G., Miao, Y., Han, Y., and Liu, Z. (2013). Guangzhou's Halfway House: A Transitional Station for Non-local Juveniles [in Chinese]. *People's Court Daily*, July 14, 2013.

Zou, Y. (2008). Current status and patterns of juvenile delinquency in Jiangxi Province [in Chinese]. *Journal of Jiangxi Administration Institute*. 10(4), 52–56.

Internet Sources

China Knowledge Resource Integrated Database (CNKI). http://oversea.cnki.net/kns55/oldnavi/n_Navi.aspx?NaviID=4. This website is the most comprehensive gateway of knowledge of China. It provides information on a wide variety of output from research and government/nongovernment reports. You will find information on China Statistical Yearbook and Law Yearbook of China. Juvenile-related statistics are also included.

Ministry of Justice. www.moj.gov.cn. You will find the Ministry of Justice's history, structure, responsibilities (such as prison administration, community correction, mandatory drug detoxification, national judicial examination, forensic analysis, lawyers and public notary administration, legal aids, etc.), and relevant research. This website also posts news from the bureaus of justice at all levels.

Ministry of Public Security. http://www.mps.gov.cn. You will find the Ministry of Public Security's history, structure, and responsibilities (such as exit and entry administration, public order management, criminal investigation, jail administration, traffic control, drug control, fire control, network security, antiterrorism, etc.). This website also posts relevant news from the bureaus of public security at all levels.

Supreme People's Court. http://www.court.gov.cn. You will find information on the Supreme People's Court's history, institutional structure, membership, jurisdiction, as well as legal processes. This website also posts relevant news from the courts at all levels.

Supreme People's Procuratorate. http://www.spp.gov.cn. You will find Supreme People's Procuratorate's history, structure, membership, jurisdiction, as well as legal processes. This website also posts relevant news from the procuratorates at all levels.

The Iranian Juvenile Criminal Justice System: An Overview

7

TAHMOORES BASHIRIYEH AND MOHAMMAD ALI RAJAB

Contents

Introduction: The Children and Juvenile Criminal Justice System in Iran 164
A Historical Overview of the Juvenile Justice System in Iran 165
   Juvenile Criminal Justice before the Revolution 165
   Juvenile Criminal Justice after the Revolution 168
Juvenile Delinquency in Iran: The Current Situation 171
   Child Delinquency in Iran: Statistical View 171
   Children and Juvenile Delinquency in Iran: Approaches and Explanations 172
Juvenile Criminal Justice in Iran: The Future 174
Conclusion 175
Review/Discussion Questions 176
References 176

FACTS ABOUT IRAN

Iran: home to one of the ancient civilizations of the world, located in southwest Asia, with an area of about 1,648,195 sq km, is a rugged, mountainous country with a central basin comprising deserts. Iran's coastline along the Persian Gulf and Caspian Sea is 2440 km; Iran shares common sea borders with Kuwait, Qatar, Bahrain, the Emirates, and Oman and land borders with Iraq, Armenia, Azerbaijan, Turkey, Afghanistan, Turkmenistan, and Pakistan. **Climate:** Iran's climate ranges from arid or semiarid to subtropical along the Caspian coast and the northern forests. **Population:** According to a 2013 estimation, Iran's population is about 75,000,000 consisting of different ethnic groups like Persians 61%, Azeris 16%, Kurds 10%, Lurs 6%, Balochis 2%, Arabs 2%, Turkmen and Turkic tribes 2%, and 1% of other groups; however, the only official language, which most people speak is Persian. **Economy:** Iran's economy is marked by statist policies and a large public sector governed by the state that is mostly inefficient and relies on oil and gas export, which provides a large share of government revenues. **Government:** The current Iranian political system, named the Islamic Republic, is an unusual amalgamation of theocratic and democratic elements based on the 1979 Constitution that comprises several intricately connected governing bodies. The leader of the Islamic Revolution ("The Supreme Leader"), as the most powerful man in the system, is the commander of military and law enforcement forces, appoints the head of the judiciary, and is responsible for the delineation and supervision of the general policies

(Continued)

FACTS ABOUT IRAN (*Continued*)

of the Islamic Republic of Iran. The Assembly of Experts in a semidemocratic way elects and can dethrone the Supreme Leader on grounds of qualification and standing. Laws deriving from both Islamic tradition and Iranian customs are adopted by the legislature (*Majlis*) and enforced by the government, which is run by the president. The president is elected by people every 4 years after a special filtering system implemented by the Guardian Council.

Introduction: The Children and Juvenile* Criminal Justice System in Iran

In this chapter, we intend first to provide a general historical background of the current juvenile justice system. Juvenile delinquency in Iran began to rise gradually as a result of industrialization and transition from traditional to modern society after the Constitutional Revolution of 1906 and throughout the twentieth century, and like other domains of the Iranian legal system became one of the arenas of conflict between tradition and modernity. The mainstream traditional legal perspective, which is strongly related to the *Shiite* jurisprudence, grants authority to religious regulations in all spheres. On the other hand, the rising modernist approach tries to focus on social and international changes. Therefore, it was not surprising that after the Islamic Revolution of 1979, the conflict turned into a more political rather than a purely legal one.

The most important principle, as the basis of the traditionalist Islamic approach, is that according to Article 4 of the Constitution of the Islamic Republic of Iran (1979), all regulations must be adopted in accordance with Islamic rules (see Box 7.1). Consequently, based on Islamic jurisprudence (*Fiqh Islami*), the basic condition for personal liability is puberty. In other words, a person becomes legally responsible and liable when he/she attains the age of puberty. Thus, accordingly, the age of criminal responsibility is 9 for females and 15 for males—a model that seems unacceptable to the modern approach.

Today, all agree that juvenile delinquency, especially in some large cities like Tehran, is one of the main social challenges and problems that the government faces and tries to resolve. However, the government has not been able to maintain its traditionalist position *vis-a-vis* domestic and international pressure in the direction of change and reform. Thus the signing and ratification of the Convention on the Rights of the Child (CRC) in 1993—despite the proviso that Islamic rules must be observed at any rate—as well as the legislature's attempt to modify regulations on child/juvenile delinquency are symbols of the conscious will of the government to face the problem squarely and move away from the traditional position (Box 7.2).

---

* According to United Nations Standard Minimum Rules for the Administration of Juvenile Justice 1985 (usually referred to as "the Beijing Rules"), "A juvenile is a child or young person who, under the respective legal systems, may be dealt with for an offence in a manner which is different from an adult"; however, as we shall see in this chapter, Iranian laws often make a difference between children who are under the age of maturity and juveniles who may be considered mature but under the age of 18. So in this chapter, we have used both terms to show this distinction.

BOX 7.1 ISLAMIC JURISPRUDENCE (FIQH)

Islamic jurisprudence (*Fiqh*) is the body of Islamic rules and laws, which are mostly derived from the Holy Quran as well as the sayings and examples (*Hadith and Sunna*) of Mohammad the Prophet, and is considered as the main source of legislation (and sometimes as the source of general norms and guidelines for legislation) in Iran after the 1979 Islamic Revolution. *Faqih* is a clergyman who derives the orders and instructions issued by God (called *hokm*) from the Islamic sources, which include a vast body of legal or juridical texts including the Holy Quran and the Prophet's *hadiths*. Iran's Constitution refers to *Shiite* jurisprudence as the source of law and as the official religion of Iran. *Shiite* Islam is based on the belief in the succession of the Prophet by Ali-ibn-Abi-Taleb and eleven of his descendants who are called the *Imam's holy leaders*. In *Shiite* jurisprudence, a great portion of legal rules (*hokm*) are derived from the Imam's sayings and examples. Although a number of new reformist approaches to *Fiqh* has risen in the last two decades, using a *hermeneutic* methodology and adopting modern Western theories of law and theology, the traditional approach continues to be dominant in Iran.

For further information on Islamic jurisprudence, see Hallaq (2009) and Weiss (2002).

BOX 7.2 NEW LEGISLATION TRENDS: PROTECTION OF CHILDREN AND JUVENILES ACT

The Protection of Children and Juveniles is another important act that, without entering into a detailed definition of the concept of child (to avoid quarrels with religious authorities) and also without making a distinction between children and juveniles, protects all persons under 18 (Article 1) by banning and making punishable all types of harmful and aggressive actions against such persons. The adoption of such laws clearly demonstrates a strong will on the part of the legislature in Iran to find a way for providing maximum protection for children and juveniles despite the ambiguity of the current codes.

A Historical Overview of the Juvenile Justice System in Iran

The social history of modern Iran can be divided into two main periods: the first from the Constitutional Revolution of 1906 to the Islamic Revolution of 1979 and the second since the Islamic Revolution and the replacement of the Pahlavi monarchy by an Islamic Republic, which is usually considered as a milestone in Iranian legal system. The revolution changed public laws and regulations such as the penal and procedural codes completely. Therefore, the first part of this chapter intends to analyze the history of juvenile delinquency in two sections: (a) before the Islamic Revolution and (b) after the revolution.

Juvenile Criminal Justice before the Revolution

With the establishment of the modern judicial and legal system in Iran from 1906, written codes inspired by Romano-Germanic and the continental European legal systems, particularly the French and Belgian systems, were adopted gradually and shaped the new judicial system in Iran particularly in the first two decades of the twentieth century (Danesh 1999). The codes included the Judicial Principles and Organization of Department of Justice Act (1907), the Criminal Procedure Act (1911), and the Penal Code (1925). With the gradual rise of modern society, delinquency began to rise particularly in major cities like Tehran, Esfahan, and Tabriz, causing the new phenomenon of the so-called street children, which was absent from traditional life.

In the above-mentioned laws, there was no explicit, or implied, reference to children and juveniles; in fact only the Penal Law, in Articles 34–39, mentioned the age of criminal responsibility. Although the laws and regulations mentioned in the preceding text were inspired by Islamic rules regarding concepts such as puberty and children's legal/mental capacity, the Penal Code sought to restrict children's criminal responsibility on the basis of age in accordance with the current approach in European legal systems—particularly the French Penal Code—the reason being that some influential legislators had been educated in European universities and/or were influenced by European ideas.

Accordingly, children under 12 years would not be punished at all; children/juveniles from 12 to 15 years who were not considered to be sexually mature enough but had sufficient mental capacity to understand good and evil actions, would be sentenced to 10 to 50 lashes for committing felonies and misdemeanors; and children between 15 and 18 years would be sentenced to imprisonment for 5 years or half of the normal legal punishments for adults committing felony or misdemeanor, respectively. The important point was that in all the above-mentioned categories, the prison term would be spent in "Houses of Correction"— places of detention where the main purpose was to reeducate and rehabilitate offenders— rather than prisons, and the offenders would be tried in misdemeanor courts (see Box 7.3).

The establishment of the University of Tehran's Faculty of Law and Political Science (1934), initially called the "School of Political Science" provided the foundation for the promotion of new criminal law reforms and the application of criminological approaches.

BOX 7.3   CORRECTIONAL INSTITUTIONS FOR CHILDREN AND JUVENILES

Correctional institutions for children and juveniles were provided in the Act of the Establishment of Children and Juvenile Offender Courts 1958 for the first time, but child and juvenile courts were formed from1966; 3 years later, the first correctional institution (housing boys only) was inaugurated in Tehran. Generally, most of the inmates were male and under 18 and were regarded as help seekers rather than prisoners to save them from social stigma. Children under 6 years resided in orphanages. The first program organized for new inmates involved a reduction in the level of fear. In addition, physical and mental tests were included. The institution has three sections: temporary maintenance, correction and treatment, and imprisonment. Some classifications have been made in the institution including one based on the inmates' age, although what happens in reality is not exactly what is intended in theory. The institution has a president, a few social workers, physicians, psychologists, and so on, performing their regular tasks every day from 6 a.m. to 8 p.m., depending on the season (Momenirad 1999, 144–147).

This became more prevalent especially after scholars and students who had graduated from European countries and later from the United States returned home.

Subsequently, the Act of the Establishment of Children/Juvenile Offender Courts (1958) ratified by Parliament led to important changes in regulations regarding children and juveniles. This act required the formation of a juvenile court in each jurisdiction unit (Article 1) and also required two counselors to attend during the trial process. The two counselors would be chosen from among retired judicial, educational, or administrative staff or from among trusted people interested in the case (Articles 2 and 3). These two counselors served only as the advisors of the judge and did not have a role in the judicial decision-making.

The 1958 act changed the Penal Code classification totally. Therefore, it required that children under 6 years of age would not be held responsible (Article 4) and also provided corrective measures, including (a) placing the children under parents' control, (b) placing them under the control of guardians requiring them to pay more and closer attention to the offenders/delinquents, or (c) dispatching them to correctional institutions according to Article 17 for juveniles between 6 and 12 years. The act also required that juveniles between 12 and 18 years be placed under close parental control, thereby obligating parents to pay more attention to the children/juveniles. If they failed to do so, parents risked being chastised by the judge or in extreme cases, children being dispatched to a correctional institution for a period ranging from 3 to 12 months or from 6 months to 5 years in the case of felony. The Penal Code specifically does not allow less than 2 years imprisonment for juveniles in the case of committing crimes with capital punishment or life imprisonment.

The differential model of punishment included in the 1958 act seems to make the act appear as advocating the "justice model"; however, there seems to be a strong tendency toward the "crime control model" in the act (see Table 1.1 in the Introduction of this textbook for a detailed summary of the models).

In their adjudication, the courts had the discretionary authority to reduce the punishment to one-fourth of the permitted sentence. Also, regulations concerning crime repetition were not applicable in the case of juvenile offenders. Thus the Supreme Court endorsed the same regulations to be applied in the case of cumulative and multiple charges.

Furthermore, regulations regarding children/juveniles were excluded from the Criminal Procedure Act to provide advantages that are not available to adults. The important point was arranging for a procedure to avoid involving them in formal judicial processes as well as keeping their information confidential, with the investigation and hearing conducted behind closed doors (Article 9). Furthermore, all investigations had to be conducted by the judge of the court instead of prosecutors and carried out in the presence of parents or guardians. Another new requirement appeared in Article 7, which allowed the judge to conduct investigations on the physical and mental and family conditions of the child by all possible means including obtaining expert (e.g., social workers) opinion in the case.

Such requirements were a great step toward creating a protective system for children and juveniles in procedural law (Moazzenzadegan 2008); such a system was complementary to protection provided by substantive laws regarding both offending and victimized juveniles and children.*

* In this period, different regulations provided support for children either by criminalizing certain actions when committed only against children or by increasing the penalties. This process continued after the revolution with some restrictions introduced on the basis of the definition of "child."

Finally, in the most recent modification of the Penal Code in 1973, in reaction to certain practical difficulties in implementing the Act of the Establishment of Courts for Juvenile Offenders,* certain procedures were adopted in places where correctional institutions could not be set up (Farzinrad 2007).

In summary, even though the juvenile justice system before the 1979 revolution was still partly impacted by the Shiite jurisprudence and had derived the concept and the age of personal criminal liability from the religious law, it gradually accepted the more secular modern and Western and international standards regarding juvenile criminal justice and eventually adopted the differential approaches. This was mostly due to the gradual adoption of regulations for establishing special courts for children and juveniles. In addition, the prerevolutionary juvenile justice system developed a new system of classification for the age of criminal responsibility for persons under 18, thus reducing the gravity of such a responsibility. Yet, it is difficult to provide a complete and realistic picture of the juvenile system at the time, because the existing statistical data and information are not sufficient, and it is practically impossible to get access to information about the rates and the various types of juvenile crimes for the period before the revolution due to radical changes in the administration of justice in the aftermath of the revolution.

Juvenile Criminal Justice after the Revolution

The change in the political system, naturally, affected the legal system particularly with regard to criminal regulations. The Islamic Republican Council, which was playing the role of Parliament in the first year after the revolution, adopted a legal bill for the establishment of general courts in 1980 and thus cancelled independent courts for child and juvenile offenders. With the establishment of the General Criminal Courts I and II,[†] child trial would be assigned to the General Criminal Courts II. Then, according to a decision by the Supreme Court, the trials of important crimes regardless of their perpetrators' age were assigned to the General Criminal Courts I. As a result of these procedural changes, no specific courts were envisaged solely for child and juvenile offenders any more (Moazzenzadegan 2008).

However, it seems that the most complicated jurisprudential question for clerical lawmakers after the revolution was how to define childhood or adulthood in terms of age limits. Traditional *Shiite* jurisprudence has been the main source of legislation after the revolution. According to *Shiite* jurisprudence, puberty suffices for considering persons mature and imposing legal responsibility on them, based on some verses of the Holy Quran and traditions (Safaei 2006; Moazzami 2009). Therefore, attaining the age of 9 for females and 15 for males according to the lunar calendar is considered as attaining puberty, thus making a person responsible for her/his actions. This definition was

---

* In fact, the act had not been implemented till 1968, when the first correctional institution opened in Tehran; cf. Danesh, T. (1999). *Trial of Offending Children in Comparative Law.* Tehran, Mizan publication.
† Criminal Courts I and II were two types or classes of criminal courts, which were established in Iran between 1985 and 1995. Criminal Court I dealt with more grave and serious offenses (which could be compared to felonies), while criminal court II was intended to deal with minor offenses (misdemeanors). These courts do not exist anymore and instead two other types of courts are instituted: General Criminal Court and State Criminal Court. However, these types are expected to change with the adoption of a new criminal procedure, which is provided by the new Criminal Procedure Code Act ratified by parliament on 23 Feb 2014 and shall be enforced after 6 months from being published in Iranian Official Gazette, i.e., 25 Oct 2014 (see Box 7.5).

adopted in the Civil Act Amendments of 1982 and the Islamic Penal Codes of 1982 and 1991. The Sharia age of puberty was also accepted as the age of criminal responsibility (without any further elaboration) by judges of criminal courts to decide the scope of criminal responsibility. Thus, underage children (under 9 years for girls and under 15 years for boys) would not be punished; they could only be "chastised" by their parents or the judges, or in exceptional cases be sent to Houses of Correction. However, children above the legal age would be responsible and could be tried in the same courts in which adults are tried.

Such an interpretation was criticized by some scholars who suggested drawing a distinction between criminal maturity on the basis of discretion capacity and puberty, thus arguing that puberty as a natural phenomenon cannot be considered as a criterion for responsibility (Rahami 2002). Even a high-ranking clerical researcher relying on a survey carried out in Tehran in the 1990s suggested that even if we accepted the puberty ages as the criterion for criminal responsibility, girls from Tehran did not mature before the age of 13 (Marashi 1994). These approaches, however, were not acceptable to the traditional scholars and clergymen who were in positions of power and policy-making. Consequently, the new proposals concerning the age of responsibility did not find their way into legislation for a long time.

In fact, the system of differential procedure, which approximates the **justice model** more than the "model of crime control" increasingly lost its feasibility and was replaced by a system of unitary procedure equally applicable to all persons who are considered as adults according to the religious definition. As a result, this resulted in the absence of a coherent and unified procedural system for child and juvenile trials for at least two decades (1980–2000).

From a procedural perspective, any kind of differentiation was removed following the adoption of the Act of the Establishment of General and Revolutionary Courts in 1994. By abolishing prosecution offices, this act radically changed the judicial system in Iran. This chaotic system continued until 1999 when under the Act of Criminal Procedure in General and Revolutionary Courts (1999), the prosecution offices were reestablished, and a relatively definite system of trial for children and juveniles came into existence. One important change was to recognize the competence of children and juvenile courts to try the so-called mature persons under 18. The intention was to give such persons priviliges and advantages which adult people enjoyed in State Courts including the trial before 5 judges. This included such procedural measures as direct hearing in the court, limitation of injunctions, compulsory access to lawyers, the possibility of revision of decisions by the same courts issuing conviction, and so on. However, in action, the courts would not apply many of these advantages to persons who were legally regarded as mature but were under the age of 18 (Khaleghi 2009).

Another important point in the act was the requirement for filing personal records (including physical, mental, and educational records) and paying closer attention to children's lifestyle, although it only has been required for minors excluding mature persons under the age of 18 (Mehra 2005).

Moreover, two other important changes were envisaged later by the decisions of the Supreme Court. The first change granted competence to children and juvenile courts regarding drug-related crimes, which was generally a matter under the Revolutionary Courts' competence and, the second change, was to assign juristic competence to State Criminal Courts in cases for which the punishment could be execution, retribution, or imprisonment for more than 10 years. The justification was to pay more attention and care in such sensitive cases.*

The most recent changes in this regard appeared in the new Islamic Penal Code passed on April 21, 2013. The 2013 code removes the burden of responsibility from those who are not mature (see Article 146) and suggests correctional measures for them according to Article 148. Nevertheless, the ages of responsibility remain the same in this act. Therefore, in the case of specific Islamic punishments including *hadd* for most crimes against chastity as well as *qisas* for crimes against personal integrity, there is no distinction made between adults and sexually mature persons under 18. Nevertheless, under the influence of some progressive scholarship, the legislator of 2013 accepted an important change. Article 91 requires that in crimes deserving *hadd* or *qisas*, if the perpetrators do not understand either the nature of the committed crime or its prohibition (*hormat*) by the religious rules, or if there is doubt with respect to the offenders' capacity of legal discretion, then they would be subject to other penalties or sanctions rather than *hadd or qisas*.

Therefore, by removing puberty as a criterion for convictions under *hadd* or *qisas*, the law allows the capacity of discretion between good and evil as the criterion for responsibility, which can be obtained through relevant experts in the capacity of forensic physicians or in any other feasible way. So, the legislator permits the courts to disallow *hadd* or *qisas* when there is any doubt regarding the perpetrator's mental and discretionary capacity, and proposes some alternatives according to Articles 88 and 89. In this context, the legislator supplies the judges with a broad variety of measures for both males and females including assigning the children/juveniles to their parents or guardians or other relevant institutions; appointing social workers, psychologists, or other experts to take care of child or juvenile offenders; taking suitable action for giving up addiction under medical supervision; curfew regulations; and so on. The measures prescribed are too broad and extensive to list here, but it should be mentioned that correctional and alternative measures have been mainly emphasized by the legislator for both juvenile and adults, providing a large extent of authority to mitigate punishments, to choose among alternative or commuted punishments, to recommend probation, or even to suspend conviction.† In addition, according to the new Penal Act, crimes committed by children and juveniles are not counted as criminal record or precedence; in this way, the legislator apparently intends to reduce further social problems for children and juveniles as a result of committing crimes.

However, it goes without saying that such an act, despite its shortcomings with regard to a coherent approach of criminal policy caught between the needs of modern society and the traditional interpretation of Islamic law, is inspired by current necessities, international obligations,‡ and the general academic literature.

---

* This court is established in the center of each province with three or five judges, depending on the sensitivity of the case; the court deals with grave offenses deserving harsh punishments such as murder and rape.
† Unlike probation, postponing and suspending the conviction is an innovation put forward in this act in the Iranian legal system.
‡ Iran has joined many international treaties and conventions in this regard such as those concerning the elimination of the worst forms of child labor and its complementary recommendation of 2001, the optional protocol to the Convention on the Rights of Children (CRC), as well as conventions regarding the sale of children, child prostitution, and child pornography (see the Introduction to this book for further discussion regarding the various international guidelines and protocols).

Juvenile Delinquency in Iran: The Current Situation

As noted earlier, in recent years, youth delinquency has risen dramatically in Iran. The increase has been attributed to the rapid urban development specifically after the war between Iraq and Iran, and currently it is considered as a major social challenge. In this section, we shall review some statistics regarding child delinquency in Iran, and subsequently we will provide a brief explanation of child delinquency in Iran based on current approaches and relevant factors.

Child Delinquency in Iran: Statistical View

The most important problem in this respect is that state organizations generally do not release statistics on the rate of crimes. In academic research works, however, some more or less reliable and valid data is available. This enables us to estimate the rate of criminality, although such data are not carefully updated and expanded.*

The data collected and presented by researchers are mostly a result of research carried out independent of official and governmental institutions. Therefore, due to limited access to official data about children and juvenile crimes, the information they provide is not always completely reliable. Thus we can only get a limited, if not a distorted, picture of children and juvenile crime rates and how the criminal justice system deals with them.

As is the case in virtually every other country, youth delinquency in Iran is the result of a wide range of factors. For example, in the 1980s, during the early phase of the revolution and in a time of war, economic and social problems were aggravated, even though correctional Institutions did not have a large number of inmates (and most of them were males).

In 1986 when the Iran–Iraq war ended, 790 cases of murder had been reported; out of these, 140 cases (18%) had been committed by persons under 19 years.

Table 7.1 shows data about juvenile offenders residing in correctional institutions in Iran in 1985 (Sheikhavandi 2007).

By contrast, Sheikhavandi (2007) has argued that the rate reported solely for the Tehran Correctional Institution was 2200 in 2003. He suggested that the rise in juvenile crime rates may be considered a result of a rise in the youth population.

The composition of the Iranian population is a relevant factor here. For instance, in 2003, the population below 14 years of age accounted for approximately 35.2% of the total

Table 7.1   Type of Offenses Committed by Incarcerated Juveniles: 1985

Crime	Drug-Related Crimes	Murder	Intentional Wounding	Theft/ Pocket Picking	Sodomy	Crimes against Chastity	Other Crimes	Total
Rate	420	37	495	871	308	371	900	3402
Percentage	12.3	1.1	14.6	25.6	9.1	10.5	26.5	100

* Some researchers point to two main problems regarding official statistics: first, lack of classification in a meaningful manner to help research work on the basis of statistical data, and second, defective and irregular release of data; cf. Ejlali, P. (2011). Looking at crime statistics in Iran. In: *Collected Articles on social issues of Iran*. Tehran, Agah publication. 349–378.

Children Delinquency Panel (2003)—the portion, which constitutes the bulk of youth population now. The rise in numbers in the last decade has increased the rate of delinquency and requires more complex amenities. According to a report in 2013, 24% of the Iranian population is under 14 and nearly 20% are between 15 and 24 years (www.cia.gov/library/publications/the-world-fact-book/geos/ir.htm).

The whole population of prisoners in the same year has been 146,134 with 1.63% being below 19 years. In the beginning of the twenty-first century, offenses committed by children/juveniles ranged from addiction and other drug-related crimes to theft and rape.

It goes without saying that the rise in youth population in recent decades has left the Iranian government unable and unprepared for the situation.

A noteworthy point is that in this period, crimes committed by girls has reached almost the same rate as that of boys. In 1998, the ratio had been 13.5 boys to 1 girl, but in the following year, the ratio was 9.5 to 1 (Shamloo 2011).

There is a remarkable report on street children in Tehran in those years (Jangholi 2011). The report divides street children into a number of groups including street workers with real or false occupations, vagrants in the shape of extortionists and beggars, and delinquents including perpetrators of theft, drug-related crimes, and sexual harassment.

More than 65% of the street children in Tehran, according to the research, are migrants, most of whom have been facing poverty, improper welfare, family dispute, and parental divorce, resulting in their attraction to gangs.

In the second half of the 2000s, the statistics from a judicial complex for children and juveniles shows meaningful trends.* "Driving without license, intentional assault, theft, rape, drinking, and possession and exchange of drugs in small amounts" demonstrate the extent of crimes committed in 2006 and 2007. Major crimes like robbery, smuggling, and blasphemy, were rare (Shamloo 2011, 151–156).

Children and Juvenile Delinquency in Iran: Approaches and Explanations

Many efforts have been made to explain child delinquency in Iran in the last two decades based on current criminological doctrines. The academic literature regarding the subject has been inspired by criminological research mostly by sociologists and international and United Nations (UN) reports and documents such as the Beijing Rules, and The Riyadh Guidelines. This theoretical literature has pursued two objectives: first, to develop a differential protective approach toward children/juveniles and second, to provide an explanation for child delinquency based on preventive criminology (Jamshidi 2003).

The various categories of criminological theories on the causes of delinquency (i.e., biological, psychological, and sociological approaches) have all been employed by Iranian scholars, particularly the second and third approaches have been emphasized more (see Box 7.4). So, in addition to dealing with factors like hereditary and health conditions, psychological disorders on the one hand and economic and social problems on the other hand have become part of the new forms of inquiry among Iranian scholars (Shami 1978).

Some studies have emphasized poverty and its role in paving the way for delinquency. Number of family members on average in Iran is 3.8, and based on a report, in the first

---

* The peculiar nature of Tehran in terms of population characteristics and its complications in terms of its pluralistic cultures should prevent us from generalizing its statistics to other cities in Iran.

BOX 7.4 SUTHERLAND AND HIRSCHI IN IRAN

A statistical research work in the last decade of the twentieth century sought to use and examine Sutherland's "differential association" theory and Hirschi's "social control" theory in a limited statistical group, including 105 offending children/juvenile delinquents with an average age of 16 and three 10-year-old children. Samples of the research, were intentionally taken from poor, densely populated density areas and low literacy families to examine the "attachment," "belief," "commitment," and "involvement" variables. The research shows that none of these theories alone can explain child delinquency and a combination of variables is needed, and that both theories together are applicable in Iran. Hence, such variables as distrust of law, negative attitude toward the police, criminal history, lack of supervision by family and school authorities, and a history of drug or alcohol abuse, all have a meaningful correlation with child delinquency.

Source: Meshkati, M. and Meshkati, Z. (2011). Measurement of family internal and external factors on juvenile delinquency (an experimental examination of social control and differential association theories combined). In: *Collected Articles on Social Issues in Iran.* Tehran, Agah Publication, 239–269.

decade of the twenty-first century, more than 12 million were below the poverty line,* creating serious social problems (Moazzami 2009) such as a decline in social welfare, nutrition issues for lower-class children, intelligence quotient (IQ) deficiency, decline in the role of the family, and finally a distorted socialization process.

Individual cultural and social incongruence, issues resulting from increasing economic growth and urbanization, immigration from villages to cities, and the rise of criminogenic suburbs are the other important factors that have been emphasized by Iranian researchers to explain child delinquency (Sheikhavandi 2007).

The total population of Iran in 2006 was about 70 million, of which 49 million has been in cities; this number increased to 53 million (out of the total population of 75 millions) in 2011. Therefore the average annual population growth in cities is 2.14%. This increasing urban population may well increase the chances for child delinquency because social and economic welfare services and amenities have not been not provided at the same pace (Iranian Statistical Center 2012).

In addition, peer group and delinquent group pressure have been considered as significant factors in child delinquency. A research in three suburban areas populated by lower-class people was conducted; the sample included 238 respondents (Moazzami 2008). The research shows that juveniles and young adults in these areas have been attracted to groups from the age of maturity because of family problems.

According to the findings of the research, the use of special slang, special clothing, extreme loyalty in friendship, intensive interest in motorcycles, drinking, hedonism, and so on, were youth characteristics of juvenile delinquency everywhere. The groups committing

---

* In the presidential election debates in 2013, candidates claimed that more than 40% of the Iranian population was below the poverty line. Although this may be an exaggeration, it can be claimed that in general, poverty in Iran has increased due to political and economic crises.

crime were not organized and lacked specific planning and committed crimes mostly for fun and adventure. The research suggested that there were some common traits among group members including disturbed relationship with parents, problems of interparental relationships, stressful family life usually because of drug abuse by parents, poor moral guidance in the family, and use of violence instead of dialogue.

On the other hand, some scholars have shown that not only lower class but also higher- and middle-class juveniles join criminal groups mostly for the resulting excitement (Moazzami 2008).

Also prevention-based theories have inspired Iranian authorities in adopting regulations compelling the government to provide education and medical treatment for all citizens concerned; the Iranian Constitution has already emphasized the role of the government in this regard. The role of the family in particular has been emphasized; the protection of the family as "the fundamental unit of Islamic society" is considered as a major duty of the government (Mehra 2005). All these aspects can be construed as major indications for government responsibility in preventing crimes from happening.

These approaches have had some impact in action. Thus in recent years, cases of judicial decision-making in a more expedient and lenient way, in some cases employing international conventions for justification, have been increasing. In many cases, harsh punishments have been avoided, and instead more lenient corrective measures or some other alternatives to punishments have been applied. However, systematic information is lacking on this interesting development.

Juvenile Criminal Justice in Iran: The Future

Based on the limited evidence available, it appears that child delinquency as a social issue has been recognized and taken seriously by the government in Iran. The Iranian government has been trying to promote the differentiated and protective judicial approaches regarding children/juveniles and has constantly modified substantive and procedural regulations, and continues to do so by taking current necessities as well as its own international commitments into account.

Accordingly, the law of "The Proceedings of Child and Juvenile Crimes" has been presented to the Parliament and has been in progress; so far the Parliament has approved the urgency of the law. The law is very significant in many respects. It envisages a special court for persons under 18 years. A special judge would be assigned for this court by the head of the judiciary; in addition, two counselors from among social workers, academicians, and educated persons familiar with juvenile subjects will have to attend the courts; in the cases where the accused is a female, the presence of a female counselor is mandatory as well. Counselors only give their recommendations to the judge and do not interfere in decision-making. The introduction to the law emphasizes the promotion of noncriminal approaches, noninterference on the part of the police, and an emphasis on taking the dignity and interests of children and juvenile very seriously. In addition, the law contains multiple regulations aimed at strengthening differentiated proceedings, avoiding public trials, securing trial information, and guarantee of protective facilities at the highest level. The other innovation of the law is a classification of punishments and alternatives to punishments, as well as correctional and societal measures. It should be noted that some of these regulations have been included in the new Penal Act of 2013 and will possibly be included

BOX 7.5   DRAFT OF THE CRIMINAL PROCEDURES ACT

The legal law of the "Proceedings of Child and Juveniles Crimes" has been added to the law of the newly proposed Iranian "Criminal Procedure Act," which is enacted by Parliament in Feb 2014 and shall be effective from Oct 2014. Some features of the new law make it look like a revival of the 1958 act, even though the experiences of the two recent decades have been taken into account to improve the act. The main model adopted is still the same differential system of proceedings and trials for children and juvenile offenders providing particular protective measures for them. Thus, the law provides that in each city, there will be a special court for children and juveniles, which will consist of a judge and two counselors who serve as mere consultants and do not directly participate in the judicial decision-making. The court shall be competent for all offenses and crimes committed by any person under the age of 18.

Some other changes are to be made in the general structure of the Iranian Criminal Justice system according to the new Code. A major change affecting the juvenile justice system will be the revival of Criminal Courts I and II that are intended to replace the current State Criminal Court and the General Criminal Court. Criminal Courts I will be instituted in the capital of every state and the Criminal Courts II in every city; the former will deal with more serious crimes deserving capital punishment, and the latter will deal with less serious ones. Criminal Court I shall consist of five and in some cases three judges. In cases when child or juvenile offenders commit a crime falling within Criminal Court I's jurisdiction, they shall be tried before the Criminal Court I but will benefit from all the protective advantages provided by the Special Court for Children and Juveniles, (including the filing of a history of the offender, the requirement for having a lawyer, confidential proceedings, limited bail amounts, etc.).

also in the Criminal Procedure Law that is in progress in the Parliament now and most likely will be adopted by the end of the year. First, this law includes provisions for the formation of a special police force for children and juveniles, although its extent of authority is not very clear; its clarification has been left to new regulations to be adopted by the head of the judiciary (see Box 7.5).

Conclusion

Child delinquency and the attitude of the Iranian criminal justice system toward it is a subject that should be considered against the general backdrop of the transition of the Iranian society from tradition to modernity. The general governmental position regarding the issue has moved toward the adoption of differentiated preventive policies with the aim of decreasing social harm affecting children and juveniles; this trend has been inspired by developments in the academic arena, which for three decades have aimed at providing a new perspective for solving the problem of child delinquency. The most important barrier in this regard is the ongoing conflict between the Iranian traditional legal system inspired by the *Sharia* law and the modern approaches to the problem inspired by current necessities and international obligations.

Nevertheless, recent developments, as well as recently adopted laws, are hopeful signs indicating that the Iranian government is moving toward a greater consideration of factual necessities and the need to heed international standards more than ever before.

Review/Discussion Questions

1. Which general juvenile justice model forms the basis of the Iranian juvenile justice system? Compare the juvenile justice system existing before and after the 1979 revolution.
2. What is the relationship between the religious laws and parliamentary laws adopted after the revolution in the field of juvenile criminal justice?
3. Which factors have had the greatest impact on the rise of juvenile delinquency in Iran?
4. How much is Hirchi's theory applicable to juvenile delinquency in Iran?
5. Which direction is the Iranian juvenile justice system heading in? Consider, for example, to what extent, if any, the influence of Islamic law/*Sharia* might have on reforms to the Iranian juvenile justice system.

References

Children Delinquency Panel. (2003). *Judiciary Legal Review*, 67(45): 7–60.

Danesh, T. (1999). *Trial of Offending Children in Comparative Law*. Tehran, Mizan Publication.

Ejlali, P. (2011). Looking at crime statistics in Iran. In: *Collected Articles on Social Pathology in Iran*. Tehran, Agah Publication, 349–378.

Farzinrad, R. (2007). Legal explanation of criminal responsibility of children and Juveniles and a Look at Police Function in Iran. *Police Studies Quarterly*, 9(1): 141–156.

Hallaq, W.B. (2009). *An Introduction to Islamic Law*. New York, Cambridge University Press.

Iranian Statistical Center. (2012). *Selected Results of Persons and Houses General Census*. Tehran, Iranian Statistical Center Publication.

Jamshidi, A. (2003). Criminal policy discourse in judicial bill of establishment of court for offender children and juvenile. *Judiciary Legal Review*, (45).

Jangholi, M. (2011). Review on street children situation. In: *Collected Articles on Social Issues in Iran*. Tehran, Agah Publication, 193–215.

Khaleghi, A. (2009). *Criminal Procedure*. Tehran, Shahre Danesh Publication.

Marashi, S.M.H. (1994). *New Approaches in Islamic Criminal Law*. Tehran, Mizan Publication.

Mehra, N. (2005). Iranian criminal regulations facing offender children: Present and future. *Theology and Law Review*, 6(20): 41–60.

Meshkati, M. and Meshkati, Z. (2011). Measurement of family internal and external factors on juvenile delinquency (an experimental examination of social control and differential association theories combined). In: *Collected Articles on Social Issues in Iran*. Tehran, Agah Publication, 239–269.

Moazzami, S. (2008). The role of peer group on juvenile delinquency groups. *Criminal Sciences Review*, 1(3): 227–264.

Moazzami, S. (2009). *Children and Juvenile Delinquency*. Tehran, Dadgostar Publication.

Moazzenzadegan, H.A. (2008). The history of protective criminal regulations regarding children and juveniles in Iran. *Judiciary Legal Review*, 72(62–63): 13–40.

Momenirad, A. (1999). Children court and securing treatment measures. *Police Studies*, (6–7): 132–149.

Rahami, M. (2002). Criminal capacity. *Faculty of Law and Political Science of University of Tehran Review*, (58): 167–198.

Safaei, S.H. and Emami, A. (2006). *Civil Law: Persons and Interdicted People*. Tehran, Samt Publication, pp. 207–213.

Shami, F. (1978). Effective factors in children and juvenile delinquency. *Judicial Monthly*, 13(150): 92–102.

Shamloo, B. (2011). *Criminal Justice and Children*. Tehran, Jangal Publication.

Sheikhavandi, D. (2007). *Sociology of Deviances and Societal Problems in Iran*. Tehran, Ghatreh publication.

Weiss, B.G. (Ed.). (2002). *Studies in Islamic Law and Society*. Leiden, Brill.

Juvenile Justice and Juvenile Crime: An Overview of Japan

8

YOKOYAMA MINORU

Contents

An Outline of Japan's History   180
The Development of Juvenile Justice in Japan   181
    Criminal Responsibility   181
    The Emergence of Juvenile Facilities   181
    Enactment of the Reformatory Law and the Juvenile Law   182
Characteristics of the Current Juvenile Law   183
    Movement for the Revision of the Juvenile Law   184
    The Revision of the Juvenile Law in 2000   185
    The Revisions of the Juvenile Law in 2007 and 2008   186
    Further Criminalization   187
The Nature and Trends of Juvenile Delinquency   188
    Juvenile Delinquency Trends after World War II   188
    Delinquency Trends   190
Profile of Juvenile Delinquents   194
    Delinquency and Gender   194
    Juvenile Delinquents by Age   195
Administration of Juvenile Justice System   195
    Preventive Activities in the Community   195
    Juvenile Guidance Centers   196
    Preventive Activities by the Police   196
    Disposition of Cases by the Police and Public Prosecutors   198
    Imposition of Criminal Punishment   199
    Family Court Probation Officers and Tentative Probation   199
    Juvenile Detention and Classification Homes   200
    Adjudication by Family Court Judges   200
    Facilities under the Child Welfare Law   202
    Juvenile Training Schools   202
    Probation and Parole   203
Conclusion   204
Review/Discussion Questions   205
References   206
Internet Sources   208

FACTS ABOUT JAPAN

Area: Japan is composed of five main islands, listed from north to south: Hokkaido, Honshu, Shikoku, Kyushu, and Okinawa. The total area is 377,955 square km. It is located from latitude 24°N to 45°N. It has one time zone. **Population:** Approximately 127.8 million in 2011 (a population density of 343 people per square km), of which 99.7% were Japanese. Ethnic Chinese made up 32.5% of the non-Japanese population followed by Koreans (26.2%) and Brazilians (10.1%). Population growth rate per 1000 declined by −2.0, and 67.3% of the population lived in urban settings. Thirteen major cities constitute a ward system, of which Tokyo is not only the largest (with a population of 13.2 million) but is also the nation's capital. The number of persons between birth and 14 years of age decreased from over 30.1 million in 1955 to 16.7 million in 2011, while those 65 and over increased from 4.8 million to 29.8 million over the same period. **Climate:** Although mostly temperate, the climate varies from north to south. For Tokyo, the average monthly temperature is 6.1°C in January and 27.4°C in August. Heavy snowfall is common along the Sea of Japan in winter. **Economy:** Soon after World War II, Japan evolved from a nation oriented to agriculture and primary industry to an industrialized and manufacturing nation. More recently, as Japan has become more developed, many people work in the tertiary industries. **Government:** Under the constitution enacted in 1946, the Emperor is a symbol of the state—a hereditary title. The sovereign power rests with the people, who elect both a member of the House of Representatives and that of the House of Councilors. The members of the Diet designate a prime minister, who organizes a cabinet. Between 1955 and 1993, the Liberal Democratic Party (LDP) was the governing group. In 1993, a political scandal brought down the LDP, ushering in an era of coalition cabinets in power. The autonomy of local governments remains limited.

An Outline of Japan's History

According to the ancient Chinese literature, the Japanese state existed in the first century AD. As early as the fourth century, emperors ruled our country. In AD 604, the first Japanese constitution with 17 articles was proclaimed, which were maxims influenced by Buddhism. In the late seventh century, a legal system was established in imitation of that in Tang China. Some of the key historical periods include

1. The **Nara** period (AD 710–793) saw the widespread influence of Buddhism under the reign of powerful emperors, although many Japanese remained believers of Shinto, a native polytheistic religion, the core of which is the worship of nature and ancestors without a creator or sacred text like other main religions.
2. The **Heian** period (AD 794–1191) witnessed the emperor gradually being deprived of political power, which resulted from internal conflicts between different factions of the court nobilities based on the manor system. Then, as a result of this internal fighting, a warrior class gained political power.
3. During the **Kamakura** period (1192–1333), two parallel legal systems coexisted, one for the court of the emperor and another for the military government of warriors that was founded by the Minamoto Shogun.

4. The **Muromachi** period (1336–1573) witnessed the weak power of the Ashikaga Shogun. For over 100 years from 1467, there were numerous wars that resulted in the complete decline of the manor system originated in the tenth century. In 1543, the Portuguese were the first Europeans to come to Japan and introduce Christianity and guns.

5. The **Edo** period (1603–1867) saw the establishment of a rigid caste system under the feudal lords. To eradicate belief in Christianity, the Tokugawa Shogunate banned any further contact with Spain or Portugal. Only the Dutch and the Chinese were allowed to trade at an artificial island in Nagasaki Harbor. In 1742, the Tokugawa Shogunate compiled the Criminal Code of One Hundred Articles. Ordinary people had to comply with a sentence without knowing the laws. In the middle of the nineteenth century, Japan was pressured by Russia and the United States to abandon its policy of isolation. This led to considerable internal squabbling over how to respond to these pressures. Consequently, the low-ranking warriors succeeded in overthrowing the Tokugawa Shogunate and restored the court of the emperor.

6. After the **Meiji Restoration** in 1868, Japan began introducing a Western legal system. In 1873, **Gustave Boissonade**, an associate of the University of Paris, was invited to help with the transition of the legal system. He succeeded in enacting the Penal Code and the Code of Criminal Procedures. The short-lived French model of the Penal Code was replaced in 1907 by a new Penal Code based on the positivist model of Germany.

7. With the defeat of Japan in the World War II (1945), the imperial regime collapsed, Japan was stripped of its empire, and the criminal justice system was democratized at the direction of the Allied Powers, with the emperor reduced to a symbolic figurehead. Following the enactment of a new constitution in 1946 and the revisions of the Penal Code in 1947, a new Code of Criminal Procedures was enacted in 1948. The code was modeled after the American system to guarantee due process.

The Development of Juvenile Justice in Japan

Criminal Responsibility

Since the late seventh century, the criminal laws for the court of the emperor had some prescriptions to exempt juveniles from penalty or to reduce sentences. This was also the case in the criminal laws for the court of warriors. For example, the Criminal Code of One Hundred Articles of 1742 allowed for the mitigation of criminal punishment for juveniles and under the age of 15.

After the **Meiji Restoration**, Western systems for juveniles were introduced. In 1872, compulsory education was instituted. In 1880, the Penal Code was enacted, which included several provisions for juvenile offenders. For example, Article 79 defined the minimum age of culpability as 12.

The Emergence of Juvenile Facilities

The Prison Rules with Illustration of Prison issued in 1872 provided for the establishment of reformatory prisons for juvenile delinquents. They were modeled after the English-style

> ## BOX 8.1   FAMILY SCHOOL ESTABLISHED BY KOSUKE TOMEOKA
>
> In 1983, the national government removed the ban on Christianity. Kosuke Tomeoka, a Christian, became a chaplain at Sorachi Penitentiary in Hokkaido, the northern island of Japan, to improve the treatment in the prison (Correctional Association 1984). He later went to the United States to learn treatment for prisoners under 30 years of age at the Concord Reformatory and the Elmira Reformatory where he was taught by Zebulon Brockway. After returning to Japan, he founded a reformatory school in Tokyo in 1899 after the model of those in Western countries.
>
> His reformatory was called a family school—Katei Gakko. A teacher and his family lived together with about 10 juveniles in an independent house. The setting was very nurturing under the affection of a married couple. For a long period, the basic model of this family school was maintained at many Child Education and Training Homes (*Kyogoin* Homes), although the Christianity atmosphere was lost. However, the system of rearing by a married couple was gradually abandoned (see Hattori 1996, for further discussion on the history and development of family schools).

prison system used in Hong Kong and Singapore. Although the intention was to provide educational programs, limited resources restricted the implementation of such provisions.

After learning more about the use of reformatory schools in Western countries, in 1883, a female priest in a sector of Shinto founded the first reformatory school. The priests of conventional religions such as Shinto and Buddhism played an important role in establishing these reformatory schools (see Box 8.1). This period saw the start of the participatory nature of our modern juvenile justice system.

Enactment of the Reformatory Law and the Juvenile Law

Given the strong support for the private reformatory schools, in 1900, the Reformatory Law was proclaimed to endorse their activities. Although the law encouraged the establishment of public reformatory schools, by 1908, only five prefectural reformatory schools were opened.

In 1907, the current Penal Code was promulgated. Article 41 prescribes that anyone under the age of 14 shall not be held criminally responsible. Confinement to the reformatory prison was abolished. In 1908, the Reformatory Law was amended to treat juveniles who had been confined in the reformatory prison.

After 9 years of debate, in 1919, the first drafts of the Juvenile Law and the Correctional School Law were completed. However, Shigejiro Ogawa, who had contributed to drafting the Reformatory Law, argued that there was not the same urgent need for the Juvenile law as in the United States. Ogawa further suggested that offenders under the age of 14 should not be adjudicated under the Juvenile law and that a correctional school similar to a juvenile prison should not be instituted in place of the well-functioning reformatory school.

In spite of such opposition, both acts passed in 1922. However, owing to budgetary restraints between 1922 and 1934, the Juvenile Law was only enforced in a few large cities such as Tokyo and Osaka. In 1933, the Juvenile Training and Education Law was enacted in place of the Reformatory Law to coordinate with the system under the Juvenile Law.

Characteristics of the Current Juvenile Law

Shortly after the Second World War, there was a sharp increase in juvenile crime in Japan. This prompted discussions of enacting the new Juvenile law. Being heavily influenced by the Allied Powers, Japan at the time was expected to place greater emphasis on child welfare for the future realization of democracy in the generations to follow.

Enacted in 1948, the new Juvenile Law, like its predecessor, followed the principle of *parens patriae*. However, to guarantee juvenile rights during adjudication, the Family Court was founded in place of the semijudicial agency for adjudication. On the other hand, to expand the welfare model, the range of cases under the Juvenile Law was expanded. The age range of juveniles the law applied to was raised from under 18 years to under 20 years. The public prosecutors lost their power to screen juvenile cases and were not qualified to appear at the Family Court. Under the current principle of *parens patriae*, the Japanese Juvenile Law is designed to provide protective educative measures that will enable juvenile delinquents to develop their individual abilities.

The post-World War II period also saw the advent of new classicists who emphasized human rights in the criminal justice system. These theorists insisted that criminal policy be carried out under the principle of legality (Yokoyama 1994). However, the Juvenile Law has been interpreted since 1922 in a manner that followed the **welfare model** and emphasized **rehabilitation** (Yokoyama 1992a). Sawanobori (1994) insists that the Juvenile Law is a welfare law because of its paternalistic orientation, while guaranteeing due process as a procedural law. In addition, referring to Table 1.1 (see Introduction), the Japanese model might also be described as representative of the **participatory model**, as many citizens have participated as volunteers in activities to realize the purpose of the Juvenile Law.

The most important provisions of the Juvenile Law include the following:

- The purpose of the law is to help ensure that juveniles are raised soundly. To this end, the law provides for protective educative measures. Paragraph 1 of Article 24 of the law prescribed three measures for juvenile delinquents: making extensive use of probation; committing them to a Home for Dependent Children or a Home to Support Children's Independence; and referring juveniles to a juvenile training school.
- *Juvenile delinquents* are defined as those under the age of 20, although the Child Welfare Law is applied to those under 18 years of age.
- The Family Court has jurisdiction over three kinds of juvenile delinquents: (a) juvenile offenders between the ages of 14 and 19, (b) law-breaking children under the age of 14, and (c) juveniles under the age of 20 who are prone to commit some criminal offense.
- Chapter 2 of the law prescribes procedures and dispositions for the protection of juveniles. In principle, they stress informality and the absence of a confrontation between the defendant and the prosecutor. The hearing in the Family Court shall be performed in a kind and friendly atmosphere under a presiding judge.
- All cases of juvenile delinquents must be referred to the Family Court. However, the Family Court judge(s) has the discretion to refer a case back to the public prosecutor. This would be analogous to transferring a youth to adult court in Western countries.

- Chapter 3 pertains to procedures and punishments in juvenile cases. The procedures are more protective than for adult offenders. In addition, the criminal punishment imposed on juveniles can be mitigated.

Movement for the Revision of the Juvenile Law

Soon after the enactment of the new Juvenile Law in 1949, the Ministry of Justice and the public prosecutors began to discuss revising the law to restore the authority and power they possessed under the old law. One principal purpose of the revision was to lower the age that the law applied to from under 20 years to under 18 years. Another was to acquire the power to express their opinion on the disposition at the Family Court from a perspective that viewed how public order was maintained.

Various initiatives taken by the Ministry of Justice resulted in several amendments to the Juvenile Law. However, these drafts encountered the severe opposition of many people including scholars of criminal law, lawyers, members of labor unions, and members of the opposition parties, who supported the welfare model prescribed under the Juvenile Law. Even the Supreme Court expressed opposition to the draft of 1966 proposing to revise the law, which prescribes that the age applied to the Juvenile Law be lowered to under 18 years of age while reserving the possibility to offer the protective measures to youths between 18 and 23 years of age. After the publicity of the interim report of the Legal System Council in 1977, Japan did not see any active movement for the revision of the Juvenile Law until the late 1990s. This was so even though Japan reached its highest peak of juvenile delinquency in 1983.

In the 1990s, lawyers participated as attendants in cases in which juveniles were referred to the Family Court for false charges. Under the Juvenile Law, there was no appropriate system to find facts on criminal behavior because of the absence of an adversarial confrontation between the defendant and the prosecutor. There were no provisions for formally declaring the innocence of juveniles found to be innocent in the adjudication. Therefore, lawyers began to consider a revision of the Juvenile Law to sufficiently guarantee juveniles' rights to due process. However, as they respected the welfare model, they were reluctant to advocate the introduction of the totality of criminal procedures to guarantee the same rights as those afforded to adult defendants. To revise the Juvenile Law, the Supreme Court, the Ministry of Justice, and the Japan Federation of Bar Association began debate in November 1996.

In 1997, a 14-year-old boy in Kobe killed two children and injured three. The media gave this incident considerable coverage as the killings were quite horrific in nature. Starting from this case, the mass media continued to report on several other murder cases committed by boys between 15 and 17 years of age. The media coverage attracted a significant degree of public attention leading to a call for the harsher punishment of juvenile offenders.

Another factor impacting the use of tougher policies has been the increasing concern for the victims of crime. The support system for the crime victims had been poor, and it was not until the late 1990s that the movement for victim support began to appear before the footlights of the public square. Some crime victims (e.g., families who had a child killed) began to insist that their rights were being neglected, while offenders' rights—above all, juvenile offenders' rights—were respected too much.

As a result of this increased media coverage, the public became increasingly critical of the Juvenile Law for being too lenient with juvenile offenders. Therefore, the ruling

LDP began to advocate the revision of the Juvenile Law, calling for tougher measures against juvenile offenders. Under pressure from the LDP, the Legal System Council hurriedly discussed a draft of the revised Juvenile Law for 6 months and submitted it to the Minister of Justice in January 1999. However, this draft did not pass a vote in the Diet owing to the political turmoil. Then, members of three ruling parties acting upon an initiative of the LDP submitted a new draft to the Diet. It was enacted at the end of November in 2000.

The Revision of the Juvenile Law in 2000

The main features of the revised Juvenile Law of 2000 are the following (Yokoyama 2003):

1. The revised Juvenile Law adds a principle of adjudication at the Family Court. During the hearing, all participants are expected to make a juvenile reflect on his/her delinquency. The Family Court is also expected to make a parent(s) or a guardian aware of their responsibility as a custodian. For this purpose, the Family Court judge(s) can give an instruction and a warning to the parent(s) or the guardian. Although this practice had informally been carried out previously, it was clearly declared as an objective in the revised law.

2. The new law guarantees a victim's right to speak to the Family Court judge or the Family Court probation officer about his/her opinion and feeling against a juvenile offender or a law-breaking child inside or outside the court. In addition, it guarantees the right to know the result of adjudication at the Family Court. In response to victims' requests, the Family Court informs him/her of the name and address of a juvenile offender or a law-breaking child, and of the result of a disposition together with the brief reasons for this disposition. A victim can request to see the original record of adjudication. However, the scope of information in the record being opened to the victim is limited to facts concerning the offense or the law-breaking behavior and the person's motivation in committing it. From the viewpoint of protecting a juvenile offender or a law-breaking child, the record on his/her personality and background is not opened.

3. The new law includes provisions to improve the procedures for finding the facts on a juvenile delinquency. In a complicated case, the court composed of three judges can adjudicate. The maximum term of the custody in the Juvenile Detention and Classification Home has been changed from 4 to 8 weeks. The Family Court can permit the public prosecutor to appear at the court in the case of a heinous offense such as a murder or robbery. In such a circumstance, a legal counselor has to appear at the court as an attendant for the juvenile offender. Furthermore, the public prosecutor can appeal to a higher court if there is a claim against the recognition of facts on juvenile delinquency by the Family Court.

4. The revision of the Juvenile Law shifted the statute's focus toward greater accountability. The minimum age of a juvenile offender, who can be referred back to the public prosecutor for a criminal charge, was lowered from 16 to 14. In cases involving juveniles over the age of 16 who have committed a homicide or a malicious offense resulting in death, the Family Court is obliged in principle to refer the case back to the public prosecutor for criminal indictment.

The Revisions of the Juvenile Law in 2007 and 2008

When the revised Juvenile Law came into force in 2000, the law prescribed that the revised items should be reviewed 5 years after its enactment. At this time, our Supreme Court compiled data on the practice relating to each revised item six times until the end of March in 2006 (Yokoyama 2009). In addition, the All Japan Labor Union of Workers at Court carried out research on the same practices on nine occasions. The Japanese Federation of Bar Association conducted surveys and interviews with member lawyers on their impressions about handling juvenile cases under the new legislation. The results of the analysis revealed that most of the respondents wanted to restore the previous laws that were reflective of the welfare model. However, despite the views and efforts of many academics, lawyers, and probation officers, the general public did not support a return to the welfare model but called for greater accountability of juvenile offenders—a shift toward a crime control model. Hence, in response to public opinion, the Juvenile Law was further revised in 2007 and in 2008.

The main contents of the revised Juvenile Law in 2007 and 2008 are as follows:

1. In July 2003, a 12-year-old male junior high school student took a 4-year-old boy whom he had sexually abused to the rooftop of a building and then threw him down to his death. In June 2004, an 11-year-old girl killed a fellow female classmate with a knife in a classroom. In both cases, the police could not conduct an investigation because the offenders were under the legal age of criminal responsibility. Unfortunately, the child consultation centers failed to conduct any researches to clarify the causes of the murders. Therefore, the police requested that they be given the power to research any serious cases involving a law-breaking child. This request was formalized in the revised Juvenile Law of 2007. The police are now able to prepare a report on any serious cases involving a law-breaking child to the child consultation center. Once received, the chief of the center should refer the case to the Family Court to determine whether the protective educative measures prescribed by the Juvenile Law should be imposed.
2. Before the revision of Juvenile Law in 2007, a law-breaking child could not be sent to a juvenile training school. However, after the occurrence of the two above-mentioned murder cases, many people began to argue that the law was too lenient with a law-breaking child. Subsequently, in response to public opinion calling for tougher policy, the Law on Juvenile Training Schools was revised to accommodate a child of over 12 years of age.
3. Juveniles placed on probation are supervised and assisted by a probation–parole officer and a volunteer officer (*Hogoshi*). If juveniles fail to observe the conditions of a probation order, they are given a warning by a chief of the probation–parole office. If a juvenile probationer neglects this warning, by the revised law of 2007, the chief can refer the probationer ignoring probationary obligations to the Family Court.
4. The revised Juvenile Law of 2008 aimed to widen the rights of crime victims. Under the revised law, crime victims are permitted to listen to adjudication in some serious cases. Before granting permission, the Family Court judge(s) is requested to hear the opinion on granting permission from a lawyer as an attendant. Another new system was introduced, under which the Family Court

explains the contents of adjudication in a closed session to victims if they so wish. In addition, the scope of victims' rights to see the original record of the result of adjudication and to take its copy has been expanded from that given under the revised law of 2000.

Further Criminalization

The leaders of the reform movement for crime victims have continued to advocate for tougher policies in the treatment of a juvenile offender who is over 14 years of age. Under the current Juvenile Law, an undetermined sentence is given to a juvenile offender in case he/she has committed a serious offense for which, in an adult case, a judge(s) should impose a sentence of over 3 years' imprisonment. Paragraph 2 of Article 52 of the Juvenile Law prescribes that the maximum length of a long-term sentence is now 10 years, while a short-term sentence is 5 years. In further response to the public outcry for tougher sentences, the Legal System Council debated the revision of the Juvenile Law in the fall of 2012 (*Asahi Shimbun* on December 19, 2012). The draft revision calls for a long-term disposition to be extended from 10 to 15 years. A short-term sentence is also extended so that it is at least half of a long-term sentence. Under the current Juvenile Law, the imprisonment sentence for a heinous juvenile offender of less than 18 years of age is mitigated to 15 years in the place of a life sentence to be imposed in an adult case. By the draft, this mitigated term is extended from 15 to 20 years. Furthermore, the scope of cases for which a public prosecutor is permitted to attend the adjudication is expanded from that prescribed under the revised law of 2000. The draft passed the Diet in April in 2014 (see Box 8.2).

BOX 8.2   CONTROVERSY ABOUT THE RESTORATION OF PUBLIC PROSECUTORS' AUTHORITY

Under the initiative of the Ministry of Justice, in which public prosecutors monopolize all key positions, several drafts for the revision of the Juvenile Law were put forth (Saito 1986). The main purpose of the revisions was the restoration of the public prosecutors' authority, which had been lost under the introduction of the welfare model resulting from the enactment of the Juvenile Law in 1948. However, legal professionals and members of the opposition parties criticized this restoration severely for being too oriented toward crime control.

Responding to the moral panic among the public that ensued in a more conservative national mood, the ruling coalition parties submitted the bill of a revised Juvenile Law to the Diet. In November 2000, it passed in spite of the opposition of the Communist Party and the Social Democratic Party. Through this enactment, the public prosecutors succeeded in acquiring competence to appear at the Family Court with the permission of a judge.

The Ministry of Justice has a draft of a revised Juvenile Law to expand the scope of cases in which public prosecutors can be permitted to appear at the court in a juvenile case. As the opposition by scholars and lawyers from the viewpoint of the Welfare Model declines, in April 2014, the draft was passed by the Diet without any serious opposition.

We see the continuation of gradual criminalization and harsher sentences in response to the opinions of grieving crime victims. In practice, many Family Court probation officers give up working as specialist case workers, in favor of serving judges as loyal servants to realize the just deserts model (Yokoyama 2012a). However, fortunately, the proposal to lower the maximum age for the application of the Juvenile Law from under 20 years to under 18 years is not included in the draft, to which the campaign by the author may have contributed (Yokoyama 2010a). As the fundamental system under the welfare model is still maintained, the author anticipates that the juvenile justice system in Japan will not shift drastically toward the **crime control model**.

The Nature and Trends of Juvenile Delinquency

The national government has strong executive powers and is able to collect various data uniformly from all over the country. Our government's statistics are considered more reliable than those in more decentralized countries. Because of the government's stable bureaucratic system, they are rarely influenced by the results of elections. Consequently, self-reports and victimization surveys, unlike Europe and North America, are not well funded, and are carried out only sporadically.

Japan has several primary sources of formal criminal justice statistics: the National Police Agency compiles crime statistics; the Ministry of Justice produces annual data on prosecution, correction, and rehabilitation; and the Supreme Court publishes judicial statistics on an annual basis. In addition to these reports, the National Police Agency, the Ministry of Justice, and the Cabinet Office publish white papers on police, crime, and children and youngsters, respectively.

Juvenile Delinquency Trends after World War II

There have been three major peaks of juvenile delinquency since World War II (Yokoyama 1986a). The first occurred in 1951 when the rate of Juvenile Penal Code offenders including law-breaking children was 9.5 per 1000 population of between 10 and 19 years of age. Given that the police had been decentralized under the decree of the Allied Powers, it seems likely that this figure represented only the tip of the iceberg. The highest rate of juvenile delinquency probably occurred in the chaos immediately after World War II when there were many poor and orphaned children. These juveniles often committed property crimes such as a theft or robbery because of absolute poverty (Yokoyama 1985).

The second peak occurred in 1964 when the rate rose to 11.9 per 1000. In the early 1960s, we gave attention to violent offenses being committed by juveniles born during the baby boom after World War II.

The third peak occurred in 1983 when the rate jumped to 17.1 per 1000. Although there were a large number of investigations, most of these were for minor offenses. The rise may reflect the "net widening" of guidance activities of the police (Yokoyama 1989) (see Box 8.3).

Subsequent to the third peak, the rate of Juvenile Penal Code offenders declined to 12.1 per 1000 in 1995. In the late 1990s, the movement for crime victims surged to advocate a harsher policy against juvenile delinquents. In response to this situation, the police increased the scrutiny and arrest of juvenile delinquents. Not surprisingly then, the rate of

BOX 8.3   "PLAY-TYPE" DELINQUENCY OR "INCIPIENT-TYPE" DELINQUENCY?

In the late 1960s, serious and violent crime declined. The police were then able to direct their resources to the less serious offenses such as a bicycle theft, embezzlement of a lost or deserted bicycle, and shoplifting (Yokoyama 1992b). Most of these crimes were committed for fun or thrills. Therefore, after 1970, the police referred to them as the "play-type" delinquency, often committed even by ordinary juveniles from middle- or upper-class families. The net-widening efforts by the police contributed to forming the third peak of juvenile delinquency in 1983.

After the research in 1981 by the National Research Institute of Police Sciences, Kiyonaga (1983) pointed out that juveniles who committed minor offenses at a younger age were prone to develop criminal tendencies toward committing a conventional theft or a violent crime. In response, the police renamed the play-type delinquency as "incipient-type" delinquency in the White Paper on Police in 1982 (National Police Agency 1982). Shoplifting, motorcycle theft, bicycle theft, and the embezzlement of a lost or deserted thing (the riding of a deserted bicycle) were categorized under this new label. However, these four offenses seem to be committed by juveniles with different motivations. For example, motorcycle theft can be committed by juveniles who admire hot-rodders, and minor shoplifting by "play-type" delinquents (see Yokoyama 2001, for further criticism).

The rate of the above-mentioned incipient-type delinquency among all juvenile Penal Code offenders increased from 36.0% in 1973 to 64.4% in 1984 and to 75.6% in 1998 (National Police Agency 1983, 1984, 1999). By advocating the category of the incipient-type delinquency, the police have carried out net-widening activities against minor offenders with little long-term criminal tendencies. In the late 1990s, such police activities contributed to warning the public against the increase in the total number of juvenile offenses. Under the moral panic engendered among the public, the Juvenile Law was revised toward partial criminalization in 2000.

The net-widening activities are still maintained. However, recently, the police stopped referring to the increase in the incipient-type delinquency in the White Paper on Police.

Juvenile Penal Code offenders rose to 15.5 per 1000 in 2003. After 2003, the rate declined constantly to reach 9.7 in 2011. However, it should also be noted that, first, the total population of children under 20 years has declined in concert with a decrease in the birth rate, and second, the system to protect children has improved especially in the area of programs for antisocial offenses. As the author foresaw some 30 years ago, Japan has developed social stability at the expense of flexibility as juveniles become too conformist under overprotection and oversupervision (Yokoyama 1986a, 112) (see Box 8.4). The percentage of Juvenile Penal Code offenders among all offenders apprehended by the police decreased from 19.7% in 2004 to 11.8% in 2011, and Japan no longer regards juvenile delinquency as a serious social problem. However, the author has argued that the protective educative measures for juvenile delinquents under the rehabilitation model are still important.

**BOX 8.4   OVERPROTECTION OF CHILDREN
IN A HIGHLY AGED SOCIETY**

Japan is becoming a highly aged society, in which children are protected more and more by adults. Every time the mass media report on a serious crime in which a child is killed or injured, parents' concern about the safety of their children surges. For example, on June 28, 2013, a man stabbed three boys with a knife in front of the gate of their elementary school (Asahi Shimbun on June 29, 2013). Concerned about such a crime, many schools have strengthened patrols around the schools, and children are accompanied to and from school in groups under the guidance of teachers and parents.

In response to the rise in concern about children's safety, the industry for a child's security develops. For example, Hanshin Railway Company has begun to sell security systems to schools (Asahi Shimbun on June 20, 2013). Under the system, pupils carrying an identity card (IC) tag are located through Global Positioning System (GPS) at a place such as the school gate or entrance gate of a train. The information on the location is immediately sent to their parents by the company. In this way, the child's security is highly protected. Under such a total supervision system, Japanese children lose their freedom, for example, their enjoyment of loitering on the way home from school.

Delinquency Trends

How has juvenile delinquency changed over time? The main trends may be described as follows:

- The main offense committed by juveniles has been and continues to be theft. During the post-World War II period, the prevailing poverty throughout the country, in all probability, contributed to the increase in thefts. However, as standards of living improved during the period of high economic growth from 1954 to 1973, juveniles committed minor thefts more frequently. In addition, the police widened the net of their guidance activities for instances of minor theft such as shoplifting or a temporary ride of a bicycle without the permission of its owner (Yokoyama 1989). This trend has continued. For example, in 2011, the total number of thefts committed by juveniles amounted to 47,776, of which 54.3% and 18.8% were for shoplifting and bicycle thefts, respectively (National Public Safety Commission and National Police Agency 2012). Unlike many Western countries, motor vehicle theft (1.1%) and theft through breaking and entering (4.3%) are infrequent. Perhaps unique to Japanese youth culture is the habit of "joyriding" of motorcycles. Motorcycle theft (10.3%) is more common than motorcar theft.
- Between 1964 and 2003, there was a sharp increase in the number of embezzlements. In Japan, this refers to crimes involving the taking of a lost or deserted thing, the most common of which is the riding of a lost or deserted bicycle. However, since 2003, the number of bicycle thefts has dropped from 38,547 in 2003 to 14,674 in 2011.

- Recently, we have witnessed a new type of a property crime committed by juveniles, who are induced by organized groups of swindlers to commit fraud though remittance soliciting. The swindlers call a senior citizen who is convinced to pay cash or to transfer money to a bank account in response to the narration of a concocted story, such as the urgent payment of money for a grandchild's traffic accident. They then ask a juvenile to receive the money directly from the deceived person or to withdraw money from the bank account. If the juvenile carries out such a job for a reward, he or she may be arrested for fraud. One such case involved the arrest, for an attempted fraud, of a 15-year-old girl wearing a man's suit when she tried to receive four million yen (US$40,000) from a deceived woman 55 years old (*Asahi Shimbun* on August 31, 2013).
- Between 1964 and 2011, Japan saw a dramatic decrease in the number of murders and robberies. The decline in all types of violent crime might be due to a very proactive campaign against violence, which was initiated in the early 1960s. However, in the late 1990s, Japan witnessed an increase in the total number of robberies. One of the common explanations for this phenomenon is the prevalence of "daddy hunting," where a group of casually gathered youngsters attack a middle-aged male to take money for recreational activity. Another reason is that the police have adopted a tough policy, especially in the aftermath of the high-profile 1997 murder case in Kobe previously referenced. The police have since arrested juveniles more frequently on serious offenses through the use of a strategy of relabeling (Spergel et al. 1982). For example, those who might have been charged previously for theft and injury were arrested for a robbery causing injury (Terao 1999). The police have continued to maintain this tough policy. However, recently, heinous offenses have declined drastically. Murders declined from 93 in 2003 to 56 in 2011, while robbery charges decreased from 1771 to 593 during the same period.
- Around 1964, school violence was considered a major social problem. Beginning in 1985, "bullying" activities—that is, minor violence in schools—drew national media attention for the first time when several victims of bullying committed suicide. It is generally felt that bullying increased as a result of intense competition in high schools. However, it is the authors' opinion that bullying became a social concern because people's tolerance levels for violent behavior has declined with the decrease of serious violent crimes. Around 1995, bullying again drew attention then the total number of those arrested as juvenile offenders, or guided as law-breaking children or preoffense juveniles, increased to 534 (National Police Agency 1999). However, by the late 1990s, media attention had shifted away from bullying, and the number of cases reported to the police dropped to 268 in 1998. In 2010, bullying drew our attention again, as some bullied juveniles committed suicide. To prevent such tragedies, the Law to Promote Preventive Measures of Bullying was enacted on June 21, 2013. While an interesting observation, it should be noted that most bullying incidents go unreported. In reality, bullying may not have increased, even at those times when mass media focused greater attention on the problem.
- The incidence of sex-related crimes such as rape and indecency have steadily decreased since 1964. Again, the campaign against violence seems to have had a positive impact on reducing sex offenses among juveniles. Another explanation may be that with the development of the economy, more youngsters had their own money, perhaps enough to buy the services of a prostitute, pornographic literature,

and so on, to satisfy their sexual appetite (Yokoyama 1995). In the late 1990s, support systems for the victims of sexual crime were improved, which helped to create greater social awareness around the issue. As a result, victims of rape reported the incidents to the police more frequently. Finally, between 2003 and 2011, the number of reported incidents of rape involving juveniles declined from 242 to 69. As herbivore boys have increased, crimes of rape have steadily declined since around 2004.

- "Hot-rodders," that is, groups of youth, who enjoy driving motorcycles and cars making a loud noise, appeared in the late 1950s (Yokoyama 1986b). The number of hot-rodder groups increased from their first appearance in the 1950s to 42,510 in 1982. As a result, amendments in the criminal laws were made to address this problem (Yokoyama 1990a). In 2011, the total number of the hot-rodder groups had decreased to 7193, of which 4,364 or 60.7% were juveniles under 20 years of age (National Public Safety Commission and National Police Agency 2012). Arguably, as juveniles are able to access more options and outlets for recreation, the number of hot-rodders has continued to decline.

- The use of such hard drugs as cocaine and heroin is not seen as a serious problem in Japan. Since the end of World War II, however, stimulant drugs composed of methamphetamines have been prevalent. Despite efforts to suppress this contamination through criminalization (Yokoyama 1991), the police have not succeeded in eradicating the drug abuse, because the *Boryokudan* (Japanese organized criminal gangs, known as *Yakuza* in foreign countries) dominate the black market for the stimulant drug (Yokoyama 1999). Owing to high prices, however, ordinary juveniles (with the exception of 18- and 19-year-old female juveniles working in bars or nightclubs) have had limited access to the stimulant drug. Recently, the number of juveniles arrested or guided on charges or offenses related to drug abuse decreased drastically. Juveniles caught for the sniffing of paint thinner or toluene decreased from 29,254 in 1982 to 112 in 2011. Juveniles committing an offense of the Stimulant Drug Control Law also declined dramatically from 2750 to 183 for the same period. In addition, in 2011, we saw only 81 juveniles arrested for an offense under the Hemp Control Law and 18 for an offense under the Narcotics and Psychotropics Control Law.

- The Japanese Police collect statistics on juveniles charged with nontraffic offenses prescribed by criminal laws except for the Penal Code. According to these statistics, the highest number of offenses were in contravention of the Swords and Firearms Control Law before 1970, as many juveniles possessed a sword or a firearm illegally. In the 1980s, we saw a greater prevalence of drug abuse, especially the sniffing of thinner or toluene among juveniles. In the place of the recent drastic drop in drug abuse offenses, we witnessed an increase in juveniles caught for some offense of the Minor Offenses Law (see Box 8.5). In 2006, the total number of juveniles caught for this offense amounted to 1626, which was more than all juveniles on charge of an offense of drug abuse.

- In Japan, people use high technology, especially information technology. Juveniles commit some crimes through the use of information technology (see Box 8.6). In turn, many juveniles are victimized by the use of information technology. Girls are more likely to be victimized by crimes such as rape and indecencies through accessing online dating websites, especially by the use of a smart phone.

BOX 8.5   RECENT NET WIDENING OF POLICE ACTIVITIES AGAINST MINOR OFFENSES

The total number of juveniles caught for an offense of the Minor Offenses Law increased drastically from 1626 in 2006 to 4672 in 2011; 59.6% of them were charged for "entering without any due reason into a prohibited place or other's field for growing rice or vegetables," followed by "obstructing other's business by a mischief" (10.2%) and "informing a public officer of a fictitious crime or disaster" (9.8%).

Some juveniles now ride a train through a checking machine by a short-distance ticket or a discounted ticket for a child. Previously, train companies treated such cases as deviant behavior. If the juveniles paid a surcharge after being caught, the railway companies would have released them without reporting to the police. However, the tolerance level of the companies has declined, and more cases are reported to the police. In addition, some police officers are enthusiastic about catching juveniles who ride trains without valid tickets because they want to increase the appearance of effectively catching and deterring juveniles who try to ride the train without buying a ticket. Police apprehending such cases cannot charge the juvenile for fraud, because he/she has not cheated any person. Thus, the police have begun to charge juveniles riding without valid tickets for the offense of "entering without any due reason into a prohibited place" under the Minor Offenses Law.

The drastic increase in offenses under the Minor Offenses Law apparent in the statistics may be brought about not by any real increase in minor offenses but by the net widening of the police activities. A juvenile offender or a law-breaking child charged for such offenses of the Minor Offenses Law are sent directly to the Family Court in the summary procedure. Until the final decision of the court, usually the decision of a dismissal without hearing, they are put under stress for 2 or 3 months, by which they may experience damage to their identity as sound and serious young persons. From a labeling perspective, the net widening of police activities against juveniles committing minor offenses should be criticized, because society suffers only a trifling damage from such minor offenses.

BOX 8.6   JUVENILE DELINQUENCY RELATED TO THE INTERNET

Juveniles are heavy users of information technology. Consequently, many juveniles become addicted to the Internet. According to the research conducted by the Ministry of Health, Labor and Welfare, the rate of such addiction among all junior and senior high school students amounted to 6% and 9%, respectively (*Asahi Shimbun* on August 2, 2013). In such situations, juveniles begin to commit some new types of offenses related to the Internet. The first type of offense is committed by juveniles proud of their ability to use high technology. An unemployed boy of 15 years of age was arrested for illegally accessing the computer of a rental server company through the use of the software Tor (*Asahi Shimbun* on April 25, 2013). A male 14-year-old junior high school student was arrested for starting a phishing site at a server in a foreign country and teaching how to create a phishing site (*Asahi Shimbun* on October 30, 2012).

(Continued)

**BOX 8.6 (*Continued*)   JUVENILE DELINQUENCY
RELATED TO THE INTERNET**

A second type of offense committed is to deprive users of some valuable items on a game site. Both a male senior high school student of 15 years in Higashi Hiroshima City and an unemployed 17-year-old juvenile in Kita Kyuushu City heard a key word from a boy at an elementary school, and deprived the boy's valuable items on the game site by the use of the key word. Although they lived at separate places, they were arrested at the same time for accessing illegally a computer of Cyber Agent, a site that is offered to about 12 million persons who enjoy chatting and games (*Asahi Shimbun* on July 6, 2012).

The third type is an offense, which juveniles commit owing to human conflict through communication resulting from the use of information technology. The most serious case occurred in June 2013. In this case A (an unemployed 16-year-old girl) slandered B (a female student at a technical special school, also 16 years old) by the use of LINE, an instant messaging application, for which the number of users reached to 230 million on August 21, 2013. B got angry and intended to murder A. B and six of her friends between 16 and 21 years of age called A up on the phone. They coerced her into a car ride, during which they attacked her. In the mountains, they continued their attack on her and she died. They were arrested for murder (*Asahi Shimbun* on August 1, 2013).

Profile of Juvenile Delinquents

Delinquency and Gender

During and subsequent to the third peak of 1983, female delinquency increased dramatically. This increase can be attributed mainly to the change in lifestyle of young girls in Japan. The number of nontraffic Penal Code offenders rose from 11,866 in 1966 to 54,459 in 1983 (Research and Training Institute of the Ministry of Justice 1975, 1984). The rate of female juvenile Penal Code offenders per all juveniles climbed to over 10% in 1971 (National Police Agency 1997). After 1976, it remained stable at a level of around 20%. However, it rose drastically to 25.4% in 1998; since then, it has remained between 25% and 18%. In 2011, it amounted to 19.2% (National Police Agency 2012). The recent increase in the rate might be attributed to the decline in tolerance levels on the part of police toward minor offenses committed by female juveniles.

The total number of female juvenile nontraffic Penal Code offenders amounted to 18,243 in 2011, of which 73.7% were charged with theft, followed by 12.8% with the embezzlement of a lost or deserted bicycle (Research and Training Institute of the Ministry of Justice 2012). Most of the thefts comprised minor shoplifting. The increase in shoplifting coincided with a growth in large-scale department stores and supermarkets that use a self-service system (National Police Agency 1976).

At the start of the new millennium, Japan witnessed a high rate of female juveniles engaged in drug abuse. In 1998, the percentage of young females among all juveniles caught for sniffing thinner or toluene amounted to 31.8%, while the corresponding percentage for those abusing stimulant drugs was 50.2% (National Police Agency 1999). The higher percentage of those abusing stimulant drugs corresponded to the increased number of young females working at night. Their increased income enabled them to buy stimulant drugs and they were often exposed to the risk of contact with members of *Boryokudan* (Yokoyama 1991). Although the juveniles apprehended for some categories of drug abuse decreased drastically, this risk seems to continue, because the illegal sale of stimulant drugs produces large revenue for the *Boryokudan*.

Juvenile Delinquents by Age

Between 1983 and 1995, the rates of juvenile delinquency among all age groups dropped. The decline may be explained by the fact that after the second baby boom in the early 1970s, Japan experienced the juvenile population decline with low birth rates, and that juveniles reared in a small family have been more protected or perhaps overprotected by adults.

Since 1966, the highest rate of juvenile nontraffic Penal Code offenders was for those children between the ages of 14 and 15. In 2011, the rates of those 14–15 years old, 16–17, and 18–19 were 45.7%, 35.5%, and 18.8%, respectively. Junior high school students of 14–15 years of age are more likely to commit minor offenses such as a theft or the embezzlement of a lost or deserted bicycle (65.3% and 15.1%, respectively).

Previously, the high delinquency rate among junior high school students was explained by the heated competition for higher education opportunities (Tokuoka and Cohen 1987). However, Harada (1995) found that students' maladjustment tends to be short term in nature. The rate of delinquency in the age group between 16 and 17 dropped because many juveniles were liberated from the stress of severe competition after graduating from a junior high school.

Administration of Juvenile Justice System

The judiciary is separate from and independent of the central and local governments. The flow of the Japanese juvenile justice administrative process involves many steps. This section outlines some of the major elements at each step in Japan's juvenile justice system.

Preventive Activities in the Community

The participatory nature of our juvenile justice system is conspicuous in the preventive measures against delinquency taken in the community (Yokoyama 2000a). Rural areas have historically relied upon strong informal control in the family and in the neighborhood to prevent juvenile delinquency. And even though the majority of the Japanese population lives in urban settings, in contrast to many Western countries, informal control is still evident even in the larger cities. The neighborhood associations carry out many activities such as festivals, the movement for traffic safety, and recreational activities for the elderly and children. These activities help to create close ties within neighborhoods and help to prevent juvenile delinquency (Yokoyama 1981).

In addition to the neighborhood associations, many citizens participate in the movement to raise young persons soundly within a positive social context. For this purpose, many local governments appoint community leaders as instructors for juveniles. For example, the total number of instructors appointed by Kanagawa Prefectural Government amounted to 5282 at the end of April in 2012 (Kanagawa Prefectural Government 2012). The instructors teach juveniles how to enjoy recreation and to play games. The national and local governments, law enforcement agencies, and juvenile justice agencies encourage and support the activities to raise juveniles in the community effectively. These activities serve to supplement formal social control.

Juvenile Guidance Centers

Two Juvenile Guidance Centers for delinquents were initially established by local citizens in Kyoto and Osaka in 1952. Soon after the second peak of juvenile delinquency in 1964, many guidance centers were established in middle-sized cities with financial assistance from the national government.

The guidance centers carry out three main activities: patrolling in neighborhood, especially in the amusement quarters to guide juveniles, counseling juveniles and their parents, and improving the social environment for rearing young persons soundly.

In the beginning of November in 1998, there were 703 juvenile guidance centers, with approximately 74,000 juvenile guidance volunteers (Cabinet Office, 1999). In small- or medium-sized cities, many Juvenile Guidance Centers are managed by the education department of the municipal government, while in large cities, the department responsible for coping with youth problems administers them. Additionally, police departments administered several Juvenile Guidance Centers in larger cities.

At the beginning of the new millennium, the police began to initiate more preventive activities for youth at risk within their communities. For example, they established the Center for Supporting Juveniles by developing their Juvenile Guidance Center under the Rules on Activities of the Juvenile Police issued in 2002 (Yokoyama 2012b). On the other hand, in 2004, the national government stopped providing subsidies to local governments to support their Juvenile Guidance Centers. As a result, the activities of the centers waned in concert with the financial difficulty of local governments. In 2010, the Cabinet Office renamed the White Paper on Juveniles as the White Paper on Children and Youngsters. The office did not mention any of the activities of the Juvenile Guidance Centers but did cite data about the activities of the Center for Supporting Juveniles. The participatory model seems to have declined as fewer volunteers participate in the activities of the Juvenile Guidance Centers managed by local governments. In March 2012, about 66,000 citizens were appointed as juvenile guidance volunteers (Cabinet Office 2011).

Preventive Activities by the Police

The police have developed their own organizations for the prevention of delinquency since 1949 when the notification on strengthening juvenile policing was conveyed to all local police organizations in Japan. In addition, numerous organizations have collaborated with the police in efforts to prevent crime.

During the second peak of juvenile delinquency in 1964, Japan directed attention to offenses committed by youths coming from rural areas after graduation from a junior high school. To prevent these youths from committing delinquency new company-police conferences were established where the police officers were in charge of delinquency prevention. At a police station, police talked with managers in charge of taking care of young employees in their district. Unfortunately, today these activities have waned, as the companies employ few teenagers.

After recovering from the economic difficulties in the aftermath of World War II, Japan began to focus on the large amount of physical violence in junior high schools. To

BOX 8.7   *KOBAN* AND *CHUZAISHO*

Soon after the World War II, the police thought that the system of *Koban* and *Chuzaisho* should be abolished for modernization. However, Bayley (1976) evaluated it highly as an effective system for the community policing in his book entitled *Forces of Order*. Since then, the Japanese police have endeavored to develop this system.

Activities at *Koban* contribute more to the juvenile prevention than those at *Chuzaisho*, as they are located in a city. Police officers at *Koban* patrol on food, by a bicycle or by a minicar in their territory. On the patrol, they sometimes question a suspicious person. In this manner, they arrested 259,514 persons on the charge of a Penal Code offense in 2011, which amounted to 84.9% among all suspects arrested by the police (National Police Agency, in 2011).

Nowadays, police officers at *Koban* guide juveniles earnestly at night to supplement the guidance activities by special police officers in charge of juvenile policing. If they find a juvenile under 18 years of age loitering after 10 p.m., especially at amusement centers, they issue a warning to him/her as a predelinquent. Therefore, juveniles found to be loitering after midnight increased from 475,594 in 2002 to 564,575 in 2011. This increase must be due to the net widening of the police guidance activities.

cope with the increased delinquency of high school students, the school–police conferences were organized. By 1969, every junior high school was required to have a teacher in charge of guiding students (Yokoyama 1981). By April 2012, there were approximately 2700 school–police conferences (Cabinet Office, in 2012).

Another police organization in the community included police boxes (i.e., *Koban*) in the urban areas and police houses (*Chuzaisho*) in rural areas (see Box 8.7). In April 2012, there were 6240 *Kobans* and 6714 *Chuzaishos* (National Public Safety Commission and National Police Agency 2012). The police officers working at *Kobans* carry out many crime prevention activities in their territory.

Within most police stations, there is a department of community safety that the special police officers in charge of juvenile policing are affiliated with. These special police officers and guidance volunteers patrol periodically at amusement centers to guide juveniles and prevent them from either committing offenses or being victimized by crime.

Finally, the police have also established three voluntary systems: the guidance volunteers, the police helpers for juveniles, and the instructors for juveniles (Yokoyama 1989). In April 2011, the total number of guidance volunteers was approximately 52,000. In addition, about 300 people, many of whom are retired police officers, work as police helpers in charge of dispersing groups of juvenile delinquents, while approximately 6700 juvenile instructors authorized by the Law on Regulation of Business Affecting Public Morals of 1985 work to protect juveniles from unsafe environments (National Police Agency, 2011). Under the Juvenile Law, the police are not qualified to supervise juveniles after providing guidance. However, recently the police have activated the aftercare treatment of predelinquents with their consent and that of their parent(s).

The police also took the initiative to introduce the Juvenile Support Team to support a problem-prone juvenile and to prevent him or her from committing further delinquent acts. The police introduced the School Supporter System to help a school to cope with a problem related to pupils' delinquency. By April 2011, the police had approximately 600 school supporters, most of whom are retired police officers in charge of juvenile policing. Ordinarily, these volunteers wait at the police station while they collect information about the delinquency in a given territory. At the request of a principal of a school, a school supporter visits the school to respond to the needs of the school.

Before the third peak, the police emphasized the necessity of early intervention for juvenile delinquents. In 1982, the National Police Agency issued a general principle enabling the police to widen their activities to control juveniles with the slogan of rearing them soundly (Ayukawa 1994). Fukuda (1988) suggested that the police have moved in the direction of placing juveniles under total control and surveillance. However, it would be more desirable if most of these activities were carried out by schools or by child welfare agencies. The author believes that the national government should assign more resources to child welfare agencies such as the Child Consultation Centers and the Juvenile Guidance Centers.

By contrast, the police have earnestly campaigned for increasing the fixed number of police officers and reinforcing their resources. In addition, every time some heinous crime occurs, the mass media point to defects in the activities of the police. Then, the police succeed in getting more financial resources to counteract these defects. For example, the police succeeded in establishing the Center for Supporting Juveniles to support both juvenile delinquents and juvenile crime victims, when the mass media more frequently reported incidents involving juveniles being victimized (Yokoyama 2010b).

Disposition of Cases by the Police and Public Prosecutors

Since the issue of the Rule on Activities of Juvenile Police in 2002, the police have become more committed to handle juveniles found to be engaging in "risky" behavior as predelinquents. If a police officer or volunteer patrolling on foot finds a predelinquent, they simply give a warning. In 2011, the total member of predelinquents guided by the police amounted to 1,013,167, of which 55.7% were guided for loitering at midnight, followed by 34.9% for smoking. As the night patrol has been strengthened, juveniles found to be loitering at midnight increased from 475,594 in 2002 to 564,575 in 2011.

According to the Juvenile Law, the category of preoffense juveniles is defined under the principle of *parens patriae*. This category has been subject to criticism by a number of legal professionals from the viewpoint of the principle of legality. They criticize the police for intervening with juveniles before they commit any offense or engage in any law-breaking behavior. Also under the law, however, police must refer all cases of preoffense juveniles to the Family Court or to the Child Consultation Center. Therefore, the police are careful when classifying a juvenile as a preoffense delinquent.

Around the second peak of juvenile delinquency, the police referred many cases of preoffense juveniles for protective purposes. In 1965, the total number of predelinquents sent to a Family Court or a Juvenile Consultation Center from the police amounted to 13,032 (National Police Agency 1970). Typically, girls who ran away from home and associated with members of *Boryokudan* were treated as preoffense juveniles. With the increase in criticism from legal professionals, since 1970, the police have hesitated to send cases as preoffense juveniles. Thus, the total number of preoffense juveniles disposed of at the Family Court declined drastically to 359 in 2011 (National Public Safety Commission and National Police Agency 2012).

Cases of law breaking by children under 14 years of age are reported to the Child Consultation Center. If the caseworker in the center determines that there is a need to impose protective educative measures under the Juvenile Law, the prefectural governor or the chief of the center may refer the child to the Family Court. In 2011, there were only 416 such referrals, of which 58 were sent compulsorily as serious cases.

The police must refer all cases of juvenile offending directly, or via public prosecutors, to the Family Court. Only a small number of cases of offenses, for which the law does not prescribe severe punishment such as imprisonment or the death penalty, are directly referred to the Family Court. The public prosecutors do not have any discretionary power to screen cases. Therefore, after an investigation, they must refer all juvenile offender cases to the Family Court. At the referral stage, they can write their opinion about disposition. However, even if they are permitted by the Family Court judge(s) to attend the hearing, they are prohibited from advocating their opinion on the disposition, because they are only expected to work as assistants to clarify the offense for the judge.

Imposition of Criminal Punishment

If Family Court judge(s) finds that a juvenile offender over 14 years of age should be punished, they can refer the offender back to the public prosecutor. In 2011, public prosecutors received 3473 juveniles for criminal indictment, of which 94.6% were for some sort of road traffic offense in order to impose a fine. Only 187 juveniles were referred back for a serious nontraffic offense such as a murder or an injury causing death.

Unlike other countries, Japan experienced a long-term trend toward making less use of punishment in juvenile criminal cases. However, this trend has reversed since 2000 when the Juvenile Law was revised for partial criminalization and the tough policy against juvenile offenders, which was instituted with the support of the general public. Nevertheless, the total number of juveniles newly committed to the prison in 2011 amounted to only 49 (Research and Training Institute of the Ministry of Justice 2012). This represents a dramatic drop from 3119 in 1951 (Research and Training Institute of the Ministry of Justice, 1989).

Owing to the low number of juveniles receiving prison terms, young adults up to the age of 26 are also being treated in a total of seven juvenile prisons throughout the country. These facilities are designed to offer many programs for vocational training and, as is the practice in many Western countries, inmates are usually granted parole before the expiration of their term of imprisonment. These practices reflect the welfare flavor evident in Japan's juvenile justice system.

Family Court Probation Officers and Tentative Probation

Since 1950, Family Courts have used probation officers who are trained in behavioral sciences (Yokoyama 2012c). Again, as in many Western countries, probation officers are responsible for processing the case, conducting background research, and providing services for protection while a juvenile delinquent is under supervision.

Before adjudication, Family Court judges can place a juvenile delinquent under **tentative probation**, which is supervised by the Family Court probation officers. In some cases, these youths are guided by volunteers or accommodated in private houses or facilities.

The total number of tentative probationary cases of some nontraffic offenses dropped from 2521 in 2000 to 1550 in 2011. One reason for this decrease is that the family court probation officers may become reluctant to work as caseworkers. The number of those who were committed to some private house or facility also decreased drastically from 338 to 127 for the corresponding period. The tentative probation by volunteers demonstrates the participatory character of our juvenile justice system. However, this system is declining as our society changes (Yokoyama 2000b). Previously, many owners of small-sized stores or factories took care of juvenile tentative probationers. Nowadays such persons have all but disappeared owing to changes in the nation's industrial structure.

After completing their tentative probation, the juveniles must appear before the Family Court for their hearing. Previously, the Family Court judges sentenced them to dismissal to avoid a double penalty (Yokoyama 1984). In 1998, the Family Courts heard 9212 juvenile tentative probationers committing some nontraffic offenses, of which nearly 80% were dismissed upon adjudication. On the other hand, of all 1550 tentative probationers in 2011, only 18.3% were dismissed before or after the adjudication, while 67.9% were placed on probation. Nowadays, the supervision system for juvenile delinquents is strengthened under the tough policy.

Juvenile Detention and Classification Homes

If crisis intervention is deemed necessary, then the Family Court judge can decide to place the juvenile in a Juvenile Detention and Classification Home. In 2011, there were 52 Juvenile Detention and Classification Homes. As the police arrested juvenile offenders more frequently in the late 1990s, the total number of juveniles newly admitted to the Juvenile Detention and Classification Homes rose to 23,063 in 2003, although more than 30,000 juveniles were accommodated at the second peak of juvenile delinquency around 1965. As juveniles become more and more conformist, they seem to commit serious offenses infrequently. Therefore, in spite of maintenance of the tough policy by the police, the total number of juveniles admitted to Juvenile Detention and Classification Homes decreased steadily to 13,189 in 2011.

In the Juvenile Detention and Classification Homes, specialists in behavioral sciences carry out many kinds of tests on inmates while observing their behavior. The test and the observation are usually completed within 4 weeks, although maximum term of custody expanded to 8 weeks under the revised Juvenile Law of 2000. In order to guarantee juveniles' their rights, the new Law on Juvenile Detention and Classification Center was enacted in June in 2014.

Adjudication by Family Court Judges

All judges in lower-class courts are professionals, although the lay judge system was introduced for judgment in serious criminal cases in 2009. Judges are appointed by the Cabinet, which follows the recommendation of the Supreme Court. Therefore, the Family Court judges are independent of any public image. However, they are not specialist judges in juvenile cases, because they are assigned to a Family Court in a rotational manner.

Previously, the Family Court judges endeavored to decide the disposition in the best interests of juvenile delinquents in consideration of the reports written by the Family Court probation officer and a specialist at a Juvenile Detention and Classification Home. However, after the murder case in Kobe (discussed earlier), many people began to question whether the rights of crime victims were neglected in the juvenile justice system, while rights of juvenile offenders were respected too much. In the light of this public pressure, it became difficult for both judges and probation officers to render decisions on the disposition without considering the impact of public opinion.

For nonserious cases, the Family Court judge can decide for dismissal without hearing from a juvenile delinquent after the initial screening by the probation officer. In other cases, the judge(s) may hear from the delinquent. Before appearing in court, the Family Court judge(s) reads not only the evidence and materials sent by the police and the public prosecutor but also reports from the Family Court probation officer and a chief of the Juvenile Detention and Classification Home. After considering all the evidence, materials, and reports, the judge(s) is obliged to hear from a juvenile delinquent and his/her parent(s) in a kind and friendly atmosphere under Paragraph 1 of Article 22. By the revision of the law in 2000, the phrase of "making a juvenile delinquents' reflect himself/herself about his/her behavior" was inserted into the paragraph. This now prompts both the Family Court judge(s) and the probation officer to inquire about the cause(s) of the delinquency before imposing any disposition. Recently, the Family Court probation officers have been compelled to work as loyal servants to the judges that are familiar with the crime control model (Yokoyama 2012a).

Based on the total number of final dispositions of juvenile nontraffic offenders, the percentage of dismissals without hearing amounted to 55.7% in 1965. This figure rose to 68.7% in 2011 (Research and Training Institute of the Ministry of Justice 2012). The increase seemed to reflect the fact that juveniles having committed minor offenses such as riding a deserted bicycle and an offense of the Minor Offenses Law were more frequently caught by the net widening of the police activities. The rate of dismissal without hearing in a case of the former and the latter is 74.1% and 71.1% respectively.

Under the Constitution, Japanese offenders are guaranteed the right to a public trial. However, in juvenile cases, the hearing is carried out in a closed court to prevent stigmatizing juveniles, although the crime victims and their relatives are permitted to listen to hearing at a court under the revised Juvenile Law of 2008. In this case, juveniles and their parent(s) or guardian can employ a legal counselor as an attendant at the hearing.

Since the 1980s, lawyers have participated in several cases to defend juveniles against a false charge. To obtain a confession, the police interrogators are apt to torture a suspect psychologically for long hours while confining him/her in a cell at a police station. The lawyers insist on the necessity of defending juveniles from false charges resulting from such interrogation, and campaign for the necessity of the legal counselor as an attendant. Under the revised Juvenile Law of 2000, the legal counselor as an attendant is obliged to appear at the adjudication of the Family Court, paid for by the state under the national budget, in a case where a public prosecutor is permitted to appear.

After the hearing, the Family Court judge(s) decides whether to impose protective educative measures or not. Many juveniles are dismissed after receiving a warning and advice at the hearing. The percentage of juveniles receiving a dismissal after a hearing was 11.8% in 2011. Only a few are released because of their innocence. However, under the principle of *parens patriae*, "the dismissal because of no fact related to any delinquency" is pronounced in the place of an "innocence" sentence.

If the Family Court judge(s) admits the necessity of protecting a juvenile delinquent, the judge imposes protective educative measures. While the old Juvenile Law of 1922 prescribed nine protective educative measures, the current Juvenile Law (Article 24) provides (as mentioned earlier) only three protective educative measures. They include probation, commitment to juvenile training schools, and commitment to facilities for children of up to 18 year of age. In 2011, the rate of juveniles placed under probation or sent to a juvenile training school was 14.6% and 3.7%, respectively.

Facilities under the Child Welfare Law

The Family Court judge(s) can also place younger juvenile delinquents in a Home for Dependent Children or a Home to Support Children's Independence. The delinquent children placed in such facilities are few in number. In 2011, the total number of those sent to such a facility amounted to 270. Almost all of these children were treated in 1 of 58 Homes to Support Children's Independency around the country, of which 2 are managed by the national government, 54 by local governments, and 2 by a private foundation. Usually the most serious cases of law-breaking children are treated in the two national Homes to Support Children's Independence; one for boys and another for girls.

In addition to compulsory commitment by the Family Court, the majority of children are accommodated on a voluntary basis in the Homes to Support Children's Independency. After getting the consent of the child's parent(s) or guardian, the prefectural governor or a director of the Child Consultation Center entrusted by the governor follows the procedure to admit him/her at the center. Unfortunately, as local governments have been assigning ordinary officers as caseworkers at the Child Consultation Centers, their knowledge and understanding of the facilities for child welfare is limited, and they often fail to obtain the consent necessary to admit such children at the Home to Support Children's Independence (Hattori 1992). Because of this, the percentage of inmates in the homes per maximum occupancy decreased from 58.7% in 1987 to 44.5% in 1991 (Hattori 1992).

To increase the number of children treated in the *Kyogoin* Homes (see Box 8.1), the Child Welfare Law was amended in 1998 by which the *Kyogoin* Homes were renamed as Homes to Support Children's Independency. The homes can also offer treatment to children with behavioral problems. However, the homes are finding it difficult to maintain the family school system owing to changes in the social structure of Japan (Hattori 1996). For example, in accordance with the Labor Law, married couples are prohibited from working with juveniles all day long and/or all year round. In a Home to Support Children's Independence, treatment under the affectionate guidance of a married couple gradually declined, although the two national homes maintain the family school system. Even after the revision of Child Welfare Law in 1998, the percentage of the total number of inmates in the homes per maximum occupancy remained low, for example, 38.5% in 2011. On the other hand, the Child Protective Home gives full accommodation to abused children as more and more abused children are given protection under the provisions of the Law to Prevent Child Abuse in 2000 (Yokoyama 2006).

Juvenile Training Schools

Until the early 1960s, juvenile training schools were overcrowded (Yokoyama 2000c). This problem contributed to the difficulty of the schools being able to offer educative treatment programs. Subsequently, judges and the Family Court probation officers distrusted the treatment offered in these schools and referred fewer cases. In addition, serious offenses by juveniles decreased after the second peak of juvenile delinquency. Therefore, the total number of juveniles newly admitted to juvenile training schools declined steadily from 8065 in 1966 to 1969 in 1974 (Research and Training Institute of the Ministry of Justice 1999).

In response to the declining juvenile inmate rate, the Ministry of Justice began to reform the system of juvenile training schools (Yokoyama 1992a). In 1977, the ministry introduced a system of short-term schools for juveniles with less advanced criminal tendencies and for serious juvenile traffic offenders. In response to the reform by the ministry, the Family Court judge began to place juveniles in the short-term schools. Therefore, the total number of juveniles sent to juvenile training schools increased to 4758 in 1983. However, after the third peak of juvenile delinquency, the numbers began to decline once again. Subsequently, to accommodate more juvenile delinquents, short-term schools with special training courses were introduced in 1991 in place of the short-term schools for juvenile traffic offenders.

Previously, juveniles admitted to the long-term juvenile training schools were treated within 2 years. However, as noted earlier, after the murder case in Kobe, the use of short-term confinement was heavily criticized. The Family Court judge(s) began to recommend correctional treatment of over a 2-year duration in the case of a juvenile having committed a heinous offense. In response to this recommendation, in 1997, the Ministry of Justice established a new special course of treatment lasting over 2 years. However, most of the inmates in the long-term schools continue to receive educative treatment for about 1 year while inmates in the general short-term schools and those in the schools with the special training courses are released after receiving treatment within 6 and 4 months, respectively.

Since the late 1990s, juvenile training schools have widened their net over juveniles who have committed less serious offenses (Yokoyama 2001). We saw a peak of inmates in 2000, when the total number of inmates amounted to 6052 (Research and Training Institute of the Ministry of Justice 2001). Of all inmates, 61.6%, 34.6%, and 3.8% were treated in the long-term schools, the general short-term schools, and the short-term schools with the special training course, respectively. Around 2000, we witnessed overcrowding in the schools.

Since 2000, more and more juveniles have become conformist, by which their delinquency, especially serious offenses, seems to have decreased. Therefore, in spite of the maintenance of the tough policy, the total number of inmates in juvenile training schools decreased to 3486 in 2011 (Research and Training Institute of the Ministry of Justice 2012).

Today, the schools continue to offer a variety of programs including academic education, vocational training, and guidance on living skills under the welfare model. The national government plans to revise the Law on Juvenile Training Schools. Japan anticipates that under the law revised in June in 2014, the programs will evolve under the Welfare Model and the rehabilitation model while also guaranteeing the rights of inmates.

Probation and Parole

One of the protective educative measures under the Juvenile Law is probation. Juvenile probationers can be placed on probation in principle until they reach 20 years of age. Between 1965 and 1983, the disposition of probation decreased. One of the reasons for this decrease might be the net widening of juvenile training schools since 1977. However, we also saw net widening in the area of probation. For example, in 1994, the Ministry of Justice adopted a new system of short-term probation for 6 or 7 months to accept more juvenile probationers.

Professional probation–parole officers are expected to work as specialists in social work activities for juvenile probationers and parolees. However, most of them work only as distributors of cases and supervisors for the volunteer probation–parole officers (*Hogoshis*). In addition to the professional officers, the Minister of Justice commissions a leader in the community to work as a *Hogoshi*. This is another example of the participatory nature of our juvenile justice system. *Hogoshis* guide, supervise, and assist almost all probationers and parolees through their experiences, that is, juvenile probationers sent from the Family Court and juvenile parolees released temporarily from a juvenile training school. They may utilize resources in the community more effectively than the professional officers who are typically transferred to another office every 2 or 3 years.

At its peak, there were a total of 52,500 *Hogoshi*s. However, in recent years it has become increasingly difficult to recruit a new *Hogoshi*, especially in urban areas. At the end of 2012, the total number of *Hogoshi*s remained at 47,975 (*Asahi Shimbun* on January 7, 2013). Today the average age of *Hogoshi*s has risen from 53.2 in 1953 to 63.0 in 2005 (Research and Training Institute of the Ministry of Justice, 2005). As a consequence, we may see a wider generation gap between *Hogoshi*s and juvenile delinquents. Recently, more females have become *Hogoshi*s. It is expected that they will have a positive influence on juveniles.

Conclusion

After the Meiji Restoration in 1868, Japan developed a juvenile justice system that was modeled after the system used in many Western countries. The objective of the newly adopted juvenile justice system was to provide juvenile delinquents with educative protective treatment to rehabilitate them. In keeping with Japanese tradition and culture, volunteers played an important role. Since the Meiji Period, we have seen the participatory nature of our juvenile justice system, although in recent years, the involvement of volunteers has been declining. In 1922, the Juvenile Law was enacted. However, owing to an insufficient budget, the juvenile justice system under this law was not covered completely throughout Japan until 1942.

After World War II, the Japanese justice system was democratized. A new Juvenile Law under the complete *welfare model* was promulgated in 1948. But, owing to limited resources and the country struggling to recover from the aftermath of the war, juvenile justice agencies had a difficult time coping with the urgent necessity of protecting many poverty-stricken juvenile delinquents. However, due to the economic recovery in the early 1950s, Japan gradually began to direct more resources toward supporting the juvenile justice system.

Then, coinciding with the growth of baby boomers after WW II, Japan experienced the second peak of juvenile delinquency in 1964. The country directed attention to an increase in violent crimes among juvenile delinquents, and increased resources were assigned to delinquency prevention activities. The police were very active with their initiatives.

By the late 1970s, the police were well equipped to guide and investigate virtually any type of delinquent behavior. As a result of the net widening of the police activities, we saw the third peak of juvenile delinquency in 1983. Then during the early 1990s, juvenile offenses decreased. This may have been partially due to the fact that young people came to be excessively protected, guided, and supervised by the surrounding adults in the aging society. During this period, heinous and violent crimes committed by juveniles decreased. However, in the late 1990s, we again witnessed an increase in official delinquency rates. This phenomenon could have been caused by the fact that the police were strengthened to widen their net against juveniles in the moral panic evident among the public, who supported the movement of crime victims.

Since the 1980s, lawyers directed increasing attention to defects in the current juvenile justice system. Their criticisms focused on the difficulty of guaranteeing due process. However, their challenges fell short of advocating the **just deserts model** as they respected the welfare model. On the other hand, after the Kobe case in 1997, Japan experienced a degree of "moral panic" about heinous juvenile crimes, especially incidents when a child was murdered. Crime victims began to insist on the guarantee of their rights in the juvenile justice system. Therefore, in 2000, conservative politicians succeeded in revising the Juvenile Law and holding juvenile offenders more accountable for their behavior. Nonetheless, in principle, the welfare/participatory model has remained, although the crime control model has been gradually adopted at the Family Court level for the adjudication of juvenile delinquent cases.

In many respects, Japan's juvenile justice practices complement the recommendations put forth in the Beijing Rules (see Box 1.1—Introduction). However, we must continue to examine the prescriptions of our juvenile law and the practice of our juvenile justice agencies in consideration of the recommendations cited in the Beijing Rules and those declared at the Ninth United Nations Congress on Prevention and Treatment. In Japan, we expect that the rights of a juvenile delinquent will be more likely be guaranteed under the new Law on Juvenile Detention and Classification Centers and the revised Law on Juvenile Training Schools enacted in June in 2014.

It is anticipated that the population of juveniles will decrease as the nation's birth rate continues to decline. Also, if the current social structures in Japan do not change drastically, then this will also in all probability contribute to a declining number of juvenile delinquents in Japan. However, if the juvenile justice agencies do not adapt to such a situation, they will not be able to maintain their current resources because the Ministry of Finance will be tempted to curtail their budgets. To prevent the process toward reduction, the juvenile justice agencies are likely to carry out additional net-widening strategies.

Net-widening ventures have produced both advantages and disadvantages for Japan. These ventures have likely contributed to the reduction in juvenile delinquency. Early intervention by the police has helped to prevent many juvenile delinquents from developing criminal tendencies. The net widening of probation and the treatment in juvenile training schools has given these young people the opportunity to receive the protective educative services that are deemed in their best interests.

Finally, as the relative proportion of young people in Japan continues to decline, we will likely see juveniles being excessively protected, guided, and supervised by adults. Previously, the author foresaw that according to Merton's (1968) typology of the modes of individual adaptation, juveniles of the retreatism type might increase (Yokoyama 2002). However, that prediction seems to be wrong, because, for example, the number of juveniles caught for some offense under the drug control laws has decreased drastically. In Japan, juveniles of overconformity and those of ritualism are prevalent. When such juveniles become adults, Japan may become a stagnant society. From this viewpoint, too, we must examine functions of the juvenile justice system in Japan.

Review/Discussion Questions

1. How have the trends and patterns of delinquency changed in Japan since World War II? What appear to have been the major contributing factors?
2. What do you consider to be the strengths and weaknesses of the Family Court within the Japanese juvenile justice system? How does it compare to other countries?
3. Japan can be characterized as trying to balance several different juvenile justice models. What are they and which model is more dominant? What are your impressions of how Japan formally deals with its juvenile delinquents?
4. Net-widening initiatives have been used extensively by the police in recent decades and have allegedly contributed to a decrease in delinquency. Do you think this is an effective approach? How does it compare to other countries?
5. Referring to other countries, how practical are the revisions to the Juvenile Law in 2000?

References

Ayukawa, J. (1994). *Sociology of Juvenile Delinquency* (written in Japanese). Kyoto: Sekai shiso-sha.

Bayley, D. (1976). *Forces of Order: Behavior in Japan and the United States.* Berkeley, CA: University of California Press.

Cabinet Office. (1999). White paper on juveniles in 1999 (written in Japanese). Tokyo: Printing Bureau of the Ministry of Finance.

Cabinet Office. (2011). White paper on children and youngsters in 2011 (written in Japanese). Tokyo: Saeki-insatsu.

Cabinet Office. (2012). White paper on children and youngsters in 2012 (written in Japanese). Tokyo: Shobi-insatsu.

Correctional Association. (1984). *Modern Development of Juvenile Correction* (written in Japanese). Tokyo: Correctional Association.

Fukuda, M. (1988). *A critical analysis of juvenile justice system in Japan.* Paper presented at the 40th Annual Meeting of American Society of Criminology. Chicago.

Harada, Y. (1995). Adjustment to school, life course transitions, and changing in delinquent behavior in Japan. *Current Perspectives on Aging and the Life Cycle*, 4:35–60.

Hattori, A. (1992). Future of the child education and training homes (written in Japanese). *Juvenile Problems* (Japan), 198:31–44.

Hattori, A. (1996). Kyogoin home in Japan. In C. B. Fields and R. H. Moore, Jr. (Eds.), *Comparative Criminal Justice*. Prospect Height, IL: Waveland Press: 573–582.

Kanagawa Prefectural Government. (2012). The instructor of juveniles (written in Japanese). http://www.pref.kanagawa.jp/cnt/f4151/p12564.html.

Kiyonaga, K. (1983). Younger juvenile delinquents—Prediction from 1983 (written in Japanese). *Crime and Delinquency* (Japan), 56:104–129.

Merton, R. (1968). *Social Theory and Social Structure* (Enlarged edition). New York: The Free Press.

Ministry of Health, Labor and Welfare. (2013). About facilities for social protection (written in Japanese). http://www.mhlw.go.jp/bunya/kodomo/syakaiteki_yougo/01.html.

National Police Agency. (1970). White paper on police in 1970 (written in Japanese). Tokyo: Printing Bureau of the Ministry of Finance.

National Police Agency. (1973). White paper on police in 1973 (written in Japanese). Tokyo: Printing Bureau of the Ministry of Finance.

National Police Agency. (1976). White paper on police in 1976 (written in Japanese). Tokyo: Printing Bureau of the Ministry of Finance.

National Police Agency. (1982). White paper on police in 1982 (written in Japanese). Tokyo: Printing Bureau of the Ministry of Finance.

National Police Agency. (1983). White paper on police in 1983 (written in Japanese). Tokyo: Printing Bureau of the Ministry of Finance.

National Police Agency. (1984). White paper on police in 1984 (written in Japanese). Tokyo: Printing Bureau of the Ministry of Finance.

National Police Agency. (1997). White paper on police in 1997 (written in Japanese). Tokyo: Printing Bureau of the Ministry of Finance.

National Police Agency. (1999). White paper on police in 1999 (written in Japanese). Tokyo: Printing Bureau of the Ministry of Finance.

National Police Agency. (2011). White paper on police in 2011 (written in Japanese). Tokyo: Saeki Insatsu.

National Police Agency. (2012). Crimes in 2011 (written in Japanese). http://www.npa.go.jp/archive/toukei/keiki/h23/h23hanzaitoukei.htm.

National Public Safety Commission and National Police Agency. (2012). White paper on police in 2012 (written in Japanese). Tokyo: Gyosei.

Research and Training Institute of the Ministry of Justice. (1975). White paper on crime in 1975 (written in Japanese). Tokyo: Printing Bureau of the Ministry of Finance.

Research and Training Institute of the Ministry of Justice. (1984). White paper on crime in 1984 (written in Japanese). Tokyo: Printing Bureau of the Ministry of Finance.

Research and Training Institute of the Ministry of Justice. (1989). White paper on crime in 1989 (written in Japanese). Tokyo: Printing Bureau of the Ministry of Finance.

Research and Training Institute of the Ministry of Justice. (1999). White paper on crime in 1999 (written in Japanese). Tokyo: Printing Bureau of the Ministry of Finance.

Research and Training Institute of the Ministry of Justice. (2001). White paper on crime in 2001 (written in Japanese). Tokyo: Printing Bureau of the Ministry of Finance.

Research and Training Institute of the Ministry of Justice. (2005). White paper on crime in 2005 (written in Japanese). Tokyo: Printing Bureau of the Ministry of Finance.

Research and Training Institute of the Ministry of Justice. (2012). White paper on crime in 2012 (written in Japanese). Tokyo: Nikkei Printing.

Riesman, D., Glazer, N., and Denney, R. (1950). *The Lonely Crowd.* New Haven, CT: Yale University Press.

Saito, T. (1986). The Japanese Juvenile Law and amendment issues. *Konan Hogaku* (Japan), 26(2/3):267–285.

Sawanobori, T. (1994). *Introduction to Juvenile Law* (written in Japanese). Tokyo: Yuhikaku.

Spergel, I.A., Lynch, J.P., Reamer, F.G., and Korbelik, J. (1982). Response of Organization and Community to a Deinstitutionalization Strategy. *Crime and Delinquency*, 28(3):426–449.

Supreme Court. (1999). Annual report of judicial statistics for 1998 (written in Japanese). Tokyo: Hoso-kai.

Supreme Court. (2012). Annual report of judicial statistics for 2011 (written in Japanese). http://www.courts.go.jp/sihotokei/nenpo/pdf/B23DSYO03~04.pdf.

Terao, F. (1999). Why do juveniles commit delinquency? (written in Japanese). In N. Araki (Ed.), *Modern Juveniles and Juvenile Law* (Japan). Tokyo: Akashi-shoten: 202–231.

Tokuoka, H. and Cohen, A.K. (1987). Japanese society and delinquency. *International Journal of Comparative and Applied Criminal Justice*, 11(1/2):13–22.

Yokoyama, M. (1981). Delinquency control programs in the community in Japan. *International Journal of Comparative and Applied Criminal Justice*, 5(2):169–178.

Yokoyama, M. (1982). *How have prisons been used in Japan?* Paper presented at the World Congress of the International Sociological Association. Mexico City, Mexico.

Yokoyama, M. (1984). *Why doesn't Japan have diversion programs for juvenile delinquents?* Paper presented at the World Congress of the International Institute of Sociology. Seattle, Washington, U.S.A.

Yokoyama, M. (1985). Criminal policy against thieves in Japan. *Kangwon Law Review* (Korea), 1:191–217.

Yokoyama, M. (1986a). The juvenile justice system in Japan. In M. Bursten, J. Graham, N. Herriger, and P. Malinowski (Eds.), *Youth Crime, Social Control and Prevention*. Wuppertal: Centaurus-Verlagsgesellschaft-Pfaffenweiler: 102–113.

Yokoyama, M. (1986b). Social control and juvenile traffic offenders in Japan. *Kangwon Law Review* (Korea), 2:142–160.

Yokoyama, M. (1989). Net-widening of the juvenile justice system in Japan. *Criminal Justice Review*, 14(1):43–53.

Yokoyama, M. (1990a). Criminalization against traffic offenders in Japan. *International Journal of Comparative and Applied Criminal Justice*, 14(1/2):65–71.

Yokoyama, M. (1990b). Criminalization against traffic offenders in Japanese criminal justice. *Kokugakuin Journal of Law and Politics* (Japan), 27(4):1–27.

Yokoyama, M. (1991). Development of Japanese drug control laws towards criminalization. *Kokugakuin Journal of Law and Politics* (Japan), 28(3):1–21.

Yokoyama, M. (1992a). Guarantee of human rights in juvenile justice system in Japan. *Kokugakuin Journal of Law and Politics* (Japan), 30(2):1–30.

Yokoyama, M. (1992b). Net-widening in juvenile justice system (written in Japanese). In the Committee for Celebrating the 70th Birthday of Professor Kuniyuki Yagi (Ed.), *Modern Development of Criminal Jurisprudence II*. Tokyo: Hogakushoin: 481–512.

Yokoyama, M. (1994). Treatment of prisoners under rehabilitation model in Japan. *Kokugakuin Journal of Law and Politics* (Japan), 32(2):1–24.

Yokoyama, M. (1995). Analysis of prostitution in Japan. *International Journal of Comparative and Applied Criminal Justice*, 19(1/2):47–60.

Yokoyama, M. (1999). Trends of organized crime by Boryokudan in Japan. In S. Einstein and M. Amir (Eds.), *Organized Crime: Uncertainties and Dilemmas*. Chicago: The Office of International Criminal Justice, the University of Illinois at Chicago: 135–154.

Yokoyama, M. (2000a). Activities for prevention of juvenile delinquency in the community in Japan. In T. Istvan (Ed.), *Tanulmanyok Vigh Jozsef 70. Szuletesnapjara*. Budapest: TLTE Allam-es Jogtudomanyi Kar: 292–307.

Yokoyama, M. (2000b). Volunteers' activities for treatment of juvenile delinquents in Japan. In the Committee for Memorizing the Retirement of Professor Han-Kyo, Lee (Ed.), *Issues and Views of Criminal Laws in Korea and in Japan*. Seoul: Whasungsa: 681–697.

Yokoyama, M. (2000c). Formation of juvenile training schools (written in Japanese). In the Committee for Celebrating the 70th Birthday of Professor Toshio Sawanobori (Ed.), *Views on Juvenile Law*. Tokyo: Gendaijinbunsha: 291–309.

Yokoyama, M. (2000d). Development of educative treatment in juvenile training schools in Japan. *Caribbean Journal of Criminology and Social Psychology*, 5(1/2):237–259.

Yokoyama, M. (2001).Tendency of juvenile delinquency in Japan and criminalization (written in Japanese). *Kokugakuin Journal of Law and Politics* (Japan), 38(4):171–205.

Yokoyama, M. (2002). Juvenile Justice and Juvenile Crime: An Overview of Japan. In W. John (Ed.), *Juvenile Justice Systems—International Perspectives* (Second edition). Toronto: Canadian Scholars' Press, Inc.: 321–352.

Yokoyama, M. (2003). Revision of the Juvenile Law toward Partial Criminalization in Japan. In A. Manganas (Ed.), *Essays in Honour of Alice Yotopoulos-Marangopoulos: Human Rights, Crime-Criminal Policy: Volume B*. Athens: Bruylant: 1545–1562.

Yokoyama, M. (2006). Early support, protection and intervention for children in Japan. *Kokugakuin Journal of Law and Politics*, 44(1):1–29.

Yokoyama, M. (2009). How has the revised juvenile law functioned since 2001 in Japan? In E. W. Plywaczewski (Ed.), *Current Problems of the Penal Law and the Criminology No.4*. Bialystok: Temida 2: 667–702.

Yokoyama, M. (2010a). Change in ideas on treatment of juvenile delinquents—Shift of the idea of protectionism related to the maximum age for application of juvenile law (written in Japanese). In T. Sawanobori and H. Takauchi (Eds.), *Ideas of the Juvenile Law*. Tokyo: Gendai Jinbun-sha: 115–139.

Yokoyama, M. (2010b). Development of guidance activities by police for prevention of juvenile delinquency in Japan. In R. Cliff, D. K. Das, and J. K. Singer (Eds.), *Police Without Borders—The Fading Distinction Between Local and Global*. Boca Raton, FL: CRC Press: 151–175.

Yokoyama, M. (2012a). Tendency of adjudication in juvenile case toward criminal trial (written in Japanese). In the Study Group on Juvenile Law (Ed.), *Progressive Activities of the Study Group on Juvenile Law for 30 Years*. Tokyo: Tokyo Colony: 74–78.

Yokoyama, M. (2012b). Police and juveniles in Japan. In P. C. Kratcoski (Ed.), *Juvenile Justice Administration*. Boca Raton, London, New York: CRC Press: 181–196.

Yokoyama, M. (2012c). Administration of Japanese juvenile justice. In P. C. Kratcoski (Ed.), *Juvenile Justice Administration*. Boca Raton, London, New York: CRC Press: 349–368.

Internet Sources

There are very few links in English that specifically address juvenile justice in Japan.
The Japan Times newspaper published in English (www.japantimes.cp.jp/).
The Japanese Ministry of Justice (http://www.moj.go.jp/ENGLISH/index.html).
The National Police Agency provides some data on juvenile crime data in English (www.npa.gp.jp/).

Child Justice in Namibia: Back to Square One?

9

STEFAN SCHULZ

Contents

A Brief Historical Overview of the Namibian (Juvenile) Justice System 210
Namibian Juvenile Delinquency Figures 212
    Children in Namibia 213
    Child Crime and Its Characteristics 213
    Diversity of Child Delinquency 214
    Age–Crime Distribution: Bimodal 215
Explaining Child Crime in Namibia 217
    Criminal Justice Research 217
    Primary Theories of (Child) Crime Causation in Namibia 218
    Between Tradition and Modernity: Social and Normative Aspects of Child
        Delinquency 219
Children in Namibia in Conflict with the Law: The Situation on the Ground 221
    Juvenile Courts 221
        Arrest (Police) and Detention 222
        Diversion 223
        Trial and Sentencing 224
        Institutionalization (Imprisonment) 227
Measuring Namibian Juvenile Justice against International Standards 227
Current Challenges Facing Namibian Youths Today 230
Looking Ahead: Moving from the Child Justice Bill to the Child Justice Act 232
Conclusion 233
Review/Discussion Questions 234
References 235
Internet Sources 236

Real generosity toward the future lies in giving it to the present.

Albert Camus

FACTS ABOUT NAMIBIA

Area: Namibia is a vast country of 823,145 km^2. It is the twelfth largest country in sub-Saharan Africa, lying on the southwest coast of the African continent between latitudes 17.5ºS and 28.5ºS and between longitudes 12ºE and 20ºE. It shares its main borders with Angola, Botswana, and South Africa. In the far northeast is the Caprivi Strip, now called Zambezi Region, an elongated panhandle consisting of tropical riverine swamplands and bordered by four countries—Angola, Botswana, Zambia, and Zimbabwe. **Population:** According to the last official census (Namibia Statistics Agency 2013), Namibia had a population of about 2.1 million with an annual growth rate (2001–2011) of about 1.4%. Namibia has a median age of 21 years, and is therefore rather "young." The average population density of the territory is only 2.6 persons per km^2 compared with 35.5 per km^2 for Africa and 47 per km^2 for the world. Although Namibia is one of the most sparsely populated regions of the world, it has a rich variety of cultures, languages, and races. While English is the official language, many languages are spoken in the country. They can be divided into three categories: the Bantu languages, spoken by the Owambos, Hereros, Kavangos, Caprivians, and Twanas; the Khoi-san languages spoken by the San and Nama/Damara; and the Indo-Germanic languages of the Afrikaans, English, and Germans. The Owambos are the biggest ethnic group, representing about 50% of Namibia's population. Windhoek is the nation's capital. Other major municipalities include Ondangwa, Oshakati, Walvisbay, Lueberitz, KatimaMulilo, Keetmanshoop, and Oranjemund. **Climate:** Namibia has a dry climate typical of a semidesert country where droughts are a regular occurrence. Days are mostly warm to very hot, while nights are generally cool. Average day temperatures in the summer vary from 20°C to 34°C and average night temperatures in the winter from 0°C to 10°C. Temperatures in the interior are lower because of the altitude, while along the coast, the cold Benguela Current has a modifying influence. Average rainfall figures vary from less than 50 mm along the coast to 350 mm in the central and 700 mm in the far northeastern regions. However, because of the high variability of rainfall, especially in the arid regions, the "annual" rainfall does not necessarily give a true picture. **Economy:** The Namibian economy continues to show the features of a dualistic production structure, that is, its main streams "comprise traditional subsistence and high-technology industry" (Kaapama et al. 2007, 1). The national economy as a whole grew annually by 4.1% between 1995 and 2007 (Sherbourne 2010, 79). The pillars of Namibia's economy are mining, fishing, tourism, and agriculture. The largest single contributor to Namibia's gross domestic product (GDP) is the government, and the largest provider of employment is agriculture. **Government:** Namibia is a unitary state, which is divided into 13 administrative regions. Namibia is ruled by a multiparty parliament and has a democratic constitution, buttressed by extensive human rights guaranties. The constitution provides for the division of power among the executive, the legislature, and the judiciary.

A Brief Historical Overview of the Namibian (Juvenile) Justice System

Prior to independence from South Africa, human rights and, with it, children's rights were not high on the agenda of the then political dispensation, the apartheid regime. But this changed fundamentally with independence in March 1990, when Namibia gave itself a democratic constitution with extended human rights guaranties. Namibia's relation with the United Nations Convention on the Rights of the Child (UNCRC) got a boost when in September 1990, the Founding President of Namibia, Sam Nujoma, led the country's delegation to the World Summit for Children, held in New York. Namibia signed and ratified the convention on September 26 and 30, 1990. Following the World Summit, an Inter-Ministerial Policy Committee was established, tasked to draft a National Programme of Action for the Children of Namibia (NPA), and "to consider steps to implement the Convention on the Rights of the Child" (Government of Namibia 2000, 26). Namibia submitted its first report to the UNCRC in 1992. Considering Namibia's country report submitted in terms of Article 44 of the CRC, the committee expressed concern as to the conformity of Namibia's justice system with, *inter alia*, the CRC, namely, its Articles 37 and 40 (see the Introduction to this book for further details regarding the articles). The committee's concerns were vindicated a short while after, when the report *A Study of Young Offenders in Namibia* (Namibian Prison Service, Legal Assistance Centre, Ministry of Youth and Sport, UNICEF 1994), based on a prison survey among young offenders carried out in January 1994, brought forth a number of inconsistencies with the CRC. The majority of young offenders had *inter alia*: (a) been sentenced to a term of imprisonment without access to a lawyer, (b) appeared in court without the presence of their parents or guardians, and (c) been subjected to pretrial detention with the average period being 3 months, to mention a few items from a longer list of observations.

In the wake of a national workshop on law reform regarding children, in July 1994, the Legal Assistance Centre (LAC), a Namibian public interest law center, was mandated to start a diversion program. This diversion program, covering only minor crimes ("petty crimes"), got under way with the permission of the prosecutor general to be conducted initially at the capital Windhoek's Magistrate's Court. The prosecutor's authority to allow diversion to take place was derived from Section 6 of the Criminal Procedure Act (CPA) (51 of 1977), a clause, which allows the prosecutor general to stop the prosecution and to withdraw criminal cases. The diversion program was soon rolled out countrywide.

In the 2000 National Report on Follow-up to the World Summit for Children, Namibia reported on the establishment of a National Inter-Ministerial Committee on Child Justice (IMC), asserting that an increasing number of juvenile offenders were being treated "according to international instruments and guidelines," and that a legal framework for the protection of children's rights was being developed. Furthermore, it was reported that a Draft Child Care and Protection Act and Draft Children Status Bill incorporating the UNCRC were at advanced stages of completion. In fact, the IMC, a multiagency task force established to oversee the establishment of structures and processes for dealing with children alleged as, accused of, or recognized as having infringed the criminal law (compare CRC Article 40 (3) and (4)) aimed at the transformation of the criminal justice system toward compliance with the CRC. A detailed plan of action for a comprehensive project was crafted and set in motion, and progress was made within a short period of time regarding all project interventions. There was a common understanding that the instrumental value of the envisaged system as a preventative and remedial tool, imbued with the principles of restorative justice, would depend in the first place on a well-developed service delivery system, based on a legislative act. Thus, in 2000, the IMC commissioned the drafting of the Juvenile Justice Bill. As reported in 2002 (Schulz 2002, 375ff), all systems appeared to be set to "go."

BOX 9.1 ROLE-PLAYERS IN THE NAMIBIAN JUVENILE/CRIMINAL JUSTICE SYSTEM	
Police	No discretionary power; investigation of child crime; transfer of dockets and evidence to the public prosecutor for decision whether to prosecute.
Public Prosecutor	*Dominus litis*; decision-making whether to dismiss, divert, or to prosecute criminal cases; discretionary power derived from Section 6 Criminal Procedure Act (51 of 1977) to stop prosecution or to withdraw charges.
	In practice, although no formal legislative framework exists, a decision to divert or withdraw considers the recommendation of the social worker after "screening" the child.
Juvenile Courts	No separate court for children in conflict with the law; adult courts double up as juvenile courts.
Youth Prison	No formal legislative framework for juvenile prisons exists. Prisons Act 17 of 1998 stipulates that children have to be kept separate from adult inmates.

Winding fast-forward to the year 2013, we would expect to find a well-installed juvenile justice system, which should have grown out of the usual teething problems. The reality could not be more different: At the 61st session (September 17–October 5, 2012), the UN Committee on the Rights of the Child (2012), considering the consolidated second and third periodic reports on Namibia (CRC/C/NAM/2-3) noted: "with concern that despite discussions for over a decade, two notable laws on children's rights, the Child Care and Protection Bill and the Child Justice Bill, have not been adopted."

In retrospect, it can be said that justice for children (including child justice) was extensively deliberated with remarkable outputs from the mids-90s until about 2005/6, when it ebbed off. Since then, not much has been achieved in terms of child justice legislation, and the CPA (51 of 1977) continues to limit the role-players in their functions when it comes to dealing with children in conflict with the law (see Box 9.1). However, in 2012, the Ministry of Gender Equality and Child Welfare (MGECW) renewed efforts to garner broader government support for the adoption of new laws on the basis of the Child Care and Protection Bill and the Child Justice Bill. A study, "Rapid Analysis: Children in Namibia in Conflict with the law" (Ministry of Gender Equality and Child Welfare 2013), was commissioned by the MGECW, which gathered as much information as was readily available. A new advocacy campaign is under way with support from the United Nations International Children's Fund (UNICEF). It may seem that we came full circle, but as the following text will show, saying that we are back at square one would not be entirely true.

Namibian Juvenile Delinquency Figures

The analysis of the data on juvenile delinquency in Namibia is hindered by many problems and limitations. One of the biggest challenges is the dearth of criminal justice data. Namibia does not publish a wide range of criminal justice data, which is due to the fact that there is no national integrated data collection system. Judicial and prosecutorial data are captured following every court date on the Namibian Court Information System (NamCIS), a computer-based digital database. Currently, it is, however, not possible to extract disaggregate data from the system. Police arrest data are captured manually on Form POL 6, at the level of police stations and sent regularly, on a monthly basis, to police headquarters in the capital, Windhoek. These data are made public on the website of the Namibian police; the set of variables used here is however limited (http://www.nampol.gov.na/). Namibian Corrections (i.e., Namibian Correctional Service [NCS]) are in the process of implementing a computer-based digital Offender Management System (OMS), which shall capture, among others, data for an extended set of variables, including those of the Level of Service/Case Management Inventory (Andrews and Bonta 2010, 319). At the point of writing, the OMS is not yet fully operational. Whether and to what extent data will be published or researchers will have access to the data sets is also not known yet. Notwithstanding these limitations, some important figures can be reported.

Children in Namibia

From the Namibian Population and Housing Census 2011 (Namibia Statistical Agency 2012a), we know that by now, approximately 910,000 children live in Namibia; 336,900 are aged 7–13 years and 185,821 are between 141 and 7 years. The median age is 21 years, with a median of 18 years in rural areas and 25 in urban areas. Child poverty is rampant in Namibia, with 34% living in poverty and a further 18.3% living in extreme poverty. The total number of orphans and vulnerable children (OVCs) today exceeds 140,000 (Namibia Statistical Agency 2012a).*

Child Crime and Its Characteristics

Annually, the Namibian police arrests about 1100 children (see Figure 9.1 and Table 9.1). The majority of child arrests take place in cities and towns, such as the capital Windhoek, the coastal towns Swakopmund and Walvisbay, and the northern towns of Oshakati and Ondangwa. The absolute number of child arrests is small, and the recorded annual crime has been stable since 2008. Estimates on the "dark figures" of child offending are difficult to estimate, and little can be said about the true dimension. This can be partially attributed to the absence of self-report studies on child delinquency, but also to the paucity of data on the volume of delinquent child behavior being dealt with in informal ways of conflict

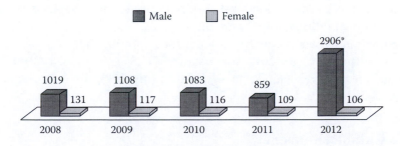

Figure 9.1 Child arrests (Namibia Police [NamPol]) 2008–2012.

* The Namibia Statistical Agency (2012b) defines the poverty incidence as the proportion of the population identified as poor: "Given a poverty line of N$377.96, the poverty incidence is the proportion of the population whose monthly consumption is less than N$377.96. Poverty Gap or the depth of poverty is the extent to which those defined as poor fall below the poverty line. The poverty gap is a measure that captures consumption shortfall relative to the poverty line across the whole population."

Table 9.1   Child Arrests (Male/Female), 2008–2012

Child Arrests	Male	Female
2008	1019	131
2009	1108	117
2010	1083	116
2011	859	109
2012	2906[a]	106

[a] Outlier due to capturing of previously accumulated unrecorded arrests.

Table 9.2   Number of Children in Correctional Detention (March, April, and May 2012)

Facilities	March 2012	April 2012	May 2012
Omaruru	5	5	6
Oluno	5	1	3
Swakopmund	1	1	2
Gobabis	25	28	28
Walvisbay	2	4	4
Hardap	10	12	13
Total	48	51	56

resolution, or absorbed by traditional courts (Hinz 2002, 198), and therefore not entering the records of the criminal justice system. Furthermore, whereas the criminal jurisdiction of the Community Courts, courts of record in terms of section 8 (1)(2)(a)(b)(c) Community Courts Act (Act 10 of 2003), comprises juvenile delinquency provided that they do not impose custodial sentences (Amoo 2008, 195), disaggregated statistics are not available.

Juvenile delinquency data are therefore direction pointers only and need to be digested with caution. We know however fairly well that children are seldom tried and sentenced, and if sentenced, very few eventually end up in prison. In the absence of disaggregated national adjudication statistics, data have been extracted for the previously mentioned MGECW-study 2012 from the court books of the Magistrate's Court, Windhoek. Throughout the entire year 2011, only six sentences against children were found, and none of the children was sentenced to unconditional imprisonment.

These numbers tally well with the national incarceration statistics of NCS. For the months of March through May 2012, for instance, NCS reported a total of 48, 51, and 56 child inmates, respectively (see Table 9.2), and in July 2013, the total number of child inmates was even below 30.

Diversity of Child Delinquency

National police arrest data suggest a diverse range of child offenses. The 2011 crime distribution shows, however, property-related crime with the highest frequency. Robbery and theft, including housebreaking with the intent of theft, and stock theft (livestock), which is important because it carries a high minimum sentence, constitute about 57% of all arrest entries, followed by assault, including assault with the intent to cause grievous bodily harm (19%) (see Table 9.3 and Figure 9.2).

Table 9.3   Child Arrest Data (NamPol), 2011

Crime	M	F
Malicious damage to property	37	12
Theft	287	44
Housebreaking + theft	162	6
Robbery	69	5
Assault, Grievous bodily harm	175	25
Murder/attempted murder	15	2
Rape	53	5
Drugs/cannabis	30	3
Fraud	2	0
Other	79	17
Total	909	119

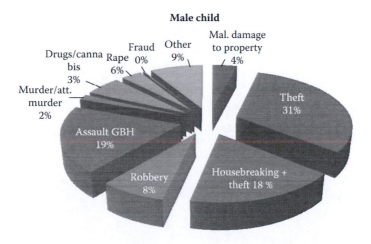

Figure 9.2 Child arrests (male/Namibia Police [NamPol]) 2011. (*Abbreviations*: Att., Attempted; Mal., Malicious.)

Age–Crime Distribution: Bimodal

Currently, there are no police data on the age–crime distribution available. To get a first picture, another manual data extraction from the court books of the Magistrate's Court, Windhoek, was undertaken in June 2013 (see Table 9.4 and Figure 9.3, respectively, Age-Crime Distribution, Windhoek 2012).

The collection of data for this analysis was triggered by the features of court data from the Magistrate's Courts of Keetmanshoop and Mariental, which had been collected for another Polytechnic of Namibia research project on the variation of the use of diversion options in Namibia (IRPC-POLY2013/8458/741). From the Mariental data on the use of

Table 9.4   Age–Crime Distribution (Windhoek Magistrate's Court, 2012)

Age/Years	Cases/Male	Cases/Female
7–13	41	2
14	14	1
15	26	3
16	92	9
17	131	7
18	158	11
19	169	9
20	187	7
21	196	11
22	**227**	19
23	204	17
24	180	12
25	198	12
26	195	23
27	**219**	14
28	203	19
29	186	15
30	159	18
31	140	19
32	139	9
33	110	14
34	107	12
35	112	8
36	108	8
37	109	10
38	82	3
39	76	7
40	36	4
41	46	4
42	53	4
43	48	5
44	39	5
45	32	6
46	36	3
47	31	4
48	26	2
49	24	4
50	20	3
51	13	1
52	13	1
53	12	0
54	11	0
55	8	0
56	9	1
57	7	1
58	6	0
59	7	0
60	3	1

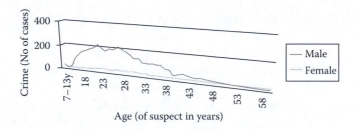

Figure 9.3 Age–crime distribution. (Windhoek Magistrate's Court, 2012.)

Table 9.5   Features of (Male) Age–Crime Distributions

Characteristics	Common Distribution	Windhoek Magistrate's Court, 2012
Mode	Unimodal: <20 years	Bimodal: 21 + 27 years
Skewness	Positively skewed: steep decline above 20 years	Positively skewed: leveling off above 27 years
Median	Approx. 20 years	26.5 years

diversion options, it appeared that the number of cases involving children was low with less than 5% of the entire 2012 case population (N = 823). More interesting perhaps is the age–crime distribution of offending youth because beyond the age of 21 years, numbers did not steeply decline but formed a plateau through age 25, peaking at age 23 (N = 45), and then only slowly declined after the age of 25 (see Table 9.5).

Comparison of the data from the districts of Mariental and Windhoek reveals some similarities in the sense that for both districts, the crime load per age group enters a plateau, which levels off only slowly beyond the age of 25. At this stage, the observation opens up more questions than it answers. We know that the median age for urban areas is 24 years, which is much higher compared with the median age of 18 years in rural areas. Comparing Mariental (rural) with Windhoek (urban) (Namibia Statistics Agency 2013), should we have expected that the age crime peak in Mariental would be lower than in Windhoek? The admittedly limited data do not support this hypothesis. Why is this so? As it stands, further investigation into the age–crime distribution in Namibia should be worthwhile.

Explaining Child Crime in Namibia

Criminal Justice Research

While many studies arising from law reform needs have been carried out, commissioned by the Namibian government, with support from international organizations (e.g., National Planning Commission 2010) and development agencies (GIZ, etc.), and there has been a host of academic perspectives (see Winterfeldt, Fox, and Mufune 2002; Ruppel 2009; Boesl, Horn, and Du Pisani 2010; Hinz 1998), genuine criminological research, including research on children and scholarly criminal justice contributions are still rare. Therefore, our government, including cabinet ministers and public servants, seem torn between policy suggestions derived from their lay perspectives on crime and child crime on the one hand and those derived from international standards for dealing with child offenders, especially the UNCRC, on the other. Recent criminal justice legislation mirrors clearly widely held preferences for retribution and deterrence, and the criminal law has indeed been given a drift toward retribution and punitiveness. While intended to maintain postindependence nominal gains in the arena of individual human rights and freedoms, the introduction—with high publicity and awareness campaigns—of stiff penalties and mandatory sentences in connection with the promulgation of legislation against sexual violence, domestic violence, and stock theft to mention a few, projected into the public mind the illusion that law enforcement could be maintained through intervention at the individual level (Ministry of Gender Equality and Child Welfare 2013).

Scientific explanations, in turn, based on Namibian data, which could guide policy-making, are not readily available. The sociology department of the traditional university, the University of Namibia (UNAM), has not grown or attracted research interested in sociology of crime or criminology. Criminal Justice research at the Polytechnic of Namibia, Namibia's university of science and technology (www.polytechnic.edu.na), has only recently taken off, and at this point in time, the existing and available data allow for no further conjectures.

Primary Theories of (Child) Crime Causation in Namibia

While our knowledge about disaggregate data remains patchy, the limited picture of our social reality makes a lot of sense against the backdrop of criminological perspectives on aggregate-level (macro-level) variations of crime rates in the tradition of Merton's explication of the anomie theory:

> [T]he theory of anomie and opportunity structure [...] holds that rates of various types of deviant behavior (not only crime) are high in a society where, as with the American dream, the culture places a high premium on economic success and upward mobility for all its members, although in brute social fact large numbers of people located in the lower reaches of the social structure have severely limited access to legitimate resources for achieving those culturally induced or reinforced goals.
>
> **Merton 1997, 519**

We recall that Merton's aim was to model how some social structures exert a definite pressure upon certain persons in the society to engage in nonconforming rather than conforming conduct. It is the underlying mechanism, which is of interest here, that is, the discrepancy between institutionalized means and cultural goals. And such a discrepancy appears to persist, if not to grow wider, in today's Namibian society (see Sherbourne 2010, 61ff; Namibia Statistical Agency 2012b). The main political goal of the liberation struggle was the self-determination of the Namibian people. However, after national independence in 1990, the establishment of a democratic society, buttressed by extensive human rights guaranties (Horn and Boesl 2008) and the enhancement of the regulatory framework for a strong market economy, added another dimension, the desire for enjoyment of the amenities of an advanced capitalist consumerist economy. It is not only the second media revolution, the Internet, which may have accelerated this process. Surely, by now via social and other media, readily available on any modern media device, like the smart phone, the tablet, and so on, the suggestion for a new social self, modeled against the requirements of a globalized economy, are transported into the most remote areas. But even earlier, the Namibian government gave the Namibian society the blueprint of a developmental vision, which wills that by 2030, the Namibian economy will be fully developed with the true *insigniae* of the knowledge economy (Government of Namibia 2004). Typical for a transitional society, the social space is impregnated with two, at least partially incompatible, value horizons, which overlap or intersect even within the same person. An indication that the above value addition has taken its grip on the Namibian society is the ever-increasing urbanization, which is fueled by a constant stream of rural–urban migration (Namibia Statistics Agency 2013, Winterfeldt 2002). At the same time however, in particular those persons who move away from the traditional lifestyle in a communal setting lack the (institutional) means to participate and to enact the aspired self with the consequence of widespread social exclusion (Mufune 2002, 179ff). The answer to the questions, whether: (a) a significant number of offenders originate from this population and (b) their involvement in criminal activities is induced by the desire to live and share the newly specified cultural goal is out there.

Regarding the category of children in conflict with the law, it seems that again conjectures inform explanation. A forthcoming issue paper, recently commissioned by UNICEF (Windhoek) in July 2013 with the intent to rekindle advocacy for Namibian child justice legislation, which would meet the standards of the CRC, puts forth two explanatory suggestions, one macro-level theory and one individual-level theory. First, it is suggested that "social disorganization in conjunction with poverty" may account for our aggregate figures of children involved in crime. Although the background assumptions have not yet been researched for Namibia, the data set of a recent replication of the 1994 Study of Young Offenders in Namibia (LAC, NPS, UNICEF 1994) by Schulz in July 2013 revealed some critical information regarding the socioeconomic environment from which the offenses of the respondent children occurred: It appeared that 50% of child inmates either never went to school or left primary school early, and an equal percentage of those children were not raised by their own parents but grew up in kinship care. At least half of the child respondents seem to have grown up living in poverty. Approximately 60% of the offenses committed by child inmates were property-related crimes like theft and/or theft of livestock, most probably motivated by the implicit opportunity to ease economic survival.

Second, Moffitt's adolescence-limited/life course-persistent offender taxonomy has been offered as an explanation (Moffit 1993, 674–701). Both theoretical approaches seem to fit well the intention to overcome any presumed or actual resistance against child justice legislation, which is compatible with international standards, and further to keep children out of the adult criminal justice system. The latter (i.e., keeping children out of the Namibian one-track criminal justice system) follows logically from the assumption of adolescence-limited offending, namely, that commonly occurring juvenile delinquency is a normal phenomenon, which can be explained by temporary association with antisocial peers and again temporary appropriation of antisocial attitudes. From here it is, however, still a long road of topical etiological research before a scientific explanation for Namibian child crime, based on Namibian data, can be sustained.

Between Tradition and Modernity: Social and Normative Aspects of Child Delinquency

Some scholars (e.g., Cohen 1985) hold that formal control efforts play a role in amplifying deviance in society. This shall explain why in so-called traditional societies with little formal measures to control deviance, deviance remains relatively underdeveloped.

If delinquency is thus related to society's social organization, the statement that the Namibian legal order does not address youth crime as a normative category, might also allow us a prediction about Namibia's society. First, a prediction about Namibia's location on a continuum between tradition and modernity, and second, something about the relative volume and extent of formal control efforts. In fact, Namibia is largely a traditional society, and the reported number of child arrests per annum is comparatively low; there seems to be a fit. Along the lines of colonialism and postcolonialism, different concepts affecting the ways in which child crime is dealt with in Namibia survived and/or emerged: There is a concept of tradition and a concept of modernity. Interestingly, the ways in which deviant/criminal behavior of children may be framed, even by the same person, depends on the situation and the merits of the case. For many readers this may seem an undesirable situation. This duality is supported however by the Namibian Constitution, which recognizes customary law as part of the law of Namibia and determines it as having the same status as common law (Namibian Constitution Art. 66).

Customary law preserves traditional principles of restorative justice, which had already existed before colonial time. Namibia, then known as German South-West Africa, became a German colony in 1884. At the time, the organization of the society was predominantly communal. The notions of what could be left to the self-help of individuals concerned and what ought to be made the concern of all as likely to imperil the orderly social existence (Elias 1956, 121) certainly formed part of the social reality of the time. But the clear distinction that makes the general law between civil and criminal matter was unknown, although under limited circumstances, for example, where blood was shed, a person could be sentenced to a punishment in the sense of the general law (Hinz 1998, 178). Yet, by and large, principles of restorative justice applied, engaging not only perpetrator and victim, but directly or indirectly also their communities and (extended) families. The family, or the community of the actors would, after negotiation before the headman's court, restore peace in the community or between communities by rendering a service or by delivery of an item of value, often heads of cattle, to one another (Hinz 1998, 178ff). In this sense, deviant behavior was considered a social disruption arising at the level of and primarily affecting the relationship between the parties involved in the matter. Until today, the principles of restorative justice remain strong pillars of problem-solving in the Namibian communities, something that the post-independent Namibian state condoned apart from the constitutional recognition of customary law with the adoption of the Traditional Authorities Act (17 of 1995) and the Community Courts Act (10 of 2003). To the extent that criminal child behavior triggers traditional conflict resolution mechanisms, it is taken care of according to the prevailing principles of restorative justice. The question to what extent customary practices attend to and solve youth behavior "under the radar" of the criminal justice system, has not been subject to systematic studies, and warrants a deeper investigation. As was mentioned elsewhere, however, the volume of such cases before the customary courts of the headmen/women is supposedly not negligible.

The second alternative perspective, the concept of modernity, is embodied in the general law under the Supreme Constitution. It also frames the concept of criminal justice. Criminal justice, first imposed by the German colonial administration, includes two aspects of the concept of criminal accountability. First is the accountability to the state as the (sole) authority to prosecute,* and second, the assumption of individual criminal responsibility often coupled with the assumption of free will (Snyman 2002), however difficult to reconcile with the concept of restorative justice prevailing in customary law (Terblanche 2007, 174ff). In terms of content and structure, the (modern) Namibian criminal justice system does not specify child crime, youth crime, or juvenile delinquency as a category of behavior, and it does not recognize children in conflict with the law as a separate category of offenders with special needs either. Two preindependence laws, the Children's Act (Act 33 of 1960) and the already-mentioned CPA (Act 51 of 1977) provide, by and large, the normative framework for dealing with children in contact with the law.

The CPA has (in principle) a bearing only on those individuals who possess criminal capacity. The lower limit of criminal capacity is 7 years, although there is a rebuttable assumption against criminal capacity, which covers the age span from 7 to 13 years. The lower limit of criminal capacity places Namibia right down at the bottom of the states on the continuum of criminal capacity (cf. Winterdyk 2002, Introduction, xii, xiii).

Section 254 CPA opens the way for a conversion of the criminal procedure into a children's court enquiry in terms of the Children's Act (33 of 1960), if it appears that the child alleged having infringed the penal law, is in "need of care." A conversion in terms of section 254 CPA, which is in the discretion of the magistrate, changes the perspective and removes the case from the criminal justice system. After assessment of the situation, the children's court will then decide on any child welfare measure provided for in the Children's Act. If a conversion is not called for or not taking place, a child is taken through the single-track criminal justice procedures, and exposed to the same imputations, assumptions, and treatments as an adult accused (Box 9.1).

Children in Namibia in Conflict with the Law: The Situation on the Ground

International Standards, under the CRC and other international documents are specifically explicit on a number of items (i.e., criminal capacity, arrest, detention, diversion, trial, sentence, and institutionalization). Owing to the MGECW 2012 study (Ministry of Gender Equality and Child Welfare 2013) on the situation of children in Namibia in conflict with the law, we have a fairly comprehensive picture both on the quality of extant child justice policies and the situation on the ground.

Juvenile Courts

In the present system, trial courts (Magistrate's Court and High Court) have jurisdiction over cases where children are accused. The relevant legislations, CPA (51 of 1977), Magistrate's Court Act (16 of 1990), and High Court Act (15 of 1990), do not provide for separate juvenile courts. However, the Magistrate's Court of Windhoek reserves administratively a specific courtroom (C-Court) for procedures against juveniles, and tries in this way to meet the

---

* S. 2 of the Criminal Procedure Act (51 of 1977) as amended, authoritatively states that the authority to prosecute is vested in the state; only when the state's prosecuting body declines to prosecute, private prosecution may be allowed.

separation requirement of CRC Article 37(c). But this does not mean that the magistrate and prosecutor serving in this court deal exclusively with juvenile cases or that they have received specific training in handling juvenile cases (Ministry of Gender Equality and Child Welfare 2013, p. 54). Juvenile cases arising within the magisterial district of Windhoek are simply concentrated in this court, which otherwise handles adult cases. As current practice has it, the sequencing of cases in the court roll on any given court day is not even systematic, and the arbitrary change from adult to juvenile cases and back makes a frequent change of mind-set necessary, because whereas adult cases are public, juvenile cases are normally in camera. Emulating the Windhoek court practice in other districts is not usually possible because many districts are much smaller than Windhoek district and are only served by a single magistrate.

Arrest (Police) and Detention

Arrest and detention are perceived as measures of choice to ensure the presence of the accused at court procedures, both during the pretrial stage and at the trial. As Amoo (2008, 125) points out: "It is inconceivable how the Police would be able to function without the power of arrest and detention." On the assumption that the accused otherwise would be absent from such procedures, release from police detention is a function of the courts. As a matter of fact, under the CPA (51 of 1977), release from police detention mostly requires payment of bail. Under certain very limited circumstances, bail may be granted by the police before the first court appearance of an accused; the police does not have the authority to release an accused on own recognizance. Since many accused persons do not have the means to pay bail or provide surety, Namibia has a huge volume of pretrial detainees. Although provided for in the Prisons Act (17 of 1998), pretrial and sentencing awaiting detention is not served in prison facilities. The consequence is that the police have to keep not only arrestees, until their first appearance before the court, but also trial-awaiting detainees in their holding cells, which leads to extreme overcrowding of certain police stations (Ombudsman of the Republic of Namibia 2006, 2008; Ruppel and Groenewaldt 2008), in particular, those located in the capital Windhoek (Central, Katutura, and Wanahenda). The time spent in police custody stretches often over months and in many cases even years. Since the police are only mandated by law to provide custody of pretrial detainees, they are ill prepared to cater to the actual volume of detainees entrusted. The situation in these facilities is unacceptable, and constitutes most of the time even a patent infringement of the dignity of the detainee (see Ombudsman of the Republic of Namibia 2006, 2008).

Where children are arrested by the police, they invariably share the same facilities as the adult accused, facilities, which apart from the administrative rules and procedures, also in terms of their physical design are not at all suitable for children. One or more of the following conditions prevail anywhere:

- In police stations with a high influx of arrestees/detainees, constant separation of children from adults is mostly impossible
- Children in detention are left on their own with virtually no appropriate adult guidance
  - Insufficient light and/or aeration
  - Ablution and shower facilities located directly in the cell without being separated
- No bedding
- Little to no cognitive/intellectual stimulation

- Overcrowding and physical design of police cells entail a lack of privacy and/or own space

It is therefore fortunate that in cases against children, the prosecution seldom requests, and the courts very seldom remand, children to pretrial detention at police stations. It still happens that about 60% of child inmates in correctional facilities reported pretrial detention in police custody longer than 1 month, and some considerably longer. But the total number of child inmates has come down to an unprecedented few. Although the quasi-informal child justice setup under the IMC almost totally disappeared after the demise of the IMC in about 2005/2006, one lesson that became anchored in the minds of the prosecution and magistracy, and has been obviously conveyed to any novice prosecutor and/or magistrate is that any form of detention in facilities of the extant criminal justice system is detrimental to the child and eventually to the criminal justice cause.

Diversion

The use of diversion refers to the general practice of dealing with children in conflict with the law without resorting to judicial proceedings or a trial. Diversion is, however, not an end in itself, and the rationale for such treatment is to deal with child offenders in effective ways, which cannot be achieved within the criminal justice system, and importantly so not in detention or in prison. As was already mentioned, in Namibia, the authority to divert is exclusively vested in the prosecutor general (s. 6 (1) CPA 51 of 1977) who may "withdraw" charges conditional to the child's acceptance of certain measures, like community service, mediation, and so forth. Although not limited by legislation, the prosecutor general has authorized to consider diversion for minor offenses only. As a consequence, where diversion otherwise would be found to be in the best interests of the child, this option has been made categorically unavailable. The Namibian police are given neither the power to divert nor to release a child on own recognizance following an arrest. Therefore, as a rule, the arrest of a child ends before a magistrate, where the prosecutor decides upon the recommendation of a social worker, whether or not to continue with the prosecution. This practice, which is currently mandated by the prevailing legislation on criminal procedure, may very well have the effect that even children without prior record or who have committed relatively minor offenses are diverted into programs, whereas they would otherwise not have entered the justice system. While the creation of awareness of this phenomenon commonly referred to as "net widening" forms part of the training curriculum for social workers in the MGECW, there is little known about the actual dimension of this effect. Besides Section 6 (1) CPA, the legal ramifications for diversion are unspecified:

- The powers of prosecutors to make diversion decisions are not regulated and reviewed, which may lead to discrimination
- Where the child complies with the condition, this does not result in a definite and final closure of the case
- Opportunity to seek legal or other assistance is practically nonexistent

Another challenge is that there are currently only two diversion options available, namely, Pretrial Community Service (PTCS) and Life Skills Programme (LSP; see Box 9.2). The use of diversion also differs greatly from region to region. According to a communication (July 2013) from the implementing Ministry of Youth, National Service, Sport and

BOX 9.2   DIVERSION IN LIMBO

Currently, there are only two diversion options practiced in Namibia, namely, Pre-trial Community Service (PTCS) and Life Skills Programme (LSP). There are implementation problems with both alternatives. There is no service delivery system for PTCS support. Since there is no list with assessed and approved placement agencies, prosecutors have to enquire themselves about placement agencies as well as their suitability; they have also ensure that a suitable supervisor is appointed. This means additional work for prosecutors who are also not well prepared for the task. Generally speaking, this does not make PTCS as a diversion option very attractive to prosecutors. The situation with regard to LSP is not much better. The Namibian LSP has been modeled after the program developed by the South African National Institute for Crime Prevention and the Reintegration of Offenders (NICRO). The responsibility for implementation of the LSP lies with the Ministry of Youth, National Service, Sport and Culture (MYNSSC). Social workers at the 13 Multi-Purpose Youth Resource Centres in the regions should conduct LSP according to a predetermined schedule. This is however often not the case either because no social worker is available or the minimum number of participant children cannot be reached. As a matter of consequence, diverted children often have to wait for lengthy periods before they can fulfill the condition for final withdrawal of the case by the prosecution.

Culture (MYNSSC), for the period June 2011 through July 2013, there are no recorded diversions into LSP for 9 out of 14 regions, namely, Erongo, Hardap, Karas, Kavango-East, Kavango-West, Kunene, Omaheke, Otjozondjupa, and Zambezi.

The incidence of screening for diversion and presentence reports across the regions also suggests that chances of getting tried or diverted are unevenly distributed across the Namibian regions. Whereas Khomas shows the highest number of screenings and the lowest number of presentence reports, with a ratio of 76:1 (1746:23), Kunene and Omaheke have a ratio of screening-to-presentence report of 1.3:1 (235:182) and 1.9:1 (146:77), respectively. This points to a **systematic discrimination** from region to region in the implementation of diversion for children in conflict with the law, in contravention of Article 2 UNCRC (see Table 9.6 and Figure 9.4).

Trial and Sentencing

The trial of children follows the law of the criminal procedure, which does not provide for much special treatment other than that proceedings of the court take place in camera. Trials against children take place in the same building and are conducted by the same officers as any other (adult) trial. In this respect, it is significant that magistrates and prosecutors, dealing with children in conflict with the law do so mostly without any systematic training in child justice (Ministry of Gender Equality and Child Welfare 2013). Criminal justice professionals dealing with children in conflict with the law are not selected on the basis of any special training in child justice. It is interesting if not ironic that Namibia aims at providing a child-friendly atmosphere, and a child-friendly procedure with regard to child witnesses/victims, including the use of closed-circuit television (CCTV) (Silungwe 2009, 27ff), but it does not offer this privilege to the child offender.

Table 9.6   Regional Distribution of Screening and Presentence Reports (2010–2013)

2010–2013	Screening	Presentence Report
Erongo	514	95
Hardap	554	32
Karas	169	17
Kavango	113	8
Khomas	**1746**	**23**
Kunene	**235**	**182**
Ohangwena	108	0
Omaheke	146	77
Omusati	145	9
Oshana	251	10
Oshikoto	152	2
Otjozondjupa	280	64
Zambesi	121	18

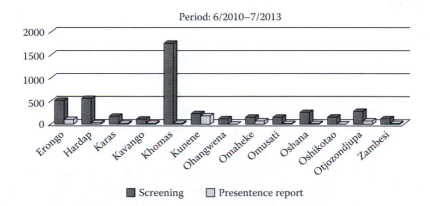

Figure 9.4 Regional distribution of screening and presentence reports (2010–2013).

Although no research has been undertaken in this regard, and no statistics are readily available, there should be some doubt as to the correct application of our rules on the criminal capacity of the child. Procedurally, if a child is below 14 years of age, criminal capacity has to be positively established by the prosecution. In the Magistrate Court, cases against children below the age of 14 are most often unconditionally withdrawn. However, where this is not the case or where diversion is envisaged, the prosecution must establish criminal capacity positively. If criminal capacity cannot be positively established, conditional withdrawal aiming at diverting the case should not be admissible. Instead, unconditional withdrawal and intervention in terms of the Children's Act would be called for. To the extent that this is not happening, this leads to net widening.

With regard to sentencing children, a number of issues may be of concern. For reasons of space, we limit the discussion to sentencing objectives, presentence reports, and community-based and restorative sentences. Sentencing principles are purely judge made and are not contained in any statute. No special set of principles or interpretation of principles

BOX 9.3   FEW CHILD INMATES FOR ELIZABETH NEPEMBA JUVENILE CENTER

At the beginning of the millennium, Elizabeth Nepemba Juvenile Center had been hailed as a milestone toward compliance of Namibian Corrections with the requirements of the Convention on the Rights of the Child (CRC), Article 44 (Schulz 2002, 368). Then the center had still been under construction, and it was planned for a total capacity of 475 children. Considering the lead time for new correctional facilities, the planned capacity seemed rational because by the end of the 1990s, there was an expectation of a further increase of child inmates, also with midterm sentences in Namibia. While the construction of the juvenile center was under way, the concerted efforts of many role-players under the guidance of the Inter-Ministerial Committee (IMC) caused a paradigm shift among criminal justice professionals, especially a heightened awareness among prosecutors and magistrates, of the plight of the child in any form of custody. Soon the number of committed children shrunk dramatically. With only a handful of child inmates, originating from diverse cultural backgrounds and geographical regions, commissioning Elizabeth Nepemba Juvenile Center to provide custody for child inmates was indefinitely deferred. Today, the continuously less than 50 child inmates are kept in correctional facilities as close as possible to their families, some of them even at Elizabeth Nepemba. But NCS is undecided about what is to be done with its oversized facility.

BOX 9.4   THE JUVENILE JUSTICE SYSTEM IN NAMIBIA—WHICH JUSTICE MODEL?

The single-track Namibian criminal justice system can be best described as being premised on the pure justice model (Winterdyk 2004). Due process, respect for individual rights, individual responsibility, and punishment are the prominent features. Nominally, since the system is a single-track system, which does not recognize a separate track for child offenders, the child justice system should also fall under the justice model. However, owing to the introduction and widespread and generally accepted practice of diversion, it may be justified to describe our actual "juvenile" justice system as falling somewhere between the "justice model" and "modified justice model." "Soft" offenders are diverted; "hard" offenders are punished. Lawyers and social workers play an important role in the process.

have evolved with regard to sentencing children, which may have to do with the fact that few child cases have so far reached our superior courts. In *S v Van Der Bergh* 2003 NR 69 (HC) it was, however, stressed that rehabilitation and not punishment should be the aim in cases involving juveniles. This goes well with CRC, Article 40 (3), which stipulates the "child's reintegration and the child's assuming a constructive role in society" as the desired outcome of the child justice process, an outcome which is also stipulated in the African Charter on the Rights and Welfare of the Child (ACRWC) Article 17 (3).

Our criminal procedure law does not require the consideration of a presentence report before sentencing. Yet, from the responses of a survey among magistrates and prosecutors

(Ministry of Gender Equality and Child Welfare 2013), it appears that nowadays presentence reports are requested as a matter of routine.

Finally, it appears that in the large majority of cases, magistrates follow as far as is justifiable, the maxim that no child should ever have to go to prison. All magistrates who returned their questionnaires responded that they "never impose a sentence of imprisonment," and "never impose a fine in respect of a child under the age of fourteen." Most magistrates indicated that they make use of community-based sentences as well as restorative sentences in terms of Section 297 CPA.

Institutionalization (Imprisonment)

With a head count often not exceeding 50 since October 2012, the fraction of child inmates in Namibian correctional facilities is dwarfed in comparison with the about 4000 adult inmates (Bruyns and Schulz, forthcoming). This can be attributed to the fact that if children are tried and sentenced, magistrates seldom hand down unconditional sentences of imprisonment. In comparison with October 2000, when 295 child inmates were reported (Schulz 2002, 369), this is clearly an impressive improvement, which comes with its own challenges for the NCS (Box 9.3).

And indeed, the earlier-mentioned recent replication of the 1994 Study of Young Offenders in Namibia suggests that children in correctional facilities are far better off than in police custody. At the same time, there is much room for improvement:

- Namibia has no separate correctional facility for children, and child inmates are concentrated in a few adult facilities (Gobabis and Walvisbay), where they are usually separated from adult inmates.
- Due to human resource shortages, total separation of children from adult inmates cannot always be guaranteed.
- Family visitations are possible, but due to a regular lack of funds of families from poor economic backgrounds, child inmates often experience long stretches between visitations.
- Intellectual stimulation (reading material, TV consumption, board games, etc.) is provided, but in limited quantity only.
- Child inmates who have not finished their schooling may continue their school education through distance with the Namibian College of Education (NamCol), but normally they have to raise the funds for their studies themselves.
- Physical exercise (e.g., soccer) is possible, mostly one hour per day, often with adult inmates.
- Correctional facilities do not seek cooperation of social workers of the local MGECW offices in preparation of child release from prison.

Measuring Namibian Juvenile Justice against International Standards

The UNCRC is the single most successful international convention in terms of the number of state parties to it. As was mentioned before, Namibia has signed and ratified the UNCRC in September 1990, as well as the ACRWC in 1999 and 2004. The way in which we deal with children in conflict with the law is therefore not just a matter of fact but it also has legal relevance.

BOX 9.5   STATE OF COMPLIANCE WITH SELECTED INTERNATIONAL OBLIGATIONS AND CHILDREN'S RIGHTS (FEBRUARY 2014)

	International Standard	Content	Current Status of Namibian Compliance (compliant; partially compliant; noncompliant; compliance doubtful)	
1	Art. 2 United Nations Convention on the Rights of the Child (UNCRC)	Nondiscrimination required; all children in conflict with the law shall be treated equally.	Partially compliant	The chances of children in conflict with the law to be tried or diverted from judicial proceedings are not equally distributed across the regions.
2	Art. 3 UNCRC; Art. 4 African Charter on the Rights and Welfare of the Child (ACRWC)	In all decisions taken within the context of the administration of child justice, the best interests of the child should be a primary consideration. Traditional objectives of criminal justice, such as repression/retribution, must give way to rehabilitation and restorative justice objectives.	Compliance doubtful	In *S v Van der Bergh* 2003 NR 69 (HC), it was stressed that rehabilitation and not punishment should be the aim in cases involving children. A recent study (Schulz 2012) suggested, however, that at the level of the magistracy, punishment still plays a dominant role.
3	Art. 40 (1) UNCRC	Treatment of children must take into account the child's age, and promotion of the child's reintegration must be upheld throughout the entire process of dealing with the child; all professionals must be knowledgeable about child development.	Noncompliant	A minority of professionals dealing with children in conflict with the law are trained in child justice and child development; such training is haphazard, nonsystematic, and erratic.
4	Art. 40 (3) UNCRC	State parties shall promote interventions without resorting to judicial proceedings (diversion) and take the necessary legislative and other measures for their implementation; the obligation of the state parties is not limited to minor offenses.	Partially compliant	In Namibia, diversion is not regulated by law and does not exist in the proper sense of the concept. Under Section 6 (a) CPA (51 of 1977), the prosecutor general has authorized provisional withdrawal from judicial proceedings for minor offenses only.
5	Art. 40 (3) UNCRC; Rule 4 Beijing Rules	State parties are required to establish a minimum age below which children shall be presumed not to have the capacity to infringe the penal law. A minimum age of criminal responsibility (MACR) below the age of 12 years, as much as the practice of allowing, by way of exception the use of a lower MACR, is considered not to be acceptable.	Noncompliant	According to the so-called doli capax/incapax rule, children in Namibia are presumed to be incapable of infringing the criminal law until the age of 6 years. This presumption may be rebutted by the state with regard to a child who has reached the age of 7 years. From the age of 14 years, a child is presumed to be criminally liable for his/her criminal behavior.
6	Art. 40 (3) UNCRC	State parties shall establish an effective organization for the administration of child justice and a comprehensive juvenile justice system.	Non-compliant	While the Namibian laws lay down a number of limited special provisions for dealing with children in conflict with the law, there does not exist a comprehensive system with specialized units within the police, the judiciary, the court system, and the prosecutor's office.

#	Provision	Standard	Compliance	Commentary
7	Art. 1 (2) Beijing Rules; Art. 9 Riyadh Guidelines, together with Arts. 3, 29, and 40 UNCRC	Prevention of child/juvenile delinquency.	Partially compliant	Namibia's multiagency plan, the National Agenda for Children (2012–2016), addresses important aspects of the prevention of child involvement in crime at primary and secondary levels. There are, however, no targeted prevention programs for "at-risk" groups, and the plan does not provide for monitoring and coordination of crime prevention at the national level.
8	Arts. 6, 37 (b) UNCRC	Arrest, detention, and/or imprisonment shall be used only as a measure of last resort. State parties should take adequate legislative and other measures to reduce the use of pretrial detention.	Partially compliant	With a few exceptions, all child inmates in correctional facilities have been held for some time in police custody while awaiting trial.
9	Art. 37 (c) UNCRC	A child deprived of his/her liberty shall not be placed in an adult prison or other facility for adults. State parties should establish separate facilities for children deprived of their liberty, which include distinct, child-centered staff, personnel, policies, and practices. Children in detention should be provided with a physical environment and accommodations, which are in keeping with the rehabilitative aims of residential placement, and due regard must be given to their needs for privacy, sensory stimuli, opportunities to associate with their peers, and to participate in sports, physical exercise, in arts, and leisure-time activities.	Noncompliant	There are no separate facilities for children, child correctional facilities, or places of detention for trial- or sentence-awaiting children in terms of Section 38 (2) Children's Act (33 of 1960). Nonseparation of child and adult detainees is a regular occurrence. Accommodations conditions, whether in police stations or correctional facilities are not conducive to child development; compare the 2006 and 2008 reports by the Ombudsman on the conditions prevailing at police cells.
10	Arts. 60–66 Riyadh Guidelines	State parties are urged to systematically collect disaggregated data relevant to the information on the practices of the administration of child justice and necessary for the development, implementation, and evaluation of policies and programs aiming at the prevention of and effective responses to child delinquency. The CRC is deeply concerned about the lack of even basic and disaggregated data on child delinquency.	Noncompliant	While invaluable criminal justice data, including those pertaining to child delinquency, are captured through the Namibian Court Information System (NamCIS), the operational database management software does not provide for disaggregated data extraction on prosecutorial or adjudication statistics. A validation of the comprehensive set of police crime/arrest data is therefore not possible.

Box 9.5 provides a summary assessment, which should be read in conjunction with the rest of this chapter.* The issues addressed in the box are highly relevant for the themes discussed in this chapter, but for reasons of space cannot be discussed in more detail; the interested reader may refer to the MGECW 2012 study (Ministry of Gender Equality and Child Welfare 2013).

The synopsis in Box 9.5 suggests that Namibia is currently not doing too well with regard to its international obligations. Arguably, on none of the criteria derived from the UNCRC does Namibia reach full compliance. Noncompliance is the norm, with partial compliance recorded for the prevention of child involvement in crime (Art. 1 (2) Beijing Rules, Art. 9 Riyadh Guidelines, with and Arts. 3, 29, and 40 UNCRC). Issues like the extremely low age of criminal responsibility, which starts under circumstances with age 7, the arrest of children, in particular, children under the age of 14, and their detention in adult facilities, the fact that none of the stages of the current criminal justice process responds appropriately to the developmental needs of the child offender, or even the fact that besides the social workers involved in screening children in preparation of prosecutorial diversion decisions, no other group of criminal justice professionals appears to receive meaningful training in the foundations and principles of child adequate justice (see Box 9.5), leaves Namibia far off target. Another particular concern is that Namibia's implementation of diversion is clearly not in line with the requirements for diversion under the UNCRC. Against the backdrop of the above, it can be said that the domestic Namibian normative (legal and policy) framework for dealing with children do not meet the requirements of the CRC.

Current Challenges Facing Namibian Youths Today

Poverty and social exclusion are serious problems for Namibians in general and Namibian youth in particular. If the Namibia Statistical Agency report on poverty (2012b) is anything to go by, unemployment and poverty are becoming intransigent challenges for Namibian youth. People are in poverty if they are continuously struggling to preserve themselves and their dependents from physical want (Mufune 2002, 181). Absolute poverty is generally understood as the inability to attain a minimum standard of living (cf. footnote †). The problem with poverty conceptually lies in defining poverty in terms of subsistence and physical want such as the bare minimum of food, clothing, and shelter. In doing so, it elevates physical needs at the expense of social needs. Mufune, therefore, prefers the concept of "relative poverty" as it refers to the idea of standards relative to time and place. What counts are the judgments by members of a particular society of what is considered a reasonable and acceptable standard of living and style of life according to the conventions of the day (Haralambos 1985, 142). This differentiation seems to be particularly important for developing societies like Namibia, with huge variations in those "standards." But to the extent that relative poverty relates to "inequality, distributive justice and power relations" (Ramprakash 1991, 49), it importantly links up with the concept of social exclusion. Social exclusion refers to a person's or group's failure to take part fully in society's affairs as a consequence of lack of capabilities and entitlements, and it stresses the process by which

---

* This table was initially prepared for the above-mentioned Issues Paper (see p. 219) and reproduced here with the permission of UNICEF.

people become poor or excluded and marginalized (Mufune 2002, 183). The complexity of social and economic reality in terms of unemployment, poverty, and exclusion prevents a deeper discussion here, but we may identify two significant factors of exclusion affecting Namibian youth (i.e., education and exclusion, and exclusion from labor-based entitlements). While the Namibian government has done extremely well in raising the enrolment ratio over the last two decades (National Planning Commission 2010), the educational system still generates exclusion among youth, through unequal access to resources, differentiating in particular between rural and urban youth and youth from lower and higher economic classes. Because youth who do not have the requisite skills remain the last to be hired and the first to be fired in the formal labor market, the economy is not growing fast enough, and as a consequence, the job market is not able to absorb as many job seekers as emerge continuously. Due to a lack of employment opportunities and limited social and marketable skills and competencies, it may be forecast that an increasing number of youth will turn to crime, prostitution, and substance abuse, among other deviant and delinquent activities. The Namibian government has appropriated considerable funds for poverty reduction and exclusion, which also includes young people (National Planning Commission 2010), but it remains to be seen whether these efforts are enough to stem the potential to generate discontent and social dislocation.

Since the beginning of the millennium, the dynamic of the HIV/AIDS pandemic changed dramatically. According to the latest UNAIDS/World Health Organization (WHO) "Epidemiological Fact Sheet on HIV/AIDS" (2009) for Namibia reports, an estimated total of the number of adults and children living with HIV/AIDS for the end of 2009 was below 200,000. The adult rate, which referred to women and men aged 15–49 years lies at approximately 13%. The incidence of new HIV infections came down from approximately 25,000 new infections around the year 2000 to far below 10,000 incidents in 2009. Equally, the number of HIV-/AIDS-related deaths decreased from above 10,000 per annum to slightly above 5,000. Another important figure is the antiretroviral treatment (ART) coverage. Today, the ART coverage includes about 90% of all infected persons. Notwithstanding gradual improvement of all indicators over the last couple of years, the HIV/AIDS pandemic remains a persistent challenge (Fox 2002, 317). Along with the development of the pandemic, Namibia faces a slow destruction of its social and cultural fabric, with the concomitant ruptures of formal and informal economic structures. At the point of writing, the number of OVCs exceeds 140,000, and the number of child-headed households has been reported as 7,671, of which 2,953 are orphan (child)-headed households (Namibia Statistical Agency 2012b). Interestingly, social exclusion, HIV/AIDS, and modernity enter into an intricate relationship, with precarious consequences, in particular for women. In 2002, Winterfeldt underlined that a larger proportion of women now engage in internal migration—despite deep-seated conservative values. Following independence, women seek the economic opportunities of employment and income, previously the preserve of men. But aspirations toward improved lifestyles also result in alternative strategies to obtain money and gifts. Sexual partners capable of supplying income and goods are deliberately sought, with "young women and mothers" being "most likely to engage in sex with affluent individuals" (USAID 2009, 22ff; Fox 2002, 325). Whether this behavior reflects a strategy to overcome limited material lifestyles or a route out of absolute deprivation, while implicitly breaking the grip of ancient patriarchal control and so gaining civil and sexual self-determination, it carries an increased risk of exposure to HIV/AIDS with the societal consequences for the prospects of juvenile delinquency discussed in the

BOX 9.6   TEENAGE PREGNANCY IN NAMIBIA

There has been an upsurge in teenage pregnancies in Namibia, throughout all Namibian regions. On November 25, 2011, however, *New Era* (Namibian Newspaper, p. 3) highlighted the Kavango Region with a prevalence rate of 34%, making it the highest in Namibia over the past 6 years. The newspaper quoted Shambyu Traditional Authority chief councilor, Mutero Sikerete, who referred to "school-going children wandering at shebeens and nightclubs, teenagers exposed to pornography, girls having sexual relations with teachers for high marks, sexual intercourse between learners, and girls having sexual relationships with sugar daddies in exchange for cash and cell phones."

preceding text (see also Box 9.6). Namibian men are not spared by the emerging cultural contradictions. In particular, young males usurp "traditional" institutions of polygamy readily, "to pit them against religious conservative values stressing monogamy and sexual abstinence" (Fox 2002, 329).

The somewhat extended discussion of HIV/AIDS at this juncture is not arbitrary. The consequences of the HIV/AIDS pandemic are tangible and certainly not negligible. At an individual level, the disappearance of parents/guardians from the life of a child (orphanage) means less guidance and less control, which according to some writers (e.g., Gottfredson and Hirschi 1990) increases the likelihood of child involvement in crime. It also means less cultural continuity/identity. At the aggregate level, the HIV/AIDS pandemic exacts a toll on the life expectancy of Namibians, which commensurate with the degree it decreases, shaves off fractions of the GDP (see Isaksen, Songstad, and Spissøy 2002).

Looking Ahead: Moving from the Child Justice Bill to the Child Justice Act

Following independence, Namibia tried to achieve compliance with the CRC, and to accommodate children's rights and entitlements, within the scope of its single-track criminal justice system. The work of the somewhat ad hoc-established IMC moved Namibia forward indeed, and a lot was achieved in a short time. But the eventual demise of the IMC several years ago may be read as the outcome of an inadvertent experiment and an answer to the implicit research question "Is CRC compliance possible without legislated policy?" So far, after a couple of years, the answer is obviously "No."

Legislated policy serves as a common point of reference and carries the authority of the democratic process. The effective coordination of stakeholders under such a normative umbrella is easily attainable, provided the necessary budget appropriation is ensured. Achieving the same without a legislated framework is much more difficult, because responding adequately to the social problem of child offending requires a multifaceted multiagency approach. The UNCRC reflects this complexity through its considerable set of state party obligations and child rights.

If Namibia has been hoping that its criminal justice system would reform somehow on its own, this hope was destroyed recently with the Concluding Observation of the

> **BOX 9.7   DEFINING THE PROPOSED CHILD
> JUSTICE SYSTEM IN NAMIBIA**
>
> The Draft Child Justice Bill, although promoting strongly a restorative justice approach, as evidenced by the provisions for family group conferences, restitution, and compensation, represents an intersectoral model, which in terms of procedures combines primarily a justice approach with welfare support mechanisms. Presumably, there are no records with a bearing on the motivation for this model. This serves the protection of the child's due process rights, which are also entrenched in Chapter 3 (Bill of Rights) of the Namibian Constitution. While reserving child justice sentences with custodial elements for serious offenders, and prescribing restorative measures for less serious cases, we may expect a dual-handling process, which may best be described as a modified justice model. The current system has, although only *de facto*, not *de lege*, been described similarly (see Box 9.4). The huge advantage of the proposed Child Justice System according to the Draft Child Justice Bill is, however, that it provides well-paced normative guidance in line with international standards like the United Nations Convention on the Rights of the Child (UNCRC), something that is almost entirely absent currently.

Committee on the Rights of the Child (Sixty-first session, October 2012). The extensive observations and recommendations put the spotlight on the deficits of the extant system. It took a while until the Namibian Government reacted, although briefly. But finally in September 2013, a review workshop on the Child Justice Bill (2004) took place with participants from the magistracy, the prosecution, civil society, and the academe, and a follow-up workshop took place in the beginning of December 2013. The workshop's objective was first, to check legislative cross-references and adjust the Bill's sections where it had become necessary since the submission of the draft in 2004, and second, to receive suggestions for amendments based on experience with the implementation of the South African Act, which by then had been in place since 2010. The envisaged new child justice legislation, once promulgated, would not only take children out of the adult criminal justice system but also shape system responses fundamentally against the backdrop of restorative justice principles (Schulz 2009; Box 9.7). The representative of the Directorate Legal Services in the Namibian Ministry of Justice was confident that the bill would be finalized and moved in Parliament within a reasonable period of time from the workshop, most probably before the end of 2014. After such a long time of inactivity, it is foreseen to go once more through a process of wide consultation in the Namibian regions to garner acceptance and support. The workshop deliberations of the draft bill suggested, however, that the bill might encounter some resistance. A number of issues under the bill did not find unanimous positions among the workshop participants, for instance, the proposed change of the age of criminal responsibility from (currently) 7 to 12 years.

Conclusion

This chapter presented an overview of the Namibian justice system and a description of how this system, not specifically conceived for handling child offenders, deals with children in conflict with the law, and provided a snapshot account of the extent and variation of juvenile delinquency in Namibia. It was noted that it is the justice model, which best characterizes the law governing the Namibian justice system, but that the actual system routines for dealing with children match the modified justice model more. It was also observed that the officially recorded juvenile delinquency has not dramatically increased in the last 5 years. It is felt that this can, in part, be explained by the fact that traditional conflict resolution mechanism at the level of traditional courts and to some extent Community Courts absorb juvenile delinquency, which therefore does not enter the police records. The chapter clarifies further that the nature of juvenile offending has not changed in recent years. The greatest part of juvenile criminality consists of age-related offenses such as property crime and assault. We discussed the socioeconomic context from which in many cases juvenile criminality emerges, namely, social disorganization and poverty. We also looked at theories, which have been put forth as an attempt to explain crime and in particular juvenile criminality in Namibia, *inter alia* Moffit's adolescence-limited life-persistent offender taxonomy. It was noted that the Namibian youth are facing persistent challenges, namely, poverty and social exclusion, and also HIV/AIDS in the context of a fast-paced change in cultural certainties. The chapter points out that Namibia does not abide by the country's obligations under the CRC. The present system does not take into account Namibia's commitment as a state party to the Convention, and therefore fails to a large extent to establish an identifiable system, which could address the special needs of children in conflict with the law. The lower limit of criminal capacity is one of the lowest in the world, and children in the system are suffering from child inadequate treatment in and by the system, and Namibia does not have a national plan for the prevention of child involvement in crime. After a lengthy period of stalled reform efforts, it seems that the Namibian juvenile justice system is again in the process of being transformed. A draft text for child justice legislation provides the foundation of a system built on internationally recognized standards, first and foremost the CRC, which may be best defined as a modified justice model.

Review/Discussion Questions

1. Why has child/juvenile justice in Namibia developed so late?
2. What factors contributed to Namibia's postindependence efforts to improve the justice system with regard to children in conflict with the law?
3. How does the current Namibian "juvenile" justice system relate to international standards, and how will the envisaged child justice legislation do in future?
4. What are the biggest challenges for the Namibian system when it comes to children in police custody?
5. The chapter highlights that the customary law of Namibia is largely imbued with the principles of restorative justice. If this is so, why should Namibia ensure that the ways in which its justice system deals with children complies with international standards?
6. Given the challenging socioeconomic and demographic features of Namibia, discuss how Namibia might be able to establish a sustainable child/juvenile justice system that meets international standards.
7. Although Namibia built the Elizabeth Nepemba Juvenile Center, the majority of the small population of child inmates is scattered throughout the correctional

facilities of the country. What may be the rationale of the Namibian Correctional Service for this practice?

8. Given the challenging socioeconomic and demographic features of Namibia, discuss how Namibia might be able to establish a sustainable child/juvenile justice system, which meets international standards.

References

Amoo, S.K. (2008). *An Introduction to Namibian Law*. Windhoek: Macmillan.

Andrews, D.A. and Bonta, J. (2010). *The Psychology of Criminal Conduct* (5th ed.). New Providence, NJ: LexisNexis.

Boesl, A., Horn, N., and Du Pisani, A. (Eds). (2010). *Constitutional Democracy in Namibia. A Critical Analysis after Two Decades*. Windhoek: Macmillan Education Namibia.

Bruyns, H.J. and Schulz, S. (forthcoming). From analysis to action: A snapshot on the Namibian inmate population.

Cohen, S. (1985). *Visions of Control: Crime, Punishment and Classification*. New Brunswick, NJ: Transaction Books.

Elias, T.O. (1956). *The Nature of African Customary Law*. Manchester: University Press.

Fox, T. (2002). The cultures of AIDS—Cultural analysis and new policy approaches. In Volker Winterfeldt, Tom Fox, and Pempelani Mufune (Eds.), *Namibia, Society, Sociology*. Windhoek: University of Namibia Press.

Gottfredson, M.R. and Hirschi T. (1990). *A General Theory of Crime*. Stanford, CA: Stanford University Press.

Government of Namibia. (2000). National Report on Follow-up to the World Summit for Children. Windhoek: Government of Namibia.

Government of Namibia. (2009). First, Second and Third Namibia Country Periodic Report on the Implementation of the United Nations Convention on the Rights of the Child. Windhoek: Government of Namibia.

Haralambos, M. (1985). *Sociology: New Directions*. London: Causeway Books.

Hinz, M. (1998). *Customary Law in Namibia: Development and Practice* (4th ed.). Windhoek: Centre for Applied Social Studies (CASS).

Hinz, M. (2002). Two Societies in one—Institutions and social reality of traditional and general law and order. In Volker Winterfeldt, Tom Fox, and Pempelani Mufune (Eds.), *Namibia, Society, Sociology*. Windhoek: University of Namibia Press.

Horn, N. and Boesl, A. (Eds.). (2008). *Human Rights and the Rule of Law in Namibia*. Windhoek: Macmillan.

Isaksen, J, Songstad, N.G., and Spissøy, A. (2002). Socio-economic Effects of HIV/AIDS in African Countries (CMI Report R 2002:10). Bergen: Chr. Michelsen Institute.

Kaapama, P., Blaauw, L., Zaaruka, B., and Kaakunga, E. (2007). *Consolidating Democratic Governance in Southern Africa: Namibia*. Johannesburg: EISA.

Merton, R.K. (1997). On the evolving synthesis of differential association and anomie theory: A perspective from the sociology of science. *Criminology*, 35:517–525.

Ministry of Gender Equality and Child Welfare. (2013). Rapid Analysis: Children in Namibia in Conflict with the Law. Windhoek: John Meinert Printing.

Moffit, T.E. (1993). Adolescence limited and life course persistent antisocial behaviour: A developmental taxonomy. *Psychological Review,* 100:647–701.

Mufune, P. (2002). Youth in Namibia—Social exclusion and poverty. In Volker Winterfeldt, Tom Fox, and Pempelani Mufune (Eds.), *Namibia, Society, Sociology*. Windhoek: University of Namibia Press.

Namibian Prison Service, Legal Assistance Centre, Ministry of Youth and Sport, UNICEF. (1994). *A Study of Young Offenders in Namibia.* Windhoek: Legal Assistance Centre.

Namibia Statistical Agency. (2012a). Namibia Household Income and Expenditure Survey Summary—June 2012. Retrieved October 15, 2012 from: http://www.nsa.org.na/files/downloads/88d_NHIES%20Executive%20Summary.pdf

Namibia Statistical Agency. (2012b). Poverty Dynamics in Namibia: A Comparative Study Using the 1993/94, 2003/4 and the 2009/10 NHIES Surveys. Windhoek: Namibian Statistical Agency.

Namibia Statistical Agency. (2013). Namibia 2011 Population and Housing Census Main Report. Windhoek: Government of Namibia.

National Planning Commission. (2010). *Children and Adolescents in Namibia 2010: A Situation Analysis.* Windhoek: John Meinert Printing (for National Planning Commission).

Ombudsman of the Republic of Namibia. (2006). Report on the Conditions Prevailing at Police Cells throughout Namibia. Windhoek: Ombudsman.

Ombudsman of the Republic of Namibia. (2008). Follow-up Report on the Conditions Prevailing at Police Cells throughout Namibia. Windhoek: Ombudsman.

Ramprakash, D. (1991). *Crushing Rural Poverty.* London: Food and Rural Development Division, Commonwealth Secretariat.

Ruppel, O.C. (Ed.). (2009). *Children's Rights in Namibia.* Windhoek: Macmillan.

Ruppel, O.C. and Groenewaldt, A. (2008). *Conditions of Police Cells in Namibia.* Windhoek: Konrad Adenauer Stiftung.

Schulz, S. (2002). Juvenile Justice in Namibia: A System in Transition. In John A. Winterdyk (Ed.), *Juvenile Justice Systems: International Perspectives* (2nd ed.). Toronto: Canadian Scholars' Press.

Schulz, S. (2009). Restorative justice: The case for a child justice act. In Oliver C. Ruppel (Ed.), *Children's Rights in Namibia* (pp. 283–326). Windhoek: Macmillan.

Sherbourne, R. (2010). *Guide to the Namibian Economy.* Windhoek: Institute for Public Policy Research.

Silungwe, A. (2009). High court of Namibia vulnerable witnesses' project. In Oliver C. Ruppel (Ed.), *Children's Rights in Namibia* (pp. 283–326). Windhoek: Macmillan.

Snyman, C.R. (2002). *Criminal Law* (4th ed.). Durban: Lexis Nexis Butterworths.

Terblanche, S.S. (2007). *Guide to Sentencing in South Africa* (2nd ed.). Durban: Lexis Nexis.

UN Committee on the Rights of the Child. (2012). Advance Unedited Version. Concluding Observations of the Committee on the Rights of the Child: Namibia. In Consideration of Reports Submitted by State Parties under Art. 44 of the Convention (61st session, September 17–October 5, 2012, CRC/C/NAM/CO/2-3).

USAID. (2009). HIV/AIDS in Namibia: Behavioural and Contextual Factors Driving the Epidemic.

Winterdyk, J.A. (2002). Introduction. In John A. Winterdyk (Ed.), *Juvenile Justice Systems—International Perspectives* (pp. XII–XIII). Toronto: CSP.

Winterdyk, J.A. (2004). Juvenile justice in the international arena. In Philip Reichel (Ed.), *Handbook of Transnational Crime and Justice* (pp. 457–469). Thousand Oaks, CA, London, New Delhi: SAGE.

Winterfeldt, V. (2002). Labour migration in Namibia—Gender aspects. In Volker Winterfeldt, Tom Fox, and Pempelani Mufune (Eds.), *Namibia, Society, Sociology.* Windhoek: University of Namibia Press.

Winterfeldt, V., Fox, T., and Mufune, P. (Eds.). (2002). *Namibia, Society, Sociology.* Windhoek: University of Namibia Press.

Internet Sources

http://www.lac.org.na/: The Legal Assistance Centre (LAC) is a public interest law center, striving to make the law accessible to those with the least access, through education, law reform, research, litigation, legal advice, representation, and lobbying, with the ultimate aim of creating and maintaining a human rights culture in Namibia.

http://namibie.chisites.org/en/t/about: LifeLine/ChildLine (LL/CL) is a nongovernmental organization (NGO), which has been in existence for 30 years in Namibia with the aim of providing essential abuse prevention and mitigation services to the children of Namibia.

http://www.nampol.gov.na/: Official website of the Namibian police, which contains also a section with Namibian Police crime statistics.

www.polytechnic.edu.na: Home site of the Polytechnic of Namibia; research projects and reports of the Department of Criminal Justice and Legal Studies are uploaded on the institutional repository (Ounongo) hosted by the institutional library.

Juvenile Justice and Juvenile Crime in the Netherlands*

10

HENK B. FERWERDA

Contents

The Dutch Perspective on Juvenile Delinquency — 240
Defining Youth Criminality in the Netherlands — 240
Juvenile Criminality in the Netherlands — 241
    Police Statistics — 241
    Self-Report Measures — 243
    Gender and Crime — 243
    Ethnicity and Crime — 244
The Different Faces of Juvenile Criminality — 245
    Hard-Core and Kick Behavior — 245
    Group Criminality — 246
    Street Gangs and Youth Gangs — 249
    The Context — 250
Background of the Dutch Juvenile Justice System — 251
Reactions to Juvenile Criminal Behavior — 253
Discussions and Developments in Delinquency and Juvenile Justice — 255
Conclusion — 258
Review/Discussion Questions — 258
References — 258
Internet Sources — 261

FACTS ABOUT THE NETHERLANDS

Area: The Netherlands is a comparatively small country of 41,543 square kilometers (of which 33,893 sq. km. is land) divided into 12 provinces. **Population:** The population is approximately 16.7 million (2012 estimate), with 3.9 million being under the age of 20. Population growth ranged from 1.9% in 1960 to 0.5% in 2011. Population density is 448 people/sq. km, which is among the highest in the world. Amsterdam is the nation's capital (population: 790.044) and The Hague (population: 502.055) is the city where the government is seated. **Climate:** The temperature is temperate and marine, with cool summers and mild winters. **Economy:** The Netherlands is a modern, industrialized, and affluent welfare state based on private enterprise. Rotterdam has one of the biggest sea harbors in the world. Unemployment is 5.3% (2012). The Netherlands has a highly sophisticated social service system, which absorbs about 25% of the domestic income. **Government:** The Dutch government is based on a parliamentary democracy with the monarch (King Willem Alexander) being a hereditary title.

---

* This chapter is an adaptation of Ferwerda, H. (2002), Youth Crime and Juvenile Justice in the Netherlands. In: Winterdyk, J. (Ed.), *Juvenile Justice Systems: International Perspectives* (2nd ed.). Canadian Scholars' Press Inc.: Toronto, 385–411.

The Dutch Perspective on Juvenile Delinquency

Until quite recently, almost everyone who was in some way involved with the phenomenon of juvenile delinquency in the Netherlands saw it as a passing element of puberty, or as a "normal" stage of adolescence. Although considered as something requiring attention, it was generally thought to be nothing to worry about. However, since 1995, when the new juvenile criminal law was introduced, juvenile criminal law has increasingly come to resemble adult criminal law. This has resulted in a number of changes such as the administration of more severe juvenile sanctions. In other words, the traditional idea of protecting juvenile offenders from strict accountability has been eroding with the new legislation (Bartels 2007). Despite these changes, juvenile public prosecutors and juvenile court judges (still) act on the principle that the sanctions imposed on juveniles should be "of a constructive character." Constructive in this respect means that, if possible, sanctions of a pedagogic character are imposed on *first-* and *second-time offenders*. However, constructive also means that more severe sanctions are imposed on recidivists, and greater emphasis is placed on the aspect of disciplining juvenile offenders. In the spring of 2012, the bill proposing the introduction of adolescent criminal law (15–23 years) generated much debate and made the issue of age limits in Dutch criminal law and changing them very topical (see van Wijk et al. 2013).

In this chapter, I will provide an overview on the issue of juvenile delinquency in the Netherlands. We will begin by defining youth criminality before examining some of the available statistics on juvenile delinquency and describing some trends and patterns of juvenile crime. The chapter will also offer an overview of the types of sanctioning and administrative measures that have been in existence and examine those that are being proposed. Finally, the chapter will conclude with an examination of some recent developments in and discussions on dealing with juvenile delinquency.

Defining Youth Criminality in the Netherlands

Every day, in the Netherlands, the regional and national media pay attention to the illegal activities committed by youths, categorically called "juvenile criminality." Even though, with some regularity, the media and public policies do not appear to differentiate the nature of illegal activities committed by a 10-year-old different from that of a 22-year-old, in legal terms it is a notable misnomer. There are distinct age limits in the Netherlands when it comes to the question of just what juvenile crime is or is not. The core of the Dutch justice system is the principle that punitive responsibility increases with age. To sum it up:

- For children under the age of 12, there are neither legal provisions for punitive responsibility nor can such youth be prosecuted for a criminal offense.
- Youth between the ages 12 and 18 fall into what is referred to as the "punitive minor years." Young persons who offend during these years are subject to the juvenile justice system.
- From 18 years on, the general justice system, also referred to as the adult justice system, applies.

When a youth under the age of 12 commits a punishable crime in the Netherlands, there is, in principle, no statement taken during the arrest.* This is the result of the content, in this case, the structure, of the juvenile justice system as we know it in the Netherlands.

Unlike in North America, it is worth noting that the juvenile criminal law is not a separate law, but a series of legal parameters within the general justice system. The Criminal Law Statute states specific parameters (Articles 77a through 77gg) regarding the category to which the juvenile justice system applies. Globally,† these are criminal minors from 12 to 18 years of age.

As previously mentioned, there is no punitive or criminal responsibility for those youths under the age of 12 years. This means that young persons under 12 years do not appear in police or judicial statistics, but in principle, the report is registered with Child Protection Services as a complaint, or child-rearing case, and not as a punitive case.‡

Like many other European countries, the Netherlands uses a graduated approach to criminal responsibility. For example, it is possible that a juvenile (usually 16 or 17 years old) is punished under the adult criminal system. This depends upon the suspect and the nature of the crime. Typically, such measures are restricted to those youths who commit serious vice crimes and extremely violent crimes such as homicide (i.e., murder and manslaughter), which are committed in a cold or calculated manner by criminal minors. The converse is also possible; that someone who is 18 or 19 years of age can also come under the juvenile justice system should their offense and character warrant it.

In spite of having a relatively precise definition of juvenile criminality, the description tends to create a general "dumping station" or "catch-all" term for juvenile crime. For example, one is just as guilty of committing a juvenile crime whether it is about a 14-year-old girl who steals cosmetics from a department store, a group of 13- or 14-year-old boys who vandalize a train car, or a 16-year-old boy who is repeatedly in the police station for breaking and entering.

The concept of juvenile criminality does not differentiate between the nature of the crimes committed and the type of offenders. Later in this chapter, juvenile crime in the Netherlands—as in other countries—will be described as being "multifacial" (Weijers and Eliaerts 2008).

Juvenile Criminality in the Netherlands

Police Statistics

Police statistics for 2008 show that in the Netherlands, the rate of juvenile offending was 24 per 1000 youths in the population. This figure is up from 1999 when the rate was (only) 16 per 1000 youths. In this respect, youth crime increased significantly until 2008. The reason for the increase may be that young people not only committed offenses more often but also that the police were more active in tackling youth crime or that victims were more inclined to report crimes (Wittebrood and Nieuwbeerta 2006; Maguire 2007). In a study into the relationship between social developments and the number of juvenile suspects

---

* This group is regarded to be 12-minors or child delinquents.
† It will later become clear why the word "globally" is used.
‡ This is consistent with the standards of the United Nations.

over the 1997–2007 period, more selective attention to youth crime was considered a likely explanation for this increase (van der Laan and Blom 2011).

However, from 2008 onward, a change has set in. Youth crime rates are decreasing. In 2008, for the first time, the number of minors arrested by the police was lower than in the preceding years. In the 2005–2009 period, the number of juvenile suspects arrested decreased from 24.5 to 20.6 per 1000 youths. The number of juvenile suspects arrested also decreased in absolute numbers (as Table 10.1 shows), as well as the number of offenses committed by them (Kalidien and Heer-De Lange 2011; van der Laan and Blom 2011).

The suspects arrested in 2009 were responsible for slightly more than 43,000 criminal offenses. Thus, on average, these suspects committed 1.8 offenses per person.

As is the case in most other parts of the world, young people in the Netherlands were mainly registered for property crime. In 2009, approximately 43% of all offenses could be classified as property crime. Shoplifting and motorcycle or bicycle theft were the offenses most often committed. A quarter of offenses could be classified as vandalism, followed by offenses in the categories of violent crime and sexual offenses (21%). In addition, a small proportion of offenses related to traffic offenses and drug-related crimes.

The offense category percentages have remained relatively stable over the past few years. However, until 2009, there was a fairly constant increase in the proportion of violent incidents (assault in particular). In 2009, this increase seemed to have come to a halt as it marked the first year since the beginning of the new millennium that there was a small decrease in the proportion of violence incidents.

The decrease in the number of suspects arrested appears to continue into the following years as well, because preliminary figures show that the total numbers of arrested suspects were 21,890 and 17,940 in 2010 and 2011, respectively. Therefore, an important policy and research question is to explain this decrease. Have young people become less delinquent? Do they spend so much time on Twitter and Facebook that there is no time left to steal a bike? Have the prevention campaigns and government policy measures been successful after all these years? Or could the decrease be ascribed to the way in which offenses are registered? As yet, it is not possible to provide a clear response.*

Table 10.1 Number of Juvenile Suspects Arrested in Absolute Numbers and per 1000 Population per Year and the Number of Offenses Committed

Year	2000	2001	2002	2003	2004	2005	2006	2007	2008	2009
Number of juvenile suspects arrested	17,150	19,220	20,920	23,360	26,440	29,370	30,630	32,230	28,540	24,400
Per 1,000 population (aged 12–17)	15,1	16,7	17,8	19,6	22,1	24,5	25,4	26,8	23,9	20,6
Total number of offenses committed by juvenile suspects arrested	39,540	41,350	44,990	50,730	55,520	60,880	62,030	65,270	55,110	43,490

Source: Central Bureau of Statistics (CBS).

* Bureau Beke is currently conducting a study in Amsterdam to find some explanations for the declining numbers of juvenile suspects in the capital city of the Netherlands.

Table 10.2   Juveniles That Reported an Offense in the Past Year by Offense Category in 2005 and 2010 in %

	2005	2010
	N = 1123	N = 2262
Violent crime	25.3	22.7
Property crime	25.3	20.7
Vandalism and offenses against law and public order	16.4	18.0
Possession of (fire)arms	5.3	3.3
Drug-related crime	2.5	2.3
All offenses	41.2	38.1

Source: Central Bureau of Statistics (CBS).

Self-Report Measures

Police statistics are not the only source of information we can use. Another way of measuring youth crime is by asking young people about their delinquent behavior and/or activities. These statistics are fairly adequate indicators of the number of young people who are not arrested for having committed an offense. For example, self-report statistics for 2010 showed that more than one-third (38%) of young people (12- to 18-years-old) committed an offense in the preceding 12 months (van der Laan and Blom 2011). This percentage is significantly higher than police statistics indicate. But the self-report data also showed a decrease across almost all crime categories. Table 10.2 shows the differences between the years 2005 and 2010.

While in 2005, 41% of 12- to 18-year-olds reported that they had been guilty of an offense, in 2010, this rate was slightly lower at 38%. The decrease can be seen, in particular, with respect to violent crime and property crime. However, the juveniles admitted to having vandalized more items compared to the juveniles in the previous research period. The causes of the decrease in self-reported offenses are unknown. However, researchers think that there is a real decline in crime and not simply a reflection of reporting or recording practices. This decline matches the decrease in the number of victims, as can be seen in victimization surveys (van der Laan and Blom 2011).

Gender and Crime

The majority of suspects arrested in the Netherlands are boys: In 2008, 80% of the juvenile suspects arrested were male and 20% were females. As is the case with their male counterparts, they are mainly registered with respect to property crimes. Girls occupy a modest place in crime statistics. Nevertheless, the proportion of girls in crime statistics has increased sharply over the years. One explanation could be that the police in particular have taken a different perspective on girls' delinquency (Mertens, Grapendaal, and Docter-Schamhardt 1998). The idea of boys committing offenses matches traditional expectations better than of girls committing offenses. Influenced by the feminist movement in the 1960s, these expectations have changed, however. Whereas previously the role of women in criminality was predominantly described from a victim's perspective, more recently more attention has been given to women as offenders. Police statistics have shown an increase in the number of crimes committed by girls since the 1960s. Girls, however, seem to stop committing criminal offenses at an earlier age than boys.

That said, the differences between delinquent boys and girls in self-report studies are much smaller than in the official records (de Vries-Bouw 2007; van der Laan and Blom 2011). This might indicate that the police treatment of offending girls differs from the way they treat offending boys. A study by Stol and Vink (2007) appears to confirm this assumption. They concluded that police contact with girls demonstrated more characteristics of a kind of (social) assistance than with boys. This seems to be logically consistent since delinquent girls have to contend with serious socio-emotional problems more frequently than boys (de Vries-Bouw 2007). Nevertheless, delinquency risk factors are mainly the same for both girls and boys. Psychological problems, early maturity, a problematic relationship with the mother, and problematic relationships with teachers seem to be risk factors specific to girls (Slotboom et al. 2011).

Ethnicity and Crime

In the past few years, more attention has been paid to crime in relation to ethnic origin in the Netherlands (Bovenkerk 1994, 2003; Kromhout and van San 2003). The central question is whether the proportion of ethnic groups in crime statistics is relatively higher than the proportion of people whose parents were both born in the Netherlands (see Box 10.1). Prudence and restraint are in order here because the risk of stigmatizing an entire ethnic group because of the criminal behavior of a minority is high.

Recent research shows that 13% of minor boys of Moroccan descent were suspected of an offense. For boys from the Netherlands Antilles, this rate was 10%. Approximately two-thirds of all Moroccan boys aged 12–23 years were arrested at least once by the police at some time or another. For Antillean boys in this age group, the rate was 55%, and of the boys whose parents were both born in the Netherlands, 25% had been arrested by the police at least once (Gijsberts, Huijnk, and Dagevos 2012).

As of 2013, much has been written on the relationship between ethnic origin and possible causes of the overrepresentation of youths from Moroccan or Antillean descent, in particular in Dutch crime statistics. Causes mentioned include a disadvantaged socio-economic position; however, native Dutch youths who are in a similar position have less often been in trouble with the police. Furthermore, many boys of Moroccan descent have problematic school careers (de Boom et al. 2010). Their time at school is characterized by skipping classes, poor results, and dropping out of high school without graduating. Consequently, their chances of entering the workforce are limited. Youths of Moroccan or Antillean descent often live in disadvantaged neighborhoods in the Netherlands where it is easy to come into contact with young people who have opted for a delinquent lifestyle (see Figure 10.1). The chances that they will enter into a criminal career themselves are very real. Moreover, parents often expect authorities such as school and police to control and

---

BOX 10.1   A MULTICULTURAL COUNTRY

Since August 1999, Statistics Netherlands has used a standard definition of foreigners. This definition states that a person is foreign if at least one parent is born abroad. In January 2012, 3.5 million foreigners (21% of the total population) lived in the Netherlands according to the standard definition. The largest groups are of Turkish, Surinam (with Dutch nationality), Moroccan, and Antillean origin.

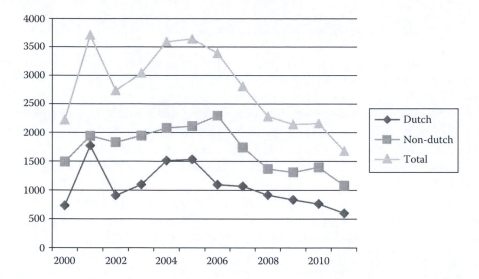

Figure 10.1 Number of juveniles in custody or placed in institutions by ethnicity from 2000 to 2011.

supervise their children. As a result, the parents themselves do not monitor the behavior of young people on the streets. For some ethnic minority youths that have no chances of acquiring wealth in a legal manner, crime is the only way to gain wealth and status. Some of them can get addicted to a "flashy life style" (van San, de Boom, and van Wijk 2006; van Wijk, Bervoets, and Stol 2003; van Wijk and Bremmers 2011).

The Different Faces of Juvenile Criminality

The term *juvenile criminality* is a catch-all term. To put it briefly, juvenile delinquents differ and offenses differ. In the Netherlands, an informal distinction is made among different types of offending youth. They include

- *At-risk youth* or juveniles who have not been guilty of committing criminal offenses as yet, but who are at risk of doing so because of several risk factors, such as problems at home, bad company, and drug abuse.
- *First offenders* or juveniles who have been arrested for an offense once. This group is responsible for a large part of all registered juvenile crime per year.
- *Multiple offenders* or juveniles who have been arrested more than once. They are also referred to as *second offenders.*
- *Repeat offenders* (also called *hardcore youth*). These juveniles frequently commit offenses (and consequently are frequent recidivists). This latter group attracts considerable media coverage. Since 2012, the Amsterdam authorities have developed a specific approach to handle this type of offenders (see Box 10.2).

Hard-Core and Kick Behavior

In general, delinquent behavior is age specific. In other words, young people may commit one or more offenses during their adolescence, but stop this kind of behavior in course of

BOX 10.2   THE AMSTERDAM TOP 600

The Top 600 is a list with the names of 600 people living in Amsterdam, the majority of whom are boys aged 18–24 years, who are responsible for a large number of serious local crimes. The police often have to deal with the same offenders. Many organizations deal with these boys alternately. The results are disappointing, as punishment or social assistance appears not to be effective for this group of offenders. The parents of these boys can hardly exert any constructive influence on them. These offenders often have mental problems or are addicted to alcohol or drugs. Since 2012, Amsterdam has worked with the Top 600, and local government, police, and the Public Prosecution Service have joined forces, together with partners from care organizations and juvenile institutions, juvenile justice institutions, and others. Delinquent behavior of these youths is met with consistent, prompt, and severe action.

time. In accordance with the typology by psychologist Moffitt (1993), only a small proportion—approximately 5% of all offenders in the Netherlands—can be labeled life course-persistent offenders. This group of offenders (i.e., repeat offenders in particular) start their criminal careers already at a young age, commit (serious) crimes very frequently, and continue to do so into late adulthood. Delinquents' life course-persistent criminal behavior can be explained as a combination of a child's problematic personality and the parents' failing (pedagogical/affective) responses to it. This "false start" may result in a negative spiral of maladjusted and antisocial behavior at a young age and a long-term criminal career into late adulthood.

By far, the majority of delinquents in the Netherlands can be classified as adolescence-limited offenders. This group consists of first and multiple offenders. Young boys commit most juvenile offenses, and it is generally considered "normal" behavior among their peers. Their behavior has been described as "kick behavior" (Ferwerda 1992). It is characterized by its short duration and is often the result of opportunity as opposed to planned behavior. Examples of opportunistic criminality are fare dodging, shoplifting, theft at school, and—preeminently—vandalism.

This form of juvenile crime is regarded as nuisance crime and is generally seen as part of young persons' "normal" development as they seek their behavioral boundaries and discover their self-control.

In the Netherlands, the philosophy on responding to this type of offenders is to react quickly and in a "pedagogical" way. Young people who have committed a minor offense are mostly given the opportunity to "pay for their crimes" ("tit for tat") without the intervention of the courts (see Box 10.3).

Group Criminality

Another characteristic of youth crime is the fact that the bulk of offenses are committed in groups (Hakkert et al. 1998; Schuyt, 1993; Sutherland, 1947). Groups are one of the most important sources of socialization for young people. Delinquent behavior is learned in these kind of social networks as well, as the esteemed sociologist Edwin H. Sutherland observed in 1947. Youth groups are often synonymous with problems, although this juxtaposition is

BOX 10.3   HALT—AN ALTERNATIVE SANCTION

Halt means "stop" in Dutch and is an acronym for *Het Alternatief* (the alternative). Halt is an organization in which local authorities join forces with the police and the judiciary to settle minor offenses quickly—such as vandalism, theft, shoplifting, or firework nuisance—committed by young people aged 12–18 years, by means of a simple sanction, in most cases, a training course or some sort of community service. In this way, young people can redeem the mistakes they made, without ending up with a criminal record (www.halt.nl).

not wholly justified. The majority of young people are members of groups of friends that do not cause any trouble, and hanging out with peer groups is part of the normal process of growing up and becoming an adult. The group's influence on the behaviors and beliefs of individual youths can be significant. As soon as youngsters go to secondary school, their parents' influence on their behaviors decreases, whereas peer groups become more and more influential (Steinberg and Silverberg 1986; Gardner and Steinberg 2005).

According to research completed by the author in 2000, young people want to be "one of the guys" and they tend to go to great lengths not to deviate from the group too much. A small proportion of them are members of groups that cause nuisance and commit offenses on the streets. Consequently, groups of youths call up negative associations in many adults. Actually, a relationship does appear to exist between being a member of a group and rule-breaking behavior. In a study of some 5000 adolescents, aged 12–18 years, the findings showed that adolescents who committed serious crimes belonged to youth groups more often than nondelinquent adolescents. The young people are members of groups and group dynamics exert a big influence on whether or not they commit offenses (Ferwerda 2000). The findings are consistent with those reported in an earlier study by Schuyt in 1993 where group delinquency was a principal characteristic of juvenile delinquency.

What can be defined as "group delinquency"? Observers are able to regard juveniles as one separate group, and/or the juveniles themselves can see themselves as one group, and they may engage in antisocial or delinquent behavior (van Wijk, Ferwerda, and Regterschot 2007). In the United States, where gangs are more or less an integral part of the street scene in certain neighborhoods, group delinquency has long been a full-fledged theme in criminology (see Chapter 15). In the Netherlands, this topic has generated attention only since the 1990s. The appearance of the first American-style gangs in the Netherlands and the individual nature of the Dutch criminal law system have definitely contributed to the fact that little attention was paid to the observation that approximately 70%–80% of juvenile crime is committed in a group context or is the result of group dynamics. There is a relationship between the nature of the offense and group activity: Some offenses are clear group crimes (e.g., public violence and vandalism), whereas others are individual crimes (e.g., household theft or theft at school and selling drugs) (see Box 10.3). Examples of offenses that may be individual as well as group crimes are bicycle theft, shoplifting, and joyriding (Ferwerda 2000).

Problematic youth groups are groups, which explicitly cause trouble and display criminal behavior in the public domain. Research in the Netherlands among 113 problematic youth groups showed that there is reason to assume that there are three types of problematic youth groups: annoying, nuisance-causing, and criminal youth groups (Beke, van Wijk, and Ferwerda 2000).

Young people who are members of *annoying groups* come together and hang around in one or more locations in their own neighborhoods. The group size varies from 10 to 20 members, for the most part, with young people aged 13–16 years, who are predominantly of native Dutch origin. The composition of these annoying youth groups is relatively stable, although these groups grow larger over time. Certain members play a leading, albeit largely implicit, role. Most of the group members go to school, and the remaining members have some kind of employment. They drink alcohol, but not as much when compared to the other two types of youth groups. Soft drugs' use is common, but Ecstasy or other drugs are consumed only rarely (see Box 10.4).

These young people have a fair number of contacts outside the group; newcomers are admitted relatively easily. On average, annoying groups last two-and-a-half years. They "specialize" in annoying behavior (e.g., hanging around, provoking shoppers, causing noise nuisance, committing minor acts of vandalism, breaking traffic rules, and sometimes committing (mainly) minor violent and property crimes), as their crime profile shows. This kind of behavior is dealt with by a so-called Halt settlement or a fine at the most. From time to time, they go too far, but they still can be corrected rather easily. This type of group has a slight tendency to challenge public authority.

Nuisance-causing groups (NCGs) also have 10–20 members in general who are just slightly older than members of annoying groups. Their level of education is also somewhat lower. Often these groups consist of young people who dropped out of school and are unemployed as well. Members of these groups are more often of different ethnic backgrounds. This type of youth group is less neighborhood bound. These young people also go out regularly, drink a lot of alcohol, and regularly use soft drugs, Ecstasy, and Speed. They engage more often in public violence and minor assault (sometimes this includes the use of weapons). They get into trouble with the police regularly, and a number of them have

---

BOX 10.4   DUTCH DRUGS POLICY

The government focuses on preventing drug use and reducing the risks to users and those around them. Toleration (i.e., exemption from prosecution) is the main thrust of Dutch policy.

Marijuana and hashish are less harmful to health than hard drugs like Ecstasy and cocaine, but they are just as illegal. This means that trafficking, selling, producing, and possessing any drugs in the Netherlands is a criminal offense.

The Netherlands pursues a policy of toleration. This means that, though possessing and selling soft drugs are misdemeanors, prosecutions are usually not brought upon the offenders.

Tolerating the sale of soft drugs within clearly defined limits and taking rigorous action against the sale of hard drugs keeps the markets for the two types of drugs separate. The sale of cannabis in coffee shops is an example of this policy. Because of such a policy, cannabis users do not need to buy their soft drugs from a dealer operating illegally, which would increase their chances of coming into contact with hard drugs.

received both a Halt settlement or penalty and a conditional, or unconditional, sentence of imprisonment.

Compared to the "annoying groups," NCGs are more closely knit, and they exist longer than "annoying groups" (4 years on average). The youths that play a central or leading role are more often recognized as leaders by the other members of the group. There tend to be few turnovers among members in the group, and membership is limited and restrictive.

NCGs do not refrain from violence and sometimes even revert to more severe forms of violence. Confrontations with public authorities occur more often and tend to be more serious than with the previous type of youth group. In this regard, the antisocial core of this group is quite evident.

Criminal groups (CGs), on average, include 30 members, and the age range is wider than for the other group types. The youngest members are approximately 12 years of age, the oldest are 20 plus. Their level of education is extremely low; a substantial part of them have not received much education beyond primary school or are in special education programs, and many of them are unemployed (Beke, van Wijk, and Ferwerda 2000). This type of youth group often consists of various ethnic groups or one single ethnic group (typically of Moroccan or Antillean descent).

CGs have the largest action radius and sometimes even operate at a regional or national level. They do so partly to visit various entertainment districts, and/or partly with criminal intent. The use of alcohol and drugs is widespread. The majority of members possess a weapon (usually a stabbing weapon or a thrust weapon), which they use whenever they see fit (Beke, van Wijk, and Ferwerda 2000). This group ranks high in all forms of annoying behavior and tend to be more involved in more serious types of crime, such as drugs dealing, assault, and robbery and assault. Crime is committed because of its gain, financial or otherwise. Apart from being fined, young people in these groups have traditionally been sentenced to imprisonment.

Street Gangs and Youth Gangs

It is also clear from the studies previously mentioned that a small number of youth groups manifest themselves as collectives. Such groups have a distinct structure and hierarchy, and decisions are weighed against the collective interest. Yablonsky (1959) called these groups *near-groups* and *groups,* also referred to as *gangs*—a term more commonly used in North America. Some researchers say gangs are characterized by their committing crimes because of financial motives; other researchers consider their level of organization a defining criterion. Sometimes, the territory aspect is referred to as well.

In a Dutch study on group crime, an inventory was made of a series of group characteristics, which can be reduced to two factors. The first factor is that "gangs" are "tightly organized versus loosely organized or unorganized," including the following five characteristics: the cohesiveness of the group structure, the degree of mutual solidarity, the degree of organization, the extent to which criminal activities are planned, and the degree/frequency of changes within the groups. The second factor used can be described as "open, nonhierarchical versus closed hierarchical," including the following three characteristics: the degree of hierarchy, the degree of internal rivalry, and the extent to which the group presents itself as a group. NGCs that score high on both dimensions are referred to as street gangs in the Netherlands; CGs that score high on these dimensions are called youth gangs (Beke, van Wijk, and Ferwerda 2000).

In late 2012, the Netherlands officially had 976 problematic youth groups. Some 731 of them could be classified as annoying, 186 as nuisance causing, and 59 as criminal. Of these groups, 10 could be classified as street gangs and 8 as youth gangs (Ferwerda and van Ham 2013). Over the years, there has been a decrease because in late 2009, there were 1760 problematic youth groups (Ferwerda and van Ham 2009). The positive effects of the joint approach (municipality, police, youth work, and the Public Prosecution Service) concerning youth groups as of 2009 thus are becoming visible.

The Context

The nuisance caused by groups of youths in the public domain is often related to the specific characteristics of the location of these young people or to the lack of facilities. Problematic youth groups, in particular those groups that cause relatively many serious problems, are often to be found in the disadvantaged neighborhoods of the large cities in the Netherlands (see Box 10.5). These neighborhoods are often characterized by social deprivation and a culture of confrontation: the young people's street culture versus the

---

BOX 10.5   SOCIAL CONTEXT: THE DIAMOND NEIGHBORHOOD OF AMSTERDAM

The Diamond neighborhood is a small area in the De Pijp district in Amsterdam with relatively small, inexpensive, thin-walled rental houses that are located on narrow streets. There are two streets with private property and there are seldom any problems there. This small neighborhood has many council houses, and there is little social cohesion among the inhabitants who come from many different sociocultural backgrounds. Social problems in this neighborhood range from quarrels between neighbors and domestic violence to poverty (debts). As one inhabitant reported: "This neighborhood does not have a problem with Moroccan youths in particular, but with inhabitants' antisocial behavior in general."

In addition, some inhabitants complain about the nuisance caused by youths on the streets. The aggressive youths from the "Diamond Group" live in the vicinity or are drawn to it. The majority of the boys from the Diamond Group have grown up in this neighborhood or its immediate surroundings, their family homes are small, and they have relatively many siblings. As a result, the streets and their friends appeal to them greatly: "At home you eat and sleep, the streets is where you live."

The mothers are the center of the family. The fathers are usually unemployed, are held in low esteem by their sons, and lack the pedagogical power to raise their children in a positive manner. The boys behave better at home than on the streets. Many of the boys do study but are frustrated because they feel that they cannot really participate in society—a sense of alienation. Boys are often refused entry to hotels, restaurants, or pubs, and for those who would like to work, it is difficult to find a job on the side or to get an internship. Some key informants indicated that the group and their families have a long-standing tradition of defiance toward organizations such as the police, judiciary, and local government, and some even harbor anti-Dutch feelings (Ferwerda 2005, 11).

Dutch bourgeois culture, also referred to as the "us versus them perspective" (Adang et al. 2006; Kop et al. 2007), young people versus older people, and young people from ethnic minorities (and sometimes their parents as well) versus the authorities. Such mechanisms and characteristics were also visible during the riots in the suburbs of Paris such as Clichy-sous-Bois and Saint Denis in 2005.

Background of the Dutch Juvenile Justice System

This section offers a concise overview of the development of juvenile justice in the Netherlands. The material is based on the work of the esteemed Dutch criminologist, Professor Josine Junger-Tas (1930–2011; Junger-Tas, 1997).

1613—First childcare measure in Amsterdam.

1666—Opening of a special courthouse and two orphanages.

1809—The Dutch Criminal Code distinguished three categories of juveniles. Children under the age of 12 could not be punished. Children aged 12–15 years could have the so-called children's punishment, and juveniles aged 15–18 years, mitigated adult punishment.

1811—Replacement of the Criminal Code by the Code Pénal (Napoleon), which did not make any distinction between children and adults.

1886—The New Penal Code added that children under the age of 10 could not be prosecuted. In this code, a separate system of sanctions for adults and children was included.

1901—The first Dutch Children's Act. This first civil law made it possible to encroach on parental authority in cases where the child was in need of protection. The second (Juvenile Penal Law) abolished the requirement of "discernment between right and wrong" as a criterion for guilt in children, and also abolished any distinction based on age. The law ruled that children could no longer be detained along with adults, but had to be placed in separate youth institutions. This law also created three special youth sanctions: reprimands, fines, and placement in a reformatory for a period of no less than 1 month and no more than 12 months. Juveniles aged 16–18 years who had committed serious crimes may be sent to prison. Mentally disturbed juveniles may be placed "at the disposal of the government" (TBS, See Box 10.9) in a treatment institution until their adulthood at the age of 21.

1922—Introduction of a separate juvenile court in civil and penal matters. The law also introduced the Supervision Order (OTS—a Supervision Order for a child).

1965—Major revision of the law in a sense that the welfare system was introduced in the juvenile justice. Its characteristics were

- Large discretionary powers, especially for the juvenile judge, based on the concept of *parens patriae*, which presumes that the judge always acts in the best interest of the child.
- Irrespective of the criminal act, the personality and the needs of the child are predominant and dictate the decision.
- An emphasis on treatment and assistance to the family and child instead of on punishment.

- Proceedings are informal—court hearings are not open to the public, all proceedings are of a confidential nature—and there are hardly any procedural safeguards because in a welfare system, these are deemed unnecessary.

1980s–1990s—Like in many other countries, the Netherlands experienced a recession, unemployment rose, immigration from trouble spots around the world increased, and the future looked insecure to many. One could say that in this period, the postwar economic boom ended and the crime picture changed. The spread of drugs and illegal immigration brought more street crime. For the first time, crime became an important political issue. There was a noticeable shift away from deterministic environmental causes of crime and a belief in education and treatment to a philosophy of free will in which juveniles are considered responsible for their actions. In these years, there was a clear shift in the juvenile justice system from a *welfare model* to a *justice model*. This change resulted in a new legislation in 1995.

1995—New Criminal Code for juveniles.

2012—Adolescent criminal law bill sent to the House of Representatives.

When we look at the development of the juvenile justice system in the Netherlands, we could say that it changed in a relatively short period of time from a *welfare model* in the 1960s and 1970s to a *justice model* in the 1990s (see Table 1.1 in the Introduction). This change also led to a renewed emphasis on punishment as well as on early detection of troublesome behavior. The trend may reflect the social and political nature of reform and a growing sentiment of conservatism in the Netherlands (see Box 10.6). Apart from this development, it is also fair to say that in the past few years, government authorities have paid considerable attention to the early detection of at-risk youth, to facilitate a customized approach (see Box 10.7).

BOX 10.6   PUBLIC DEMAND FOR MORE SEVERE PUNISHMENT

On January 14, 2012, 15-year-old Winsie Hau was stabbed to death in the hallway of her family home in the city of Arnhem. Because of an argument over some gossip on Facebook with her former 16-year-old best friend Polly, the latter concluded that Winsie had to die. Polly and her 17-year-old boyfriend sent the then 14-year-old Jinhua from Rotterdam to Arnhem to stab Winsie to death. Five days after having been stabbed by Jinhua, Winsie died of her injuries in hospital. On Monday, August 20, 2012, the Arnhem court public prosecutor demanded the maximum sentence for Jinhua: 1 year of juvenile detention and 2 years of youth custody. This youth custody can be extended to a maximum of 7 years. The next day, a regional newspaper asked its readers what they thought of the following statement: "Maximum sentences for juvenile delinquents should be increased significantly"; 975 readers responded, and 92% voted in favor of the statement. On September 3, 2012, the judge sentenced the juvenile offender in accordance with the prosecution's demand.

Source: Dagblad de Gelderlander, September 2012.

> ## BOX 10.7   A CUSTOMIZED APPROACH FOR EVERY YOUNG PERSON
>
> Since 2012, the so-called National Toolset for the Juvenile Criminal Law Chain (NTJ) has been applied in the Netherlands. This toolset was developed by a group of academics (van der Put et al. 2011) and is meant for young people aged 12–18 years who have gotten into trouble with law enforcement authorities. The NTJ calculates the risk of recidivism and draws a profile of existing protective and risk factors and indications of care needed, if any. On these grounds, it is determined which criminal law approach and what care, if any, juveniles need. At this moment, the NTJ is tested in several areas and will subsequently be introduced nationally.

Reactions to Juvenile Criminal Behavior

In general, it can be said that the Dutch are reserved when it comes to imposing heavy sanctions such as imprisonment and rather gravitate toward using alternative measures. The Dutch approach toward its justice model tends to emphasize prevention over custody. Therefore, unless the offense committed is "serious," the police are inclined to use the so-called pedagogical sanctions before using alternative measures such as community service or some other measure.

In the Netherlands, there are various possibilities to punish juvenile delinquents. The most common ones are listed here (van Wijk, Appelman, Ferwerda, and Bremmers 2013):

Halt—This is an alternative type of punishment imposed on juveniles who have been arrested by the police for having committed less serious offenses (e.g., shoplifting or vandalism) for the first time. In general, Halt sanctions include performing assigned tasks, making apologies to the victim, and paying back the damage they caused (see Box 10.3).

Community service and training program sanctions—Such sanctions can be imposed instead of a major penalty (a conditional or unconditional sentence of imprisonment or a fine). In fact, a combination of community service and training program sanctions can be imposed to a maximum of 240 hours of service.

A fine—A fine can be a separate penalty, but can also be imposed in combination with another penalty (e.g., a conditional sentence of imprisonment). Depending on the offense, fines may range from 3 to 3900 euro.

Conditional sentence of imprisonment—A conditional sentence of imprisonment should mainly be regarded as a judicial "wake-up call." This sanction is often imposed, combined with another sanction (assistance and support).

Youth custody—The unconditional sentence of imprisonment called youth custody can be imposed in the case of a (serious) criminal offense. The length of youth custody varies from a minimum of 1 day to a maximum of 2 years (custody in a youth detention center).

Behavioral interventions—These measures fill the gap between a conditional sentence and detention. If a conditional sentence is too mild and detention too harsh, a judge can decide to impose a behavioral intervention. Consequently, these measures are meant for multiple offenders, repeat offenders, and "hard-core youth" with behavior problems in particular (Drost, van de Grift, and Jongebreur 2010). Behavioral interventions may include social skills training and aggression management training. These measures are imposed for a period of 6–12 months.

Placement in a juvenile institution (PJI)—In addition to the aforementioned sanctions, Dutch juvenile criminal law also includes a number of (correctional) measures. These are meant for minors who—in the eyes of the law—not only need to be punished for felonies but also need to be treated psychologically to prevent recidivism (e.g., in the case of psychopathological juvenile delinquents). The most important criminal law measure meant for minors is placement in a juvenile institution (for a maximum stay of 6 years).

Mandatory contact with youth rehabilitation services—In addition to punishment and (correctional) measures, the instrument of mandatory contact with youth rehabilitation services (for counseling) can also be used. This type of sanction is imposed in the case of rather mild offenses, and in those cases where young offenders show a wider range of problem behaviors, and opportunities for "assistance and support" appear to exist. In these cases, the Dutch Child Welfare Council may conduct a study, an OTS may be imposed, or the youths concerned may be subjected to other forms of mandatory assistance. Counseling by youth rehabilitation services is possible both before and after appearance in court.

In the past few years, the number of juveniles in custody or institutions has decreased considerably (see Figure 10.2).

A recent Halt Netherlands annual report showed that in 2011, a total of 16,526 young people were referred to their offices by police, school attendance officers, or other authorities for some sort of punishment (Halt Nederland, 2011). This number was slightly lower than in previous years and was in line with the national trend of falling crime rates. It turns out that the number of juveniles in detention decreased by more than 50%—from approximately 5000 in 2005 to 2000 in 2010. It also turns out that judges most often sentenced minor suspects to community service (working for the benefit of the community

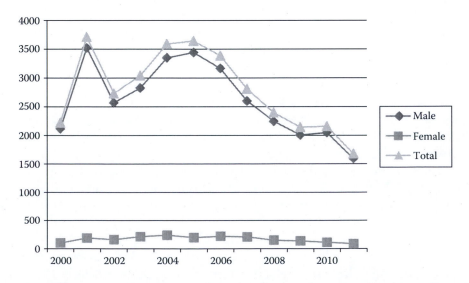

Figure 10.2 Number of juveniles in custody or placed in institutions by sex from 2000 to 2011.

BOX 10.8   THE CLOSING DOWN OF JUVENILE JUSTICE INSTITUTIONS

In 2007, the Dutch government spent 320 million euro on juvenile justice institutions; in 2012, it spent 272 million euros. This reduction was mainly caused by the decline in youth crime. Recently, the Department of Justice has reduced the number of juvenile justice institutions from 14 to 10, and residential treatment has been reduced by more than 50% to a capacity of 1244 beds. The State Secretary for Security and Justice intends to reduce this number further to 950. The increasing number of unfilled vacancies in juvenile justice institutions is also caused by the fact that young people are more often sentenced to other types of dispositions such as community service and training program sanctions. The Ministry of Security and Justice estimates the current costs of the unfilled vacancies at 100 million euro per year.

---

and educational penalties). In 2010, more than 7000 community sentences were imposed. The data also show that the proportion of community sentences increased steadily from 2005 to 2010. In 2010, nearly three-quarters of all juvenile delinquents were sentenced to some sort of community sentence; about one-quarter was sentenced to a detention facility. Based on available data for 2010, fines only accounted for approximately 5% (N = 450) of all sanctions imposed on minors (see Box 10.8).

Discussions and Developments in Delinquency and Juvenile Justice

Since the beginning of the new millennium, there have been a number of important developments and debates in the Netherlands that should be mentioned here.

Ever since the publication of the "Tenacious and Effective" (*Vasthoudend en Effectief*) report in 2002, Dutch policy-makers have particularly focused on a joint approach of tackling youth crime, and young people's behavior and the application of approved behavioral interventions have played a major role in this respect. This view was also expressed in the action program "Justice to Young People" (Jeugd Terecht), which the Balkenende II government presented in 2002. The key focus points included more goal-oriented action in the investigation phase, a quick and coherent response, effective punishment, and emphasis on resocialization. This aspect of resocialization in particular constituted a change compared to previous measures. In addition, differential approaches were proposed for at-risk youth, first offenders, multiple offenders, and repeat offenders (Minisiterie van Justitie 2002). Also, a distinction was made among groups (i.e., annoying, NCGs, and CGs), youth under the age of 12, and young people from ethnic minorities. It is striking that the action program paid so much attention to risk factors. Special efforts were made to reintegrate young people back into society.

This personalized approach, with its focus on risk factors at both individual and family levels, was continued in the 2008 program "Tackling Juvenile Crime" (*Aanpak Jeugdcriminaliteit*) (Minisiterie van Justitie 2008). In addition, a quick and consistent youth chain, early intervention, and appropriate aftercare remained key action points. An example from this program is the way at-risk youth are dealt with in secure homes. In dealing with these youths, care and punishment are combined to create a personalized approach aimed at changing behavior, reducing recidivism, and enhancing delinquents' quality of life. A preliminary assessment of these secure homes showed that coordination between parties and the coherence of interventions has increased significantly, just as early detection and correctional action have improved (Rovers 2011). Moreover, a National Toolset for the Juvenile Criminal Law Chain (NTJ) was developed as a result of this program. With this toolset, an appropriate offender-focused approach can be realized for every youth considered at risk.

In 2011, the Rutte government (liberal/conservative) not only focused on action against annoying and nuisance-causing youth groups but also against criminal youth groups (Ministerie van Veiligheid and Justitie 2011). The "Criminal Youth Groups" action program stated that criminal youth groups were the most serious category of youth groups who committed serious types of crimes, such as armed robbery and assault. The seriousness of the offenses and their far-reaching consequences for society combined with the public's feelings of safety prompted the government to decide that the CGs should be dealt with. Effective action would entail a combination of penalties and measures, and taking away profits resulting from criminal activities had to be encouraged. Effective action also meant that a quick criminal law response was essential. In this respect, a "tit for tat" approach was considered paramount. To realize a quick response, the importance of close cooperation of all parties involved—police, local government, and the Public Prosecution Service in particular—was emphasized. Examples of measures that could be effectively combined included behavioral measures, restraining orders ("stay away" or "no contact" provisions), the duty to report oneself to the authorities on given days and times, rehabilitation measures, community sentences, detention, and summary justice. Also, attention was required for the further development of adolescent criminal law.

As mentioned earlier, Dutch juvenile criminal law applies to young people aged 12 (lower limit) to 18 (upper limit) years. It is possible, however, to sentence 16- and 17-year-olds under adult criminal law. And it is also possible to apply juvenile criminal law to 18- to 21-year-olds. The age limits have always been the subject of debate. Recently, the Dutch government presented a bill on the introduction of separate criminal law for adolescents, which could be applied to 15- to 23-year-old offenders. Should the House of Representatives and the Senate adopt this bill, then in the future, judges will determine—on the basis of the young person's personal development—the type of criminal law that is applicable (juvenile, adolescent, or adult criminal law) (Doreleijers, Ten Voorde, and Moerings 2010).

The reasons for the government to draft such a bill include the findings of recent neurobiological research (de Graaf-Peters and Hadders-Algra 2006; Spear 2013). These findings clearly demonstrate that neurological development is not complete in 18-year-olds. Essential developments actually take place at a later age, for example, the ability to control impulses, emotion management, empathy, and the ability to make long-term plans. At approximately 24 years of age, these abilities are fully developed. For that reason, one might say that juvenile offenders are not fully accountable for their actions given their "limitations." Brain development may thus be an important explanation for delinquent youth desisting crime in adulthood. In other words, there is a relationship between the not-fully developed brain and criminal behavior, which in most cases can be characterized as an age-specific phenomenon.

Another reason for the Dutch government to introduce adolescent criminal law is the fact that adolescents are well represented in crime statistics. According to various officials, they should be punished more efficiently and in an evidence-informed manner.

For example, one proposal entails making use of electronic supervision more often and making possible temporary placement in an institution for juvenile offenders if a young person refuses to participate in measures aimed at influencing behavior. With the new adolescent criminal law, the government not only intends to create a more efficient and effective punishment, but also to ensure greater accountability for the legal transgressions of juvenile offenders. To quote the government: "A coherent set of sanctions for 15- to 23-year-olds which focuses on tough and, in particular, consistent action towards at-risk youth." According to the proposal, the maximum length of juvenile detention will be increased from 2 to 4 years, and serious crimes such as sexual or violent offenses cannot be settled with a community sentence. If the convict is still (considered) dangerous at the end of a PJI-order, the court can change that measure into detention at the Government's pleasure (TBS) (see Box 10.9).

Several Dutch professors have been very critical of this proposed adolescent criminal law (see e.g., Doreleijers, Ten Voorde, and Moerings 2010). In a national newspaper article, they stated that the number of juvenile offenders is decreasing. Meanwhile various juvenile justice institutions have been closed because of too few delinquents being directed or placed in these facilities (see Box 10.8). The experts fear that the effects of tougher action against juvenile delinquents will be counterproductive, in particular with respect to 16- and 17-year-olds. The findings of neurobiological research should, on the contrary, lead to a less repressive punishment regime.

The Council for the Administration of Criminal Justice and Protection of Juveniles is also very critical of the proposed bill on adolescent criminal law and advises against it (Raad voor Strafrechtstoepassing en Jeugdbescherming 2012). In the council's view, one objection is that the measures proposed are neither substantiated by academic research nor is it clear whether they will contribute to making the Netherlands safer and more secure. It is suggested that tougher and more repressive measures against juvenile delinquents would be more effective and would contribute to reducing recidivism. The council, however, argued that research literature irrefutably shows that tougher and more repressive measures are not conducive to safety and security, but may even be counterproductive, and will result—in any case in the long term—in more rather than less recidivism. The council argues in favor of separate criminal law for all young adults aged 18–24 years and more emphasis on the pedagogic basis of juvenile criminal law.

BOX 10.9   DETENTION AT THE GOVERNMENT'S PLEASURE, OR TBS

The Dutch abbreviation TBS stands for detention at the government's discretion. It is a treatment order that the court imposes on people who have committed serious crimes and are suffering from a mental illness or psychiatric disorder. This disorder influences their behavior to a greater or lesser extent. Therefore, the court does not hold them fully accountable for their offenses. For the part of the offense for which the perpetrator can indeed be held accountable, the court can impose a prison sentence; this is a so-called combined sentence (e.g., 2 years in prison plus TBS). One of the reasons for imposing TBS is to treat the disorder and to prevent the perpetrator from reoffending (recidivism). All this is done to protect society.

Conclusion

In the Netherlands, youth crime is—as in many other countries—predominantly committed by boys. Girls are "catching up," however. The extent of youth crime appears to be declining, although it is not exactly clear why this is the case. Dutch crime statistics also indicate that ethnic minority youths are disproportionately represented; in particular, boys of Moroccan and Antillean descent commit more (group) crimes.

Over the past few decades, Dutch juvenile criminal law has evolved from a welfare model into a justice model. Despite the fact that much attention is paid to the offender's background characteristics in the Netherlands, the current trend is one of more severe punishment. In the past few years, this development has been illustrated by the introduction of the NTJ, which focuses on risk assessment and a customized approach for juvenile offenders with, on the one hand, a joint customized approach in dealing with juvenile delinquents and, on the other hand, tough action against criminal youth groups.

The recent proposal to introduce adolescent criminal law is also reflective of this growing ambiguity. At this time, individual characteristics of the juvenile offender are taken into account (e.g., intelligence and vulnerability) to facilitate a customized approach. However, several proposals that are currently discussed imply more severe sanctions for juveniles who have committed serious offenses. Therefore, it appears that the Dutch juvenile justice system is in a state of considerable flux. It is almost certain that juvenile criminal law will change in the Netherlands in the near future. What these changes will involve, however, is not clear as yet.

Review/Discussion Questions

1. Do you consider the introduction of adolescent criminal law—as is intended in the Netherlands—useful? Please explain your answer.
2. Explain why you feel that adolescents in the Netherlands get either less or more associated with hard drugs compared to juveniles/young offenders of your country, perhaps.
3. What is your opinion on the National Toolset for the Juvenile Criminal Law Chain (NTJ), which is developed in the Netherlands? Please explain your answer.
4. Notwithstanding the fact that suspects in the case of Winsie Hau (Box 10.6) received the maximum sentence, citizens tended to disagree with this penalty. Please explain how this can be interpreted.
5. Juvenile crime often is committed in groups. In the Netherlands, three types of problematic youth groups are distinguished. What is your opinion on this typology of problematic youth groups and do you consider such a typology to be applicable in your country? Please explain your answer.

References

Adang, O., N. Kop, H. Ferwerda, J. Heijnemans, W. Olde Nordkamp, P. de Paauw, and K. van Woerkom. (2006). *Omgaan met conflictsituaties: Op zoek naar goede werkwijzen bij de politie.* Politieacademie/Bureau Beke: Apeldoorn.

Bartels, J. (2007). *Jeugdstrafrecht*. Kluwer Juridisch: Deventer.

Beke, B., A. van Wijk, and H. Ferwerda. (2000). *Criminaliteit in groepsverband ontrafeld. Tussen rondhangen en bendevorming*. SWP: Amsterdam.

Bovenkerk, F. (1994). Een misdadige tweede generatie immigranten? Verklaringen voor de omvang, aard en oorzaken van jeugdcriminaliteit in verschillende etnische groepen. *Jeugd en Samenleving,jrg.* 24 (7/8), 387–404.

Bovenkerk, F. (2003). Over de oorzaken van allochtone misdaad. In: F. Bovenkerk, M. Komen, and Y. Yesilgöz (Eds.), *Multiculturaliteit in de strafrechtspleging*. Boom Juridische Uitgevers: Den Haag, 29–58.

de Boom, J., A. Weltevrede, P. van Wensveen, M. van San, and P. Hermus. (2010). *Marokkaanse Nederlanders 2010. Een nulmeting van hun positie op de terreinen van onderwijs, arbeid en uitkering en criminaliteit in 22 gemeenten*. Risbo, Erasmus Universiteit: Rotterdam.

de Graaf-Peters, V.B. and M. Hadders-Algra. (2006). Ontogeny of the human central nervous system: What is happening when? *Early Human Development*. 82 (4), 257–266.

de Vries-Bouw, M. (2007). Meisjes en delinquentie. In: A. van Wijk, E. Bervoets and W. Stol (Eds.), *Politie en jeugd. Inleiding voor de praktijk*. Elsevier: Den Haag, 127–138.

Doreleijers, T., J. Ten Voorde, and M. Moerings. (2010). *Strafrecht en forensische psychiatrie voor 16- tot 23-jarigen*. Boom Juridische Uitgevers: Den Haag.

Drost, V., M. van de Grift, and W. Jongebreur. (2010). *Impact van de gedragsbeïnvloedende maatregel ruim twee jaar na invoering*. Significant B.V.: Barneveld.

Ferwerda, H. (1992). *Watjes en ratjes. Een longitudinaal onderzoek naar het verband tussen maatschappelijke kwetsbaarheid en jeugdcriminaliteit*. Wolters-Noordhof B.V.: Groningen.

Ferwerda, H. (2000). Jeugdcriminaliteit en de rol van de groep. De groep als negatieve voedingsbodem. *J*—Tijdschrift over jongeren*. 1 (1), 34–44.

Ferwerda, H. (2002). Youth Crime and Juvenile Justice in The Netherlands. In: Winterdyk, J. (Ed.), *Juvenile Justice Systems: International Perspectives* (2nd ed.). Canadian Scholars' Press Inc.: Toronto, 385–411.

Ferwerda, H. (2005). *De Diamantgroep: De aanpak gebundeld*. Bureau Beke: Arnhem.

Ferwerda, H. and T. van Ham. (2009). *Problematische jeugdgroepen in Nederland: Omvang, aard en politieproces beschreven*. Bureau Beke: Arnhem.

Ferwerda, H. and T. van Ham. (2013). *Problematische jeugdgroepen in Nederland: Omvang en aard in het najaar van 2012*. Bureau Beke: Arnhem.

Gardner, M. and L. Steinberg. (2005). Peer influence on risk taking, risk preference, and risky decision making in adolescence and adulthood: An experimental study. *Developmental Psychology*. 41 (4), 625–635.

Gijsberts, M., W. Huijnk, and J. Dagevos. (2012). *Jaarrapport integratie 2011*. Sociaal en Cultureel Planbureau: Den Haag.

Hakkert, A., A. van Wijk, H. Ferwerda, and T. Eijken. (1998). *Groepscriminaliteit: Een terreinverkenning op basis van literatuuronderzoek en een analyse van bestaand onderzoeksmateriaal, aangevuld met enkele interviews met sleutelinformanten en jongeren die tot groepen behoren*. Stafbureau Informatie, Voorlichting en Publiciteit. Directie Preventie, Jeugd en Sanctiebeleid. Ministerie van Justitie: Den Haag.

Halt Nederland. (2011). *Jaarbericht Halt-sector*. Leiden.

Junger-Tas, J. (1997). Juvenile delinquency and juvenile justice in The Netherlands. In: J.A. Winterdyk (Ed.), *Juvenile Justice Systems: International Perspectives*. Canadian Scholars' Press: Toronto, 55–75.

Kalidien, S. and N. Heer-de Lange. (2011). *Criminaliteit en rechtshandhaving 2010. Ontwikkelingen en samenhangen*. Boom Juridische uitgevers: Meppel.

Kop, N., M. Euwema, M.M.V., H. Ferwerda, E. Giebels, W. Olde Nordkamp, and P. de Paauw. (2007). *Conflict op straat, strijden of mijden?: Marokkaanse en Antilliaanse jongeren in interactie met de politie*. Apeldoorn.

Kromhout, M. and M. van San. (2003). *Schimmige werelden. Nieuwe etnische groepen en jeugdcriminaliteit*. BJU: Den Haag.

Maguire, M. (2007). Crime data and statistics. In: Maguire, M., R. Morgan, and R. Reiner (Eds.), *Oxford Handbook of Criminology* (3rd ed.). Oxford University Press: New York.

Mertens, N., M. Grapendaal, and B. Docter-Schamhardt. (1998). *Meisjescriminaliteit in Nederland*. WODC: Den Haag.

Ministerie van Justitie. (2002). *Jeugd terecht—aanpak jeugdcriminaliteit 2003-2006*. Den Haag.

Ministerie van Justitie. (2008). *Programma Aanpak Jeugdcriminaliteit 2008-2010*. Den Haag.

Ministerie van Veiligheid and Justitie. (2011). *Actieprogramma criminele jeugdgroepen*. Den Haag.

Moffitt, T. (1993). Adolescence-limited and life-course-persistent antisocial behavior: A developmental taxonomy. *Psychological Review*. 100 (4), 674–701.

Raad voor Strafrechtstoepassing en Jeugdbescherming. (2012). *Wetsvoorstel adolescentenstrafrecht. Een gemiste kans*.

Rovers, B. (2011). Eerst de beren, dan de honing. Resultaten van Veiligheidshuizen. *Secondant*. 25 (3/4), 58–63.

Schuyt, C. (1993). Jeugdcriminaliteit in groepsverband. *Delikt en Delinkwent*. 23 (6), 499–510.

Slotboom, A., T. Wong, C. Swier, and T. van der Broek. (2011). *Delinquente meisjes, achtergronden, risicofactoren en interventies*. Boom Juridische uitgevers: Den Haag.

Spear, L. (2013). Adolescent neurodevelopment. *Journal of Adolescent Health*. 52 (2), S7–S13.

Steinberg, L. and S. Silverberg. (1986). The vicissitudes of autonomy in early adolescence. *Child Development*. 57 (4), 841–851.

Stol, W. and N. Vink. (2007). Interacties op straat tussen politie en jeugd. In: A. van Wijk and E. Bervoets, and W. Stol (Eds.), *Politie en jeugd. Inleiding voor de praktijk*. Elsevier: Den Haag, 301–316.

Sutherland, E. (1947). *Principles of Criminology* (4th ed.). Harper and Row, Publishers, Inc.: New York.

van der Laan, A. and M. Blom. (2011). *Jeugdcriminaliteit in de periode 1996–2010. Ontwikkelingen in zelfgerapporteerde daders, door de politie aangehouden verdachten en strafrechtelijke daders op basis van de Monitor Jeugdcriminaliteit 2010*. WODC: Den Haag.

van der Put, C., H. Spanjaard, L. van Domburgh, T. Doreleijers, H. Lodewijks, H. Ferwerda, R. Bolt, and G. Stams. (2011). Ontwikkeling van het landelijk instrumentarium jeugdstrafrechtketen (LIJ). In: *Kind and Adolescent Praktijk*. 2 (June), 76–83.

van San, M., J. de Boom, and A. van Wijk. (2006). *Verslaafd aan een flitsende levensstijl. Aard en omvang van de criminaliteit onder Antillianen in Rotterdam*. RISBO: Rotterdam.

van Wijk, A., T. Appelman, H. Ferwerda, and B. Bremmers. (2013). Helpt straffen? Een essay over straffen van jeugddelinquenten en de effecten daarvan. In: Goldenbeld, C., A. van Wijk, and J. Mesken (Eds.), *Straffen in het verkeer: Wetenschappelijke beschouwingen over straffen in en buiten het verkeer*. SWOV: Leidschendam.

van Wijk, A., E. Bervoets, and W. Stol. (2003). *Ik ben geen slechte jongen, ik doe alleen slechte dingen. Een inventarisatie van de problemen rond Antillianen in Nijmegen*. Elsevier: Den Haag.

van Wijk, A. and B. Bremmers. (2011). *Snelle jongens: Een onderzoek naar drugsrunners en daaraan gerelateerde problematiek in Limburg-Zuid* (Beke reeks). Bureau Beke: Arnhem.

van Wijk, A., H. Ferwerda, and H. Regterschot. (2007). Problematische Jeugdgroepen en groepscriminaliteit. In: A. Van Wijk and E. Bervoets (Eds.), *Politie en jeugd: Inleiding voor de praktijk*. Politieacademie Onderzoeksreeks, Elsevier: Overheid, 217–233.

Weijers, I. and C. Eliaerts. (2008). *Jeugdcriminologie. Achtergronden van Jeugdcriminaliteit*. Boom Juridische Uitgevers: Den Haag.

Wittebrood, K. and P. Nieuwbeerta. (2006). Een kwart eeuw stijging in geregistreerde criminaliteit. Vooral meer registratie, nauwelijks meer criminaliteit. *Tijdschrift voor Criminologie*. 48 (3), 227–242.

Yablonsky, L. (1959). The delinquent gang as a near-group. *Social Problems*. 7 (2), 108–117.

Internet Sources

Bureau Beke—http://www.beke.nl
Central Bureau of Statistics - http://www.cbs.nl
Halt Nederland—http://www.halt.nl/
Ministry of Health, Welfare, and Sports—http://www.government.nl/ministries/vws
Ministry of Security and Justice—http://www.government.nl/ministries/venj
Netherlands Youth Institute—http://www.youthpolicy.nl/yp/Youth-Policy/Youth-Policy-subjects/
    Child-protection-and-welfare/Juvenile-justice-policy
Public Prosecution Service—http://www.om.nl/vast_menu_blok/english/
Police in the Netherlands (in Dutch)—http://www.politie.nl/
The Research and Documentation Centre (WODC) of the Ministry of Justice—http://english.wodc.nl/
The Trimbos Institute, the Netherlands Institute of Mental Health and Addiction—http://www.trim-
    bos.org/

The Scottish Juvenile Justice System: Policy and Practice

11

LESLEY McARA AND SUSAN McVIE

Contents

Introduction	264
The Development of Juvenile Justice in Scotland	265
Punishment, Deterrence, and Reform: Juvenile Justice in the Nineteenth and Early Twentieth Centuries	265
The Triumph of Welfarism: 1968–1995	266
The Incursion of Populism: 1995–2007	268
Penetration of Public Interest Discourse into the Hearings	268
Social Inclusion and Social Control	269
The Era of Compassionate Justice: 2007 Onward	270
The Structure and Operation of the Juvenile Justice System	272
The Children's Hearings System	272
Referrals to the System	272
The Reporter	274
Grounds for Referral	274
The Hearing	274
Compulsory Supervision Orders	275
Secure Accommodation	276
Age of Children Dealt with by the Hearings System	277
Child Offenders and the Courts	277
Youth Courts in Scotland	277
Criminal Courts: Children Aged under 16	278
Criminal Courts: Young People Aged 16–17	278
Extent and Pattern of Youth Crime	279
The Official Picture	280
Offense Referrals to the Reporter	280
Court Proceedings	281
Imprisonment	283
Evidence from the Edinburgh Study of Youth Transitions and Crime	283
Implications of the Data on Youth Crime in Scotland	289
Current Issues in Juvenile Justice	289
Age of Criminal Responsibility in Scotland	289
Transition between the Juvenile and Adult Justice Systems	289
Police Stop and Search	290
Conclusion	291
Review/Discussion Questions	291
References	291
Internet Sources	294

FACTS ABOUT SCOTLAND

Area: Scotland has an area of 78,470 sq km/30,297 sq m. **Major Cities:** The major cities are Edinburgh (capital city), Glasgow, Dundee, Aberdeen, and Inverness. **Climate:** The climate is temperate. **Economy:** Scotland has seen a decline in traditional heavy industry such as mining and steel making. Main industries currently include electronics, oil, natural gas, chemicals, textiles, clothing, printing, paper, food processing, tourism, banking, and finance. **Population:** At the time of the 2011 census, the population stood at 5,295,400. The number of young people has been declining over the past 30 years: the number of 16 year olds, for example, fell by 36% from 95,000 in 1981 to 60,437 in 2011. **Structure of Government:** Since the union in 1707, Scotland has been part of the United Kingdom (which also comprises England, Wales, and Northern Ireland). Although governed by the UK Parliament at Westminster between 1707 and 1998, Scotland always had a separate legal and education system. From 1999, Scotland has had its own parliament for devolved, domestic matters (including justice, education, and health). For other UK-wide issues, it is still subject to the UK Parliament at Westminster. There are currently 32 elected local authorities in Scotland, which are responsible for the administration of, *inter alia*, education and social work. Unlike many other parliamentary democracies, there is no written constitution. However, the European Convention on Human Rights was incorporated into Scots law (Human Rights Act 1998). A referendum on Scottish independence is to be held in 2014.

Introduction

Society is, we believe, seriously concerned to secure a more effective and discriminatory machinery for interventions for the avoidance and reduction of juvenile delinquency.

Kilbrandon Committee 1964, 75

A principal aim of comparative criminal justice research is to explore the relationship between the characteristics of different criminal justice systems and the specific cultural contexts within which they are located (see Nelken 1994, 1997). The Scottish system of juvenile justice provides a useful point of comparison with other Western juvenile justice systems primarily because the distinctive nature of Scottish civic and political culture has enabled the system to resist the trends evident in many other Western systems toward populist punitiveness (see McAra 2008).

The above quotation is particularly apt in the context of the issues that we will be exploring in this chapter. It comes from the report of the Kilbrandon Committee set up in the 1960s to review the then-existing juvenile justice system. Although written almost 50 years ago, it continues to be indicative of the key aspects of Scottish civic culture—in particular, the sense of *common ownership* with regard to the problems posed by youth offending and the continued commitment to the development of effective practice. Aside from a short period during the 1970s and 1980s, the quotation also reflects a recurrent preoccupation of key policy elites that existing structures of juvenile justice are inadequate to the task of reducing offending among children and young people and require to be reformed. Indeed, it is the interplay between the concerns of such policy elites and broader political and cultural processes, which we will suggest in the course of this chapter, determines the precise character of the juvenile justice system at any particular juncture.

This chapter is divided into four linked, but quite distinct, sections. The first section provides an overview of the development of the Scottish juvenile justice system over the past two centuries and explores the manner in which social, political, and cultural processes have impacted the evolution of institutions for dealing with troubled and troublesome children. The second section describes the system as it currently operates; the characteristics of cases that go through the system and the nature of contemporary disposals for child offenders. The third section focuses on empirical data relating to the nature and pattern of offending among young people in Scotland. In addition to data taken from official sources, it draws on the findings of the Edinburgh Study of Youth Transitions and Crime (the Edinburgh Study), a longitudinal program of research on pathways into and out of offending.* We conclude the chapter with a review of a number of key issues currently facing the system.

The Development of Juvenile Justice in Scotland

While welfarism has remained a cornerstone of the Scottish juvenile justice system, debates around the appropriate treatment of child offenders have always been bifurcated between a welfarist perspective (focused on the needs of the individual child) and what may be termed a public interest perspective (i.e., focused on what are conceived as broader societal concerns or the concerns of the general public) (see McAra 1999).

In this section of the chapter, we are going to suggest that the history of the Scottish juvenile justice system can be divided into four distinct periods, which we have termed: (a) the era of punishment, deterrence, and reform, (b) the triumph of welfarism, (c) the incursion of populism (detartanization), and (d) the era of compassionate justice (retartanization). The first of these periods was characterized by a high degree of tension between welfarist and public interest perspectives; during the second period, welfare principles came to dominate institutional responses to offending; by contrast, the third period saw a resurgence of the public interest perspective and a shift away from a purely child-centered institutional ethos; while in the final period, efforts have been made to link the public interest to a distinctively Scottish vision of justice, predicated on welfarist imperatives. Our argument is that the system has changed in response to both macro social, economic, and cultural change over the course of the twentieth and early twenty-first century and shifts in the interests of elite groups who have had a key role to play in shaping the policy agenda within Scotland.

Punishment, Deterrence, and Reform: Juvenile Justice in the Nineteenth and Early Twentieth Centuries

Although there is little surviving historical documentation about the emergence of separate institutions for dealing with child offenders in Scotland, that which does exist suggests that

---

* The Edinburgh Study has been funded by the Economic and Social Research Council, the Nuffield Foundation, and the Scottish government. The authors of this chapter are codirectors of the program. For further information about the study, see http://www.esytc.ed.ac.uk/.

developments in the nineteenth and early twentieth centuries paralleled those in England and Wales (see Bruce 1982; Murphy 1992; Smout 1972). Early institutions of juvenile justice emerged in a rather piecemeal way and included reformatories for offenders and industrial schools for children of the "perishing classes."

Formal separation of the adult and juvenile justice systems in both Scotland and England and Wales occurred in 1908 with the passage of the Children Act. As a result of this act, courts in Scotland were required to act as juvenile courts on certain days of the week. Although court procedures were modified to try to ensure that children could understand what was happening, no fundamental changes were made to the principles of criminal procedure (see Morris and McIsaac 1978). It was not until the 1930s that specially constituted juvenile courts staffed by "suitably qualified justices" appeared in Scotland. These courts were enabled by the Children and Young Persons (Scotland) Act of 1932, which also imposed a duty on the courts to have consideration for the welfare of the child. Only four juvenile courts were ever established in Scotland, and most cases of juvenile offenders continued to be dealt with in Sheriff and Burgh courts. The age of criminal responsibility was set at age eight by the Children and Young Persons (Scotland) Act 1937.

These early developments were underpinned by a fundamental ambivalence toward juvenile offenders. On the one hand, there was an explicit recognition that the welfare of the child should have a key role to play in decision-making, and many of the disposals available to the courts were reformative in orientation. On the other hand, many of these disposals were quite punitive in effect. While the 1908 act did institute some restrictions on the use of imprisonment for young offenders, this was to ensure that prison did not lose its deterrent effect by being used too soon (see Gelsthorpe and Morris 1994). Furthermore, periods of penal servitude were retained as an incapacitative measure for the "truly depraved and unruly" to minimize their "evil influence" on others. The act also made provision for the retention of corporal punishment (whipping) as a disposal.

The piecemeal approach to reform continued during the 1930s and in the immediate postwar (Second World War) era, with only a gradual growth in child-centered services, such as school psychological services and child guidance clinics for children with behavioral difficulties. Additionally, police liaison schemes were instituted in some areas, in which specially trained police officers worked at a community level with young offenders, and the Children Act 1948 created local authority children's departments with an "obligation to consider the needs and abilities of children in their care." Although many of these new initiatives were welfarist in orientation, the juvenile justice system continued to be torn between welfarist and criminal justice imperatives. This was principally because, *in the case of offenders*, the gatekeeper to many of the new services continued to be criminal justice agencies. The tensions that beset the juvenile court, in particular, between the requirement to look after the needs of the child and also act as a formal court of law within a predominantly public interest perspective was one of the precipitating factors for the review of juvenile justice in Scotland conducted by the Kilbrandon committee in the early 1960s. It was this review that laid the groundwork for the new Children's Hearings System.

The Triumph of Welfarism: 1968–1995

The period between 1968 and 1995 can be seen as the high point of welfarism in juvenile justice in Scotland. This is in direct contrast to the system in England and Wales in which there was a major retreat from welfarist principles (Cavadino and Dignan 1997).

The primacy of the welfare principle was set in motion by the Social Work (Scotland) Act 1968, which had far-reaching consequences for both the adult and juvenile justice systems in Scotland principally because it placed social work at the heart of the criminal justice enterprise. The act, *inter alia*, abolished the probation service in Scotland and handed over responsibility for criminal justice to the newly constituted local authority social work department, in contrast to other jurisdictions where such intervention remained the responsibility of criminal justice agencies (see McAra and Young 1997). Importantly the act also abolished the existing juvenile courts and established a new institutional framework for juvenile justice, the Scottish Children's Hearings System, which remains largely in force today.

These structural changes were driven by a coherent vision of criminal justice known as the "Kilbrandon philosophy," named after the chairman of the committee set up to examine the problems of the existing system of juvenile justice in Scotland. It stressed that juvenile offending and other troublesome behaviors should be regarded as manifestations of deeper social and psychological malaise and/or failures in the normal upbringing process (Kilbrandon Committee 1964). The overall aim of the new juvenile justice system was to deal with the child's needs (whether referred on offense or care and protection grounds), with the *best interests* of the child to be paramount in decision-making. To achieve this, the Kilbrandon Committee recommended that a new tribunal be set up—the Children's Hearing—one, which was not staffed by experts but by ordinary members of the public. The system (implemented in April 1971) was to be administered by a new official, the Reporter. Procedures were to be informal with the aim of involving children and their families in the decision-making process (see the section "The Structure and Operation of the Juvenile Justice System" for a more detailed discussion of the operation of the Hearings System). Importantly, however, the Crown reserved the right to prosecute children who had committed the most serious offenses (such as rape, serious assault or homicide) in the adult court system (see McAra 2002).

The drive toward welfarism in the context of the Children's Hearings System set the Scottish juvenile justice system on a different trajectory from that in England and Wales. A review of juvenile justice in England and Wales (conducted by the Ingleby and Longford committees, respectively, in the late 1950s and early 1960s) had recommended a similar commitment to welfare principles, which were enshrined in the subsequent Children and Young Persons Act 1969. This act, however, was never fully implemented, and the 1970s saw a major increase in youth custody with a concomitant retreat from welfare concerns (see Gelsthorpe and Morris 1994).

The very different fates of the 1968 Social Work (Scotland) Act (fully implemented) and the 1969 Children and Young Person's Act (partially implemented) again have to be understood against the backdrop of broader political, social, and penal change. The retreat from welfarism in England and Wales was precipitated by a number of processes including the election of a Conservative government committed to law and order principles, the resistance of key players in the criminal justice system to the main precepts of the act (in particular magistrates and the police), and, finally, a growing moral panic about youth crime in the context of a broader penal crisis linked to the decline in faith in rehabilitation and prison overcrowding (see Cavadino and Dignan 1997; Gelsthorpe and Morris 1994; Morris and McIsaac 1978).

By contrast, in Scotland, the new institutions of juvenile justice had the support of key elites within the Scottish Office and the criminal justice system itself. In addition, there was a concerted media campaign extolling the uniqueness of the new institutions of juvenile justice that helped garner public support (see Morris and McIsaac 1978). However, one of the principal factors marking out Scotland from England and Wales was the distinctive nature of Scottish civic culture that had emerged by the 1960s. This culture stemmed from a strong democratic tradition in key civic institutions such as the education system and the church, accompanied by a growing dominance of socialist and communitarian principles at local government level (see McAra 1999). This civic culture enabled the Scottish justice system to resist the siren voices proclaiming the decline of the rehabilitative ideal in other Western jurisdictions and served to shore up and reproduce the predominantly welfare-based penal culture, which underpinned both the adult and juvenile justice systems in Scotland during the 1970s and 1980s (see McAra 1999).

The Incursion of Populism: 1995–2007

Most of the institutional arrangements set up by the Social Work (Scotland) Act remain in force today. However, a number of new policy developments from the mid-1990s arguably laid the groundwork for a third phase of juvenile justice, one that we refer to as "detartanization" (see McAra 2006). This new phase was characterized by a gradual penetration of public interest discourse into the Hearings System itself. It was also characterized by a massive increase in the panoply of controls over children and their families, as issues of juvenile justice became increasingly caught up in the new Labour government's social inclusion and social crime prevention agendas. The effect of this was a gradual narrowing of the differences between the Scottish juvenile justice system and that existent in England and Wales; hence the reference to this phase as an era of detartanization.*

Penetration of Public Interest Discourse into the Hearings

The penetration of public interest discourse into the Hearings System was marked most explicitly by a number of changes introduced by the Children (Scotland) Act 1995. The passage of this act was the culmination of a major review of the Children's Hearings System, which occurred in the wake of two major child protection inquiries (see Edwards and Griffiths 1997) and increased concern about persistent offending (McAra and Young 1997). This act enabled the Hearings System to place the principle of public protection above that of the best interests of the child in cases where the child presented a significant risk to the public. It also empowered sheriffs to substitute their own decision for that of the hearing in disputed (and appealed) cases, whereas previously they could only require reconsideration by a hearing or discharge a case.

What the first of these developments suggests is that the hearings were being *explicitly* directed to work within a bifurcated discursive framework: considering public protection questions in "high-risk" (to the public) cases and the welfare needs of the child in low-risk and other child protection cases. The second of the developments (the increased powers of the sheriff) indicates a greater concern for due process rights of children and their families as well as the growing importance accorded to a public interest perspective in the hearings (see Cleland 1995).

---

* This is not to say that that the Scottish system replicated all aspects of the new juvenile justice system in England and Wales, merely that the ethos of the two systems came closer together.

Social Inclusion and Social Control

The public interest perspective became even more firmly entrenched within the juvenile justice system as a result of the Labour Government's commitment to social inclusion and to social crime prevention strategies. A key aspect of these strategies was to reduce youth crime by promoting safer communities; confronting the causes of crime as they relate to such factors as poor parenting, unemployment, and social isolation; providing support for victims of crime; promoting early intervention prior to the establishment of a pattern of offending; and developing effective programs to assist established offenders to change their behavior. This was exemplified in the policy documents *Partnership for Scotland* (Scottish Executive 1999a), *Safer Communities in Scotland* (Scottish Executive 1999b), and in the *Invest to Save* pilot projects, in which at-risk families were targeted by the interventions (see Hogg 1999).

While these policies did display a continued commitment to welfare values (e.g., through their emphasis on the promotion of behavioral change and community integration for offenders), they were driven as much by a community and victim-centered ethos as the child-centered ethos that characterized the system between 1968 and the mid-1990s. Moreover, the social inclusion agenda was underpinned by a fundamental paradox. On the one hand, policies were aimed at devolving responsibility for crime control to communities, parents, and offenders themselves, while, on the other hand, the effect of these policies was to increase both formal and informal mechanisms of social control. Children identified as being at risk of offending became subject to high levels of scrutiny and surveillance as did their families and the communities in which they were living. Thus, the Scottish system came to reflect changes in the English and Welsh juvenile justice system wrought by the Crime and Disorder Act (1998).

The drive toward detartanization and the narrowing of the differences between Scotland and England and Wales gained momentum in the early years of the twenty-first century. A key commonality between the Scottish and English and Welsh systems was the increased level of managerialism evident in each jurisdiction. In Scotland, this included the introduction of national standards for youth justice and the creation of a new bureaucratic infrastructure to take the youth justice agenda forward, including multiagency youth justice teams. Another convergent trend was the embracing of restorative principles exemplified by the expanding number of victim–offender mediation schemes, conferencing, and police restorative cautioning initiatives. Both jurisdictions also focused on reducing persistent offending and antisocial behavior by legislating to enable the use of civil orders to tackle low-level crime and disorder (antisocial behavior and parenting orders).* Finally, a youth court model was piloted in Scotland in 2003, and then continued in 2005 at which point the then Justice Minister, Cathy Jamieson, stated, "Punishment is a key part of the youth justice process" (Scottish Executive 2005a).

Detartanization arose, we would suggest, from a number of complex processes. First, the newly elected Labour Government in 1997 was more in tune with Scottish political and civic culture than the previous Conservative administration. The emphasis on community safety and civic participation, for example, was broadly in keeping with the communitarian values that we have argued characterized Scottish civic culture during the latter half

---

* In Scotland, antisocial behavior orders (ASBOs) for 12- to 15-year-olds and parenting orders were enabled by the Anti-Social Behaviour (Scotland) Act 2004.

of the twentieth century. As such, it provided a generally acceptable framework on which to reconstruct key elements of penal policy. Second, the process of devolution allowed the development of an integrated policy strategy exemplified by the gradual elision between the social inclusion and the youth justice agendas. Third, changes were precipitated by a loss of faith among key elites (in particular the judiciary, the police, and central government) in the effectiveness of the Children's Hearings System in dealing with persistent offenders (Hallet et al. 1998; McAra 1998).

The shift toward detartanization has also to be understood against the backdrop of more macro social, economic, and cultural change. Scholars have argued that Western penal systems underwent profound change in response to the social and economic processes associated with late modernity, in particular the rise of the risk society, globalization, and the accompanying loss of state sovereignty (see Douglas 1992; Garland 1996; O'Malley 1992). The incursion of the risk discourse into crime control and penal practice, it is claimed, led to more rigorous policing of both socially included and excluded groups, accompanied by a shift away from rehabilitation to the management of potentially dangerous populations (Bauman 2000; Lianos and Douglas 2000; Pratt 2000). Commentators suggest that advanced liberal societies were no longer able to sustain their role as the principal provider of security within their own territorial boundaries and, as a consequence, increasingly devolved responsibility for crime control and community safety onto active individuals and onto communities themselves (so-called responsibilization strategies) (see Garland 1996; Rose 1999).

McAra has argued that Scotland was initially resistant to some of these penal trends due to the strength and influence of elite policy networks and to the characteristics of Scottish civic culture, which continued to valorize community integration and mutual support in the face of increased polarization and marginalization (see McAra 2005). Within Scotland, she suggested that risk management and "responsibilization strategies," far from leading to a decline in rehabilitation, were reconstructed into core components of effective practice with offenders. At the beginning of the twenty-first century, this appeared to change, and Scotland embraced a more fragmented and contradictory penal discourse in which notions of public protection, individual rights and responsibilities, together with community dynamics, increasingly came to challenge rather than complement the welfare ethos. A key focus of this new discourse was, of course, youth crime. This change occurred because of a need for the new devolved administration to build political capacity in a manner akin to governing through crime (McAra 2011; Simon 2007). Enhanced democratization within Scotland under the devolved settlement weakened the power of penal elites as government ministers responded to the perceived demands of the electorate. Looking south and west for evidence, they embarked on a new "tough on crime" agenda.

The Era of Compassionate Justice: 2007 Onward

From this conflicted and punitive third phase, there is evidence that juvenile justice in Scotland has moved into a fourth phase characterized by a renewed emphasis on prevention and early intervention within the framework of a compassionate approach to justice, a move, we suggest, toward "retartanization." This change was heralded during the final term of the Labour/Liberal Democrat coalition government with the publication of *Getting it Right for Every Child: Proposals for Action* (Scottish Executive 2005b). This document, which arose following a review of the Children's Hearings System in 2004, set out a vision for high-quality children's services (including those for child offenders) somewhat at odds with the more populist political rhetoric on youth crime described in the previous section. It placed primary emphasis on individual well-being, recognizing the need to improve outcomes for vulnerable children through early identification of needs and risks and the timely provision of integrated universal services aimed at minimizing the necessity for later crisis management, which reflected in large part, the original principles of the Kilbrandon Report (1964).

Adopted by the incoming Scottish National Party (SNP) Government in 2007, the Getting It Right for Every Child (GIRFEC) model has underpinned all subsequent policy decisions relating to juvenile justice in Scotland. This includes the first major policy document on youth crime produced by the SNP, *Preventing Offending by Young People: A Framework for Action* (Scottish Government 2008a), which set out a strategic approach to preventing offending through early and effective intervention (EEI) and diversion from prosecution. The proposals for EEI included a nationally agreed process for timely, supportive, and appropriate intervention aimed at directing universal services toward individual needs. A key focus was placed on diverting those aged 8–17 years away from prosecution so as to facilitate the successful transition from childhood to adulthood, particularly during the vulnerable period between 16 and 21 years.

Juvenile justice in Scotland underwent a major transformation in 2011 when the Scottish Government rolled out a new "Whole System Approach" (WSA) for young people who offend in all 32 local authorities. Building on GIRFEC and the 2008 Framework for Action, the WSA represents a major shift away from punitive, risk-focused measures toward policies focused on welfare delivered through multiagency response, a key focus being to maximize the use of diversion and keep 16- and 17-year-olds out of the criminal justice system. Unlike policy developments during the populist phase, the WSA was founded on strong empirical evidence from research, including the Edinburgh Study, that the long-term outcomes for young people involved in offending behavior would be better served by diverting them away from statutory measures, prosecution, and custody and instead implementing early intervention and robust community alternatives (McAra and McVie 2007), and that persistent serious offending was strongly associated with victimization and social adversity, which needed to be addressed alongside offending behaviors (McAra and McVie 2010a).

The WSA aims to achieve positive outcomes for the most vulnerable young people in Scotland, helping them to fulfill their potential and become valuable contributors to their communities. The implementation strategy involves putting in place streamlined and consistent planning, assessment, and decision-making processes for young people who offend, to make sure they receive the right help at the right time. A raft of guidance documents has been produced by the Scottish government to support local authorities to implement the WSA, and early evaluation has indicated that the response to the initiative has been largely positive (MacQueen and McVie 2013). There is overwhelming support for, and acceptance of, the key underlying ethos and agreement in principle to embrace multiagency strategic working practices. And early indications suggest that it may have been successful in reducing youth crime in Scotland, since the number of young people committing crime between 2011 and 2012 fell by 9% and offense referrals to the children's Reporter over the same period dropped by 31%. It remains to be seen, however, whether concerns about financial resources to support the development of new initiatives and achieving participation from all the key agencies might hamper implementation of the WSA in some local authorities.

Other significant changes in recent years have further transformed the landscape of juvenile justice in Scotland. The minimum age of prosecution was increased from 8 to 12 years by the Criminal Justice and Licensing (Scotland) Act 2010, although the age of criminal responsibility in Scotland remained at 8 years, one of the lowest internationally (see Table 1.1 in the Introduction to this book). And the Children's Hearings (Scotland) Act 2011 legislated that offenses admitted during children's hearings could be classified as alternatives to prosecution rather than convictions, as they were previously. Scottish ministers also specified that only a small number of very high tariff offenses could be disclosed as criminal convictions to employers or others authorized to seek such information, as previously all admitted offenses were potentially disclosable up to age 40. Currently, the Scottish government is developing a Children and Young People Bill, which proposes to enshrine in law key elements of the GIRFEC approach. Importantly, all of the changes during this fourth phase reflect a degree of political capacity building whereby governance has been manifested as a positive and inclusive process based on a broader vision of Scotland as a compassionate nation.

To summarize, a consistent feature of juvenile justice policy has been the manner in which debates have been bifurcated between a welfare perspective and public interest perspective. The trend in the early twenty-first century was for the public interest perspective to penetrate more deeply into the aspects of the system that (at least since the instigation of the Children's Hearings System) were the sole preserve of welfarism. The changing character of the system has been shaped both by broader social, political, and economic change and, more recently, by the need for the devolved Scottish administration to assert its authority and build its legitimacy.

Having set out the history and development of juvenile justice in Scotland, we will now turn to a more detailed description of the system as it operates today. In the following section, we will provide an overview of the role of the Children's Hearings System and the courts in juvenile justice, before going on to examine the nature of disposals, which are available for young offenders in Scotland.

The Structure and Operation of the Juvenile Justice System

The Children's Hearings System

The Children's Hearings System was recently reformed by the Children's Hearings Scotland Act 2011, which has resulted in a number of changes to its structure and operation, although the basic principles underlying the system remain the same. The biggest change to the system has been the creation of a new national panel, which is led by a National Convenor and supported by a dedicated body called Children's Hearings Scotland. The number and types of cases dealt with by the Children's Hearings System and the range of decisions made can be seen from Figure 11.1. This shows the numbers of cases that passed through the system in 2012/13 (the latest year for which published statistics are available) and it also illustrates usefully the various stages of the system.

Referrals to the System

As can be seen, in 2012/13, there were 22,561 children referred to the Hearings System, which represents 2.5% of all children and young people aged under 16 in Scotland. A total of 36,298 referrals were made, which means that many children were referred on more than

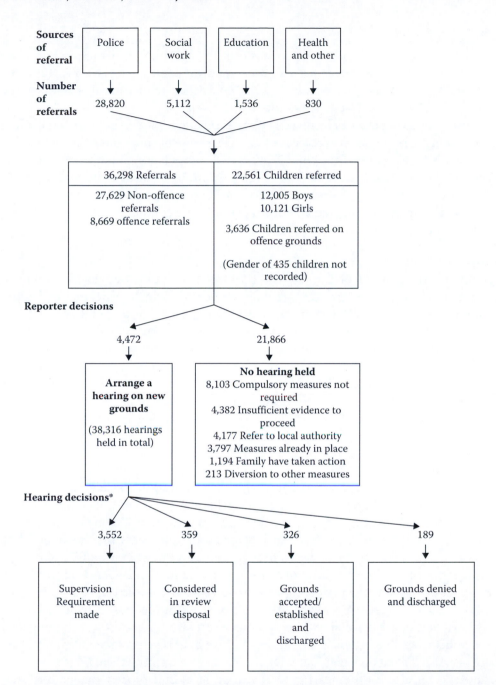

Figure 11.1 Children's hearings statistics 2012/13. *Figures show the primary decisions for hearings arranged on new grounds in 2012/13 (a child may be referred to and dealt with by a hearing on more than one occasion in the year). (Scottish Children Reporters Administration. (2013). Online Statistical Dashboard 2012/13. http://www.scra.gov.uk/cms_resources/Online%20 annual%20dashboard%202012-13.swf (accessed 11 November 2013).)

one occasion. The bulk of all referrals were nonoffense related, while 24% were made on the grounds that the child had committed an offense. Of those children who were referred, 16% were referred on offense grounds.

The Reporter

The Reporter is the paid official who presides over the children's hearings. While anyone can refer a case to the Reporter, in practice most referrals come from the police (79% of all referrals and 99.7% of offense referrals, in 2012/13), with a smaller number of cases being referred by social workers, teachers, or other individuals.

The task of the Reporter is to investigate referrals and, on the basis of the evidence, decide whether there is a prima facie case that at least one of the grounds for referral to a hearing has been met *and* that the child is in need of compulsory measures of care. As can be seen from Figure 11.1, the majority of referrals result in *no* hearing being held (83% in 2012/13) because compulsory measures are not considered or proved to be necessary, other measures to deal with the child are already in place, or the child is diverted away from the system for more informal measures of support.

Grounds for Referral

The Children's Hearings (Scotland) Act 2011 set out 17 grounds on which a child could be referred to a hearing (see Box 11.1).* These grounds are principally concerned with (a) the child as being at risk of harm from others (through lack of parental care, potential exposure to sexual or physical abuse, or requiring special accommodation or measures of support) and (b) the child's behavior (such as offending, school truancy, misuse of drugs or alcohol, poor conduct, or lack of control). For a hearing to proceed, the child and the parents must accept the grounds for referral. For children referred on offense grounds, this means admitting guilt. Where the grounds are disputed, the case is referred to the Sheriff Court for a proof hearing and, provided the court finds that the grounds are established, the case will be brought back for another hearing.

The Hearing

The hearing itself is a private legal meeting, which is arranged to consider and make decisions about the lives of children or young people who may be in need of compulsory measures of care. It consists of three people (including at least one man and one woman) who act as lay tribunals, called panel members. Panel members are volunteers and should be selected from a wide range of occupations, social backgrounds, and neighborhoods. The representativeness of panels has been a matter of concern in the past, with evidence suggesting that women, older people, and the middle class were overrepresented (see Hallet et al. 1998; Reid 1998). Panel members are expected to either live or work in the area in which they sit on hearings so that they are familiar with the local area in which the children and young people they see at hearings live. After selection, they receive extensive preservice training before they are permitted to sit on a panel, and regular in-service training thereafter.

The Reporter attends the hearing to advise on legal and procedural matters and to record the reason for the panel's decision. Children and their parents or guardian are normally expected to attend and participate in the hearing. They can be accompanied by a representative who may be a lawyer. The overall task of the panel is to decide whether compulsory measures of care are necessary. The three main principles on which panel member decisions should be based are the following: the welfare of the child throughout childhood should be the paramount consideration; taking account of the age and maturity of the

---

* The Social Work (Scotland) Act 1968 initially set out 8 grounds for referral, which was increased to 12 by the Children (Scotland) Act 1995.

BOX 11.1   GROUNDS FOR REFERRAL—CHILDREN'S HEARINGS (SCOTLAND) ACT 2011

1. The child is likely to suffer unnecessarily or be seriously impaired in his/her health or development, due to lack of parental care.
2. A Schedule 1 offense has been committed in respect of the child.*
3. The child has, or is likely to have, a close connection with a person who has committed a Schedule 1 offense.
4. The child is, or is likely to become, a member of the same household as a child in respect of whom a Schedule 1 offense has been committed.
5. The child is being, or is likely to be, exposed to persons whose conduct is (or has been) such that it is likely that the child will be abused or harmed, or the child's health, safety, or development will be seriously adversely affected.
6. The child has, or is likely to have, a close connection with a person who has carried out domestic abuse.
7. The child has, or is likely to have, a close connection with a person who has committed an offense under Part 1, 4, or 5 of the Sexual Offences (Scotland) Act 2009.
8. The child is being provided with accommodation by a local authority under Section 25 of the 1995 Act, and special measures are needed to support the child.
9. A permanence order is in force in respect of the child, and special measures are needed to support the child.
10. The child has committed an offense.
11. The child has misused alcohol.
12. The child has misused a drug (whether or not a controlled drug).
13. The child's conduct has had, or is likely to have, a serious adverse effect on the health, safety, or development of the child or another person.
14. The child is beyond the control of a relevant person.
15. The child has failed without reasonable excuse to attend school regularly.
16. The child: (a) is being, or is likely to be, subjected to physical, emotional, or other pressure to enter into a marriage or civil partnership, or (b) is, or is likely to become, a member of the same household as such a child.

* A Schedule 1 offense is a physical, emotional, or sexual offense against a child as listed in the first schedule of the Criminal Procedure (Scotland) Act 1995.

child, the child should be given the opportunity to express his/her views and have these views taken into account; and no supervision requirement or order should be made unless the hearing considers it absolutely necessary. The only aspect of the legislation, which is not consistent with the welfare principle is where it is considered necessary to protect the public from serious harm, whereby the child's welfare is to be of primary rather than paramount consideration (s.25 of the 2011 Act).

Compulsory Supervision Orders

When the Children's Hearings System came into being in 1971, panel members were given discretionary power (but not an obligation) to make a Supervision Requirement if they considered that a child was in need of compulsory measures of supervision. In June 2013, the Supervision Requirement was replaced by the Compulsory Supervision Order (CSO), which means that a named Local Authority is responsible for supporting the child or young person and it ensures that they are allocated a supervising social worker. Various conditions or "measures" can be attached to the CSO by panel members, including a requirement of residence at a specified place; prohibited disclosure of the child's place of residence; restriction of the child's movements; placement in secure accommodation; provision of medical or other treatment or examination; regulation of contact between the child and a specified person or class of persons; requirement that the child comply with any other conditions made by the hearing; and a requirement that the named Local Authority carry out specific duties in relation to the child (see s.83, Children's Hearings (Scotland) Act 2011). Guidance issued by the Scottish government (2013) states that a CSO should be issued "if the nature of the child's circumstances is such that it is necessary for the protection, guidance, treatment or control of the child" (p. 39).

In 2012/13, 12,514 children and young people were subject to a Supervision Requirement on the census date of March 31, 2013, which amounts to 1.4% of all young people in Scotland. Of these, 48% had a Home Supervision Requirement (HSR), which means they were resident at home with a parent or relevant carer, while the remaining 52% had a condition of residence (to be looked after by someone other than a parent) attached. According to the principle of minimal intervention, the hearing must be satisfied that making the order will be more beneficial for the child than making no order at all. In fact, research has shown that children who were subject to an HSR were typically known to social work services for several years before being placed on compulsory supervision (Gadda and Fitzpatrick 2012). Their families experienced multiple, chronic problems such as domestic violence, drug and alcohol abuse, mental health problems, and financial difficulties; and children who were subject to an HSR experienced a great deal of instability, both in terms of placements and people. This study also found evidence that children who were on an HSR were subject to compulsory supervision for most of their childhoods. In addition, evidence from the Edinburgh Study has shown that young people engaged in offending who were made subject to Supervision Requirements were less likely to desist from offending when compared to a group of similar young offenders who did not receive such intervention (McAra and McVie 2007).

Secure Accommodation

Measures aimed at restricting the movement of children or placing them in secure accommodation can only be imposed on a child if he/she is deemed to be at high risk of absconding (potentially with a history of absconding) and that his/her physical, mental, and moral welfare would be in danger as a result, or if the child is engaging in self-harming behavior or likely to cause injury to another person. On average, over the last 10 years, around 270 children have been detained in secure accommodation annually (with approximately 100 places available at any one time). In 2011/12, just over 16,000 children were looked after in total (representing 2% of all children in Scotland), with 237 admissions to secure care during that time, at an average cost of £5160 (approx. $8300) per bed per week. There has been little detailed research on the types of work undertaken with offenders in secure care, although previous research found a lack of focused interventions and recommended the further development of programs based on social skills training and cognitive behavioral methods (Hogg 1999). Moreover, little is known about the longer-term effects of such detention on offending behavior; however, a recent review by the Scottish Children's Reporter Administration (SCRA) (Whitehead et al. 2010) found that while the lives of 24% of young people receiving secure care were said to have improved, the majority of young people who had been placed in secure accommodation continued to offend and struggle with drug and alcohol misuse, and mental health problems. Findings from the Edinburgh Study also showed that 77% of those who had been in residential care by the age of 16 received criminal convictions, and 31% had experienced at least one period of imprisonment, by age 22 (which compares with 9% and 0.3%, respectively, of cohort members with no care history by age 16).

Age of Children Dealt with by the Hearings System

The majority of children dealt with by the Children's Hearings System are under the age of 16. As the age of criminal responsibility in Scotland is 8 years, only children aged 8 or over can be referred on offense grounds. Children can be kept in the Hearings System until they reach 18 years through the extension of their supervisory orders; however, in practice, most offenders between the ages of 16 and 18 are dealt with by the adult criminal justice system. Courts do have the power to remit such cases to the Hearings System for advice and/or disposal and, indeed, must do so if the child is subject to supervision. As noted earlier, the new WSA which was rolled out nationally in 2011 aims to divert as many 16- and 17-year-olds away from prosecution as possible. Nevertheless, in 2011/12, 16- and 17-year-olds represented only 2.5% of referrals to the Hearings System and less than five referrals in total were received from the sheriff courts. Previous research evidence has suggested that sheriffs consider the Hearings System as too soft an option for the majority of 16- to 17-year-olds and will only remit cases in which the welfare element far outweighs the seriousness of the offense (McAra 1998). Historically, the Hearings System has been reluctant to retain 16- and 17-year-olds, with most Supervision Requirements being terminated just prior to the child's 16th birthday (Waterhouse et al. 1999).

Child Offenders and the Courts

Youth Courts in Scotland

In 2003, two pilot youth court projects were created in Scotland to deal with persistent offenders (charged with summary offenses) aged 16 and 17 and children aged 15 who would otherwise have been dealt with in the sheriff summary court. The criterion for referral to the youth court was three or more police referrals to the Procurator Fiscal (PF) in a 6-month period. The youth courts did not have an easy gestational period. While the government-sponsored evaluation of the pilots (McIvor et al. 2006) was largely positive, a controversial "minority report," published in the journal *Youth Justice* (Piacentini and Walters 2006), claimed that the fast-track proceedings undermined human rights. The two youth courts continued to operate until 2009, when a further review concluded that they had failed to achieve several of their objectives (Scottish Government 2009a). Analysis revealed that reconviction rates were no different in the youth courts to those processed in the normal Sheriff summary courts; the specific features of the youth courts (such as having a separate court and the multiagency approach) had no clear impact on offending behavior; and the youth courts were not cost-effective. As a result, the Scottish government began a phased withdrawal of funds from the two youth courts in 2012/13.

Table 11.1   Persons Aged under 16 with a Charge Proved, 2011/12

Disposal	Children Aged under 16 (Percent) (n = 47)
Remit to children's hearings	47
Admonishment or absolute discharge	21
Community sentence (includes Community Payback Order, probation, and Restriction of Liberty Order)	15
Custody (including secure accommodation)	13
Financial penalty	4

Source: Scottish Government. (2013). Scottish Government Criminal Proceedings Database. Personal communication, 3rd October 2013.

Criminal Courts: Children Aged under 16

Children aged between 12 and 15 can come before the criminal courts when they have been accused of an extremely serious crime such as rape or homicide or (in the case of children aged 15 or over) for certain driving offenses. The number of children aged under 16 dealt with by the courts is extremely small. In 2011/12, only 47 children (45 males and 2 females) had at least one charge proved against them, which represents a significant drop since 1998 when 140 children were convicted. Table 11.1 reveals that the majority of these children were either remitted to the children's hearings for disposal or received an admonishment or absolute discharge. Children who are sentenced to a period of custody will normally serve their time in secure care, although, once they reach the age of 16, they may be transferred to a young offender's institution.

Criminal Courts: Young People Aged 16–17

With the exception of those dealt with by the youth courts in Scotland, which offer a range of alternative disposals, the majority of offenders aged between 16 and 17 years are subject to the same procedures as adult offenders. Their cases are referred by the police to the PF, who then decides whether there is sufficient evidence to prosecute and whether it is in the public interest to proceed. If it is deemed appropriate to proceed, the PF will then decide in which court and under which procedure (solemn or summary) the case should be dealt with.

As shown in Table 11.2, there were similarities and differences with regard to court disposals for males and females aged 16–17 in 2011/12. A large proportion of 16- to 17-year-olds are dealt with by means of a community sentence. Around a third of both males and females were dealt with in this way, most commonly by means of a Community Payback Order.* Other common disposals were an absolute discharge or admonishment. These were the most common types of disposal for females (39%), although almost a quarter of males also received these disposals. Around a quarter of both males and females received a financial penalty (either a fine or a compensation order). Custodial sentences were not commonly used for 16- to 17-year-olds, but males were five times more likely than females

* Community Payback Orders were introduced to Scotland by the Criminal Justice and Licensing (Scotland) Act 2010, and came into force in February 2011. They replace provisions for community service orders, probation orders, and supervised attendance orders, and provide sentencers with a range of options from which they can choose one or more to make up a bespoke order tailored specifically to each offender based on the nature of the offense and the underlying issues, which cause him/her to offend. Options include unpaid work in the community, completion of intensive supervision, and alcohol, drug, or behavior programs.

Table 11.2 Persons Aged 16–17 with a Charge Proved, 2011/12

Court Disposal	Males Aged 16–17 (Percent) (n = 13,083)	Females Aged 16–17 (Percent) (n = 1,948)
Remit to children's hearings	4	3
Admonishment or absolute discharge	23	39
Community sentence (includes Community Payback Order, probation, and Restriction of Liberty Order)	32	31
Custody (including secure accommodation)	15	3
Financial penalty	26	23
Other	*	*

Source: Scottish Government. (2013). Scottish Government Criminal Proceedings Database. Personal communication, 3rd October 2013.

* Less than 1%.

to receive a custodial disposal at this age, which is likely to reflect the more serious and persistent patterns of offending, which male offenders present, rather than being indicative of any particular leniency towards females. Note, however, that very few 16- and 17-year-olds were remitted back to be dealt with by the Children's Hearings System.

Having explored the structure and operation of the system and the nature of disposals available to deal with young people who offend, we now need to look at patterns of youth crime in Scotland to show in more detail the scope of the problems with which the juvenile justice system has to deal.

Extent and Pattern of Youth Crime

It is notoriously difficult to obtain accurate statistics on levels of offending among children and young people in Scotland. Unlike some other jurisdictions, there is no national survey of offending and, therefore, trend data can only be obtained from official sources, such as the routine statistics collated by Police Scotland,* the SCRA, Scottish courts, and the Scottish Prison Service. These data vary enormously in terms of their focus, structure, and content. Commentators on juvenile justice in Scotland are generally in agreement that young people are responsible for a disproportionately large amount of crime. The most recent estimate suggested that 43% of all crimes and offenses in Scotland were committed by young people aged under 21, with 48% of that being attributed to those aged between 18 and 21 years (DTZ Pieda 2005). This represents an increase on an earlier figure of 37% estimated by the Prince's Trust (1997); however, it should be noted that a consistent picture has emerged over the last 10 years of a general decrease in youth crime.

The most reliable "official" measures available are statistics on referrals to the Children's Hearings System (published by SCRA), statistics on criminal proceedings in the Scottish courts, and imprisonment statistics (published by the Scottish Government). Each of these has major limitations, however. As shown earlier, the majority of referrals to the Children's Hearings System come from the police, and decisions to refer a case to the Reporter at

* In April 2013, the eight territorial police forces in Scotland and the Scottish Crime and Drug Enforcement Agency were merged to create a new national force, Police Scotland. Previously, statistics had to be collected from each police force individually and combined by the Scottish government. Police Scotland now has the responsibility for collating all policing statistics in Scotland.

any given time will be as much a reflection of the level of available resources, patterns of agency activity, and shifts in policy (particularly in light of the introduction of the Whole Systems Approach), as a reflection of the levels of youth crime. Similarly, statistics on court proceedings and imprisonment rates are partly a product of the decision-making practices at earlier stages of the criminal justice process, which serve to filter out many cases before they reach the courts (which would include young people diverted away from prosecution). As such, these statistics can only provide a partial account of the levels of youth crime in Scotland.

To supplement the official statistics used in this section, we will draw on findings from the Edinburgh Study. As was noted, this is a major longitudinal program of research exploring pathways into and out of crime for a cohort of 4300 children who started secondary school in August 1998. The findings from this self-report study provide additional information about the nature and pattern of offending among a cohort of young people, as well as giving some indication as to the mechanisms and processes, which lead to offending among both girls and boys.

We will begin this section with an overview of trends in official statistics relating to referrals to the Reporter, criminal proceedings, and imprisonment. We will then set out in more detail the findings from the Edinburgh Study. The section will conclude by assessing the implications of these findings for the nature and operation of the juvenile justice system in Scotland.

The Official Picture

Offense Referrals to the Reporter

The total number of young people referred to the Reporter on offense grounds has changed dramatically over the last decade, as shown in Figure 11.2. From the mid-1990s to 2002/3, the number of referrals remained relatively stable at around 14,500 per year; however, between 2002/03 and 2005/6, there was an 18% increase in the number of children referred on offense grounds. This rise coincided with the period of detartanization in Scottish policy, described earlier, and reflects a distinct policy drive to target persistent young offenders

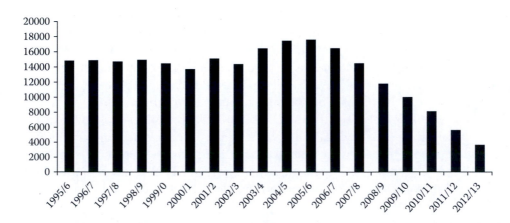

Figure 11.2 Number of people aged under 18 referred to the Reporter on offense grounds. (McAra, L. and McVie, S. (2010b). Youth crime and justice in Scotland. In Croall, H., Mooney, G., and Munro, M. (Eds.), *Criminal Justice in Scotland*. Oxon, Willan Publishing.)

in Scotland. In a misguided effort by the Labour/Liberal Democrat coalition to reduce the number of persistent young offenders by 10% over this period, the strong police focus on targeting "at-risk" youths served to drive up the number of referrals to the Children's Hearings System. As can be seen, however, toward the end of that phase of youth justice in 2006/7, the number of children referred to the Reporter on offense grounds started to fall and has continued to do so annually ever since. In fact, there has been an 80% reduction in the number of children referred to the Reporter on offense grounds since it peaked in 2005/6 to 2012/13.

Part of the explanation may be due to underlying changes in the population of young people (as noted at the start of this chapter, the population of young people has declined by around a third over the last three decades). However, when referral patterns are examined as a rate per 1000 of the population aged under 16 years, a similar downward trend is observed. It is also possible that this fall in referrals reflects a real drop in offending among young people, although this is impossible to verify due to lack of independent data. It seems most likely that this downward trend reflects the major policy changes that have occurred in Scotland, underpinned by GIRFEC, which have resulted in an increase in early intervention aimed at diverting children and young people from the Hearings System, as discussed earlier.

Court Proceedings

As noted earlier, a specific aim of recent policy developments in Scottish juvenile justice has been to divert as many 16- and 17-year-olds away from prosecution as possible. The trend in the number of 16- and 17-year-olds who were proceeded against in the Scottish courts is revealed in Figure 11.3, shown as a rate per 1000 of the population to adjust for changes in population size. This chart shows that the rate of conviction among both 16- and 17-year-olds fell toward the end of the 1990s before flattening off and then starting to

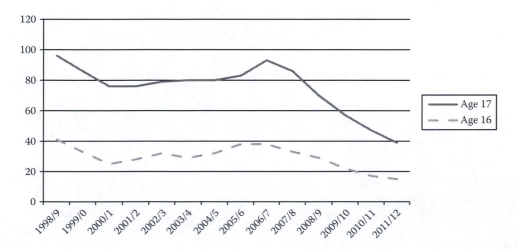

Figure 11.3 Number of 16- and 17-year-olds proceeded against in the Scottish courts per 1000 population. (Scottish Government. (2009b). *Criminal Proceedings in Scotland 2007–08*. Edinburgh, Scottish Government National Statistics Publication; Scottish Government. (2012a). *Criminal Proceedings in Scotland 2011–12*. Edinburgh, Scottish Government National Statistics Publication.)

incline slightly during the early 2000s. Following a peak in rates around 2006/7, trends have declined for both age groups over the last 5 years.

The decline in criminal proceedings amongst 17-year-olds is particularly pronounced, which suggests that aspects of the GIRFEC policy model may have been particularly successful in driving this trend. A review of PF data provides no strong evidence that prosecutorial decision-making practices have driven changes in criminal proceedings through greater use of alternatives to prosecution. The available case-processing statistics suggest that between 2008/9 and 2011/12, there was an overall drop in total court disposals of around 15%; however, there was also a fall of around 25% in the number of cases that resulted in no further action, and the proportion of cases receiving a noncourt disposal fell by about 8% in 2010/11 before returning to its previous level. These data are not disaggregated by age; however, all things being equal, they do not suggest that a significant shift in prosecutorial practice is driving down court proceedings.

Other significant legislative changes during this period may have impacted on the number of young people proceeded against in court. This includes the implementation of the Antisocial Behaviour, etc. (Scotland) Act 2004, which led to the introduction of police Fixed Penalty Notices in 2007. These have been identified as driving down prosecutions for minor offenses including breach of peace and public order offenses (Cavanagh 2009). In addition, the Criminal Proceedings etc. (Reform) (Scotland) Act 2007 introduced changes to several aspects of summary justice reform, including an increased use of direct measures for low-level offenses to keep them out of the courts. Again, there is no publicly available data on the extent to which these measures have impacted on young people specifically; however, given the nature of the offenses that they are targeted at (including vandalism and breach of the peace), it seems likely that they have had some impact on the trends shown in Figure 11.3.

Unlike SCRA data, criminal proceedings statistics do give information on the nature of offenses for which young people have been convicted. Unfortunately, the available data groups all young people together under the age of 21 rather than breaking the numbers down into separate years. Table 11.3 shows the types of crimes and offenses for which males and females were convicted in 2011/12, broken down according to the five crime

Table 11.3 Males and Females with a Charge Proved in 2011/12 by Crime and Offense Type

Crime/Offense	Males under 21 (Percent) (n = 13,128)	Females under 21 (Percent) (n = 1,950)
Nonsexual crimes of violence	4	2
Crimes of indecency (includes crimes relating to prostitution)	1	*
Crimes of dishonesty	12	12
Fire raising and vandalism, etc.	6	4
Other crimes (includes drugs and crimes against justice)	21	16
Miscellaneous offenses (includes simple assault, breach of peace)	36	49
Motor vehicle offenses	19	17

Source: Scottish Government. (2012a). *Criminal Proceedings in Scotland 2011–12.* Edinburgh, Scottish Government National Statistics Publication.

* Represents less than 1%.

and two offense groups used to classify crimes in Scotland. As can be seen, convictions for serious violent and sexual crimes are rare, with most offenders being convicted of miscellaneous offenses (such as breach of peace or minor assaults) and, to a slightly lesser extent, other crimes (mainly shoplifting) and motor vehicle offenses. Therefore, while justice reforms aim to keep more minor crimes and offenses out of the courts, the data presented in Table 11.3 indicate that these types of behavior are still the main driver of conviction for young people in Scotland.

Imprisonment

Statistics relating to the imprisonment of young people in Scotland have also shown a fluctuating pattern over the past decade or so. Despite an extensive and continual growth in the annual prison population, Figure 11.4 shows that the average daily prison population for those aged under 21 declined at a steady rate between 1998/9 and 2004/5, before rising again during the period when the Labour/Liberal Democrat coalition's focus on youth offending was at its peak. Interestingly, however, this rise continued well into the period when the SNP government took over in 2007 and introduced a raft of new policies aimed at reducing the number of young people in the system. Indeed, it is only since 2010/11 that we have started to see a decline in the average number of people aged under 21 who are being imprisoned in Scotland. These figures are particularly interesting, given the dramatic fall in the number of 16- and 17-year-olds being proceeded against in Scottish courts and may indicate that the behavior of sentencers, while moving in the right direction, has been much slower to respond to recent policy shifts than other parts of the juvenile and adult criminal justice system.

Evidence from the Edinburgh Study of Youth Transitions and Crime

An alternative data resource that allows us to look at the extent of crime among one cohort of young people growing up in Scotland is the Edinburgh Study, a large-scale prospective

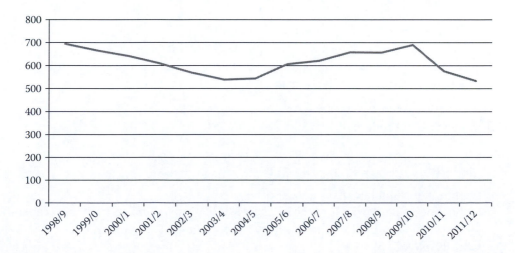

Figure 11.4 Average daily prison population of prisoners aged under 21 in Scotland. (Scottish Government. (2008b). *Prison Statistics Scotland 2007/08*. Edinburgh, Scottish Government National Statistics Publication; Scottish Government. (2012b). *Prison Statistics and Population Projections Scotland 2011–12*. Edinburgh, Scottish Government National Statistics Publication.)

longitudinal study of youth offending, which began in 1998 with a cohort of over 4000 young people (Smith and McVie 2003). It is important to note that this study cannot tell us about how young people have changed over time; however, it can give us insights into how individual young people's behavior changes as they mature and develop with age. The main aims and methods have been summarized in Box 11.2.

Between the ages of 12 and 17, annually administered self-completion questionnaires were used to collect data about young people's involvement in a range of offending behaviors, ranging from trivial forms of antisocial behavior to more serious forms of crime. Table 11.4 presents a summary of the offending behavior reported by these young people, giving separate results for males and females. In common with other self-report studies undertaken in Scotland (see Anderson et al. 1994; Jamieson, McIvor, and Murray 1999), the Edinburgh Study findings suggest that the experience of offending is quite common-place among the cohort.

Between age 12 and 17, a large proportion of young people admitted being involved in at least one act of antisocial or offending behavior. Three-quarters of the young people stated that they had been involved in some form of violence, although this mainly

---

BOX 11.2   THE EDINBURGH STUDY OF YOUTH TRANSITIONS AND CRIME

Aims of the program

- To investigate the factors leading to involvement in offending and desistance from it
- To examine the striking differences between males and females in criminal offending
- To explore the above in three contexts:
  - Individual development
  - Interactions with formal agencies of control
  - The social and physical structures of neighborhoods
- To develop new theories explaining offending behavior and contribute to practical policies targeting young people

Overview of Methods

- Longitudinal study of all children in Edinburgh who started secondary school in the city of Edinburgh in August 1998 (n = 4300): annual self-completion questionnaire from age 12 to 17
- Collection of data from a range of agencies having formal contact with the cohort including Children's Hearings System and social work and criminal records office
- In-depth interviews with subsamples of children at ages 13 and 17
- A study of the social geography of Edinburgh
- Case studies of two neighborhoods

Table 11.4 Prevalence of Self-Reported Offending among the Edinburgh Study Cohort (Age 12–17)

	Males (%)	Females (%)	All (%)
Violence (assault, robbery, and animal abuse)	86	63	75
Antisocial behavior (being rowdy or unruly in public)	71	65	68
Theft (shoplifting, vehicle thefts, and housebreaking)	60	49	55
Property crime (vandalism, fire raising)	57	32	45
Serious offending (vehicle theft, joyriding, housebreaking, fire raising, possession of a weapon, robbery, and >5 assaults)	66	40	52
Persistent serious offending (more than 10 incidents in any 1 year)	34	14	24

Source: McAra, L. and McVie, S. (2010b). Youth crime and justice in Scotland. In Croall, H., Mooney, G., and Munro, M. (Eds.), *Criminal Justice in Scotland*. Oxon, Willan Publishing.

consisted of minor and infrequent physical assaults. Engagement in antisocial behavior in public was also fairly common. Around half of the young people said they had committed at least one act of theft during the 6 years, while just under a half said they had vandalized or set fire to someone else's property. Again, around half of the young people in this study reported committing at least one serious offense* at some point between the age of 12 and 17, although only a quarter were persistent serious offenders (committing more than 10 of these offenses in any 1 year). As shown in Table 11.4, females were significantly less likely to be involved in offending, particularly of a serious or persistent nature, than males.

Looking in more detail at those who committed serious offenses, Figure 11.5 shows the longitudinal trend in the percentage of young people involved in any serious offending and persistent serious offending between age 13 and 17, according to self-reports. The trend lines show that, at age 13, around a quarter of young people reported committing at least one serious offense and just under 1 in 10 were persistent serious offenders. Serious offending peaked in terms of prevalence at age 14 and then declined steadily to age 17, by which time around 15% were still reported to be involved in some serious offending and 5% were self-reported persistent serious offenders.

To determine whether the young people who were involved in serious offending differed from other young people, Table 11.5 compares serious offenders to other nonserious offenders and nonoffenders on a range of characteristics at age 14 (the peak age of offending). On almost every characteristic, serious offenders tended to be significantly different from those involved in nonserious offending and those who did not offend at age 14. Serious offenders were significantly more likely to be male and to be living in conditions associated with higher social deprivation or poverty. Serious offenders were also less likely to be living with both birth parents, which is an indication of family disruption, and gave lower scores on average in response to a series of questions on parental supervision (such as parental knowledge about where they went, who they were with, and what time they would return home when going out).

Differences among the serious offenders, the nonserious offenders, and the nonoffenders were particularly marked in terms of their involvement in other types of "risky"

---

* This includes theft of/from a motor vehicle, riding in a stolen vehicle, carrying an offensive weapon, housebreaking, fire raising, robbery, and six or more incidents of violence.

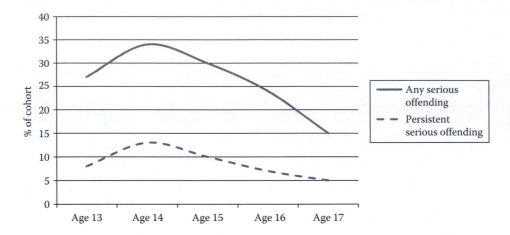

Figure 11.5 Serious and persistent offending amongst the Edinburgh Study cohort (age 13–17). (McAra, L. and McVie, S. (2010b). Youth crime and justice in Scotland. In Croall, H., Mooney, G., and Munro, M. (Eds.), *Criminal Justice in Scotland*. Oxon, Willan Publishing.)

Table 11.5 Comparing the Characteristics of Serious Offenders, Nonserious Offenders, and Nonoffenders in the Edinburgh Study at Age 14

Domain	Characteristics	Nonoffender (n = 1007)	Nonserious Offender (n = 1729)	Serious Offender (n = 1426)
Sex	% male	44	41	67
Social deprivation	% with parents in unemployment/ manual work	37	41	52
	Mean neighborhood deprivation score (0–14)	2.9	3.4	3.7
	% entitled to free school meals	15	18	26
Family dynamics	% living with both birth parents	72	67	57
	Mean score on parental supervision scale (0–9)	7.4	6.3	5.4
Risky behaviors	% who drink alcohol weekly	3	13	33
	% who took drugs in last year	3	13	44
	% who hang out most days	31	50	72
	% truanting from school >5 times in last year	1	7	23
	% belong to a "gang"	6	17	33
Personality	Mean self-esteem score (0–24)	16.0	15.2	15.2
	Mean impulsivity score (0–24)	9.2	12.9	15.0
	Mean risk-taking score (0–24)	3.5	6.8	9.6
Vulnerability	% victims of violence in last year	6	18	40
	% victim of violence with a weapon in last year	1	4	23
	% who self-harmed in last year	5	10	25
	% victims of bullying at least once a week	17	18	22

Source: McAra, L. and McVie, S. (2010b). Youth crime and justice in Scotland. In Croall, H., Mooney, G., and Munro, M. (Eds.), *Criminal Justice in Scotland*. Oxon, Willan Publishing.

behavior. Nonserious offenders were around three times as likely to drink alcohol regularly or to have taken drugs in the last year compared to nonoffenders, whereas, serious offenders were around two to three times more likely to have used alcohol or drugs than nonserious offenders. Serious offenders were also the most likely group to say that they would frequently hang around the streets and truant from school. Around 4 in 10 serious offenders reported that they belonged to a group they considered to be a "gang," compared to only 22% of nonserious offenders and 9% of nonoffenders.

In terms of their personality characteristics, serious offenders were not significantly different from other nonserious offenders in terms of their level of self-esteem (although self-esteem was higher among those who did not offend at age 14); however, serious offenders did have significantly higher scores than other young people on a scale of impulsivity and a scale of risk-taking behavior.

Those engaged in serious offending were also a highly vulnerable group, which is indicated by a range of indices. Four in 10 serious offenders at age 14 had been a victim of violence within the last year, and around a quarter had been assaulted with a weapon. One in four also reported that they had self-harmed, often by cutting themselves, and around the same proportion reported being victims of bullying behavior on a weekly basis. Aspects of vulnerability, including crime victimization, self-harming, and risk-taking behaviors, were found to be strongly predictive of involvement in violence among boys and girls at age 15 even when controlling for a broad range of other factors (McAra and McVie 2010a). In addition, there appear to be causal links between violence and vulnerability that run in both directions, as early violence was found to predict later self-harming behavior and vice versa.

Taken together, these findings on the links between serious offending, vulnerability, and social adversities provide strong support for the Kilbrandon ethos—in particular, its core contention that offending behaviors are symptoms of deeper-seated needs. This contention was explored further to determine whether those young people who were most in need of support and intervention from the Children's Hearings System were in fact the ones who received it, and what impact this had on their longer-term outcomes. Quasi-experimental analysis of the Edinburgh Study data was carried out to determine whether the offending outcomes for young people who had contact with different stages of the juvenile justice system were improved compared to matched individuals who had no system contact (McAra and McVie 2007). The results showed that those who experienced some system contact but were diverted away from formal intervention reported levels of serious offending similar to their matched groups 1 year later; however, those who were subject to compulsory measures of care within the Children's Hearings System were engaged in significantly higher levels of serious offending 1 year later compared to a group of children who were matched on a broad range of indicators but who did not have a hearing. The authors suggest that minimal intervention and maximum diversion is likely to be successful in terms of reducing crime among many young people in their mid-teenage years.

As noted earlier, a key component of contemporary juvenile policy is EEI, which is very much predicated on a risk factor paradigm. Findings from the Edinburgh Study suggest, however, that there could be major problems for agencies in identifying from an early age those specific individuals who will turn out to be chronic serious offenders in the teenage years (McAra and McVie 2010a). Combining self-report data on offending with official records of juvenile justice involvement revealed that the majority of those who were classified as violent, persistent, and serious offenders at age 17 were never known to social work agencies or the Children's Hearings System and, therefore, could not have been subject to intervention. Worryingly, however, those who were convicted by the courts at age 17 were far more likely to be known to the formal agencies from an early age, and there was strong evidence that early system contact had done little to stem the involvement of these young people in offending behavior.

Rather than focusing the gaze of criminal justice on the early years, evidence from the Edinburgh Study suggests that policy-makers should focus more firmly on critical moments in the mid-teenage years (McAra and McVie 2010a). Using criminal convictions data, semiparametric group-based modeling was used to identify trajectories of conviction amongst the study cohort, and it revealed three key offending groups, as shown in Figure 11.6. There are two early-onset groups, whose first conviction occurred at around age 9/10: one of these is a "chronic group" whose probability of conviction rises steeply in the early to mid-teenage years before starting to decline in their early 20s, while the other is a "desister group" whose probability of conviction declines from about age 15/16 and stops completely by about age 20. Growth in the probability of conviction for the third "later-onset" group starts at around age 15/16 and peaks at around age 20 before declining again. Analysis revealed that there were important changes in the lives of cohort members who experienced criminal convictions in their teenage years, and these changes occurred primarily between age 13 and 15. In particular, the factors that most strongly predicted a rising and sustained probability of conviction were school truancy, exclusion, adversarial police contact, and formal intervention from the juvenile justice system. In terms of theorizing why such factors may impact adversely on young people's conviction trajectories, McAra and McVie (2012) have argued that the cultural practices of formal orders (including those imposed by schools, the police, and the Children's Hearings System) play a key role in processing and labeling young people in such a way that it undermines their capacity to negotiate, limits their autonomy, and constrains their choices, rendering them more likely to absorb the offending identities ascribed to them with damaging consequences in terms of their offending behavior.

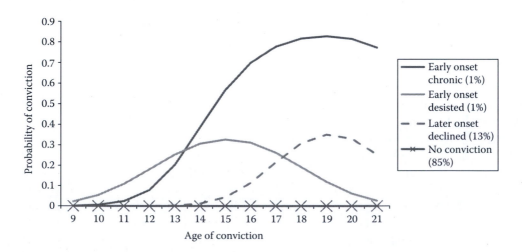

Figure 11.6 Semiparametric group-based trajectories of criminal conviction among the Edinburgh Study cohort (N = 3855). (McAra, L. and McVie, S. (2010a). Youth crime and justice: Key messages from the Edinburgh Study of Youth Transitions and Crime. *Criminology and Criminal Justice* 10(2):179–209.)

Implications of the Data on Youth Crime in Scotland

To conclude this section, the official statistics on youth crime in Scotland suggest that the number of young people entering both the juvenile and adult justice systems has declined significantly in recent years. Much of the juvenile offending that comes to the attention of official agencies tends to be fairly petty in nature, and it is likely that changes to the juvenile justice landscape within the last decade have played a considerable role in reducing the number of young people receiving convictions. Crimes are overwhelmingly committed by boys, according to both self-report data and official statistics, and there is strong evidence that a small number of young people (mainly boys) who are serious and persistent offenders are responsible for a disproportionate amount of the crimes that are attributed to young people. However, the lack of published information (e.g., on the age and gender of children reported to the police) and national survey data on offending makes it difficult to estimate with any degree of accuracy the actual nature and scale of youth offending across Scotland and the degree to which changing trends are due to changes in organizational policy and practice as opposed to behavior. The Edinburgh Study has provided valuable contextual information about the way in which individual behavior changes with age, the characteristics and background of those who engage in the most serious and persistent offending, the relationship between self-reported offending and conviction histories, and the significant impact that formal regulatory mechanisms can have on individual behavior.

Current Issues in Juvenile Justice

In this final section of the chapter, we consider some of the key issues, which are currently facing the juvenile justice system in Scotland. These relate to the age of criminal responsibility in Scotland; key transitions between juvenile and adult justice; and the use of police stop and search on young people.

Age of Criminal Responsibility in Scotland

Despite an increase in the age of criminal prosecution in Scotland, the age of criminal responsibility remains at 8 years. This is the first age at which children can be referred to the Children's Hearings System on offense grounds (unruly behavior on the part of children under the age of 8 can result in a referral to the Reporter but this would be on nonoffense grounds—see Box 11.1, earlier, for a list of grounds). Scotland has one of the lowest ages of criminal responsibility worldwide (putting it on par with countries such as Indonesia and Kenya) and the lowest in Europe. The debate about age, stage of maturity, and criminal responsibility is a complex and controversial one. As stated in the Kilbrandon Report, whatever age is chosen will inevitably prove to be rather arbitrary. There continue to be calls from youth organizations for the Scottish government to raise the age of criminal responsibility in Scotland, on the basis that the current legislation labels children effectively as criminals; however, to date, there has not been any legislative move in this direction.

Transition between the Juvenile and Adult Justice Systems

The normal point of transition from the juvenile to adult justice systems occurs at age 16. Despite some changes within the current system, Scotland remains out of kilter with many

European countries, which place the transition point at age 18. There is a consensus among many commentators that the transition between the Children's Hearings System and the adult courts is too abrupt and that young offenders find it difficult to adjust to the very different ethos of the latter. Those in favor of raising the point of transition argue that the adult criminal justice system is not geared to dealing with the needs of 16- to 17-year-old offenders. Despite the establishment of Pilot Youth Courts in Scotland in 2003, there was no clear evidence that the outcomes for young people aged 16 and 17 attending these courts was significantly different from those who attended adult courts. Many offenders at this age present with problems relating to substance misuse, high levels of victimization, or family relationship difficulties, and many are immature and emotionally underdeveloped (see Hogg 1999; McAra and McVie 2007). As such, they would benefit far more from the more holistic approach offered by the Children's Hearings System.

Those in favor of retaining 16 years as the point of transition argue that it is an age when young people generally do reach a sufficient degree of maturity. It is both the legal age of marriage in Scotland and also the school-leaving age. Moreover, it is argued that the nature and scale of offending among many 16-year-olds makes the criminal courts a more appropriate forum than the Children's Hearings System (see Hallet et al. 1998). The Edinburgh Study findings reported earlier, however, indicate that those who engage in offending at age 16 and 17 are a particularly vulnerable group and often in need of diversionary strategies that provide meaningful alternatives to court disposals and address the many social, economic, and personal adversities underlying their criminal behavior.

Police Stop and Search

Finally, the use of police stop and search for young people in Scotland is a particularly controversial topic at present. Rates of stop and search have increased enormously in some parts of Scotland in the last 5 years alone, to the extent that the rate of stop searches in the Strathclyde region (where the practice has been particularly heavily implemented) is more than double that of the Metropolitan Police in London (Murray 2013). McAra and McVie (2005) found that adversarial police contact was directed predominantly at a group of "usual suspects," namely, young males from low socioeconomic backgrounds and living in areas of multiple deprivation and that the impact of such practice was to label and criminalize many young people. Murray's research also found that police stop searches were disproportionately directed at young males in their mid-teenage years, and reveals that the success of such searches in terms of positive detection (of a weapon, e.g.) was far lower than for older age groups. She argues that the sharp discrepancy between the pattern of searches and persons charged in "proactive policing" areas, coupled with low detection rates, indicates that stop and search in some areas of Scotland has resulted in the "overpolicing" of young people.

Since the establishment of the new single police force in April 2013, it appears that the policy on stop and search previously implemented in the legacy Strathclyde force has been rolled out to the rest of Scotland and, contrary to other parts of the United Kingdom, the rate of police stop and search is on the increase. Police Scotland have claimed that major reductions in recorded violent crime in the Strathclyde area in recent years are due in large part to the implementation of intelligence-led stop search policing tactics (Scottish Police Authority 2013). However, there are concerns that such specific targeting of young disenfranchised groups may breach certain aspects of the Human Rights Act 1998, such as

Articles 5 (Right to Liberty and Security) and 8 (Respect for Private and Family Life), and that it is contrary to the principles of procedural justice and police fairness advocated by scholars such as Tyler (1990). In addition, the increased use of stop and search for young people is at odds with the development of a WSA in dealing with young people, which is premised on a minimal intervention approach.

Conclusion

Within Scotland, policy on juvenile offenders has always been bifurcated between a public interest and welfarist perspective. The precise interplay between the concerns of key policy elites and broader social and cultural processes has determined which of these perspectives has triumphed at any particular juncture. After a period in which welfarism was in ascendance, the immediate postdevolution years saw the public interest perspective increasingly coming to challenge dominant modes of discourse within the system. The elision between the youth justice and social inclusion agenda contributed to this process, heralding an era of protective tutelage, which threatened to undermine rather than strengthen key aspects of the Kilbrandon philosophy. More recently, the SNP administration has attempted to build political capacity through the concept of compassionate justice, an ethos that is much more in keeping with the original Kilbrandon vision of juvenile justice.

To return to the quotation at the beginning of the chapter, Scottish society still seems concerned to secure a more effective and discriminatory machinery for dealing with children and young people who offend. Changes to the juvenile justice system in recent years, based strongly on evidence of what works, have moved very much in the right direction. There remains, however, some concern about the potential for tension between policing strategies that target particular young people and the more diversionary aspects of Scotland's new WSA to juvenile justice.

Review/Discussion Questions

1. What were the reasons for the divergence of the Scottish and English systems of juvenile justice during the 1970s and 1980s?
2. How much youth crime is there in Scotland and how has it changed over time?
3. What is the appropriate age at which young offenders should make the transition to the adult criminal justice system?
4. What are the implications of the Edinburgh Study of Youth Transitions and Crime for the best ways of dealing with persistent young offenders?

References

Anderson, S., Kinsey, R., Loader, I., and Smith, C. (1994). *Cautionary Tales: Young People, Crime and Policing in Edinburgh*. Aldershot, Avebury.

Bauman, Z. (2000). Social Issues of Law and Order. *British Journal of Criminology* 40(2):205–221.

Bruce, N. (1982). Historical background. In Martin, F. and Murray, K. (Eds.), *The Scottish Juvenile Justice System*. Edinburgh, Scottish Academic Press. 3–12.

Cavadino, M. and Dignan, J. (1997). *The Penal System: An Introduction*, second edition. London, Sage.

Cavanagh, B. (2009.) *A Review of Fixed Penalty Notices for Antisocial Behaviour*. Edinburgh, Scottish Government.

Cleland, A. (1995). Legal solutions for children: Comparing Scots law with other jurisdictions. *Scottish Affairs* (10): 6–24.

Douglas, M. (1992). *Risk and Blame: Essays in Cultural Theory*. London, Routledge.

DTZ Pieda. (2005). *Measurement of the Extent of Youth Crime in Scotland*. Edinburgh, Scottish Executive.

Edwards, L. and Griffiths, A. (1997). *Family Law*. Edinburgh, Green/Sweet and Maxwell.

Gadda, A. and Fitzpatrick, J.P. (2012). Home Supervision Requirements: Messages from Research. Glasgow, Centre for Excellence for Looked After Children in Scotland. Briefing Paper RB-2-12-03.

Garland, D. (1996). The limits of the sovereign state. *British Journal of Criminology* 36(4):445–471.

Gelsthorpe, L. and Morris, A. (1994). Juvenile Justice 1954–1992. In Maguire, R., Morgan, R., and Reiner, R (Eds.), *The Oxford Handbook of Criminology*, first edition. Oxford, Oxford University Press. 890–949.

Hallet, C., Murray, C., Jamieson, J., and Veitch, B. (1998). *The Evaluation of the Children's Hearings in Scotland, Volume 1: Deciding in Children's Interests*. Edinburgh, The Scottish Office Central Research Unit.

Hogg, K. (1999). *Youth Crime in Scotland: A Scottish Executive Policy Unit Review*. http://www.scotland.gov.uk/Resource/Doc/158950/0043190.pdf.

Jamieson, J., McIvor, G., and Murray, C. (1999). *Understanding Offending Among Young People*. Edinburgh, The Scottish Executive Central Research Unit.

Kilbrandon Committee. (1964). *Report on Children and Young Persons, Scotland*. Edinburgh, Her Majesty's Stationery Office.

Lianos, M. and Douglas, M. (2000). Dangerization and the end of deviance: The institutional environment. *British Journal of Criminology* 40(2):261–278.

MacQueen, S. and McVie, S. (2013). The Whole System Approach for Children and Young People Who Offend: An Evaluation of Early Stage Implementation. Glasgow, University of Edinburgh. SCCJR Briefing Paper 01/2013.

McAra, L. (1998). *Social Work and Criminal Justice, Volume 2: Early Arrangements*. Edinburgh, The Stationary Office.

McAra, L. (1999). The politics of penality: An overview of the development of penal policy in Scotland. In Duff, P. and Hutton, N. (Eds.), *Criminal Justice in Scotland*. Aldershot, Dartmouth. 355–380.

McAra, L. (2002). The Scottish juvenile justice system: Policy and practice. In Winterdyk, J. (Ed.), *Juvenile Justice Systems: International Perspectives*, second edition. Toronto, Canadian Scholars Press.

McAra, L. (2005). Negotiated order: Gender, youth transitions and crime. *British Society of Criminology e-Journal*. 6:1–19. http://www.britsoccrim.org/volume6/005.pdf.

McAra, L. (2006). Welfare in crisis? Youth justice in Scotland. In Muncie, J. and Goldson, B. (Eds.), *Comparative Youth Justice*. London, Sage. 127–145.

McAra, L. (2008) Crime, criminal justice and criminology in Scotland. European Journal of Criminology. 5(4):481–504.

McAra, L. (2011). The impact of multi-level governance on crime control and punishment. In Crawford, A. (Ed.), *International and Comparative Criminal Justice and Urban Governance: Convergence and Divergence in Global, National and Local Settings*. Cambridge: Cambridge University Press. 276–303.

McAra, L. and McVie, S. (2005). The usual suspects? Street-life, young people and the police. *Criminal Justice* 5(1):5–35.

McAra, L. and McVie, S. (2007). Youth justice? The impact of system contact on patterns of desistance from offending. *European Journal of Criminology* 4(3):315–345.

McAra, L. and McVie, S. (2010a). Youth crime and justice: Key messages from the Edinburgh Study of Youth Transitions and Crime. *Criminology and Criminal Justice* 10(2):179–209.

McAra, L. and McVie, S. (2010b). Youth crime and justice in Scotland. In Croall, H., Mooney, G., and Munro, M. (Eds.), *Criminal Justice in Scotland*. Oxon, Willan Publishing.

McAra, L. and McVie, S. (2012). Negotiated order: Towards a theory of pathways into and out of offending. *Criminology and Criminal Justice* 12(4):347–376.

McAra, L. and Young, P. (1997). Juvenile justice in Scotland. *Criminal Justice* 15(3):8–10.

McIvor, G., Barnsdale, L., Brown, A., Eley, S., Macrae, R., Malloch, M., Murray, C., Murray, L., Piacentini, L., Popham, F., and Walters, R. (2006). *Evaluation of the Airdrie Sheriff Youth Court Pilot*. Edinburgh, Scottish Executive Social Research.

Morris, A. and McIsaac, M. (1978). *Cambridge Studies in Criminology, Volume 39: Juvenile Justice? The Practice of Social Welfare*. Cambridge, Heinemann.

Murphy, J. (1992). *British Social Services: The Scottish Dimension*. Edinburgh, Scottish Academic Press.

Murray, K. (2013). *Stop and Search in Scotland: The Proactive Turn*. Glasgow, SCCJR Bulletin.

Nelken, D. (1994). Whom can you trust? The future of comparative criminology. In Nelken, D. (Ed.), *The Futures of Criminology*. London, Sage.

Nelken, D. (1997). Understanding criminal justice comparatively. In Maguire, R., Morgan, R., and Reiner, R. (Eds.), *The Oxford Handbook of Criminology*, second edition. Oxford, Oxford University Press.

O'Malley, P. (1992). Risk, power and crime prevention. *Economy and Society* 21(3):252–275.

Piacentini, L. and Walters, R. (2006). The politicization of youth justice in Scotland and the rise of the "Burberry Court." *Youth Justice* 6(1):43–59.

Pratt, J. (2000). The return of the wheelbarrow men; or the arrival of postmodern penalty. *British Journal of Criminology* 40(1):127–145.

The Prince's Trust. (1997). *Young People and Crime in Scotland*. The Prince's Trust.

Reid, B. (1998). Panels and hearings. In Lockyer, A. and Stone, F. (Eds.), *Juvenile Justice in Scotland: Twenty-Five Years of the Welfare Approach*. Edinburgh, T & T Clark.

Rose, N. (1999). *Powers of Freedom: Reframing Political Thought*. Cambridge, Cambridge University Press.

Scottish Children Reporters Administration. (2013). Online Statistical Dashboard 2012/13. http://www.scra.gov.uk/cms_resources/Online%20annual%20dashboard%202012-13.swf (accessed 11 November 2013).

Scottish Executive. (1999a). *Partnership for Scotland*. Edinburgh, HMSO.

Scottish Executive. (1999b). *Safer Communities in Scotland: Guidance for Community Safety Partnerships*. Edinburgh, HMSO.

Scottish Executive. (2005a). Scotland's first youth court opens. Press release: http://www.scotland.gov.uk/News/Releases/2005/06/15112358.

Scottish Executive. (2005b). *Getting it Right for Every Child: Proposals for Action*. Edinburgh, Scottish Government.

Scottish Government. (2008a). *Preventing Offending by Young People: A Framework for Action*. Edinburgh, Scottish Government.

Scottish Government. (2008b). *Prison Statistics Scotland 2007/08*. Edinburgh, Scottish Government National Statistics Publication.

Scottish Government. (2009a). *Review of the Hamilton and Airdrie Youth Courts Report*. Edinburgh, Scottish Government.

Scottish Government. (2009b). *Criminal Proceedings in Scotland 2007-08*. Edinburgh, Scottish Government National Statistics Publication.

Scottish Government. (2012a). *Criminal Proceedings in Scotland 2011-12*. Edinburgh, Scottish Government National Statistics Publication.

Scottish Government. (2012b). *Prison Statistics and Population Projections Scotland 2011-12*. Edinburgh, Scottish Government National Statistics Publication.

Scottish Government. (2013). Scottish Government Criminal Proceedings Database. Personal communication, 3rd October 2013.

Scottish Government. (2013). *Training Resource Manual, Volume 1: Legislation and Procedures*. Edinburgh, Scottish Government.

Scottish Police Authority. (2013). Keeping People Safe through Stop and Search. Ayr, Scotland. Briefing Paper for SPA Authority Meeting, held August 21, 2013.

Simon, J. (2007). *Governing through Crime*. Oxford: Oxford University Press.

Smith, D. and McVie, S. (2003).Theory and method in the Edinburgh Study of Youth Transitions and Crime. *British Journal of Criminology* 43(1):169–195.

Smout, T. (1972). *A History of the Scottish People 1560–1830*. London, Collins/Fontana.

Tyler, T.R. (1990). *Why People Obey the Law*. New Haven, Yale University Press.

Waterhouse, L., McGhee, J., Loucks, N., Whyte, B., and Kay, H. (1999). *The Evaluation of the Children's Hearings in Scotland, Volume 3: Children in Focus*. Edinburgh, The Scottish Executive Central Research Unit.

Whitehead, I., Henderson, G., McNiven, G., and Lamb, D. (2010). Secure authorisations in Scotland's Children's Hearings System. Stirling, Scottish Children's Reporter Administration.

Internet Sources

Children's Hearings Scotland website, which describes the roles and responsibilities of the children's panel—http://www.chscotland.gov.uk

Edinburgh Study of Youth Transitions and Crime website, which provides information on the study and lists publications—http://www2.law.ed.ac.uk/cls/esytc/

Kilbrandon Report, which outlines the rationale for the establishment of the Children's Hearing System—http://www.scotland.gov.uk/Resource/Doc/47049/0023863.pdf

Police Scotland website—http://www.scotland.police.uk

Scottish Centre for Crime and Justice Research website, which highlights research on crime and justice in Scotland—http://www.sccjr.ac.uk Scottish Children's Reporter Administration website, which explains the Children's Hearing System and the role of the Reporter—http://www.scra.gov.uk/home/index.cfm

Scottish Children's Reporter Administration Statistical Dashboard, which provides valuable statistical data on referrals to and disposals from hearings—http://www.scra.gov.uk/cms_resources/Online%20statistical%20dashboard%202011-12.swf

Scottish courts website, which provides information on the structure and administration of courts in Scotland—http://www.scotcourts.gov.uk

Scottish Government website pages, which explain the nature of the youth justice system in Scotland, including the Whole Systems Approach and Early and Effective Intervention—http://www.scotland.gov.uk/Topics/Justice/crimes/youth-justice

Scottish Government website pages, which provide information about and access to crime statistics in Scotland—http://www.scotland.gov.uk/Topics/Statistics/Browse/Crime-Justice

Scottish Parliament Justice Committee website—http://www.scottish.parliament.uk/parliamentary-business/currentcommittees/29845.aspx

Scottish Prison Service website, which lists the prisons in Scotland and explains how they are managed and organized—http://www.sps.gov.uk/home/home.aspx

Juvenile Justice in Slovakia

12

DAGMAR KUSA AND
ANNE M. NURSE

Contents

Historical Profile   296
Historical Overview of the Juvenile Justice System   297
A Brief History of Social Evolution/Evolution of Thought   298
Current Legislation/Situation   299
    Criminal Offenses and Clearance Rates   299
    Pretrial   301
    Court and Sentencing   302
    Custody   304
Alternatives to the Traditional System   308
    Reeducation   308
    Waiver of Punishment   308
    Diversion   308
    Mediation   309
    Probation   309
    Community Service   310
Juvenile Crime Trends   310
Special Issues   313
    Prevention of Criminality   313
    The Roma   314
    Child Trafficking   315
Conclusion   315
Acknowledgment   316
Review/Discussion Questions   316
References   317
Internet Sources   319

FACTS ABOUT THE SLOVAK REPUBLIC

Area: The Slovak Republic is a country in east-central Europe. It is bordered by the Czech Republic, Poland, Ukraine, Hungary, and Austria. Slovakia is landlocked and has a total area of 18,928 square miles (49,035 square kilometers). The Carpathian Mountains occupy most of the northern half of the country. **Population:** The population is approximately 5.5 million. The capital, Bratislava, is located on the Danube in southwestern Slovakia and is home to about 430,000 people. **Climate:** Generally the weather is temperate with cool summers and cold, cloudy, and humid winters. There can be significant weather differences between the southern part of the country and the mountainous region in the north. **Economy:** From 1948 to 1990, the Slovak Republic had a centrally planned economy. Today they have an advanced, market-driven economy. The 2000s have seen rapid economic growth in Slovakia. The Slovak Republic joined the European Union in 2004 and adopted the euro in 2009. Of all the countries in the European Union, Slovakia had the highest gross domestic product growth in 2007, 2008, and 2010 (Slovakia 2013). At the same time, the country has not been immune to the economic recession and recently has had a relatively high level of unemployment (currently 14%) (Passell 2013). **Government:** Slovakia is a parliamentary democratic republic with a multiparty system. The Slovak head of state is the president who is elected by direct popular vote for a 5-year term. Andrej Kiska was elected president in March of 2014. Most of the executive power lies with the prime minister (currently Mr. Robert Fico).

Historical Profile

Prior to 1918, the territory of modern-day Slovakia was part of the Austro-Hungarian Empire. The region seceded in 1918 and became part of the democratic Czechoslovak Republic. For 6 years during the Second World War, Slovakia operated as a quasi-independent state, propped up by Nazi Germany, but then it rejoined Czechoslovakia. The Communist Party assumed power in 1946 and remained at the helm for over four decades. The fifties were an era of a Stalinist rule, accompanied by the nationalization of property, forced collectivization, staged political trials, labor camps, and so on. Totalitarian rule was milder in the 1960s, when the regime, under the leadership of Alexander Dubček, attempted a series of progressive reforms. Those reforms were abruptly halted by the invasion of the Moscow-led Warsaw Pact armies in 1968. The '70s and '80s were referred to as the era of "normalization." Communist rule was in effect until a peaceful revolution (commonly known as the Velvet Revolution) in 1989. The Communist Party of Czechoslovakia relinquished power, and democratic elections were held in 1990.

The transition period was accompanied by rampant nationalism that soon burdened the political discourse and Czech–Slovak relations. In 1993, a political agreement was reached that separated the Czech Republic and the Slovak Republic. This split, sometimes referred to as the "the Velvet Divorce" was achieved peacefully, although only a minority of the public was in favor of it at the time (Slovakia 2013). There is some debate over the primary reasons for the split (especially given public opinion), but most historians agree that it involved both economic and cultural differences between the regions. Additionally, Czech and Slovak politicians had difficulty reconciling their visions of a unified state. The populism and nationalism that accompanied the transition period in both Slovak and Czech parts of the common country also played a role in the divorce. Slovakia has since then been on its own transition path toward democracy, experiencing ups and downs connected with privatization, populism, a semiauthoritarian era in the '90s, as well as economic boom, integration into European structures, and gradual reforms in all spheres of society.

Historical Overview of the Juvenile Justice System

The foundations of the Czechoslovak Penal Code lie in its predecessors in the Austro-Hungarian Empire. Following the lead of the Western countries, the Austro-Hungarian Penal Code was gradually modernized. The introduction of Dualism in 1867* was problematic as it meant that Austrian laws were implemented in the Czech lands, and Hungarian in the Slovak lands (Luprichová 2008). This continued for some years after the establishment of the Czechoslovak Republic.

The Hungarian Penal Code was passed in 1880 and was significantly amended in 1908. These amendments formed the backbone for criminal proceedings against juveniles, as they stipulated that youth could receive special sentencing reductions and that judges could employ small modifications of normal criminal proceedings. In 1913, a separate legal article on criminal proceedings against juveniles was passed, thereby introducing juvenile courts in each royal district. The courts decided that sentences could take the form of incarceration, a fine, or a corrective reeducative measure.

After the formation of Czechoslovakia in 1918, lawmakers attempted to harmonize legislation by adopting new common legislative measures and practices (Luprichová 2008, 7–8). In 1931, Czechoslovakia adopted the Juvenile Criminal Judiciary Act No. 48/1931 Coll., which established a youth penal code and a juvenile court system. This law was seen as very progressive for its time as it brought the term "juvenile" into the language of the criminal code and set up a distinctive sentencing structure for juveniles. The act also mandated specialized training of juvenile judges. Accused juveniles appeared before panels composed of both the new juvenile judges and lay judges at the district court level. The law underscored corrective and reeducative measures over punishment, and raised the age of criminal responsibility from 12 to 14 years of age. Persons under the age of 14 were considered children and not responsible under the penal code. Juveniles between the ages of 14 and 18 could be reprimanded or sentenced to placement in a foster family or protective supervision, or provided therapy. If the crime was punishable with the death penalty or a life sentence under the penal code, the juvenile could be sentenced to protective care in a reeducational or therapeutic institution (Luprichová 2008).

In 1948, when the communists seized power in Czechoslovakia, a totalitarian regime was instituted. At first, the new regime simply layered various new laws—often repressive—on top of the existing laws. In 1950, the government adopted a new criminal code, based on Soviet law. The age of criminal responsibility was set at 15, and juvenile courts were abolished. This criminal code was particularly harsh, although some modifications to the most repressive parts were made during the 1950s. At the same time, the numbers in reeducation centers dropped sharply. These two seemingly countervailing

---

* In 1867, the Austro-Hungarian Empire was federalized, giving the Hungarians more freedom and power in administration and legislation over their territories, including current Slovakia.

tendencies stemmed, at least partly, from the communist ideology itself—communism assumed that the establishment of socialism would eventually lead to the elimination of criminality and other social problems.* Violent crime was considered doubly serious, as it was perceived not only as a trespassing against the penal code but also as being against the communist ideology and revolution. At the same time, the regime tried to contribute actively toward the decrease in criminality by reforming *the prison system* and emphasizing alternative forms of punishment. These changes did not, however, achieve a decrease in crime rate (Marešová and Válková 1994, 3).

The government adopted a new constitution in 1960 followed by an updated criminal code in 1961. The new code was similar to the previous one but made several changes including the establishment of "people's courts" for low-level offenses as well as statutes mandating better treatment of inmates. The 1961 Criminal Code again failed to establish juvenile courts; juveniles were simply handled by special provisions in the general criminal law (Karabec et al. 2011). Amendments passed in 1965 (Regulation No. 56/1965 Coll.) specify, again within the penal code (Act No. 140/1961), that the penalties for juveniles under the age of 18 were to be carried out in "correctional-educational" facilities. Depending on the length of the sentence and severity of the crime, youth could continue to be held in these facilities after they reached the age of 18. Sentences could be mitigated, or canceled, by the court due to good behavior or when the juvenile reached the age of 18, and the court could also decide to erase the crime from the record. Criminal proceedings against juveniles were only slightly amended after 1989. An amendment passed in the year 2000 (Act No. 85/2000 Coll.) introduced a special section on treatment of juveniles in its Head VII, a document which summarizes the criminal proceedings and sentencing and carrying out of the sentences in the cases of juveniles.

In 2005, Slovakia enacted a new criminal code. This code, which is still in effect today, is significantly different from those that came before. The new criminal code lessens penalties for minor crimes while simultaneously increasing penalties for serious and violent crimes. New features of the law include the option of plea bargains, more specific drug laws intended to distinguish personal use from trafficking, and provisions making racial motivation an aggravating circumstance. The new law also allows for work punishment rather than incarceration for some categories of juveniles and adults. In terms of juveniles, the most important change in this law is a shift in the age of criminal responsibility back from 15 to 14. As in the old system, however, juveniles are covered by the same criminal code and judicial system as adults. The new code does allow age to be considered as a mitigating circumstance and the code contains special provisions for juveniles. For example, a judge can declare a less serious misdemeanor "noncriminal" if the offender is a juvenile (Hičárová et al. 2010).

A Brief History of Social Evolution/Evolution of Thought

Slovak criminal law and sentencing, like that found in many other countries, contains conflicting strains. On the one hand, there are strong punitive aspects in the new criminal code, exemplified by increased penalties on many types of serious crime. Slovakia also has three-strikes sentencing, which means that a life sentence is automatically imposed when

---

* For example, the strength of the oldest reeducation center dropped in 1948 from the original 240 (and having reached the maximum occupancy at 720) to just 60 juveniles (History of the School 2013).

a person has committed three serious crimes. While a later amendment allowed for 20–25 year sentences in place of life, Slovakia's legislation still stands out as unusually harsh. Apart from Hungary, Slovakia is the only other country in the European Union to have this kind of three-strikes legislation. Notably, Slovak law allows a serious crime committed by a juvenile to count as a first strike.

While the punitive aspects of the new Slovak Criminal Code stand out, the law also contains important rehabilitative and progressive aspects. For example, it lessens sentences for minor crimes and allows home confinement for adults and work punishment for either adults or juveniles. There is also a move toward instituting elements of restorative justice, specifically mediation, into criminal matters. It is also important to note that the punitive aspects of the new law have not been accepted uncritically. There has been a current of protest from some politicians, judges, and academics against the more punitive measures, especially the three-strikes legislation (Šutková 2007).

Looking specifically at juveniles, the new criminal code generally takes a rehabilitative tone. It cites the goal of punishment for young offenders as threefold: reeducation, protection of society, and reintegration into the family and society. In theory, youth are supposed to be confined only in extreme circumstances. When confinement is the only option, it is required to be in the least restrictive setting. On the other hand, there are also punitive features of the law with regard to young offenders. As described, the age of criminal responsibility was lowered from 15 to 14 years. While the law mandates a psychological evaluation of maturity for anyone under 15 years of age, the age shift reflects an increasing willingness to assign blame and punish youth. A report from the United Nations' Committee on the Rights of the Child (2006, 19), reflecting on the reasons behind the change in the minimum age commented: "Most [child] psychologists and [child] psychiatrists hold the view that the acceleration of mental and physical development of youth in recent decades has had the consequence of juveniles of at least 14 years of age being, in fact, capable of distinguishing and assessing the consequences of their actions and the related criminal consequences in all crimes."

Slovakia, like many countries, does not fit neatly into any one model of juvenile justice. It most closely resembles a modified justice model, however. As is clear from the new criminal code as well as from long-established practice, there is an emphasis put on both the diagnosis/treatment of problems and on punishment. The Ministries of Education and Social Affairs are involved with troubled youth, as are the courts. The fact that the Slovak Republic continues to deal with juveniles through special provisions in the law also suggests that they view youth as simply having reduced culpability and responsibility. All of these features are consistent with a modified justice model.

Current Legislation/Situation

Criminal Offenses and Clearance Rates

Slovak police and criminal courts handle a fairly large number of cases each year. Table 12.1 shows the number of criminal offenses committed between 2003 and 2012. The figures combine adult and juvenile perpetrators; we present juvenile crime separately later in the chapter.

Figure 12.1 shows the crime-type data for selected years as a proportion of the total.

Table 12.1 Proportion of Different Types of Crime in General Crime in the Years 2003–2012

	2003	2004	2005	2006	2007	2008	2009	2010	2011	2012
Total crime rate of which:	111,893	131,244	123,563	115,152	110,802	104,759	104,905	95,252	92,873	90,351
General crimes	83,420	100,417	88,951	84,107	80,400	74,751	71,655	64,904	61,203	55,988
Property crimes	61,034	77,098	65,306	63,077	60,045	54,755	52,399	47,408	43,176	39,944
Violent crimes	13,724	13,755	12,906	10,896	9,620	9,030	8,337	7,532	7,002	6,607
Moral crimes	835	875	794	798	805	840	791	678	1,041	841
Other crimes	7,827	8,689	9,945	9,336	9,930	10,126	10,128	9,286	9,984	8,596
Economic crimes	14,863	16,414	19,245	19,168	17,895	16,974	19,518	16,781	18,145	16,681
Remainder crimes	13,610	14,413	15,367	11,877	12,324	12,932	13,638	13,518	13,500	17,660

Source: Office of Statistics of the Slovak Republic. (2013). Demography. http://portal.statistics.sk (accessed on May 13, 2013).

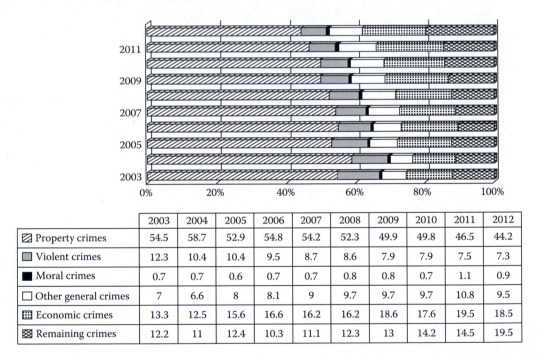

	2003	2004	2005	2006	2007	2008	2009	2010	2011	2012
Property crimes	54.5	58.7	52.9	54.8	54.2	52.3	49.9	49.8	46.5	44.2
Violent crimes	12.3	10.4	10.4	9.5	8.7	8.6	7.9	7.9	7.5	7.3
Moral crimes	0.7	0.7	0.6	0.7	0.7	0.8	0.8	0.7	1.1	0.9
Other general crimes	7	6.6	8	8.1	9	9.7	9.7	9.7	10.8	9.5
Economic crimes	13.3	12.5	15.6	16.6	16.2	16.2	18.6	17.6	19.5	18.5
Remaining crimes	12.2	11	12.4	10.3	11.1	12.3	13	14.2	14.5	19.5

Figure 12.1 Crime type as a proportion of the total, selected years 2003–2012. (Office of Statistics of the Slovak Republic. (2013). Demography. http://portal.statistics.sk (accessed on May 13, 2013).)

In Figure 12.2, we show the total number of reported offenses compared to the number cleared by arrest between 2007 and 2011. The number of reported offenses has declined, while the number of crimes cleared by arrest has stayed more or less stable. This may indicate that the police are becoming more efficient as they are clearing a higher proportion of crimes over time.

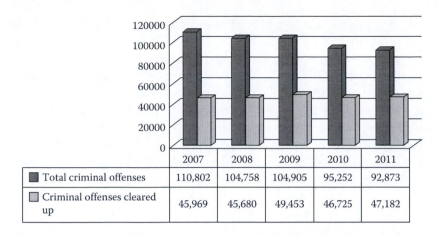

	2007	2008	2009	2010	2011
■ Total criminal offenses	110,802	104,758	104,905	95,252	92,873
☐ Criminal offenses cleared up	45,969	45,680	49,453	46,725	47,182

Figure 12.2 Reported criminal offenses and offenses cleared by arrest 2007–2011. (Office of Statistics of the Slovak Republic. (2013). Demography. http://portal.statistics.sk (accessed on May 13, 2013).)

Pretrial

There is a significant population of pretrial (remand) prisoners in Slovakia, including a fairly large number of juveniles. This is because the average time to trial is quite high—estimates from the United Nations suggest that juveniles wait an average of about 12 months, but that some are held as long as 4 years (Hazel 2008). This lengthy time to trial is the most frequent complaint heard about Slovakia at the European Court of Human Rights in Strasbourg, France. Judges have at least partial control over the length of pretrial custody as they decide the original terms of custody, and the law requires them to reexamine custody cases every 6 months. To be held pretrial, the accused must be judged to meet at least one of three criteria: flight risk, likelihood of committing more crime, or likelihood of trying to influence witnesses. While it is not entirely clear why the time to trial takes so long, it is possibly because there are too few judges, investigators, and prosecutors to handle the caseloads. Additionally, because defense lawyers are paid more than prosecutors, they have an incentive to appeal verdicts. The fact that Slovak law has been changing rapidly makes it difficult for the system to keep up, resulting in a backlog of cases. Finally, several different Slovakian ministries have control over juvenile delinquents, and this can lead to miscommunication, lack of information, and administrative shuffling, which also increases time to trial.

Remand prisoners are held in special wards of regular prisons. The United Nations has expressed concerns about the conditions under which they live because the "standard regime" offered them can involve being locked up to 23 hours in a cell with no activities or programming (Council of Europe 2010). Education, although compulsory for juveniles until they turn 16, can only be provided through individual study. Slovakia has begun offering a "mitigated regime" to some prisoners and especially to juvenile offenders. Under this new option, remand prisoners are allowed to move around in a corridor or go to a television room during certain hours of the day. They can also attend short-term educational programs, usually lectures on various topics. In recent years, some of the topics have included the adoption of the euro in Slovakia, sexual education, reverence to senior citizens, Easter traditions, and legal regulations about incarceration (Krošláková 2011). The United Nations has strongly recommended that juvenile remand prisoners be given more education and regular programming than what is currently being provided (Council of Europe 2010).

While in most Slovak prisons, pretrial juveniles are held in a separate ward from adults, this is not always the case. There is one prison where juveniles are housed with adults. In another, the remand juveniles are not put in rooms with adults, but can associate with them during the day (Council of Europe 2010). These conditions have caused the United Nations to express concern, as this policy conflicts with their recommendation that juveniles and adults always be kept separate. Some Slovakian officials believe, however, that housing youth among adults can discourage the formation of gangs and that youth can benefit with contact with some of the older stable prisoners (Council of Europe 2010).

Juveniles have somewhat different rights from adults in the pretrial phase of criminal proceedings. For example, they have the right to an attorney during all pretrial procedures. Only adults who are charged with a crime carrying a sentence of greater than 5 years have this same right. Additionally, pretrial juveniles can only be placed in solitary confinement for 14 days, as opposed to 30 days for adults. They can receive visits from close relatives once a week, whereas adults can only receive them every 3 weeks (Mihalovič 2006).

Court and Sentencing

As described, the criminal code was significantly revamped in 2005 and further amended in 2006. One of the important areas of change involved strengthening the adversarial court system. While cases are decided by a judge, both the victim and the accused have the right to an attorney, and the state provides the attorney for indigent defendants (US Department of State 2011). Judges, however, uphold a good deal of power as they can determine what evidence is admissible.

While the criminal code tried to create conditions of an independent judiciary, it remains mired in problems. This is regularly noted in various governance and human rights reports on Slovakia (e.g., United States Department of State 2013a). The Report on Slovakia for the year 2012, for example, highlights problems of abuse of power by judicial figures, a lack of checks and balances within the judicial system, and continued societal discrimination and violence against Roma (also referred to as "gypsies") (see Box 12.1). Other human rights problems included prison overcrowding and targeting of the press for civil defamation suits by members of the political and business elite. The government investigated reports of abuses by members of the security forces and other government institutions, but some officials engaged in corrupt practices with impunity.

In terms of sentencing, judges generally assign juveniles half of an adult sentence. The longest juvenile sentences are 7 years except in very serious cases where a penalty of up to 15 years can be imposed. Slovakian law allows for life sentences for juveniles, although they are rarely given. Life sentences do allow for the possibility of release. The European Committee for the Prevention of Torture and Inhuman or Degrading Treatment or Punishment has criticized the life sentence policy and argues that it is not in line with the Convention on the Rights of the Child (CRC) because juveniles with life sentences are not provided any education and/or training that would prepare them for release. These juveniles are also not given regular progress reviews (Council of Europe 2010).

Figure 12.3 shows sanctions imposed by criminal courts against juveniles between the years of 2000 and 2010. We see that while there is a long-standing preference for the conditional suspension of a prison sentence, the use of this sanction declined by almost 10% throughout the decade. There is also a slight decline in the use of unconditional

**BOX 12.1   CASES OF TORTUROUS, DEGRADING, OR
INHUMANE TREATMENT OF CHILDREN AND JUVENILES**

Slovakia has a high rate of abusive, degrading, or inhumane treatment of children and juveniles. While hard data do not exist, there are frequent reports of such treatment from the ranks of official institutions charged with protection of children.

Among the most notorious cases was the inhumane and degrading abuse of power by the police in Košice-Juh in 2009. Officers brought in six Roma boys between the ages of 10 and 16 after they were accused of robbing and injuring an elderly woman. The officers then threatened the boys with a service weapon, used service dogs to inflict fear, and ordered the boys to slap each other and strip naked. One of the officers forced a boy to lick his boot. The incident was videotaped and the video was leaked to the public 1 month after the incident, causing a public sensation. The trial was lengthy and controversial. Six of the seven initially implicated officers were immediately dismissed from service and indicted for the abuse of power and blackmail by a public official. The general prosecutor indicted 10 other officers on the same counts in 2009. Some of the acts were qualified as motivated by racial and ethnic hatred (Courts 2010). The court trial of the indicted officers was postponed several times. In 2012, not a single one of the accused police officers attended the trial, and several witnesses were missing as well, citing loss of an identity (ID) card, illness, and so on. The court case has been postponed multiple times but is scheduled to be resolved in 2014. (Case of bullying of Roma boys 2012).

The most recent public discussion of degrading treatment of juvenile offenders was connected to the monitoring conducted by the ombudsperson J. Dubovcová in the Reeducation Center in Hlohovec. She found individual and systemic failures there, leading to a situation where basic human rights of juveniles in the care of the center could not be guaranteed. The juveniles reported physical punishment, use of solitary confinement as punishment, hunger, and verbal abuse (Office of the Ombudsman 2013).

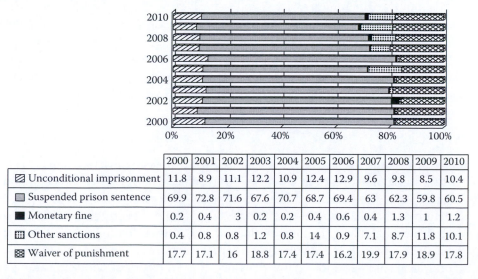

	2000	2001	2002	2003	2004	2005	2006	2007	2008	2009	2010
▨ Unconditional imprisonment	11.8	8.9	11.1	12.2	10.9	12.4	12.9	9.6	9.8	8.5	10.4
▥ Suspended prison sentence	69.9	72.8	71.6	67.6	70.7	68.7	69.4	63	62.3	59.8	60.5
■ Monetary fine	0.2	0.4	3	0.2	0.2	0.4	0.6	0.4	1.3	1	1.2
▦ Other sanctions	0.4	0.8	0.8	1.2	0.8	14	0.9	7.1	8.7	11.8	10.1
▩ Waiver of punishment	17.7	17.1	16	18.8	17.4	17.4	16.2	19.9	17.9	18.9	17.8

Figure 12.3 Sanctions imposed by criminal courts against juveniles in the years 2000–2010. (Vráblová, M. (2012). *Criminological and Legal Aspects of Criminal Activities of Juveniles.* Plzeň: Vydavatestvo Aleš Čeněk.)

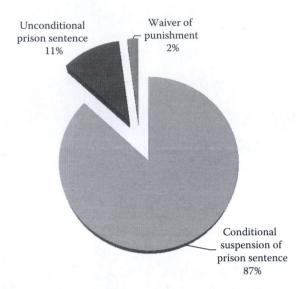

Figure 12.4 Structure of sanctions used against convicted juveniles in Čadca and Trnava between 2004 and 2006. (Vráblová, M. (2007). Juvenile justice system in the Slovak Republic—Empirical results. In *Days of Public Law Conference Proceedings*. Brno: Tribun EU. http://www.law.muni. cz/sborniky/Days-of-public-law/files/pdf/trest/Vrablova.pdf (accessed on August 26, 2013).)

imprisonment. On the other hand, there is a notable growth in the use of other (alternative) sanctions. These types of sanctions increased from 0.4% in 2000 to 10.1% in 2010. The use of monetary fines remains low, having grown from 0.2% to 1.2% during the observed years. Punishment was consistently waived in about 18% of the cases.

It is important to note that Figure 12.3 contains national data and may not be representative of every region of the country. Vráblová's (2007) work shows the variety of sanctions given in the different areas of Slovakia. In Figure 12.4 in the following text, she presents data from court decisions in the towns of Čadca and Trnava between 2004 and 2006. Although similar to the rest of the country, suspended prison sentences were more common (imposed about 87% of the time). A prison sentence was imposed in 11% of the cases and the court decided to waive punishment in 2% of the cases. Monetary punishment was very seldom used; hence, it does not appear in the figure (Vráblová 2007, 4).

Custody

Slovak law requires that juvenile offenders be assigned the least restrictive sanctions possible. Accordingly, the first level of intervention for troubled youth is not custody, but rather family therapy. Once a juvenile and his or her family have completed treatment, there is an assessment by a social worker of whether rehabilitation has been achieved. If the social worker determines that it has, the intervention can end. Other possible low-level sanctions include fines (if the juvenile is employed) or a verbal warning (Karabec et al. 2011).

A second level intervention for juveniles involves educational children's homes and centers. These institutions are run by the Ministry of Education and are intended for children under the age of 18 who are too troubled to be handled at home or in community schools. The government described the population served in these homes as "children with social and moral disruptions where deficiencies in social adaptability, personality features, and character development are so serious that their education cannot be provided in other establishments" (Council of Europe 2006, 11). Children are generally placed in these homes for 6 months, although they can have weekend passes to go home. The state is able to mandate children to go to these homes. Interestingly, parents are able to place their children there as well. These "welfare institutions" house a considerable number of children and youth—in 2005, for example, there were 834 children in residence (Council of Europe 2006).

Diagnostic Centers are places designed for youth who have committed serious infractions or for whom family therapy has been ineffective. These centers are operated by the Ministry of Education, but the Ministry of Social Affairs determines which children are placed there and when the children are released. This results in some tension between agencies as the staff in the center have little control over placement decisions. The Diagnostic Centers look like educational homes in that they have low security and are often just large houses. Resident youth attend school in the center, although some are allowed to go to the local community schools (see Box 12.2).

Prisons are the most severe sanctions Slovakian juvenile offenders face. As described, juvenile remand prisoners are held in the same prisons as adults. After trial, however, juveniles are housed in a special juvenile prison in Sučany (formerly in Košice). Incarcerated youth are separated into two groups (A and B) on the basis of their intellectual abilities and an assessment of their potential for rehabilitation. All prisoners under the age of 16 have a right to complete their compulsory education. To accomplish this, the prison hires on-site pedagogical staff. Secondary school, however, is not covered by the mandatory education provision of the law, and incarcerated youth who are interested can only participate individually through correspondence courses. Youth who began college prior to their incarceration are also allowed to continue their education via correspondence courses. As of February 2013, there were 63 male juvenile prisoners and 1 female juvenile prisoner (Prison and Court Guard 2013).

Women and incarcerated juveniles are each given 4 square meters of living space (Council of Europe 2006). This stands in contrast to the mandatory 3.5 square meters for adult males. As described, juveniles are not generally housed with adults. Like adults, they are also not put in the same room with members of different religious groups, nor are first-time offenders and recidivists housed together. Juvenile offenders can only be held in solitary confinement for 10 days as opposed to 20 for adults (Council of Europe 2006, 19).

In recent years, Slovakia has increased its efforts to help juvenile prisoners maintain family ties. For example, visitation was increased from one to two times a month (Council of Europe 2006). Additionally, incarcerated youth can list five close relatives on their visiting list. Like adults, they can make phone calls to approved people using a prepaid calling card. The Council of Europe (2010) points out, however, that some inmates cannot afford such cards. Another way that Slovakia encourages the maintenance of family ties is by allowing some juveniles to take leave from the prison for up to 10 hours, a privilege not afforded to adults (Council of Europe 2006, 19). However, monitoring of the conditions in juvenile reeducation and Diagnostic Centers is lacking, and the existing inspection is conducted by internal inspection bodies (see Box 12.3).

BOX 12.2   LIFE IN A DIAGNOSTIC CENTER

In 2012, the authors of this chapter visited a Diagnostic Center for males aged 15–18. It was housed in a large building in a quiet residential neighborhood about 20 minutes outside Bratislava. There were a total of 28 beds, although only 24 of them were in the normal housing units. The other four were in the health center and the isolation ward. When we visited, the house was not at full strength and the director said that they are rarely full. Most of the boys who stay at the diagnostic center live there from 3 to 6 months. In total, the center treats about 70 boys each year. They try to maintain a 1:1 ratio of staff to youth, but because the staff members work in shifts, there are not an equal number of staff and youth in the building at any one time. The emphasis of the center is on ethics and skills building. Central to their philosophy is a community system in which everyone is required to attend twice-daily meetings to talk about their behavior and feelings. Behavior is also monitored through a point system run by the staff. Youth are able to gain points for good behavior, but do not lose them for bad. The rewards for earning points include the right to go for a walk in the neighborhood or a weekend pass home. The staff base decisions about points on youth activity, cooperation, and discipline.

Because this diagnostic center is the only one for 15- to 18-year-old males in Slovakia, the residents come from all over the country. They live in groups of eight, four to a room with a common room in between. The rooms are very simple. The boys each have a wardrobe in which they can keep their belongings. At the time of our visit, the rooms and bathrooms were clean.

When there is sufficient funding, youth at the Diagnostic Center are able to go on trips and do team-building activities. Some examples include rock climbing, farming, and biking. The doors to the Diagnostic Center are not locked but the director told us that they rarely have problems with runaways. There are, however, sometimes problems with kids getting out of control. The director pointed out the lock-down isolation room, but we could not look inside because it was occupied.

The director cautioned us not to assume that this diagnostic center was the same as others in Slovakia. Because of its proximity to the capital, this center was better funded and more progressive than others. At the same time, he reported that staff turnover is extremely high because of low rates of pay for workers.

We were both struck by the wide range of youth who were housed in the center. The director told us that in some cases, kids live there because their parents wish to punish them or because the parents deem them out of control. He told us that one girl ended up in the center because her parents reported that she "filled up her bathtub too much and listened to music." Parents can have kids placed in a diagnostic center for 60 days. At the same time, other kids end up in the center for quite serious crimes. All of the juveniles except those with mental disabilities are housed and schooled together. As the director pointed out, sometimes children who entered the system with relatively few problems leave the system much worse off.

BOX 12.3   INSTITUTIONAL CHALLENGES IN JUVENILE JUSTICE

Legislation designed both to prosecute and protect juveniles in the area of criminal justice has progressed significantly over the country's two decades of independence. This is also true of Slovak legislation designed to protect and implement human rights in general. At the same time, Slovakia is behind in terms of its actual implementation of legislation, and it has failed to build a strong institutional human rights architecture. Annual reports by nongovernmental organizations and by monitoring bodies attached to international human rights covenants that Slovakia is a party to regularly point out these shortcomings.

Within Slovakia, there are very few reports and studies on the topic of juvenile prisoners or juveniles placed in reeducation centers. Some information from 2009 can be found in the *Report on the Implementation on the Rights of the Child* (Guráň and Rusňkov, 2010) released by the National Center for Human Rights. An earlier version of the report was released in 2007. Its main conclusions are that there is a need to supplement existing legislation to resolve the issue of lack of differentiation of placement (currently, children are not placed in special programs on the basis of the severity of the crime, mental disabilities, or other conditions) and there is a need for much greater coordination between the Ministries of Education, Justice, Labor, Social Work and Family, and Health in providing care for juveniles. Despite partial improvement in some of the centers, the overall situation is one of continuing stagnation. As the 2010 Report concludes, there still is "an urgent need for fundamental changes in the philosophy, conception, and differentiation of the institutions tasked with reeducation of juveniles" (Guráň and Rusňáková 2010, 33). Unfortunately, our own visit to the reeducation center in Záhorská Bystrica in 2012 showed us that the situation has remained practically unchanged since the time of the first monitoring in 2005.

Slovakia has initiated and led the efforts to draft the United Nations Optional Protocol to the Convention on the Rights of the Child on a communications procedure in the year 2011 (this protocol allows the Committee on the Rights of the Child overseeing the implementation of the convention to receive and investigate individual complaints from children). However, reports of international monitoring bodies point out that Slovakia has so far failed to introduce an independent representative for the rights of the child—an institution mandated by the convention, further stipulated in General Comment n. 2 on the role of national human rights institutions and founded upon the full application of the Paris Principles. The Third Optional Protocol on communications procedure underscores the importance of independent monitoring of all spaces and institutions where children are placed.

The Slovak institutional architecture generally lacks independent monitoring bodies. Monitoring of the condition in prisons, for example, is carried out by an inspection under the Ministry of Interior. This pattern of internal inspection is characteristic of other departments as well. Therefore, the draft of an upcoming first *National Strategy for Protection and Promotion of Human Rights* stresses the importance of focusing energy especially on the area of institutional design and implementation of human rights, including the area of juvenile justice. Additionally, the current Ombudsman is proactive about the issue of restrictive custody and has visited several juvenile centers. She has also released six reports from working groups, these are available on her webpage (Office of the Ombudsman, 2013).

Alternatives to the Traditional System

Vráblová's work (2007, 2012) provides some information about the use of alternative sanctions in Slovak juvenile justice. She reports that in the first years of the new penal code, the courts were reluctant to use alternative sentences because they felt the law was not clear. Specifically, the law did not stipulate exactly how a person who failed to fulfill the terms of an alternative sentence would be reassigned to prison. Additionally, the mechanisms for monitoring people with alternative sentences were not clearly specified. Use of alternative sentences does, however, appeared to be increasing.

In the following text, we describe different types of alternatives available for juvenile offenders and present some limited data on how often they are employed. Unfortunately, few official records are available.

Reeducation

Reeducation is an option that the prosecutor can give youth at or prior to a trial. According to the penal code, it can consist of such restrictions as probationary supervision, reaching a settlement with the victim, restitution, community service, drug treatment, and social skills training. As described in the 'Custody' subsection above, the youth can also be placed in an educational home.

Waiver of Punishment

The court has the power to grant a conditional waiver of punishment for juvenile offenders. To be eligible, they must meet at least one out of a set of criteria. First, the juvenile may "show signs of repentance and willingness to be rehabilitated." It is also possible to receive a waiver if a judge feels that the process from arrest to court appearance has already caused the youth to rehabilitate. The court can waive punishment if there is a responsible person who volunteers to help rehabilitate the juvenile. Juveniles who are judged to be of diminished sanity can be assigned a mental health treatment plan in lieu of punishment (Lulei and Galbavy 2008).

When punishment is waived, the youth is assigned to probation, and the court is charged with overseeing his/her behavior for up to 1 year. The juvenile must enter into an agreement with the court whereby he/she promises to abide by certain standards of behavior. If juveniles do not live up to the terms of the agreement, the court can decide to warn them and keep the current probation arrangement or they can assign punishment. The court also has the option to add new reeducation measures or extend the probation period for another year. One year after the probation period is complete, the offense disappears from the juvenile's record (Slovak Criminal Code 2005, Section 101). This type of sanction assumes that a juvenile offender has the cognitive ability to understand the terms of the agreement he/she is entering. This assumption is consistent with the new lowered age of criminal responsibility (from 15 to 14 years) as it also presupposes the competence of juveniles.

Diversion

Slovakia's law allows for the possibility of diversion. This means that adults or juveniles accused of low-level crimes are allowed to plead guilty prior to trial and, instead of receiving a traditional sanction, they create a plan for rehabilitation/treatment or community service.

If they complete the agreement, they do not have a permanent criminal record. If they fail to complete the agreement, they have to come back to court and go through the traditional judicial process. The first diversion program was piloted in 1994, but the options for its use were expanded in the new penal code. It appears, however, that diversion is underutilized because there are not enough investigators and parole officers to do the initial investigation required. There are also concerns about the ability of the system to protect the rights of the accused, particularly juveniles. It is possible that young people are not capable of understanding the repercussions of an admission of guilt (Válkova, Hulmáková, and Vráblová 2010). Data on the use of diversion are lacking, but Vráblová's study (2007) of the juvenile justice system found that, in 2006, diversion was used between 12% and 14.6% of the time (Vráblová 2007, 6).

Mediation

The Slovakian government created the Probation and Mediation Services in 2002 with a pilot project in three court districts. Probation officers and mediators are civil servants who work for the court. Based on the success of the pilots, probation and mediation were codified in 2004 and were extended to all regional courts. Mediation is a voluntary and informal system that happens in lieu of a court hearing. It is now binding under the law. According to Mražek (2010) at the Ministry of Justice, the mediation programs are an attempt to bring restorative justice principles to Slovak law. He said, "The new legal regulations result from a principle concerning the auxiliary role of criminal repression, namely that coercion must only be applied by the state in connection to criminal measures when there is no other solution to achieve accord between the behavior of the people and the law. The currently valid criminal law promotes the application of probation and mediation as new methods which belong to the trend of restorative justice" (Mražek 2010, 285).

Mediation can be requested for a broad range of minor and medium criminal issues. Referrals to mediation can come from judges, probation officers, prosecutors, victims, or offenders. Both the victim and accused must agree to mediation and, when juveniles are involved, their legal representative must also agree to the proceedings. Today, the use of mediation varies widely between jurisdictions (Dolanská and Michančová 2010). In 2010, there were only 79 probation/mediation officers working in the country (CEP 2010, 2). Current reliable national data on the number of cases resolved by mediation are not available, and the lack of a systemic approach is acknowledged by the Minister of Justice. In a statement from November 2012 (Borec 2012), he announced the formation of two new commissions. These commissions are intended to work on amendments of the criminal law and penal code and to prepare administrative rules that will improve the process of implementing criminal justice in practice. Among other provisions, the minister stated the need to "jumpstart" the Council for Mediation and Probation to use this institution in criminal proceedings more frequently and systematically.

Vráblová's (2007) examination of the outcomes of juvenile cases found that an out-of-court settlement (via mediator) was used 10 times less often than a conditional suspension, but that its use appears to be increasing.

Probation

Probation services in the Slovak Republic are housed with mediation. Unlike mediation, probation is generally imposed after a court hearing and is assigned in place of either incarceration or a fine. People on probation usually have restrictions on their activities (like visits to sporting events or other mass events, the use of alcoholic drinks and other addictive substances, consorting with accomplices, or participating in gambling games) (Lulei and Galbavy 2008). In addition, they have duties like looking for work, paying monetary compensation to the victim, or attending therapy. Probation can be combined with home confinement or community service. While probation is on the rise in Slovakia, it is still underutilized in many districts, and workers have identified a number of problems with the law as it currently stands (CEP 2010).

Community Service

The community service program was added to Slovakian sentencing options in 1995 and was expanded in 2006. Community service can be assigned for a period of up to half the maximum length of a custodial sentence. The work itself must be conducted for a state agency or a nonprofit organization. When a juvenile offender is involved, their legal representative must be informed and must agree to this alternative sanction. If a young offender fails to comply with the terms of their community service, he/she is sentenced to 1 day of incarceration for each 2-hour period of service they fail to perform (Karabec et al. 2011).

Juvenile Crime Trends

During the communist regime, juvenile crime in Slovakia was suppressed, and levels remained low and fairly stable. It is difficult to get accurate estimates of the actual level of youth criminality, but the available data suggests that during the years 1975–1989, youth aged 15–17 years committed between 14% and 17% of all crime in the country (Válkova, Hulmáková, and Vráblová 2010, 1251).

After the fall of communism, there was an official increase in both adult and youth criminality. Between 1989 and 1998, for example, Slovakia's juvenile crime rate jumped by about 60% (UNICEF 2000, 85). There are many possible reasons for this. First, it is likely that more crime was reported and recorded. It is also possible that the enormous social changes and new market-based economy led to decreases in social cohesion and, in turn, to more crime. Unemployment rose, and many youth programs were dismantled, leaving large numbers of young people at a loose end. Sociological studies show that young people who experienced long-term unemployment during the era of transition had significantly more problems, including criminality, than others (Mason, Orkeny, and Sidorenko-Stephenson 1997). Increased crime was also a result of the influx of new drugs into a society that previously had little drug use. Increasing crime caused considerable trouble during this period, especially because the police forces and courts did not have adequate resources to address the increased caseload (UNICEF 2000).

Levels of youth criminality are difficult to summarize—both because there is not a clear trend and because of data limitations. Figure 12.5 shows the total number of reported juvenile crimes between 2006 and 2012.

Figure 12.6 indicates that there is a general decrease in youth criminality over the period, but there are also a number of peaks and valleys. The proportion of child and adolescent criminality as compared to total crime fell, however, between 1998 and 2006—from a high of 27% to about 15%. Some of this reduction, however, may have

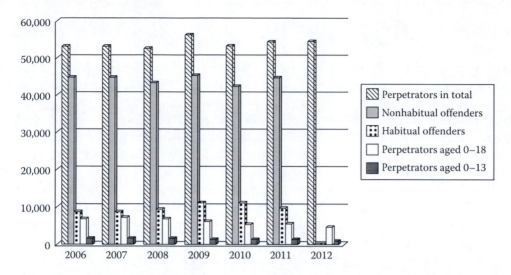

Figure 12.5 Number of arrested offenders in Slovakia, 2006–2012. (Office of Statistics of the Slovak Republic. (2013). Demography. http://portal.statistics.sk (accessed on May 13, 2013).)

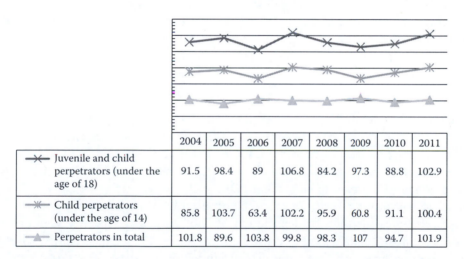

	2004	2005	2006	2007	2008	2009	2010	2011
Juvenile and child perpetrators (under the age of 18)	91.5	98.4	89	106.8	84.2	97.3	88.8	102.9
Child perpetrators (under the age of 14)	85.8	103.7	63.4	102.2	95.9	60.8	91.1	100.4
Perpetrators in total	101.8	89.6	103.8	99.8	98.3	107	94.7	101.9

Figure 12.6 Crime rate 2004–2011 for child/juvenile combined, child alone, and total. (Office of Statistics of the Slovak Republic. (2013). Demography. http://portal.statistics.sk (accessed on May 13, 2013).)

been a result of the government's reclassification of several types of crimes commonly committed by juveniles rather than a true decrease in crime (Válkova, Hulmáková, and Vráblová 2010, 1251). Adding another layer of confusion, in 1993, the two republics separated, and everything, including police, the judiciary, and the prison system changed. This makes it difficult to know how consistent criminal justice policy or record keeping was across the period, especially during the transition. Additionally, all of the data should be read with care as the total number of juvenile offenders is low enough that a small change strongly affects the rate, resulting in seemingly large swings from year to year. Figure 12.6 shows the crime rates for child/juveniles as compared to all perpetrators.

BOX 12.4   MARIJUANA AND YOUTH

Both possession and distribution of marijuana are currently illegal in Slovakia and the majority of Slovaks support retaining prohibition. In 2011, the percentage of Slovakians who supported marijuana legalization was much lower than the European Union average (Klobucký 2012). At the same time, a fairly high percentage of youth report using marijuana. In 2007, almost 45% of 15- to 18-year-olds reported that they had tried marijuana at least once. Over 50% said that marijuana was easily obtainable (Klobucký 2012, 37–38).

In 2012, it was reported that the Ministry of Justice was working on developing alternative punishments for recreational marijuana use and was considering declassifying it as a criminal offense. Prime Minister Robert Fico, who announced the new plans, discussed the current law making marijuana a crime. He was quoted as saying "Young people risk 3-year sentences, 5-year sentences. Everyone is getting stoned anyway, smoking marijuana, so what good does it do?" (Boyd 2012). While, to date, the law has not been changed, it appears that the Slovak Republic may be moving in the direction of legalization.

In May 2013, the criminal law was amended, making it more possible for judges to use probation for possession of small amounts of drugs (less than 10 individual doses) and lessening the minimum sentence for drug possession above this limit from 4 to 3 years of prison sentence (*SME*, May 22, 2013).

Slovakia is like many other countries in that males are overrepresented in criminality. Only about 5% of arrested juveniles are girls (Válkova, Hulmáková, and Vráblová 2010, 1257). The gender disparity in criminal involvement is also reflected in incarceration statistics. As described in subsection 'Custody', in 2013, there were 63 male juveniles in prison and only 1 female (Prison and Court Guard 2013).

The most common category of crime committed by Slovakian juveniles is property crime. This includes the theft or destruction of another person's property. Robbery and assault are the most frequent violent crimes. Murders by adolescents are fairly rare—with only three to nine cases each year between 1997 and 2006. Rapes are also fairly rare, with 4 to 22 reported cases each year during the same period (Válkova, Hulmáková, and Vráblová 2010, 1255). It should be noted, however, that there is evidence suggesting that rapes are seriously underreported (United States Department of State 2011).

Drug crimes are relatively common in Slovakia as it is one of the stops for Southwest Asian heroin on its way to Western Europe. Slovakia is also a producer of synthetic drugs for a regional market. It is, of course, difficult to estimate the true scope of the drug problem as it is likely that most of the activity goes undetected. Official data suggest that there is variability over time in the amount of drug-related crime, although this may simply reflect changing levels of prosecution or detection (see Box 12.4). For example, the number of youth apprehended for drug crimes between 1997 and 2006 varied widely, with 102 in 1997, 37 in 1999, and a high of 138 in 2005. Adolescents only make up between 0.6% and 2.9% of people charged with drug crimes (Válkova, Hulmáková, and Vráblová 2010, 1256). The relatively low involvement of juveniles in drug crime is likely because much of the drug trade is controlled by adult-organized crime syndicates.

Special Issues

Prevention of Criminality

The Slovak government emphasizes prevention of criminality as one of its priorities. In a section of the 2006 Program Statement of the Government entitled *The Prison System*, they indicate renewed attention to the prison system and to juvenile justice. Specifically, they discuss two goals: humanizing the conditions of prisons and improving crime prevention. The document goes on to say that special care is to be devoted to juvenile offenders and convicts, with an eye on activating a special regime promoting education and work. Importantly, there is to be a focus on prevention (Program Statement 2006).

Based upon this program statement, a new law on crime prevention came into force in 2009 (Act No. 583/2008 Coll.). This law, for the first time, outlines the roles and responsibilities of actors engaged in crime prevention. The aim of the law is to bring a greater balance between repressive and preventive measures. The law also establishes an Information Center for Combatting Human Trafficking and for Crime Prevention tasked with collecting data on crime and established guidelines for funding projects focusing on crime prevention by the existing Government Council for the Prevention of Criminality.

The government has formulated a national strategy for crime prevention since 1999. The Strategy for Crime Prevention and Other Antisocial Activities for the Years 2012–2015 notes that in the past, attention has been given primarily to repressive and judicial measures and it highlights the need to focus on the prevention of criminality among children and youth (Strategy for Crime Prevention 2012).

To coordinate crime prevention initiatives, the Ministry of Justice has sponsored the Government Council for the Prevention of Criminality. This body is composed of a range of representatives including deputy ministers (of education and other areas) as well as members of the police force and the Association of Cities and Villages. It also includes the plenipotentiary for the Roma community and one representative of a nongovernmental organization. This means that the implementation of crime prevention policies is horizontally spread across ministries and relevant departments. Their task is to coordinate the Strategy for Crime Prevention, which is implemented on three levels—government, district, and local levels.

Slovak prevention of criminality is commonly divided into three types: primary, secondary (i.e., establishment of various crisis or counseling centers, asylum centers, integration programs, e.g., for Roma minority members and requalification trainings for unemployed), and tertiary (i.e., activities of mediation and probation officers, postpenitentiary care, monitoring, etc.) (Bubelíni 2001). The Strategy for Crime Prevention utilizes this division and applies it to three types of crime prevention: social prevention (general prevention of all types of criminality and antisocial activities, primarily through socialization and social integration activities, focusing especially on positive influence on children and youth), situational prevention (focusing on specific types of crime that arise in certain conditions, areas, or locations), and victim prevention (services for at-risk populations, training, counseling) (Strategy for Crime Prevention 2012).

In terms of prevention of juvenile criminality, the key target area should be social prevention of primary type. In reality, however, Slovak educational and social care praxis still focuses primarily on secondary and tertiary prevention. The governmental strategy pushes for more involvement of actors on the community level; however, it cannot dictate to cities and villages what, or how many, initiatives in crime prevention should be taken.

Thus, some communities that have strong cooperation between schools, police, and city officials have started implementing vigorous educational programs of crime prevention. An example of this type of cooperation is the Safe Košice Program in the Eastern Slovak town of Košice. In other areas, however, coordinated prevention efforts have been sparse.

Critics of the crime prevention programs claim that there is a lack of transparency due to the horizontal dispersion of responsibility across so many agencies and organizations. They also point out that there is a missing focus on early primary prevention. For example, "a smart and responsible state should realize that subsequent prevention is more costly than primary prevention and that repression is more costly than prevention" (Čečot and Kotrecová 2007, 10). Finally, critics say that while some of the factors influencing criminality in juveniles are known and there has been an institutional framework for crime prevention for some time, there has been no significant decline in criminality among juveniles in recent years (see Box 12.3).

The Roma

Slovakia, by law, does not maintain statistics on ethnicity.* Between 1986 and 2001, however, between 3.9% and 5.8% of arrested youth claimed Roma origin (Válkova, Hulmáková, and Vráblová 2010, 1257). Census records suggest that about 1.5% of the Slovakian population is Romani (Vaňo 2001), but it is likely that the true percentage is closer to 10 (Erlanger 2000). Census records about Slovakian ethnicity cannot be trusted as many Roma choose to self-identify as Hungarian or other ethnicities. The problem of self-identification exists for the arrest data as well, and scholars believe that Roma are overrepresented in both arrests and in incarceration. For example, the government reported that in 2005, 42 of 77 incarcerated youth were members of various ethnic minorities, primarily Roma (Council of Europe 2006, 7).

As is the case in most of the former Eastern bloc countries, there is a long history of anti-Roma prejudice in Slovakia. The living situation for the Roma, however, became worse after the fall of communism. Jobs were no longer guaranteed, employers were unwilling to hire Roma people, and unemployment consequently soared. Additionally, in the 1990s, there was an increase in the number of Slovakian skinhead and Neo-Nazi groups (Erlanger 2000). In 2007, the United Nations noted that Slovakia was engaged in efforts to improve both the material conditions of the Roma and the attitudes toward them. They made particular note of new policies to help Roma with housing, health, and human rights (United Nations 2007). Another important milestone occurred in 2012, when a Slovakian regional court passed a law banning segregation of Roma children in schools. At the same time, however, Amnesty International noted that deep problems persisted. In particular, they expressed concern about instances of forced evictions, torture, and forced sterilizations of Roma women (Amnesty International 2012).

As regards juvenile justice and the Roma, in Box 12.1, we described a widely publicized 2009 incident involving six arrested Roma juveniles. Today, all Slovak police officers are required to undergo psychological testing every fifth year and must attend training on

* Slovak law holds that collecting data on ethnicity would be discriminatory. However, the lack of any data on ethnicity (e.g., in education or crime, in prisons, and in health services and facilities) has caused many debates in the last few years, as it prevents rigorous analysis of social problems, prognostics, or identification of key trends and possible solutions. There are efforts, particularly from the third sector arena, to devise a sensitive yet accurate measure of ethnicity in the public sector.

dealing with minorities (Council of Europe 2010). It is apparent, however, that more needs to be done to ensure that Roma youth are handled fairly by juvenile justice authorities.

Child Trafficking

The US Department of State (2013b) reports that the Slovak Republic is a source, destination, and transit location for the trafficking of children and adults. Slovakian women and girls are used as sex workers both within the country and in other countries. In addition, girls and women are routed for sex trade through Slovakia from countries including Moldova, Ukraine, Bulgaria, the Balkans, the Baltics, and China. They are sent to a wide range of countries including Germany, the United Kingdom, the Czech Republic, Switzerland, Sweden, Italy, the Netherlands, and Spain. Traffickers also place victims in forced labor like domestic servitude or cannabis cultivation. Children are often forced to beg in the streets and hand over their earnings. A relatively recent form of trafficking is called "benefits fraud" and it occurs when a person (often a child) is taken and fraudulently registered for welfare benefits by their trafficker (CEOP 2011).

Because so much trafficking is hidden, it is difficult to get reliable estimates of its prevalence. A study conducted in the United Kingdom in 2011 found that between January and September, 202 victims of child trafficking were identified; 12 of these victims were from the Slovak Republic. The majority were female and between the ages of 14 and 16 (CEOP 2011). The United Kingdom is similar to other European countries in that the Slovak children who are trafficked are disproportionately Roma. Here is an example, taken from report of the Child Exploitation and On-line Protection Centre (CEOP 2011), of Slovak children trafficked to the United Kingdom:

> In one case, a family was approached in a village and groomed for trafficking by a group of men travelling from village to village, claiming that they could arrange travel documents, work, accommodation and transport to the UK. The family were trafficked by bus to London, and then onto another city in the UK. From there, control of the family passed to another group of men who forced them to work in a factory. They were not paid for their work, and were told that their wages would be confiscated to cover the costs of their accommodation and food. They were threatened with violence if they attempted to leave their accommodation or did not comply with instructions. This group of men also withheld their identity documents, claiming to arrange for benefits on their behalf (2011, 15).

The Slovak government has laws against trafficking and operates a shelter for minors who enter the country without family. The government also provides antitrafficking information in schools and has a public outreach campaign. In 2011, they were upgraded by the U.S. Department of State from a "tier 2" to a "tier 1" country to recognize the progress they had made. At the same time, they are still criticized for not being proactive enough in their antitrafficking work (United States Department of State 2013b).

Conclusion

The Slovak Republic is at an important juncture in terms of juvenile justice. The passage of the 2005 criminal code allows for more flexibility and innovation in dealing with juveniles. At the same time, Slovakia has instituted a number of punitive measures and still retains problematic remnants of its older system, including the reeducation centers. The challenge will be to move forward in a consistent direction in this time of budgetary strain. Slovakia currently resembles a modified justice model—but this is more a result of conflicting strains in Slovak thought about juvenile crime than a guiding framework. Slovakia's membership in the European Union may help make the change since the country is under increased scrutiny and pressure to comply with international standards. EU membership also makes Slovakia eligible for multicountry initiatives and conferences that might promote change in its practices.

The state of juvenile justice is to be understood within the broader context of justice and human rights issues in Slovakia. The Slovak judiciary is among the least trusted public institutions, cases and issues are often politicized, trials take an exorbitant amount of time, and judges are often viewed as partial and corrupt (Anderson and Gray 2007; World Bank and USAID 2000). There is an overall lack of awareness of human rights, often perceived as something imposed upon Slovakia from outside. Juvenile justice then, and the status or rights of juveniles within the system, is a reflection of the broader problems that Slovakia is grappling with on its path of transition from communism to the present.

The situation is unlikely to improve significantly in the near future. There is a lack of awareness and interest in the topic of juvenile justice. Without the push for amelioration of the situation from the public, there is little chance that there will be more systematic placement of juveniles into diagnostic or rehabilitation centers or prison. It is also unlikely that there will be greater cooperation among responsible institutions and ministries that provide services related to juvenile justice, or that there will be more than lip service paid to crime prevention and youth education.

Acknowledgment

The authors are grateful to their research assistant Paige Ambord for her tireless work on this chapter. They also acknowledge the Global Liberal Arts Alliance of the Great Lakes Colleges Association for the grant funding that enabled a trip from the United States to Slovakia.

Review/Discussion Questions

1. The Slovak Republic differs from many other countries in the European Union (and in the world) because it does not have a separate juvenile court. What do you think are the advantages and disadvantages of the combined court model?
2. Roma youth continue to face discrimination at various points in the criminal justice process. What safeguards should be put in place? Are other countries better able to protect the Roma who are in their criminal justice systems?
3. Slovakia has a lower crime rate than many other postcommunist states. What factors might have contributed to this?
4. Several elements of Slovakian law seem to assume that juveniles have the same cognitive capabilities as adults. What do you think of this assumption?
5. Slovakia has a unique organization of residential placement. Describe and critique its multilayered system.

References

Amnesty International. (2012). Annual Report 2012: Slovakia. Amnesty International, London: Amnesty International publisher information. http://www.amnesty.org/en/region/slovak-republic/report-2012 (accessed on March 11, 2013).

Anderson, J. and Gray, C. (2007). Transforming judicial systems in Europe and Central Asia. In *Annual World Bank Conference on Development Economics Regional 2007: Beyond Transition*, edited by Francois Bourguignon and Boris Pleskovic. Washington DC: World Bank Publications, 329–355.

Borec: A More Just Criminal Law and a More Effective Penal Code Will Be Prepared. (2012, November 22). http://www.justice.gov.sk/Lists/Aktuality/DispForm.aspx?ID=1676 (accessed on August 26, 2013).

Boyd, J. (2012). Marijuana use should now only be a misdemeanor. *The Daily.SK.* Issue no. 1167. http://www.thedaily.sk/marijuana-use-should-now-be-only-a-misdemeanour/ (accessed on August 13, 2013).

Bubelíni, J. (2001). *Prevention of Criminality: Introduction to Crime Prevention and Preventology and Their Application to Action.* Bratislava: Ministry of Interior, Secretariat of the Council for Prevention of Criminality of the Government of the Slovak Republic. pp. 12–13.

Case of bullying of Roma boys: After two years another trial! (2012, November 9). *Nový čas.* www.cas.sk (accessed on August 26, 2013).

Čečot, V. and Kotrecová, A. (2007). How to proceed with prevention of juvenile criminality? In *Social Prevention*, Bratislava: National Cultural Centre, Vol. 2. pp. 9–11.

CEOP (Child Exploitation and Online Protection Center). (2011). Child Trafficking Update. http://ceop.police.uk/Documents/ceopdocs/child_trafficking_update_2011.pdf (accessed on August 13, 2013).

CEP (Conférence Permanente Européenne de la Probation). (2010). Summary Information on Probation in Slovakia. www.cepprobation.org (accessed on March 11, 2013).

Council of Europe. (2006). Questionnaire on Juvenile Offenders Deprived of their Liberty or Subject to Community Sanctions or Measures: Slovakia. Strasbourg: European Council on Crime Problems.

Council of Europe. (2010). Report to the Government of the Slovak Republic on the Visit to the Slovak Republic Carried out by the European Committee for the Prevention of Torture and Inhuman or Degrading Treatment or Punishment (CPT). Stasbourg, France: Council of Europe. www.cpt.coe.int/documents/svk/2010-01-inf-eng.pdf (accessed on March 11, 2013).

Courts: Policemen from the case of the torture of Roma children did not testify in court. (2010, November 5). *SITA.* www.sita.sk (accessed on August 26, 2013).

Dolanská, R. and Michančová, S. (2010). Mediation Country Report: Slovak Republic. JAMS International ADR Center. London: JAMS International. www.adrcenter.com/ (accessed on March 12, 2013).

Erlanger, S. (2000, April 3). The gypsies of Slovakia: Despised and despairing. *The New York Times.* http://www.nytimes.com (accessed on March 11, 2013).

Guráň, P. and Rusňáková, E. (2010). Report on Implementation of the Rights of Children in Slovakia for the Year 2009. Bratislava: Slovak National Center for Human Rights.

Hazel, N. (2008). Cross-national Comparison of Youth Justice. United Kingdom: Youth Justice Board. http://www.academia.edu/1621782/Cross-national_comparison_of_youth_justice (accessed on January 23, 2013).

Hičárová, T., Kiššová, L., Očenášová, Z., Miklíková, S., Škařupová, K., Vavrinčíková, L., Krošláková, M., Kuropková, K., Rojčeková, J., Staroňová, K., and Dolejš, M. (2010). Summary Final Report: Project to evaluate selected drug-possession provisions of Act No 300/2005 Criminal Code of the Slovak Republic. Bratislava: Nadácia otvorenej spoločnosti—Open Society Foundation.

History of the School. (2013, March 30). Reeducation Center. http://rchlohovec.edupage.org (accessed on April 10, 2013).

Karabec, Z., Vlach, J., Diblíková, S., and Zeman, P. (2011). *Criminal Justice System in the Czech Republic*. Prague: Institute of Criminology and Social Prevention.

Klobucký, R. (2012). Research Report: Drug Policy in Slovakia after the Fall of the Communist Regime. Institute for Sociology, Slovak Academy of Sciences. Bratislava: Slovak Academy of Sciences. http://www.sociologia.sav.sk/cms/uploaded/1540_attach_drug_policy_slovakia.pdf (accessed on August 13, 2013).

Krošláková, D. (2011). Overview of the Prison System in the Slovak Republic. Paper presented at the European Prison Association, Malta Branch, September 2011. http://www.epeamalta.org/course-2011-presentations.html (accessed on March 12, 2013).

Lulei, M. and Galbavy, L. (2008). Slovakia. In *Probation in Europe*, edited by Anton M. van Kalmthout and Ioan D. Nijmegen. The Netherlands: Wolf Legal Publishers (WLP). pp. 937–966.

Luprichová, P. (2008). Historical and legal aspects of special regulations on penalizing youth delinquents. In *Conference of Young Lawyers: Conference Proceedings*, edited by Jiří Valdhans, Radovan Dávid, Martin Orgoník, Jan Neckář, David Sehnálek, and Jaromír Tauchen. Brno: Masarykova Univerzita, 1088–1098.

Marešová, A. and Válková, J. (1994). *On Alternative Punishment*. Prague: Institute of criminology and social prevention.

Mason, D., Orkeny, A., and Sidorenko-Stephenson, S. (1997). Middle class: Increasingly fond memories of a grim past. *Transitions Online, 3* (5):3–21.

Mihalovič, R. (2006). Questionnaire on Juvenile Offenders Deprived of Their Liberty or Subject to Community Sanctions or Measures. European Committee on Crime Problems. Strasbourg, France: Council of Europe. http://www.coe.int/t/dghl/standardsetting/prisons/Replies%20to%20questionnaire/pc-cp_2006_08%20rev%203%20-%20e_questionnaire_Slovakia.pdf.

Mražek, P. (2010). Victim offender mediation and mediators in the Republic of Slovakia. In *European Best Practices of Restorative Justice in the Criminal Procedure Conference Publication*, edited by Melinda Gyokos and Krisztina Lanyi. Budapest: Ministry of Justice and Law Enforcement for the Republic of Hungary, pp. 209–212. http://www.restorativejustice.org/articlesdb/articles/10140 (accessed on March 12, 2013).

Office of Statistics of the Slovak Republic. (2013). Demography. http://portal.statistics.sk (accessed on May 13, 2013).

Office of the Ombudsman. (2013). Report from Investigation of Upholding Basic Rights and Freedoms of Minors in the Reeducation Center, Hlohovec. Bratislava: Office of the Ombudsman, Slovak Government. http://www.vop.gov.sk/files/Reedukacne%20centrum%20Hlohovec-sprava%20VOP.pdf (accessed on August 26, 2013).

Passell, P. (2013, January 2). Slovakia showcases the benefits of the European Union. *U.S. News and World Report*. http://www.usnews.com/opinion/blogs/economic-intelligence/2013/01/02/slovakia-showcases-the-benefits-of-the-european-union (accessed on January 20, 2013).

Prison and Court Guard. (2013). Statistics of Incarcerated Juveniles. www.zvjs.sk (accessed on June 24, 2013).

Program Statement of the Government of the Slovak Republic. (2006). http://static.cream.sk/zbierka.sk/webroots/www/content/mediagallery/zbierka_document/file/example/file/2.pdf (accessed on April 12, 2013).

Slovak Criminal Code. (2005). Act 300/2005 Coll. of 20 May 2005.

Slovakia: Birth of a nation. (2013, January 1). *The Economist*. http://www.economist.com/blogs/easternapproaches/2013/01/slovakia (accessed January 20, 2013).

SME. (2013, May 22). *MPs passed lesser punishments for drugs*. www.sme.sk (accessed on August 26, 2013).

Strategy for Crime Prevention and Other Antisocial Activities for the Years 2012-2015. (2012, February). Bratislava: Ministry of Interior of the Slovak Republic.

Šutková, V. (2007, June 4). Ministry wants shorter sentences: Draft proposed shorter sentences for serious crimes. *The Slovak Spectator*. http://spectator.sme.sk/articles/view/27836/2/ (accessed on January 25, 2013).

UNICEF. (2000). Young People in Changing Societies. Regional Monitoring Report No. 7. Florence: UNICEF Innocenti Research Centre.

United Nations. (2006). Committee on the Rights of the Child: Second Periodic Report. CRC/C/SVK/2, 21 September. Geneva, Switzerland: United Nations.

United Nations. (2007). Committee on the Rights of the Child: Forty-fifth Session. Consideration of Reports Submitted by States Parties under Article 44 of the Convention. Concluding Observations: Slovakia. Slovakia: UN Committee on the Rights of the Child (CRC). www.unhcr.org/refworld/pdfid/469f12252.pdf (accessed on March 11, 2013).

United States Department of State. (2011). 2010 Human Rights Report: Slovakia. Bureau of Democracy, Human Rights, and Labor. Washington DC: US Department of State. http://www.state.gov/j/drl/rls/hrrpt/2010/eur/154450.htm (accessed on March 12, 2012).

United States Department of State. (2013a). Country Reports on Human Rights Practices for 2012: Slovakia. Washington DC: US Department of State. http://www.state.gov/j/drl/rls/hrrpt/humanrightsreport/index.htm#wrapper (accessed on May 20, 2013).

United States Department of State. (2013b). Trafficking in Persons Report. Office to Monitor and Combat Trafficking in Persons. Washington DC: US Department of State. http://www.state.gov/documents/organization/210741.pdf (accessed on August 13, 2013).

Válkova, H., Hulmáková, J., and Vráblová, M. (2010). Slovakia. In *Juvenile Justice Systems in Europe: Current Situation and Reform Developments*, Vol. 3, edited by Frieder Dünkel, Joanna Grzywa, Philip Horsfield, and Ineke Pruin. Forum Verlag Godesberg GmbH: Mönchengladbach, Germany, pp. 1245–1262.

Vaňo, B. (2001). *The Demographic Characteristics of Roma Population in Slovakia*, translated by Frantisek Bernadic. Bratislava: INFOSTAT—Institute of Informatics and Statistics Demographic Research Centre. www.infostat.sk/slovakpopin/pdf/romeng.pdf (accessed on March 11, 2013).

Vráblová, M. (2007). Juvenile justice system in the Slovak Republic—Empirical results. In *Days of Public Law Conference Proceedings*. Brno: Tribun EU, 856–876. http://www.law.muni.cz/sborniky/Days-of-public-law/files/pdf/trest/Vrablova.pdf (accessed on August 26, 2013).

Vráblová, M. (2012). *Criminological and Legal Aspects of Criminal Activities of Juveniles*. Plzeň: Vydavateľstvo Aleš Čeněk.

World Bank and USAID. (2000). Corruption in Slovakia—Results of Diagnostic Surveys. http://pdf.usaid.gov/pdf_docs/pnacw367.pdf (accessed on August 12, 2013).

Internet Sources

Ministry of Justice of the Slovak Republic—http://wwwold.justice.sk/a/wf.aspx

Ministry of Labor, Social Affairs, and Family of the Slovak Republic—http://www.employment.gov.sk/en.html

The Open Society Foundation Bratislava—http://www.opensocietyfoundations.org/about/offices-foundations/open-society-foundation-bratislava

Slovak National Centre for Human Rights—http://www.snslp.sk/?locale=en

Statistical Office of the Slovak Republic—http://portal.statistics.sk/showdoc.do?docid=359

South Africa's New Child Justice System

13

ANN SKELTON AND
R. MORGAN COURTENAY

Contents

Introduction   322
Brief History of South Africa and Its Legal System   323
The Development of Child Justice in South Africa   323
The Child Justice Act   325
   Scope and Application of the CJA   326
   Age and Criminal Capacity   326
   Police Power and Duties   328
   Pretrial Detention and Release   329
   Diversion   330
   Preliminary Inquiry   332
   Child Justice Court   333
   Sentencing   333
   Legal Representation   334
   Automatic Review of Certain Sentences   334
   Expungement of Criminal Records   335
Specific Areas of Interest and Debate   335
   Possible Change to the Minimum Age of Criminal Capacity   335
   Detention as a Measure of Last Resort   336
   Children and Sexual Offenses   337
   Violence in Schools   338
Conclusion   338
Review/Discussion Questions   339
References   339
Case Law   340
Internet Sources   341

The government will, as a matter of urgency, attend to the tragic and complex question of children and juveniles in detention and prison. The basic principles from which we will proceed from now onwards is that we must rescue the children of the nation and ensure that the system of criminal justice must be the very last resort in the case of juvenile offenders.

Nelson Mandela, First Address to the Democratically Elected Parliament, 1994

FACTS ABOUT SOUTH AFRICA

Area: South Africa is a medium-sized country, with a total land area of 1,219.912 sq. km. The total area is divided into nine provinces. The country lies between 22° and 35° south, bounded by the Atlantic Ocean to the west and the Indian Ocean to the east. Its borders meet Namibia, Botswana, Zimbabwe, Swaziland, and Mozambique. Lesotho is a landlocked country within the boundaries of South Africa. **Population:** The population was in excess of 51 million people in 2011. According to Census 2011, the population breakdown is approximately 79.2% black African, 8.9% colored, Indian/Asian 2.5%, and 8.9% white. Females make up just over half (51.3%) of the population, and males 48.7%. **Languages:** South Africa is a multilingual country. The country's constitution recognizes 11 official languages. According to Census 2011, IsiZulu is the most common home language spoken (22.7%). It is followed by IsiXhosa (16%), Afrikaans (13.5%), English (9.6%), Sepedi (9.1%), Setswana (8%), and Sesotho (7.6%). The remaining four official languages are spoken at home by less than 5% of the population each. Most South Africans can speak English, which is fairly ubiquitous in official and commercial public life. **Economy:** South Africa's currency is known as the rand. The country has shifted from a primary and secondary economy to an economy driven primarily by the tertiary sector, which accounts for an estimated 65% of the gross domestic product. The country's economy is reasonably diversified with key economic sectors including mining, agriculture and fisheries, vehicle manufacturing and assembly, food processing, clothing and textiles, telecommunication, energy, financial and business services, real estate, tourism, transportation, and wholesale and retail trade. **Climate:** The country's subtropical location, moderated by the ocean on three sides of the country and the altitude of the interior plateau, accounts for South Africa's warm and temperate conditions. **Government:** South Africa is a constitutional democracy. The constitution provides national, provincial, and local spheres of government. The national government is mainly responsible for policy, while the provincial and local spheres are mainly responsible for implementation. Each of the nine provinces has an elected legislature, and there are almost 850 local government structures in South Africa. The ruling party is the African National Congress, which has a 5-year term.

Introduction

South Africa has a new system for child offenders, which has been ushered in by the Child Justice Act (CJA) 75 of 2008. Prior to that time, there was no separate legislation, though there were sections in the criminal law that provided a limited number of special procedures for accused or convicted persons below the age of 18 years. South Africa never fully embraced the welfarist approach to juvenile justice, even though many of the "child-saving" ideas did make their way to South Africa in the late 1800s, particularly the introduction of reformatories and industrial schools (Skelton 2011). Early legal frameworks allowed for children to be referred from the criminal justice system to the care system in suitable cases, and these measures continue to the present day. The system prior to the new act could best be described as a justice model, but the new approach is a modified justice model. The following features identify it as such: Although the child justice system is located within a justice framework, it focuses on diversion of children away from the criminal justice system as far as possible, and no offenses are completely excluded from the possibility of diversion. The system also features a preliminary inquiry—a semi-informal pretrial procedure chaired by a presiding officer of the child justice court (a magistrate), which maximizes truth telling and promotes diversion. There is an emphasis on avoidance of detention, both as a pretrial measure and as a sentence. However, children charged with more serious crimes, where diversion is less likely, will mostly be tried in a child justice court, represented by a lawyer, provided at state expense if necessary. If sentenced, any child 14 years or older could face imprisonment. There is no life sentence for children, the maximum sentence is 25 years, and early parole is a possibility after half of the sentence has been served. There is no referral to adult court.

Brief History of South Africa and Its Legal System

Hunter-gatherers known as the San and pastoralists known as the Khoi originally populated South Africa. Farmers from east and central Africa joined them about 1700 years ago. Prior to colonization, peoples' interactions were governed by customary law, which still survives in rural parts of the country today and is recognized by the constitution (Bennett 2004). In 1652, the country was colonized by the Dutch and later by the British. In 1948, the National Party came to power and, during its ensuing reign, initiated the policy of apartheid. The struggle against apartheid took place over decades, a conflict in which children themselves were involved. Formal negotiations began in 1990 when Nelson Mandela and other political leaders were released, and a negotiated settlement was finally reached in 1994, saving South Africa from a violent revolution, which had at times seemed inevitable. In April 1994, South Africa held its first democratic elections, and in 1996, the final South African Constitution was adopted.

The civil and criminal justice systems in South Africa are primarily based on Roman–Dutch law, with strong influences from the English common law system. All laws, however, are subject to the Bill of Rights in the South African Constitution, and the Constitutional Court is the highest court in the land. Most criminal matters are heard in the magistrates' courts. South African magistrates are professional people, all of whom hold law degrees or diplomas. Depending on the severity of the case, certain criminal matters are heard in the high court, presided over by judges. Under the new CJA, any court before which a child appears is a "child justice court."

The Development of Child Justice in South Africa

South Africa's predominant focus during the struggle against apartheid was the establishment of basic human rights and a democratic society. The need to develop a fair and equitable child justice system only came to the fore during the early 1990s. In 1992, various nongovernmental organizations (NGOs) initiated a campaign in an effort to raise awareness, both nationally and internationally, about the predicaments facing children in conflict with the law (Skelton and Tshehla 2008). They issued a report, which called for the creation of a comprehensive child justice system, for humane treatment of young people in conflict with the law, for the diversion of minor offenses away from the criminal justice system, and for systems that humanized rather than brutalized young offenders (Juvenile Justice Drafting Consultancy 1994).

A further initiative, launched in 1992 by the National Institute for Crime Prevention and Rehabilitation of Offenders (NICRO), was an important milestone in the development of child justice. NICRO negotiated with prosecutors to offer diversion and alternative sentencing options that aimed to promote the emerging restorative justice concepts specifically focused on youth (see Box 13.1). Despite the fact that no legal framework existed in South Africa for diversion, the 1990s nevertheless saw a steady increase in the number of children being diverted away from the criminal justice system (Skelton and Tshehla 2008).

The death of Neville Snyman in 1992 proved to be the watershed moment for the child rights movement working toward the reform of South Africa's child justice system. Neville was only 13 years old when he and a group of friends broke into a local shop in Robertson and stole sweets and sodas. Neville was arrested and detained in police cells with other offenders under the age of 21. While detained, his cellmates bludgeoned him to death. While NGOs had been raising the issue of children in the criminal justice system and calling for reform for some time, until this happened, their calls had fallen on deaf ears (Community Law Centre 2005). Neville's tragic death led to a public outcry, and the government took action by setting up a national working committee on children in detention.

Meanwhile, NGOs redoubled their efforts. Lawyers for Human Rights ran a campaign called "Free a child for Christmas," which resulted in the release of 260 children by Christmas, 1992. The NGOs also decided that legislative reform was necessary, and in 1993, they set about drafting proposals for a new child justice system. The NGOs published *Juvenile Justice for South Africa: Proposals for Policy and Legislative Change* in 1994. The new system was based on restorative justice principles and centered on the procedure of family group conferencing (Juvenile Justice Drafting Consultancy 1994), an idea taken from a New Zealand model (Pinnock, Skelton, and Shapiro 1994). This new vision influenced future developments, in particular, the rights-based approach—which would later formed the bedrock of the Child Justice Act 75 of 2008 (the "Act")—and the principles of restorative justice.

The coming to power of the first democratically elected government in 1994 was accompanied by a renewed focus on the need to protect children in conflict with the law and the development of a child justice system (Badenhorst 2011). The introduction of the constitution further set the stage for a new approach to child justice. Chief among these is

BOX 13.1   NATIONAL INSTITUTE FOR CRIME PREVENTION AND REHABILITATION OF OFFENDERS

The National Institute for Crime Prevention and Rehabilitation of Offenders (NICRO) was founded by Justice Mr. J de Villiers Roos on September 6, 1910, as the South African Prisoners' Aid Association, the first countrywide organization of its kind providing assistance and after-care support services to prisoners and their families. More than 100 years later, NICRO has changed its name and image, pioneered diversion and noncustodial sentencing in South Africa, and helped launch probation services and community service.

the introduction of Sections 28(1)(g) and 28(2) of the Constitution. Section 28(1)(g) provides that every child has the right not to be detained except as a measure of last resort, and where the detention is necessary, he/she may then be detained only for the shortest appropriate period of time and in a manner that takes account of his or her age. Section 28(2) provides that a child's best interests are of paramount importance in every matter concerning the child.

These provisions in the constitution had been influenced by South Africa's ratification of the United Nations Convention on the Rights of the Child (CRC) in 1995. Mindful of these international and constitutional obligations, the Minister of Justice requested the South African Law Commission to include an investigation regarding "juvenile justice" in its program. This led to the appointment of a project committee, which began its work in the beginning of 1997. The Juvenile Justice Project Committee commenced its work almost immediately, releasing a discussion paper with a draft bill for comment in 1999. The project committee followed an extensive consultative process, holding workshops and receiving written submissions from a range of criminal justice role-players. Children were also consulted on the bill while it was being developed (Community Law Centre 2000). The final report of the committee was completed and handed to the Minister of Justice in August 2000 (South African Law Commission 2000). The Child Justice Bill was approved by the cabinet in 2001 for introduction into the parliament and was introduced in August 2002. Although the parliamentary process was fraught with significant delays, and many ideological skirmishes, the bill survived reasonably intact and was eventually assented to on May 7, 2009 (Skelton and Gallinetti 2008).

The Child Justice Act

On April 1, 2010, a historic day for children's rights in South Africa, the CJA was officially launched at the Walter Sisulu Child and Youth Care Centre in Soweto. The Act aims to establish a system that has as a central feature the possibility of diverting matters away from the criminal justice system. The Act expands and entrenches the principles of restorative justice, while ensuring that children are held responsible and accountable for the offenses they commit. It further recognizes the need to be proactive in crime prevention by placing an increased emphasis on the effective rehabilitation and reintegration of children to minimize the potential for reoffending, and balances the interests of children and those of society with due regard for the rights of the victims (Preamble to the Child Justice Act). The Act also creates special mechanisms, processes, or procedures for children in conflict with the law by

- Amending the common law pertaining to criminal capacity by raising the minimum age of criminal capacity for children from 7 to 10 years of age
- Ensuring that the individual needs and circumstances of all children in conflict with the law are assessed by a probation officer shortly after apprehension
- Providing for special processes or procedures for securing attendance at court, the release or detention, and placement of children
- Providing for appearance in a preliminary inquiry, which is an informal, inquisitorial, pretrial procedure, designed to facilitate the best interests of children by allowing for the diversion of matters involving children away from criminal proceedings in appropriate cases

- Providing for the adjudication of matters involving children, which are not diverted in child justice courts
- Providing for a wide range of appropriate sentencing options specifically suited to the needs of children (Badenhorst 2011)

The Act is described in a high court judgment as having introduced a comprehensive system of dealing with children in conflict with the law that represents a decisive break with the traditional criminal justice system (*S v CKM* (unreported)). The traditional pillars of punishment, retribution, and deterrence are replaced with continued emphasis on the need to gain an understanding of a child caught up in law-transgressing behavior by assessing his or her personality, determining whether the child is in need of care, and correcting errant actions as far as possible by diversion, community-based programs, the application of restorative justice processes, and reintegration of the child into the community (*S v CKM* (unreported)) (see Figure 13.1).

Scope and Application of the CJA

The Act applies to any person under the age of 18 who is alleged to have committed an offense (s. 4(1) of the CJA). In this regard, the act distinguishes between two groups of children to whom it applies:

First, it applies to children who commit offenses while under the age of 10 years (s. 4(1)(a) of the CJA). These children lack criminal capacity, and are therefore incapable of being prosecuted. The Act nevertheless seeks to establish the cause of the behavior and to provide remedial action where necessary (s. 4(1)(a) read with s. 9 of the CJA). This may include the referral of the child to the children's court for care and protection proceedings to be instituted (s. 9(3)(a)(i) of the CJA); the referral of the child for counseling or therapy (s. 9(3)(a)(ii) of the CJA); the referral of the child to an accredited program (s. 9(3)(a)(iii); or arrangement of support service for the child (s. 9(3)(a)(iv) of the CJA). Any action taken against the child does not, however, imply that the child is criminally liable for the incident (s. 9(3)(b) of the CJA). Any such action taken therefore does not amount to a criminal prosecution.

Second, the Act applies to children aged 10 years and older but younger than 18 years at the time that they were handed a written notice to appear in court, were served with a summons, or were arrested (s. 4(1)(b) of the CJA). The date relevant for the determination of whether or not the Act applies is pegged at the time of the notice, summons, or arrest, rather than the date of the commission of offense. The rationale for this is to avoid the anomalous situation where a child commits an offense and is only arrested many years later.

Once it is established that the Act operates in a particular case, the protections afforded by the Act continue to find application until the finalization of the matter, irrespective of whether the child subsequently turns 18.

Age and Criminal Capacity

Under South African law, a person may only be held responsible for criminal conduct if the prosecution proves, beyond reasonable doubt, that at the time the offense was perpetrated, the person possessed criminal capacity (Burchell 2011). Criminal capacity is understood to mean the ability of a person to appreciate the difference between right and wrong, at

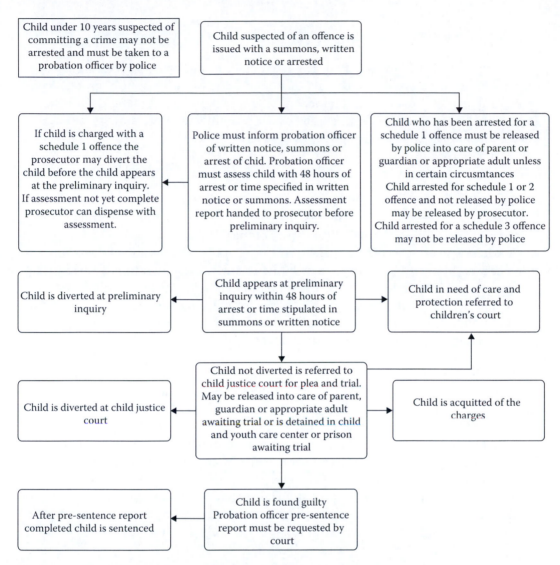

Figure 13.1 Systemic overview of Child Justice Act. (Gallinetti, J. (2009). Getting to Know the Child Justice Act. University of the Western Cape: Cape Town.)

the time of the commission of the offense, and act in accordance with such appreciation (Burchell 2011).

Children may, in certain circumstances, lack criminal capacity as a result of their youthfulness. In this regard, the Act distinguishes between the following groups of children:

- Children who have not yet completed their 10th year at the time of the commission of the offense: In these cases, the child is irrefutably presumed to lack criminal capacity and therefore cannot be prosecuted (s. 7(1) of the CJA).
- Children between the ages of 10 and 14 years at the time of the commission of the offense: There is a presumption that such children lack criminal capacity (s. 7(2) of the CJA). However, this presumption is rebuttable and weakens as a child approaches the age of 14. In instances where the state fails to prove, beyond a

BOX 13.2   AGE DETERMINATION BECOMING LESS OF A PROBLEM

Uncertainty about age used to be a major problem in South Africa, but in recent years, this has improved due to the fact that many benefits, such as social grants and school attendance, can only be obtained upon proof of a child's registration of birth. In addition, in 2012, the government introduced facilities at clinics and hospitals to enable the online registration of births as soon as possible.

reasonable doubt, that the child has criminal capacity, the Act prescribes that, where it is in his or her best interests, he or she must be treated in the same manner as children below the age of 10 (s. 11(5) of the CJA).

- Children who are 14 years and older at the time of the commission of the offense: Once a child has attained the age of 14, he or she is presumed to have criminal capacity and is regarded in law as being no different from an adult with regard to the question of criminal capacity (s. 7(3) of the CJA). However, the CJA does treat all children below the age of 18 years as child offenders. There is no "waiver" or referral to adult court under any circumstances.

Where the age of a child is uncertain for any reason, the Act provides that certain procedures must follow. In this regard, the Act differentiates between the responsibilities of the police (s. 12 of the CJA), the probation officer (s. 13 of the CJA), and the inquiry magistrate or child justice court (s. 14 of the CJA). The mechanisms for estimating age are the functions of the probation officer who will give an age estimate based on statements made by the parent or appropriate adult; statements made by the child; estimation by a medical practitioner; and any official documentation, which may assist the probation officer in making the determination. Once the probation officer has made an estimation of the age of the child, such a report must be forwarded to the inquiry magistrate for him/her to make a finding. That finding is presumed to be the age of the child until any different evidence is placed before a child justice court (see Box 13.2).

Police Power and Duties

One of the primary aims of the Act is to prevent children being exposed to the adverse effects of the formal criminal justice system (s. 2(c) of the CJA). One of the ways in which this is achieved is through the promotion of alternatives to arrest. These alternatives include the handing of a written notice to the child warning him or her to appear before a preliminary inquiry and the serving of a summons on a child (Sections 18 and 19 of the CJA). To ensure that the alternatives to arrest are given priority by the South African Police Service (SAPS), the Act provides—in no uncertain terms—that a child may not be arrested for a petty offense unless compelling reasons exist, justifying the arrest (s. 20(1) of the CJA).

If a child has been arrested, or an alternative to arrest has been effected, the police official is required to notify the child's parent and a probation officer of the arrest or the use of an alternative within 24 hours (Sections 18(4)(b), 19(3)(b), and 20(4)(a) of the CJA). In the case of a child who has been arrested and who is not released, such a child must be brought before a preliminary inquiry within 48 hours thereof (s. 20(5) of the CJA) (see Box 13.3).

BOX 13.3   IMPLEMENTATION CHALLENGES

In the first year of implementation 75,435 children were "charged" by the South African Police Service (SAPS) (Department of Justice and Constitutional Development 2011). This translates roughly to about 6,286 children per month, which is substantially lower than the approximately 10,000 children arrested per month that was reported to the parliament in 2008 (Badenhorst 2011). In the second year of implementation, a total of 57,592 children were charged by the SAPS. This in turn translates to roughly about 4799 children per month; a decrease of 23% on the previous year's statistics and a decrease of approximately 52% on 2008.

In the first 2 years that the Act has been in operation, various reasons have been advanced by the implementing departments for this decrease. These include the following: the SAPS making use of alternative methods of policing children, a general decrease in crime due to the 2010 World Cup; and the possibility of a natural drop in the winter months owing to the cyclical nature of crime (Badenhorst 2012). None of the reasons are convincing, especially considering the further decrease witnessed in the year 2011/2012. A more plausible explanation emanating from experts in the child justice sector is that members of the SAPS have all been informed about the Act, but have not received adequate training on its provisions. The uncertainty caused by the lack of training is in all likelihood the reason for the drastic drop of numbers in the system. Most SAPS members may err on the side of caution, and in their zeal not to arrest, they fail to use alternative measures to secure the child's attendance at the preliminary inquiry (Badenhorst 2012). This has led to concern that children are not being linked with the appropriate services to address the issues that give rise to children resorting to crime.

Pretrial Detention and Release

In the past, South Africa had a significant number of children in prison awaiting trial. For a number of years, the number of pretrial detentions was disproportionately high compared to the number of custodial sentences. Nine children died in custody during the decade between 1997 and 2007, most of them in police cells (Skelton and Potgieter 2002; Centre for Child Law 2007) (see Box 13.4). For these reasons, the reduction of detention, and particularly pretrial detention, was a major aim of the new law.

The Act provides for a number of principles that are to be considered by any person who makes a decision regarding the detention or release of a child. Chief among these is the injunction that "[w]hen considering the release or detention of a child who has been arrested, preference must be given to releasing the child" (s. 21(1) of the CJA). If detention cannot be avoided, the least restrictive form of detention appropriate to the child and the circumstances must be selected. In this regard, the Act makes provision for the further detention in either a child and youth care center or a prison (Sections 29 and 30 of the CJA).

Importantly, a child can only be remanded to a prison to await trial if certain prerequisites are met, namely: the child is 14 years of age or older; the child is accused of having committed a serious offense (e.g., murder, rape, or armed robbery); the detention is necessary in the interests of justice or the safety and protection of the community or the child

BOX 13.4   DEATH OF CHILD IN POLICE CELLS

In 2006, 14-year-old Leon Booysen, awaiting trial on a minor charge, died in the Heidelberg police cells. The Centre for Child Law insisted on formal inquest proceedings and represented the family at the inquest. Although the inquest court determined that suicide was probably the cause of death, the magistrate criticized various government officials for their failure to protect young Leon (Centre for Child Law 2011).

or another child in detention; and there is a likelihood that the child, if convicted, could be sentenced to imprisonment (s. 30(1) of the CJA). The net effect of these requirements is that children are, where necessary, detained in child and youth care centers rather than prisons. Child and youth care centers fall under the Department of Social Development rather than under the Department of Correctional Services. They are managed in terms of the Children's Act 38 of 2005.

The provisions, together with a number of practical actions, have resulted in a further reduction of children in pretrial detention, complementing a process to reduce pretrial detention that was introduced prior to the Act. This is discussed more fully in the following text, and the figures are illustrated in Table 13.1.

Diversion

Diversion may be defined as the channeling of children away from the formal criminal justice system into reintegrative programs. If a child acknowledges responsibility for a wrongdoing, in certain circumstances, he or she can be diverted to such a program, thereby avoiding the stigmatizing and even brutalizing effects of the mainstream criminal justice system. Diversion further provides children with the opportunity to avoid a criminal record, while at the same time ensuring that they remain accountable and responsible for their actions (Badenhorst 2011).

Under the Act, the provision of diversion services now forms a central feature in the child justice process. The Act provides for a range of innovative diversion options set out in two varying levels of intensity. Level one applies to petty offenses and may include options such as a compulsory school attendance order; a family time order; a good behavior order; community service order, and so forth (s. 53(3) read with s. 53(1) of the CJA). These orders allow children to remain in their homes while providing a backup to parents and families having difficulty in guiding their children through adolescence. Level two options, on the other hand, may include compulsory attendance and even residence at a specified center or place for a specific vocational, educational, or therapeutic purpose (s. 53(5) of the CJA). This level of diversion services applies to any child who has committed a serious and/or violent offense (s. 53(2) of the CJA) (see Box 13.5).

Probation officers, tasked with the compulsory assessment of each child who has been arrested or in respect of whom an alternative to arrest was used, may make a recommendation regarding diversion, which is recorded on an assessment report. This report is referred to the relevant prosecutor. Upon consideration of the recommendation, the prosecutor may exercise power to withdraw the charges if the charge is a minor one, or must arrange for

Table 13.1   Pretrial Detention of Children

Year	Economical	Aggressive	Sexual	Narcotics	Other	Total
1994/1995	734	443	103	21	58	1359
1995/1996	436	289	99	10	37	871
1996/1997	768	518	196	18	64	1564
1997/1998	1232	893	353	31	76	2495
1998/1999	1244	944	449	27	73	2737
1999/2000	1788	1364	557	30	127	3866
2000/2001	1627	1451	534	30	113	3755
2001/2002	1709	1511	521	28	118	3887
2002/2003	1804	1641	536	35	125	4141
2004/2005	1346	1484	436	33	115	3414
2005/2006	809	1147	344	21	78	2399
2006/2007	720	1020	289	21	99	2149
2007/2008	714	965	280	27	90	2076
2009/2010	462	668	257	19	89	1475
2010/2011	287	451	199	11	31	979
2011/2012	Unknown	Unknown	Unknown	Unknown	Unknown	553

Source: Muntingh, L. and Ballard, C. (2012). Children in Prison in South Africa. Community Law Centre: Cape Town.

BOX 13.5   DECLINE IN DIVERSION SERVICES RENDERED

Despite the centrality of diversion in the new child justice order, it appears from information available that there has been a sharp decline in the numbers of children being diverted. A trend analysis conducted by the Intersectoral Committee for Child Justice revealed that a comparative analysis of the periods April 2009–December 2009 and April 2010–December 2010 showed a decrease of 24% (Department of Justice and Constitutional Development 2011). This is confirmed by civil society organizations offering diversion services and programs (Badenhorst 2012). The numbers further decreased in the second year of implementation by a staggering 44% (Badenhorst 2012).

The reasons for the drastic drop in referrals for diversion is almost certainly linked to the drop in children being brought into the system, and is thus also probably attributable to the fact that the police, who are the gatekeepers to the system, are insufficiently trained. This is evident if one considers that in the first year of implementation, the South African Police Service (SAPS) provided training to 15,891 members on the Act (Department of Justice and Constitutional Development 2011). In the second year of implementation, the SAPS provided training to 14,060 members. In total, only a small percentage of SAPS members have been trained, the overall figure sitting at a mere 29,951 or 19% of the total members. The fact that so few SAPS members have been trained, highlights a serious gap for the successful implementation of the Act.

the opening of a preliminary inquiry to consider diversion in more serious cases (Sections 41 and 52 of the CJA) (see Table 13.2). In instances where diversion is not considered at the early stages of the legal proceedings, a child justice court may nevertheless order that a child be diverted at any stage during the trial but before the state closes its case (s. 67 of the CJA).

Table 13.2   Diversions Referred to NICRO during 2009/2010 and 2010/2011*

Referral Source	2009/2010	2010/2011
Prosecutor	4274	2848
Probation officer	4469	2673
Magistrate	552	305
Total	9295	5826

Source: Badenhorst, C. (2012). Second Year of the Child Justice Act's Implementation: Dwindling Numbers. University of the Western Cape: Cape Town.

* NICRO (the National Institute for Crime Prevention and Rehabilitation of Offenders) is but one of several accredited diversion service providers in South Africa. The total therefore does not represent all children diverted in South Africa during the periods identified.

Preliminary Inquiry

In contrast to the adversarial nature of conventional criminal proceedings, the Act mandates that all children should first attend a preliminary inquiry. A preliminary inquiry envisages a compulsory inquisitorial pretrial procedure, which is presided over by an inquiry magistrate, involving the child, the parents, the prosecutor, and the probation officers (s. 43(1) of the CJA). The objectives of the preliminary inquiry are to

- Consider the assessment report of the probation officer
- Establish whether the child can be diverted before plea
- Identify a suitable diversion option, where applicable
- Establish whether the matter should be referred to the children's court for care and protection proceedings to commence
- Ensure that all the available information relevant to the child, his/her circumstances, and the offense are considered to make a decision regarding diversion or release or detention
- Ensure that the views of all present, including the child, are taken into consideration before a decision is made
- Encourage the participation of the child and his/her parent and an appropriate adult or guardian in decision concerning the child
- Determine the release or placement of child where such child is detained (s. 43(2) of the CJA)

Once the inquiry magistrate has considered all the information gathered at the preliminary inquiry, he or she may make one of three orders (Gallinetti 2009). The first is that the child be diverted (s. 49(1)(a) of the CJA). The second is a referral to the care and protection system. The third is that, if not diverted, the child must be referred to the child justice court for plea and trial (s. 49(2) of the CJA). In instances where the child is in detention, the inquiry magistrate must consider whether release is appropriate (s. 49(2)(b) of the CJA). If pretrial detention is deemed necessary, the inquiry magistrate determines whether the child is to be detained in a child and youth care center or prison.

BOX 13.6   THE CASE OF THE BOY CHARGED WITH
THE MURDER OF EUGENE TERRE BLANCHE

In the case of *Media 24 Limited v National Prosecuting Authority in re: S v Mhlangu* (2011 (2) SACR 321 (GNP)), the court found that the media representatives could not sit in the courtroom as it would affect the child offender's rights. However, due to the public interest in this case, which dealt with the murder of prominent right-wing leader Eugene Terre Blanche, the judge did allow media representatives to sit in another room at the court and view the proceedings via closed-circuit TV, provided the face of the child accused was blurred. The press was also prohibited from directly or indirectly identifying him. Unfortunately, the boy's details were released to the press after he turned 18—due to a misinterpretation of the legal provision in question—resulting in him being named by local and international media houses. In the end, he was acquitted of murdering Eugene Terre Blanche, but because of his identity being revealed, he had to relocate and assume another identity.

Child Justice Court

A child justice court is any court that deals with the bail application, plea, trial, or sentencing of a child (s.1 of the CJA). In some of the major urban areas, there are a sufficient number of children being charged with offenses to warrant the establishment of designated child justice courts staffed by specialized personnel. Any court is a child justice court if a child accused appears before it.

In instances where an adult and child are tried together, the court must apply the Act in respect of the child and the Criminal Procedure Act 51 of 1977 in respect of the adult (s. 63(2)).

To ensure that the fair trial rights of a child are upheld, specifically the ability to testify freely, and promote the future reintegration of the child into society, the Act prohibits any person whose presence is not necessary from sitting in on the hearing (s. 63(5) of the CJA). The Act further prohibits the publication of any information that reveals or may reveal the identity of the child (s. 63(6) of the CJA) (see Box 13.6).

Sentencing

The Act provides for a wide range of sentencing options. These include

- Community-based sentences, which do not involve a residential requirement and which allow a child to remain in his or her community (s. 72 of the CJA).
- Restorative justice sentences, such as referral of the child to a family group conference or victim–offender mediation (s. 73 of the CJA).
- Fines or alternatives to fines, which may be paid as compensation to persons or to a community organization, charity, or welfare organizations (s. 74(2)(b) of the CJA). The Act also envisages the use of symbolic restitution rather than the payment of a specified sum of money (s. 74(2)(a) of the CJA) and the provision of services by the child to a specified person and/or community (s. 74(2)(c) of the CJA). A child may not be imprisoned for nonpayment of a fine.

Table 13.3   Breakdown of Sentences Handed Down, 2011/2012

Type of Sentence	2011/2012
Community-based sentence	795
Restorative justice sentence	405
Fines/alternatives to fines	37
Correctional supervision	302
Referral to a child and youth care center	353
Imprisonment	94

Source: Department of Justice and Constitutional Development. (2012). Annual Report on the Implementation of the Child Justice Act. Government Printers: Pretoria.

- Correctional supervision, which may be suspended or postponed on the condition that a child be placed under the supervision of a probation officer or correctional official and that the child perform a service to the benefit of the community (s. 75 of the CJA).
- Referral to a child and youth care center (s. 76 of the CJA) or a prison (s. 77 of the CJA).
- The postponement or suspension of any sentence, with or without conditions (s.78 of the CJA).

The Act does not permit the imposition of a life sentence on a child who was under the age of 18 at the date of sentencing (s. 77(4) of the CJA), and sets the maximum length of imprisonment at 25 years (with opportunity for earlier parole) (see Table 13.3).

Legal Representation

The Act provides that any child who appears before a child justice court is entitled to have a legal representative of his or her own choice, at own expense. If the child's family cannot retain such services, then a legal representative must be provided by the state (s. 82 of the CJA). A child may not waive his or her right to legal representation (s. 83(1) of the CJA). An unusual feature of the Act is that where a child does not wish to have a legal representative or declines to give instructions to an appointed legal representative, the court must, regardless of the child's wishes, appoint a legal representative to assist the court in upholding the fair trial rights of the child (s. 83(2) of the CJA) (see Box 13.7).

Automatic Review of Certain Sentences

A protective feature of the new Act provides for automatic review of magistrate's court sentences by a high court (see Box 13.8). This has been expansively interpreted by the high courts to include all cases regardless of sentence in cases of children below 16 years and all cases of children 16 years or older regarding a sentence of imprisonment that is not wholly suspended (Skelton 2013). Appeals may also be noted in such matters, but appeals require legal representation, whereas review does not. The matter is automatically referred to a high court judge who generally reviews the sentence in chambers, though more complex matters may be set down in court for argument.

BOX 13.7   LEGAL AID SOUTH AFRICA

Legal Aid South Africa derives its mandate from Section 35 of the Constitution. In the terms of this section, every person who is arrested, detained, or accused has a right to a fair trial, which includes the right to have a legal practitioner by the state and at state expense. Legal Aid South Africa's role is therefore to provide legal aid to those who cannot afford their own legal representation. This includes poor people and vulnerable groups such as children. Under its obligations in terms of the Child Justice Act (CJA), Legal Aid South Africa represented in 2010/2011 25,586 children and in 2011/2012 a further 22,376 children.

BOX 13.8   IMPORTANCE OF THE AUTOMATIC REVIEW PROCESS

In two recent high court cases, the judges noted the importance of automatic review and highlighted its usefulness in ensuring that children should be detained as a measure of last resort and for the shortest period of time as required by the constitution and Section 37 of the Convention on the Rights of the Child (CRC). See the cases of *S v FM* 2013 (1) SACR 57 (GNP) and *S v LM* 2013 (1) SACR 188 (WCC) for the courts' reasoning in this regard.

Expungement of Criminal Records

The system for the expungement of criminal records is based on the type of offense. In minor offenses, the record can be expunged after 5 years and in more serious offenses, after 10 years. The young person must apply for a certificate of expungement, which will be supplied provided the person has not committed a crime of the same or a more serious nature during the 5- or 10-year period. However, convictions for very serious crimes such as murder, rape, and armed robbery are never expunged. As the Act has only been in operation since 2010, it is too early to assess how effective these provisions will be in practice. It is concerning that the expungement is not automatic, and it may be difficult to ensure that that these provisions work for impoverished and poorly educated young people who were convicted as children.

Specific Areas of Interest and Debate

Possible Change to the Minimum Age of Criminal Capacity

Although South Africa's CJA is relatively new, discussion is already underway about possibly changing the provisions regarding age and capacity. In fact, when the bill was being debated in the parliament, there were submissions from various civil society organizations urging a higher age than 10 years, particularly in the light of the United Nations Committee on the Rights of the Child's General Comment no. 10 (2007), in which states were urged to set a minimum age of no less than 12 years of age. The parliament stopped short of doing that, but nevertheless included an unusual clause in the Act. Section 8 provides that to determine whether or not the age of capacity should be raised, the Minister of Justice must submit a report to the parliament within 5 years of the Act coming into operation (which will be in 2015). The report will include information about the nature and prevalence of crimes committed by children between the ages of 10 and 14 years. Skelton and Badenhorst (2011) have pointed to various practical difficulties in the individual assessment of children, especially in the light of South Africa's limited number of qualified professionals who can assess capacity. They promote the introduction of a single age of criminal capacity—12 years—to replace the current system, which is based on the *doli incapax* approach. This accords with General Comment no. 10 (UN Committee on the Rights of the Child 2007), which urges states to set a minimum age at no lower than 12 years of age.

Detention as a Measure of Last Resort

The Bill of Rights in South Africa's Constitution contains a provision that mirrors article 37(b) of the CRC: A child must be detained only as a measure of last resort and for the shortest appropriate period of time. Although this was included in the Bill of Rights in 1996, it took some time for this to bring any real results for children. The number of children being held in prison awaiting trial was of great concern. In the year 2000, the number of children awaiting trial was 2176. By 2010, when the CJA came into operation, that number had come down dramatically to 979 (Muntingh and Ballard 2012) (see Table 13.1). In the first 2 years of the Act's life, a further reduction in children awaiting trial has been noted. This success story—is due in part to concerted efforts by the inter-ministerial committee on child justice, to reduce the numbers of children awaiting trial through intersectoral cooperation. Secure care alternatives to prison (run by the Department of Social Development) were introduced from the late 1990s, which provided courts with another option, albeit a custodial one. Constant monitoring by a vibrant and well-informed civil society has assisted in ensuring this drop in numbers (Muntingh and Ballard 2012).

The story of sentenced children has also been an interesting one. The courts have strongly upheld the "last resort" principle, showing recognition of the CRC, the United Nations Standard Rules for the Administration of Juvenile Justice, and the Rules for the Protection of Juveniles Deprived of their Liberty. In the case of *Centre for Child Law v Minister for Justice and Constitutional Development* 2009 (6) SA 632 (CC), a law that aimed to draw 16- and 17-year-olds into the ambit of minimum sentences (including life imprisonment) was successfully challenged. The majority of the constitutional courts found that the minimum sentencing regime was at odds with detention as a measure of last resort. They held that the minimum sentencing legislation limited the discretion of sentencing officers by directing them to hand down long sentences (including life imprisonment) as a first resort. Furthermore, the legislation discouraged the use of noncustodial options, it prevented courts from individualizing sentences, and was likely to cause longer prison sentences. The court found that children should be treated differently from adults not for sentimental reasons, but because of their greater physical and psychological vulnerability and the fact that they were more open to influence and pressure from others. The court considered it to be vitally important that child offenders are generally more capable of rehabilitation than adults. The court also gave a useful description of what is meant by "the shortest appropriate period:" "If there is an appropriate option other than imprisonment,

---

BOX 13.9   THE CENTRE FOR CHILD LAW

The Centre for Child Law is a specialized law clinic based in the Law Faculty at the University of Pretoria. It was officially launched in October 1998 and is headed by Professor Ann Skelton. The Centre contributes to the promotion of the best interests of children in the South African community through research, advocacy, and litigation. The center employs test litigation specialists who take cases to court on a wide range of children's issues, with the aim of developing legal precedents that advance children's rights.

---

the Bill of Rights requires that it be chosen. In this sense, incarceration must be the sole appropriate option. But if incarceration is unavoidable, its form and duration must also be tempered, so as to ensure detention for the shortest possible period of time" (para 31) (see Table 13.1 in the preceding text and see Box 13.9).

Children and Sexual Offenses

Around the same time that the CJA was introduced, South Africa also brought into law the Criminal Law (Sexual Offences and Related Matters) Amendment Act 32 of 2007 (hereafter, Sexual Offences Act). This comprehensive piece of legislation broadened the common law concept of rape to "penetrative sexual violation" which is now gender-neutral and includes a wide range of penetrative acts into any orifice, with various parts of the body or with objects. A central aim of the act is to protect children from sexual offenses, but an unforeseen consequence of the law has been to draw child "offenders," particularly adolescents, within its ambit. It is a fact that many sexual offenses against children are committed by other children—partly because they spend a lot of time with children. Furthermore, many of them do not understand sexual "rules" or "norms" as in many cultures it is taboo to discuss sex with children.

Internationally, concern has been expressed about how new, tough sexual offense laws have a disproportionately harsh impact on child offenders (Human Rights Watch 2013). Most modern juvenile justice or youth justice systems focus on early intervention measures such as diversion and emphasize treatment-based approaches to young sex offenders. However, the new sexual offenses legislation tends to be punitive and exclusionary, and draws young offenders within its net. Many such laws expand the definitions of sexual offenses that, in some instances, criminalize behavior, which is not harmful. Practices such as taking a picture of oneself naked on a cell phone camera and sending it via SMS to a girlfriend or boyfriend has suddenly become "manufacturing and distributing child pornography." Legislators appear to overlook the fact that while it is wrong for adults to be sexually interested in children, children and adolescents being sexually interested in one another is normal. Of course, an unwanted sexual act is an offense, whether between children or adults, but many of these sexual offenses laws also criminalize consensual sexual activity between children and adolescents.

In South Africa, a constitutional challenge has declared unconstitutional a section of the Sexual Offences Act that included a requirement that when children who are both between the ages of 12 and 16 years indulge in any consensual sexual act (penetrative or nonpenetrative) and a decision is taken to prosecute, then both must be prosecuted. In the case of *Teddy Bear Clinic and Another v Minister of Justice and Constitutional Development and Others* 2014 (2) SA 168 (CC), the Constitutional Court handed down a unanimous judgment, which found the impugned provisions infringed adolescents' rights of dignity and privacy and further violated the best interests of the child principle. The judgment underlined the dignity of children, describing the law as having placed youthful transgressors in a state of disgrace for behavior that was developmentally normative.

The Sexual Offences Act also introduced a sex offender register aimed at preventing persons convicted of sexual offenses from being permitted to work with children. In *J v National Director of Public Prosecutions 2014 (2) SACR 1 (CC)* the Constitutional Court declared the automatic inclusion of the names of child offenders (below 18 years at the date of offense) in the sex offenders register unconstitutional. The court suspended the order of invalidity to allow parliament time to redraft the law and bring it in line with the constitution.

Violence in Schools

School-based violence continues to be an area of concern in South Africa. In a recent study conducted by the Centre for Justice and Crime Prevention, it was estimated that 22.2% or 1,020,597 secondary school learners had been victims of some form of violence (threats of violence, assault, sexual assault, and robbery) while at school (Burton and Leoschut 2013). In the same study, it was estimated that if the incidences of theft were included in this figure, the overall victimization rate increased to 53.2% or 2,445,756 secondary school learners (Burton and Leoschut 2013). This percentage increased further when the experiences of cyber violence were included, the overall victimization rate soaring to 58.7% or 2,698,606 secondary school learners (Burton and Leoschut 2013).

The Department of Basic Education has, together with other stakeholders, initiated several strategies designed to curb and ultimately eradicate the high incidences of school-based violence. While the strategies will take some time to come to fruition, it is concerning that most of these programs are targeted at the learners themselves and do not address the systemic issues and social ills prevalent in the immediate communities. Furthermore, the violence is not one sided. Despite the fact that South Africa outlawed corporal punishment in schools in 1996, in the General Household Survey 2013, 15.8% of all learners had experienced corporal punishment in schools in 2012. This figure amounts to approximately 2.2 million. Clearly, South Africa has a long way to go in the development of a culture of nonviolence.

Conclusion

During its colonial and apartheid eras, South Africa did not have a separate law dealing with child offenders. South Africa became a constitutional democracy in 1994. The ratification of the CRC and the introduction of the Bill of Rights in the constitution led to far-reaching law reform initiatives for the protection of children.

The CJA was signed into law in 2008 and came into operation in April 2010. It introduced a comprehensive system of dealing with children in conflict with the law that represents a decisive break with the traditional criminal justice system. The traditional pillars of punishment, retribution and deterrence are replaced with continued emphasis on the need to gain an understanding, through an assessment, of a child caught up in behavior transgressing the law, determining whether the child is in need of care and correcting errant actions as far as possible by diversion, community-based programs, the application of restorative justice processes, and reintegration of the child into the community. The Act minimizes the use of detention through alternatives to arrest and limitations on pretrial custody. The Act does retain imprisonment—up to a maximum of 25 years—in the most serious cases involving offenders 14 years and older. Life imprisonment is not available, and there is no waiver of cases to the adult court. Compulsory legal representation, automatic review of sentences by the high court, and the expungement of records are additional protections.

This chapter illustrates the description of the Act with case law, facts, and figures. It concludes with a consideration of contemporary issues such as a reconsideration of the minimum age of criminal capacity, and the way in which the "detention as a measure of last resort" principle has been used to protect child offenders.

This chapter acknowledges that South Africa's new child justice system is in its infancy, and that some problems have been experienced in the early years of its operation. It is evident that investment in the training of child justice officials, particularly members of the police service, will benefit its effective implementation.

Review/Discussion Questions

1. What are the main aims of the Child Justice Act?
2. Which children fall within the scope of the Child Justice Act?
3. What is the legal status of diversion?
4. How is the child justice court different from any other court?
5. What other specific safeguards are there for child offenders in the Child Justice Act?
6. Describe the debates about the minimum age of criminal capacity in South Africa.
7. How has the South African Constitutional Court interpreted "measure of last resort and for the shortest appropriate period of time"?

References

Badenhorst, C. (2011). *Overview of the Implementation of the Child Justice Act, 2008 (Act 75 of 2008): Good Intentions, Questionable Outcomes.* Open Society Foundation for South Africa: Cape Town.

Badenhorst, C. (2012). *Second Year of the Child Justice Act's Implementation: Dwindling Numbers.* University of the Western Cape: Cape Town.

Bennett, T. (2004). *Customary Law in South Africa.* Juta: Cape Town.

Burchell, J. (2011). *South African Criminal Law and Procedure (Vol. 1: General Principles of Criminal Law)* (4th ed.). Juta: Claremont.

Burton, P. and Leoschut, L. (2013). *School Violence in South Africa: Results of the 2012 National School Violence.* Monograph 12, Study Centre for Justice and Crime Prevention: Cape Town.

Centre for Child Law. (2007). Death of child in police cells. Annual Report available at www.centre-forchildlaw.co.za

Centre for Child Law. (2011). Inquest into death of 14 year old boy in police cells. Annual Report available at www.centreforchildlaw.co.za

Community Law Centre. (2000). *What the Children Said*. University of the Western Cape: Cape Town.

Community Law Centre. (2005). *Law, Practice, and Policy: South African Juvenile Justice Today*. University of Cape Town: Cape Town.

Department of Justice and Constitutional Development. (2011). *Annual Report on the Implementation of the Child Justice Act*. Government Printers: Pretoria.

Department of Justice and Constitutional Development. (2012). *Annual Report on the Implementation of the Child Justice Act*. Government Printers: Pretoria.

Gallinetti, J. (2009). *Getting to Know the Child Justice Act*. University of the Western Cape: Cape Town.

Human Rights Watch. (2013). *Raised on the Registry: The Irreparable Harm of Placing Children on Sexual Offences Registries in the US*. Human Rights Watch: United States of America.

Juvenile Justice Drafting Consultancy. (1994). *Juvenile Justice for South Africa: Proposals for Policy and Legislative Change*. Allies Printers: Cape Town.

Muntingh, L. and Ballard, C. (2012). *Children in Prison in South Africa*. Community Law Centre: Cape Town.

Pinnock, D., Skelton, A., and Shapiro, R. (1994). New juvenile justice legislation for South Africa: Giving children a chance. *South African Journal of Criminal Justice*, 7(3): 338–347.

Skelton, A. (2011). From Cook County to Pretoria: A long walk to justice for children. *Northwestern Journal of Law and Social Policy*, 6: 414–427.

Skelton, A. (2013). The automatic review of child offenders' sentences. *Southern Africa Crime Quarterly*, 44: 37–44.

Skelton, A. and Badenhorst, C. (2011). *The criminal capacity of children in South Africa: International developments and considerations for a review*. Child Justice Alliance and Open Society Foundation: Cape Town.

Skelton, A. and Gallinetti, J. (2008). A long and winding road: The child justice bill and civil society advocacy. *Southern Africa Crime Quarterly*, 25: 3–10.

Skelton, A. and Potgieter, H. (2002). Juvenile justice in South Africa. In Winterdyk, J. (Ed.) *Juvenile Justice Systems: International Perspectives*. Canadian Scholars Press: Toronto. pp. 477–502

Skelton, A. and Tshehla, B. (2008). *Child Justice in South Africa*. Monograph 150, Institute for Security Studies: Pretoria.

South African Law Commission. (2000). *Report on Juvenile Justice*. South African Law Commission: Pretoria.

UN Committee on the Rights of the Child. (2007). General Comment No. 10. Children's Rights in Juvenile Justice (Forty-fourth session). U.N. Doc. CRC/C/GC/10 (2007).

Case Law

Centre for Child Law v Minister for Justice and Constitutional Development 2009 (6) SA 632 (CC).

Media 24 Limited v National Prosecuting Authority in re: S v Mhlangu (2011 (2) SACR 321 (GNP)).

S v FM (Centre for Child Law as Amicus Curiae) 2013 (1) SACR 57 (GNP).

S v LM (Faculty of Law, University of the Western Cape: Children Rights Project of the Community Law Centre and Another as Amici Curiae) 2013 (1) SACR 188 (WCC).

Teddy Bear Clinic and Another v Minister of Justice and Constitutional Development and Others 2014 (2) SA 168 (CC)

J. v National Director of Public Prosecutions 2014 (2) SACR 1 (CC)

Internet Sources

http://www.centreforchildlaw.co.za—The Centre for Child Law is based at the University of Pretoria. The Centre contributes the promotion of the best interests of children in South Africa through education, research, advocacy and litigation. The website contains useful information about cases involving children, including cases taken to court by the Centre in order to achieve its objectives.

http://www.childjustice.org.za/default.htm—A website operated by the Child Justice Alliance which is dedicated to providing practitioners and advocates with resources and information on child justice. Special attention is given to the Child Justice Act the successful implementation thereof.

http://www.communitylawcentre.org.za/projects/childrens-rights-project—This is the website of the Children's Rights Project by the Community Law Centre (an NGO) at the University of the Western Cape. It provides information about the project, contains South African case and judgments involving children and also a number of valuable links to child related sites.

http://www.nicro.org.za—NICRO is a national organisation, with its head office situated in Cape Town. Through people centred development and services to victims, offenders and communities NICRO strengthens a human rights culture and a safer South Africa. To this end NICRO engages in lobbying and advocacy, capacity building, direct service delivery and research. The website describes the programmes and services it offers.

Juvenile Justice: England and Wales

14

LORAINE GELSTHORPE AND
VICKY KEMP

Contents

Introduction 344
An English and Welsh Perspective on Juvenile Delinquency 345
The YJS in England and Wales: An Overview 346
Youth Crime and Youth Victimization 346
    Youth Justice Statistics 348
    Youth Victimization and the Crime Survey 350
Developments in the YJS 350
    The Children Act 1908—Juvenile Justice: The Beginning 351
    Children and Young Persons Act 1933 351
    Politics and Juvenile Justice—1945 to 1970 351
    Children and Young Persons Act 1963 352
    Children and Young Persons Act 1969: The Eclipse of Welfare? 352
    Criminal Justice Act 1982: The "Moment of Crime Control" 353
    Children Act 1989: A Return to Consensus? 354
    Criminal Justice and Public Order Act 1994: A Punitive Turn? 354
    CDA 1998: Reforming the YJS 355
    Youth Justice and Criminal Evidence Act 1999 356
    Criminal Justice and Immigration Act 2008 357
Whither Youth Justice? New Shifts in Thinking and Contemporary Issues and
      Pressures 358
    Legal Aid, Sentencing, and Punishment of Offenders Act 2012 358
    Gender and the YJS 360
    Young People and the 2011 "Riots" 360
    The YJS in Times of Austerity 361
    The YJS and International Standards on the Rights of the Child 362
Juvenile Justice in Northern Ireland 363
Whither Youth Justice? Summary 364
Review/Discussion Questions 365
References 365
Internet Sources 368

FACTS ABOUT THE UNITED KINGDOM

Area: With an area of 244,820 sq. km. the United Kingdom of Great Britain comprises England, Wales, Scotland, and Northern Ireland. It is one of the 28 member states of the European Union, which it joined in 1973. **Population:** Britain is densely populated with over 63 million people. The proportion of the population aged 65 and over has increased by 0.5% while the younger population, aged 15 and under, has decreased by 1% over the past decade. The older population, aged 65 years and older has more than tripled, from 5% in 1911 to 16% in 2011. Over the centuries, many people from overseas have settled in Britain either to escape political or religious persecution or in search of economic opportunities. It is worth noting that since 1981, there had been a tightening of immigration law, something that has made it much more difficult for foreign nationals to settle in Britain. However, over the past decade, the borders in Europe have been relaxed, which has led to Britain becoming more ethnically diverse. This has led to the ethnic minority population (other than "white British") more than doubling in number since 1991 from 3 to 7 million (increasing from 5.5% to 14% of the total population). Although Britain has been predominantly Christian since the early Middle Ages, today most of the world's other religions are represented. Britain's Hindu, Sikh, and Jewish communities each number around 817,000, 423,000, and 263,000, respectively. The Muslim community has changed significantly over the past decade, increasing from 1.6 million in 2001 to 2.2 million in 2011. **Economy:** Historically, Britain was one of the leading industrialized countries, but in recent years, the economic and industrial pattern has altered considerably. Service industries have become increasingly important, accounting for around 80% of the employees. Financial and other business services had also grown in significance during the 1980s, but recent problems in these services has led to the UK economy becoming weak and the growth being flat since 2010. **Government:** Britain is a parliamentary democracy with a constitutional monarch—currently Queen Elizabeth II—as head of State. Unlike many other parliamentary democracies, it has no written constitution outlining the rights and obligations of government or citizens. Instead, it is ruled according to laws passed by Parliament, decisions made in the higher judicial courts, and (perhaps more importantly) tradition. Parliament, Britain's legislature, comprises the House of Commons, the House of Lords, and the Queen in her constitutional role. General elections to choose members of parliament must be held at least every 5 years. The government is formed by the party with the majority support in the Commons. The last general election was held in May 2010 that, for the first time since the Second World War, led to a coalition government with the Conservatives and Liberal Democrats sharing power. The Labour Party forms the official opposition, with its own leader and shadow cabinet. The opposition has a duty to challenge government policies and to present alternatives.

Introduction

In the little world in which children have their existence, whosoever brings them up, there is nothing so finely perceived and so finely felt, as injustice.

Charles Dickens, 1812–1870

This chapter is primarily concerned with youth justice in England and Wales, though we include a brief outline of the legal framework and issues of Northern Ireland, one of the other jurisdictions of the United Kingdom (see Box 14.1 in the following text); youth justice in Scotland, the remaining legal jurisdiction in the United Kingdom is considered in a separate chapter (Chapter 11). Occasionally, Parliament passes similar legislation in respect of all its jurisdictions, but, as we hope to make clear, different arrangements exist for dealing with young offenders in the three jurisdictions: Scotland, Northern Ireland, and England and Wales.

Since its inception, youth justice in the United Kingdom has evolved as a particularly complex and volatile area of criminal justice, reflecting shifting ideas and anxieties about young people and social disorder. The social, political, and cultural context in which the youth justice system (YJS) has taken shape is important for any understanding of the content of responses.

In the first section of this chapter, we provide a short description of perspectives on juvenile delinquency. In the second section, we provide an overview of the YJS and its working. In the third part, we give an outline of crime committed by young people and point toward new knowledge about their victimization. The fourth part provides a brief historical summary before outlining more recent changes, which have led to the current system of youth justice. The fifth part of the chapter focuses on new shifts in thinking and contemporary issues and pressures.

An English and Welsh Perspective on Juvenile Delinquency

As in other countries, an English and Welsh understanding of youth crime is inevitably shaped by historical and contextual specificities and by a reflection of the social conditions of the time. Childhood during Victorian times, for instance, was at the same time idealized, worshipped, and protected, and feared, regulated, and punished. Hendrick (1990) identifies no less than five versions of childhood, which were articulated during the Victorian era: the Romantic child, the Evangelical child, the Factory child, the Delinquent child, and the Schooled child. The twentieth century saw the emergence of the Psycho-medical child and the Welfare child (Brown 1998) reflecting the rise of the psycho-medical profession and the establishment of the welfare state whose aim, during the 1960s, at least, was to support families, the "troublesome" child being a "troubled child" whose family deserved help. Since the 1950s, perceptions of youth crime have also revolved around youth cultures, gangs and subcultures, and "style" as crime (with rave and club cultures seen to be encouraging crime, for instance, particularly drug misuse and disorder through excessive consumption of alcohol).

It is arguable that since the 1970s and 1980s, social and economic conditions for many young people have become much tougher, and youth unemployment has now become a permanent feature of the social landscape (Morgan and Newburn 2012). As a consequence, lifestyles have become dominated by consumption rather than work, with notions that young people are "amusing themselves to death" (Postman 1987). Moreover, alongside recognition that an escalation of violent and sexual material broadcast through electronic media is corrupting children to the point that they are losing their childhood altogether, moral panics around youth abound, and "feral youth" continue to be a focus for political attention. The existence of "gang culture" remains contested (Hallsworth and Silverstone 2009), but this has not stopped governments identifying the emergence of gangs as a key prompt for youthful delinquency.

Broadly, on the political right, it is viewed that crime among young people has increased and that childhood innocence has been lost, that young people are somehow worse than their predecessors in previous generations, and that the best way to address the problems is to impose tougher penalties. Individuals and their families should be made responsible for crime. On the political left, there is some acknowledgment that social conditions can prompt crime and that there is need to shore up civil society so as to facilitate resilience against crime. There is also recognition that moral panics are socially constructed. In practice, these different perspectives have merged in the operational policies of successive governments. In academia, there is some sophisticated research which has explored the nature of gangs (Pitts 2008), involvement in "public disorder" and links with disaffection among young people (notably the August street disorder of 2011) (Lewis et al. 2011), and work that is trying to integrate individual factors and social contextual factors (Wikström et al. 2012), as well as important investigations of youth lifestyles, youth crime and ethnicity, the associations among young people, drugs, alcohol, and crime, and young women and crime. There is certainly no one theoretical perspective on the causes of youth crime, but rather a mixture of ideas and evidence.

The YJS in England and Wales: An Overview

The YJS in England and Wales works to prevent offending and reoffending by children and young people under the age of 18. At the heart of modern youth justice is the notion that children's offending should be treated differently from that of adults because of their immaturity and undeveloped capacity to constrain their impulses. The system is different from the adult system and is structured to address the needs of young people, taking into account perceptions of their lesser responsibility. The Youth Justice Board (YJB) is the executive nondepartmental public body that oversees the YJS in England and Wales. In addition, there are currently 160 multiagency youth offending teams (YOTs) or youth offending services (YOSs) as they are known in some local authority areas (a local authority area is a local unit of government).* There have been recent debates about incorporating the YJB into the Ministry of Justice more centrally, but for the moment, the notion of a separate YJB has been retained (Ministry of Justice 2013a).

The YJS was transformed by the Crime and Disorder Act (CDA) 1998. In our earlier chapter, we had included two figures (5.1 and 5.2), which provided an outline of the YJS both prior to and following implementation of the 1998 Act (Gelsthorpe and Kemp 2002, 129 and 146). There have been further changes to the YJS, and Figure 14.1 gives an outline of the current YJS in England and Wales.

Youth Crime and Youth Victimization

Interestingly, while concerns about youth crime continue to abound (Pearson 1983), the number of young people in the YJS, as in many other parts of the world, has been in

---

* A youth offending team (YOT) or youth offending service (YOS) usually comprises at least a social worker, probation officer, police officer, person nominated by the local health authority, person nominated by the local education authority, and a YOT or YOS manager.

APPREHENSION AND CHARGE

Parents are expected to prevent their children from committing offenses and, in the circumstances, if their child does offend, they can be placed on a "parenting order" under which they are required to attend parenting classes (they can be fined or imprisoned for failing to attend).

In addition to the police apprehending or having youngsters reported to them, children under 10 years who have broken a local curfew or committed an offense can be dealt with under a child safety order in the family proceedings court, and such an order can lead to care proceedings.

BAIL

The contents of bail support programs vary. Support can include programs, which seek to reintroduce youngsters back to school or assist in finding training or employment. The lack of accommodation is generally recognized as a major factor influencing bail, with some teams seeking to increase provision.

The 1998 act requires that every local authority must ensure, to such extent as is appropriate for their area, that there is provision for the support of children and young persons remanded or committed on bail while awaiting trial or sentence.

DIVERT

On issuing a youth caution, or youth conditional caution, the police have to notify the youth offending team (YOT), and an intervention is normally expected. This can be by way of a "change program" and/or a restorative outcome.

Replacing the statutory final warning scheme are youth cautions and youth conditional cautions for 10-to 17-year-olds as well as community resolution.

Doli incapax is no longer available for young offenders aged 10 to 13 years.

These out-of-court disposals do not need parents' consent.

YOUTH OFFENDING TEAM (OR YOUTH OFFENDING SERVICE)

Out-of-Court Disposals	Community Sentences	Civil/Criminal Orders		Custody	Others
Community resolution Youth caution Youth conditional caution [10- to 17-year-olds]	Rehabilitation order [10- to 17-year-olds]	ASBO Sex offender order	[10- to 17-year-olds]	Detention and training order* [12- to 17-year-olds]	Referral order Fine Discharges Compensation or bind-over
		Child safety order	[Under 10 years]		[10- to 17-year-olds]
		Parenting order	For parents and guardians		

Figure 14.1 Outline of the youth justice system in England and Wales in 2013. *Detention and training orders were included in the 1998 act and implemented on April 1, 2000, replacing young offender institutions and secure training orders. The orders can be for 4–24 months with half the order served in custody and the other half under supervision. Section 53 Children and Young Persons Act 1933 (concerning provision for children who have committed grave crimes) is retained.

decline since the beginning of the twenty-first century. The number of known young offenders began to increase from the 1930s and rose sharply (with some fluctuations) during the Second World War. Increases during the war have often been attributed to family disruption, high wages for youth labor, and the closure of schools and youth clubs (Bailey 1987). In the late 1940s and 1950s, with the advent of the welfare state, there was expectation that crime would return to a prewar lower level. Instead, the youth crime rate continued to rise quite sharply right through to the 1990s. Thus, the decline since the mid-2000s is all the more significant. Reductions have been seen in the number entering the system for the first time as well as reductions in those receiving disposals in and out of court, including those receiving custodial sentences. To provide further illustration, since 2008/09, there have been 54% fewer young people coming into the YJS, 32% fewer young people (under 18) in custody, and 14% fewer reoffenses by young people. While the rate of reoffending has been broadly stable over the last decade, the frequency rate fell by 8% between 2000 and 2010/11 (Youth Justice Board and Ministry of Justice 2012). This sounds like a success story, but of course there are a number of critical questions to ask about the apparent "crime drop." Is it a *crime-specific* drop, for example, because of technological improvements to prevent car theft, burglary, or shoplifting? Is the crime drop due to the falling value of stealable goods or to increasing intolerance of violence or reductions in the use and misuse of alcohol or drugs? Or, can it be attributed to better policing and crime prevention or even to an increased use of Xboxes,* which means that young people have little time to be committing crimes? We would also have to consider a shift in patterns of crime, from simple crime to cybercrime perhaps, or even whether there are fewer opportunities for debut crime. Moreover, does the apparent crime drop reflect shrinkage in the number of new entrants to crime or shrinkage in the intensity of offending by established young offenders?

It is very likely that elements of all of these possible explanations are true, combined with changes in counting rules regarding the criminal statistics, and so we have to be content with speculation. But it is worth noting that the crime drop within the criminal statistics is mirrored by experience as reported in the Crime Survey England and Wales (a victim survey) (http://www.crimesurvey.co.uk/).

Youth Justice Statistics

Drawing on the Youth Justice/Ministry of Justice Youth Justice Statistics for England and Wales (2013) helps to give some sense of scale to youth crime.

In 2010/11, there were 1,360,451 arrests in England and Wales of which 201,660 were of people aged 10–17 years. Thus, 10- to 17-year-olds accounted for 15.5% of all arrests, but were 10.7% of the population of England and Wales of offending age. Overall, there were 137,335 proven offenses by young people in 2011/12, down 22% from 2010/11 and down 47% since 2001/02. In the last year, there has been a notable reduction in offenses committed by young people, in particular; criminal damage (down 28%), public order (down 27%), theft and handling (down 23%), and violence-against-the-person offenses (down 22%).

Of those offenses dealt with by the police, there were 40,757 reprimands, final warnings, and conditional cautions (collectively called youth cautions and signifying precourt diversion from court) given to young people in England and Wales in 2011/12. This is a decrease of 18% on 2010/11 figures and a decrease of 57% on the 94,836 given in 2001/02. Shown in Figure 14.2 are trends in youth cautions by gender from 2001/02 to 2011/12.

One question that emerges here of course is whether young people were sent to court instead. But before we address that question, we should also consider other "out-of-court" disposals, which can be given by the police. There were 5571 Penalty Notices for Disorders (PNDs) given to 16- to 17-year-olds in 2011/12, and in 2011, there were 375 Anti-Social

* The Xbox is a sixth-generation video game console manufactured by Microsoft.

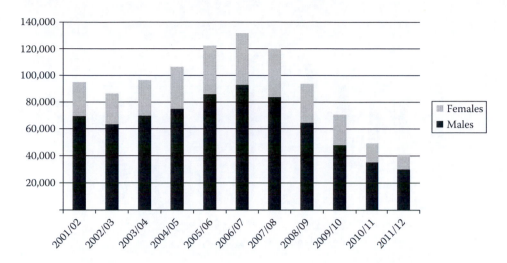

Figure 14.2 Trends in Reprimands, Final Warnings, and Conditional Cautions by Gender, 2001/02–2011/12. (Youth Justice Board and Ministry of Justice. (2013). *Youth justice statistics: England and Wales 2011/12*. London: Ministry of Justice.)

Behavior Orders (ASBOs) given to young people. In the last year, the number of PNDs given to young people has gone down by 26% and the number of ASBOs down 30%.*

While for most offense types, there was a decrease in the number of out-of-court disposals given to young people from 2006/07, there was a small increase for robbery and sexual offenses; however, these numbers are small and tend to fluctuate year to year. As shown in Figure 14.3 in the following text, there has similarly been a drop in the number of first-time entrants into the YJS, falling by 59% from 88,984 in 2001/02 to 36,677 in 2011/12. Since its peak in 2006/07 (as shown in the figure below), the number of first-time entrants has fallen by 67% and, in the last year alone, there has been a fall of 20%.

Were more people sent to court instead of out-of-court or pre-court disposals? The answer is a very clear no. In terms of court disposals, the official youth justice statistics reveal that in 2011/12, there were 59,335 court disposals (sentences) given to young people aged 10–17 in England and Wales. The total number of disposals given to young people at the courts has fallen by 18% in the last year. The number of custodial disposals fell 6% in 1 year, from 2010/11 to 2011/12 (4128 to 3925). This type of disposal has fallen 48% since 2001/02, when 7485 custodial sentences were given to young people. The custody rate was 6.6% in 2011/12, and this has fluctuated between 5% and 8% for the last decade. It is important not to confuse a drop in the number of young people in custody with the proportion of young people in custody though, and while the former has been encouraged (Morgan and Newburn 2012), the latter continues to be a cause for concern.

* Anti-Social Behavior Orders (ASBOs) are civil orders introduced in the 1998 Crime and Disorder Act (CDA). The common criterion is that the child or adult has acted "in a manner that caused or was likely to cause harassment, alarm or distress" to one or more persons outside the family (CDA 1998, ss. 1(1)(a) and 12(3)(c)). The ASBO must last for not less than 2 years. They can be awarded by magistrates in their civil jurisdiction, or, under the Police Reform Act 2002, imposed by the criminal courts against individuals convicted of a criminal offense. These orders are sometimes referred to as Criminal Anti-Social Behavior Orders (CRASBOs). Penalty Notices for Disorder (PNDs) were introduced for adults only by the Criminal Justice and Police Act 2001, but later extended by the Anti-Social Behaviour Act 2003 to cover 16- and 17-year-olds.

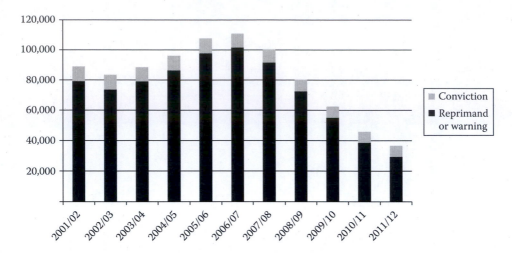

Figure 14.3 Trends in First-Time Entrants into the Youth Justice System, 2001/02–2011/12.
(Youth Justice Board and Ministry of Justice. (2013). *Youth justice statistics: England and Wales 2011/12*. London:
Ministry of Justice.)

Youth Victimization and the Crime Survey

The Crime Survey for England and Wales (previously called the British Crime Survey) was
first introduced in 1988; since 2009, the survey also includes interviews (approximately
4000 per year) with 10- to 15-year-olds. This addition to the survey reflects the growing
interest in developing more effective ways to prevent crime both against and by young people. Important new information has emerged as a result of the 10- to 15-year-olds' survey.
For example, we now know that 10- to 15-year-olds are more likely to be victims of violent
crime than adults are; a finding that would not otherwise have been highlighted.

The 10- to 15-year-olds' survey is much shorter than the adult survey taking just 15–20
minutes to complete; within this are questions on experience of crime, bullying, thoughts
on the police, and steps taken to keep belongings safe. There is a section where the young
person will type their answers directly onto the laptop, which covers cyberbullying, tru-
anting from school, alcohol and drugs, and carrying knives and street gangs. The crime
survey suggests that just under a quarter of children had contact with the police in 2009/10
(23%) and 22% reported having been bullied in that year in a way, which either frightened
or upset them, of whom around a quarter reported "cyberbullying" (i.e., having been sent
unwanted and nasty email or texts) (Morgan and Newburn 2012, 504).

Developments in the YJS

One of the most striking features of juvenile justice in England and Wales is the range of
agencies that are involved. The system has emerged on an ad hoc basis over the past hundred years. Indeed, one feature of juvenile justice is the range of competing approaches
to the problem of youth crime in the country. Here we provide a summary of historical developments before turning to the substance of this section, which revolves around

contemporary developments (for a more detailed history, see Gelsthorpe and Kemp 2002). We begin with a summary of the changes brought about by legislation, and then turn to other important events, which have implications for the YJS.

The Children Act 1908—Juvenile Justice: The Beginning

For much of its history, there has been relatively little formal differentiation between adult and juvenile offenders in the conception and delivery of criminal justice. However, following the emergence of a discourse on juvenile delinquency as a distinct social problem, the expansion of summary jurisdiction, and the expansion of reformatory and industrial schools, this changed through the Children Act 1908, which established the principle of dealing with juvenile offenders separately from adult offenders. Essentially, the act was founded upon three principles that are often taken to mark the beginnings of a welfare perspective within British juvenile justice:

- Juvenile offenders should be kept *separate* from adult criminals and should receive *treatment* differentiated to suit their special needs
- Parents should be made more responsible for the wrongdoing of their children
- The imprisonment of juveniles should be abolished

But the introduction of the juvenile court* reflected a primarily *symbolic* change in attitudes toward the juvenile offender. Juvenile courts remained *criminal* courts, and the procedures were essentially the same as for adults. Close scrutiny of matters suggests that the act reflected ideas and principles derived from concerns about criminal justice and crime control. From its inception, conflict and ambivalence were embedded in the concept of the juvenile court.

Children and Young Persons Act 1933

The juvenile courts retained their original character and structure until the 1933 act when there were some significant developments, namely, that there be a specially selected panel of magistrates to deal with juveniles and that the age of criminal responsibility be raised from the age of 7 to 8. The act also dictated that magistrates were to have consideration for "the welfare of the child." The juvenile court was to act in *loco parentis*, establishing itself as the forum capable of adjudicating on matters of family socialization and parental behavior, even if no "crime" as such had been committed (see Morris and McIsaac 1978; Rutherford 1986). A combination of **crime control** and **welfare** perspectives thus informed juvenile justice.

Politics and Juvenile Justice—1945 to 1970

Between 1945 and 1970, Britain experienced both Labour (1945–1951 and 1964–1970) and Conservative (1951–1964) administrations and reflected broad political consensus. One feature of this consensus was the creation of a postwar welfare state. This was the context

---

* Juvenile courts were initially special sittings of the magistrates' courts from which the public were excluded.

for a new phase in juvenile justice as it provided a backdrop for consensus with regard to criminal and juvenile justice policy. Nevertheless, despite the emergence of a welfare perspective in general and a sympathetic, child-oriented perspective in particular (Rose 1989), the war years had seen a new clamor for an unequivocally punitive perspective toward young offenders. Thus a concern for the welfare of the child coexisted with a tougher outlook, that is, a **crime control model** (see Table 1.1, in the Introduction to this book for further explanation of the model).

Labour Party criticisms emerged in *Crime-A Challenge to Us All*, the report of a Labour Party study group, published some months before the Labour Party came to power in 1964. A fundamental principle underlying the report was that "delinquents are to some extent a product of the society they live in and of the deficiencies in its provision for them" (Labour Party 1964, 28). One further issue was clear: juveniles had no personal responsibility for their offenses. The aim was to take juveniles out of the criminal courts and the penal system and to treat their problems in a family setting through the establishment of family advice centers, a family service and, for a minority, a family court. The subsequent report *The Child, the Family and the Young Offender* (Home Office 1965) proposed the abolition of the juvenile court and its replacement by a nonjudicial **family council**, linked to a unified **family service**. But there was concerted opposition to these proposals (from magistrates, lawyers, and probation officers who, commentators believe, did not want to lose the chance of working with young offenders) (Pitts 1988). In response to this opposition, the Labour Government produced a second report: *Children in Trouble* (Home Office 1968).

Children and Young Persons Act 1963

Key events in the postwar history of juvenile justice included the call from penal reformers, social work thinkers, and others for an urgent need to reorientate social services toward the maintenance of the family, not least because they believed juvenile crime often resulted from family breakdown. A government-led review subsequently proposed that the age of criminal responsibility be raised from 8 to 12 years; however, thereby replacing criminal with care proceedings for the younger age group. In the 1963 act, as a legislative compromise, the age of criminal responsibility was raised to 10.

Children and Young Persons Act 1969: The Eclipse of Welfare?

The culmination of this period of political activity was the 1969 Children and Young Persons Act. This dictated that juveniles under 14 were not to be referred to the juvenile court solely on the grounds that they had committed offenses (thus bringing Britain into line with many other European countries). Criminal proceedings were to be possible against juveniles aged 14–16 who had committed offenses, but only after mandatory consultation had taken place between the police and social service departments. The expectation was that these juveniles would be dealt with under care and protection proceedings and be dealt with by social workers in the main. There was also an attempt in the 1969 act to curtail magistrates' power to make use of custodial sentences. Further, detention centers and attendance centers were to be replaced by a new form of treatment—intermediate treatment (IT)—and the form, which this would take was also to be determined by social services (Bottoms et al. 1990).

Overall, the general aim of the act was to make the commission of an offense no longer a sufficient ground for intervention. That is, to **decriminalize** the court's jurisdiction; to reduce the number of juveniles appearing before the juvenile court—to *divert* juveniles wherever possible; and to abolish detention centers and Borstals and replace them with community measures—to encourage *deinstitutionalization*. Put very simply, the juvenile court was to become a welfare-providing agency, but also an agency of last resort: referral to the juvenile court was to take place only where voluntary and informal agreement could not be reached among social workers, juveniles, and their parents (Morris and McIsaac 1978).

The 1969 act brought latent tensions to the surface. The Conservative Party depicted the lawbreaker as choosing to commit offenses and as doing so from personal iniquity and from "demands" or "desires" exacerbated by the welfare state rather than from social inequality. Consequently, juvenile offenders were viewed as personally responsible for their actions although, depending on their age, parents might share in this responsibility, in that they had failed both to discipline their young and to inculcate in them basic values. Thus "family responsibility" was given a different force and meaning from that found in comparable Labour Party writings. More broadly, two opposing trends—first, an increase in punitive dispositions generally and in custodial dispositions in particular, and second, an increase in the use of diversion—occurred in the 1970s. Neither are overtly linked with welfare; the opposite, in fact. Indeed, there was a decline in the use of welfare-oriented dispositions despite the intentions underlying the act (see Gelsthorpe and Morris (1994) for more detailed analysis).

Criminal Justice Act 1982: The "Moment of Crime Control"

In the 1980s in England and Wales, as elsewhere, there was an explicit revival of traditional criminal justice values—a model of **crime control**. It is no accident that this coincided with and was fueled by the electoral campaigns and eventual election of a Conservative Government with a large majority. In electoral campaigns, the Conservative Party took a strong stand against crime, in contrast to the Labour Party, which was presented as excusing crime and as being sympathetic to offenders.

The Conservative Government's Criminal Justice Act 1982—hit at the root of the social welfare perspective underlying the 1969 act, although there was some endorsement for the expansion of diversion and a reduction in the minimum period of custody for which a boy could be held in a detention center. Clearly, there were moves toward the notion of personal responsibility, punishment, and parental responsibility. In brief, the 1982 act made available to magistrates three new powers of disposal: youth custody, care orders with certain residential requirements, and community service. Further, there were three major changes to existing powers: periods in detention centers became shorter, restrictions on activities as part of supervision orders became more common, and it was to become normal practice to fine the parents rather than the juvenile.

Changes in the 1982 act also required changes in social work practice. They forced social workers and probation officers to reconsider the provision and content of social enquiry reports (court reports) and to reform the provision and content of IT. Though the original form of IT continued to be available (as part of a supervision order), a new format was also introduced in the 1982 act—the supervised activity requirement. The significance of this was that the control and content of the order shifted to magistrates. This was an explicit attempt to increase the magistrates' confidence in such orders as realistic alternatives to custody.

Children Act 1989: A Return to Consensus?

The first significant event of the 1990s was the implementation of the 1989 Children Act. This represented a major structural alteration to the law concerning the welfare of juveniles and covered an enormous range of matters previously dealt with in different legislations. The law affecting juveniles who offend was only touched upon, but the resulting changes, together with the act's underlying sentiments about the nature of the relationship among the state, children, and their parents had significant implications for juvenile offenders.

The most important of these was the cessation of the use of the care order as a disposal available to the court in criminal proceedings and the removal of the offense condition in proceedings justifying state intervention in the life of a family. These changes at once recognized the enormous decline in the use made of the care order, the inappropriateness of a care order in criminal proceedings, the principle of determinacy in sentencing, and the importance that the government gave to parental responsibility. New rules also provided for the transfer of care proceedings from the juvenile court. These were shifted to a renamed "Family Proceedings" court, the newly named "Youth Court" dealing only with criminal proceedings.

Criminal Justice and Public Order Act 1994: A Punitive Turn?

The 1990s saw a dramatic repoliticization of youth justice. In part, this was fueled by the murder of 2-year-old James Bulger by two 10-year-old boys in 1993 (see Box 14.1) and by media-generated anxieties about serious and persistent young offenders (notwithstanding a lack of evidence to support the level of anxiety; Hagell and Newburn 1994).

The 1994 act supported a "toughening up" of penalties for young offenders (e.g., by increasing the maximum length of a sentence of detention for an offender 15–17 years [inclusive] in a young offenders' institution from 12 months to 2 years). The act also made further attempts to strengthen parental responsibility by making clear that in a parental bindover, the parent should ensure that the offender complies with the requirements of a community sentence. As a result of court cases in 1994 and 1995 (most notably the Bulger case), the principles governing the criminal responsibility of children between the ages of 10 and 13 were reviewed. As previously stated, the age of criminal responsibility

---

BOX 14.1   THE CASE OF JAMES BULGER

Two-year-old James Bulger was abducted from a shopping center and murdered by two 10-year-old boys in 1993. With sensationalized media reports, both nationally and internationally, this event was to trigger a moral panic that led to widespread moral outrage and concerns that the youth justice system (YJS) was failing to protect the public (see Smith and Sueda 2008). The government responded by embracing "populist punitive" (Bottoms 2002) rhetoric and introducing a package of measures, at the center of which was the reassertion of the centrality of custody (see Morgan and Newburn 2012, 508).

in England and Wales is 10 years, and children under that age could not be found guilty of a criminal offense. Children between 10 and 13 are presumed in law to be incapable of criminal intent and this presumption must be rebutted by the prosecution before they can be convicted. To rebut the presumption, the prosecution must show beyond all reasonable doubt that the child appreciated that what he or she did was "seriously wrong" as opposed to merely naughty or mischievous. Nevertheless, following the review, the principle of *doli incapax* was upheld on the grounds that there is wisdom in protecting young children against the full rigor of the criminal law because of the need to acknowledge varying rates of child development and maturity.

CDA 1998: Reforming the YJS

Throughout their opposition years 1979–1997, the Labour Party argued that youth crime and youth justice would be a priority if elected. A number of documents setting out the proposed reforms were published both prior to and following the election of the Labour Government (Labour Party 1996; Home Office 1997a, 1997b, 1997c, 1997d). The intention of the concomitant legislation, the CDA 1998, was described as a "comprehensive and wide-ranging reform programme" (Home Office 1997a, 1) and as "the biggest shake-up for 50 years in tackling crime" (Travis 1997). The legislation appeared to favor punishment to signal society's disapproval of criminal acts and deter offending. At the same time, however, it remained faithful to its commitment to be "tough on crime, tough on the causes of crime" by referring at times to social factors, which contribute to crime, and by proposing to prevent reoffending through an interventionist, welfare approach reminiscent of interventions in the 1960s and 1970s. The act also contained provisions that underlined support for the government's belief in restorative justice principles (through reparation orders, for instance). Therefore, while this juvenile justice model largely represented a **corporatist model** (see Table 1.1—Introduction), it is unclear where the balance lay between crime control and welfare.

In a way, none of this was unexpected. If the mood of the early 1990s can be characterized by the public response to the James Bulger case and fears about persistent young offenders, the shape of the CDA 1998 reflects a concern to control crime, to strike at the causes of crime through preventative measures and at the same time address the needs of victims.

The 1998 CDA was significant in all sorts of ways. The setting up of a national and local administrative framework for the YJS in England and Wales (via the YJB and YOTs/YOSs) itself can be seen as reflection of a managerialist thrust, which had been on the horizon in the 1980s. One major change brought about by the 1998 Act was to hold children to account for their criminal acts in the same way as adults. This was despite an earlier review, considered in relation to the 1994 Criminal Justice and Public Order Act, which upheld the rebuttable presumption of *doli incapax*; this was repealed by s. 34 of CDA 1998. British (excluding Scotland) children are almost alone in Europe in being regarded as criminals at the age of 10! The legislation of 1998 no longer shared the pure characteristics of a **corporatism model**, therefore, but may be described as a system, which reflected "juvenile penal law" (Walgrave and Mehlbye 1998) or even one which was "explicitly correctionalist" (Bottoms 2002).

The CDA 1998 adopted a scaled approach to youth justice by progressively indicating tougher and more intrusive penalties. This was a rigid scheme, which adopted an "escalator" or stepwise approach when dealing with 10- to 17-year-olds; for a first offense, there would be a reprimand and for a second offense, a final warning or criminal charges depending on the seriousness of the offense. Any further offending following a final warning would normally be dealt with at court (a second warning could only be given in very limited circumstances). A final warning initiated a referral to the local YOT/YOS for an assessment of what intervention may be required under programs of rehabilitative intervention. New court orders were also introduced, including the Reparation Order, the Drug Treatment and Testing Order, Action Plan Orders, and Curfew Orders.* Separate custody sentences were also replaced by the 1998 act with a generic Detention and Training Order. While the legislation made this custodial sentence available for all 10- to 17-year-olds, it is only effective for 12- to 17-year-olds at present.

Youth Justice and Criminal Evidence Act 1999

In addition to the 1998 act setting up a new range of sentences, the 1999 Youth Justice and Criminal Evidence Act introduced the **Referral Order**, which required the court to adopt a restorative approach when dealing with first-time offenders (aged 10–17 years) who pleaded guilty and for whom the court was not intending to impose a custodial sentence, hospital order, or absolute discharge. Essentially, the referral order involved the young offender being referred to the "youth offender panel" within the local YOT.† The panel then sought to reach an agreement with the offender for a program of activity based on a restorative justice approach, and which was also intended to prevent reoffending.‡ If the panel and offender did not agree on a contract, the case would return to the youth court for sentence, but otherwise the panel had continuing jurisdiction for the length of the contract. The referral order has been described as the "jewel in the crown" in the New Labour's youth justice reforms (Morgan and Newburn 2012, 519); however, an early assessment found that only a very small proportion of cases resulted in the active participation of victims (see Crawford and Newburn 2003), which arguably diminished the restorative justice component.

Altogether, the YJS was subjected to a massive shake-up, and while the aim was to make things clearer, responses to crime and antisocial behavior earlier, firmer, and more effective, it is not entirely clear whether it achieved its objectives (Morgan and Newburn 2012). What is unmistakable is that it resulted in more and more young people being drawn into the YJS, but there are other surrounding developments, which fueled the expansion in the number of children and young people being drawn into the YJS too. These include

---

* Other community sentences included community punishment orders and community punishment and rehabilitation orders. For details of the postcriminal court system sanctions available following the 1998 act, see Gelsthorpe and Kemp (2002, 147–151). An Intensive Supervision and Surveillance Programme was also introduced in 2001, a program, which was targeted at relatively serious and persistent offenders as an alternative to custody.

† The panel comprises a person from the YOT and two volunteers from the local community, the offender, the offender's parents/guardian, or local authority representative if under the care of the local authority, the victim (if s/he wishes to attend), the offender's friend (any person over 18—including a lawyer, although there is no provision for legal aid), the victim's friend, and any person thought "capable of being a good influence on the offender."

‡ The "youth offender contract" may require the offender to be at home at specified times, to attend school/work, to attend specified programs, to make restitution or reparation to their victim based on a restorative justice approach, and/or to attend victim–offender mediation schemes, and/or to perform unpaid community work.

- The introduction of a police performance target to bring more offenses to justice. By 2002, concerns were raised over police performance due to a low detection rate for offenses reported by members of the public. Within the new *managerial* ethos, the government published proposals for *Narrowing the Justice Gap* (CPS 2002). The report stated, "Bringing offenders to justice is the best way of demonstrating to criminals that their crimes will not go unpunished" (CPS 2002, Foreword). It was also noted at that time that "only a fifth of crimes reported to the police result in their perpetrator being brought to justice. We can and must do better" (CPS 2002, Foreword). From 2002, the police were given a target to increase the number of detections; this was then a contributing factor in the dramatic increase in the number of offenders drawn into the YJS from 2002 to 2006/07 (see Figures 14.1 and 14.2 above) (Padfield, Morgan, and Maguire 2012). From 2007, the performance target was revised to encourage the police to concentrate their efforts on more serious types of offenses. Subsequently, in 2010, the new Coalition Government abandoned this target and replaced it with a national police target to reduce crime (Greenwood 2010).
- From 2004, in addition to reprimands and warnings, the police were able to use **PNDs** for 16- and 17-year-olds (see footnote on p. 349). There is no requirement for the police to conduct an interview, and no admission of guilt is required. For a recordable offense, however, PNDs are recorded on the Police National Computer and can be disclosed on an Enhanced Criminal Records Disclosure issued by the Criminal Records Bureau.
- The CDA 1998 introduced the **ASBO** to take a stand against bad behavior (Home Office 2003; footnote on p. 349). In 2000, over half of those sentenced in court for breach received a custodial sentence (Campbell 2002).

These measures reflected broader "remoralization" and "respect" agendas as well as an aim to be more effective. Indeed, the Home Office had proposed that further civil penalties be imposed on children and their parents for antisocial behavior via education and housing law. There was also a government-led "Respect Unit" and a Youth Taskforce to stamp our antisocial behavior. One particular proposal in *Youth Matters* (DfES 2005) was to create equal opportunities to allow young people to be "included" in society, but in a negative and ironic twist outlined in the Respect Action Plan (Home Office 2006), there was a message that those who display antisocial behavior were to be denied any opportunities for social inclusion. Thus "tough on crime, tough on the causes of crime" was quickly becoming empty rhetoric and social disadvantage perhaps leading to social exclusion rather than inclusion. A Barnardo's report *Children in Trouble* (Monaghan, Moore, and Hibbert 2003, 6) indicated that we were witnessing "a tendency to criminalise children unnecessarily and at younger ages, and a corresponding tendency to treat them as adults too soon." Explicitly using the voices of a group of working-class young people who have been defined as a "social problem," France, Bottrell, and Armstrong (2012) emphasize how criminal identities and pathways are strongly influenced by the interactions embedded in political ecological systems and relationships.

Criminal Justice and Immigration Act 2008

The **Youth Rehabilitation Order** was introduced as a new generic community sentence under the 2008 act, replacing previous sentences in the community. Instead of having a range of different sentencing options, there is now a menu of 18 requirements that can be attached to this order to provide different types of intervention as required (including, e.g., a curfew, supervision, unpaid work, electronic monitoring, drug treatment, mental health treatment, education requirements, and restorative justice).

Whither Youth Justice? New Shifts in Thinking and Contemporary Issues and Pressures

We have witnessed some important shifts in thinking in recent years. The Criminal Justice and Immigration Act 2008 initiated a move away from the "prevention of offending and reoffending" to emphasize more clearly reform and rehabilitation, the protection of the public, reparation, and punishment. Other recent changes include a response to criticisms of the "scaled approach" adopted under the CDA 1998, which led to a dramatic expansion in the number of children and young people drawn into the formal YJS (Haines and Case 2012).

Legal Aid, Sentencing, and Punishment of Offenders Act 2012

The 2012 act has reduced and simplified the out-of-court landscape, simultaneously reflecting a push toward greater flexibility. Instead of the rigid approach adopted under the Final Warning scheme, the act introduces three new out-of-court disposals for juveniles: **community resolutions, youth cautions, and youth conditional cautions** (in which disposals can be used in any order rather than in an incremental fashion). A community resolution is intended to provide an informal response to low-level offending or antisocial behavior where the offender has been identified. It is primarily aimed at first-time offenders who have expressed remorse and, if agreed upon both by the offender and the victim, the offense can be resolved through an informal agreement between the parties instead of the police taking formal action. A community resolution can be delivered either with or without the use of restorative justice techniques.

Before taking formal action and imposing either a youth caution or youth conditional caution, the police must interview the young person (with at least one parent or guardian present).* Following the interview, if the offense is denied, the police must seek to prove the case in court or drop the matter. Where the police have sufficient evidence to charge the child or young person with an offense, and where the offense is admitted, they can decide to take *no further action* or informal action (community resolution for minor offenses), or impose a youth caution or youth conditional caution. These disposals are issued by a police officer in the presence of an appropriate adult and formally recorded. This means that these actions can be cited in court if the young person offends again in the future.

Youth cautions and youth conditional cautions are intended to be used as alternatives to prosecution for young offenders. The conditions that can be attached to the youth conditional caution can be reparative, rehabilitative, or punitive in nature. Having imposed a youth caution, the police have a statutory duty to refer the young offender to the

---

* If it is not possible for a parent or guardian to be present, then the police must arrange for "an appropriate adult" (e.g., a social worker or a "specialist" or "volunteer" provided through a professional or voluntary service) to accompany the child.

YOT/YOS. For a second or subsequent youth caution, or where a young person has previously received a youth conditional caution, the YOT has a statutory duty to carry out an assessment of the young offender and consider putting in place an intervention program aimed at preventing reoffending. When considering a youth conditional caution, the police have to refer the offender to the YOT, as an assessment is required before advising on the appropriate conditions.

The 2012 act also has implications for cases dealt with at court. While magistrates were previously required to impose a referral order for all first-time offenders (unless the offense was so minor as to warrant a discharge or so serious that custody was being considered), the act now encourages the court to discharge or fine young offenders in cases where it is proportionate to do so. Magistrates also have flexibility in appropriate cases to impose a referral order repeatedly.

The 2012 act also gives practitioners working with juveniles on court orders more flexibility when deciding on appropriate programs of intervention. This change is in contrast to the "scaled approach" which, from 2008, had required practitioners to adopt a tiered approach to interventions to reduce the likelihood of reoffending. Based on an assessment of their risks and needs, this approach had aimed to ensure that interventions were tailored to the individual. This involved the development of a risk-based assessment "tool," known as *Asset*, which gauged the risk of reoffending by children and young people. However, the scaled approach and its reliance on "risk factor" research has been much criticized, and its value on reducing reoffending has been called into question. Indeed, analysis of reconviction rates relating to the scaled approach found a significant increase in youth reconviction. This led Haines and Case (2012) to conclude that the "scaled approach is a failed approach."

With the election of the Coalition Government, there has been seen to be a move away from the centralist and prescriptive approach to youth justice management. In the Green Paper, *Breaking the Cycle*, for example, it was stated by the Coalition Government, "Professionals in the public, private and voluntary community sectors will be given much greater discretion" (Ministry of Justice 2010, para. 37). In April 2012, the Ministry of Justice revised the Youth Justice National Standards for Youth Offending Teams and Services. The one-year "Youth Justice Board Trial National Standards 2012" thus provided an opportunity to test and evaluate whether YOTs can have the "freedom and flexibility to adapt their practice" (Youth Justice Board 2012, 3). Subsequently, the Ministry of Justice (2013b) has published materials encouraging "Innovation and Evaluation in Youth Justice." These include resources and materials designed to assist youth justice practitioners in developing practice and programs and evaluating practice to measure its effectiveness.

This seems to be a departure from the centralist youth justice policies of the recent past, and as Briggs (2013, 28) notes, tends to "hark back to the more decentralized and localized practices." He also comments, "Only time will tell whether the Government's youth justice policy rhetoric will come to fruition."

So what type of model is now emerging? Arguably one, which is managerialist in approach, with cutting costs to the YJS being a priority, but also one in which there is more flexibility.

We have witnessed some important shifts in thinking in recent years. There have also been some sharp critiques of the seeming ineffectiveness of the elaborate YJS devised under Labour (Independent Commission on Youth Crime and Antisocial Behaviour 2010) with the damning conclusion that, at the very least, the system should seek to "do no harm"; the system should be based on principles of effectiveness, using problem-solving approaches. And there has been new thinking about the costs of it all. Thus the interventionist approaches under Labour have been increasingly questioned because of two related risks of criminalization: stigmatization and escalation through the criminal justice tariff. Indeed, a Youth Justice Board /Ministry of Justice Report (2012) has suggested that nearly 68% of all children and young people given ASBOs between 2000 and 2010 were breached, with 25% resulting in a custodial sentence for breach of conditions.

As indicated in Figures 14.1 and 14.2 in the preceding text, following the 1998 reforms, there was a marked rise in the number of young people being drawn into the system. Having examined the YJS, next explored are current issues facing young people in the YJS today.

Gender and the YJS

With a significant increase in the number of first-time entrants into the YJS, one consequence was that it became "silted up" with low-level offenders (Morgan and Newburn 2012). This is particularly the case with regard to girls and young women, despite there being no evidence of increase in self-reported offending by girls and young women (Phillips and Chamberlain 2006). The increasing criminalization of girls and young women has certainly caused concern (Gelsthorpe and Sharpe 2006; Howard League 2012); yet there is much scope to challenge the simplistic and demonizing popular representations of "bad" girls (Sharpe 2012). In essence, girls have been criminalized in courts when no intervention was needed or when they could be diverted to other services. This reflects magistrates' confusion regarding high welfare needs and high risk of reoffending, with resultant increases in the severity of sentences or "up-tariffing" girls.

Young People and the 2011 "Riots"

The early August 2011 public disorder in England and Wales (widely described as "riots") have perhaps given all YJS players pause for thought, since the evidence suggests that both children and young people participated (Downes and Morgan 2012). Will this result in more localized services to address their needs? Only time will tell. At the time of the riots, the prime minister commented on the lack of "responsibilization" of young people (see Box 14.2).

BOX 14.2   *THE TELEGRAPH*: UK RIOTS: DAVID CAMERON'S STATEMENT IN FULL

When we see children as young as 12 and 13 looting and laughing, when we see the disgusting sight of an injured young man with people pretending to help him while they are robbing him, it is clear that there are things that are badly wrong with our society. For me, the root cause of this mindless selfishness is the same thing I have spoken about for years. It is a complete lack of responsibility in parts of our society, people allowed to feel the world owes them something that their rights outweigh their responsibilities and their actions do not have consequences. Well, they do have consequences. We need to have a clearer code of standards and values that we expect people to live by and stronger penalties if they cross the line (Cameron 2011).

In the preceding text, we note how the Legal Aid, Sentencing and Punishment of Offenders Act 2012 provides increased opportunities for diverting juveniles from court and adopts a more flexible approach to court sentences, as well as being designed to reduce the number of juveniles sent to custody. However, with media-generated anxieties over the "riots" and "youth violence," the act also reflects a punitive approach with the creation of a new offense of "knife crime." The offense is "threatening with an article with blade or point or offensive weapon in public or on school premises," which attracts a deterrent-based sentence involving a mandatory minimum sentence of 4 months custody for 16- and 17-year-olds (with a maximum custodial sentence of 4 years). Thus, while there has been a shift toward diversionary policies in the 2012 act, there is also the adoption of harsher and more punitive penalties.

The YJS in Times of Austerity

As indicated, the Legal Aid, Sentencing and Punishment of Offenders Act 2012 has incorporated measures designed to introduce a more flexible approach to juvenile offenders (these include increased opportunities for diverting juveniles from court, e.g., and also adopting a more flexible approach to court sentences, designed to reduce the number of juveniles sent to custody). One explanation for this shift in policy is the current economic climate. Certainly, the funding and remit of youth justice is under scrutiny at present, alongside major structural changes with regard to many other areas of public policy, which have an impact on children's services (e.g., police, health, and education). These public sector policy reforms have been linked to the notion of the "Big Society" introduced by the Conservative Party in their party political manifesto—a flagship idea designed to empower local communities and roll back state responsibility. Morgan (2012) has suggested that behind the "Big Society" lurks the "big market" and indeed, the current government is encouraging new partnerships among the state and commercial and third sector (voluntary) organizations via "social investment" and "payment by results" to incentivize such new players. How far these developments will impinge on provision for young offenders, again, remains to be seen.

Since 2010, *parsimony* has become the new watchword in youth justice, with the concomitant result that we can see a rolling back of the criminalizing tendencies of previous governments. There have been increases in the use of out-of-court disposals, reductions in the number of young people coming into the courts, and a reduction in the number (if not the proportion) of young people being given custodial sentences. Such measures have undoubtedly been fueled by the incoming Coalition Government's dramatic public spending cuts from 2010. But new debates have also been prompted by sharp critiques of the continued high use of custody (and the high costs associated with this [£300m for 3% of offenses]), the possibility of racial discrimination in custodial sentencing, and the very poor quality and effectiveness of custodial care (including concerns about the use of restraints [Goldson 2011; Stone 2012; Morgan and Newburn 2012]). Indeed, it is arguable that the push toward restorative justice, better crime prevention, and better integration of young people outlined in the Independent Commission's report *Time for a Fresh Start* (2010), which acknowledges that the restorative justice that has been underplayed in the system, is not nearly radical enough (Goldson 2011). Haines and Case (2012), in particular, suggest that what is really needed is a system, which places children's rights and entitlements at the center of all initiatives and which addresses children's "needs" rather than "risks."

BOX 14.3   INNOVATIONS IN YOUTH JUSTICE

1. Putting Children First—An experiment in Wales, which has involved a policy to give emphasis to children's rights and entitlements (Case and Haines 2009).
2. Restorative Justice—Examples of restorative justice abound:
    a. Whether implemented by the police: see The Use of Community Resolutions (including Restorative Justice) guidelines, endorsed by the Association of Chief Police Officers: http://www.acpo.police.uk/documents/criminal justi ce/20/12/201298CJBAComResandRJ.pdf
    b. Or promoted within custody: http://www.justice.gov.uk/downloads/youth-justice/working-with-victims/restorative-justice/RJActionPlan25_10.pdf
3. In Plymouth, the youth offending services (YOSs) invite the public to suggest projects for reparative purposes—www.plymouth.gov.uk/homepage/education/lifelonglearning/youthservices/youthoffending/restorativejustice.htm.
4. The Youth Justice Board (YJB) has published guidance on key elements of effective restorative justice—http://yjbpublications.justice.gov.uk/en-gb/Resources/Downloads/KEEP_Restorative%20Justice.pdf—Other innovations revolve around the dissemination of good practice via the national YJB.
5. An Effective Practice Library—http://www.justice.gov.uk/youth-justice/effective-practice-library.
6. Effective Practice Toolkits—http://www.justice.gov.uk/youth-justice/toolkits—The toolkits, developed following direct work with services across England and Wales, enable youth offending teams (YOTs) to identify and address areas of underachievement, risk, or change. They are designed to help YOTs arrive at a clear understanding of the causes and contributory factors, select from a range of potential solutions that can be tailored to local circumstances, and learn from the best practice available.

Set out in Box 14.3 are examples of some recent innovations in youth justice.

Notwithstanding innovations and support for putting children first or adopting community-based resolutions, there are continuing concerns relating to the neglect of the rights of the child in a UK context.

The YJS and International Standards on the Rights of the Child

In 1989, the United Nations (UN) resolved to recognize specific children's rights worldwide through the Convention on the Rights of the Child (CRC). This was ratified by the United Kingdom in 1991—in relation to anyone under the age of 18. The CRC (Article 2) entitles every child "without regard to race, sex, language, religion, political or other opinion, national, ethnic or social origin, property, disability, birth or other status" to have resort to 40 specific rights ranging from the need for all actions relating to children to be in "their best interests" to "no child shall be deprived of his or her liberty unlawfully or arbitrarily." However, many of the principles underpinning the CRC are best known in the breach, and the United Kingdom is no exception here. The punitive framework for juvenile justice, which dominates policy certainly seems to be in contradiction to children's "best interests." The shift toward criminalization and retribution is telling (Muncie 2008). Eight states have been specifically criticized for merging the distinctions between adults and juveniles in custodial provisions, for example, the United Kingdom included. Overrepresentation of immigrant and minority groups under arrest or in detention has also drawn criticism. Indeed, some of the most punitive elements of juvenile justice appear to be increasingly used/reserved for the punitive control of immigrant or minority populations (Muncie 2008). The Ministry of Justice (2011) Section 95 report on race and criminal justice statistics shows an alarming rate of police stops and searches in relation to black and minority groups. Per 1000 of the population, for example, black persons were stopped and searched seven times more than white people in 2009/10 compared to six times more in 2006/07. The United Kingdom has shown considerable ambivalence in relation to the principles embodied in the CRC and thus far has resisted incorporating the principles into domestic legislation. The low age of criminal responsibility (10) continues to attract criticism from the UN Committee, which reviews compliance with the CRC articles as does the "offender first, child second" approach, although important distinctions should be recognized between the different legal jurisdictions in the United Kingdom and between England and Wales, with Wales taking steps toward a "children first" approach.

There are other international standards for children and young people involved in the YJS, which have been adopted by the UN. These include the UN Standard Minimum Rules for the Administration of Juvenile Justice (1985: "the Beijing Rules"); the UN Rules for the Protection of Juveniles Deprived of their Liberty (1990: "the Havana Rules"); and the UN Guidelines for the Administration of Juvenile Delinquency (1990: "the Riyadh Guidelines"). However, as found more generally within the YJS, there are tensions within these Conventions due to the potential for conflict between "just deserts" and "welfarist" imperatives (Putt and Walgrave 2006; McAra 2010, 291). In an exchange between the UN Committee and the Labour government in the late 1990s, it could be seen how the UNCRC, and other conventions, could be flouted. This dispute involved the UN Committee being critical of the government in England and Wales for intensifying modes of intervention into the lives of children and young people aimed at preventing crime under the CDA 1998. In response, the government had claimed that early intervention is an entitlement and that such preemptive policies contribute to "the right of children to develop responsibility for themselves" (UK Government 1999). Thus, as Muncie and Goldson (2006, 38) point out, the government in England and Wales was to appropriate a discourse of rights, which was to justify degrees of authoritarianism that were far removed from UN intentions.

Before presenting our summary and conclusions, we would like to offer a few words about juvenile justice in Ireland.

Juvenile Justice in Northern Ireland

Northern Ireland shared the same legal system as England and Wales until devolution in 1998 and was shaped by the same broad legislative and policy developments (McVie 2011). A Criminal Justice Review led to the Justice (Northern Ireland) Act 2002 and subsequently to some major transformations, including the setting up of a Youth Justice Agency—an executive agency which has strong parallels with the YJB in England and Wales, to oversee the YJS—giving national direction and structure, and maintaining a monitoring function. This was the first major legislative reform for juveniles since 1908; law and practice had attracted a good deal of criticism because of the low age of criminal responsibility at 7 years and overemphasis on institutionalization as well failure to comply with the CRC guidelines even though Northern Ireland ratified the CRC in 1992. Indeed, until the 1960s, juvenile crime was not seen to be a pressing issue. But with some excitement, the complex religious geopolitics in Northern Ireland ("the Troubles" and subsequent "Peace Agreement")* have given developments there a distinctive character, giving priority to restorative justice practices delivered by the voluntary sector, but very clearly promoted by the police (Jacobson and Gibbs 2009). The 2002 act enshrined in statute a wide-ranging youth conferencing model based firmly on restorative justice principles (Criminal Justice Review Group 2002, para. 68) with considerable police support (Jacobson and Gibbs 2009). It should be noted that the 2002 act embraced such measures as community-based penalties and other alternatives to detention, perhaps suggesting that the reforms reflect a number of "best practice" initiatives, and not just a commitment to restorative justice. Despite their shared histories, therefore, there are now sharp divergences between Northern Ireland and England and Wales. Notwithstanding concerns that the difficult social and economic climate is limiting full implementation of new initiatives, it is anticipated that conferencing will continue to be the primary response for almost all young people in Northern Ireland (O'Mahony and Campbell 2008). Critics of the system in England and Wales have looked on with envy, although there is recognition that the rhetoric and reality of restorative justice on the ground may be very different.

Whither Youth Justice? Summary

The history of juvenile justice in England and Wales shows increased politicization of issues and the criminalization of young people. There has been a clear departure from a welfare-based model, the adoption of a route through crime control and corporatist models, and now the development of a bifurcated model (with an expansion in precourt measures to divert young people from court) and tough measures (of custody) for the most serious offenders. The model is now one, which is explicitly correctionalist. Thus while there is positive endorsement of out-of-court options (e.g., restorative justice), there is also suspicion that cost considerations are the key drivers of the turn away from the court.

Moreover, although there has been a push for the increased use of community-based resolutions (including restorative justice), there are continuing concerns about the high use of custody and about the use of restraints within (Travis 2013) as well as the high reoffending rates upon release. Thus, the reversal of Labour's expansionist program and a push for less criminalization and punishment does not necessarily mean a restatement of new values for children and young people in trouble or fundamental rethinking of the shape of youth justice. What is clear is that the future direction of youth justice is *not yet clear*. There are ongoing debates about the age of criminal responsibility, and there is periodic recognition that what might be needed is a problem-solving approach rather than a punitive one, but there is governmental ambivalence. In many ways, we might describe the current situation as a "moment of ambivalence"; there is concern and quest for change with

---

* The Northern Ireland Peace Agreement or The Good Friday Agreement or Belfast Agreement as it is sometimes known, was a major political development in the Northern Ireland peace process of the 1990s. Northern Ireland's present devolved system of government is based on the agreement.

regard to making youth justice more child centered and problem-solving in orientation, but resistance to moving too far away from punitive rhetoric and practice.

Review/Discussion Questions

1. How can we best understand the volatile nature of youth justice policy in England and Wales? How do developments compare with what has happened in other countries?
2. What are your main criticisms of the current youth justice system in England and Wales?
3. How does the youth justice systems in England and Wales and Northern Ireland (see Chapter 11 for Scotland) fare in the context of European human rights and more particularly, children's rights?
4. Where next for youth justice in England and Wales and Northern Ireland? What can these countries within the United Kingdom learn from other countries?
5. What should youth justice look like?

References

Bailey, V. (1987). *Delinquency and Citizenship: Reclaiming the Young Offender 1914-1948*. Oxford: Clarendon Press.

Bottoms, A. (2002). On the decriminalisation of English juvenile courts. In J. Muncie, G. Hughes, and E. McLaughlin (Eds.), *Youth Justice, Critical Readings* (pp. 216–227). London: Sage.

Bottoms, A., Brown, P., McWilliams, B., McWilliams, W., and Nellis, M. (1990). *Intermediate Treatment and Juvenile Justice: Key Findings and Implications from a National Survey of Intermediate Treatment Policy and Practice*. London: HMSO.

Briggs, D. (2013). Conceptualising risk and need: The rise of actuarialism and the death of welfare? *Youth Justice: An International Journal*, 13(1): 17–30.

Brown, S. (1998). *Understanding Youth and Crime*. Buckingham: Open University Press.

Cameron, D. (2011, August 10). UK riots: David Cameron's statement in full. *The Telegraph*. Retrieved from: http://www.telegraph.co.uk/news/uknews/crime/8693134/UK-riots-David-Camerons-statement-in-full.html.

Campbell, S. (2002). *A Review of Anti-social Behaviour Orders*. Home Office Research Study 236. London: Home Office Research, Development and Statistics Directorate.

Case, S. and Haines, K. (2009). Putting children first in Wales: The evaluation of extending entitlement. *Social Work Review*, (3–4): 22–30.

CPS (Crown Prosecution Service). (2002). *Narrowing the justice gap*. London: CPS.

Crawford, A. and Newburn, T. (2003). *Youth Offending and Restorative Justice: Implementing Reform in Youth Justice*. Cullompton: Willan.

Criminal Justice Review Group. (2002). *Review of the Criminal Justice System in Northern Ireland: A Guide*. Belfast: HMSO.

DfES (Department for Education and Skills). (2005). *Youth Matters* (Command 6629). London: HMSO.

Downes, D. and Morgan, R. (2012). Overtaking on the left? The politics of law and order and the Big Society. In M. Maguire, R. Morgan, and R. Reiner (Eds.), *The Oxford Handbook of Criminology* (5th ed.) (pp. 182–205). Oxford: Clarendon Press.

France, A., Bottrell, D., and Armstrong, D. (2012). *A Political Ecology of Youth and Crime*. Basingstoke: Palgrave Macmillan.

Gelsthorpe, L. and Kemp, V. (2002). Comparative juvenile justice: England and Wales. In J. Winterdyk (Ed.), *Juvenile Justice Systems: International Perspectives* (2nd ed.) (pp. 127–169). Toronto: Canadian Scholars' Press.

Gelsthorpe, L. and Morris, A. (1994). Juvenile justice. In M. Maguire, R. Morgan, and R. Reiner (Eds.), *The Oxford Handbook of Criminology* (2nd ed.) (pp. 949–993). Oxford: Clarendon Press.

Gelsthorpe, L. and Sharpe, G. (2006). Gender, youth crime and justice. In B. Goldson and J. Muncie (Eds.), *Youth Crime and Justice* (pp. 47–62). London: Sage.

Goldson, B. (2011). Time for a fresh start, but is this it? A critical assessment of the report of the Independent Commission on Youth Crime and Antisocial Behaviour. *Youth Justice: An International Journal*, 11(1): 3–27.

Greenwood, C. (2010, June 29). Theresa May axes police performance targets. *The Independent*. Retrieved from: http://www.independent.co.uk/news/uk/home-news/theresa-may-axes-police-performance-targets-2013288.html.

Hagell, A. and Newburn, T. (1994). *Persistent young offenders*. London: Policy Studies Institute.

Haines, K. and Case, S. (2012). Is the Scaled Approach a Failed Approach? *Youth Justice: An International Journal*, 12(3): 212–228.

Hallsworth, S. and Silverstone, D. (2009). "That's life innit:" A British perspective on guns, crime and social order. *Criminology and Criminal Justice*, 9(3): 359–377.

Hendrick, H. (1990). Constructions and reconstructions of British childhood: An interpretive survey, 1800 to the present. In A. James and A. Roud (Eds.), *Constructing and Reconstructing Childhood: Contemporary Issues in the Sociological Study of Childhood* (pp. 33–60). London: Falmer Press.

Home Office. (1965). *The Child, the Family and the Young Offender* (Command 2742). London: HMSO.

Home Office. (1968). *Children in Trouble* (Command 3601). London: HMSO.

Home Office. (1997a). Tackling youth crime (Consultation paper). London: HMSO.

Home Office. (1997b). Tackling delays in the youth justice system (Consultation paper). London: HMSO.

Home Office. (1997c). New national and local focus on youth crime (Consultation paper). London: HMSO.

Home Office. (1997d). *No More Excuses: A New Approach to Tackling Youth Crime in England and Wales* (Command 3809). London: HMSO.

Home Office. (2003). *A Guide to Anti-Social Behaviour Orders and Acceptable Behaviour Contracts*. London: Home Office.

Home Office. (2006). *Respect action plan*. London: Home Office. Retrieved from: http://webarchive.nationalarchives.gov.uk/20060116185058/http://homeoffice.gov.uk/documents/respect-action-plan?view=Binary.

Howard League. (2012). Inquiry on girls: From courts to custody. (All Party Parliamentary Group on Women in the Penal System. Briefing paper). London: The Howard League for Penal Reform.

Independent Commission on Youth Crime and Antisocial Behaviour. (2010). *Time for a Fresh Start: The Report of the Independent Commission on Youth Crime and Antisocial Behaviour*. London: Police Foundation.

Jacobson, J. and Gibbs, P. (2009). *Making amends: Restorative justice in Northern Ireland*. London: Prison Reform Trust.

Labour Party. (1964). *Crime: A challenge to us all. Report of a Labour Party Study Group* (Chaired by F. Longford: the 'Longford Report'). London: Labour Party.

Labour Party. (1996). *Tackling Youth Crime, Reforming Youth Justice: A Consultation on an Agenda for Change*. London: Labour Party.

Lewis, P., Newburn, T., Taylor, M., Mcgillivray, C., Greenhill, A., Frayman, H., and Proctor, R. (2011). *Reading the Riots: Investigating England's Summer of Disorder*. London: London School of Economics and Political Science and the Guardian.

McAra, L. (2010). Models of youth justice. In D. Smith (Ed.), *A New Response to Youth Crime* (pp. 287–317). Cullompton: Willan.

McVie, S. (2011). Alternative models of youth justice: Lessons from Scotland and Northern Ireland. *Journal of Children's Services*, 6(2): 106–114.

Ministry of Justice. (2010). *Breaking the Cycle—Government Response*. London: HMSO.

Ministry of Justice. (2011). *Statistics on race and the criminal justice system 2010*. London: Ministry of Justice.

Ministry of Justice. (2013a). *Triennial review of the Youth Justice Board for England and Wales. Stage one report*. London: Ministry of Justice.

Ministry of Justice. (2013b). *Innovation and evaluation in youth justice*. Retrieved from: http://www. justice.gov.uk/youth-justice/improving-practice/innovation-and-evaluation-in-youth-justice

Monaghan, G., Moore, S., and Hibbert, P. (2003). *Children in Trouble: Time for Change*. Barkingside: Barnardo's.

Morgan, R. (2012). Crime and justice in the Big Society. *Criminology and Criminal Justice*, 12(5): 463–481.

Morgan, R. and Newburn, T. (2012). Youth crime and justice: Rediscovering devolution, discretion, and diversion? In M. Maguire, R. Morgan, and R. Reiner (Eds.), *The Oxford Handbook of Criminology* (5th ed.) (pp. 490–530). Oxford: Clarendon Press.

Morris, A. and McIsaac, M. (1978). *Juvenile Justice?* London: Heinemann.

Muncie, J. (2008). The 'punitive' turn in juvenile justice: Cultures of control and rights compliance in Western Europe and the USA. *Youth Justice: An International Journal*, 8(2): 107–121.

Muncie, J. and Goldson, B. (2006). *Youth Crime and Justice*. London: Sage.

O'Mahony, D. and Campbell, C. (2008). Mainstreaming restorative justice for young offenders through youth conferencing—The experience of Northern Ireland. In J. Junger-Tas and S. Decker (Eds.), *International Handbook of Juvenile Justice* (pp. 93–116). New York: Springer.

Padfield, N., Morgan, R., and Maguire, M. (2012). Out of court, out of sight: Criminal sanctions and non-judicial decision-making. In M. Maguire, R. Morgan, and R. Reiner (Eds.), *The Oxford Handbook of Criminology* (5th ed.) (pp. 955–985). Oxford: Oxford University Press.

Pearson, G. (1983). *Hooligan: A History of Respectable Fears*. London: Macmillan.

Phillips, C. and Chamberlain, V. (2006). *MORI five year report: An analysis of youth justice data*. London: Youth Justice Board.

Pitts, J. (1988). *The Politics of Juvenile Justice*. London: Sage.

Pitts, J. (2008). *Reluctant Gangsters: The Changing Face of Youth Crime*. Cullompton: Willan.

Postman, N. (1987). *Amusing Ourselves to Death*. York: Methuen.

Putt, J. and Walgrave, L. (2006). Belgium: From protection towards accountability. In J. Muncie and B. Goldson (Eds.), *Comparative Youth Justice* (pp. 111–126). London: Sage.

Rose, N. (1989). *Governing the Soul: The Shaping of the Private Self*. London: Routledge.

Rutherford, A. (1986). *Growing Out of Crime*. Harmondsworth: Penguin.

Sharpe, G. (2012). *Offending Girls. Young Women and Youth Justice*. London: Routledge.

Smith, D. and Sueda, K. (2008). The killing of children by children as a symptom of national crisis: Reactions in Britain and Japan. *Criminology and Criminal Justice*, 8(1): 5–25.

Stone, N. (2012). Legal commentary 'A sorry tale': Forcible physical restraint of children in custody. *Youth Justice: An International Journal*, 12(3): 245–257.

Travis, A. (1997, September 26). Straw to combat crime-breeding excuse culture. *The Guardian*, p. 9.

Travis, A. (2013, March 14). MPs alarmed at rising use of force to restrain young offenders in detention. *The Guardian*. Retrieved from: http://gu.com/p/3edh6.

UK Government. (1999). *Convention on the rights of the child: Second report to the UN Committee on the Rights of the Child by the United Kingdom*. London: HMSO.

Walgrave, L. and Mehlbye, J. (1998). An overview: Comparative comments on juvenile offending and its treatment in Europe. In J. Mehlbye and L. Walgrave (Eds.), *Confronting Youth in Europe: Juvenile Crime and Juvenile Justice* (pp. 21–53). Copenhagen: AKF Forlaget.

Wikström, P.-O., Oberwittler, D., Treiber, K., and Hardie, B. (2012). *Breaking rules: The Social and Situational Dynamics of Young People's Urban Crime*. Oxford: Oxford University Press.

Youth Justice Board. (2012). *National Standards trial April 2012—April 2013*. Retrieved from: http://www.justice.gov.uk/downloads/youth-justice/national-standards-trial/national-standards-trial-2012.pdf.

Youth Justice Board and Ministry of Justice. (2012). *Youth justice statistics: England and Wales 2010/11*. London: Ministry of Justice.

Youth Justice Board and Ministry of Justice. (2013). *Youth justice statistics: England and Wales 2011/12*. London: Ministry of Justice.

Internet Sources

Council of Europe: Commissioner on Human Rights: See thematic reports on children's rights—http://www.refworld.org/publisher/COECHR.html (filter thematic reports on children's rights).

Howard League for Penal Reform: Offers a wide range of briefing papers and critiques on youth justice—http://www.howardleague.org/.

National Association for the Care and Resettlement of Offenders: Offers briefing and research papers on youth justice law, policy and practice—https://www.nacro.org.uk/publications/publications/list-resources.html.

Prison Reform Trust: Offers critical and accessible commentary on developments in criminal justice policy—http://www.prisonreformtrust.org.uk/.

Youth Justice Board for England and Wales: Offers a full description of the system, publications and statistics—http://www.justice.gov.uk/about/yjb.

Juvenile Justice in the United States

15

PETER J. BENEKOS AND
ALIDA V. MERLO

Contents

Introduction	370
Historical Developments	370
Prevailing Delinquency Theories	376
The Juvenile Justice and Delinquency Prevention Act of 1974	377
Detention	378
The U.S. Supreme Court and Youth	379
Capital Punishment and Life without Parole Sentences for Youth	381
Evidence-Based Practice	384
Juvenile Justice Models	385
Protection of Children and Youth	386
Adolescence and Psychological Development	387
Continuing and Future Issues	387
Review/Discussion Questions	390
References	390
Internet Sources	394

FACTS ABOUT THE UNITED STATES

Area: By land mass, the United States is the third-largest country and includes 50 states and the nation's capital, the District of Columbia, encompassing 3.79 million square miles (9.83 million square kilometers). **Population:** The national population in 2012 (estimate) was 313,914,040, with 23.5% of the population under 18 years. About 17% of the population was Hispanic or Latino and 13% was African American. With a population of 8.3 million (estimate), New York City is the largest city in the United States, followed by Los Angeles, California (3.8 million), and Chicago, Illinois (2.7 million). Population growth ranged from approximately 1.6% in 1960 to 7% in 2011. Population density is about 87.4 people per square mile. **Climate:** The overall climate of the United States is temperate, but varies considerably with the seasons of the year. There are nine distinct regional climates and they combine both tropical and colder climates. **Government:** Washington is the nation's capital (population: 4.1 million). The United States is a federal democracy with three branches of government: legislative, judicial, and executive. The bicameral legislative branch includes 435 members of the House of Representatives and 100 members of the Senate. The judicial branch includes a nine-member Supreme Court and 11 United States Courts of Appeal. The

(Continued)

FACTS ABOUT THE UNITED STATES (*Continued*)

president heads the executive branch of government and is elected for a 4-year term, and may be elected a second term. **Economy:** In 2012, the United States had an estimated gross domestic product (GDP) of $15.7 trillion (€12.10 trillion) with a *per capita* GDP of $49,600 (€38,300). The GDP by sector is about 1% agriculture, 19% industry, and 80% services. The main export partners are Canada (19%), Mexico (13%), China (7%), and Japan (5%). Unemployment is 8.2% (United States Census Bureau 2014).

Introduction

Juvenile justice in the United States is not one system but rather 51 systems that are legislated by each state and the federal government. The respective systems are guided by policies and philosophies that reflect state and regional differences while also maintaining some continuity with established national guidelines and judicial opinions and mandates. In 2012, there were approximately 314 million people living in the United States, and about 74 million were youth under the age of 18 (OJJDP Statistical Briefing Book 2013). This chapter identifies general themes and developments, and presents characteristics that reflect prevailing views and policies of juvenile justice in the United States. The information includes consideration of the United Nations Standard Minimum Rules for the Administration of Juvenile Justice ("the Beijing Rules") adopted in 1985 and how they are (or are not) reflected in U.S. policies and practices. Several of "the Beijing Rules" that will be referenced in this chapter are listed in Table 15.1.

Some of the ideals and guidelines presented in "the Beijing Rules" are evident in the objectives and priorities legislated in the Juvenile Justice and Delinquency Prevention (JJDP) Act of 1974, which established "core protections" for the treatment and handling of youth. This was lauded as a "landmark" legislation, which mandated reforms that refocused juvenile justice on protection and rehabilitation of juvenile offenders.

This chapter provides a brief history of the founding and evolution of the juvenile court, a review of models and philosophies that have guided juvenile justice practice, contemporary developments including legislative reforms and judicial decisions, and future issues in juvenile justice. The authors identify salient features of juvenile justice in the United States and describe characteristics that demonstrate how juvenile offenders experience justice in the United States.

Historical Developments

In the late 1880s, the original framers of the court envisioned a special court where juvenile proceedings would be confidential, and judges and court personnel would act in the best interests of the child. Juveniles were to be accorded different care and treatment than their adult counterparts. In brief, youth were considered to be malleable and capable of being reformed. Although the child savers focused their attention primarily on poor children, their commitment was unwavering. Their efforts resulted in An Act to Regulate the Treatment and Control of Dependent, Neglected, and Delinquent Children, which was passed unanimously by the Illinois legislature in April of 1899 (Tanenhaus 2004, 22).

Table 15.1   Selected Rules from the United Nations Standard Minimum Rules for the Administration of Juvenile Justice ("the Beijing Rules") Adopted in 1985

7. Rights of Juveniles

7.1 Basic procedural safeguards such as the presumption of innocence, the right to be notified of the charges, the right to remain silent, the right to counsel, the right to the presence of a parent or guardian, the right to confront and cross-examine witnesses, and the right to appeal to a higher authority shall be guaranteed at all stages of proceedings.

13. Detention Pending Trial

13.4 Juveniles under detention pending trial shall be kept separate from adults and shall be detained in a separate institution or in a separate part of an institution also holding adults.

15. Legal Counsel, Parents and Guardians

15.1 Throughout the proceedings, the juvenile shall have the right to be represented by a legal adviser or to apply for free legal aid where there is provision for such aid in the country.

17. Guiding Principles in Adjudication and Disposition

17.1 (b) Restrictions on the personal liberty of the juvenile shall be imposed only after careful consideration and shall be limited to the possible minimum.

Source: UN General Assembly. (1985). United Nations Standard Minimum Rules for the Administration of Juvenile Justice ("the Beijing Rules"): Resolution/Adopted by the General Assembly. A/RES/40/33. http://www.refworld.org/docid/3b00f2203c.html (accessed May 10, 2013).

According to Tanenhaus (2004, 22), the court's principal proponents, Lucy Flower and Julia Lathrop, "succeeded in writing their ideals about childhood innocence and public responsibility into law."

In the intervening 115 years, the court has undergone a series of transformations resulting in the "adultification" of youth. The decade of the 1990s represented a dramatic shift in perceptions of youth and in policy reactions to delinquent offending. Perhaps the most noteworthy changes occurred when legislatures drafted new statutes, which facilitated the transfer of more youth to adult criminal court. As indicated in Figure 15.1, more juveniles were waived to adult court for "person offenses" (e.g., homicide, rape, aggravated assault, or armed robbery) in 2010 than in 1985, but judicial waivers have decreased since the mid-1990s, most likely offset by statutory exclusion and decreased crime rates.

Although judicial waiver had been the primary method to determine whether youth should be retained in the juvenile system, changes in state statutes authorized that certain youth could be automatically excluded from the juvenile court if they engaged in specified offenses. As Adams and Addie (2010, 2) noted, "Legislatures in nearly every state revised or rewrote their laws to broaden the scope of transfer-lowering age and/or offense thresholds, moving away from individual and toward categorical handling, and shifting authority from judges to prosecutors." In 11 states, prosecutors were granted more authority. By amending or enacting existing concurrent jurisdiction statutes, legislators made it possible for prosecutors (alone) to decide which youth would be waived to adult court in specified cases (Adams and Addie 2010, 2). These expanded transfer provisions suggest that the juvenile court might be less willing to deal with delinquent youth today than in the past.

Judicial waiver also was used more frequently in the 1990s. In terms of volume, 1994 was the peak year for judicially waived cases to be transferred to adult court. According to Puzzanchera, Adams, and Hockenberry (2012, 40), that year, represented a 91% increase

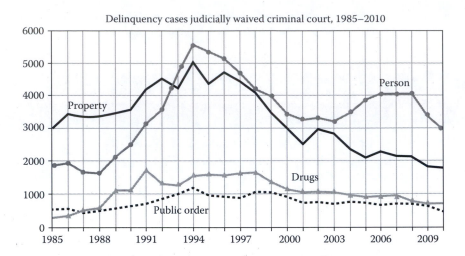

Figure 15.1 Trends in juvenile waiver in the United States, 1985–2010. (OJJDP [Office of Juvenile Justice and Delinquency Prevention] Statistical Briefing Book. (2013). http://www.ojjdp.gov/ojstatbb/population/qa01101.asp (accessed June 26, 2013).)

over the number of delinquency cases waived in 1985. In brief, not only did the range of waiver mechanisms expand but there was also greater utilization of existing mechanisms.

Overall, more youth are being processed through the juvenile justice system. It is clear that a more formal approach to youth has evolved. For example, as illustrated in Figure 15.2, in 2010, 1,369,151 cases were processed by the juvenile courts compared to 405,000 in 1960. Although that number represents a decrease from the peak year (1997), there has been a shift toward more youth being referred to court. Puzzanchera, Adams, and Hockenberry (2012) report that in 2010, juvenile courts processed about 3700 delinquency cases on a daily basis compared to 1100 in 1960.

Decisions to refer youth to the juvenile justice system might seem like a benevolent approach. However, there is little evidence to support that position. Research by Petrosino, Turpin-Petrosino, and Guckenberg (2010, 38) examined 29 experimental studies conducted on juveniles over a 35-year period and found that "system processing results in more subsequent delinquency." In a 20-year longitudinal study, Gatti, Tremblay, and Vitaro (2008, 996) found evidence of the "inefficacy of the juvenile justice system and also its iatrogenic effects."

Legislators also determined that maintaining closed juvenile court proceedings and shielding youth from having their names publicized in the media were no longer consistent with the court's mission. By the end of 2004, legislators in 14 states authorized juvenile court hearings to be open to the public, and in another 21 states, they enacted statutes that allowed open delinquency proceedings for certain types of offenses (Snyder and Sickmund 2006, 108). Similarly, juvenile records, which were once treated as confidential were no longer perceived to be "off limits." In fact, Snyder and Sickmund (2006, 109) reported that all states now make certain parts of the record available to various individuals from schools to the public. Although it is not an automatic release of the information, it is a distinct change in policy from previous years.

These punitive policies are inconsistent with the framers' perspectives on the best interests of wayward youth who would benefit from the benevolent juvenile court attention and concern for child welfare. By contrast, they demonstrate a more intolerant attitude toward

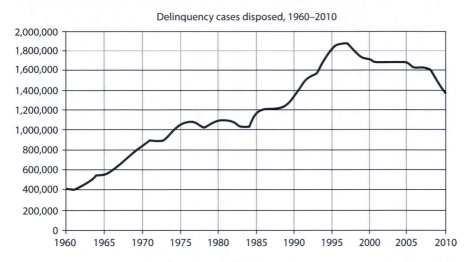

Figure 15.2 Number of delinquency cases handled by the courts, 1960–2010. (OJJDP [Office of Juvenile Justice and Delinquency Prevention] Statistical Briefing Book. (2013). http://www. ojjdp.gov/ojstatbb/population/qa01101.asp (accessed June 26, 2013).)

youth. Despite these trends and a system, which is now more focused on accountability, there are also indications that the juvenile court is not yet ready to cast rehabilitation and the child's best interests adrift. There are developments which indicate a continuing commitment to children. Rather than suggest that the court has adopted entirely punitive or rehabilitative philosophies, it seems the court has adopted a more ambivalent approach toward youth than when it first emerged in Cook County, Illinois, in 1899.

Progressive Era advocates made significant contributions to juvenile justice policy. During the 1920s, they drafted Juvenile-Court Standards, which provided a model that states could employ to assess how well their policies adhered to the philosophy of the early court. The standards included "broad and exclusive jurisdiction until at least age eighteen, private hearings, confidential records, and individualized treatment" (Tanenhaus 2004, 132). These tenets characterized the juvenile justice system and the Standards prevailed until the 1950s.

The juvenile court ideals shifted slowly in the 1960s, when there was greater attention to due process protections and a more formal juvenile system. Beginning in the late 1970s and 1980s, a punitive model evolved with calls for greater accountability. Three dimensions, namely, increased media attention directed at violent youth and crime, a more conservative ideology, and the influence of politics affected juvenile justice policy (Benekos and Merlo 2006). The current system reflects the punitive approach while simultaneously incorporating some elements of the original ideals.

Although the incidence of youth involvement in violent crimes peaked in the mid-1990s and subsequently declined, some of the get tough policies that emerged during that time have continued. The declining arrest trends, however, have coincided with a softening of punitive juvenile justice policies.

Data from the Federal Bureau of Investigation (FBI) indicate that arrests of youth under age 18 years declined from 1,382,486 in 2002 to 962,452 in 2011, a 30% decrease. As indicated in Table 15.2, from 2002 to 2011, juvenile arrests for violent crimes declined 28.5% (56,681–41,940). In fact, from 2002 to 2011, juvenile arrests for all index offenses decreased (Federal Bureau of Investigation 2012, Table 32). With attention to increased

Table 15.2 Juvenile Arrests for Index Offenses: Ten-Year Trends (2002–2011)

Offense Charged	Number of Persons Arrested								
	Total All Ages			Under 18 Years of Age			18 Years of Age and Over		
	2002	2011	Percent Change	2002	2011	Percent Change	2002	2011	Percent Change
TOTAL*	8,608,479	7,994,216	−7.1	1,382,486	962,542	−30.4	7,225,993	7,031,674	−2.7
Murder and nonnegligent manslaughter	7,630	6,752	−11.5	679	500	−26.4	6,951	6,252	−10.1
Forcible rape	17,293	12,069	−30.2	2,814	1,735	−38.3	14,479	10,334	−28.6
Robbery	67,523	67,791	+0.4	15,339	14,360	−6.4	52,184	53,431	+2.4
Aggravated assault	305,232	258,765	−15.2	39,849	25,345	−36.4	265,383	233,420	−12.0
Burglary	189,315	193,993	+2.5	56,995	40,253	−29.4	132,320	153,740	+16.2
Larceny-theft	755,039	840,187	+11.3	227,824	172,003	−24.5	527,215	668,184	+26.7
Motor vehicle theft	86,046	40,876	−52.5	26,324	8,301	−68.5	59,722	32,575	−45.5
Arson	10,790	7,385	−31.6	5,616	3,210	−42.8	5,174	4,175	−19.3
Violent crime†	397,678	345,377	−13.2	58,681	41,940	−28.5	338,997	303,437	−10.5
Property crime†	1,041,190	1,082,441	+4.0	316,759	223,767	−29.4	724,431	858,674	+18.5
Other assaults	802,791	808,239	+0.7	148,787	123,198	−17.2	654,004	685,041	+4.7
Forgery and counterfeiting	76,770	45,543	−40.7	3,454	1,017	−70.6	73,316	44,526	−39.3
Fraud	217,608	112,059	−48.5	5,953	3,531	−40.7	211,655	108,528	−48.7
Embezzlement	13,289	11,075	−16.7	996	296	−70.3	12,293	10,779	−12.3

Stolen property; buying, receiving, possessing	81,686	61,880	-24.2	17,234	8,907	-48.3	64,452	52,973	-17.8
Vandalism	178,566	158,679	-11.1	70,119	45,901	-34.5	108,447	112,778	+4.0
Weapons; carrying, possessing, etc.	100,878	95,423	-5.4	22,175	17,727	-20.1	78,703	77,696	-1.3
Prostitution and commercialized vice	44,376	34,936	-21.3	906	677	-25.3	43,470	34,259	-21.2
Sex offenses (except forcible rape and prostitution)	60,154	46,198	-23.2	12,587	8,400	-33.3	47,567	37,798	-20.5
Drug abuse violations	968,518	954,164	-1.5	117,610	94,134	-20.0	850,908	860,030	+1.1
Gambling	4,214	2,691	-36.1	316	133	-57.9	3,898	2,558	-34.4
Offenses against the family and children	86,762	67,591	-22.1	6,025	2,287	-62.0	80,737	65,304	-19.1
Driving under the influence	857,295	765,635	-10.7	13,543	6,612	-51.2	843,752	759,023	-10.0
Liquor laws	430,374	327,482	-23.9	99,260	61,610	-37.9	331,114	265,872	-19.7
Drunkenness	398,859	370,093	-7.2	12,648	7,959	-37.1	386,211	362,134	-6.2
Disorderly conduct	418,153	367,175	-12.2	121,555	88,744	-27.0	296,598	278,431	-6.1
Vagrancy	16,059	17,700	+10.2	1,427	1,190	-16.6	14,632	16,510	+12.8
All other offenses (except traffic)	2,319,481	2,268,214	-2.2	258,673	172,891	-33.2	2,060,808	2,095,323	+1.7
Suspicion	2,873	932	-67.6	1,092	90	-91.8	1,781	842	-52.7
Curfew and loitering law violations	93,778	51,621	-45.0	93,778	51,621	-45.0	—	—	—

Source: From Federal Bureau of Investigation. (2012). Uniform Crime Reports, 2011. http://www.fbi.gov/about-us/cjis/ucr/crime-in-the-u.s/2011/crime-in-the-u.s.-2011/tables/table-32 (accessed June 24, 2013).

* Does not include suspicion.

† Violent crimes are offenses of murder and nonnegligent manslaughter, forcible rape, robbery, and aggravated assault. Property crimes are offenses of burglary, larceny-theft, motor vehicle theft, and arson.

fiscal constraints and evidence of successful interventions, the decline in juvenile crime
has created opportunities to reexamine assumptions and perspectives on juvenile justice
policy.

Prevailing Delinquency Theories

In the context of juvenile justice policy, several theories of delinquency have guided philosophies and legislative reforms in the United States. For example, Cloward and Ohlin (1960)
elaborated on the concepts of anomie in their treatise, *Delinquency and Opportunity*, in
which they examined the relationship between illegitimate opportunities and delinquency.
Their work was considered a catalyst for a massive delinquency prevention program,
Mobilization for Youth, and was also considered instrumental in the social reform movement known as the War on Poverty (Stricker 2007).

The intent of this section is not to review the exhaustive literature on delinquency
theory but rather to focus attention on a few theories that remain salient in explaining
delinquency and guiding policies and intervention strategies. For more detailed information on crime and delinquency theories, consider *The Juvenile Justice System: Delinquency,
Processing, and the Law* by Champion, Merlo, and Benekos (2013), and *Introduction to
Criminology: Theories, Methods, and Criminal Behavior*, by Hagan (2012).

From a classic perspective, understanding delinquency has often reflected class and
race bias focused on studying lower-class, urban youth. With attention to urban settings
with their concentrations of poverty and heterogeneous populations, social disorganization
theory (Shaw and McKay 1972) recognizes that youth in certain areas are disproportionately at risk for exposure to delinquency influences and limited legitimate opportunities.
This theory examines delinquency in an environment of family disunity, limited social
resources, underfunded schools, and deteriorated facilities. These factors and conditions
generate a street culture, which is transmitted to youth and perpetuated through social
learning. The principles of differential association (Sutherland 1951) explain how the street
values and behaviors are transmitted or learned; the theory of lower-class focal concerns
identifies the "codes" that are learned and reinforced (Miller 1958). Miller identified trouble, toughness, smartness, excitement, fate, and autonomy as six core concerns or characteristics of delinquents growing up in inner cities.

These principles continue to influence the understanding of this population of delinquents. In his book, *Code of the Street*, Anderson (1999) described the informal rules that
have replaced the rule of law, and help to explain the prevalence of violence and the justification for antisocial behaviors. A related perspective that complements this explanation of
delinquency is the strain theory. From Durkheim to Merton to Agnew, there is a strong tradition of explaining delinquency as an adaptation to blocked opportunities, hopelessness,
and alienation (Champion, Merlo, and Benekos 2013, 97). These motivational theories (i.e.,
social disorganization, lower-class focal concerns, strain, and differential association) continue to offer explanations for why and how youth engage in delinquent behavior. A more
contemporary model of delinquency, which reflects the neoclassical approach of "rational
choice" and situational explanations is the routine activities theory (Felson and Cohen
1979). This theory explains the occurrence of delinquency as a confluence of motivated
offender, suitable target, and lack of guardianship. The model lends itself to delinquency
prevention by supporting target hardening and deterrence efforts.

While the motivational theories explain why youth commit delinquency, there are also theories that look at why youth resist opportunities and avoid the situations that increase the risk of delinquency. The idea that youth would become delinquent if they could, suggests some restraining influences to prevent delinquency. Hirschi (1969) explained that prosocial bonds could serve to control youth. This social control theory included four bonds: attachments to family and emotional links to respected others; commitment and enthusiasm to relationships; belief in moral rightness of certain conduct; and involvement with others in conventional conduct and activities (Champion, Merlo, and Benekos 2013, 101). The theory characterizes delinquents as youth with weak bonds to conventional society, which increase susceptibility to delinquent peers and their negative influences.

In an effort to specify the delinquency theory further, Gottfredson and Hirschi (1990) developed another control explanation, which attributed delinquency to low self-control resulting from poor parenting. This was an attempt to explain all criminality by the low level of internalized control developed by individuals at a young age, which put them on a trajectory toward delinquency. As an effort to develop a "general theory" of crime, the self-control theory of delinquency has been criticized for its characterization of families (especially the role of women) and for its implications of family regulation policies (Hagan 2012).

Delinquency is a complex phenomenon that has produced numerous theoretical explanations. The theories noted earlier provide a sense of some of the social antecedents and conditions that are linked to delinquency. Essentially, delinquency is an epiphenomenon of adolescence, but very few youth become violent, serious offenders. Nonetheless, it is the minority of adolescents that generate the most media attention and policy reactions including punitive legislation. Fortunately, there are strategies to prevent and reduce delinquency, and some theories provide foundations for developing programs and interventions.

The Juvenile Justice and Delinquency Prevention Act of 1974

As previously noted, in 1974, Congress enacted the JJDP Act (see Box 15.1). There were two specific goals: the deinstitutionalization of status offenders and the sight and sound separation of youth in adult institutions (OJJDP n.d.). In 1980, Congress amended the legislation to include the removal of youth from adult jails. The directive to remove status offenders

BOX 15.1   THE JUVENILE JUSTICE AND DELINQUENCY PREVENTION ACT

When Congress enacted The Juvenile Justice and Delinquency Prevention (JJDP) Act in 1974, the legislation included provisions for the creation of the Office of Juvenile Justice and Delinquency Prevention in the Department of Justice. This legislation enabled the federal government to engage more actively in juvenile justice policy and to aid states in developing initiatives to prevent or reduce delinquency and to enhance the juvenile justice system. Key tenets included the removal of status offenders from custodial institutions intended for youth who had been adjudicated delinquent and the sight and sound separation of youth from adult offenders in adult institutions. Several amendments to the legislation have occurred in the intervening years, including removal of youth from adult jails, a federal mandate to address disproportionate minority confinement (later amended to contact), and gender-specific programming.

from institutions designed to hold delinquent youth signaled a major shift in policy in the United States. Youth referred to the juvenile court for offenses like school truancy, running away, curfew violation, or incorrigibility could no longer be subjected to the same sanctions as youth who were adjudicated delinquent for acts that would be crimes if committed by adults (OJJDP n.d.).

The second goal, sight and sound separation, was designed to prevent youth from any contact with adult offenders (OJJDP Legislation n.d.). Youth alleged to be delinquent or adjudicated delinquent were not to be held in an adult institution where they would have contact with adult offenders. The original legislation, and its subsequent amendment in 1980 regarding removal of juveniles from adult jails, established the separation of juveniles from adults, both by sight and sound, and the importance of processing cases in a timely manner (Champion, Merlo, and Benekos 2013, 191). The federal government encouraged states to refrain from placing youth handled by the juvenile court in any jail or adult lockup institution. Although this legislation was not legally binding on the 50 states, compliance was linked to federal funding of state programs and initiatives.

Since the 1980s, Congress amended the legislation to address evolving issues pertaining to children and youth. For example, subsequent provisions focused on disproportionate minority confinement in 1988 and new programming for girls to address gender bias in 1992. In 2002, Congress expanded disproportionate minority confinement to disproportionate minority contact (DMC) (OJJDP Legislation n.d.). To facilitate implementation, the federal government provided both technical assistance and funding to prevent or reduce critical problems. For example, in 2002, the federal government provided a minimum of $600,000 to each state. However, a state's allocations were reduced by 20% for every core requirement when the state was not in compliance with the legislation's directives (Juvenile Justice and Delinquency Prevention Allocation to States 2002).

In efforts to reduce DMC, state legislatures have employed various strategies and policy initiatives (Brown 2012). In Connecticut, a statute authorizes a commission to develop special training for court personnel, including judges, on how to address specific issues like disproportionate minority confinement. A Washington State law requires the court administrator to develop a curriculum designed to promote understanding diversity and its impact on working with youth and their families (Szymanski 2012). Although there is no uniform curriculum in the 50 states, recognition of the importance of training juvenile justice personnel in cultural and racial diversity has become more prominent.

Detention

Rule 13.1 of the United Nations Standard Minimum Rules for the Administration of Juvenile Justice ("the Beijing Rules"—also, see the Introduction in this collection) discusses juvenile detention. Specifically, detention is the last resort for youth, and the stay should be as brief as possible (UN General Assembly 1985). Ideally, youth who must be held are to be placed in alternative settings rather than a juvenile detention facility or an adult jail while waiting for court appearances. Juvenile detention policy in the United States reflects this rule. In most cases, youth are in the community rather than in juvenile detention centers while their case proceeds. For example, Knoll and Sickmund (2012) reported that 79% of youth referred to the court for delinquent conduct in 2009 were not detained. In addition, juvenile detention is short term, and statutes stipulate that a judge must conduct a detention hearing within a specific time period soon after the youth is detained.

BOX 15.2   SOLITARY CONFINEMENT

While systematic data of the number of adolescents held in solitary confinement are not available, a report by the American Civil Liberties Union and Human Rights Watch (2012, 63) found that some jails and prisons "hold 100 percent of youth in solitary confinement," while other facilities rarely use the practice. The New York City Department of Corrections reports that about 14% of youth between 16 and 18 years of age are confined in solitary for some portion of their pretrial detention. About 11% of adolescent and youthful offenders (under age 21) are held in solitary confinement in Pennsylvania. The length of time spent in solitary isolation varies from 1 day to over 365 days. The American Civil Liberties Union and Human Rights Watch found that most of the youth in their study were confined between 1 and 6 months. While in solitary confinement, youth are denied family contacts and access to education, and experience anxiety, psychological stress, and physical symptoms, and are also denied access to medical treatment. The report concludes that "solitary confinement of youth is itself a serious human rights violation and can constitute cruel, inhuman, or degrading treatment under international human rights law" (2010: 5).

Rule 13.4 of "the Beijing Rules" adopted in 1985 addresses issues associated with the confinement of youth in detention (UN General Assembly 1985). In particular, this rule stipulates the need to hold youth in separate (youth only) institutions or to ascertain that they will be kept separate from adults while they are being held. Provisions of the JJDP Act indicate consensus on conditions for youth in detention. In the United States, this issue has been partially resolved through state legislation.

Nonetheless, states utilize jails to hold juveniles. At midyear 2012, the U.S. Department of Justice reported that there were over 5000 juveniles in adult jails on a given day in June. Of these, 900 were being processed as juveniles, and over 4000 were being detained as adults (Minton 2013). In this context, the Governor of Colorado signed legislation banning the use of jails for youth awaiting court appearances even if they were waived to adult criminal court (Equal Justice Initiative 2012). As Colorado illustrates, individual state statutes establish whether youth who have been waived to adult court can be incarcerated in jail or in juvenile detention facilities pending trial. Similarly, many states determine that youth detained in jail pending court appearances are to be separated from adult offenders through sight and sound. In other states, individual facilities determine the best approach (American Civil Liberties Association and Human Rights Watch 2012). In their report, the American Civil Liberties Union and Human Rights Watch (2012) reviewed the negative consequences of solitary confinement, which may be used as a sanction when youth are held in adult institutions (see Box 15.2).

The U.S. Supreme Court and Youth

The U.S. Supreme Court was silent regarding juvenile justice processes for the first 67 years of the juvenile court's existence. However, beginning in 1966 with the case, *Kent v. United States*, the Supreme Court reviewed and determined that a number of informal policies of the juvenile court violated the U.S. Constitution (*Kent v. United States* 1966). In *Kent,* the majority of the justices established that youth have certain rights associated with the waiver or transfer process, including the right to counsel. In the following year, the justices ruled that specific protections including the right to notice of the charges, right to counsel, the right to confront and cross-examine witnesses, and the privilege against self-incrimination associated with the adjudicatory hearing were applicable to juveniles (*In re Gault* 1967). Subsequently, the court established that the standard of evidence necessary to determine the youth's involvement in delinquency should be the same as adults (i.e., proof beyond a reasonable doubt [*In re Winship* 1970]).

The U.S. Supreme Court decided *Gault* before the United Nations formally adopted "the Beijing Rules" in 1985. However, the General Principles of Rule 7 concerning the rights of juveniles address rights, which are consistent with the court's decision (i.e., the principle stipulates that youth have the right to notice of the charges, the right to counsel, the right to remain silent, and the right to confront and cross-examine witnesses). "The Beijing Rules" also reference appeal and note that youth have the right to an appeal. By contrast, in *Gault*, the justices refrained from mandating the right to appeal for juveniles. Rather, it was left to individual states to determine whether youth could appeal their cases.

Similarly, Rule 15 highlights the importance of the right to counsel for youth. It reiterates that youth should have counsel available during all the proceedings. This is not necessarily the case in the United States. Furthermore, Rule 15 notes the importance of free legal services to youth in countries where it is available. In the United States, there are provisions for free legal assistance for youth (see Box 15.3). Unfortunately, research suggests that this is one area where youth have been adversely affected (see, e.g., Feld and Schaefer 2010; Sterling 2009).

In 2009, a special commission in Pennsylvania, the Interbranch Commission on Juvenile Justice, was appointed to make recommendations for future policies on access to defense counsel following a scandal in which youth were routinely denied access to counsel at delinquency proceedings. One prominent recommendation focused on ensuring access to counsel. The Interbranch Commission on Juvenile Justice (2010, 48) reiterated "Pennsylvania's obligation to enforce a child's constitutionally guaranteed right to counsel in delinquency proceedings" and "the constitutional requirements of due process and the right to counsel for juveniles." Not surprisingly, issues surrounding the right to counsel and due process occur in a number of states (see Feld and Schaefer 2010; Jones 2004).

Concerns about due process rights for juvenile offenders were also evident in the state-level analysis conducted by Willison et al. (2009). They found that "measures extending procedural due process also figured prominently on many states' agendas" (Willison et al.

BOX 15.3   CONSTITUTIONAL RIGHTS

During 2001 to 2011, "nine States provided for the constitutional right of defense counsel in juvenile proceedings: Kentucky, Louisiana, Maryland, Mississippi, North Dakota, Tennessee, Texas, Utah, and Virginia" (pp. 6–7). These legislatures emphasized concern for protecting the due process rights of juveniles. In addition to requiring defense counsel, Pennsylvania also requires judges to articulate rationale for imposing their sentences. In the context of more punitive sanctioning of youthful offenders, and questions of juvenile competency, states have demonstrated initiatives to preserve and protect rights of youth.

2009, 41). Mississippi, for example, had provisions in its Juvenile Delinquency Prevention Act of 2006 relating to the quality of counsel (Willison et al. 2009, 52). The researchers noted California for its Youth Bill of Rights, which included due process provisions on the right to counsel and required that the Bill of Rights be presented in age-appropriate and developmentally appropriate language (Willison et al. 2009, 52).

The National Conference of State Legislatures (2010) also reported that some states have been focused on due process rights of juveniles. Montana, Maine, and North Dakota (National Conference of State Legislatures 2010, para. 2) all recognized the importance of ensuring quality defense counsel for youth. Maine, for example, provided that indigent juvenile defendants would receive "efficient, high quality services." North Dakota and Mississippi required that juveniles have counsel at all stages of juvenile court proceedings. In the National Conference of State Legislatures' (2010, para. 2) assessment, "Policymakers understand that, too often, youth waive their right to an attorney and accept plea offers without understanding their actions."

While these initiatives recognize that youth are not as capable of providing "informed consent about legal proceedings as adults" and therefore need to be represented with legal counsel, Kempf-Leonard (2010, 361) cautions that it is not just the presence of counsel that is important, but the effectiveness of representation. In spite of the court's decision in *In re Gault* (1967) that juveniles require due process protections, Kempf-Leonard questions the quality of assistance that youth receive in court. This critique suggests that the availability and quality of legal representation vary and may be insufficient to navigate the juvenile justice system effectively. In brief, monitoring legal representation of youth might be an issue that both "the Beijing Rules" and the United States could prioritize.

Capital Punishment and Life without Parole Sentences for Youth

On the question of capital punishment, the U.S. Supreme Court has ruled on the constitutionality of the death penalty for youth under the age of 18 (*Roper v. Simmons* 2005) and found it to be in violation of the Eighth Amendment ban on cruel and unusual punishment. Rule 17.2 of the 1985 Beijing Rules expressly prohibits the use of capital punishment for juveniles. As noted, the court's decision was about 20 years later. The *Roper* case demonstrates the shift in attitudes toward capital punishment for youth in the United States. Previously, the court determined in *Stanford v. Kentucky* (1989) that capital punishment was constitutional for youth who were 16 years of age at the time of the crime. Clearly, *Roper* represents a significant shift, which brings U.S. policy on capital punishment in line with "the Beijing Rules" and other developed countries' positions. After *Roper* established that youth are different, the majority of the justices ruled that a youth cannot be sentenced to life without the possibility of parole for a nonhomicide offense (*Graham v. Florida* 2010), and that youth cannot be sentenced to a mandatory life without the possibility of parole sentence for a homicide offense (*Miller v. Alabama* 2012). Table 15.3 notes these four cases.

In these decisions, the justices clearly noted that youth are different from adults and should not be subject to the severe punishments of death, life without parole (LWOP) for nonhomicide offenses, and *mandatory* LWOP for homicide offenses. In *Roper v. Simmons* (2005), the Court ruled (5-4) that the evolving "standards of decency" preclude the use of capital punishment for offenders who were under the age of 18 when their crimes were committed. Taking into consideration a growing state consensus that the death penalty

Table 15.3   U.S. Supreme Court Decisions on Capital Punishment and Life without Parole

Stanford v. Kentucky 1989

States can execute youth aged 16 or older at the time of the offense

Roper v. Simmons 2005

States cannot execute youth for offenses committed under the age of 18

Graham v. Florida 2010

States cannot sentence a youth under the age of 18 to life without parole for a nonhomicide offense

Miller v. Alabama 2012

States cannot sentence a youth under the age of 18 to mandatory life without parole sentence for a homicide offense

was inappropriate and used disproportionately for minority offenders, the court also cited international opinion on the rights and treatment of children in determining that execution of minors was not consistent in modern society.

In addition to the evolving standards of decency, the court relied on scientific evidence on adolescent brain development to affirm the vulnerability, immaturity, and impulsivity of youth and to recognize diminished culpability for youth under age 18. This acknowledgement that cognitive functioning in adolescents was underdeveloped was significant in reaffirming the rationale that children should not be treated the same as adults and therefore they warrant different consideration. In their research, Scott and Steinberg (2008) examined cognitive brain functioning of youth and concluded that the immature judgment of adolescents should result in less blameworthiness for their criminal activity (see Box 15.4).

Using arguments similar to those presented in *Roper*, the Supreme Court ruled in *Graham v. Florida* (2010) that sentencing offenders under the age of 18 years to LWOP for nonhomicidal offenses was a violation of the Eighth Amendment prohibition of cruel and unusual punishment. One issue in the court's deliberation was the "categorical" exclusion of minors, which further delineated adolescence as a status requiring different and less punitive consideration. The court's reference to international opinion reflects a distinctive status for children, which is articulated in the Convention on the Rights of Children (CRC), which was adopted in 1989 by the General Assembly of the United Nations. The CRC recognizes that childhood is a special status, which requires governments to ensure the protection and care of children and to seek their best interests. Article 3, Section 1 captures the goal of the convention:

In all actions concerning children, whether undertaken by public or private social welfare institutions, courts of law, administrative authorities or legislative bodies, the best interest of the child shall be a primary consideration (see United Nations Office of High Commissioner for Human Rights; www.unhchr.ch/html).

In reviewing *Graham*, Liles and Moak (2011, 9) concluded that, in effect, the court's rationale reiterated that juveniles are different from adults and therefore "should be treated differently in court." The authors were optimistic that the decision demonstrated a growing consensus about youthful offenders that reinforces the original intent of the juvenile

BOX 15.4   ADOLESCENT BRAIN DEVELOPMENT

Steinberg's research illustrates that maturation of the brain occurs later than earlier studies suggested. As a result, adolescents have less impulse control than adults. For example, they are unlikely to plan or to anticipate the consequences of their behavior. They are also more influenced by peers. As youth mature from adolescence to early adulthood, changes occur in the prefrontal cortex. During adolescence, youth experience heightened arousal and low self-control. This delayed brain development contributes to their greater vulnerability (Steinberg 2012).

court (Liles and Moak 2011, 10). While the court took a categorical approach (e.g., age) in *Graham*, the ruling left some questions unanswered: What is a "meaningful opportunity" for youth serving life sentences to have their cases reviewed?

In 2012, the U.S. Supreme Court returned to the issue of sentencing youth who have been convicted in adult court to mandatory life in prison without the possibility of parole (LWOP). In *Miller v. Alabama*, the justices consolidated two cases: *Jackson v. Hobbs* (No. 10-9647 2004) and *Miller v. Alabama (No. 10-9646 2012)*. Both Jackson and Miller were 14 years of age when they were convicted and sentenced to LWOP in Alabama and Arkansas, respectively. The justices determined that these sentencing statutes violated the Eighth Amendment ban on cruel and unusual punishment. In part, the justices noted (*Miller v. Alabama* 2012, 3):

> The mandatory penalty schemes at issue here, however, prevent the sentencer from considering youth and from assessing whether the law's harshest term of imprisonment proportionately punishes a juvenile offender. This contravenes Graham's (and also Roper's) foundational principle: that imposition of a State's most severe penalties on juvenile offenders cannot proceed as though they were not children.

In *Graham*, the justices indicated that the inability of the sentencer to consider "the mitigating qualities of youth" in mandatory life without the possibility of parole cases is unconstitutional in view of the court's earlier decisions regarding death penalty cases (*Miller v. Alabama* 2012, 3). When judges sentence offenders in capital crimes, they have to consider mitigating circumstances. Therefore, these same individualized sentencing decisions would be required in juvenile cases (*Miller v. Alabama* 2012, 3).

The court's decision prompted state legislatures to draft new sentencing laws for youth convicted in adult courts of homicide, to consider establishing procedures to review retroactively those youth who are serving LWOP as a result of mandatory sentencing and to review options for possible parole consideration. In some states, youth who were previously sentenced to LWOP are having their sentences commuted by governors to a specific number of years. Other states are exploring or enacting different sanctions for youth below the age of 15 or 16 at the time of the offense versus those who were age of 15 or 16 when charged. For example, as an alternative to mandatory LWOP for juveniles, Pennsylvania has legislated that youth who were 14 years or younger at the time of their offense can receive a minimum of 25 years to life, while those aged 15–17 can be sentenced to a minimum of 35 years to life, both eligible for parole review at the minimum dates (Juvenile Law Center 2013).

Evidence-Based Practice

As noted earlier, one of the significant developments in juvenile justice has been the advancement of scientific research to demonstrate which strategies and programs are effective in preventing and reducing delinquency. The general initiative of best practices and data-driven policy in criminal justice is reflected in the ideological shift from "nothing works" (Martinson 1974) to "what works" (Cullen and Gilbert 2012; Cullen and Gendreau 2001).

In his 1974 article, Martinson concluded that he could find little evidence to support the effectiveness of rehabilitation strategies in reducing recidivism. In context of the then rising crime rates, conservative politics, and a mentality of get tough on crime, Martinson's message helped to shift policies away from the medical model and rehabilitation toward the deterrence model and punishment. The pessimism that offenders could not be rehabilitated, and therefore such programs should be abandoned, overshadowed the efforts to determine what could change offender behaviors and reduce recidivism (Warren and Crime and Justice Institute 2007).

In addition to public policy, which distanced itself from therapeutic intervention and rehabilitation, simultaneous criticisms of the ability of the juvenile justice system to respond adequately to youthful offenders, and specifically violent youth, raised concern about the viability of the future of juvenile justice (Feld 1997).

In the intervening years, the question "What works?" has generated considerable research and scholarship that demonstrate successful and cost-effective programs and strategies to rehabilitate offenders and reduce recidivism (Greenwood and Welsh 2012; Lipsey and Cullen 2007; Latessa, Cullen, and Gendreau 2002). The state of rehabilitation policy in the 2000s is decidedly more optimistic, based on scientific evidence that shows which treatments can change offender behaviors and reduce recidivism (Cullen 2012, 98). In addition to the empirical support for rehabilitation, Clear (1994) argues that the "penal harm" movement has been eroded by fiscal constraints, overcrowded institutions, and evidence that punishments alone do not work to reduce reoffending.

With over 15 years of evidence, several programs have been demonstrated to be successful and cost-effective in reducing delinquency. Three popular programs are listed in Table 15.4. Greenwood and Welsh (2012) identified seven progressive states that have made serious commitments to evidence-based practice in juvenile justice and have adopted such "brand-name" programs as Functional Family Therapy (FFT), Multidimensional Treatment Foster Care (MTFC), and Multisystemic Therapy (MST). Of the seven states (California, Connecticut, Florida, Maryland, New York, Pennsylvania, and Washington), the authors identify Connecticut and Pennsylvania as "early adopters" in evidence-based practice in delinquency prevention and going to "scale" with proprietary strategies. This early adopter status reflected that these states implemented at least two of the prevailing

Table 15.4 Three Major Evidence-Based Programs for Youth

Functional Family Therapy (FFT)

Multidimensional Treatment Foster Care (MTFC)

Multisystemic Therapy (MST)

Research demonstrates success and cost-effectiveness in reducing delinquency.

programs (e.g., FFT, MST, MTFC) and trained a number of therapy teams to serve the juvenile population (Greenwood and Welsh 2012, 502).

Information about evidence-based programs is easily accessible and includes the Blueprints for Healthy Youth Development (formerly Blueprints for Violence Prevention) from the Institute of Behavioral Science, University of Boulder Colorado, Center for the Study and Prevention of Violence (http://www.colorado.edu/cspv/blueprints/); Crime Solutions sponsored by the U.S. Office of Justice Programs (http://www.crimesolutions.gov/); and the Model Programs Guide (MPG) sponsored by the Office of Juvenile Justice and Delinquency Prevention (http://www.ojjdp.gov/mpg/search.aspx). In her critique of evidence-based practice, Bishop (2012, 484) recognized the importance of the federal role in providing funding for "experimental evaluation research" and in the commitment to ensuring accessibility of the information for practitioners with the goal of "informing juvenile justice policy and practice."

Not to discourage this resurgence and enthusiasm for therapeutic interventions in juvenile justice in the United States, Greenwood and Welsh (2012, 508) caution that "evidence-based practice in delinquency prevention has a long way to go." They cite a 2007 study by Hennigan et al. (2007, 508), which estimated that "only approximately 5%" of potentially eligible youth were participants on evidence-based programs.

Juvenile Justice Models

It is probably safe to acknowledge, however, that rehabilitation has been reaffirmed (Cullen and Gilbert 2012), and evidence-based practice has been incorporated into juvenile justice. More specifically, the emergent approach of juvenile justice in the United States may be characterized by using dimensions of Reichel's (2012) typology, which distinguishes between the "legalistic model" with elements such as due process and the "welfare model" that includes treatment and child protection. A "balance" of these models suggests an approach, which accepts therapeutic intervention while maintaining concern for juvenile crime and public safety. As presented by Winterdyk in the Introduction to this volume, the "Modified Justice Model" incorporates features of crime control and treatment (see Table 1.1). This model recognizes the diminished responsibility of youth and provides for treatment but also sanctions the behaviors.

In Pennsylvania, for example, the Balanced and Restorative Justice (BARJ) model has been adopted to guide policies in three areas: public safety; accountability to the victim; and offender competency (Griffin 2006). While holding delinquents accountable for the harm they have done to the victim and community, the model encompasses strategies (e.g., evidence-based practice) to help juveniles overcome at-risk factors and to develop skills and capabilities to avert subsequent offending. With a partnership between the John D. and Catherine T. MacArthur Foundation and the Juvenile Justice and Delinquency Prevention Committee, reform in Pennsylvania is known as the *Models for Change* and includes efforts to improve screening and assessment; diversion; education and aftercare; family involvement; and indigent defense (Schwartz 2013, 31). In addition to supervision and treatment, initiatives also emphasize "strategies to identify and refer youth with behavioral health and mental health needs to appropriate services"(Schwartz 2013, 26).

This approach and the elements of the BARJ model are consistent with the principles and spirit of "the Beijing Rules," which seek a "comprehensive framework of social justice" that recognizes the importance of both the well-being of juveniles and the protection of public order (UN General Assembly 1985, Section E, 4). The essential statement in Rules 1.1–1.6, "Fundamental Perspectives," addresses broad social policy that includes continuing improvement of juvenile justice practices and efforts to reduce delinquency. Rule 17.1 (b) is more specific by stating that "strictly punitive approaches (to juvenile cases) are not appropriate" (UN General Assembly 1985, Section E, 12). The progressive model described earlier (i.e., BARJ) appears to demonstrate this principle by moving away from the strictly punitive model and incorporating both therapeutic strategies and accountability.

Protection of Children and Youth

In addition to principles for the treatment of juvenile offenders, "the Beijing Rules" also provide commentary on the importance of protecting youth from "harmful influences and risk situations" (UN General Assembly 1985, Section E, 1). At the federal level in the United States, in 2010, the U.S. Attorney General, Eric Holder, established the Defending Childhood Initiative to examine the causes and consequences of "children exposed to violence" (CEV). In addition to being victims of abuse, neglect, and crime, the Department of Justice reported that children who witness violence and are exposed to violent conditions also experience negative effects that impact emotional well-being and mental health of children and adolescents (Defending Childhood n.d.). Together with caring for the well-being of children, the relationship between childhood victimization and adolescent offending is not overlooked in this policy, especially the link between exposure to violence and violent offending (Lin, Cochran, and Mieczkowski 2011).

While the punitive model of juvenile justice has not disappeared, the CEV national initiative and the BARJ model in Pennsylvania and other jurisdictions (OJJDP 1998) can be viewed as efforts to underscore and promote delinquency prevention and treatment, and to advance the welfare model and rehabilitative mission of juvenile justice. This model suggests that when juveniles are victims of trauma, a trauma-informed approach to juvenile programs has resulted in strategies to "heal the hurt" and treat the delinquent (Center for Nonviolence and Social Justice n.d.). The approach is the Sanctuary Model, which represents an evidence-supported therapeutic environment to develop four domains to help youth overcome trauma and to prepare them for a successful posttreatment life. The acronym S.E.L.F. represents a "nonlinear organizing framework" to provide *Safety*, to develop

---

BOX 15.5   SANCTUARY MODEL

Without identifying specific individual traumatic events, the Sanctuary curriculum for S.E.L.F. (Safety, Emotions, Loss, Future) is a psychoeducational approach for assessing problems that have resulted from exposure to violence (Center for Nonviolence and Social Justice n.d.). Using a group setting, the discussions focus on how to think differently about the problems, how to organize changes that are needed to manage problems better, how to develop recognition for the patterns that present problems related to past experiences, and how to provide strategies for the process of recovery. Creating a safe, nonthreatening group setting is crucial to the success of the psychodynamics of the Sanctuary Model, which helps clients learn, grow, and change.

Emotional management, to deal with *Loss* and grief, and to prepare for the *Future* (Center for Nonviolence and Social Justice n.d.) (see Box 15.5). Sanctuary uses cognitive behavioral techniques to facilitate recovery and adjustment in a supportive, nurturing culture while holding youth accountable and helping them and their families overcome trauma and to plan for a better future.

This approach clearly recognizes that juveniles should not only be viewed as youth who come in conflict with the law but also as youth who have been victims. In the context of Rule 5 of "the Beijing Rules," which identifies promotion of the well-being of juveniles (UN General Assembly 1985, Section E, 6), Sanctuary is more therapeutic and child centered and attempts to provide a milieu for juveniles to overcome adverse childhood experiences and begin healthy development toward positive futures.

Adolescence and Psychological Development

As scientific research has provided evidence of effective programs and intervention strategies, research on brain development has presented a better understanding of the psychological maturation of adolescents and how their cognitive capacities contribute to delinquency (Scott and Steinberg 2008). While recognizing that youth are exposed to "psychosocial and emotional influences" that affect judgment, Scott and Steinberg have described four developmental features that modify reasoning and understanding. The immature judgments that characterize adolescents are influenced by a lack of future orientation; "susceptibility to peer influence"; risk–reward assessment that minimizes risks and maximizes benefits; and low impulse control (Scott and Steinberg 2008, 20–21). Based on developmental immaturity characteristic of underdeveloped prefrontal cortex, Scott and Steinberg conclude that adolescents have "diminished decision-making capacity" that qualifies them for less culpability.

As previously noted, these scientific conclusions on adolescent brain development were prominent in the U.S. Supreme Court decisions that negated capital punishment (*Roper v. Simmons* 2005) and mandatory LWOP (*Miller v. Alabama* 2012) for offenders who were under age 18 when they committed their crimes. The court reasoned that youth are not able to discern risks and consequences properly due to immaturity, impulsivity, and impetuosity (*Miller v. Alabama* 2010). In the *Miller* decision, the Court reaffirmed that juveniles are different and should therefore be treated differently. The psychological perspective of juveniles presented by Scott and Steinberg distinguishes between developmental immaturity in thinking processes and characterological issues that can affect criminality. It recognizes the malleability of youth and provides rationale for treatment to develop skills and competencies for better decision-making and delinquency prevention.

Continuing and Future Issues

This section reviews selected issues briefly that continue to challenge the juvenile justice system. Concerns about victimization of youth while in custody, DMC, and persistent adultification policies are considered.

As the narrative in this chapter indicates, juvenile justice in the United States has transitioned through different eras beginning with rehabilitation and best interests of the child, to get tough with youthful offenders, and back to concerns about how youth are treated in the legal system. Bernard and Kurlychek (2010) described that juvenile justice policies have undergone cycles from lenient treatment to harsh punishment, suggesting that responses to delinquency are influenced by social, economic, and political forces. They observe that policies are usually limited in their effectiveness because they rarely consider the antecedents of delinquency but rather respond to prevailing exigencies.

If the current era of juvenile justice can be characterized as a "rethinking" of policy with a shift toward softening strategies and more compassionate principles for handling youthful offenders, there are still concerns about the supervision and treatment of youth in the juvenile justice system. In a study sponsored by the Office of Juvenile Justice and Delinquency Prevention (OJJDP) of youth in custody, *The Survey of Youth in Residential Placement*, Sedlak, McPherson, and Basena (2013) found significant evidence of victimization of youth in custody. They reported that 46% of youth had been victims of theft and 1 in 10 had been forced to engage in sexual activity (Sedlak, McPherson, and Basena 2013, 10). Risk of violent victimization was also characteristic of residential placement, and youth often lacked effective grievance procedures. The authors identified facility policies and management practices as contributing factors to a climate that aggravated victimization and concluded that "traditional policies and longstanding practices" are resistant to change and present challenges if conditions of confinement are to be improved (Sedlak, McPherson, and Basena 2013, 11).

In a similar study focusing on sexual victimization of youth in juvenile facilities, Beck et al. (2013) also found that about 10% of adjudicated youth in confinement reported experiencing "one or more incidents of sexual victimization by another youth or staff" (Beck et al. 2013, 11). Their report, *Sexual Victimization in Juvenile Facilities Reported by Youth, 2012*, also documented physical and sexual abuse perpetrated by facility staff. While the rates of incidents varied by state and facility, the authors identified conditions of confinement that were conducive to victimization and placed youth at greater risk.

Both studies coincide with the efforts of the Department of Justice to address the issues and consequences of CEV and to promote the attorney general's initiatives of defending childhood with promising practices that "mitigate the negative effects experienced by children exposed to violence" (Defending Childhood n.d.). The findings that youth in custody are at risk for exposure to violence certainly contradicts these efforts as well as "the Beijing Rules," and provide evidence that deinstitutionalization and decarceration remain salient concerns in juvenile justice and represent an area that continues to require reform.

A second issue concerns the "school to prison pipeline" where school authorities and school-based police officers rely on suspensions, expulsions, and criminalization as responses to student misconduct (see Box 15.6). Known as "zero tolerance," these disciplinary policies not only criminalize minor youth misconduct that has historically been handled administratively, but the increased number of students that have been suspended or arrested also contributes to school dropout and increased likelihood of justice system contact (New York City School–Justice Partnership Task Force 2013). A study in New York City, *Keeping Kids in School and Out of Court*, concluded that most suspensions were for minor discretionary infractions such as disorderly conduct, which were annoying and disruptive, but did not reach the level of criminal behavior (New York City School–Justice Partnership Task Force 2013).

The increased number of arrests and summonses represents one aspect of the punitiveness toward students; the overrepresentation of suspensions and arrests of students of color demonstrates the continuing concerns of DMC. In the New York City study, black students

BOX 15.6   SCHOOL TO PRISON PIPELINE

In a recent study of students in the New York City school system, data indicate that the incidence of school violence reported to the Department of Education decreased, but that the number of school suspensions increased (New York City School–Justice Partnership Task Force 2013). The research also suggests that the number of suspensions is not spread evenly across schools; that is, some schools rely extensively on this sanction for minor misbehavior. The uneven use of school suspensions highlights the need for alternative strategies for misbehavior that are less punitive and less likely to adversely affect student retention, academic success, graduation rates, and delinquent activity.

"represented 28 percent of the student population" but were "four times more likely to be suspended than white students" and "accounted for almost 63 percent of the arrests" (New York City School–Justice Partnership Task Force 2013, 7–8). These trends and patterns are not so much a function of youth misbehavior as of adult responses and institutional policies (New York City School–Justice Partnership Task Force 2013, iv). While encouraging initiatives to implement alternative sanctions have been implemented, the issue of DMC continues to plague the juvenile justice system.

Since 1988 when the issue of DMC was first presented to Congress, the OJJDP has developed and promoted numerous opportunities for technical support, training, and funding for system improvement strategies to reduce DMC (OJJDP DMC n.d.). Strategic innovations that have been used in targeted states have demonstrated effective progress in improving collaborative participation in reducing disparities. For example, when alternatives to detention and commitment are developed, more community-based programs are made available that reduce minority confinement. In Pennsylvania, one of the model states, the following reforms have been undertaken: "improved data gathering and analysis, increased cultural competence, implementation of objective screening instruments, development of alternatives to detention and out-of-home placement, improved probation practices, work with the faith-based community, and training and collaboration with law enforcement" (Shoenberg 2012, 2).

Finally, the continued use of exclusionary policies to transfer youth to adult court remains a vestige of the "get tough" era of public policy, which places youth at risk and has doubtful impact on crime reduction. In their study of the effects of transfer, Mulvey and Schubert (2012) found that in comparison to juvenile court, transferring youth to adult court had detrimental effects including longer sentences, increased potential for victimization, and disruptions in personal development. In 2009, there were approximately 7600 juvenile cases waived to adult criminal court. In 1994, the peak year in terms of the number of transfers, there were over 13,000 juvenile cases waived to adult court (Adams and Addie 2012). The researchers caution that these experiences are unduly harsh for most youthful offenders and the influence of "prisonization" adversely affects identify formation and social development (Adams and Addie 2012, 5). Furthermore, while some incapacitation effect may be realized, transferred youth are more likely to recidivate, to recidivate more quickly, and to recidivate more frequently (Adams and Addie 2012, 7). Mulvey and Schubert (2012, 7) find that the research indicates that "juvenile transfer policies uniformly produce negative outcomes."

While outcomes are variable with different types of offenders, the use of transfer, especially statutory exclusion, demonstrates the persistence of punitive policy that overshadows the principles of individualized treatment of delinquents. While the cycle of juvenile justice identified by Bernard and Kurlychek may have some softening, the punitive elements are also manifest. Even as the Supreme Court has reaffirmed that youth are different and have the potential for rehabilitation, some states have not rescinded punitive sanctions that require mandatory transfer of jurisdiction and longer sentences (Adams and Addie 2010). The juvenile justice system essentially reflects bifurcated strategies: While promoting prevention programs, evidence-based practices, risk reduction, and therapeutic intervention, the get tough response characterized by deterrence and incapacitation with lengthy sentences runs parallel.

Tremendous strides as well as impediments in juvenile justice policy have both been evident in the United States in the last 115 years. Ideology and practice have not incorporated the best interests of the child and the least restrictive intervention consistently. With the current emphasis on research, there is optimism that a return to the rehabilitative ideal and a transition to a more prevention-based and early intervention model will continue to emerge. In this review and analysis, the authors demonstrated that juvenile justice policies in the United States do not encompass all "the Beijing Rules." Nonetheless, current practices and trends including the ban on the death penalty for offenders under the age of 18 and the restriction on mandatory LWOP are important benchmarks. In conjunction with concern for youth victimization, initiatives by the federal government to prevent maltreatment of youth are laudable. Simultaneously, there appears to be an ongoing emphasis on due process and a greater awareness that youth differ from adults. These developments bode well for the future of juvenile justice in the United States and signal a more responsive rather than reactive course of action.

Review/Discussion Questions

1. How would you describe the juvenile justice system in the United States?
2. What is your response to the Supreme Court decision (*Roper v. Simmons* 2005) that banned the death penalty for youth under the age of 18?
3. What are the characteristics of the Sanctuary Model? Do you think this model is appropriate for juvenile offenders? Explain your rationale.
4. What is the status of life without parole sentences for juvenile offenders in the United States? What is your response to life without parole sentencing?

References

Adams, B. and S. Addie. (2010). *Delinquency cases waived to criminal court, 2007*. Washington, DC: Office of Juvenile Justice and Delinquency Prevention, U.S. Department of Justice.

Adams, B. and S. Addie. (2012). *Delinquency cases waived to criminal court, 2009*. Washington, DC: Office of Juvenile Justice and Delinquency Prevention, U.S. Department of Justice.

American Civil Liberties Association and Human Rights Watch. (2012). *Growing up locked down: Youth in solitary confinement in jails and prisons across the United States*. New York: Human Rights Watch.

Anderson, E. (1999). *Code of the Street: Decency, Violence, and the Moral Life of the Inner City*. New York: W.W. Norton and Company.

Beck, A., D. Cantor, J. Hartge, and T. Smith. (2013). *Sexual victimization in juvenile facilities reported by youth, 2012*. Washington, DC: Bureau of Justice Statistics.

Benekos, P. J. and A. V. Merlo. (2006). *Crime Control, Politics and Policy*, 2nd Edition. Cincinnati, OH: Anderson Publishing Co.

Bernard, T. J. and M. C. Kurlychek. (2010). *The Cycle of Juvenile Justice*. New York: Oxford University Press.

Bishop, D. M. (2012). Evidence-based practice and juvenile justice. *Criminology and Public Policy* 11(3):483–489.

Brown, S. A. (2012). *Trends in Juvenile State Legislation: 2001–2010*. Washington, DC: National Conference of State Legislatures.

Center for Nonviolence and Social Justice. (n.d.). The Sanctuary Model. http://www.sanctuaryweb. com/center.php (accessed May 7, 2013).

Champion, D. J., A. V. Merlo, and P. J. Benekos. (2013). *The Juvenile Justice System: Delinquency, Processing, and the law*, 7th Edition. Boston, MA: Pearson.

Clear, T. R. (1994). *Harm in American Penology: Offenders, Victims, and their Communities*. Albany, NY: SUNY Press.

Cloward, R. and L. Ohlin. (1960). *Delinquency and Opportunity: A Theory of Delinquent Gangs*. Glencoe, IL: Free Press.

Cullen, F. T. (2012). Taking rehabilitation seriously: Creativity, science, and the challenge of offender change. *Punishment and Society* 14(1):94–114.

Cullen, F. T. and P. Gendreau. (2001). From nothing works to what works: Changing professional ideology in the 21st century. *Prison Journal* 81(3):313–338.

Cullen, F. T. and K. E. Gilbert. (2012). *Reaffirming Rehabilitation*, 2nd Edition. Cincinnati, OH: Anderson.

Defending Childhood. (n.d.). The United States Department of Justice. http://www.justice.gov/ defendingchildhood/ (accessed May 7, 2013).

Equal Justice Initiative. (2012). States Retreat from Laws that Prosecute Children as Adults. http:// www.eji.org/node/672 (accessed June 19, 2013).

Federal Bureau of Investigation. (2012). Uniform Crime Reports, 2011. http://www.fbi.gov/about-us/ cjis/ucr/crime-in-the-u.s/2011/crime-in-the-u.s.-2011/tables/table-32 (accessed June 24, 2013).

Feld, B. C. (1997). Abolish the juvenile court: Youthfulness, criminal responsibility, and sentencing policy. *The Journal of Criminal Law and Criminology* 88(1):68–136.

Feld, B. C. and S. Shaefer (2010). The right to counsel in juvenile court: Law reform to deliver legal services and reduce justice by geography. *Criminology and Public Policy* 9(2):327–356.

Felson, M. and L. Cohen. (1979). Social change and crime rate trends: A routine activity approach. *American Sociological Review* 44(4):588–608.

Gatti, U., R. E. Tremblay, and F. Vitaro. (2008). Iatrogenic effect of juvenile justice. *The Journal of Child Psychology and Psychiatry* 50(8):991–998.

Gottfredson, M. R. and T. Hirschi. (1990). *A General Theory of Crime*. Stanford, CA: Stanford University Press.

Graham v. Florida, 560 U.S—(Docket No. 08-7412) (2010).

Greenwood, P. W. and B. C. Welsh. (2012). Promoting evidence-based practice in delinquency prevention at the state level: Principles, progress, and policy directions. *Criminology and Public Policy* 11(3):493–513.

Griffin, P. (2006). *Ten years of balanced and restorative justice in Pennsylvania*. Harrisburg, PA: Pennsylvania Commission on Crime and Delinquency.

Hagan, F. E. (2012). *Introduction to Criminology: Theories, Methods, and Criminal Behavior*, 8th Edition. Thousand Oaks, CA: Sage.

Hennigan, K., K. Kolnick, J. Poplawski, A. Andrews, N. Ball, C. Cheng, and J. Payne. (2007). *Juvenile justice data project. Phase I: Survey of interventions and programs: A continuum of graduated responses for juvenile justice in California*. Los Angeles: Center for Research on Crime, University of Southern California.

Hirschi, T. (1969). *Causes of Delinquency*. Berkeley, CA: University of California Press.

In re Gault, 387 U.S. 1 (1967).

In re Winship, 397 U.S. 358 (1970).

Interbranch Commission on Juvenile Justice. (2010). *Report*. Philadelphia, PA: Administrative Office of Pennsylvania Courts.

Jackson v. Hobbs, No. 10-9647 (2004).

Jones, J. B. (2004). *Access to counsel*. Washington, DC: Office of Juvenile Justice and Delinquency Prevention, U.S. Department of Justice.

Juvenile Justice and Delinquency Prevention Allocation to States. (2002). Catalog of Federal Domestic Assistance. https://www.cfda.gov/?s=programandmode=formandtab=step1andid=c7809db1858ebf00f723ec4f908197ab (accessed July 8, 2013).

Juvenile Law Center. (2013). Juvenile Life without Parole in Pennsylvania. http://jlc.org/current-initiatives/promoting-fairness-courts/juvenile-life-without-parole/jlwop-pennsylvania (accessed June 22, 2013).

Kempf-Leonard, K. (2010). Does having an attorney provide a better outcome? The right to counsel does not mean attorneys help youths. *Criminology and Public Policy* 9(2):357–363.

Kent v. United States, 383 U.S. 541 (1966).

Knoll, C. and M. Sickmund. (2012). *Delinquency cases in juvenile court, 2009*. Washington, DC: Office of Juvenile Justice and Delinquency Prevention.

Latessa, E. J., F. T. Cullen, and P. Gendreau. (2002). Beyond correctional quackery: Professionalism and the possibility of effective treatment. *Federal Probation* 66(2):43–49.

Liles, A. and S. Moak. (2011). Evolving standards of decency involving juvenile offenders: A review of *Graham v. Florida*. *ACJS Today* 35(3):4–11.

Lin, W. H., J. K. Cochran, and T. Mieczkowski. (2011). Direct and vicarious violent victimization and juvenile delinquency: An application of general strain theory. *Sociological Inquiry* 81(2):195–222.

Lipsey, M. W. and F. T. Cullen. (2007). The effectiveness of correctional rehabilitation: A review of systematic reviews. *Annual Review of Law and Social Science* 3:297–320.

Martinson, R. (1974). What works? Questions and answers about prison reform. *The Public Interest* 35(Spring):22–54.

Miller v. Alabama, 132 S. Ct. 2455, 183 L. Ed. 2d 407 (2012).

Miller, W. (1958). Lower class culture as a generating milieu of gang delinquency. *Journal of Social Issues* 14(3):5–19.

Minton, T. D. (2013). *Jail inmates at midyear 2012—Statistical tables*. Washington, DC: Bureau of Justice Statistics.

Mulvey, E. P. and C. A. Schubert. (2012). *Transfer of juveniles to adult court: Effects of a broad policy in one court*. Washington, DC: Office of Juvenile Justice and Delinquency Prevention.

National Conference of State Legislatures. (2010). 2009 Juvenile Justice State Legislation. http://www.ncsl.org/?tabid=19713 (accessed May 31, 2013).

New York City School–Justice Partnership Task Force. (2013). *Keeping kids in school and out of court*. Albany, NY: New York State Permanent Judicial Commission on Justice for Children. http://www.courts.state.ny.us/IP/justiceforchildren/PDF/NYC-School-JusticeTaskForceReportAndRecommendations.pdf (accessed June 15, 2013).

OJJDP (Office of Juvenile Justice and Delinquency and Prevention). (1998). *Guide for Implementing the Balanced and Restorative Justice Model*. Washington, DC: U. S. Department of Justice.

OJJDP (Office of Juvenile Justice and Delinquency Prevention) DMC. (n.d.). A disproportionate minority contact (DMC) chronology: 1988 to date. http://www.ojjdp.gov/dmc/chronology.html (accessed June 16, 2013).

OJJDP (Office of Juvenile Justice and Delinquency Prevention). (n.d.). The Juvenile Justice and Delinquency Prevention Act of 1974. http://ojjdp.gov/compliance/jjdpchronology.pdf (accessed June 16, 2013).

OJJDP (Office of Juvenile Justice and Delinquency Prevention) Legislation. (n.d.). http://www.ojjdp. gov/about/legislation.html (accessed June 20, 2013).

OJJDP (Office of Juvenile Justice and Delinquency Prevention) Statistical Briefing Book. (2013). http://www.ojjdp.gov/ojstatbb/population/qa01101.asp (accessed June 26, 2013).

Petrosino, A., C. Turpin-Petrosino, and S. Guckenberg. (2010). *Formal system processing of juveniles: Effects on delinquency. Campbell Systematic Reviews* 1:1–88.

Puzzanchera, C., B. Adams, and S. Hockenberry. (2012). *Juvenile Court Statistics 2009*. Pittsburgh, PA: National Center for Juvenile Justice.

Reichel, P. L. (2012). *Comparative Criminal Justice Systems: A Topical Approach*, 6th Edition. Upper Saddle River, NJ: Pearson/Prentice Hall.

Roper v. Simmons, 543 U.S. 551 (2005).

Schwartz, R. G. (2013). *Pennsylvania and MacArthur's models for change: The story of a successful public-private partnership*. Philadelphia, PA: Juvenile Law Center.

Scott, E. S. and L. Steinberg. (2008). Adolescent development and the regulation of youth crime. *The Future of Children* 18(2):15–33.

Sedlak, A. J., K. S. McPherson, and M. Basena. (2013). *Nature and risk of victimization: Findings from the survey of youth in residential placement*. Washington, DC: Office of Juvenile Justice and Delinquency Prevention.

Shaw, C. R. and H. D. McKay. (1972). *Juvenile Delinquency and Urban Areas*, Revised Edition. Chicago: University of Chicago Press.

Shoenberg, D. (2012). *Innovation Brief: Reducing racial and ethnic disparities in Pennsylvania*. John D. and Catherine T. MacArthur Foundation. Models for Change. http://www.modelsforchange. net/publications/351 (accessed June 16, 2013).

Snyder, H. and M. Sickmund. (2006). *Juvenile offenders and victims: 2006 national report*. Washington, DC: Office of Juvenile Justice and Delinquency Prevention, U.S. Department of Justice.

Stanford v. Kentucky, 492 U.S. 361 (1989).

Steinberg, L. (2012). Adolescent brain development: What parents, teachers, and teens need to know. Ardmore, PA: Lower Merion High School Lecture.

Sterling, R. W. (2009). *Role of juvenile defense counsel in delinquency court*. Washington, DC: National Juvenile Defender Association.

Stricker, F. (2007). *Why America Lost the War on Poverty—And How to Win It*. Chapel Hill, NC: The University of North Carolina Press.

Sutherland, E. H. (1951). *Principles of Criminology*. Philadelphia, PA: Lippincott.

Szymanski, L. A. (2012). Must judges and other court personnel receive special training with respect to preventing and controlling juvenile crime? *NCJJ Snapshot*. Pittsburgh, PA: National Center for Juvenile Justice.

Tanenhaus, D. S. (2004). *Juvenile Justice in the Making*. New York: Oxford University Press.

UN General Assembly. (1985). United Nations Standard Minimum Rules for the Administration of Juvenile Justice ("the Beijing Rules"): Resolution/Adopted by the General Assembly. A/RES/40/33. http://www.refworld.org/docid/3b00f2203c.html (accessed May 10, 2013).

United Nations Office of High Commissioner for Human Rights. (n.d.). Convention on the Rights of Children. http://www.ohchr.org/EN/ProfessionalInterest/Pages/CRC.aspx (accessed June 12, 2014).

United States Census Bureau. (2014, May 27). The 2012 Statistical Abstract. http://www.census.gov/compendia/statab/ (accessed June 12, 2014).

Warren, R. and Crime and Justice Institute. (2007). *Evidence-based practice to reduce recidivism: Implications for state judiciaries*. Washington, DC: U.S. Department of Justice, National Institute of Corrections.

Willison, J. B., D. P. Mears, T. Shollenberger, C. Owens, and J. A. Butts. (2009). *Past, present, and future of juvenile justice: Assessing the policy options (APO). Final report*. Washington, DC: The Urban Institute. http://www.urban.org/url.cfm?ID=412247 (accessed May 26, 2013).

Internet Sources

American Civil Liberties Union—http://www.aclu.org/

The Annie E. Casey Foundation—http://www.aecf.org/

Campaign for Youth Justice—http://www.campaignforyouthjustice.org/

Center for the Study and Prevention of Violence, Institute of Behavioral Science, University of Colorado Boulder—http://www.colorado.edu/cspv/blueprints/

Department of Justice Defending Childhood—http://www.justice.gov/defendingchildhood/

Equal Justice Initiative—http://eji.org/

Federal Bureau of Investigation—www.fbi.gov

John D. and Catherine T. MacArthur Foundation Models for Change—http://www.modelsfor-change.net/index.html

National Center for Juvenile Justice—www.ncjj.org

Office of Juvenile Justice and Delinquency Prevention—http://www.ojjdp.gov/

Office of Juvenile Justice and Delinquency Prevention Statistical Briefing Book—http://www.ojjdp.gov/ojstatbb/

Supreme Court of the United States—http://www.supremecourt.gov/

Index

A

Aboriginal youth, 131
ACT, *see* Australian Capital Territory
Acts of infraction (*atos infracionais*), 96
Age–crime distribution, Namibia, 215–217
Alive Youth Plan (*Plano Juventude Viva*), Brazil, 102
Antiretroviral treatment (ART), Namibia, 231
Anti-Social Behavior Orders (ASBOs), England and Wales, 348–349
Atos infracionais, see Acts of infraction
Australasian Juvenile Justice Administrators (AJJA), 63
Australia; *see also* Youth justice and crime, Australia
   ACT, 70–71
   Department of Health and Human Services (DHHS), Australia, 77
   New South Wales, 70–73
   Northern Territory, 73–74
   Queensland, 74
   South Australia, 75–76
   Tasmania, 77
   Victoria, 78–79
   Western Australia, 79–80
   young offenders, 63–68
   youth justice systems, 69–70
Australian Bureau of Statistics (ABS), 66
Australian Capital Territory (ACT), 70–71
Austria; *see also* Juvenile Justice Framework, Austria
   Constitutio Criminalis Carolensia from 1532, 30
   criminal responsibility, 29
   economy, 27
   history, 26–28
   Jugend im Recht, 49
   Juvenile Court Act, 1928, 30
   Juvenile Court Act, 1961, 30–31
   Juvenile Court Act, 1988, 31–32
   juvenile justice model, 50–51
   police-reported alleged offenders, 41
   public trial and formal conviction, 31
Austrian Juvenile Court Act 1988 (*Jugendgerichtsgesetz*), 28

B

Bail support program, Australia, 74
Beijing Rules
   Brazilian context, 100–101
   fundamental perspectives, 14
   international documents, 48–49
   juvenile justice, United States, 370
   Standard Minimum Rules, 4
   UNICEF, 8
Bimberi Youth Detention Centre, Australia, 71
Boston Gun Project, 128
Brazil, *see* Juvenile justice administration, Brazil

C

Canada, *see* Juvenile justice, Canada
Canadian Centre for Justice Statistics (CCJS), 115
Capital punishment, United States, 381–383
Child crime, Namibia
   criminal justice research, 217–218
   primary theories, 218–219
   child delinquency, 219–221
Child Justice Act, Namibia, 232–233
Child Justice Act (CJA), South Africa
   Act creation, 325–326
   age and criminal capacity, 326–328
   automatic review, 334–335
   child justice court, 333
   diversion, 330–332
   expungement of criminal records, 335
   legal representation, 334
   police power and duties, 328–329
   preliminary inquiry, 332–333
   pretrial detention and release, 329–330
   scope and application, 326
   sentencing options, 333–334
The Child Savers, Brazil, 94
Child Welfare Law, Japan, 202
Children Act 1908, England and Wales, 351
Children Act 1989, England and Wales, 354
Children Aid Panels and Screening Panels, Australia, 59
Children and Young Persons Act 1933 and 1963, Engleand and Wales, 351, 352
Children's hearings system, Scotland
   age of children, 277
   compulsory measures, 275–276
   grounds for referral, 274
   hearings, 274–275
   referrals, 272–273
   Reporter, 274
   secure accommodation, 276–277
   welfare principle, 267

China Statistical Yearbook, 139
China's juvenile justice
    adjudication, 156–157
    age restrictions, 150
    arrest, 155
    crime statistics, 138–139
    crime control model, 150
    cultural and social contexts, 143–145
    defense attorney, 154
    development, 158–159
    historical evolutions, 145–147
    juvenile delinquency and crime, 148–149
    legal representation, 154
    operational mechanisms, 149–150
    overview, 138
    patterns, 140–143
    police powers, 151–152
    pretrial detention, 154–155
    procuratorate system, 152–153
    prosecution, 155–156
    rehabilitation, 157–158
    sentencing, 156–157
    trends, 139–140
Closed-circuit television (CCTV), Namibia, 224
Communist Party of Czechoslovakia, 296
Community Courts Act, Namibia, 214, 220
Community-based resolutions, England and Wales,
        364–365
Comparative studies
    methodological and epistemological
        challenges, 19
    rationale for, 17–19
Confucianism, 143–144
Convention on the Rights of the Child (CRC)
    Namibia, 226
    Slovakia, 302
    South Africa, 335
Conviction
    suspended sentencing decision, 34–35
    without sentence, 34
Corporatist model, 355
Correctional institutions for children and juveniles,
        Iran, 166
Court dispositions, Austria, 46, 47
Crime and Disorder Act (CDA) 1998, England and
        Wales, 355–356
Crime control model, England and Wales, 352
Crime Severity Index (CSI), Canada, 116–117
Criminal courts, Scotland
    children aged 12–15, 278
    young people aged 16–17, 278–279
Criminal groups (CGs), Netherlands, 249
Criminal Procedures Act, (CPA), Namibia, 1977,
        211, 221
Criminal Procedures Act, Iran, 175
Criminal punishment, Japan, 199
Cultural and social contexts, China, 143

Current Juvenile Law, see Juvenile Law
Custodial Youth Justice Services, Australia, 77
Customary law, Namibia, 220
Cyberbullying, 129
Czechoslovak Penal Code, 297

D

DCYFS, see Disability, Child, Youth and Family
        Services
Defense attorney and legal representation,
        China, 154
Delinquency problem, Canada
    causes of youth crime, 120–121
    crime committee, 118
    criminal code violations, 118–120
    dimensions, 115–116
    official trends, 116–117
    repeat offenders, 121–122
    victimization, 120
Delinquency theory, United States
    detention, 378–379
    JJDP Act, 377–378
    motivational theories, 377
    principles, 376
    solitary confinement, 379
    War on Poverty, 376
Delinquency trends, Japan, 190–194
Delinquency, international, 3–6
Disability, Child, Youth and Family Services
        (DCYFS), Australia, 77
Disproportionate minority contact (DMC),
        United States, 378
Dual track system, Australia, 78
Dutch Children's Act, 251

E

Early and effective intervention (EEI),
        Sxotland, 271
ECA, see Estatuto da Criança e do Adolescente
Edinburgh Study, 283–288
EEI, see Early and effective intervention
Empire's criminal code, 92–93
Epidemiological Fact Sheet on HIV/AIDS,
        Namibia, 231
Era of compassionate justice (2007), Scotland,
        270–272
Estatuto da Criança e do Adolescente (ECA),
        Brazil, 95

F

Family and Youth Welfare Law, Austria, 36–37
Family courts, Japan
    adjudication, 200–201
    Child Welfare Law, 202

criminal punishment, 199
Juvenile Detention and Classification Home, 200
probation officers and tentative probation,
    199–200
FBI, *see* Federal Bureau of Investigation
Federal Bureau of Investigation (FBI), United States,
    Female offenders, Canada, 130–131
Fetal alcohol spectrum disorder (FASD), Canada, 131
The Fifteen Points on Juvenile Trials, 146
Financial burden, 122

G

Getting It Right for Every Child (GIRFEC) model,
    Scotland, 271
Global phenomenon, *see* Juvenile crime
Global Positioning System (GPS), 190
Gross domestic product (GDP), 27

H

Habitual young offenders, Australia, 61
Hardcore offenders, Netherlands, 245
Havana Rules, 4
Hirschi's "social control" theory, Iran, 173
Historical evolution, China
    approaches, 147
    developments, 145–146
    further struggles, 146–147
    origins, 145
HIV/AIDS, Namiba, 231
Hogoshis, Japan, 203–204

I

IMC, *see* Inter-Ministerial Committee
Incursion of populism (1995–2007), Scotland
    Hearings System, 268
    social inclusion and control, 269–270
Institutionalization (imprisonment), Namibia, 227
Inter-Ministerial Committee (IMC), Namibia, 226
International standards, Namiba, 227–230
Incipient-type delinquency, *see* Play-type
    delinquency
Information technology, Japan, 193–194
Informal and formal interventions, Austria
    diversion, 33–34
    fines and imprisonment, 35
    nonpunitive reactions, 36–37
    sentence without conviction, 34
    sentencing decision with conviction, 34–35
    traditional sanctions, 32–33
Indigenous and non-indigenous young people,
    Australia, 67–68
Intensive Supervision Program (ISP), Australia, 80
Iranian juvenile criminal justice system; *see also*
    Juvenile justice system, Iran

Criminal Procedures Act, 175
features, 174–175
juvenile delinquency, 171–174
overview, 163–164
social history, 165–170
traditional Islamic approach, 164–165
Islamic jurisprudence (Fiqh), Iran, 165

J

Japan, juvenile delinquency and crime
    age of offense, 195
    case disposals, 198–199
    Child Welfare Law, 202
    criminal punishment, 199
    criminalization, 187–188
    delinquency trends, 190–194
    detention homes, 200
    family court decisions, 200–201
    gender, 194–195
    guidance centers, 196
    information technology, 193–194
    Minor Offenses Law, 193
    police action, 196–198
    preventive measures, 195–196
    probation and parole, 199–200, 203–204
    punishment, 199
    training schools, 202–203
    World War II, 188–190
JJDP Act, *see* Juvenile Justice and Delinquency
    Prevention
Judges and prosecutors, Austria, 38
Justice approach, Australia, 58–60
Juvenile Aid Panels, Australia, 59
Juvenile Court Act, 1928, 1961, 1988, Austria, 30,
    31–32
Juvenile courts, Namiba
    arrest and detention, 222–223
    Criminal Procedure Act, 211, 221
    diversion, 223–224, 225
    institutionalization (imprisonment), 227
    Magistrate's Court, 221–222
    trial and sentencing, 224–227
Juvenile crime, 18–19
Juvenile criminal law, Brazil, 102
Juvenile criminal procedure, Australia
    avoidance of arrest/pretrial detention, 38
    financial burdens, 39
    offender protection, 38
    principle of publicity, 39
    procedural provisions, 38–39
    youth inquiry reports, 39
Juvenile delinquency and crime, China; *see also*
    China's juvenile justice
    area of, 148–149
    legislative attempts, 148

Juvenile delinquency, Austria
  causal factors, 40
  coming-of-age period, 41
  conviction rates, 41–43
  imprisonment, 46, 48
  pretrial detention and imprisonment rate, 44–45
  public preparedness, 40–41
  sanctions system, 45–46
  trends, 43–44
  typical offenses, 44
Juvenile delinquency, England and Wales, 345–346
Juvenile delinquency, international arena, 8–12
Juvenile delinquency, Iran
  child delinquency, 172–173
  statistical view, 171–172
Juvenile delinquency, Japan
  age, 195
  delinquency trends, 190–194
  gender, 194–195
  information technology, 193–194
  Minor Offenses Law, 193
  World War II, 188–190
Juvenile delinquency, Namibia; *see also* Juvenile
    courts, Namiba
  age–crime distribution, 215–217
  child crime and characteristics, 213–214
  children, 213
  diverse range, 214–215
  NamCIS, 212–213
Juvenile delinquency, Netherlands, *see* Juvenile
    justice and crime, Netherlands
Juvenile Delinquency Prevention Law, China, 148
Juvenile Delinquents Act (JDA), Canada, 109–110
Juvenile Guidance Centers, Japan, 196
Juvenile justice administration, Brazil
  adolescent population, 90–91
  custody infrastructure, 91–92
  historical overview, 91–95
  irregular situation, 95
  liberty, 91–92
  models, 99–101
  overview, 89–90
  procedure, 96–99
  protection measures, 96
  trends, 101–104
Juvenile justice and crime, Japan
  criminal responsibility, 181
  Current Juvenile Law, 183–188
  delinquents, 188–195
  historical periods, 180–181
  juvenile facilities, 181–182
  juvenile justice system, 195–204
  Juvenile Law, 182
  overview, 180
  Reformatory Law, 182
Juvenile justice and crime, Netherlands
  context, 250–251

  customized approach, 253
  developments and debates, 255–257
  different types, 245–251
  ethnicity and crime, 244–245
  gender and crime, 243–244
  group criminality, 246–249
  hard-core offenders, 245–246
  juvenile delinquency, 240
  overview, 251–252
  police statistics, 241–242
  reactions, 253–255
  self-report measures, 243
  street and youth gangs, 249–250
  youth criminality, 240–241
Juvenile Justice and Delinquency Prevention (JJDP)
    Act, United States, 370, 377–378
Juvenile Justice Framework, Austria
  conviction rates, 41–43
  factors for juvenile delinquency, 40
  history, 30–37
  imprisonment (condition), 46–48
  imprisonment rate and pretrial detention,
    44–45
  international recommendations, 48–49
  legislation and practice, 50
  overview, 28–30
  pretrial detention, 49–50
  procedural provisions, 37–39
  public preparedness, 40–41
  rules, 39–40
  sanctioning practices, 45–46
  trends, 43–44
  typical offenses, 44
  in Vienna, 50
  young adult delinquency, 41
Juvenile justice, Canada
  Aboriginal youth, 131
  chronological overview, 110–111
  delinquency problem, 115–122
  female offenders, 130–131
  overview, 108
  runaway/street-involved youth, 128. 130
  street/youth gangs, 128
  teenage suicide, 130
  YCJA, 114–115
  Young Offenders Act, 109–110, 111–114
  youth justice process, 122–127
Juvenile justice, England and Wales
  community-based resolutions, 364–365
  contemporary issues and pressures, 358–363
  development of YJS, 350–358
  juvenile delinquency, 345–346
  overview, 344–345
  United Kingdom, facts, 344
  YJS overview, 346
  youth crime and victimization, 346–350
Juvenile Justice, international arena

"child-saving" movement, 1–2
child-rearing practices, 1–2
comparative studies, 17–19
country profiles, 8–12
delinquent youth, 2–3
disease and illness, 2
international delinquency, 3–6
models, 7–8
overview, 19–20
Juvenile justice, Northern Ireland, 363–364
Juvenile justice, Slovakia
    child trafficking, 315
    children and juveniles, 303
    court and sentencing, 302–304
    crime trends, 310–312
    criminal offenses and clearance rates, 299–301
    custody, 304–307
    Czech–Slovak relations, 296
    Diagnostic Center, 306
    historical profile, 296–297
    institutional human rights, 307
    overview, 297–298
    pretrial (remand) prisoners, 301–302
    prevention of criminality, 313–314
    Roma origins, 314–315
    Slovak Republic, 296
    social evolution/evolution, 298–299
    traditional system, 308–310
Juvenile justice, United States
    adolescence and psychological development, 387
    bifurcated strategies, 390
    capital punishment, 381–383
    children and youth protection, 386–387
    core protections, 370
    delinquency theories, 376–379
    evidence-based practice, 384–385
    historical developments, 370–376
    international recommendations, 48–49, 370
    issues, 387–388
    models, 385–386
    OJJDP, 388–389
    overview, 369–370
    prison pipeline, 388–389
    progress, 390
    Sanctuary Model, 386
    school-based police officers, 388
    supreme court and youth, 379–381
    traditional policies and longstanding
        practices, 388
Juvenile justice system, China
    case procedure, 151
    components, 150–151
    defense attorney and legal representation, 154
    policing, 151–152
    procuratorate system, 152–153
Juvenile justice system, Iran
    after Islamic revolution, 168–170

hadd or qisas, 170
    before Islamic revolution, 165–168
Juvenile justice system, Japan
    adjudication, 200–201
    Child Welfare Law, 202
    criminal punishment, 199
    detention homes, 200
    Family Courts, 199–200
    Guidance Centers, 196
    police activities, 196–198
    preventive activities, 195–196
    probation and parole, 203–204
    public and police prosecutors, 198–199
    training schools, 202–203
Juvenile justice system, Namibia
    Child Justice Act, 232–233
    criminal justice research, 217–218
    Criminal Procedures Act, (CPA), 1977, 211, 221
    historical overview, 210–212
    international convention, 227–230
    juvenile courts, 221–227
    juvenile delinquency figures, 212–217
    overview, 210
    primary theories, 218–219
    tradition and modernity, 219–221
    youth challenges, 230–232
Juvenile justice system, Scotland
    age of criminal prosecution, 289
    child offenders and courts, 277–279
    children's hearings system, 272–277
    development, 265
    Era of compassionate justice (2007), 270–272
    piecemeal approach, 266
    police stop and search, 290–291
    Populism (1995–2007), 268–270
    punishment, deterrence and reform, 265–266
    transition, 289–290
    Welfarism (1968–1995), 266–268
Juvenile Law, Japan
    crime control model, 188
    criminalization, 187–188
    Family Court, 185
    Juvenile Law, 183–184
    Juvenile Law, 2000, 185
    Juvenile Law, 2007 and 2008, 186–187
    movement, 184–185
    overview, 182
    participatory model, 183
    public prosecutors, 187
    welfare model, 183
Juvenile proceedings, China
    adjudication and sentencing, 156–157
    arrest warrant, 155
    pretrial detention, 154–155
    prosecution, 155–156
    rehabilitation, 157–158
Juvenile Protection Law, China, 148

K

Koban and *Chuzaisho*, Japan, 197

L

Laboratory for the Analysis of Violence
　　(LAV-UERJ), 102
Legal aid, sentencing, and punishment of
　　offenders Act 2012, England and
　　Wales, 358–360
Legal Assistance Centre (LAC), Namibia, 211
Lex mitior principle, Austria, 42
Liberal Democratic Party (LDP), Japan, 180
Loosely coupled system, Canada, 112

M

Magistrate's Court Act, Namibia, 221–222
Magistrate's Court, Australia, 77
Maoism, 143–144
Meiji restoration, Japan, 181
Migrant/floating population, China, 143
Ministry of Gender Equality and Child Welfare
　　(MGECW), Namibia, 212
Minor Offenses Law, Japan, 193
Modified justice model
　　Austrian juvenile criminal law, 50
　　juvenile justice, United States, 385
　　tough-on-crime approach, Canada, 112
　　young offender system, Canada, 123
Moment of Crime Control, *see* Criminal
　　Justice Act 1982
Multisystemic Therapy (MST) model, Australia, 80

N

Namibian Correctional Service (NCS), 213–214
Namibian Court Information System (NamCIS),
　　212–213
Namibian juvenile justice system
　　Child Justice Act, 232–233
　　criminal justice research, 217–218
　　Criminal Procedures Act, (CPA), 1977, 211, 221
　　historical overview, 210–212
　　international convention, 227–230
　　juvenile courts, 221–227
　　juvenile delinquency figures, 212–217
　　overview, 210
　　primary theories, 218–219
　　tradition and modernity, 219–221
　　youth challenges, 230–232
National Crime Prevention Centre (NCPC),
　　Canada, 128
National Institute for Crime Prevention and
　　Rehabilitation of Offenders (NICRO),
　　South Africa, 324

National Inter-Ministerial Committee on Child
　　Justice (IMC), Namibia, 211
National Programme of Action for the Children of
　　Namibia (NPA), Namibia, 211
National Toolset for the Juvenile Criminal Law
　　Chain (NTJ), Netherlands, 253
The Netherlands; *see also* Juvenile justice and crime,
　　Netherlands
　　context, 250–251
　　definition, 240–241
　　ethnicity and crime, 244–245
　　gender and crime, 243–244
　　groups criminality, 246–249
　　hard-core offenders, 245–246
　　overview, 239
　　police statistics, 241–242
　　self-report measures, 243
　　street and youth gangs, 249–250
New Millennium, Canada, 114–115
New Qing Imperial Criminal Code, China, 145
New South Wales (NSW), 71–73
Nongovernmental organizations (NGOs), South
　　Africa, 323–325
Northern Ireland, *see* Juvenile justice, Northern
　　Ireland
Nuisance-causing groups (NCGs), Netherlands, 248

O

Offender Management System (OMS), Namibia, 213
Operational mechanisms, China, 149–150
Orphans and vulnerable children (OVCs),
　　Namibia, 213

P

Penal and Procedural Laws, Austria, 28
Penalty Notices for Disorders (PNDs), England and
　　Wales, 348
Penalty ranges, Austria, 35–36
People's Republic of China (PRC), 146
Piecemeal approach, Scotland, 266
Placement in a juvenile institution (PJI),
　　Netherlands, 254
Plano Individual de Atendimento (PIA), Brazil,
　　98–99
Play-type delinquency, Japan, 189
PNDs, *see* Penalty Notices for Disorders
Police and public prosecutors, Japan, 198–199
Politics and Juvenile Justice, 1945 to 1970, England
　　and Wales, 351–352
PRC, *see* People's Republic of China
Pre-trial Community Service (PTCS), Namibia,
　　223–224
Preventative measures, Austria, 36
Preventive activities, Japan, 196–198

Primary theories, Namibia, 218–219
Prison Rules, Japan, 181–182
Probation–parole officers, *see* Hogoshis
"The Proceedings of Child and Juvenile Crimes, Iran," 174–175
Protecting infants doctrines, China, 144
Protection and socio-educational measures, Brazil, 96–97
Protection of Children and Juveniles Act, Iran, 165
Public prosecutors' decisions, Austria, 45–46, 47

R

Rationale for comparative studies
   "age of responsibility," 17
   cross-cultural comparisons, 18
   global phenomenon, 18–19
   nonlinear model, 17
   sentencing polices, 18
   youth crime, 17–18
Rebuttable presumption, 62
Reformatory Law, Japan, 182
Republican penal code, Brazil, 93
Responsibilization strategies, Scotland, 270
Restorative justice approach, Australia, 60–62
Riyadh Guidelines, 4

S

Sanctions system, *see* Informal and formal interventions
Scottish juvenile justice system
   issues, 289–291
   juvenile justice system, 265–272
   overview, 264–265
   structure and operation, 272–279
   youth crime, 279–289
Scottish National Party (SNP), 271
Screening and presentence reports, Namibia, 224–225
Security Administration Sanction Law, China, 143
Sentencing Act, 7
Sentencing polices, 18
Serious Young Offenders Review Panel (SYORP), Australia, 72
Sharia law, 175
Shiite jurisprudence, 168
SINASE Act, Brazil, 98–99
Slovakia; *see also* Juvenile justice, Slovakia
   crime trends, 310–312
   crime-type data, 300
   criminal law, 298–299
   history, 296–297
   police and criminal courts, 299–300
   reports of offenses, 300–301
   sanction structure, 304

Social context, Netherlands, 250
Social inclusion and control, Scotland, 269–270
Social Learning Theory, Canada, 121
Social Work (Scotland) Act, 267
Solitary confinement, United States, 379
South Africa; *see also* Child Justice Act (CJA)
   age and capacity, 335–336
   child justice development, 323–325
   detention, 336–337
   historical profile, 323
   overview, 322–323
   sexual offenses, 337–338
   school-based violence, 338
South African Police Service (SAPS), 329, 331
Status offenses, Austria, 30
Structured discretion, Canada, 115
Suspension of fines or imprisonment, Austria, 35
Sutherland's "differential association" theory, 173
Swords and Firearms Control Law, Japan, 192
Systematic discrimination, Namibia, 224

T

Teenage pregnancies, Namibia, 232
Teenage suicide, Canada, 130
Tentative probation, Japan, 199–200
Tough-on-crime approach, Canada, 112–113
Traditional Authorities Act, Namibia, 220
Traditional societies, Namibia, 219–220
Traditional system, Slovakia
   community service, 310
   conditional waiver of punishment, 308
   diversion, 308–309
   mediation programs, 309
   probation, 309–310
   reeducation, 308
Traditional youth gangs, Canada, 128
Traditional Islamic approach, Iran, 164–165
Trafficking, Slovakia, 315
Welfarism (1968–1995), Scotland, 266–268

U

UCR, *see* Uniform Crime Reporting
UNAM, *see* University of Namibia
UNCRC, *see* United Nations Convention on the Rights of the Child
UNICEF, *see* United Nations Children's Fund
Uniform Crime Reporting (UCR), Canada, 116
United Kingdom, *see* Juvenile justice, England and Wales
   Criminal Justice Act 1982, United Kingdom, 353–354
   Criminal Justice and Immigration Act 2008, 357–358
United Nations Children's Fund (UNICEF), 8

United Nations Convention on the Rights of the
        Child (UNCRC)
    features, 5–6
    highlights, 12–17
    international problem, 5
    international standards, Namiba, 227–230
    Namibian relationship, 211
    treatment, 3–4
    youth justice and welfare, 4
United Nations International Children's Fund
        (UNICEF), 212
United States; *see also* Juvenile justice, United States
    administration rules, 371
    adolescent brain development, 383
    adultification of youth, 371
    constitutional right, 380
    FBI data, 373–375
University of Namibia (UNAM), 218

V

Victim's and Suspect's rights, Austria, 38
Vienna Guidelines, 4, 50

W

Wales, *see* Juvenile justice, England and Wales
Welfare approach, Australia, 57–58
Welfare model, Brazil, 100
Welfare of Minors, Brazil, 94–95
Welfare-oriented model, Austria, 50–51
Whole System Approach (WSA), Scotland, 271

Y

YCJA, *see* Youth Criminal Justice Act (YCJA), 2004
YJB, *see* Youth Justice Board
YOSs, *see* Youth offending services
YOTs, *see* Youth offending teams
Young offender procedural rights, Austria, 38
Young Offenders Act (YOA), 1984, Canada, 109,
        111–114
Young offenders, Australia
    causes, 63–64
    children's/youth courts, 66
    detention, 66–67
    features, 80–81
    overrepresentation, 67–68
    under supervision, 67
    type of, 65–66
    youth justice systems, 64–65
Young offenders, Canada
    criminal code violations, 118–120
    chronological overview, 110–111
    YOA, 111–114

Youth bail service and intensive supervision
        program, Australia, 80
Youth Courts, Scotland, 277–278
Youth crime and victimization,
        England and Wales
    crime-specific, 348
    justice system, 346–348
    statistics, 348–350
    survey, 350
Youth Criminal Justice Act (YCJA), 2004
    public reaction, 3, 7
    Canada, 109, 114–115
Youth justice and crime, Australia
    criminal responsibility, 62–63
    fascinating laboratory, 57
    justice approach, 58–60
    overview, 56
    restorative justice approach, 60–62
    welfare approach, 57–58
Youth Justice and Criminal Evidence Act 1999,
        England and Wales, 356–357
Youth Justice Board (YJB), England and
        Wales, 346
Youth justice process, Canada
    court, 125–126
    criminal justice system, 122–123
    custody, 126–127
    financial burden, 122
    graphic representation, 123
    initial contact, 124
    sentencing options, 125
    youth courts, 124–125
Youth justice system (YJS), Australia, 69–70
Youth justice system (YJS), England and Wales
    Children Act 1908—juvenile justice, 351
    Children Act 1989, 354
    Children and Young Persons Act 1933, 351
    Children and Young Persons Act 1963, 352
    Children and Young Persons Act 1969,
        352–353
    Crime and Disorder Act (CDA) 1998, 355–356
    Criminal Justice Act 1982, 353–354
    Criminal Justice and Immigration Act 2008,
        357–358
    Criminal Justice and Public Order Act 1994,
        354–355
    context, 345
    gender issues, 360
    historical developments, 350–351
    international standards, 362–363
    legal aid, sentencing, and punishment of
        offenders Act 2012, 358–360
    Politics and Juvenile Justice,1945 to 1970,
        351–352
    youth crime and victimization, 346–350

Youth Justice and Criminal Evidence Act 1999,
    356–357
Youth offending services (YOSs), England and
    Wales, 346
Youth offending teams (YOTs), England and Wales,
    346
Youth Rehabilitation Order, England and Wales,
    357–358

Youth transitions and crime, Scotland
    court proceedings, 281–283
    Edinburgh Study, 283–288
    extent and pattern, 279–280
    implication, 289
    imprisonment, 283
    methods, 284
    offense referrals, 280–281